JAVA™

An Introduction to Computer Science & Programming

Third Edition

WALTER SAVITCH

PEARSON

Prentice
Hall

PEARSON EDUCATION, INC.
Upper Saddle River, NJ 07458

Library of Congress Cataloging-in-Publication Data
CIP data on file

Vice President and Editorial Director, ECS: *Marcia Horton*
Publisher: *Alan R. Apt*
Associate Editor: *Toni D. Holm*
Editorial Assistant: *Patrick Lindner*
Vice President and Director of Production and Manufacturing, ESM: *David W. Riccardi*
Executive Managing Editor: *Vince O'Brien*
Assistant Managing Editor: *Camille Trentacoste*
Production Editor: *Lakshmi Balasubramanian*
Copyeditor: *Rebecca Pepper*
Director of Creative Services: *Paul Belfanti*
Creative Director: *Carole Anson*
Art Director: *Heather Scott*
Cover Designer: *Heather Scott*
Art Editor: *Xiaohong Zhu*
Manufacturing Manager: *Trudy Pisciotti*
Manufacturing Buyer: *Lisa McDowell*
Marketing Manager: *Pamela Shaffer*
Marketing Assistant: *Barrie Reinhold*

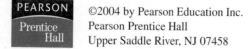

©2004 by Pearson Education Inc.
Pearson Prentice Hall
Upper Saddle River, NJ 07458

The author and publisher of this book have used their best efforts in preparing this book. These efforts include the development, research, and testing of the theories and programs to determine their effectiveness. The author and publisher make no warranty of any kind, expressed or implied, with regard to these programs or the documentation contained in this book. The author and publisher shall not be liable in any event for incidental or consequential damages in connection with, or arising out of, the furnishing, performance, or use of these programs.

Printed in the United States of America
10 9 8 7 6 5 4 3 2 1

ISBN 0-13-101378-5

Pearson Education Ltd., *London*
Pearson Education Australia Pty. Ltd., *Sydney*
Pearson Education Singapore, Pte. Ltd.
Pearson Education North Asia Ltd., *Hong Kong*
Pearson Education Canada, Inc., *Toronto*
Pearson Educación de Mexico, S.A. de C.V.
Pearson Education—Japan, *Tokyo*
Pearson Education Malaysia, Pte. Ltd.
Pearson Education, Inc., *Upper Saddle River, New Jersey*

TRADEMARK INFORMATION

ANSI is a registered trademark of American National Standards Institute.
CodeWarrior is a registered trademark of Metrowerks, Inc.
Java, Duke, and all Java based trademarks and logos are trademarks or registered trademarks of Sun Microsystems, Inc. in the United States and other countries.
JBuilder and JBuilder Foundation are trademarks of Inprise/Borland.
Mac, Macintosh, and MacOS are trademarks of Apple Computer, Inc.
Netscape and Netscape Navigator are trademarks of Netscape Communications, Inc.
TextPad is a trademark of Helios Software Solutions.
UNIX is a trademark of UNIX System Laboratories.
Windows, WindowsNT, and Internet Explorer are trademarks or registered trademarks of Microsoft Corporation.
FrontPage (Microsoft Corportation)
DreamWeaver (Maacromedia, Inc.)
GoLive (Adobe Systems Inc.)

To Christina

FEATURES OF THIS TEXT

FAQ: Why Do We Need new?

When new is used in an expression such as the following, you can think of it as creating the instance variables of the object.

```
SpeciesFirstTry speciesOfLastMonth = new SpeciesFirstTry();
```

An object of a class type, such as speciesOfLastMonth, can have smaller variables inside of it, namely, the instance variables of the object. The new places these instance variables inside of the object. We will explain this use of new more completely in Section 4.3.

◀ **FAQ**
Provides students answers to frequently asked questions within the context of the chapter.

Gotcha ▶

Helps students identify possible programming pitfalls.

▲ *Gotcha*

Variables Declared in a Block

When you declare a variable within a block, that variable becomes a local variable for the block. This means that you cannot use the variable outside of the block. If you want to use a variable outside of a block, you must declare it outside of the block. Declaring the variable outside of the block will let you use the variable both outside and inside the block. △

◀ **Quick Reference**
Provides concise, user-friendly reference for key programming concepts.

Quick Reference: Method Invocation (Calling a Method)

You **invoke** a method by writing the calling object followed by a dot, then the name of the method, and finally a set of parentheses that may (or may not) have information to pass to the method.

Java Tip ▶

Gives students helpful information about the Java programming language.

■ **Java Tip**
Use of return in void Methods

A void method returns no value and so is not required to have any return statement. However, there is a kind of return statement that you may sometimes want to use in a void method. A return statement within a void method has the form

```
return;
```

◀ **Remember**
Reinforces concepts presented in the chapter.

Remember: Two Kinds of Methods

There are two kinds of methods: (1) those that return a single value and (2) those that perform some action other than return a value. Methods that perform some action other than returning a value are called void **methods.**

? Self-Test Questions

Self-Test Questions ▶

Provides students the opportunity to practice skills learned in the chapter.

1. Consider the program in Display 4.4. Suppose you wanted to add another species object called speciesOfTheYear, and suppose you wanted the user to give it data, specifically a name, population, and growth rate. What code do you need to add to the program? (*Hint:* It requires only three or four lines of code.)

2. Suppose Employee is a class with a void method named readInput and dilbert is an object of the class Employee. So dilbert was named and created by the following:

```
Employee dilbert = new Employee();
```

PREFACE FOR INSTRUCTORS

This book was designed to be used in a first course in programming and computer science. It covers programming techniques, as well as the basics of the Java programming language. It is suitable for courses as short as one quarter or as long as one full academic year. No previous programming experience is required, nor is any mathematics, other than a little high school algebra. The book can also be used for a course designed to teach Java to students who have already had another programming course, in which case the first few chapters can be assigned as outside reading. (For students who have had previous programming experience in C or C++, there is an appendix that explains some of the differences between Java and C or C++.)

All of the code in the book has been tested with Java 2 from Sun Microsystems (version 1.4). To be fully compatible with the material presented, the Java used in your class should be version 1.4 or higher. The coverage of Java was carefully arrived at by class testing and is a concise, accessible introduction for beginners.

Changes in This Edition

If you have not used the second edition of this text, you can skip this subsection. If you have used the second edition, this subsection will tell you how this third edition differs from that edition.

For instructors, the transition from the second edition of the text to this third edition is easy: You can teach the same course, with basically the same topics presented, in the same order and with only very minor changes in the material covered.

In addition to technical changes in the material, which we discuss shortly, we have completely gone over and refined the presentation for this edition. Without abandoning our student-friendly, easy-to-understand style, we have redone the entire text to make it more concise. Some have complained about the quality of the copyediting in the previous edition. We have gone to great pains to obtain a copy editor we have used before and know to be an excellent editor. Here are the main differences between this and the previous edition:

We have added coverage of the new assertion-checking facility now built into Java. This topic is covered in Chapter 4.

Binary file I/O is now covered using the classes `ObjectInputStream` and `ObjectOutputStream`, rather than the classes `DataInputStream` and `DataOutputStream`. For I/O of primitive types and strings, the details are the same in either case. For I/O of class objects, `ObjectInputStream` and `ObjectOutputStream` are more object oriented and, even more important, are easier to use and perform better.

The previous edition allowed for covering either text files first or binary files first. This required some repetition of material. Many instructors disliked the repetition, and as far as we can now tell, nobody was choosing the option of covering binary files first. This edition requires that text files be covered before binary files. As a result, the discussion is more concise and is organized in the way that instructors prefer. (You can, of course, skip coverage of binary files completely if you wish.)

This edition adds coverage of the Unified Modeling Language (UML). All UML coverage is optional (even though it is not labeled as such).

The material on JOptionPane that was in Chapter 2 of the second edition has been moved to Appendix 10 in this edition. Instructors told us that they did not cover the material, so we removed it from Chapter 2 to simplify that chapter. For any instructors who do want to teach the material, we left it in an appendix that can be covered anytime after Chapter 2.

Chapter 15, which covered more advanced graphics techniques, such as drawing pictures, advanced color manipulation, and control of fonts, has been eliminated. Instructors told us that they never used the material and that they would prefer a shorter book. Chapters 12, 13, and 14 still include extensive coverage of Swing windowing interfaces and applets.

The CD in the book now comes with Java 2 SDK edition, version 1.4, for Windows and Linux and with Sun ONE Studio 4, Community Edition Integrated Development Environment IDE (formerly Forte for Java 4, Community Edition), for Windows and Linux. The CD also contains a simpler shareware IDE named TextPad, which runs under Windows and which beginners may find more friendly and easier to learn. Because we have added Sun ONE Studio 4 (aka Forte), there was no longer any need for JBuilder, so we have omitted the trial version of JBuilder from the CD for this edition. JBuilder is a fine IDE and will work well with the text, but we felt that a third IDE choice might be too confusing for beginning students. If you prefer JBuilder, you can have your students download a trial version from Borland's Web site (http://www.borland.com/ as we went to press).

Latest Java Coverage

This edition has been updated to use the latest features of Java, including assertion checking and the updated versions of the Swing and file I/O classes. As we wrote the book, we checked all code on Sun's Java 2 version 1.4.

Flexible Sequence of Topics

If you are an instructor, this book adapts the material presented to the way you teach, rather than making you adapt to the material. The book does not tightly prescribe the order in which your course must cover topics, nor does it prescribe the specialized libraries that must be used in your course. You can easily change the order in which you cover chapters and sections. The details about rearranging material are explained in a dependency chart following the acknowledgements section. More details are given in a "Prerequisites" section at the start of each chapter.

Since Java does not include any simple console input, most texts (even those which are more advanced) provide a class for console input. This book adds only one simple class for console input, thus requiring as little nonstandard software as possible. Even that one class, which is included early in the book, becomes an understandable programming example for students well before the end of the book. All of the remaining software is from standard Java libraries that should be part of any Java installation.

Coverage of Problem-Solving and Programming Techniques

The book is designed to teach students basic problem-solving and programming techniques and is not simply a book about Java syntax. Numerous case studies and programming tips, as well as many other sections, explain important problem-solving and programming techniques, such as loop design techniques, debugging techniques, style techniques, abstract data types, and basic object-oriented programming techniques, including UML and event-driven programming, as well as other computer science topics.

Object-Oriented and Traditional Techniques

Any course that really teaches Java must teach classes early, since everything in Java involves classes. A Java program is a class. The data type for strings of characters is a class. Even the behavior of the equals operator (==) depends on whether it is comparing objects from classes or simpler data items. Classes cannot be avoided, except by means of absurdly long and complicated "magic formulas." Accordingly, the book introduces classes fairly early. Some exposure to using classes is given in Chapters 1 and 2. Chapter 4 covers how to define classes. All of the basic information about classes—including inheritance—is presented by the end of Chapter 7 (even if you omit Chapter 6). However, some topics regarding classes (including inheritance) can be postponed to later in a course.

Although the book introduces classes early, it does not neglect traditional programming techniques, such as top-down design and loop design techniques. These older topics may no longer be glamorous, but they are information that all beginning students need.

UML Coverage

New to this edition is the coverage of UML, which starts in Chapter 4. Instructors who would prefer to leave UML coverage to a later course can skip the material without losing continuity of the text.

Swing GUIs and Applets

Starting with the first version of Java 2, Java comes with an improved graphical user interface (GUI) library known as Swing that allows programmers to design portable GUIs. This book uses Swing to teach students to produce professional-looking windowing interfaces. In the process, students learn event-driven programming, as well as receiving a lot of practice with object-oriented programming.

As we class-tested this material and gathered the views of instructors, we found that regular Swing GUIs were a more accessible way than applets to teach students object-oriented programming. Thus, we place greater emphasis on regular Swing GUIs in this text. Such an emphasis makes sense, since almost all advanced applet tools are really general Swing tools. However, for those who want to cover applets early, Chapter 1 has an optional section that previews them. Chapter 13 covers applets in detail and may be presented much earlier than the chapter number suggests. You may choose to introduce GUIs early, late, or not at all.

In addition to the optional GUI material in Chapter 1, there are three full chapters on GUIs, thus giving thorough coverage of Swing GUIs and applets.

Language Details and Sample Code

The book teaches programming technique, rather than simply the Java language. However, neither students nor instructors would be satisfied with an introductory programming course that did not also teach the programming language. Until you calm a student's fears about language details, it is often impossible to focus her or his attention on bigger issues. For this reason, the book gives complete explanations of Java language features and lots of sample code. Programs are presented in their entirety, along with sample input and output. In many cases, there are even extra complete examples on the CD, in addition to the complete examples in the text.

Self-Test Questions

Self-test questions are spread throughout each chapter. These questions have a wide range of difficulty levels. Some require only a one-word answer, whereas others require the reader to write an entire nontrivial program. Complete answers to all the self-test questions, including those requiring full programs, are given at the end of each chapter.

Class Tested

The material in the book has been fully class tested. Much of the material and many of the methods of presentation were revised in response to this testing.

Support Material

The support materials described here that are not included with the book can be obtained from the publisher or over the Internet.

Companion CD

Each book contains a CD that includes all the programs and classes in the volume. The CD also includes Sun Microsystems' Java 2 SDK edition, version 1.4, for Windows and Linux and Sun ONE Studio 4, Community Edition (formerly Forte for Java 4, Community Edition), for Windows and Linux. The CD also includes a copy of TextPad, a simpler shareware IDE that runs under Windows and that may be easier for students to deal with than the Sun ONE Studio 4 IDE (previously known as Forte).

Instructor's Resource Guide and Companion Web Site

The instructor's tools include a chapter-by-chapter *Instructor's Resource Guide* that contains numerous teaching hints, quiz questions with solutions, and solutions to many programming exercises. The companion Web site includes code, PowerPoint slides, and other teaching resources. Instructors should contact their Prentice Hall sales representative to obtain a copy of the *Instructor's Resource Guide* and to receive information on how to access the companion Website. For the name and number of your sales representative, call Prentice Hall Faculty Services at 1-800-526-0485. Additional information on this book and other Prentice Hall products can be found on Prentice Hall's Web site at

`http://www.prenhall.com/`

Other Resources

There are many Java resources available from other vendors which we do not supply, but which you may wish to purchase. One such resource is the JJ environment from Public Static Void Main. This environment includes a simple IDE as well as course administration software all accessed via the Internet. The JJ environment has been setup to be highly compatible with this book. In particular, the `SavitchIn` class, which is used for keyboard input in this book, is an installed library class in JJ. For more information see their website:

`http://www.LearnJavaNow.org/`

Walter Savitch
`wsavitch@ucsd.edu`
`http://www.cse.ucsd.edu/users/savitch`

PREFACE FOR STUDENTS

This book is designed to teach you the Java programming language and, even more importantly, to teach you basic programming techniques. It requires no previous programming experience and no mathematics other than some simple high school algebra. However, to get the full benefit of the book, you should have a version of Java available on your computer, so that you can practice with the examples and techniques given. You should have a version of Java called Java 2. That "2" is not a version number, but something more like a generation number. The version number will be of the form 1.n.x, such as 1.2.x or 1.4.x. The "x" is another number and may not even be there. To be fully compatible with the book, your Java version number should be 1.4.x or higher. (The exact number that is filled in for the "x" is not critical. Indeed, the "x" need not even be present. If software says only "version 1.4," that is fine.)

If You Have Programmed Before

You need not have any previous programming experience to use this book. It was designed for beginners. Nonetheless, you can still use the book to learn Java if you happen to have had experience with some other programming language—but allow us to give you a few words of advice. Do not assume that Java is the same as the programming language(s) you are accustomed to using. All languages are different, and the differences, even if small, are large enough to give you problems. Read at least the boxed material in Section 1.3 of Chapter 1 and all of the boxed material in Chapters 2 and 3. These boxed sections are labeled "Quick Reference," "Remember," and "FAQ." By the time you reach Chapter 4, you would be wise to read the entire chapter.

If you have programmed before in either C or C++, the transition to Java can be troublesome. At first glance, Java may seem almost the same as C or C++. However, Java is very different from these languages, and you need to be aware of the differences. Appendix 11 presents a comparison of Java and C++ that will help you see what the differences are.

Copies of the Programs in the Text

Accompanying the book is a CD that includes all the programs and other software examples given in the volume, so that you can practice with these examples without having to type them into your computer.

Obtaining a Copy of Java

The version of Java you use depends somewhat on what operating system you are using. Be sure to consult the subsection which follows that corresponds to your operating system.

Microsoft Windows

The CD that comes with this text contains a copy of the Java 2 SDK edition, version 1.4, and the Sun ONE Studio 4 (also known as Forte). The Java 2 SDK includes the Java compiler. The Sun ONE Studio 4 (also called Forte) is an IDE that includes an editor from which you can compile and run Java programs. Install both pieces of software, and you will have all you need to write and run Java programs.

The CD also contains a trial version of the TextPad IDE as an alternative to the Sun ONE Studio 4 (also called Forte). Both IDEs are good in their own way, and you may, of course, use either one, but our preference is for the TextPad IDE, which is simpler to use and has all you need to work with the material in the text. If you are in a course, take your instructor's advice on what IDE you should use. If the choice is yours, we suggest that you use the TextPad IDE. Note that in order to use TextPad, you must still install the Java software from Sun described in the previous paragraph.

Macintosh Operating Systems

A recent version of Java for the Mac OS X can be downloaded from the Apple website. When this book went to press, the URL was:

```
http://developer.apple.com/java/
```

As we went to press this Mac Java was Java 1.3.1, which should be fine for almost all the code in this book. When the version 1.4.1 Java for the Mac comes out, we suggest that you change to it.

Another good alternative is to purchase a version of CodeWarrior from Metrowerks, Inc. It works well with the Mac operating system.

Linux Operating System

The CD that comes with this text contains a copy of the Java 2 SDK edition, version 1.4, and the Sun ONE Studio 4 (also known as Forte). The Java 2 SDK includes the Java compiler. The Sun ONE Studio 4 (also called Forte) is an IDE that includes an editor from which you can compile and run Java programs. Install these pieces of software, and you will have all you need to write and run Java programs. (Note that, if you prefer, you may use an editor other than the Sun ONE Studio 4 (Forte).)

UNIX Operating Systems (Other than Linux)

If you are in a course using UNIX, then, in all likelihood, Java has already been installed on the course computer for you. If Java has not been installed, visit the Sun Web site to download a suitable version of Java. At the time this book went to press, the URL was

```
http://java.sun.com/
```

Self-Test Questions

Each chapter contains numerous self-test questions. Complete answers to all the questions are given at the end of the chapter. One of the best ways to practice what you are learning is to do the self-test questions *without looking at the answers*. Look at the answers only after you have answered the questions.

This Text Is Also a Reference Book

In addition to using this book as a textbook, you can and should use it as a reference. When you need to check a particular point that you may have forgotten or that you hear mentioned by somebody, but have not yet learned yourself, just look in the index. Many index entries give a page number for "quick reference." Turn to this quick-reference page. It will contain a short entry, usually set off in a box, that gives all the essential points on that topic. You can consult the quick-reference page to check details of the Java language, as well as details on programming techniques.

Boxed sections in every chapter give you a quick summary of the main points in that chapter. These boxed sections are labeled "Quick Reference," "Remember," and "FAQ." You can use these boxes to review the chapter, preview the chapter, or check details of the Java language.

We Want Your Opinions

This book was written for you, and I would like to hear any comments you have on it. You can contact me via e-mail at the following address:

wsavitch@ucsd.edu

Unfortunately, I cannot provide you with answers to the programming exercises. Only instructors who adopt the book can receive (selected) answers from the publisher. For help with the programming exercises, you will have to contact your instructor. (Even if you are not enrolled in a class, I still cannot provide answers to programming exercises.) But remember that there are answers to all the self-test questions at the end of each chapter.

Walter Savitch
http://www.cse.ucsd.edu/users/savitch

Acknowledgments

I thank the Computer Science and Engineering Department of the University of California, San Diego (UCSD), which is my home department and the place that I tested much of the material covered in this book. Many students in my classes were kind enough to help correct preliminary versions of the book. These students' comments and the comments of instructors who class-tested the book were a tremendous help in shaping the final text. In particular, I extend a special thanks to Carole McNamee of California State University, Sacramento, and to Paul Kube of UCSD; their feedback and class-testing of earlier editions or drafts of the book were a great help to me in producing this edition.

I also thank all the reviewers who took the time to read drafts of this or the previous editions of the book. They provided invaluable detailed comments and suggestions. In alphabetical order within each group, they are as follows:

Reviewers for this third edition:

Robert P. Burton—Brigham Young University
Steve Cater—Kettering University
Gobi Gopinath—Suffolk County Community College.
Rob Kelly—SUNY, Stony Brook
Michele Kleckner—Elon College
Mike Litman—Western Illinois University
Michael Olan—Stockton State
Ken Slonneger—University of Iowa
Boyd Trolinger—Butte College

In addition, the following individuals were kind enough to provide helpful responses to a survey done in preparation for this third edition:

Martin Chelten—Moorpark Community College
Tom Cortina—SUNY, Stony Brook
Adel Elmaghraby—University of Louisvile

Gopal Gupta—University of Texas, Dallas
Ricci Heishman—North Virginia Community College
Blayne Mayfield—Oklahoma State University
Subramanian Vijayarangam—University of Massachusetts, Lowell

Reviewers for the second edition:

Jim Buffenbarger—Idaho State University
Martin Chetlen—Moorpark Community College
Tom Cortina—SUNY, Stony Brook
Prasun Dewan—University of North Carolina
Laird Dornan—Sun Microsystems, Inc.
H. E. Dunsmore—Purdue University, Lafayette
Adel Elmaghraby—University of Louisville
Gopal Gupta—New Mexico State University
Le Gruenwald—University of Oklahoma
Ric Heishman—North Virginia Community College
Rob Kelly—SUNY, Stony Brook
Blayne Mayfield—Oklahoma State University
Alan Saleski—Loyola University, Chicago

Reviewers for the first edition:

Michael Clancy—University of California, Berkeley
Michael Godfrey—Cornell University
Robert Herrmann—Sun Microsystems, Inc., Java Soft
Robert Holloway—University of Wisconsin, Madison
Lily Hou—Carnegie Mellon University
John Motil—California State University, Northridge
James Roberts—Carnegie Mellon University
Nan C. Schaller—Rochester Institute of Technology
Ryan Shoemaker—Sun Microsystems, Inc.
Donald E. Smith—Rutgers University

I also thank all the individuals at Prentice Hall who organized the reviewing and production of this book. In particular, I thank Toni Holm for her work in coordinating things between offices and I thank both Lakshmi Balasubramanian and Xiaohong Zhu for their fine job of converting my manuscript into a published book. Thanks also to Patrick Lindner, Heather Scott, and Jake Warde. All these wonderful people cheerfully did a great job. I extend a special thanks to my publisher, Alan Apt, for his invaluable support and advice throughout the writing and production process.

Lew Rakocy prepared the programming solutions for the instructor's guide, Brian Durney prepared the PowerPoint slides and the test bank questions. I thank both of them for their conscientious work.

I thank Rebecca Pepper for an excellent job of copyediting the manuscript. Since I had final approval on all corrections, any problems that remain in the text are my fault.

I thank Sun Microsystems for allowing me to use the Duke icon in a number of my GUI examples and for permitting us to include Java software on the CD.

Finally, I give a special thanks to Christina for her help and inspiration.

W.S.

Dependency Chart

This chart shows the prerequisites for the chapters in the book. If there is a line between two boxes, the material in the higher box should be covered before the material in the lower box. Minor variations to the chart are discussed in the "Prerequisites" section at the start of each chapter. These variations usually provide more, rather than less, flexibility than what is shown on the chart.

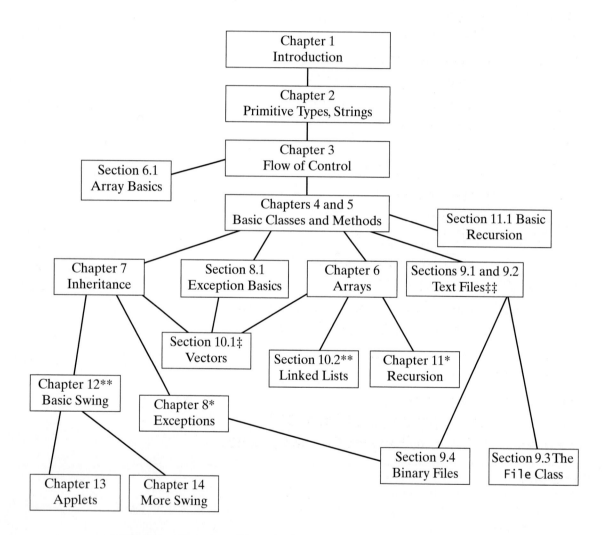

* Note that some sections of these chapters can be covered sooner. Those sections are given in this chart.

** See the chapter's "Prerequisites" section for full details.

‡ Most of Section 10.1 ("Vectors") can be covered before covering inheritance.

‡‡ Also requires Section 8.1 of Chapter 8.

BRIEF TABLE OF CONTENTS

TABLE OF CONTENTS

CHAPTER 14 More Swing 823

Chapter

1

Introduction to Computers and Java

It is by no means hopeless to expect to make a machine for really very difficult mathematical problems. But you would have to proceed step-by-step. I think electricity would be the best thing to rely on. -Charles Sanders Peirce (1839–1914)

This chapter gives you a brief overview of computer hardware and software. Our discussion of software will include a description of a methodology for designing programs known as object-oriented programming. Much of this introductory material applies to programming in any language, not just to programming in Java. Section 1.3 introduces the Java language and explains two simple Java programs. An optional section at the end of this chapter gives some sample applets, which are Java programs that can be run from an Internet Website.

OBJECTIVES

Give you a brief overview of computer hardware and software.

Introduce you to the basic techniques of program design in general and object-oriented programming in particular.

Give you an overview of the Java programming language.

PREREQUISITES

This first chapter does *not* assume that you have had any previous programming experience, but it does assume that you have access to a computer. To get the full value from the chapter, and from the rest of this book, you should have a computer that has the Java language installed, so that you can try out what you are learning. The Preface discusses some ways to obtain a free copy of the Java language for your computer.

If you prefer, you may intersperse the reading of this first chapter with your reading of the next five chapters of the book. However, you should read at least Section 1.3 before moving on to Chapter 2. You can read Section 1.3 before reading Sections 1.1 and 1.2. (In fact, you can read Sections 1.1, 1.2, and 1.3 in any order.)

1.1 COMPUTER BASICS

The Analytical Engine has no pretensions whatever to originate anything. It can do whatever we know how to order it to perform. It can follow analysis; but it has no power of anticipating any analytical relations or truths. Its province is to assist us in making available what we are already acquainted with. -Ada Augusta, Countess of Lovelace (1815–1852)

hardware
software
program

Computer systems consist of **hardware** and **software.** The hardware is the physical machine. A set of instructions for the computer is called a **program.** All the different kinds of programs used to give instructions to the computer are referred to as software. In this book, we will be discussing software, but in order to understand the software, it does help to know a few basic things about computer hardware.

Hardware and Memory

Most computers available today have the same basic components, configured in basically the same way. They all have input devices, such as a keyboard and a mouse. They all have output devices, such as a display screen and a printer. They also have two or three other basic components, usually housed in some sort of cabinet, where they are not so obvious. These other components are a processor and two kinds of memory, known as main memory and auxiliary memory.

The **processor** is the device inside your computer that follows a program's instructions. (The processor is also called the **CPU,** which stands for **central processing unit.**) If you buy a PC, you will be told what kind of chip it has. The **chip** is the processor. Currently, one of the better-known chips is the Pentium processor. The processor follows the instructions in a program, but it can carry out only very simple instructions, such as moving numbers or other items around from one place in memory to another and performing some simple arithmetic operations like addition and subtraction. The power of a computer comes from its speed and the intricacies of its programs. The basic design of the hardware is relatively simple.

processor
CPU
chip

A computer's **memory** holds data for the computer to process, and it holds the result of the computer's intermediate calculations. The computer has two basic kinds of memory, known as main memory and auxiliary memory. All of the various kinds of disk drives, diskettes, and compact discs that are used with computers are types of **auxiliary memory.** They are the (more or less) permanent memory. (Auxiliary memory is also called **secondary memory.**) The working memory that your program uses for intermediate calculations (and for holding the program you are currently running) is called the **main memory.** It is the character of the main memory that you most need to be aware of when you are writing programs. Main memory holds the current program and much of the data that the program is manipulating.

memory

auxiliary memory

main memory

To make this more concrete, let's look at an example. You may have heard a desktop computer (PC) described as having, say, 256 megabytes of RAM and a 20-gigabyte hard drive (or some other numbers for RAM and hard drive storage). **RAM** (short for random access memory) is the main memory, and the hard drive is the principal (but not the only) form of auxiliary memory. A byte is a quantity of memory. So 256 megabytes of RAM is approximately 256 million bytes of memory, and a 20-gigabyte hard drive has approximately 20 billion bytes of memory. So what exactly is a byte? Read on.

RAM

A **bit** is a digit that can assume only the two values 0 and 1. (Actually, any two values will do, but the two values are typically written as 0 and 1.) A **byte** is eight bits of memory—that is, a quantity of memory capable of holding eight digits, each either 0 or 1. Both main memory and auxiliary memory are measured in bytes. In main memory, the organization of the bytes is very important. The computer's main memory consists of a long list of numbered locations, each of which can hold one byte of information. The number of a byte is called its **address.** A piece of data, such as a number or a keyboard character, can be stored in one of these bytes. When the computer needs to recover the data later, it uses the address of the byte to find the data item.

bit

byte

address

Data of various kinds, such as letters, numbers, and strings of letters, are encoded as a series of zeros and ones and placed in the computer's memory. As it turns out, one byte is just large enough to store a single keyboard character. This is one of the reasons that a computer's memory is divided into these 8-bit bytes, instead of into pieces of some other size. However, in order to store a large number or a string of letters, the computer needs more than a single byte. When the computer needs to store a piece of data that cannot fit into a single byte, it uses a number of adjacent bytes. These adjacent bytes are then considered to be a single, larger **memory location,** and the address of the first byte is used as the address of the entire larger memory location. Display 1.1 shows how a typical computer's main memory might be divided into memory locations. The boundaries between these locations are not fixed by the hardware. The size and location of the boundaries will be different when different programs are run.

memory location

Recall that main memory is used only when the computer is running a program. Auxiliary memory is used to hold data in a more or less permanent form. Auxiliary memory is also divided into bytes, but these bytes are then grouped into much larger units known as **files.** A file may contain (in an encoded form) almost any sort of data, such as a program, a letter, a list of numbers, or a picture. The important characteristics of a file are that it has a name and that it can hold data. When you write a Java program, you will store the program in a file. The file is stored in auxiliary memory (typically some kind of disk storage), and when you want to run the program, the program is copied from auxiliary memory to main memory.

file

■ DISPLAY 1.1   **Main Memory**

byte 3021   11110000 ⎤ 2-byte memory location at address 3021
byte 3022   11001100 ⎦
byte 3023   10101010 ⎤ 1-byte memory location at address 3023
byte 3024   11001110 ⎤
byte 3025   00110001 ⎬ 3-byte memory location at address 3024
byte 3026   11100001 ⎦
byte 3027   01100011 ⎤ 2-byte memory location at address 3027
byte 3028   10100010 ⎦
byte 3029   01111111
byte 3030   10000001
byte 3031   10111100

Files are often organized into groups of files known as **directories** or **folders.** *Folder* and *directory* are two names for the same thing. Some computer systems use one name, and some use the other.

directory
folder

FAQ:[1] Why Just Zeros and Ones?

Computers use zeros and ones because it is easy to make a physical device that has only two stable states. However, when you are programming, you normally need not be concerned about the encoding of data as zeros and ones. You can program as if the computer directly stored numbers, letters, or strings of letters in memory.

There is nothing special about the digits zero and one. We could just as well use any two names, such as *A* and *B* or *true* and *false*, instead of *zero* and *one*. The important thing is that the underlying physical device has two stable states, such as on versus off or high versus low voltage. Calling these two states *zero* and *one* is simply a convention, but it's one that is almost universally followed.

Quick Reference: Bytes and Memory Locations

A **byte** is a memory location that can hold eight digits, each either 0 or 1. A computer's main memory is divided into numbered bytes. The number of a byte is called its **address.** To store a piece of data that is too large to fit into a single byte, the computer uses a number of adjacent bytes. These adjacent bytes are considered to be a single larger memory location, and the address of the first byte is used as the address of the entire larger memory location.

Programs

You probably have some idea of what a program is. You use programs all the time. For example, text editors and word processors are programs. A bank ATM machine is really a computer that is running a program. A **program** is simply a set of instructions for a computer to follow.

program

Display 1.2 shows two ways to view the running of a program. To see the first way, forget the dashed lines that form a box. What's left is what really happens when you run a program. Note that when you run a program, there are (normally) two kinds of input to a computer. The program is one kind of input; it contains the instructions that the computer will follow. The other kind of input is often called the **data** for the program. It is the information that the computer program will process. For example, if the program is a simple spelling check program, the data would be the text that needs to be checked. As far as the computer is concerned, both the data and the program itself are input. The output is the result (or results) produced when the computer follows the program's instructions. If the program checks the spelling of some text, the output might be a list of words that are misspelled. When you give the computer a program and some data and tell the computer to follow the instructions in the program, that is called **running** the program on the data, and the computer is said to **execute** the program on the data.

data

running or executing

---

1. FAQ stands for frequently asked question.

■ DISPLAY 1.2   **Running a Program**

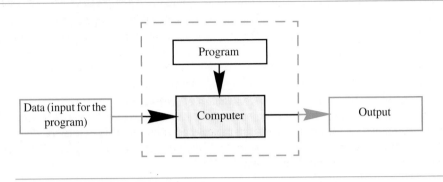

This first view of running a program is what really happens, but it is not always the way we think about running a program. Another view is to think of the data as the input to the program. In this second view, the computer and the program are considered to be one unit that takes the data as input and produces the output. In this view, the combined program–computer unit is indicated by the box with the dashed outline. When we take this view, we think of the data as input to the program and the output as output from the program. Although the computer is understood to be there, it is presumed just to be something that assists the program. Programmers find this second view to be more useful when they design a program.

There are more programs on your computer than you might think when you first begin using your computer. Much of what you think of as "the computer" is actually a program rather than hardware. When you first turn on a computer, you are already running and interacting with a program. That program is called the **operating system.** The operating system is a kind of supervisory program that oversees the entire operation of the computer. If you want to run a program, you tell the operating system what you want to do. The operating system then retrieves and starts the program. The program you run might be a text editor, a program to surf the World Wide Web, or some program that you wrote using the Java language. You might tell the operating system to run the program by clicking an icon with your mouse, by choosing a menu item, or by typing in a simple command. Thus, what you probably think of as "the computer" is really the operating system. Some common operating systems are DOS, Microsoft Windows, Apple's (Macintosh) Mac OS, Linux, and UNIX.

operating system

FAQ: **What Exactly Is Software?**

The word *software* simply means programs. Thus, a software company is a company that produces programs. The software on your computer is just the collection of programs on your computer.

Programming Languages and Compilers

Most modern programming languages are designed to be (relatively) easy for people to write and to understand. These programming languages that are designed for people to use are called **high-level languages.** Java is a high-level language. Most of the programming languages you are likely to have heard of, such as Pascal, FORTRAN, C, C++, BASIC, and Visual Basic, are also high-level languages. Unfortunately, computer hardware does not understand high-level languages. Before a program written in a high-level language can be run, it must be translated into a language that the computer can understand. The languages that the computer can (more directly) understand are called **low-level languages.** The translation of a program from a high-level language, like Java, to a low-level language is performed by another program known as a **compiler.**

When you run a program written in a high-level language, such as a Java, you are actually running a low-level-language translation of that program. Thus, before you run a high-level-language program, you must first run the compiler on the program. When you do this, you are said to **compile** the program.

The low-level languages produced by compilers are usually referred to as **machine languages** or **assembly languages.** The language that the computer can directly understand is called machine language. Assembly language is almost the same thing as machine language, but it needs some minor additional translation before it can run on the computer. Normally, this additional translation is done automatically and need not be of concern to you. In practice, it will look as though you are running the program produced by the compiler.

One disadvantage of the translation process we just described for high-level languages is that, with most programming languages, you need a different compiler for each type of computer and each operating system. If you want to run your high-level-language program on three different types of computers, you need to use three different compilers and must compile your program three different times. Moreover, if a manufacturer comes out with a new type of computer, a team of programmers must write a new compiler for that computer. This is a problem because compilers are very large programs that are expensive and time consuming to produce. Despite this cost, this is the way most high-level-language compilers work. Java, however, uses a slightly different and much more versatile approach to compiling. We discuss the Java approach to compiling in the next subsection.

When you use a compiler, the terminology can get a bit confusing, because both the input to the compiler program and the output from the compiler program are programs. Everything in sight is a program of some kind or other. To help avoid confusion, we call the input program, which in our case will be a Java program, the **source program,** or **source code.** The translated low-level-language program that the compiler produces is often called the **object program,** or **object code.** The word **code** just means a program or a part of a program.

high-level language

low-level language

compiler

compile

machine language

source code
object code

code

Quick Reference: Compiler

A **compiler** is a program that translates a high-level-language program, such as a Java program, into a program in a simpler language that the computer can more or less directly understand.

Java Byte-Code

The Java compiler does not translate your program into the machine language for your particular computer. Instead, it translates your Java program into a language called **byte-code.**   *byte-code*

Java Virtual
Machine

interpreter

Byte-code is not the machine language for any particular computer. Byte-code is the machine language for a hypothetical computer that is something like the average of all computers. This hypothetical computer is called the **Java Virtual Machine.** The Java Virtual Machine is not exactly like any particular computer, but it is similar to all typical computers. Thus, it is very easy to translate a program written in byte-code into a program in the machine language for any particular computer. The program that does this translation is called an **interpreter.** The interpreter works by translating each instruction of byte-code into instructions expressed in your computer's machine language and then executing those instructions on your computer. Thus, an interpreter translates and executes the instructions in the byte-code one after the other, rather than translating the entire byte-code program at once. However, the only detail that you really need to know is that the interpreter somehow allows your computer to run Java byte-code.[2]

In order to run your Java program on your computer, you proceed as follows: First, you use the compiler to translate your Java program into byte-code. Then you use the byte-code interpreter for your computer to translate each byte-code instruction to machine language and to run the machine-language instructions. The whole process is diagrammed in Display 1.3.

It sounds as though Java byte-code just adds an extra step in the process. Why not write compilers that translate directly from Java to the machine language for your particular computer? That could be done, and it is what is done for most other programming languages. Moreover, that technique would produce machine-language programs that typically run faster. However, Java byte-code gives Java one important advantage, namely, portability. After you compile your Java program into byte-code, you can use that byte-code on any computer. When you run your program on another type of computer, you do not need to recompile it. This means that you can send your byte-code over the Internet to another computer and have it run easily on that computer. That is one of the reasons Java is good for Internet applications.

Portability has other advantages as well. When a manufacturer comes out with a new type of computer, the creators of Java do not have to design a new Java compiler. One Java compiler works on every computer. This means that Java can be added to a new computer very quickly and very economically. Of course, every type of computer must have its own byte-code interpreter in order to translate byte-code instructions into machine-language instructions for that particular computer, but these interpreters are simple programs compared to a compiler.

Quick Reference: **Byte-Code**

The Java compiler translates your Java program into a language called **byte-code**. This byte-code is not the machine language for any particular computer, but is a language that is similar to the machine language of most common computers and that is very easy to translate into the machine language of any particular computer. Each type of computer will have its own translator (called an interpreter) that translates from byte-code instructions to machine-language instructions for that particular computer.

---

2. Sometimes people use the term *Java Virtual Machine* (JVM) to refer to the Java byte-code interpreter (as well as to refer to the underlying hypothetical machine that the interpreter is based on).

■ DISPLAY 1.3   Compiling and Running a Java Program

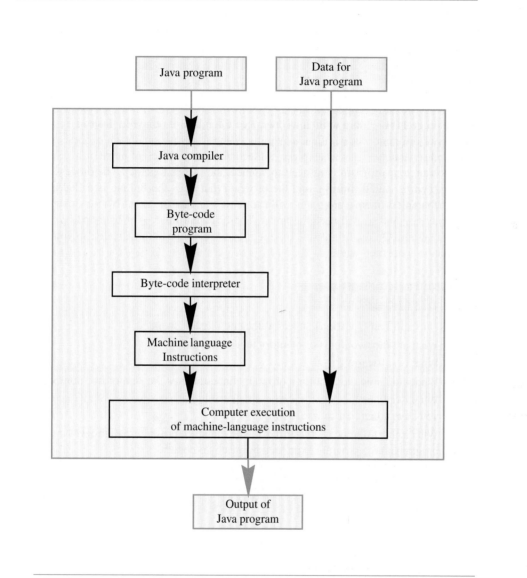

It is important to know about Java byte-code, but in the day-to-day business of programming, you will not even be aware of the fact that there is byte-code for your program.
You normally give two commands, one to compile your program (into byte-code) and one
to run your program. The **run command** executes the Java byte-code interpreter on the
byte-code. This run command might be called "run" or something else, but is unlikely to
be called "interpret." You will come to think of the run command as running whatever the
compiler produces, and you will not even think about the fact that it is byte-code rather
than machine language.

run command

FAQ: Why Is It Called "Byte-Code"?

Programs in low-level languages, such as byte-code and machine-language code, consist of instructions, each of which can be stored in a few bytes of memory. This is presumably why byte-code was given its name. To the designers of Java, byte-code must have looked like "a bunch of bytes."

Linking

linking

A Java program is seldom written as one piece of code all in one file. Instead, it typically consists of different pieces, often written by different people, and each of these pieces is compiled separately. Thus, each piece is translated into a different piece of byte-code. In order to run your program, you need to connect the pieces together. The process of connecting them is called **linking,** and the program that does the linking is called a **linker.** Even the simplest of Java programs will use some standard pieces of byte-code written by somebody else and so will need the linker. These standard pieces of byte-code come with the Java system. On the bright side linking is typically done automatically, so you usually need not be concerned with it.

? Self-Test Questions

Answers to Self-Test Questions appear at the end of each chapter.

1. What are the two kinds of memory in a computer?
2. What is software?
3. What would be the data for a program that computes the sum of two numbers?
4. What would be the data for a program that computes the average of all the quizzes you have taken in a course?
5. What is the difference between a machine-language program, a high-level-language program, and a program expressed in Java byte-code?
6. Is Java a high-level language or a low-level language?
7. Is Java byte-code a high-level language or a low-level language?
8. What is a compiler?
9. What is a source program?
10. What do you call a program that translates Java byte-code instructions into machine-language instructions?

1.2 DESIGNING PROGRAMS

'The time has come,' the Walrus said,
'To talk of many things:
Of shoes–and ships–and sealing wax–
Of cabbages–and–kings...' -Lewis Carroll, Through the Looking Glass

Programming is a creative process. We cannot tell you exactly how to write a program to do whatever task you may want it to perform. However, we can give you some techniques that experienced programmers have found to be extremely helpful when designing programs. In this section, we discuss some of these techniques. The techniques are applicable to programming in almost any programming language and are not particular to Java.

Object-Oriented Programming

Java is an **object-oriented programming** language, abbreviated **OOP.** What is an OOP? The world around us is made up of objects, such as people, automobiles, buildings, trees, shoes, ships, sealing wax, cabbages, kings, and so forth. Each of these objects has the ability to perform certain actions, and each of the actions has some effect on some of the other objects in the world. OOP is a programming methodology that views a program as similarly consisting of objects that interact with one another by means of actions.

OOP

This approach is easier to understand if the program simulates something in the real world. For example, consider a program that simulates a highway interchange in order to analyze traffic flow. The program would have an object to simulate each of the automobiles that enter the interchange, perhaps other objects to simulate each lane of the highway, and so forth.

Object-oriented programming comes with its own terminology. The objects are called, appropriately enough, **objects.** The actions that an object can take are called **methods.** Objects of the same kind are said to have the same *type* or, more often, are said to be in the same **class.** For example, in a simulation program, all the simulated automobiles might belong to the same class, probably called the `Automobile` class. All objects within a class have the same methods. Thus, in a simulation program, all automobiles have the same methods (or possible actions), such as moving forward, moving backward, accelerating, and so forth. This does not mean that all simulated automobiles are identical. They can have different characteristics, which the program indicates by associating some data (that is, some information) with each particular automobile object. For example, the data associated with an automobile object might consist of a word telling the make of the automobile and a number indicating its current speed. (All this will become clearer when you start to define classes yourself, using the Java programming language.)

object

method
class

Quick Reference: Objects, Methods, and Classes

An **object** is a program construction that has data (that is, information) associated with it and that can perform certain actions. When the program is run, the objects interact with one another in order to accomplish whatever the program is designed to do. The actions performed by objects are called **methods.** A **class** is a type or kind of object. All objects in the same class have the same kinds of data and the same methods.

As you will see, this same object-oriented methodology can be applied to any sort of computer program and is not limited to simulation programs. Object-oriented programming is not a new methodology, but its use in applications outside of simulation programs did not become popular until the early 1990s.

Object-oriented programming uses classes and objects, but it does not use them in just any old way. It uses them while following certain design principles. The following are three of the main design principles of object-oriented programming:

Encapsulation

Polymorphism

Inheritance

We will discuss each of these principles briefly in this chapter and more fully at appropriate places later in the book.

Quick Reference: **Object-Oriented Programming**

Object-oriented programming (OOP) is a programming methodology that views a program as consisting of objects that interact with each other by means of actions (known as **methods**). Object-oriented programming uses objects while following certain design principles. The main design principles of object-oriented programming are encapsulation, polymorphism, and inheritance.

Encapsulation

encapsulation

Encapsulation sounds as though it means putting things into a capsule, or, to say it another way, packaging things up. This intuition is correct as far as it goes. The most important part of encapsulation, however, is not simply that things are put into a capsule, but that only part of what is in the capsule is visible. Let's look at an example.

Suppose you want to drive an automobile. What is the most useful description of the automobile? It clearly is not a description of how many cylinders the automobile has and how they go through a cycle of taking in air and gasoline, igniting the gasoline–air mixture, and expelling exhaust. You don't need such details to learn how to drive an automobile. Indeed, knowing those details would be of no real help.

To a person who wants to learn to drive, the most useful description of an automobile consists of information such as the following:

If you press your foot on the accelerator pedal, the automobile will move faster.

If you press your foot on the brake pedal, the automobile will slow down and eventually stop.

If you turn the steering wheel to the right, the automobile will turn to the right.

If you turn the steering wheel to the left, the automobile will turn to the left.

There are other details to describe, but these are perhaps the main ones and are enough to illustrate the concept of encapsulation.

The principle of encapsulation says that, when describing an automobile to somebody who wants to learn to drive, you should provide something like the previous list. In the context of programming, encapsulation means the same thing. It means that when you produce a piece of software, you should describe it in a way that tells other programmers how to use your piece of software, but that omits all the details of how the software works. In particular, if your piece of software is 10 pages long, the description given to another programmer who uses the software should be much shorter than 10 pages, perhaps only a half page long. Of course, that is possible only if you write your software in such a way that it lends itself to this sort of short description.

Note that encapsulation hides the fine detail of what is inside the "capsule." For this reason, encapsulation is often called **information hiding.**

information hiding

Another analogy that may help is that an automobile has certain things that are visible, like the pedals and steering wheel, and other things that are hidden under the hood. The automobile is encapsulated so that the details are hidden under the hood and only the controls needed to drive the automobile are visible. Similarly, a piece of software should be encapsulated so that the details are hidden and only the necessary controls are visible.

Encapsulation is important because it simplifies the job of the programmer who uses the encapsulated software to write more software.

Quick Reference: Encapsulation

Encapsulation is the process of hiding (encapsulating) all the details of how a piece of software was written and telling only what a programmer needs to know in order to use the software. Put another way, encapsulation is the process of describing a class or object by giving only enough information to allow a programmer to use the class or object.

Polymorphism

Polymorphism comes from a Greek word meaning "many forms." The basic idea of polymorphism is that it allows the same program instruction to mean different things in different contexts. Polymorphism commonly occurs in English, and its use in a programming language makes the programming language more like a human language. For example, the English instruction "Go play your favorite sport" means different things to different people. To one person, it means to go play baseball. To another person, it means to go play soccer.

polymorphism

In a programming language such as Java, polymorphism means that one method name, used as an instruction, can cause different actions, depending on the kind of objects that perform the action. For example, there can be a method named `output` that will output the data in an object. But which data and how many data items it outputs depend on the kind of object that carries out the action. There is a bit more to explain about polymorphism, but this brief introduction will give you the general idea. (We will explain polymorphism more fully in Chapter 7.)

If polymorphism is an everyday occurrence in languages like English, why is it a big deal in programming languages? The reason is that early programming languages had very little polymorphism. When it was introduced into programming languages, polymorphism was a big deal because it made programs easier to read and understand.

Quick Reference: Polymorphism

In a programming language such as Java, **polymorphism** means that one method name, used as an instruction, can cause different actions, depending on the kind of object that performs the action.

Inheritance

inheritance

Inheritance refers to a way of organizing classes. The name comes from the notion of inheritance of traits like eye color, hair color, and so forth, but it is perhaps clearer to think of it in terms of a classification system. An example of such a system is shown in Display 1.4. Note that at each level the classifications become more specialized: The class Vehicle includes the classes Automobile, Motorcycle, and Bus; the class Automobile includes the classes Family Car and Sports Car.

The class Vehicle has certain properties, like possessing wheels. The classes Automobile, Motorcycle, and Bus "inherit" the property of having wheels, but add more properties or restrictions. For example, an Automobile has four wheels, a Motorcycle has two wheels, and a Bus has at least four wheels.

Note that as you go higher in the diagram, the classes are more inclusive. A School Bus is a Bus. Since it is a Bus, a School Bus is also a Vehicle. However, a Vehicle is not necessarily a School Bus. A Sports Car is an Automobile and is also a Vehicle, but a Vehicle is not necessarily a Sports Car.

In programming languages like Java, inheritance is used to organize classes in the manner just described. This type of organization has the advantage of allowing the programmer to avoid repeating the same set of programming instructions for each class. For example, everything that is true of every Vehicle, such as "has a motor," is described only once, and it is inherited by the classes Automobile, Motorcycle, and Bus. Without inheritance, descriptions like "has a motor" would have to be repeated for each of the classes Automobile, Motorcycle, Bus, School Bus, Luxury Bus, and so forth.

Inheritance is very important to object-oriented programming and to the Java language. However, it is a bit difficult to understand without concrete programming examples. We will discuss inheritance in the Java language in Chapter 7. At that point, we will explain the notion of inheritance more fully and more clearly.

■ DISPLAY 1.4   **An Inheritance Hierarchy**

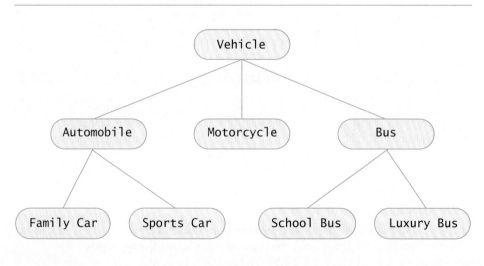

If You Know Some Other Programming Language

If Java is your first programming language, you should skip this subsection. If you know some other programming language, the discussion that is to follow may help you understand objects in terms of things you already know about. If you are already familiar with some other object-oriented programming language, such as C++, Smalltalk, or Borland's Turbo Pascal or Delphi, then you have a good idea of what objects, methods, and classes are. They are basically the same in all object-oriented programming languages, although some other languages use the words *function* or *procedure* to mean the same thing as *method*. You may be familiar with an older programming language that does not use objects and classes, in which case objects can be described in terms of other, older programming constructs. If you know about variables and functions, you can think of an object as a variable that has multiple pieces of data and its own functions. Methods are really the same thing as what are called *procedures* or *functions* in older programming languages.

Algorithms

Objects interact with one another by performing actions (called methods). You as a programmer need to design these actions by giving instructions for carrying out the actions. The hardest part of designing the actions is not figuring out how to express your solution in Java (or whatever programming language you are using). The hardest part is coming up with a plan or strategy for carrying out the action. This strategy is often expressed as something called an algorithm.

An **algorithm** is a set of instructions for solving a problem. To qualify as an algorithm, the instructions must be expressed so completely and so precisely that somebody could follow the instructions without having to fill in any details or make any decisions that are not fully specified in the instructions. An algorithm can be expressed in English or in a programming language such as Java. However, when we use the word *algorithm*, we usually mean that the instructions are expressed in English or something like English.

algorithm

An example may help to clarify the notion of an algorithm. Our first sample algorithm determines the total cost for a list of items. For example, the list of items might be a shopping list that includes the price of each item. The algorithm would then determine the total cost of all the items on the list. The algorithm is as follows:

Algorithm that determines the total cost of a list of items

1. Write the number 0 on the blackboard.
2. Do the following for each item on the list:
   > Add the cost of the item to the number on the blackboard.
   > Replace the old number on the blackboard with the result of this addition.
3. Announce that the answer is the number written on the blackboard.

This algorithm uses a blackboard to store intermediate results. Most algorithms need to store some intermediate results. If the algorithm is written in the Java language and run on a computer, intermediate results are stored in the computer's main memory.

Quick Reference: **Algorithm**

An **algorithm** is a set of instructions for solving a problem. To qualify as an algorithm, the instructions must be expressed so completely and precisely that somebody could follow the instructions without having to fill in any details or make any decisions that are not fully specified in the instructions.

? Self-Test Questions

11. What is a method?
12. What is the relationship between classes and objects?
13. Do all objects of the same class have the same methods?
14. What is encapsulation?
15. What is information hiding?
16. What is polymorphism?
17. What is an algorithm?

Reusable Components

When you first start to write programs, you can easily get the impression that each program that is produced is a completely separate project that is designed from scratch. That is not the way good software is produced, however. Most programs are created by combining components that already exist. Doing so saves time and money. Also, since the software being reused has probably been used many times, it is likely to be better tested and therefore more reliable than newly created software.

For example, a highway simulation program might include a new highway object to model a new highway design, but would probably model automobiles by using an automobile class that was already designed for some other program. To ensure that the classes you use in your programs are easily reusable, you must design them to be reusable. You must specify exactly how objects of that class interact with other objects. This is the principle of encapsulation that we discussed earlier. But encapsulation is not the only principle you must follow. You must also design your class so that the objects are general and not designed in an ad hoc way for one particular program. For example, if your program requires that all simulated automobiles move only forward, you should still include a reverse in your automobile class, because some other simulation may require automobiles to back up. (We will return to the topic of reusability after we learn some details about the Java language and have some examples to work with.)

Testing and Debugging

The best way to write a correct program is to carefully design the objects your program will need and the algorithms for the methods the objects will use and then to carefully translate everything into Java code (or into whatever programming language you are using). In other words, the best way to eliminate errors is to avoid them in the first place. However, no matter how carefully you proceed, your program might still contain some errors. When you finish writing a program, you should test it to see whether it performs correctly and then fix any errors you may find.

A mistake in a program is called a **bug.** For this reason, the process of eliminating mistakes in your program is called **debugging.** There are three commonly recognized types of bugs or errors: syntax errors, run-time errors, and logic errors. Let's consider them in that order.

A **syntax error** is a grammatical mistake in your program. There are very strict grammar rules for how you write a program. If you violate one of these rules—for example, by omitting a required punctuation mark—that is a syntax error. The compiler will catch syntax errors and output an error message telling you that it has found the error and indicating what it thinks the error is. If the compiler says you have a syntax error, you probably do have an error. However, the compiler is only guessing at what the error is, so it could be incorrect in its diagnosis of the problem.

bug

debugging

syntax error

Quick Reference: Syntax

The rules for the correct way to write a program or part of a program (the grammar rules for a programming language) are called the **syntax** of the language.

An error that is detected when your program is run is called a **run-time error.** If your program contains a run-time error, the computer will output an error message when the program is run. The error message may or may not be easy to understand, but at least it lets you know that something is wrong. Sometimes it can even tell you exactly what the problem is.

If there is some mistake in the underlying algorithm for your program, or if you write something in Java that is incorrect, but still valid, your program will compile and run without any error message. You have written a valid Java program, but you have not written the program you want. The program runs and produces output, but the output it produces is incorrect. In this case, your program contains a **logic error.** For example, if you were to mistakenly use the addition sign in place of the subtraction sign, that would be a logic error. You could compile and run your program with no error messages, but the program would give the wrong output. Logic errors are the hardest kind of error to locate, because the computer does not give you any error messages.

run-time error

logic error

▲ *Gotcha*
Coping with "Gotchas"

gotcha

Any programming language has details that can trip you up in ways that are surprising or hard to deal with. These sorts of problems are often called pitfalls, but a more colorful and more commonly used term is *gotchas*. The term stems from the fact that the problems, or pitfalls, or gotchas, are like traps waiting to catch you. When you get caught in the trap, the trap has "got you," or, as it is more commonly pronounced, "gotcha."

In this book, we have sections like this one, with the heading "Gotcha:" that warn you about many of the most common gotchas and tell you how to avoid them or cope with them. △

▲ *Gotcha*

Hidden Errors

Just because your program compiles and runs without any errors and even gives reasonable-looking output, does not mean that your program is correct. You should always run your program with some test data for which you know what the output is supposed to be. To do this, choose some data for which you can compute the correct output, with pencil and paper, by looking up the answer, or by some other means. Even this testing does not guarantee that your program is correct, but the more testing you do, the more confidence you can have in your program. △

? Self-Test Questions

18. What is a syntax error?

19. What is a logic error?

20. What kinds of errors are likely to produce error messages that will alert you to the fact that your program contains an error?

21. Suppose you write a program that is supposed to compute which day of the week (Sunday, Monday, and so forth) a given date (like December 1, 2004) will fall on. Now suppose that you forget to account for leap years. Your program will then contain an error. What kind of program error is it?

1.3   A SIP OF JAVA

Java. An Island of Indonesia, 48,842 square miles in area, lying between the Indian Ocean and the Java Sea.
java n. Informal. Brewed coffee. [From Java.] - The American Heritage Dictionary of the English Language, First Edition

In this section, we describe some of the characteristics of the Java language and examine a simple Java program.

History of the Java Language

Java is widely viewed as a programming language for Internet applications. However, this book, and many other books and people, view Java as a general-purpose programming language that can be used without any reference to the Internet. At its birth, Java was neither of these things, but it eventually evolved into both.

The history of Java goes back to 1991, when James Gosling and his team at Sun Micro-systems began designing the first version of a new programming language that would become Java (though it was not yet called that). The first version of Java was intended to be a programming language for programming home appliances, like toasters and TVs. That sounds like a humble engineering task, but in fact, it's a very challenging one. Home appliances are controlled by a wide variety of computer processors (chips). The language that Gosling and his team were designing needed to work on all these different processors. Moreover, a home appliance is typically an inexpensive item, so the manufacturer would be unwilling to invest large amounts of time and money into developing complicated compilers (programs that would translate the appliance language programs into a language the processor could understand). In this appliance language that the team was designing, and now in the Java language into which it has evolved, programs are first translated into an **intermediate language** that is the same for all appliances (or all computers). Then a small, easy-to-write, and hence inexpensive program translates the intermediate language into the machine language for a particular appliance or computer. The intermediate language is called Java byte-code or simply byte-code, as we discussed in an earlier section. The plan for programming appliances with this first version of Java never caught on with appliance manufacturers, but that was not the end of the story.

intermediate language

byte-code

In 1994, Gosling realized that his language would be ideal for developing a Web browser that could run (Java) programs over the Internet. The Web browser was produced by Patrick Naughton and Jonathan Payne at Sun Microsystems and has evolved into the browser that is today known as HotJava. That was the start of Java's connection to the Internet. In the fall of 1995, Netscape Incorporated decided to make the next release of its Web browser capable of running Java programs. Other companies associated with the Internet have followed suit and have developed software that accommodates Java programs.

FAQ: Why Is the Language Named "Java"?

The question of how Java got its name does not have a very interesting answer. The current custom is to name programming languages in pretty much the same way that parents name their children. The creator of the programming language simply chooses any name that sounds good to her or him. The original name of the language was "Oak." Later the creators realized that there already was a computer language named Oak, so they needed another name, and "Java" was chosen. One hears conflicting explanations of the origin of the name "Java." One traditional, and perhaps believable, story is that the name was thought of when, after a fruitless meeting in which they tried to come up with a new name, the development team went out for coffee, and the rest is, as they say, history.

Applets

There are two kinds of Java programs: applets and applications. An **application** is just a regular program. An **applet** sounds as though it would be a little apple, but the name is meant to convey the idea of a little application. Applets and applications are almost identical. The difference is that an application is meant to be run on your computer, like any other program, whereas an applet is meant to be sent to another location on the Internet and run there.

applet
application

Once you know how to design and write either applets or applications, it is easy to learn to write the other of these two kinds of programs. This book emphasizes applications rather than applets. The reason is that you need to know a number of things about the World Wide Web and Web sites in order to use applets in the way they were intended to be used, and we did not want to cover that whole other topic here. However, if you want to write applets right away, we've given some sample applets later in this chapter in the sub-section entitled "Preview Examples of Applets *(Optional)*." Applets are also covered in detail in Chapter 13 of the book.

A First Java Application Program

Our first Java program is shown in Display 1.5. Below the program, we show two screen dialogs that might be produced when a person runs and interacts with the program. The person who interacts with a program is called the **user.** The text typed in by the user is shown in color. If you run this program (and you should do so), both the text displayed by the program and the text you type will be the same color on your computer screen. The user may or may not be the person who wrote the program. In a programming class, they very often are the same person, but in a real-world application, they are usually different people.

The person who writes the program is called the **programmer.** This book is teaching you to be the programmer, and one of the first things you need to learn is that the user of your program cannot be expected to know what you want her or him to do. For that reason, your program must give the user understandable instructions, as we have done in the sample screen dialogs.

At this point, we just want to give you a feel for the Java language by providing a brief, informal description of the sample program shown in Display 1.5. In Chapters 2 and 3, we will explain the details of the Java features used in the program. *Do not worry if some of the details of the program are not completely clear on this first reading.* They will be clarified in Chapters 2 and 3. This is just a preview of things to come.

For now, ignore the following few lines that come at the start of the program:

```
public class FirstProgram
{
    public static void main(String[] args)
    {
```

These opening lines set up a context for the program, but you need not worry about them yet. Instead, you can think of them as being Java's way of writing "Begin the program named `FirstProgram`."

The next three lines are the first actions the program performs:

```
System.out.println("Hello out there.");
System.out.println("Want to talk some more?");
System.out.println("Answer y for yes or n for no.");
```

Each of these lines begins with `System.out.println`. Each one causes the quoted string given within the parentheses to be output to the screen. For example, consider

```
System.out.println("Hello out there.");
```

user

programmer

■ DISPLAY 1.5   **A Sample Java Program**

```java
public class FirstProgram
{
    public static void main(String[] args)
    {
        System.out.println("Hello out there.");
        System.out.println("Want to talk some more?");
        System.out.println("Answer y for yes or n for no.");

        char answerLetter;
        answerLetter = SavitchIn.readLineNonwhiteChar();
        if (answerLetter == 'y')
            System.out.println("Nice weather we are having.");

        System.out.println("Good-bye.");

        System.out.println("Press Enter key to end program.");
        String junk;
        junk = SavitchIn.readLine();
    }
}
```

In order to run this program, you must have both of the files FirstProgram.java *and* SavitchIn.java *in the same directory (folder) and must compile them both. Read the subsection "Compiling a Java Program or Class" later in this chapter.*

Sample Screen Dialog 1

```
Hello out there.
Want to talk some more?
Answer y for yes or n for no.
y
Nice weather we are having.
Good-bye.
Press Enter key to end program.
```

Sample Screen Dialog 2

```
Hello out there.
Want to talk some more?
Answer y for yes or n for no.
n
Good-bye.
Press Enter key to end program.
```

This code causes the line

    Hello out there.

to be written to the screen.

For now, you can consider these lines, which begin with `System.out.println`, to be a funny way of saying "Output what is shown in parentheses." However, we can tell you a little about what is going on here.

As we discussed earlier, Java programs work by having things called objects perform actions. The actions performed by an object are called methods. `System.out` is an object used for sending output to the screen; `println` is the method (that is, the action) that this object carries out in order to send what is in parentheses to the screen. When an object performs an action using a method, it is said to **invoke** the method (or **call** the method). In a Java program, you write such a method invocation by writing the object name, followed by a period (called a **dot** in computer jargon), followed by the method name and some parentheses that may or may not have something inside them. The item or items inside the parentheses are called **arguments** and provide the information the method needs to carry out its action. In each of these first three lines, the method is `println`. The method `println` writes something to the screen, and the argument (a string in quotes) tells it what it should write.

Margin notes:
`System.out. println`

invoke

dot

argument

Quick Reference: **Classes, Objects, and Methods**

A Java program works by having things called **objects** perform actions. The actions are known as **methods**. All objects of the same kind are said to be in the same class. Thus, a **class** is a category of objects. (If you want to know more details about classes and objects, read the subsection entitled "Object-Oriented Programming," earlier in this chapter.) When the object performs the action for a given method, it is said to **invoke** the method (or **call** the method).

In some special cases, a class can serve the same role as an object—that is, the class can perform the action (invoke the method)—but that level of detail need not worry you yet. Just note that things called objects and things called classes can both perform actions and the actions are called methods.

The next line of the program, shown here, says that `answerLetter` is the name of a variable:

    `char answerLetter;`

*variable
char*

A **variable** is something that can store a piece of data. The `char` says that the data must be a single character; `char` is an abbreviation for *character*.

The next line reads a character that is typed in at the keyboard and stores this character in the variable `answerLetter`:

    `answerLetter = SavitchIn.readLineNonwhiteChar();`

SavitchIn

`SavitchIn` is a class designed for users of this text. The class `SavitchIn` is used to obtain input from the keyboard. This class contains the method `readlineNonwhite-Char`, which reads a single nonblank character from the keyboard. If the user types some input on a single line and presses the Enter key (also called the Return key), the method will read the first nonblank character on that line of keyboard input and discard everything else on the line.

The expression

```
SavitchIn.readLineNonwhiteChar( );
```

is a method invocation. This method invocation simply reads the first nonblank character, which is `'y'` in the first dialog, and dumps the character at the location of the invocation. The beginning of the line tells what is to happen to this character `'y'`. It says to make the character the value of the variable `answerLetter`:

```
answerLetter = SavitchIn.readLineNonwhiteChar( );
```

The equals sign is used differently in Java than in everyday mathematics. In the preceding program line, the equals sign does not mean that `answerLetter` *is equal to* `SavitchIn.readLineNonwhiteChar( )`. Instead, the equals sign is an instruction to the computer to *make* `answerLetter` *equal to* `SavitchIn.readLineNonwhiteChar( )`; that is, it tells the computer to store the character it has read from the keyboard in the variable `answerLetter`.

equal sign

As it turns out, `SavitchIn` is not really an object, but a class. However, in this context, we are using the class `SavitchIn` as if it were an object. For some special methods, you can use the name of a class rather than the name of an object when you invoke the method. In Chapter 5, we explain the significance of this distinction, but those details need not concern you now. At this point, you could even consider the following as a peculiarly spelled instruction that tells the computer to read one character and store that character in the variable `answerLetter`:

```
answerLetter = SavitchIn.readLineNonwhiteChar( );
```

As we will explain more fully later, `SavitchIn` does not automatically come with the Java language. The programmer must define the class `SavitchIn` (or some similar class). To get you started, however, we have defined it for you and placed it on the CD that comes with this text.

The next two lines of the program make a decision to do or not to do something, on the basis of what the user types at the keyboard. Together, these lines perform a test for equality, using the double equals sign. In Java, the double equals sign acts as what you might think of as an ordinary equals sign. The following two program lines first check to see whether the character stored in the variable `answerLetter` is equal to the character `'y'`. If it is, they write `"Nice weather we are having."` to the screen.

double equal sign

```
if (answerLetter == 'y')
    System.out.println("Nice weather we are having.");
```

If the character stored in `answerLetter` is anything other than `'y'`, these two lines do not write anything to the screen.

Notice that one sample dialog outputs the string `"Nice weather we are having."` and one does not. That is because, in the first run of the program, the character `'y'` is stored in the variable `answerLetter`, and in the second run of the program, the character `'n'` is stored in `answerLetter`.

The following three lines at the end of the program are there to stop the screen output from going away before you can read it:

```
System.out.println("Press Enter key to end program.");
String junk;
junk = SavitchIn.readLine();
```

Some systems will erase the screen as soon as the program ends. These three lines make the program, and the screen, wait for the user to press the Enter (Return) key. If pressing the Enter (Return) key one time does not end the program, just press it a second time. This detail can vary a little from one system to another. Although you can use the preceding three lines without understanding them, we should explain a bit more about what they do.

The line

```
String junk;
```

declares a variable named `junk`. The type `String` means that `junk` can hold an entire string of characters. If the user enters a line of text and ends the line by pressing the Enter (Return) key, the following line will read the entire line of text and make it as the value of `junk`:

```
junk = SavitchIn.readLine();
```

Simply pressing the Enter (Return) key will still cause the computer to read the blank line of input, so all the user needs to do is press the Enter key. The variable is named `junk` because the value stored in it is not used for anything.

The method `readLine` is similar to the method `readLineNonwhiteChar`, except that `readLine` reads in an entire line of input rather than a single character. You could end the program in Display 1.5 by typing in the words

```
So long for now.
```

all on one line and then pressing the Enter key. The entire line of text would be stored in the variable `junk`. However, all we really need the user to do to end the program is press the Enter key.

The only things left to explain in this first program are the final semicolons on each line and the braces } at the end of the program. The semicolon acts as ending punctuation, like a period in an English sentence. A semicolon ends an instruction to the computer. The

statements

foregoing instructions are called **statements.** The braces } at the end simply signal the end of the program.

Of course, there are precise rules for how you write each part of a Java program. These rules form the grammar for the Java language, just like the rules for the grammar of the English language, but the Java rules are more precise. The grammar rules for a program-

syntax

ming language (or any language) are called the **syntax** of the language.

Quick Reference: Method Invocation

A **method** is an action that an object is capable of performing. When you ask an object to perform the action of a method, that is called **invoking** or **calling** the method. In a Java program, you invoke a method by writing the object name (or, in some special cases, the class name), followed by a period (called a **dot**), followed by the method name, followed by the arguments enclosed in parentheses. The **arguments** are information given to the method.

Examples:

```
System.out.println("Hello out there.");
answerLetter = SavitchIn.readLineNonwhiteChar();
```

In the first example, `System.out` is the object, `println` is the method, and `"Hello out there"` is the argument. If there is more than one argument, the arguments are separated by commas.

In the second example, the class `SavitchIn` serves the same role as an object, the method is `readLineNonwhiteChar`, and there are no arguments. In some cases, such as the methods of the class `SavitchIn`, you can use a class name in place of an object name when you write a method invocation.

In a program, a method invocation is typically followed by a semicolon.

? Self-Test Questions

22. What would the following statement, used in a Java program, cause to be written to the screen?

    ```
    System.out.println("Java is great!");
    ```

23. Give a statement or statements that can be used in a Java program to write the following to the screen:

    ```
    Java for one.
    Java for all.
    ```

24. Suppose that `mary` is an object of a class named `Person`, and suppose that `increaseAge` is a method for the class `Person` that uses one argument, an integer. How do you write an invocation of the method `increaseAge` for the object `mary`, using the argument 5? The method `increaseAge` will change the data in `mary` so that it simulates `mary` aging by five years.

25. What is the meaning of the following line, which appears in the program in Display 1.5?

    ```
    answerLetter = SavitchIn.readLineNonwhiteChar();
    ```

26. Write a complete Java program that uses `System.out.println` to output the following to the screen when the program is run:

    ```
    Hello World!
    ```

    Your program does nothing else, but, if the output goes away before you get a chance to read it, you should add the following to the end of the program:

    ```
    System.out.println("Press Enter key to end program.");
    String junk;
    junk = SavitchIn.readLine();
    ```

Note that you do not need to fully understand all the details of the program in order to write it. You can simply follow the model of the program in Display 1.5. (You do want to understand all the details eventually, but that may take a few more chapters.)

Compiling a Java Program or Class

A Java program is divided into smaller parts called classes, and normally each class definition is in a separate file. Before you can run a Java program, you must translate these classes into a language that the computer can understand. This translation process is called compiling. (There is more information on classes in the subsection "Object-Oriented Programming" earlier in this chapter. There is more information on compiling in the subsection entitled "Programming Languages and Compilers," also earlier in the chapter.)

A Java program can consist of any number of class definitions. The program in Display 1.5 consists of two classes. The first is the class named FirstProgram, which is shown in Display 1.5. Every program in Java is a class as well as a program. The other class used in this first program is the class SavitchIn, which has already been defined for you. At this point, you would not understand the definition of the class SavitchIn, but you can still obtain a copy of the class, compile it, and use it. A copy of the class SavitchIn is provided on the CD that accompanies this book, along with the other classes defined in this book.

There are, in fact, two other classes used in the program in Display 1.5: the classes named System and String. However, these two classes are automatically provided for you by Java, and you need not worry about compiling either of them. As a rule, you do not need to compile the classes that are provided for you as part of Java. You normally need compile only the classes that you yourself write. So why do you have to compile the class SavitchIn? The reason is that *you* are supposed to write the definition of the class SavitchIn. SavitchIn is not provided as part of Java. However, to make things easier for you, we have written the definition of the class SavitchIn for you. By the time you finish most of this text, you will be fully capable of writing the definition of classes such as SavitchIn.

Before you can compile a Java program, each class definition used in the program (and written by you, the programmer) should be in a separate file. Moreover, the name of the file should be the same as the name of the class, except that the file name has .java added to the end. The program in Display 1.5 is a class called FirstProgram, so it should be in a file named FirstProgram.java. The program in Display 1.5 uses the class SavitchIn. Therefore, the class definition of SavitchIn should be in a file named SavitchIn.java.

.java files

Before you can run the program in Display 1.5, you must compile both the class SavitchIn, which is in the file SavitchIn.java, and the class FirstProgram, which is in the file FirstProgram.java. (If you are in a course, your instructor may have configured the system so that SavitchIn is already compiled for you, but later on, when you define your own classes, you will need to compile the classes.)

If you are using a system that has a special environment for Java, you will have a menu command that can be used to compile a Java class or Java program. (You use the same command to compile any kind of Java file.) You will have to check your local documentation to see exactly what this command is, but it is bound to be simple. (In the TextPad environment, which is provided on the CD that comes with the text, the command is Compile Java on the File menu.)

If your operating system expects you to type in a one-line command, that is easy to do. We will describe the commands for the Java system distributed by Sun Microsystems (usually called "the SDK," "the JDK," or "Java 2"). If you have some other version of Java, these commands might be different.

To compile a Java class, the command is `javac`, followed by the name of the file containing the class. Suppose you want to compile a class named `MyClass`. It will be in a file named `MyClass.java`. To compile the class, you simply give the following command to the operating system:

javac

```
javac MyClass.java
```

Thus, to compile all the classes needed to run the program in Display 1.5, you would give the following two commands (on two separate lines):

```
javac SavitchIn.java
javac FirstProgram.java
```

Remember, if you have an environment that lets you compile with a menu command, you will find it easier to use the menu command rather than the preceding commands.

When you compile a Java class, the translated version of the program, produced by the compiler, is called byte-code. The resulting byte-code for that class is placed in a file of the same name, except that the ending is changed from `.java` to `.class`. So when you compile a class named `MyClass` in the file `MyClass.java`, the resulting byte-code is stored in a file named `MyClass.class`. When you compile the class file named `SavitchIn.java`, the resulting byte-code is stored in a file named `SavitchIn.class`. And, of course, when you compile the class file named `First-Program.java`, the resulting byte-code is stored in a file named `FirstProgram.class`. (There is more information on byte-code in the subsection entitled "Java Byte-Code" earlier in the chapter.)

.class files

Running a Java Program

running a Java
program

A Java program can involve any number of classes, but when you run a Java program, you run only the class that you think of as the program. You can recognize this class because it will contain words identical to or very similar to

```
public static void main(String[] args)
```

These words will probably (but not necessarily) be someplace near the beginning of the file. The critical words to look for are `public static void main`. The remaining portion of the line might be spelled slightly differently in some cases.

If you are using a system that has a special environment for Java, you will have a menu command that can be used to run a Java program. You will have to check your local documentation to see exactly what this command is. (In the TextPad environment, which is provided on the CD that comes with this text, the command is Run Java Application on the File menu.)

If your operating system expects you to type in a one-line command, then (on most systems) you can run a Java program by giving the command `java`, followed by the name of the class you think of as the program. For example, to run the program in Display 1.5, you would give the following one-line command:

```
java FirstProgram
```

Note that when you run a program, you use the class name, such as `FirstProgram`, without any `.java` or `.class` ending. And remember that if you have a menu command for running a Java program, then that is an easier way to run your Java program.

(When you run a Java program, you are actually running the Java byte-code interpreter on the compiled version of your program. When you run your program, the system will automatically link in any classes you need and run the byte-code interpreter on those classes as well.)

In the preceding discussion, we assumed that the Java compiler and other system software was already set up for you. We also assumed that all the files were in one directory, or folder. If this is not the case, and you need to set up the Java compiler and system software, consult the manuals that came with the software. If you wish to spread your class definitions across multiple directories, that is possible and not difficult, but we will not concern ourselves with that detail now.

? Self-Test Questions

27. Suppose you define a class named `SuperClass` in a file. What name should the file have?

28. Suppose you compile the class `SuperClass`. What will be the name of the file with the resulting byte-code?

29. Is the class `SavitchIn` part of the Java language, or does the programmer have to define the class?

Preview Examples of Applets *(Optional)*

applet

An **applet** is special kind of Java program that can be displayed as part of an Internet site so that it can be sent across the Internet to another user's computer and run on that user's computer. Applets have windowing interfaces, so they are typically more flashy than the kind of program we created in Display 1.5. In this section, we will give you a brief look at how two Java applets were written. This is just a preview; we will not be able to fully explain the applets we show you. (We discuss applets in detail in Chapter 13.)

Display 1.6 shows a simple applet program and the window display that it produces. Let's look at the details.

Swing

The line

```
import javax.swing.*;
```

says that this program uses the Swing library (package). Applets use software in the Swing library.

`PreviewApplet1` is the name of this applet, and the words `extends JApplet` indicate that we are dealing with an applet.

The part that begins

```
public void init( )
```

specifies the way the applet looks. The words `public void` will have to remain a mystery for now, but they are required. The word `init` is an abbreviation for "initialization" and indicates that this part describes how the applet is initialized.

The line

```
JLabel myFirstLabel = new JLabel("Hello out there!");
```

creates a label named `myFirstLabel`. A **label** is simply some text that can be added to   label
the applet window. In this case, the text says `"Hello out there!"`. The next line adds
the label `myFirstLabel` to the applet window:

```
getContentPane( ).add(myFirstLabel);
```

The portion `getContentPane( )` produces the inside of the applet window, so this line
says to place the label `myFirstLabel` inside the applet window.

Below the applet code in Display 1.6 is a view of what the applet display looks like
when the applet is run. **GUI** stands for **graphical user interface,** the term used for win-   GUI
dowing interfaces. So the applet window shown in Display 1.6 is a GUI.

■ DISPLAY 1.6   **A Sample Java Applet**

```
import javax.swing.*;

public class PreviewApplet1 extends JApplet
{
    public void init( )
    {
        JLabel myFirstLabel = new JLabel("Hello out there!");
        getContentPane( ).add(myFirstLabel);
    }
}
```

Resulting GUI

Click here with your mouse and the applet display will end.

Applets can contain pictures. The applet in Display 1.7 is similar to the one in Display 1.6, with two differences, one small and one significant. The label in Display 1.7 has the text "Java is fun!" instead of "Hello out there!". That's the small difference. What is really new to this second applet is the addition of a picture, which is done with the following lines:

```
ImageIcon dukeIcon = new ImageIcon("duke_waving.gif");
niceLabel.setIcon(dukeIcon);
```

■ DISPLAY 1.7   **An Applet with an Icon Picture**

```
import javax.swing.*;

public class PreviewApplet2 extends JApplet
{
    public void init()
    {
        JLabel niceLabel = new JLabel("Java is fun!");
        ImageIcon dukeIcon = new ImageIcon("duke_waving.gif");
        niceLabel.setIcon(dukeIcon);
        getContentPane().add(niceLabel);
    }
}
```

Resulting GUI[3]

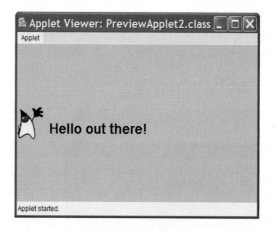

3. Java, Duke, and all Java-based trademarks and logos are trademarks or registered trademarks of Sun Microsystems, Inc. in the United States and other countries. (Duke is the figure waving.)

The first line creates an **icon** (a small picture) from the picture file `duke_waving.gif`. The file `duke_waving.gif` contains a digital version of a picture of Duke, the guy waving in the GUI shown in Display 1.7. The second of the previous two lines adds this icon to the label named `niceLabel`. (Duke is a trademark of Sun Microsystems and serves as a mascot for the Java programming language.)

The preceding two applets simply display something for the user; they do not allow any interaction. Other applets that we will consider in Chapter 13 will interact with the user, but the two we have seen will do as an introduction to applets.

An applet is compiled in the same way as any other Java program, but it is run in a different way.

An applet is designed to run from a Web site, but you need not know how to embed an applet in a Web site in order to run it. There are ways to run applets directly. One way is to use an **applet viewer.** The easiest way to do this is to run the applet from an IDE (integrated development environment), such as Forte for Java (also know as Sun ONE Studio) or the TextPad environment, both of which are included on the CD that comes with this text. (In the TextPad environment, the command is Run Java Applet on the Tools menu. If a window pops up asking you to choose a file, answer "No". This environment command will automatically invoke an applet viewer.) If you do not have an IDE or cannot find the right command for the applet viewer, consult a local expert.

The way that you end an applet depends on how you are running it. If you are using an applet viewer (or are running it from an environment), you end the applet display by clicking the close-window button with your mouse. The close-window button will probably be as shown in Display 1.6, but it might be in a different location, depending on your computer and operating system. If the close-window button is not as shown in Display 1.6, it will likely be in the same place as the close-window button on other windows on your computer. If you are running the applet from a Web site, the applet stays until you close or navigate away from the page it is on.

icon

running an applet

applet viewer

ending an applet

CHAPTER SUMMARY

■ A computer's main memory holds the program that is currently being executed, and it also holds many of the data items that the program is manipulating. A computer's main memory is divided into a series of numbered locations called bytes.

■ A computer's auxiliary memory is used to hold data in a more or less permanent way.

■ A compiler is a program that translates a program written in a high-level language like Java into a program written in a low-level language. The Java compiler translates your Java program into a program in the byte-code language. When you give the command to run your Java program, this byte-code program is translated into machine-language instructions, and the machine-language instructions are carried out by the computer.

■ An object is something that has data associated with it and that can perform certain actions. The actions performed by objects are called methods. A class defines a type of object. All objects in the same class have the same methods.

■ Three of the main principles of object-oriented programming are encapsulation, polymorphism, and inheritance.

■ An algorithm is a set of instructions for solving a problem. To qualify as an algorithm, the instructions must be expressed so completely and precisely that somebody could follow them without having to fill in any details or make any decisions that are not fully specified in the instructions.

■ In a Java program, a method invocation is specified by writing the object name (or class name), followed by a period (called a dot), the method name, and, finally, the arguments in parentheses.

✔ Answers to Self-Test Questions

1. Main memory and auxiliary memory.

2. Software is just another name for programs.

3. The two numbers to be added.

4. All the grades on all the quizzes that you have taken in the course.

5. A machine-language program is written in a form the computer can execute directly. A high-level-language program is written in a form that is easy for a human being to write and read. A high-level-language program must be translated into a machine-language program before the computer can execute it. Java byte-code is a low-level language that is similar to the machine language of most common computers. It is relatively easy to translate a program expressed in Java byte-code into the machine language of almost any computer.

6. Java is a high-level language.

7. Java byte-code is a low-level language.

8. A compiler translates a high-level-language program into a low-level-language program such as a machine-language program or a Java byte-code program. When you compile a Java program, the compiler translates your Java program into a program expressed in Java byte-code.

9. The high-level-language program that is input to a compiler is called the source program.

10. A program that translates Java byte-code instructions to machine-language instructions is called an interpreter. It is also often called the Java Virtual Machine.

11. A method is an action that an object is capable of performing. (In some other programming languages, methods are called functions or procedures.)

12. A class is a category of objects. All objects in the same class have the same kind of data and the same methods.

13. Yes, all objects of the same class have the same methods.

14. Encapsulation is the process of hiding all the details of an object that are not necessary to understanding how the object is used. Put another way, encapsulation is the process of describing a class or object by giving only enough information to allow a programmer to use the class or object.

15. "Information hiding" is another term for "encapsulation."

16. In a programming language, such as Java, polymorphism means that one method name, used as an instruction, can cause different actions, depending on what kind of object performs the action.

17. An algorithm is a set of instructions for solving a problem. To qualify as an algorithm, the instructions must be expressed so completely and precisely that somebody could follow the instructions without having to fill in any details or make any decisions that are not fully specified in the instructions.

18. A syntax error is a grammatical mistake in a program. There are very strict grammar rules for how you write a program. If you violate one of these rules—by omitting a required punctuation mark, for example—that is a syntax error.

19. A logic error is a conceptual error in a program's algorithm. If your program runs and gives output, but the output is incorrect, that means you have a logic error.

20. Syntax errors and run-time errors.

21. A logic error.

22. `Java is great!`

23.
```java
System.out.println("Java for one.");
System.out.println("Java for all.");
```

24. `mary.increaseAge(5);`

25. This statement skips over blank spaces until it reaches the first nonblank character, and then it reads that nonblank character (`'y'` or `'n'` in the sample dialogs) and stores it in the variable `answerLetter`.

26.
```java
public class ExerciseProgram1
{
    public static void main(String[] args)
    {
        System.out.println("Hello World!");

        System.out.println("Press Enter key to end program.");
        String junk;
        junk = SavitchIn.readLine();
    }
}
```

Some details, such as identifier names, may be different in your program. Be sure you compile and run your program.

27. The file with the class named `SuperClass` should be named `SuperClass.java`.

28. `SuperClass.class`.

29. The class `SavitchIn` is not part of the Java language. The programmer (probably you) is supposed to define a class similar to `SavitchIn`. To get you started, we have defined it for you, but think of it as a class that you have defined.

● **Programming Projects**

1. Obtain a copy of the file `SavitchIn.java`, which contains the definition of the class `SavitchIn`. (It is on the CD that accompanies this book. In a course, your instructor may provide you with a copy. It is also in Appendix 4, but it would be a pain to type the whole thing from there.) Compile the class `SavitchIn` so that you get no compiler errors. Next, obtain a copy of the Java program shown in Display 1.5. (That program is also on the CD that comes with the book.) Name the file `FirstProgram.java`. Compile the program so that you receive no compiler error messages. Finally, run the program in `FirstProgram.java`. If you are in a class and your instructor has already compiled the class `SavitchIn` for you, you can skip that part.

2. Modify the Java program that you entered in Programming Exercise 1 so that if the user types the letter `'n'` in response to the question

   `Want to talk some more?`

   the program will output the phrase

   `Too bad. You seem like such a nice person.`

   The program should behave the same as in Display 1.5 if the user enters `'y'` instead of `'n'`. Compile and run the modified program. (*Hint:* Include a second statement that begins with `if` and that tests whether `answerLetter` is equal to `'n'`.)

3. Modify the Java program that you wrote in Programming Exercise 2 to include a third option to the question

   `Want to talk some more?`

   In addition to the responses to `'y'` and `'n'`, if the user enters `'m'` for "maybe," the program will output the phrase

   `Sorry, but I can't wait for your decision.`

4. Both color monitors and your eyes use just three colors—red, blue and green—to create all other colors. In particular, yellow is made by combining red and green, magenta (a shade of purple) by combining red and blue, and cyan by combining green and blue. Write a program that asks the user which of the three colors—yellow, magenta, or cyan—to break down into its two components. If the user enters the letter `'y'` for "yellow," the following message is displayed

   `Yellow is made by combining red and green.`

   Similarly, if the letter `'m'` for "magenta" is entered, the following message is displayed.

   `Magenta is made by combining red and blue.`

and if the letter `'c'` for "cyan" is entered, the following message is displayed,

```
Cyan is made by combining green and blue.
```

5. Write a complete Java program that will ask the user for the initials of the user's first and last names and then output a greeting that says "Hello", followed by the user's initials and an exclamation mark. For example, if the user's initials are "J" and "B", then the output greeting would be

```
Hello J B!
```

If the user's initials are stored in the two variables `firstInitial` and `lastInitial`, both of type `char`, the above output can be produced by the following statement:

```
System.out.println("Hello " + firstInitial
                        + ' ' + lastInitial + '!');
```

There is no significance to the fact that we typed the statement on two lines; if it fits on one line, you can type it all on one line. Be sure to note that the blank symbol is output after `firstInitial`. The use of the plus sign in this way is discussed in Chapter 2, but you do not need to read those details before doing this exercise.

Chapter

2

Primitive Types, Strings, and Console I/O

primitive adj. 1. Not derived from something else; primary or basic. string n. 1. A cord usually made of fiber, used for fastening, tying or lacing. …6. Computer Science. A set of consecutive characters treated by a computer as a single item. - The American Heritage Dictionary of the English Language, Third Edition

In this chapter, we explain enough about the Java language to allow you to write simple Java programs. You do not need any programming experience to understand this chapter. If you are already familiar with some other programming language, such as C, C++, Pascal, BASIC, or FORTRAN, much of what is in Section 2.1 will already be familiar to you. However, even if you know the concepts, you should learn the Java way of expressing them.

OBJECTIVES

Become familiar with the Java data types used for numbers, characters, and similar simple data. These types are called primitive types.

Learn about the assignment statement and expressions.

Find out about the Java data type used for strings of characters and learn how to do simple string processing. This will also serve to familiarize you with the notation used for classes, methods, and objects.

Learn about simple keyboard input and screen output.

PREREQUISITES

If you have not read Chapter 1, you should read at least the subsection of Chapter 1 entitled "A First Java Application Program" to familiarize yourself with the notions of class, method, and object.

As with all optional sections, you do *not* need to cover the subsection of Chapter 1 entitled "Preview Examples of Applets *(Optional)*" before reading this chapter or any other chapter of this book.

2.1 PRIMITIVE TYPES AND EXPRESSIONS

Once a person has understood the way variables are used in programming, he has understood the quintessence of programming. -E. W. Dijkstra, Notes on Structured Programming

In this section, we explain how simple variables and arithmetic expressions are used in Java programs.

Variables

Variables in a program are used to store data such as numbers and letters. They can be thought of as containers of a sort, The number, letter, or other data item in a variable is called its **value.** This value can be changed, so that at one time the variable contains, say, 6, and at another time, after the program has run for a while, the variable contains a different value, such as 4. In the program in Display 2.1, numberOfBaskets, eggsPer-Basket, and totalEggs are variables. For example, when this program is run with the input shown in the sample dialog, eggsPerBasket has its value set to 6 with the following statement, which reads a number from the keyboard.

```
eggsPerBasket = SavitchIn.readLineInt();
```

Later, the value of the variable eggsPerBasket is changed to 4 when the program executes the following statement:

```
eggsPerBasket = eggsPerBasket - 2;
```

We will explain these two statements in more detail shortly.

■ DISPLAY 2.1   **A Simple Java Program** *(Part 1 of 2)*

```java
public class EggBasket
{
    public static void main(String[] args)
    {
        int numberOfBaskets, eggsPerBasket, totalEggs;

        System.out.println("Enter the number of eggs in each basket:");
        eggsPerBasket = SavitchIn.readLineInt();
        System.out.println("Enter the number of baskets:");
        numberOfBaskets = SavitchIn.readLineInt();

        totalEggs = numberOfBaskets * eggsPerBasket;

        System.out.println(eggsPerBasket + " eggs per basket.");
        System.out.println(numberOfBaskets + " baskets.");
        System.out.println("Total number of eggs is " + totalEggs);

        eggsPerBasket = eggsPerBasket - 2;
        totalEggs = numberOfBaskets * eggsPerBasket;

        System.out.println("Now we take two eggs out of each basket.");
        System.out.println(eggsPerBasket + " eggs per basket.");
        System.out.println(numberOfBaskets + " baskets.");
        System.out.println("Total number of eggs is " + totalEggs);

        System.out.println("Press Enter key to end program.");
        String junk;
        junk = SavitchIn.readLine();
    }
}
```

■ DISPLAY 2.1   **A Simple Java Program** *(Part 2 of 2)*

Sample Screen Dialog

```
Enter the number of eggs in each basket:
6
Enter the number of baskets:
10
6 eggs per basket.
10 baskets.
Total number of eggs is 60
Now we take two eggs out of each basket.
4 eggs per basket.
10 baskets.
Total number of eggs is 40
Press Enter key to end program.
```

variables in
memory

In Java, variables are implemented as memory locations. (Chapter 1 discussed memory locations.) Each variable is assigned one memory location. When the variable is given a value, this value (encoded as a string of zeros and ones) is placed in the variable's memory location.

The rules for naming variables follow the spelling rules given for Java identifiers in the next subsection. Besides following those rules, you should also choose variable names that are helpful. Variable names should suggest their use or indicate the kind of data they will hold. For example, if a variable is used to count something, you might name the variable count. If the variable is used to hold the speed of an automobile, you might call the variable speed. You should almost never use single-letter variable names like x and y. Somebody reading the following would have no idea of what the program is really adding:

    x = y + z;

variable
declarations

declare

In order to run your program, the computer must be given some basic information about each variable in your program. It needs to know the name of the variable, how much computer memory to reserve for the variable, and how the data item in the variable is to be coded as strings of zeros and ones. All this information can be obtained, provided that the compiler (and so ultimately the computer) is told the name of the variable and what type of data are stored in the variable. You give this information by **declaring** the variable. Every variable in a Java program must be declared before it is used. For example, the following line from Display 2.1 declares numberOfBaskets, eggsPerBasket, and totalEggs to be variables of type int:

    int numberOfBaskets, eggsPerBasket, totalEggs;

A variable declaration consists of a type name, followed by a list of variable names separated by commas. The declaration then ends with a semicolon. All the variables named in the list are declared to have the type given at the start of the declaration.

The type `int` is the most commonly used type for variables that hold whole numbers, such as 42, –99, 0, and 2001. The word `int` is an abbreviation of *integer*.

int

A variable's **type** determines what kind of value the variable can hold. If the type is `int`, the variable can hold whole numbers. If the type is `double`, the variable can hold numbers with a decimal point and a fractional part after the decimal point. If the type is `char`, the variables can hold any one character from the computer keyboard.

type

A variable declaration tells the computer what type of data the variable will hold. Different types of data are stored in the computer's memory in different ways, so the computer must know the type of a variable in order to know how to store and retrieve the value of the variable from the computer's memory.

Quick Reference: Variable Declarations

In a Java program, a variable must be declared before it can be used. Variables are declared as follows:

Syntax:

Type   Variable_1 ,   Variable_2 ,   . . . ;

Examples:

```
int styleNumber, numberOfChecks, numberOfDeposits;
char answer;
double amount, interestRate;
```

There are two main kinds of types in Java: class types and primitive types. As the name implies, a **class type** is a type for a class, that is, a type for objects with both data and methods. A **primitive type** is simpler. Values of a primitive type are simple, indecomposable values, such as a single number or a single letter. The type `SavitchIn` is a class type. `String` is another class type. The types `int`, `double`, and `char` are primitive types. By convention, class type names begin with an uppercase letter and primitive type names begin with a lowercase letter, but variable names of both class and primitive types begin with a lowercase letter. Variable names for class and primitive types are declared in the same way, but there are different mechanisms for storing values in variables of class types and in variables of primitive types. In this and the next chapter, we will confine our attention primarily to primitive types. We will occasionally use variables of a class type, but only in contexts where they behave pretty much the same as variables of a primitive type. In Chapter 4, we will explain class type variables in more detail.

class type

primitive type

Every variable in a Java program must be declared before the variable can be used. Normally, a variable is declared either just before it is used or at the start of a section of your program that is enclosed in braces {}. In the simple programs we have seen so far, this means that variables are declared either just before they are used or right after the lines

location of declarations

```
public static void main(String[] args)
{
```

Quick Reference: Syntax

The rules for the correct way to write a program or part of a program (the grammar rules for a programming language) are called the **syntax** of the language.

Many of the boxes in this text describe Java syntax using **syntactic variables**. For example, in the box entitled "Variable Declarations" earlier in this chapter, we used the following:

Syntax:

> *Type* *Variable_1* , *Variable_2* , . . . ;

The words *Type*, *Variable_1*, and *Variable_2* are examples of syntactic variables. They are written in a different font, appear in a special color, and use underscore symbols, so that it will be easy for you to recognize them. Syntactic variables are not meant to be words that might appear in a Java program. Instead, they are a kind of blank that is meant to be filled in by an appropriate Java word (or words). *Type* can be replaced by any Java type. For example, *Type* can be replaced by int, double, char, or any other type name. *Variable_1* and *Variable_2* can each be replaced by any variable name. For example, *Variable_1* can be replaced by styleNumber, *Variable_2* can be replaced by numberOfChecks, and the . . . indicates that the list of variables can be of any length. Thus,

> *Type* *Variable_1* , *Variable_2* , . . . ;

can, for example, be replaced by

> int styleNumber, numberOfChecks, numberOfDeposits;

to obtain a valid variable declaration that can be used in a Java program. To help clarify these syntax expressions, they are usually followed by one or more examples of the Java item they specify.

Remember: Syntactic Variables

Remember that when you see something in this book like *Type*, *Variable_1*, or *Variable_2*, these words do not literally appear in your Java code. They are syntactic variables, which means that you replace them with something of the category that they describe. For example, *Type* can be replaced by int, double, char, or any other type name. *Variable_1* and *Variable_2* can each be replaced by any variable name.

Java Identifiers

identifier

case sensitive
upper- and
lowercase

The technical term for a name in a programming language, such as the name of a variable, is an **identifier.** In Java, an identifier (a name) may contain only letters, digits (0 through 9), and the underscore character (_), but the first character in a name cannot be a digit.[1] In particular, no name can contain a space or any other character such as a dot (period) or an asterisk (*). There is no limit to the length of a name. (Well, in practice, there is always a limit, but there is no official limit, and Java will accept even absurdly long names.) Java is **case sensitive**. This means that uppercase and lowercase letters are considered to be different characters. For example, Java considers mystuff, myStuff, and MyStuff to be

---

1. Java does allow the dollar sign symbol $ to appear in an identifier, but these identifiers have a special meaning, so you should not use the $ symbol in your identifiers.

three different names, and you could have three different variables (or other items) with these three names. Of course, it is very poor programming practice to have two names that differ only in their capitalization, but the Java compiler would be happy with them. Within these rules, you can use any name you want for a variable or for a class that you define or for any other item you define in a Java program. But there are some style guidelines for choosing names.

Our somewhat peculiar use of uppercase and lowercase letters, such as `numberOfBaskets`, deserves some explanation. It would be perfectly legal to use `NumberOfBaskets` or `number_of_baskets` instead of `numberOfBaskets`, but these other names would violate some well-established conventions about how you should use uppercase and lowercase letters. By convention, we write names using only letters and digits. We "punctuate" multiword names using uppercase letters (since we cannot use spaces). The following are all legal names that also follow this well-established convention:

   `inputStream    YourClass    CarWash    hotCar    theTimeOfDay`

The following are all illegal names in Java, and the compiler will complain if you use any of them:

   `My.Class    netscape.com    go-team    7eleven`

The first three contain illegal characters, either a dot or a hyphen. The last name is illegal because it starts with a digit.

Notice that some of the legal names start with an uppercase letter and others, such as `hotCar`, start with a lowercase letter. We will always follow the convention that the names of classes start with an uppercase letter and the names of variables, objects, and methods start with a lowercase letter.

Of course, there are words in a Java program, such as the word `if`, that do not name a variable, a class, or an object. Some words, such as `if`, are called **keywords** or **reserved words.** These keywords have a special predefined meaning in the Java language and cannot be used as the names of classes or objects or anything else other than their intended meaning. A full list of keywords for Java is given in Appendix 1, but it is easier to learn them by use. Beginning in this chapter, keywords, such as `public`, `class`, `static`, and `void`, are in a special color when they appear in displayed code, as you can see in Display 2.1. Some other words, such as `main` and `println`, have a predefined meaning, but are not keywords. That means you can change their meaning, but it is a bad idea to do so, because it could easily confuse you or somebody else reading your program.

keyword
reserved word

Quick Reference: Names (Identifiers)

The name of something in a Java program, such as a variable, class, method, or object, must not start with a digit and may contain only letters, digits (0 through 9), and the underscore character (_). Uppercase and lowercase letters are considered to be different characters. (The symbol $ is also allowed, but it is reserved for special purposes, and so you should not use $ in a Java name.)

Names in a program are often called **identifiers**.

Although it is not required by the Java language, the common practice, and the one followed in this book, is to start the names of classes with uppercase letters and to start the names of variables, objects, and methods with lowercase letters. These names are usually spelled using only letters and digits.

▲ *Gotcha*

Java Is Case-Sensitive

Do not forget that Java is case sensitive. If you use an identifier, like `myNumber`, and then in another part of your program you spell the identifier `MyNumber`, Java will not recognize them as being the same identifier. To be seen as the same identifier, they must use exactly the same capitalization. △

Primitive Types

integer

floating-point number

All the Java primitive types are given in Display 2.2. Notice that there are four types for integers, namely, `byte`, `short`, `int`, and `long`. The only differences among the various integer types is the range of integers they can store and the amount of computer memory they use. If you cannot decide which integer type to use, use the type `int`.

A whole number, such as 0, 1, −1, 2, or −2, is called an **integer.** A number with a fractional part, such as 9.99, 3.14159, −5.63, or 5.0 is called a **floating-point number.** Notice that 5.0 is a floating-point number, not an integer. If you ask the computer to include a fractional part and that fractional part happens to be zero, that does not change the type of the number. If it has a fractional part, even if the fractional part is zero, it is a floating-point number. As shown in Display 2.2, Java has two types for floating-point numbers, `float` and `double`. For example, the following code declares two variables, one of type `float` and one of type `double`:

```
float cost;
double capacity;
```

If you cannot decide between the types `float` and `double`, use `double`.

■ DISPLAY 2.2   **Primitive Types**

Type Name	Kind of Value	Memory Used	Size Range
`byte`	*integer*	*1 byte*	−128 to 127
`short`	*integer*	*2 bytes*	−32768 to 32767
`int`	*integer*	*4 bytes*	−2147483648 to 2147483647
`long`	*integer*	*8 bytes*	−9223372036854775808 to 9223372036854775807
`float`	*floating-point number*	*4 bytes*	$\pm 3.40282347 \times 10^{+38}$ to $\pm 1.40239846 \times 10^{-45}$
`double`	*floating-point number*	*8 bytes*	$\pm 1.76769313486231570 \times 10^{+308}$ to $\pm 4.94065645841246544 \times 10^{-324}$
`char`	*single character (Unicode)*	*2 bytes*	*all Unicode characters*
`boolean`	`true` *or* `false`	*1 bit*	*not applicable*

The primitive type `char` is used for single characters, such as letters or the percent sign. For example, the following declares the variable `symbol` to be of type `char`, stores the character for uppercase A in `symbol`, and then writes that value to the screen so that an A would appear on the screen:

```
char symbol;
symbol = 'A';
System.out.println(symbol);
```

Note that when we give a character in a Java program, we enclose the character in single quotes, as in `'A'`. Note also that there is only one single-quote symbol. The same quote symbol is used on both sides of the character. That one symbol serves as both the left and right quote symbol. Finally, remember that uppercase and lowercase letters are different characters. For example, `'a'` and `'A'` are two different characters.

single quotes

The last primitive type we have to discuss is the type `boolean`. There are two values of type `boolean`, namely, `true` and `false`. This means we can use a variable of type `boolean` to store the answer to a true/false question such as "Is `myTime` less than `yourTime`?" We will have more to say about the type `boolean` in the next chapter.

Assignment Statements

The most straightforward way to give a variable a value or to change its value is to use an **assignment statement.** For example, if `answer` is a variable of type `int` and you want to give it the value 42, you would use the following assignment statement:

assignment
statement

```
answer = 42;
```

The equal sign, =, is called the **assignment operator** when it is used in an assignment statement. It does not mean what the equal sign means in other contexts. The assignment statement is an order telling the computer to change the value stored in the variable on the left-hand side of the assignment operator to the value of the expression on the right-hand side. Thus, an assignment statement always consists of a single variable followed by the assignment operator (the equal sign) followed by an expression. The assignment statement ends with a semicolon. So assignment statements take the form

assignment
operator

Variable = *Expression*;

The expression can be another variable, a number, or a more complicated expression made up by using arithmetic operators, such as + and *, to combine variables and numbers.

For example, the following are all examples of assignment statements:

```
amount = 3.99;
firstInitial = 'B';
score = numberOfCards + handicap;
eggsPerBasket = eggsPerBasket - 2;
```

(All the names, such as `amount`, `score`, and `numberOfCards`, are variables. We are assuming that the variable `amount` is of type `double`, `firstInitial` is of type `char`, and the rest of the variables are of type `int`.)

When an assignment statement is executed, the computer first evaluates the expression on the right-hand side of the assignment operator (=) to get the value of the expression. It then uses that value to set the value of the variable on the left-hand side of the assignment operator (=). You can think of the assignment operator (=) as saying, "Make the value of the variable equal to what follows."

For example, if the variable numberOfCards has the value 7 and handicap has the value 2, the following makes 9 the value of the variable score:

```
score = numberOfCards + handicap;
```

The following line from the program in Display 2.1 is another example of an assignment statement:

```
totalEggs = numberOfBaskets * eggsPerBasket;
```

is multiply

This assignment statement tells the computer to set the value of totalEggs equal to the number in the variable numberOfBaskets multiplied by the number in the variable eggsPerBasket. The asterisk character (*) is the symbol used for multiplication in Java.

same variable both sides of =

Note that a variable can meaningfully occur on both sides of the assignment operator (=) and can do so in ways that may at first seem a little strange. For example, consider

```
count = count + 10;
```

This does not mean that the value of count is equal to the value of count plus 10, which, of course, is impossible. Rather, the statement tells the computer to add 10 to the *old* value of count and then make that the *new* value of count, which means that the statement will increase the value of count by 10. Remember that when an assignment statement is executed, the computer first evaluates the expression on the right-hand side of the assignment operator and then makes that value the new value of the variable on the left-hand side of the assignment operator.

As another example, consider the following assignment statement from Display 2.1:

```
eggsPerBasket = eggsPerBasket - 2;
```

constant

This assignment statement will decrease the value of eggsPerBasket by 2.

The number 2 in the preceding assignment statement is called a **constant.** It is called a constant because, unlike a variable such as eggsPerBasket, the value of 2 cannot change. (Constants are sometimes also called **literals.**) Constants need not be numbers. The characters 'A', 'B', and '$' are three constants of type char. Their values cannot change, but they can be used in an assignment statement to change the value of a variable of type char. For example, the following changes the value of the variable firstInitial to 'B':

literals

```
firstInitial = 'B';
```

In this assignment statement, the variable firstInitial would normally be of type char.

Similarly, the following changes the value of the variable price to 9.99:

```
price = 9.99;
```

In this assignment statement, the variable price would normally be of type double (although it could also be of type float). It cannot be of type int or char. As the saying goes, "You can't put a square peg in a round hole," and you can't put a double value in a variable of type int.

Quick Reference: Assignment Statements with Primitive Types

An assignment statement with a variable of a primitive type on the left-hand side of the equal sign causes the following action: First, the expression on the right-hand side of the equal sign is evaluated, and then the variable on the left-hand side of the equal sign is set to this value.

Syntax:

> *Variable* = *Expression*;

Example:

```
score = goals - errors;
interest = rate * balance;
number = number + 5;
```

Specialized Assignment Operators

You can combine the simple assignment operator (=) with an arithmetic operator, such as +, to produce a kind of special-purpose assignment operator. For example, the following will increase the value of the variable amount by 5:

```
amount += 5;
```

This statement is really just shorthand for

```
amount = amount + 5;
```

This is hardly a big deal, but it can sometimes be handy.

You can do the same thing with any of the other arithmetic operators: −, *, /, and %. (We cover the % operator later, in the subsection "Arithmetic Operators.") For example, consider the following line:

```
amount = amount*25;
```

This line could be replaced by the following equivalent line:

```
amount *= 25;
```

Simple Input and Output

Now we will give you a brief overview of input and output—just enough to allow you to write and understand programs like the one in Display 2.1. Section 2.3 will continue the discussion of input and output that we start here.

As we noted in Chapter 1, System.out is an object and println is a method of this object that sends output to the screen. So

```
System.out.println(eggsPerBasket + " eggs per basket.");
```

outputs the value of the variable eggsPerBasket (to the screen) followed by the phrase " eggs per basket." Notice that the + sign is not being used for arithmetic here. It is a kind of "and." You can read the preceding output statement as an instruction to output the value of the variable `eggsPerBasket` *and* then to output the string `" eggs per basket."`

readLineInt

Next, we consider input. In particular, consider the following line from Display 2.1:

```
numberOfBaskets = SavitchIn.readLineInt( );
```

This is an assignment statement that sets the value of the variable `numberOfBaskets` equal to the value returned by the expression

```
SavitchIn.readLineInt( )
```

This expression invokes the method `readLineInt( )` of the class `SavitchIn`. As we said in Chapter 1, a method is an action, and invoking a method causes that action to take place. The action performed by the method `readLineInt` is to read a single integer from a line of input and deliver that value to the program. In this case, the value becomes the new value of the variable `numberOfBaskets`.

There are a few technical details you need to know when invoking the method `readLineInt`. First, there should be a pair of empty parentheses after the name `readLineInt`. Second, the user must input the integer on a line with nothing else on the line, except possibly blank space before or after the number. The value produced by an invocation of the method `readLineInt` (or any similar method) is usually referred to as the **value returned** by the method invocation.

value returned

The following line from Display 1.5 in Chapter 1 is similar to the invocation of `readLineInt` that we just discussed:

readLine-
NonwhiteChar

```
answerLetter = SavitchIn.readLineNonwhiteChar( );
```

The class `SavitchIn` has a number of different methods for reading different kinds of data. The method `readLineNonwhiteChar` reads a single nonblank keyboard character, whereas the method `readLineInt` reads a single integer. Otherwise, the two methods `readLineInt` and `readLineNonwhiteChar` are similar. `SavitchIn` also has a method named `readLineDouble` that can be used to read a value of type `double`—that is, to read a number that contains a decimal point.

We will say more about this kind of input and output in Section 2.3 of this chapter.

Quick Reference: Returned Value

An expression like `numberOfBaskets * eggsPerBasket` produces a value. If `numberOfBaskets` has the value 2 and `eggsPerBasket` has the value 10, the number produced is 20. In computer parlance, this is called the **value returned.** So instead of saying, "The number produced is 20.", we would say, "The value returned is 20."

The same terminology is used with method invocations. If a method produces a value, we say that the method returns the value. For example, in the last of the following program statements, the method invocation `SavitchIn.readLineInt( )` produces a value—namely, the value read from the keyboard. We refer to this as the value returned by the method invocation `SavitchIn.readLineInt( )`.

```
int myNumber;
System.out.println("Enter an integer:");
myNumber = SavitchIn.readLineInt( );
```

FAQ: What If the Screen Display Goes Away Too Quickly?

Some systems make your program output go away as soon as the program ends. Because computers are fast, this means that the screen dialog can disappear before you get a chance to read it. If this happens on your system, you can add the following to your programs, so the screen display will remain visible until the user presses the Enter (Return) key:

```
System.out.println("Press Enter key to end program.");
String junk;
junk = SavitchIn.readLine();
```

You insert the preceding three lines at the end of your program, as we did in Display 1.5 and Display 2.1. However, we will not add these three lines to programs in the rest of this book. Your program may or may not need the lines, depending on your particular Java environment.

Number Constants

A variable can have its value changed. That is why it is called a variable: its value *varies*. A literal number like 2 cannot change. It is always 2. It is never 3. Literal values like 2 or 3.7 are called **constants** because their values do not change. Literal expressions of types other than number types are also called constants. So, for example, `'Y'` is a constant of type char. There is essentially only one way to write a constant of type char, namely, by placing the character in single quotes. On the other hand, some of the rules for writing numeric constants are more complicated.

constant

Constants of integer types are written the way you would expect them to be written, such as 2, 3, 0, −3, or 752. An integer constant can be prefaced with a plus or minus sign, as in +12 and −72. Numeric constants cannot contain commas. The number expression 1,000 is *not* correct in Java. Integer constants cannot contain a decimal point. Numbers with a decimal point are floating-point numbers.

integer constant

Floating-point constant numbers may be written in either of two forms. The simple form is like the everyday way of writing numbers with digits after the decimal point. The other, slightly more complicated, form is similar to a notation commonly used in the physical sciences.

floating-point constant

The more complicated notation for floating-point constants is frequently called **e notation, scientific notation,** or **floating-point notation.** For instance, consider the number 865000000.0. This number can be expressed more clearly in the following notation, which is used in mathematics and physics, but not in Java:

scientific (e) notation

$$8.65 \times 10^8$$

Java has a similar notation, but because keyboards have no way of writing exponents, the 10 is omitted and both the multiplication sign and the 10 are replaced by the letter **e**. So, in Java, 8.65×10^8 is written as `8.65e8` (or in the less convenient form 865000000.0). The two forms, `8.65e8` and 865000000.0, are equivalent in a Java program.

Similarly, the number 4.83×10^{-4}, which is equal to 0.000483, could be written as `4.83e−4` in Java. The **e** stands for *exponent*, since it is followed by a number that is thought of as an exponent of 10.

Because multiplying by 10 is the same as moving the decimal point in a number, you can think of the number after the e as telling you to move the decimal point that many digits to the right. If the number after the e is negative, you move the decimal point that many digits to the left. For example, 2.48e4 is the same number as 24800.0, and 2.48e−2 is the same number as 0.0248.

The number before the e may be a number with or without a decimal point. The number after the e cannot contain a decimal point

---

FAQ: What Is "Floating" in a Floating-Point Number?

Floating-point numbers got their name because, with the e notation we described in this subsection, the decimal point can be made to "float" to a new location by adjusting the exponent. You can make the decimal point in 0.000483 float to after the 4 by expressing this number as the equivalent expression 4.83e-4. Computer language implementers use this trick to store each floating-point number as a number with exactly one digit before the decimal point (and some suitable exponent). Because the implementation always floats the decimal point in these numbers, they are called floating-point numbers. (The numbers are actually stored in base 2, rather than as the base 10 numerals we used in our example, but the principle is the same.)

Assignment Compatibilities

As we mentioned previously, trying to put a value of one type into a variable of another type is like trying to put a square peg in a round hole. You cannot put an int value like 42 in a variable of type char. You cannot put a double value like 3.5 in a variable of type int. You cannot even put the double value 3.0 in a variable of type int. You cannot store a value of one type in a variable of another type unless the value is somehow converted to match the type of the variable. However, when dealing with numbers, this conversion will sometimes (but not always) be performed automatically for you. The conversion will always be done when you assign a value of an integer type to a variable of a floating-point type, such as

```
double doubleVariable;
doubleVariable = 7;
```

Slightly more subtle assignments, such as the following, also perform the conversion automatically:

```
int intVariable;
intVariable = 7;
double doubleVariable;
doubleVariable = intVariable;
```

More generally, you can assign a value of any type in the following list to a variable of any type that appears further down in the list:

```
byte-->short-->int-->long-->float-->double
```

For example, you can assign a value of type long to a variable of type float or to a variable of type double (or, of course, to a variable of type long), but you cannot assign a value of type `long` to a variable of type `byte`, `short`, or `int`. (Note that this is not an arbitrary ordering of the types. As you move down the list from left to right, the types become more complex, either because they allow larger values or because they allow decimal points in the numbers.)

You can assign a value of type `char` to a variable of type `int` or to any of the numeric types that follow `int` in our list of types. However, we do not advise doing so, because the result could be confusing.[2]

If you want to assign a value of type `double` to a variable of type `int`, you must change the type of the value using a type cast, as we explain next.

Quick Reference: Assignment Compatibilities

You can assign a value of any type on the following list to a variable of any type that appears further down on the list:

```
byte-->short-->int-->long-->float-->double
```

In particular, note that you can assign a value of any integer type to a variable of any floating-point type.

Type Casting

The title of this subsection has nothing to do with the Hollywood notion of typecasting. In fact, it is almost the opposite. In Java (and in most programming languages), a **type cast**   type cast
involves changing the type of a value from its normal type to some other type—for example, changing the type of `2.0` from `double` to `int`. In the previous subsection, we described when you could assign a value of one type to a variable of another type and have the type conversion occur automatically. In all other cases, if you want to assign a value of one type to a variable of another type, you must perform a type cast. Let's see how this is done in Java.

Suppose you have the following:

```
double distance;
distance = 9.0;
int points;
points = distance;
```

This is an illegal assignment.

---

2. Readers who have used certain other languages, such as C or C++, may be surprised to learn that you cannot assign a value of type `char` to a variable of type `byte`. This is because Java uses the Unicode character set rather than the ASCII character set, and so Java reserves two bytes of memory for each value of type `char`, but naturally reserves only one byte of memory for values of type `byte`. This is one of the few cases in which you might notice that Java uses the Unicode character set. However, if you convert from an `int` to a `char` or vice versa, you can expect to get the usual correspondence of ASCII numbers and characters.

As the note indicates, the last statement is illegal in Java. You cannot assign a value of type `double` to a variable of type `int`, even if the value of type `double` happens to have all zeros after the decimal point and so is conceptually a whole number.

In order to assign a value of type `double` to a value of type `int`, you must place `(int)` in front of the value or the variable holding the value. For example, you can replace the preceding illegal assignment with the following and get a legal assignment:

```
points = (int)distance;
```

This is a legal assignment.

The expression `(int)distance` is called a type cast. This does not change the value stored in the variable `distance`, but it does change the value returned by the expression. Thus, in the assignment

```
points = (int)distance;
```

neither `distance` nor the value stored in `distance` is changed in any way. But the value stored in `points` is the "int version" of the value stored in `distance`. If the value of `distance` is `9.0`, the value of `distance` remains `9.0`, but `9` is the value assigned to `points`.

It is important to note that a type cast does not change the value of the source variable in an expression like `(int)distance`. An expression like `(int)25.36` or `(int)distance` is an expression that *produces* an `int` value. So if the value of `distance` is `25.36`, then the value of `(int)distance` is `25`, but the value of `distance` is still `25.36`. The situation is analogous to computing the number of (whole) dollars you have in an amount of money. If you have $25.36, the number of dollars you have is 25, but the $25.36 has not changed; it has merely been used to produce the whole number 25. For example, consider the following code:

```
double dinnerBill;
dinnerBill = 25.36;
int dinnerBillPlusTip = (int)dinnerBill + 5;
System.out.println(
        "The value of dinnerBillPlusTip is " + dinnerBillPlusTip);
```

The expression `(int)dinnerBill` produces the value 25, so the output of this code would be

```
The value of dinnerBillPlusTip is 30
```

But the variable `dinnerBill` still contains the value `25.36`.

Be sure to note that when you type cast from a `double` to an `int` (or from any floating-point type to any integer type), the amount is not rounded. The part after the decimal point is simply discarded. This is known as **truncating.** For example, consider the following:

truncating

```
double dinnerBill;
dinnerBill = 26.99;
int numberOfDollars;
numberOfDollars = (int)dinnerBill;
```

This does not set `numberOfDollars` to 27. It sets `numberOfDollars` to 26. The result is *not rounded.*

As we mentioned previously, when you assign an integer value to a variable of a floating-point type (such as a variable of type double), the integer is automatically type cast to the type of the variable. For example, consider

```
double point;
point = 7;
```

This assignment statement is equivalent to

```
point = (double)7;
```

The type cast (double) is implicit in the first version of the assignment.

Quick Reference: **Type Casting**

In many situations, you are not allowed to store a value of one type in a variable of another type. In these situations, you must use a **type cast** that converts the value to an "equivalent" value of the target type.

Syntax:

(*Type_Name*) *Expression*

Example:

```
double guess;
guess = 7.8;
int answer;
answer = (int)guess;
```

The value stored in answer will be 7. Note that the value is truncated, *not rounded*. Note also that the variable guess is not changed in any way. The assignment statement affects only the value stored in answer.

■ **Java Tip**
Type Casting a Character to an Integer

Java sometimes treats values of type char as integers, but the assignment of integers to characters has no connection to the meaning of the characters. For example, the following type cast will output the int value corresponding to the character '7':

```
char symbol;
symbol = '7';
System.out.println((int)symbol);
```

You might expect the preceding to output 7 to the screen, but it does not. It outputs the number 55. Java (and all other programming languages) use an arbitrary numbering of characters so as to produce an integer corresponding to each character. In this correspondence, there is nothing special about the digits; they are just characters the same as the letters or the plus sign. Thus, no effort was made to have the digits correspond to their intuitive values. Basically, they just wrote down all the characters and then numbered them in the order they were written down. The character **'7'** just happened to get 55. (This numbering system is called the Unicode system, which we discuss later in the chapter. If you have heard of the ASCII numbering system, the Unicode system is the same as the ASCII system for the characters of the English language.) ☐

● **Programming Tip**
Initialize Variables

uninitialized
variable

A variable that has been declared, but that has not yet been given a value by an assignment statement (or in some other way), is said to be **uninitialized.** If the variable is a class variable, it literally has no value. If the variable is a variable of a primitive type, it may have some default value. However, your program will be clearer if you explicitly give the variable a value, even if you are simply reassigning the default value. (The exact details on default values have been known to change and should not be counted on.)

One easy way to ensure that you do not have an uninitialized variable is to initialize it within the declaration. Simply combine the declaration and an assignment statement, as in the following examples:

```java
int count = 0;
double taxRate = 0.075;
char grade = 'A';
int balance = 1000, newBalance;
```

Note that you can initialize some variables and not initialize others in a declaration.

Sometimes the compiler may complain that you have failed to initialize a variable. In most cases, that will indeed be true. Occasionally, though, the compiler is mistaken in giving this advice. However, the compiler will not compile your program until you convince it that the variable in question is initialized. To make the compiler happy, initialize the variable when you declare it, even if the variable will be given another value before it is used for anything. In such cases, you cannot argue with the compiler. ○

Quick Reference: **Combining a Variable Declaration and an Assignment**

You can combine the declaration of a variable with an assignment statement that gives the variable a value.

Syntax:

Type Variable_1 = Expression_1, Variable_2 = Expression_2, ...;

Example:

```java
int numberSeen = 0, increment = 5;
double height = 12.34, prize = 7.3 + increment;
char answer = 'y';
```

▲ *Gotcha*

Imprecision in Floating-Point Numbers

Floating-point numbers are stored with a limited amount of accuracy and so are, for all practical purposes, only approximate quantities. For example, the floating-point number `1.0/3.0` is equal to

    0.3333333...

where the three dots indicate that the 3s go on forever. The computer stores numbers in a format somewhat like the decimal representation on the previously displayed line, but it has room for only a limited number of digits. If it can store only 10 digits after the decimal, then `1.0/3.0` is stored as

    0.3333333333 (and no more 3s)

Thus, `1.0/3.0` is stored as a number that is slightly smaller than one-third. In other words, the value stored as `1.0/3.0` is only approximately equal to one-third. In reality, the computer stores numbers in binary notation, rather than in base 10, but the principles are the same and the same sorts of things happen. Some floating-point numbers lose accuracy when they are stored in the computer.

Floating-point numbers (like numbers of type `double`) and integers (like numbers of type `int`) are stored differently. As we indicated in the previous paragraph, floating-point numbers are, in effect, stored as approximate quantities. Integers, on the other hand, are stored as exact quantities. This difference sometimes can be subtle. For example, the numbers 5 and `5.0` are conceptually the same number. But Java considers them to be different. The whole number 5 is of type `int` and is an exact quantity. The number `5.0` is of type `double` because it contains a fractional part (even though the fraction is 0), and so `5.0` is stored with only a limited degree of accuracy. △

? Self-Test Questions

1. Which of the following may be used as variable names in Java?

   `rate1, 1stPlayer, myprogram.java, long, TimeLimit, numberOfWindows`

2. Can a Java program have two different variables with the names `aVariable` and `avariable`?

3. Give the declaration for a variable called `count` of type `int`. The variable should be initialized to zero in the declaration.

4. Give the declaration for two variables of type `double`. The variables are to be named `rate` and `time`. Both variables should be initialized to zero in the declaration.

5. Write the declaration for two variables called `miles` and `flowRate`. Declare the variable `miles` to be of type `int` and initialize it to zero in the declaration. Declare the variable `flowRate` to be of type `double` and initialize it to `50.56` in the declaration.

6. Write a Java assignment statement that will set the value of the variable `interest` to the value of the variable `balance` multiplied by `0.05`.

7. Write a Java assignment statement that will set the value of the variable `interest` to the value of the variable `balance` multiplied by the value of the variable `rate`. The variables are of type `double`.

8. Write a Java assignment statement that will increase the value of the variable `count` by 3. The variable is of type `int`.

9. What is the output produced by the following lines of program code?

```
char a, b;
a = 'b';
System.out.println(a);
b = 'c';
System.out.println(b);
a = b;
System.out.println(a);
```

10. In the Java Tip entitled "Type Casting a Character to an Integer," you saw that the following does not output the integer 7:

```
char symbol;
symbol = '7';
System.out.println((int)symbol);
```

Thus, `(int)symbol` does not produce the number corresponding to the digit in `symbol`. Can you give an expression that will work to produce the integer that intuitively corresponds to the digit in `symbol` (assuming that `symbol` contains one of the 10 digits `'0'`, `'1'`, ..., `'9'`)? *Hint*: The digits do correspond to consecutive integers, so if `(int)'7'` is 55, then `(int)'8'` is 56.

11. What is the output produced by the following code?

```
int result = 10;
result *= 3;
System.out.println("result is " + result);
```

Arithmetic Operators

In Java, you can form arithmetic expressions involving addition (+), subtraction (−), multiplication (*), and division (/) in basically the same way that you would form them in ordinary arithmetic or algebra. You can combine variables or numbers by using the arithmetic operators +, −, *, and /. The meaning of such an expression is basically what you expect it to be, but there are some subtleties about the type of the result and, occasionally, even about the value of the result. All of the arithmetic operators can be used with numbers of any of the integer types, any of the floating-point types, and even with numbers of differing types. The type of the value produced depends on the types of the numbers being combined.

mixing types

Let's start our discussion with simple expressions that combine only two variables, two numbers, or a variable and a number. If both operands (i.e., each number or variable) are of the same type, then the result is of that type. If one of the operands is of a floating-point type and the other is of an integer type, the result is of the floating-point type. For example, consider the expression

```
amount - adjustment
```

If the variables `amount` and `adjustment` are both of type `int`, the result (the value returned) is of type `int`. If either `amount` or `adjustment`, or both, are of type `double`, then the result is of type `double`. If you replace the operator – with any of the operators +, *, or /, the type of the result is determined in the same way.

Larger expressions using more than two operands can always be viewed as a series of steps, each of which involves only two operands. For example, to evaluate the expressions

```
balance + (balance*rate)
```

you (or the computer) evaluate `balance*rate` and obtain a number, and then you combine that number with `balance`, using addition. This means that the same rule we used to determine the type of an expression with two operands can also be used for more complicated expressions: If all of the items being combined are of the same type, the result is of that type; if some of the items being combined are of integer types and some are of floating-point types, then the result is of a floating-point type.

Knowing whether the value produced is of an integer type or a floating-point type is typically all that you need to know. However, if you need to know the exact type of the value produced by an arithmetic expression, you can determine it as follows: The type of the value produced is one of the types used in the expression. Of all the types used in the expression, it is the last type (reading from left to right) on the following list:

```
byte-->short-->int-->long-->float-->double
```

Note that this is the same sequence as the one used to determine automatic type conversions.

The division operator (/) deserves special attention, because the type of the result can affect the value produced in a dramatic way. When you combine two numbers with the division operator and at least one of the numbers is of type `double` (or of some other floating-point type), the result is what you would normally expect of a division. For example, `9.0/2` has one operand of type `double`, namely, `9.0`. Hence, the result is the type `double` number `4.5`. However, when both operands are of an integer type, the result can be surprising. For example, `9/2` has two operands of type `int`, so it yields the type `int` result 4, not `4.5`. The fraction after the decimal point is simply lost. Be sure to notice that when you divide two integers, the result *is not rounded*; the part after the decimal point is discarded (truncated), no matter how large it is. So, `11/3` is 3 (not `3.6666`...). If there is nothing but a zero after the decimal point, that decimal point and zero after the decimal point are still lost, and even this seemingly trivial difference can be of some significance. For example, `8.0/2` evaluates to the type `double` value `4.0`, which is only an approximate quantity. However, `8/2` evaluates to the `int` value 4, which is an exact quantity. The approximate nature of `4.0` can affect the accuracy of any further calculation that is performed with this result.

The % **operator** can be used with operands of integer types to recover something equivalent to the fraction after the decimal point. When you divide one integer by another, you get a result (which some call a quotient) and a remainder. For example, 14 divided by 4 yields 3 with a remainder of 2. To rephrase it, 14 divided by 4 is 3 with 2 left over. The % operation gives the remainder—that is, the amount left over— after doing the division. So `14/4` evaluates to 3, and `14%4` evaluates to 2, because 14 divided by 4 is 3 with 2 left over.

division

integer division

the % operator

The % operator has more applications than you might at first suspect. It allows your program to count by 2s, 3s, or any other number. For example, if you want to do something to every other integer, you need to know whether the integer is even or odd, so you can perform the action on every even integer (or alternatively, on every odd integer). An integer n is even if n%2 is equal to 0, and the integer is odd if n%2 is equal to 1. Similarly, if you want your program to do something to every third integer, then your program can step through all the integers, using an int variable n to store the integer, and can test n%3. In this case, your program might perform the action only when n%3 is equal to 0.

Parentheses and Precedence Rules

parentheses

Parentheses can be used to group items in an arithmetic expression in the same way that you use parentheses in algebra and arithmetic. With the aid of parentheses, you can tell the computer which operations are performed first, second, and so forth. For example, consider the following two expressions that differ only in the positioning of their parentheses:

```
(cost + tax) * discount
cost + (tax * discount)
```

To evaluate the first expression, the computer first adds cost and tax and then multiplies the result by discount. To evaluate the second expression, it multiplies tax and discount and then adds the result to cost. If you use some numbers for the values of the variables and carry out the two evaluations, you will see that they produce different results.

If you omit the parentheses, the computer will still evaluate the expression. For example, consider the following assignment statement:

```
total = cost + tax * discount;
```

This is equivalent to

```
total = cost + (tax * discount);
```

precedence rules

When parentheses are omitted, the computer performs multiplication before addition. More generally, when the order of operations is not determined by parentheses, the computer will perform the operations in an order determined by the **precedence rules** shown in Display 2.3. (Display 2.3 shows all the operators we will use in this chapter. More precedence rules will be given in Chapter 3, and an even more complete list of precedence rules is given in Appendix 2.) Operators that are listed higher on the list are said to have **higher precedence.** When the computer is deciding which of two operations to perform first and the order is not dictated by parentheses, it performs the operation of higher precedence before the operation of lower precedence. Some operators have equal precedence, in which case the order of operations is determined by the left-to-right order of the operators. Binary operators of equal precedence are performed in left-to-right order. Unary operators of equal precedence are performed in right-to-left order.

unary operator

A **unary operator** is an operator that has only one argument (one thing that it applies to), like the operator − in the assignment statement

```
bankBalance = −cost;
```

■ DISPLAY 2.3   **Precedence Rules**

Highest Precedence

First: the unary operators: +, −, ++, −−, and !
Second: the binary arithmetic operators: *, /, and %
Third: the binary arithmetic operators: + and −

Lowest Precedence

A **binary operator** has two arguments, like the operators + and * in

    total = cost + (tax * discount);

binary operator

Note that the same operator symbol can sometimes be used as both a unary and a binary operator. For example, the − and + symbols can serve as either binary or unary operators.

These precedence rules are similar to the rules used in algebra classes. However, except for some very standard cases, it is best to include the parentheses, even if the intended order of operations is the one indicated by the precedence rules. The parentheses make the expression clearer to a person reading the program code. One standard case in which it is normal to omit parentheses is a multiplication within an addition. Thus,

    balance = balance + (interestRate*balance);

would usually be written

    balance = balance + interestRate*balance;

Both forms are acceptable, and the two forms have the same meaning.

When writing arithmetic expressions, you can include spaces before and after operations or you can omit them. Similarly, you can include or omit spaces around parentheses.

spacing

Display 2.4 shows some examples of how you write arithmetic expressions in Java and indicates some of the parentheses that you can normally omit.

■ DISPLAY 2.4   **Arithmetic Expressions in Java**

Ordinary Mathematical Expression	Java Expression (Preferred Form)	Equivalent Fully Parenthesized Java Expression
$rate^2 + delta$	rate*rate + delta	(rate*rate) + delta
$2(salary + bonus)$	2*(salary + bonus)	2*(salary + bonus)
$\dfrac{1}{time + 3mass}$	1/(time + 3*mass)	1/(time + (3*mass))
$\dfrac{a-7}{t+9v}$	(a − 7)/(t + 9*v)	(a − 7)/(t + (9*v))

Case Study
Vending Machine Change

Vending machines often have small computers to control their operation. In this case study, you will write a program that handles one of the tasks that such a computer would need to perform. The input and output will be performed via the keyboard and screen. To integrate this program into a vending machine computer, you would have to embed the code from the program into a larger program that takes its data from someplace other than the keyboard and sends its results to someplace other than the screen, but that's another story. In this case study, the user enters an amount of change from 1 to 99 cents. The program responds by telling the user one combination of coins that equals that amount of change.

For example, if the user enters 55 for 55 cents, the program tells the user that 55 cents can be given as two quarters and one nickel (i.e., two 25-cent coins and one 5-cent coin). You decide that the dialog should read like the following example, which you write out to see how it looks before coding the program:

```
Enter a whole number from 1 to 99.
I will output a combination of coins
that equal that amount of change.
87
87 cents in coins:
3 quarters
1 dime
0 nickels and
2 pennies
```

data

The program will need variables to store the amount of change and the number of each type of coin. So it will need at least the following variables:

```
int amount, quarters, dimes, nickels, pennies;
```

That takes care of some routine matters, and now you are ready to tackle the heart of the problem. You need an algorithm to compute the number of each kind of coin. You come up with the following algorithm:

pseudocode
first try

Algorithm to determine the number of coins in `amount` cents:

Read the amount into the variable `amount`.

Set the variable `quarters` equal to the maximum number of quarters in `amount`.

Reset `amount` to the change left after giving out that many quarters.

Set the variable `dimes` equal to the maximum number of dimes in `amount`.

Reset `amount` to the change left after giving out that many dimes.

Set the variable `nickels` equal to the maximum number of nickels in `amount`.

Reset `amount` to the change left after giving out that many nickels.

```
pennies = amount;
```
Output the original amount and the numbers of each coin.

pseudocode

This algorithm is expressed in **pseudocode,** which is any convenient combination of Java and English used to express an algorithm before the algorithm is translated into Java.

When you look at your pseudocode, you realize that the algorithm changes the value of amount. However, you want to have the original amount at the end so that you can output it. So you use one more variable, called originalAmount, to save the original amount. You modify the pseudocode as follows:

Algorithm to determine the number of coins in amount cents:

Read the amount into the variable amount.

```
originalAmount = amount;
```
Set the variable quarters equal to the maximum number of quarters in amount.

Reset amount to the change left after giving out that many quarters.

Set the variable dimes equal to the maximum number of dimes in amount.

Reset amount to the change left after giving out that many dimes.

Set the variable nickels equal to the maximum number of nickels in amount.

Reset amount to the change left after giving out that many nickels.

```
pennies = amount;
```
Output originalAmount and the numbers of each coin.

pseudocode
revised

You now need to produce Java code that does the same thing as your pseudocode. Much of it is routine. The first line of your pseudocode simply calls for prompting the user and then reading input from the keyboard. You produce the following Java code for this first line of pseudocode:

coding

```
System.out.println("Enter a whole number from 1 to 99.");
System.out.println("I will output a combination of coins");
System.out.println("that equals that amount of change.");

amount = SavitchIn.readLineInt();
```

The next line of pseudocode, which sets the value of originalAmount, is already Java code, so you need not do any translating.

Thus far, the main part of your program reads as follows:

```
public static void main(String[] args)
{
    int amount, originalAmount,
        quarters, dimes, nickels, pennies;

    System.out.println("Enter a whole number from 1 to 99.");
    System.out.println("I will output a combination of coins");
    System.out.println("that equals that amount of change.");
```

```
        amount = SavitchIn.readLineInt( );
        originalAmount = amount;
```

Next, you need to translate the following to Java code:

Set the variable `quarters` equal to the maximum number of quarters in `amount`.

Reset `amount` to the change left after giving out that many quarters.

integer division
/ and %

You give this some thought and decide to try an example. For 55 cents, there are 2 quarters, because 55 divided by 25 is 2 with a remainder of 5. Ah! You realize that the operators / and % can be used for this kind of division. For example,

    55/25 is 2 (the maximum number of 25s in 55)
    55%25 is 5 (the remainder)

Replacing 55 with `amount` and changing to Java syntax, you produce the following:

```
    quarters = amount/25;
    amount = amount%25;
```

You realize that dimes and nickels are treated in a similar way, so you next produce the following code:

```
    dimes = amount/10;
    amount = amount%10;
    nickels = amount/5;
    amount = amount%5;
```

The rest of the program coding is straightforward. You produce the program shown in Display 2.5 as your final program.

testing

After producing your program, you need to test it on a number of different kinds of data. You decide to test it on each of the following inputs: 0 cents, 4 cents, 5 cents, 6 cents, 10 cents, 11 cents, 25 cents, 26 cents, 35 cents, 55 cents, 65 cents, and a number of other cases. This sounds like a lot of different inputs, but you want to try cases that give zero values for all possible coin values, and you want to test values near change points, like 25 and 26 cents, which changes from all quarters to quarters and another coin. All your tests are successful, but the grammar for the output is not exactly correct. For 26 cents, you get the output

```
    26 cents in coins:
    1 quarters
    0 dimes
    0 nickels and
    1 pennies
```

The output is correct, but would read a lot better if it said `1 quarter` instead of `1 quarters` and `1 penny` instead of `1 pennies`. The techniques you need to produce this nicer looking output will be presented in the next chapter. For now, let's end this project here. The output is correct and understandable. ■

■ DISPLAY 2.5   **Change-Making Program**

```java
public class ChangeMaker
{
    public static void main(String[] args)
    {
        int amount, originalAmount,
            quarters, dimes, nickels, pennies;

        System.out.println("Enter a whole number from 1 to 99.");
        System.out.println("I will output a combination of coins");
        System.out.println("that equals that amount of change.");

        amount = SavitchIn.readLineInt();
        originalAmount = amount;

        quarters = amount/25;
        amount = amount%25;
        dimes = amount/10;
        amount = amount%10;
        nickels = amount/5;
        amount = amount%5;
        pennies = amount;

        System.out.println(originalAmount
                        + " cents in coins can be given as:");
        System.out.println(quarters + " quarters");
        System.out.println(dimes + " dimes");
        System.out.println(nickels + " nickels and");
        System.out.println(pennies + " pennies");
    }
}
```

25 goes into 87 three times with 12 left over.
87/25 is 3.
87%25 is 12.
87 cents is three quarters with 12 cents left over.

Sample Screen Dialog

```
Enter a whole number from 1 to 99.
I will output a combination of coins
that equals that amount of change.
87
87 cents in coins can be given as:
3 quarters
1 dimes
0 nickels and
2 pennies
```

12. What is the output produced by the following lines of program code?

```
int quotient, remainder;
quotient = 7/3;
remainder = 7%3;
System.out.println("quotient = " + quotient);
System.out.println("remainder = " + remainder);
```

13. What is the output produced by the following lines of program code?

```
double result;
result = (1/2) * 2;
System.out.println("(1/2) * 2 equals " + result);
```

14. Consider the following statement from the program in Display 2.5:

```
System.out.println(originalAmount
                + " cents in coins can be given as:");
```

Suppose that you replaced the preceding line with the following:

```
System.out.println(amount
                + " cents in coins can be given as:");
```

How will this change the sample dialog in Display 2.5?

15. What is the output produced by the following code?

```
int result = 11;
result /= 2;
System.out.println("result is " + result);
```

Increment and Decrement Operators

The increment and decrement operators can be used to increase or decrease the value of a variable by 1. They are very specialized operators, and you (and Java) could easily get along without them. But they are sometimes handy, and they are of cultural significance because programmers use them. So to be "in the club," you should know how to use them. Even if you do not want to use them yourself, you need to be familiar with these operators so you can understand them when you see them in another programmer's code.

increment
operator ++

The **increment operator** is written as two plus signs (++). For example, the following will increase the value of the variable count by 1:

```
count++;
```

This is a Java statement. If the variable count has the value 5 before this statement is executed, it will have the value 6 after the statement is executed. You can use the increment operator with variables of any numeric type, but they are used most often with variables of integer types (such as the type int).

The **decrement operator** is similar, except that it subtracts 1 rather than adds 1 to the value of the variable. The decrement operator is written as two minus signs (−−). For example, the following will decrease the value of the variable count by 1:

```
count--;
```

If the variable count has the value 5 before this statement is executed, it will have the value 4 after the statement is executed.

Note that

```
count++;
```

is equivalent to

```
count = count + 1;
```

and

```
count--;
```

is equivalent to

```
count = count - 1;
```

As you can see, the increment and decrement operators are really very specialized. Why does Java have such specialized operators? It inherited them from C++ (and C++ inherited them from C). In fact, this increment operator is where the ++ came from in the name of the C++ programming language. Why was it added to the C and C++ languages? Because adding or subtracting 1 is a very common thing to do when programming.

More about the Increment and Decrement Operators

Although we do not recommend doing so, the increment and decrement operators can be used in expressions. When used in an expression, these operators both change the value of the variable they are applied to and return a value.

In expressions, you can place the ++ or −− either before or after the variable, but the meaning is different, depending on whether it is before or after the variable. For example, consider the code

```
int n = 3;
int m = 4;
int result;
result = n * (++m);
```

After this code is executed, the value of n is unchanged at 3, the value of m is 5, and the value of result is 15. Thus, ++m both changes the value of m and returns that changed value to be used in the arithmetic expression.

In the previous example, we placed the increment operator in front of the variable. If we place it after the variable m, something slightly different happens. Consider the code

```
int n = 3;
int m = 4;
int result;
result = n * (m++);
```

In this case, after the code is executed, the value of n is 3 and the value of m is 5, just as in the previous case, but the value of `result` is 12, not 15. What is the story?

The two expressions n * (++m) and n * (m++) both increase the value of m by 1, but the first expression increases the value of m *before* it does the multiplication, whereas the second expression increases the value of m *after* it does the multiplication. Both ++m and m++ have the same effect on the final value of m, but when you use them as part of an arithmetic expression, they give a different value to the expression. If the ++ is *before* the m, then the value of m is increased *before* its value is used in the expression. If the ++ is *after* the m, then the value of m is increased *after* its value is used in the expression.

The −− operator works the same way when it is used in an arithmetic expression. Both −−m and m−− have the same effect on the final value of m, but when you use them as part of an arithmetic expression, they give a different value to the expression. If the −− is *before* the m, the value of m is decreased *before* its value is used in the expression. If the −− is *after* the m, the value of m is decreased *after* its value is used in the expression.

The increment and decrement operators can be applied only to variables. They cannot be applied to constants or to more complicated arithmetic expressions.

? Self-Test Questions

16. What is the output produced by the following lines of program code?

```
int n = 2;
n++;
System.out.println("n == " + n);
n--;
System.out.println("n == " + n);
```

2.2 THE CLASS String

Words, words, mere words, no matter from the heart. -William Shakespeare, *Troilus and Cressida*

String

Strings of characters, such as `"Enter the amount:"`, are treated slightly differently from values of the primitive types. There is no primitive type for strings in Java. However, there is a class called `String` that can be used to store and process strings of characters. In this section, we introduce you to the class `String`.

String Constants and Variables

You have already been using constants of type `String`. The quoted string

```
"Enter a whole number from 1 to 99."
```

which appears in the following statement from the program in Display 2.5, is a string constant:

```
System.out.println("Enter a whole number from 1 to 99.");
```

A value of type `String` is one of these quoted strings. That is, a value of type `String` is a sequence of characters treated as a single item. A variable of type `String` can name one of these string values.

The following declares `greeting` to be the name for a `String` variable:

```
String greeting;
```

The following sets the value of `greeting` to the `String` value `"Hello!"`:

```
greeting = "Hello!";
```

These two statements are often combined into one, as follows:

```
String greeting = "Hello!";
```

Once a `String` variable, such as `greeting`, has been given a value, you can write it out to the screen as follows:

```
System.out.println(greeting);
```

If the value of `greeting` has been set as we just described, this statement will cause

```
Hello!
```

to be written on the screen

Concatenation of Strings

You can connect two strings using the + operator. Connecting ("pasting") two strings together to obtain a larger string is called **concatenation.** So when it is used with strings, the + symbol is sometimes called the **concatenation operator.** For example, consider the following:

+ operator
concatenation

```
String greeting = "Hello";
String sentence;
sentence = greeting + "my friend.";
System.out.println(sentence);
```

This will set the variable `sentence` to `"Hellomy friend."` and will write the following on the screen:

```
Hellomy friend.
```

Notice that no spaces are added when you concatenate two strings by means of the + operator. If you wanted `sentence` set to `"Hello my friend."`, you could change the assignment statement to

```
sentence = greeting + " my friend.";
```

Notice the space before the word `"my"`.

You can concatenate any number of `String` objects with the use of the + operator. You can even connect a `String` object to any other type of object via the + operator. The result is always a `String` object. Java will figure out some way to express any object as a string when you connect it to a string with the + operator. For simple things like numbers, it does the obvious thing. For example,

```
String solution = "The answer is " + 42;
```

will set the `String` variable `solution` to `"The answer is 42"`. This is so natural that it may seem as though nothing special is happening, but it does require a conversion from one type to another. The constant 42 is a number, whereas `"42"` is a string consisting of the character '4' followed by the character '2'. Java converts the number constant 42 to the string constant "42" and then concatenates the two strings "The answer is " and "42" to obtain the longer string "The answer is 42".

Quick Reference: **Using the + Sign with Strings**

You can concatenate two strings by connecting them with the + sign.

Example:

```
String name = "Chiana";
String greeting = "Hi " + name;
System.out.println(greeting);
```

This sets `greeting` to the string "Hi Chiana" and then outputs the following to the screen:

```
Hi Chiana
```

Note that we needed to add a space at the end of "Hi ".

Classes

class

Classes are central to Java, and you will soon be defining and using your own classes much more than we do in these first few chapters. However, this discussion of the class `String` gives us an opportunity to introduce some of the notation and terminology used for classes.

object

A **class** is a type whose values are objects. **Objects** are entities that store data and can take actions. For example, objects of the class `String` store data consisting of strings of charac-

method

ters, such as "Hello". The actions that an object can take are called **methods.** Most of the methods for the class `String` return, or produce, some value. For example, the method `length( )` returns the number of characters in a `String` object. So "Hello".length( ) returns the integer 5 and can be stored in an `int` variable as follows:

```
int n = "Hello".length( );
```

method call or
method invocation

As indicated by the example "Hello".length( ), you call a method into action by writing a name for the object, followed by a dot, followed by the method name, and ending with parentheses. When you call a method into action, you are (or your code is) said

calling object

to **invoke** the method or **call** the method, and the object before the dot is known as the **calling object.**

Although you can call a method with a constant object, as in "Hello".length( ), it is more common to use a variable that names an object as the calling object, as illustrated by the following:

```
String greeting = "Hello";
int n = greeting.length( );
```

Information for the method invocation is given in the parentheses. In some cases, such as the method `length`, no information is needed (other than the data in the calling object), and the parentheses are empty. In other cases, as you will see soon, some information must be provided inside the parentheses. The information in parentheses is known as an

argument

argument (or arguments).

All objects within a class have the same methods, but each object can have different data. For example the two `String` objects `"Hello"` and `"Good-Bye"` have different data—that is, different strings of characters. However, they have the same methods. Thus, since we know that the `String` object `"Hello"` has the method `length( )`, we know that the `String` object `"Good-Bye"` must also have the method `length( )`.

Quick Reference: **Objects, Methods, and Classes**

An **object** is a program construction that has data (that is, information) associated with it and that can perform certain actions. The actions performed by objects are called **methods.** A **class** is a type or kind of object. Different objects in the same class can have different data, but all objects in the same class have the same kinds of data and the same methods. When an object performs the action of a method, the object is said to **invoke** the method or **call** the method. The syntax for a method invocation is to write down a name for the object, followed by a dot, and then ending with a possibly empty set of parentheses. The parentheses enclose some information to use when the method is invoked. This information in parentheses is known as the method's **argument(s)**.

You have now seen two kinds of types in Java: primitive types and class types. The main difference you have seen between these two kinds of types is that classes have methods and primitive types do not have methods. A smaller difference is that all the primitive types are spelled using only lowercase letters, but by convention, class types are spelled with their first letter in uppercase, as in `String`. Later you will see more differences between classes and primitive types.

String Methods

A `String` variable is not just a simple variable, as a variable of type `int` is. A `String` variable is a variable of a class type that can name an object, and an object has methods as well as a value. These `String` methods can be used to manipulate string values. A few of the `String` methods are described in Display 2.6. As with any method, you call (or invoke) a `String` method by writing a dot and the name of the method after the object name. In this section, the object name will always be a variable of type `String`. Any arguments to the method are given in parentheses. Let's look at some examples.

■ DISPLAY 2.6   **Methods in the Class `String` (Part 1 of 4)**

Method	Description	Example
`length( )`	*Returns the length of the `String` object.*	`String greeting = "Hello!";` `greeting.length( )` *returns* 6.

`equals(Other_String)`	*Returns* `true` *if the calling object string and the Other_String are equal. Otherwise, returns* `false`.	`String greeting =`
		`  SavitchIn.readLine( );`
		`if (greeting.equals("Hi"))`
		`System.out.println(`
		`  "Informal Greeting.");`

■ DISPLAY 2.6   **Methods in the Class** `String` *(Part 2 of 4)*

Method	Description	Example

`equalsIgnoreCase(`
Other_String`)`
	Returns `true` *if the calling object string and the* Other_String *are equal, considering uppercase and lowercase versions of a letter to be the same. Otherwise, returns* `false`.	*If a program contains*
		`String s1 = "mary!";`
		then after this assignment,
		`s1.equalsIgnoreCase("Mary!")`
		returns `true`.

`toLowerCase()`	*Returns a string with the same characters as the calling object string, but with all characters converted to lowercase.*	`String greeting = "Hi Mary!";`
		`greeting.toLowerCase()`
		returns
		`"hi mary!"`

`toUpperCase()`	*Returns a string with the same characters as the calling object string, but with all characters converted to uppercase.*	`String greeting = "Hi Mary!";`
		`greeting.toUpperCase()`
		returns
		`"HI MARY!"`

`trim()`	*Returns a string with the same characters as the calling object string, but with leading and trailing whitespace removed.*	`String pause = "    Hmm     ";` `pause.trim()` *returns* `"Hmm"`
`charAt(`*Position*`)`	*Returns the character in the calling object string at* Position. *Positions are counted 0, 1, 2, etc.*	`String greeting = "Hello!";` `greeting.charAt(0)` *returns* `'H'`. `greeting.charAt(1)` *returns* `'e'`.
`substring(`*Start*`)`	*Returns the substring of the calling object string from position* Start *through to the end of the calling object. Positions are counted 0, 1, 2, etc.*	`String sample = "AbcdefG";` `sample.substring(2)` *returns* `"cdefG"`.

■ DISPLAY 2.6   **Methods in the Class** String *(Part 3 of 4)*

Method	Description	Example
substring(*Start*, *End*)	*Returns the substring of the calling object string from position Start through, but not including, position End of the calling object. Positions are counted 0, 1, 2, etc.*	`String sample = "AbcdefG";` `sample.substring(2, 5)` *returns* `"cde"`.
indexOf(*A_String*)	*Returns the position of the first occurrence of the string A_String in the calling object string. Positions are counted 0, 1, 2, etc. Returns −1 if A_String is not found.*	`String greeting = "Hi Mary!";` `greeting.indexOf("Mary")` *returns 3.* `greeting.indexOf("Sally")` *returns −1.*
indexOf(*A_String*, *Start*)	*Returns the position of the first occurrence of the string A_String in the calling object string that occurs at or after position Start. Positions are counted 0, 1, 2, etc. Returns −1 if A_String is not found.*	`String name =` `"Mary, Mary quite contrary";` `name.indexOf("Mary", 1)` *returns 6. The same value is returned if 1 is replaced by any number up to and including 6.* `name.indexOf("Mary", 0)` *returns 0.* `name.indexOf("Mary", 8)` *returns −1.*
lastIndexOf(*A_String*)	*Returns the position of the last occurrence of the string A_String in the calling object string. Positions are counted 0, 1, 2, etc. Returns −1 if A_String is not found.*	`String name =` `"Mary, Mary, Mary quite so";` `name.lastIndexOf("Mary")` *returns 12.*

■ DISPLAY 2.6   **Methods in the Class** `String` *(Part 4 of 4)*

Method	Description	Example
`compareTo(`*A_String*`)`	*Compares the calling object string with A_String to see which comes first in the lexicographic ordering. Lexicographic ordering is the same as alphabetical ordering when both strings are either all uppercase or all lowercase. If the calling string is first,* `compareTo` *returns a negative value. If the two strings are equal, it returns zero. If the argument is first, it returns a positive number.*	`String entry = "adventure";` `entry.compareTo("zoo")` *returns a negative number.* `entry.compareTo("adventure")` *returns zero.* `entry.compareTo("above")` *returns a positive number.*

length

> As we've already noted, the method `length` can be used to find out the number of characters in a string. For example, suppose we declare `String` variables as follows:

```
String command = "Sit Fido!";
String answer = "bow-wow";
```

Then `command.length( )` returns 9 and `answer.length( )` returns 7. Notice that spaces, special symbols, and repeated characters are all counted when computing the length of a string.

You can use a call to the method `length` anywhere that you can use a value of type `int`. For example, all of the following are legal Java statements:

```
int count = command.length( );
System.out.println("Length is " + command.length( ));
count = command.length( ) + 3;
```

position

index

> Many of the methods for the class `String` depend on counting **positions** in the string. Positions are counted starting with 0, not with 1. So in the string "Hi Mom", 'H' is in position 0, 'i' is in position 1, the blank character is in position 2, and so forth. A position is usually referred to as an **index** in computer parlance. So it would be more normal to say 'H' is at index 0, 'i' is at index 1, the blank character is at index 2, and so forth. Display 2.7 illustrates how index positions are numbered in a string.

The method `indexOf` will return the index of the substring given as its one argument. If the substring occurs more than once, `indexOf` returns the index of the first occurrence of its substring argument. For example, consider

```
String phrase = "Time flies like an arrow.";
```

After this declaration, the invocation `phrase.indexOf("flies")` will return 5 because the 'f' of "flies" is at index 5. (Remember, the first index is 0, not 1.)

■ DISPLAY 2.7   **String Indices**

The twelve characters in the string `"Java is fun."` have indices 0 through 11. The index of each character is shown above it.

0	1	2	3	4	5	6	7	8	9	10	11
J	a	v	a		i	s		f	u	n	.

Note that the blanks and the period count as characters in the string.

String Processing

Many reference books on the Java language say that objects of type `String` cannot be changed. In a sense, this is true, but it is a misleading statement. Notice that none of the methods in Display 2.7 changes the value of the `String` object. There are more `String` methods than those shown in Display 2.7, but none of them lets you write statements that say things like "Change the fifth character in the calling object string to `'z'`". This is not an accident. It was done intentionally in order to make the implementation of the `String` class more efficient—that is, to make the methods execute faster and use less computer memory. There is another string class, however, that has methods for altering the string object. It is called `StringBuffer`, but we will not discuss it here because we do not need it.

Although there is no method that allows you to change the value of a `String` object, such as `"Hello"`, you can still write programs that change the value of a `String` variable, which is probably all you want to do anyway. To make the change, you simply use an assignment statement, as in the following example:

```
String name = "D'Aargo";
name = "Ka " + name;
```

The assignment statement in the second line changes the value of the `name` variable from `"D'Aargo"` to `"Ka D'Aargo"`. Display 2.8 shows a sample program that demonstrates how to do some simple string processing that changes the value of a `String` variable. Part of that program is explained in the next subsection.

Escape Characters

Suppose you want to output a string that contains quotation marks. For example, suppose you want to output the following to the screen:

quotes in quotes

```
The word "Java" names a language, not just a drink!
```

The following will not work:

```
System.out.println(
    "The word "Java" names a language, not just a drink!");
```

■ DISPLAY 2.8   **Using the** `String` **Class**

```java
public class StringDemo
{
    public static void main(String[] args)
    {
        String sentence = "Text processing is hard!";
        int position;

        position = sentence.indexOf("hard");
        System.out.println(sentence);
        System.out.println("01234567890123456789 0123");
        System.out.println("The word \"hard\" starts at index "
                                    + position);

        sentence = sentence.substring(0, position) + "easy!";
        System.out.println("The changed string is:");
        System.out.println(sentence);
    }
}
```

The meaning of `\"` *is discussed in the subsection entitled "Escape Characters."*

Sample Screen Dialog

```
Text processing is hard!
01234567890123456789 0123
The word "hard" starts at index 19
The changed string is:
Text processing is easy!
```

This will produce a compiler error message. The problem is that the compiler sees

```
"The word "
```

as a perfectly valid quoted string. Then the compiler sees `Java"`, which is not anything valid in the Java language (although the compiler might guess that it is a quoted string with one missing quote or guess that you forgot a + sign). The compiler has no way to know that you mean to include the `'"'` symbol as part of the quoted string, unless you tell it that you mean to do so. You tell the compiler that you mean to include the quote in the string by placing a backslash (\) before the troublesome character, like so:

backslash \

```java
System.out.println(
    "The word \"Java\" names a language, not just a drink!");
```

Display 2.9 lists some other special characters that are indicated with a backslash. These are often called **escape sequences** or **escape characters,** because they escape from the usual meaning of a character, such as the usual meaning of the double quote.

escape
sequence or
character

It is important to note that each escape sequence is a single character, even though it is written as two symbols. So the string `"Say \"Hi\"!"` contains 9 characters (`'S'`, `'a'`, `'y'`, the blank character, `'\"'`, `'H'`, `'i'`, `'\"'`, and `'!'`), not 11 characters.

Including a backslash in a quoted string is a little tricky. For example, the string `"abc\def"` is likely to produce the error message "Invalid escape character." To include a backslash in a string, you need to use two backslashes. The string `"abc\\def"`, if output to the screen, would produce

```
abc\def
```

The escape sequence \n indicates that the string starts a new line at the \n. For example, the statement

```
System.out.println("The motto is\nGo for it!");
```

will write the following to the screen:

```
The motto is
Go for it!
```

It may seem that there is no need for the escape sequence \', since it is perfectly valid to include a single quote inside a quoted string, such as `"How's this?"`. But you do need to use \' if you want to indicate the constant for the single-quote character, as in

```
char singleQuote = '\'';
```

The Unicode Character Set

Most other programming languages use the ASCII character set, which is given in Appendix 3. The **ASCII** character set is simply a list of all the characters normally used on an English-language keyboard, together with a standard number assigned to each character. Java uses the Unicode character set instead. The **Unicode** character set includes the entire ASCII character set, plus many of the characters used in languages that have an alphabet different from English. As it turns out, this is not likely to be a big issue if you are using an English-language keyboard. Normally, you can just program as though Java were using

ASCII

Unicode

■ DISPLAY 2.9   **Escape Characters**

```
\"  Double quote.
\'  Single quote.
\\  Backslash.
\n  New line. Go to the beginning of the next line.
\r  Carriage return. Go to the beginning of the current line.
\t  Tab. Add whitespace up to the next tab stop.
```

the ASCII character set, because the ASCII character set is a subset of the Unicode character set. Thus, Appendix 3 can be thought of as listing the ASCII character set or as listing a subset of the Unicode character set. The advantage of the Unicode character set is that it makes it easy to handle languages other than English. The disadvantage is that it sometimes requires more computer memory to store each character than it would if Java used only the ASCII character set.

? Self-Test Questions

17. What is the output produced by the following?

```
String greeting = "How do you do";
System.out.println(greeting + "Seven of Nine.");
```

18. What is the output produced by the following?

```
String test = "abcdefg";
System.out.println(test.length());
System.out.println(test.charAt(1));
```

19. What is the output produced by the following?

```
String test = "abcdefg";
System.out.println(test.substring(3));
```

20. What is the output produced by the following?

```
System.out.println("abc\ndef");
```

21. What is the output produced by the following?

```
System.out.println("abc\\ndef");
```

22. What is the output produced by the following?

```
String test = "Hello John";
test = test.toUpperCase();
System.out.println(test);
```

23. What is the output produced by the following?

```
String s1 = "Hello John";
String s2 = "hello john";
if (s1.equals(s2))
    System.out.println("Equal");
System.out.println("End");
```

If you do not understand the if, see Display 1.5 in Chapter 1.

24. What is the output produced by the following?

```
String s1 = "Hello John";
String s2 = "hello john";
s1 = s1.toUpperCase();
```

```
        s2 = s2.toUpperCase( );
        if (s1.equals(s2))
            System.out.println("Equal");
        System.out.println("End");
```

If you do not understand the if, see Display 1.5 in Chapter 1.

2.3 KEYBOARD AND SCREEN I/O

Garbage in, garbage out. -Programmer's saying

Input and output of program data are usually referred to as **I/O.** There are many different ways that a Java program can perform I/O. In this section, we present some very simple ways to handle text input typed in at the keyboard and text output sent to the screen. In later chapters, we will discuss more elaborate ways to do I/O.

I/O

In order to do I/O in Java, you almost always need to add some classes to the language. Sometimes these are classes that, although not part of the language proper, are nonetheless provided in all implementations of Java. Other times, these classes are not provided along with the language, and you must write the classes yourself (or obtain them from whoever wrote the class definitions). In this section, we will do output using a class provided automatically with the Java language. However, Java does not provide a class that handles simple keyboard input, so we will do input using the class SavitchIn, which is not provided with the Java language, but was written expressly for readers of this text.

Screen Output

We have been using simple output statements since the beginning of this book. This section will simply summarize and explain what we have already been doing. In Display 2.5, we used statements such as the following to send output to the display screen:

System.out. println

```
        System.out.println("Enter a whole number from 1 to 99.");
                    . . .
        System.out.println(quarters + " quarters");
```

System.out is an object that is part of the Java language. It may seem strange to spell an object name with a dot in it, but that need not concern you at this point.

The object System.out has println as one of its methods. So the preceding output statements are calls to the method println of the object System.out. Of course, you need not be aware of these details in order to use these output statements. You can simply consider System.out.println to be one rather peculiarly spelled statement. However, you may as well get used to this dot notation and the notion of methods and objects.

In order to use output statements of this form, simply follow the expression System.out.println with what you want to output, enclosed in parentheses, and then follow that with a semicolon. You can output strings of text in double quotes, like "Enter a whole number from 1 to 99." or " quarters"; variables, like quarters;

numbers, like 5 or 7.3; and almost any other object or value. If you want to output more than one thing, simply place an addition sign between the things you want to output. For example,

```
System.out.println("Lucky number = " + 13
                        + "Secret number = " + number);
```

If the value of `number` is 7, the output will be

```
Lucky number = 13Secret number = 7
```

Notice that no spaces are added. If you want a space between the 13 and the word `Secret` in the preceding output (and you probably do), you should add a space at the beginning of the string

```
"Secret number = "
```

so that it becomes

```
" Secret number = "
```

Notice that you use double quotes, not single quotes, and that the left and right quotes are the same symbol. Finally, notice that it is OK to place the statement on two lines if it is too long. However, for readability, you should indent the second line, and you should break the line before or after a + sign. You cannot break a line in the middle of a quoted string or a variable name.

You can also use the `println` method to output the value of a `String` variable, as illustrated by the following:

```
String greeting = "Hello Programmers!";
System.out.println(greeting);
```

This will cause the following to be written on the screen:

```
Hello Programmers!
```

Every invocation of `println` ends a line of output. For example, consider the following statements:

```
System.out.println("One, two, buckle my shoe.");
System.out.println("Three, four, shut the door.");
```

These two statements will cause the following output to appear on the screen:

```
One, two, buckle my shoe.
Three, four, shut the door.
```

print versus println

If you want two or more output statements to place all of their output on a single line, use `print` instead of `println`. For example,

```
System.out.print("One, two,");
System.out.print(" buckle my shoe.");
System.out.println(" Three, four,");
System.out.println(" shut the door.");
```

will produce the following output:

```
One, two, buckle my shoe. Three, four,
  shut the door.
```

Notice that a new line is not started until you use a `println`, rather than a `print`. Notice also that the new line starts *after* the items specified in the `println` have been output. This is the only difference between `print` and `println`.

That is all you need to know in order to write programs with this sort of output, but we can still explain a bit more about what is happening. Consider the following statement:

```
System.out.println("The answer is " + 42);
```

The expression inside the parentheses should look familiar:

```
"The answer is " + 42
```

In the section on the class `String`, we said that you could use the + operator to concatenate a string, such as `"The answer is "`, and another item, such as the number constant 42. The + operator inside these `System.out.println` statements is the same + operator that performs string concatenation. In the preceding `System.out.println` statement, Java converts the number constant 42 to the string `"42"` and then uses the + operator to obtain the string `"The answer is 42"`. The `System.out.println` statement then outputs the string `"The answer is 42"`. The `println` method always outputs strings. Technically speaking, it never outputs numbers, even though it looks as though it does.

Quick Reference: `println` Output

You can output one line with `System.out.println`. The items that are output can be quoted strings, variables, constants such as numbers, or almost any object you can define in Java.

Syntax:

```
System.out.println(Output_1 + Output_2 + ... + Output_Last);
```

Example:

```
System.out.println("Hello out there!");
System.out.println("Area = " + theArea + " square inches");
```

Quick Reference: `println` Versus `print`

`System.out.println` and `System.out.print` are almost the same method. The only difference is that with the `println` method, the *next* output goes on a *new line*, whereas with the `print` method, the next output will be placed on the *same line*.

Example:

```
System.out.print("one ");
System.out.print("two ");
System.out.println("three ");
System.out.print("four ");
```

will produce the following output

```
one two three
four
```

(The output would look the same whether the last line read `print` or `println`.)

Input Using `SavitchIn`

In order to do simple input in Java, you need to use some class that is defined for you (or that you define). In this section, we will handle input using the class `SavitchIn`, which is in the file `SavitchIn.java` provided with this text. `SavitchIn` is an extremely simple class, and once you learn a little more Java, you will have no problem understanding the code for this class definition. However, in the current section, we will not explain the definition of `SavitchIn`. We will explain only how to use the class `SavitchIn`.

It is very easy to obtain a copy of the class definition for `SavitchIn`. The definition is given in Appendix 4. However, there is no need to type it in. Simply copy the file `SavitchIn.java`, which is on the CD provided with this text, into the directory in which you keep your Java programs, and compile the class `SavitchIn.java`. At this point, you need not even read the definition of the class `SavitchIn`. Although it may seem strange at first to use a class definition without reading it, this is a common thing to do. A class definition is just another piece of software, and you use all kinds of software without reading their code. For example, you use an editor without ever seeing the code for the editor, you use the Java compiler without ever seeing the code for the Java compiler, and you use the Java classes `String` and `System` (as in `System.out`) without reading their definitions.

The class `SavitchIn` has methods that read a piece of data from the keyboard and return that data. When you place an invocation of one of these methods in an assignment statement, your program can read from the keyboard and place the data it reads into the variable on the left-hand side of the assignment operator. For example, the following statement from the program in Display 2.5 will read in one integer and make that integer the value of the variable `amount`:

```
amount = SavitchIn.readLineInt( );
```

You may be wondering why there is nothing in the parentheses after the name `readLineInt`. This is because the method `readLineInt` does not use any arguments. You must still include the parentheses, however.

`readLineInt`

The method `readLineInt` expects the user to input one integer (of type `int`) on a line by itself, possibly with space before or after it. If the user inputs anything else, then an error message is output to the screen and the user is asked to reenter the input. Input is read only after the user starts a new line, so nothing happens until the user presses the Enter key.

`readLine-`
`Double`

What if you want to read in a number of some type other than `int`? The methods `readLineLong`, `readLineFloat`, and `readLineDouble` work in exactly the same way as `readLineInt`, except that they read in values of type `long`, `float`, and `double`, respectively. For example, the following will read a single number of type `double` and store that number in the variable `measurement`:

```
double measurement;
measurement = SavitchIn.readLineDouble( );
```

You can use the method `readLineNonwhiteChar` to read in a single nonwhitespace character, as in the following example:

```
char symbol;
symbol = SavitchIn.readLineNonwhiteChar( );
```

Any whitespace characters at the start of the line will be ignored, and the first non-whitespace character on the line will be read. If there is more than one nonwhitespace character on the line, readLineNonwhiteChar will read the first such character and discard the rest of the input line. **Whitespace** characters are all characters that print as whitespace if you output them to paper (or to the screen). The only whitespace character you are likely to be concerned with at first is the blank space character. (The start of a new line and the tab symbol are also whitespace characters, but those details are not likely to concern you yet.)

whitespace

There is a slight difference between readLineNonwhiteChar and the methods that read a single number. For the methods readLineInt and readLineDouble, the input number must be on a line with nothing before or after the number, except possibly whitespace. The method readLineNonwhiteChar allows anything to be on the line after the first nonwhitespace character, but it ignores the rest of the line. That way, when the user enters a word such as yes, readLineNonwhiteChar can read the first letter, like 'y', and ignore the rest of the word yes.

If you want to read in an entire line, you would use the method readLine (without any Int or Double or such at the end). For example,

```
String sentence;
sentence = SavitchIn.readLine();
```

reads in one line of input and places the string that is read into the variable sentence.

The class SavitchIn also has other methods, some of which are discussed in the next subsection.

The equal sign in a statement such as the second of the two that follow is the assignment operator:

```
int number;
number = SavitchIn.readLineInt();
```

As we pointed out earlier, you can combine a declaration of a variable and an assignment of a value to that variable into one longer statement. So the previous two lines of code can be expressed more compactly as

```
int number = SavitchIn.readLineInt();
```

Remember: **SavitchIn Is Not Part of the Java Language**

The class SavitchIn is not part of the Java language and does not come with the Java language. You must add the class yourself. This class was defined by the author for readers of this book. It is named SavitchIn to remind you that it was written by Savitch and is not part of the Java language. The class SavitchIn is given in Appendix 4, and a copy is provided on the CD that accompanies the book.

Why do we use the class SavitchIn? Why don't we simply use the classes provided with the Java language? Unfortunately, the Java language does not provide any classes for simple keyboard input. If you want to read simple input from the keyboard, you must add some class or classes that can do so.

Remember: **Treat** `SavitchIn.java` **like Code That You Wrote**

Since the class `SavitchIn` is not part of the Java language, you must treat it just like code that you yourself wrote. You must compile the class `SavitchIn.java`, and you (or some software that runs automatically) must link it with your program. If you obey the following rules, you should not have any problems with `SavitchIn`: Place a copy of `SavitchIn.java` in the same directory (the same folder) as your Java program, compile both `SavitchIn.java` and your program, and then run your program.

Quick Reference: **Input Using** `SavitchIn`

You use methods in the class `SavitchIn` to read values from the keyboard. When you invoke one of these methods, you use the class name `SavitchIn` as if it were the calling object. In other words, a typical method invocation has the form

Variable = `SavitchIn.`*Method_Name*`( );`

Although there are other methods in `SavitchIn`, you should normally use the methods that include the word "`Line.`" These methods each read a single value, such as a number, on a line by itself. The value may have whitespace before or after it, but other characters should not be on the line. (The method `readLineNonwhiteChar` is an exception and does allow nonwhitespace to follow the character that it reads.) There is a different method for each type of value you want to read from the keyboard. You need to use the method that matches the type of the value to be read, such as `int` for a whole number or `char` for a single character.

(The method invocation `SavitchIn.readLineInt( )` returns an `int` value and can be used anyplace that an `int` value is allowed, such as in an arithmetic expression. The method invocation does not have to be used in a simple assignment statement as described shortly, but that is its most common usage. Similar remarks apply to the other methods, except that the type of the value returned is different for each method.)

Syntax:

```
Int_Variable = SavitchIn.readLineInt( );
Long_Variable = SavitchIn.readLineLong( );
Float_Variable = SavitchIn.readLineFloat( );
Double_Variable = SavitchIn.readLineDouble( );
Char_Variable = SavitchIn.readLineNonwhiteChar( );
String_Variable = SavitchIn.readLine( );
```

Example:

```
int count;
count = SavitchIn.readLineInt( );
long bigOne;
bigOne = SavitchIn.readLineLong( );
float increment;
increment = SavitchIn.readLineFloat( );
double distance;
distance = SavitchIn.readLineDouble( );
char letter;
letter = SavitchIn.readLineNonwhiteChar( );
```

```
String wholeLine;
wholeLine = SavitchIn.readLine();
```

More Input Methods

All the methods in the class SavitchIn that begin with readLine, such as readLine and readLineInt, always read an entire line of text. That is why their names start with "read line." But sometimes you do not want to read a whole line. For example, let's say you are given the input

```
2 4 6
```

You might want to read these three numbers with three statements that put the numbers into three different variables. You can do this with the method readInt. For example, the following might appear in a program:

```
System.out.println("Enter 3 numbers on one line:");
int n1, n2, n3;
n1 = SavitchIn.readInt();
n2 = SavitchIn.readInt();
n3 = SavitchIn.readInt();
```

The user will be given the prompt

```
Enter 3 numbers on one line:
```

Suppose that, in response to the prompt, the user enters the following, all on one line, and then presses the Enter key:

```
2 4 6
```

The program will give n1 the value 2, n2 the value 4, and n3 the value 6.

After an integer is read with readInt, the input continues on the same line (unless it happens to have reached the end of the line). For example, if the user enters

```
10 20 30
```

then the following code will set n equal to 10 and will set theRest equal to the string "20 30":

```
int n;
n = SavitchIn.readInt();
String theRest;
theRest = SavitchIn.readLine();
```

Remember: Prompt for Input

Always prompt the user when your program needs the user to input some data, as in the following example:

```
System.out.println("Enter the number of trolls:");
int trolls = SavitchIn.readLineInt();
```

Two other, similar methods in `SavitchIn` that read less than a whole line are `read-Double` and `readNonwhiteChar`. The only difference between these and `readInt` is that with `readDouble`, a value of type `double` is read, and with `readNonwhiteChar`, a nonwhitespace character is read. Recall that whitespace characters are blanks, tabs, and the new-line character. For the sort of simple things we will be doing, the only whitespace that will be relevant is the blank character.

whitespace

The methods `readInt`, `readDouble`, and `readNonwhiteChar` each require that the input items be separated by one or more blank spaces. Moreover, these methods do not prompt the user if the input format is incorrect. When using these methods, you need to be certain that the input will be entered correctly the first time.

The last method from the class `SavitchIn` that we will consider here is `readChar`. The method `readChar` reads whatever single character is next in the input stream. For example, consider the following:

```
char c1, c2, c3;
c1 = SavitchIn.readChar();
c2 = SavitchIn.readChar();
c3 = SavitchIn.readChar();
```

If the user enters

```
a b c d e f g h i
```

where `'a'` is the first thing on the line, then `c1` will be set to the value `'a'`, `c2` will have its value set to the blank character, and `c3` will have its value set to `'b'`. Any further reading would begin with the blank after the letter `'b'`.

As indicated in the next Gotcha section, it is safer to use the methods that begin with `readLine` and that read a whole line, and to use the other methods sparingly and with caution.

▲ *Gotcha*

readInt and readDouble

The methods `readLineInt` and `readLineDouble` in the class `SavitchIn` will prompt the user to reenter the input if the user enters it in an incorrect format. The methods `readInt` and `readDouble`, on the other hand, have no such recovery mechanism. If the user enters the input in an incorrect format, the program will crash. For this reason, you should try to use the methods `readLineInt` and `readLineDouble` and avoid using the methods `readInt` and `readDouble`. The methods `readInt` and `read-Double` should be reserved for when you are certain the input will be in the correct format. For most of our applications, you cannot count on the user entering the input in the correct format.

The methods `readChar` and `readNonwhiteChar` also do no checking for the format of the input, but they are less dangerous, because they will process almost any kind of input the user enters. After all, any input consists of characters of some sort. Even the input 178, which might be considered an integer, can be processed as the three-character input `'1'`, followed by `'7'`, followed by `'8'`. △

FAQ: **Why Aren't `readInt` and `readDouble` Better?**

Why don't `readInt` and `readDouble` prompt the user to correctly reenter input that is incorrect? They could easily be written that way, but then they might confuse the user. The reason is that such prompts are likely to be in confusing places. The operating system always reads an entire line and then gives the entire line to Java. If the user enters four items, such as numbers, on a line, and there is a format mistake in the second item, the operating system will read the whole line before Java notices that something is wrong. So the prompt to reenter the input would come after the user entered the fourth item, not after the second one. It would be possible to design `readInt` and `readDouble` so that they prompted the user to reenter input correctly and in an understandable way, but it would be neither simple to write nor simple to understand. Moreover, many input methods in many languages behave like `readInt` and `readDouble`, so you should be made aware of such problems.

● **Programming Tip**
Echo Input

You should output all input, so that users can check whether they entered their input correctly. This practice is called **echoing the input.** For example, the following two statements from the program in Display 2.1 echo the two input values that were read into the variables `eggsPerBasket` and `numberOfBaskets`:

echoing input

```
System.out.println(eggsPerBasket + " eggs per basket.");
System.out.println(numberOfBaskets + " baskets.");
```

It may seem that echoing input is not needed. After all, when the user enters input, it appears on the screen as it is entered. Why bother to write it to the screen a second time? There are several reasons for this. First, the input might be incorrect, even though it looks correct. For example, the user might type a comma instead of a decimal point or the letter "O" in place of a zero. Echoing the input will reveal such problems. Also, the echoed input gets the user's attention. Some users do not look at the screen as they type in input. In an ideal program, the user should even be given the opportunity to reenter the input if it is incorrect, but we don't have enough tools to do that yet. However, when something is wrong with the input, we do want the user to at least be aware that there is a problem. ○

? Self-Test Questions

25. Write Java statements that will cause the following to be written to the screen:

    ```
    Once upon a time,
    there were three little programmers.
    ```

26. What is the difference between `System.out.println` and `System.out.print`?

27. Write a Java statement that will set the value of the variable `number` equal to the number typed in at the keyboard. Assume that `number` is of type `int` and that the input is entered on a line by itself.

28. Write a Java statement that will set the value of the variable `amount` equal to the number typed in at the keyboard. Assume that `amount` is of type `double` and that the input is entered on a line by itself.

29. Write a Java statement that will set the value of the variable `answer` equal to the first nonwhitespace character typed in at the keyboard. The rest of the line of input is discarded. The variable `answer` is of type `char`.

30. What are the whitespace characters?

31. Is the class `SavitchIn` part of the Java language, or does the programmer have to define the class?

32. Write some Java code that will read a line of text and then output the line with all lowercase letters changed to uppercase.

2.4 DOCUMENTATION AND STYLE

"Don't stand there chattering to yourself like that," Humpty Dumpty said, looking at her for the first time, *"but tell me your name and your business."*
"My name *is Alice, but—"*
"It's a stupid name enough!" Humpty Dumpty interrupted impatiently. *"What does it mean?"*
"Must a name mean something?" *Alice asked doubtfully.*
"Of course it must," Humpty Dumpty said with a short laugh: *"my* name means the shape I am— and a good handsome shape it is too. With a name like yours, you might be any shape, almost."
-Lewis Carroll, *Through the Looking Glass*

A program that gives the correct output is not necessarily a good program. Obviously, you want your program to give the correct output, but that is not the whole story. Most programs are used many times and are changed at some point either to fix bugs or to accommodate new demands by the user. If the program is not easy to read and understand, it will not be easy to change, and it might even be impossible to change with any realistic effort. Even if the program is going to be used only once, you should pay some attention to readability. After all, you will have to read the program in order to debug it.

In this section, we discuss four techniques that can help make your program more readable: meaningful names, indenting, documentation, and defined constants.

● **Programming Tip**
Use Meaningful Names for Variables

As we mentioned earlier, the names x and y are almost never good variable names. The name you give to a variable should be suggestive of what the variable is used for. If the variable holds a count of something, you might name it `count`. If the variable holds a tax rate, you might name it `taxRate`.

In addition to giving variables meaningful names and giving them names that the compiler will accept, you should choose names that follow the normal practice of programmers. That way, your code will be easier for others to read and to combine with their code, should you work on a project with more than one programmer. By convention, variable names are made up entirely of letters and digits. If the name consists of more than one word, "punctuate" it by using capital letters at the word boundaries, as in `taxRate`, `numberOfTries`, and `timeLeft`. Also, start each variable with a lowercase letter, as in the examples we just gave. The practice of starting with a lowercase letter may look strange at first, but it is a convention that is commonly used, and you quickly get used to it. We use names that start with an uppercase letter for something else, namely, for class names like `String` and `SavitchIn`.

Documentation and Comments

The documentation for a program tells what the program does and how it does it. The best programs are **self-documenting.** This means that, thanks to a very clean style and very well-chosen variable names (and other names), what the program does and how it does it will be obvious to any programmer who reads the program. You should strive for such self-documenting programs, but your programs may also need a bit of additional explanation to make them completely clear. This explanation can be given in the form of comments.

self-documenting

Remember: Write Self-Documenting Code

A **self-documenting** program (or other piece of code) is a program that uses well-chosen variable names (and other names) and has a style so clear that what the program does and how it does it will be obvious to any programmer who reads the program, even if the program has no comments. To the extent that it is possible, you should strive to make your programs self-documenting.

Comments are notes that you write into your program to help a person understand the program, but that are ignored by the compiler. In Java, there are two ways to insert comments. The first way is to use the two symbols `//` at the beginning of a comment. Everything after these symbols up to the end of the line is treated as a comment and is ignored by the compiler. This technique is handy for short comments, such as

`//`
comments

```
String sentence; //Spanish version
```

If you want a comment of this form to span several lines, then each line must contain the symbols `//` at the beginning of the comment.

The second kind of comment can more easily span multiple lines. Anything written between the matching symbol pairs `/*` and `*/` is a comment and is ignored by the compiler. For example,

`/* */`
comments

```
/*
This program should only
be used on alternate Thursdays,
except during leap years when it should
only be used on alternate Tuesdays.
*/
```

This is not a very likely comment, but it does illustrate the use of `/*` and `*/`.

Many text editors automatically highlight comments by showing them in a special color. In this book, we will also write comments in a different color, as illustrated by the following comment:

```
/**
 This program should only
 be used on alternate Thursdays,
 except during leap years when it should
 only be used on alternate Tuesdays.
*/
```

Notice that this comment uses two asterisks rather than one in the opening /**. This is not required to make it a comment, but it will be needed when we use a program named java-doc that automatically extracts documentation from Java software. We will discuss java-doc later in this book, but we will start using the double asterisks now.

It is difficult to explain just when you should and when you should not insert a comment. Too many comments can be as bad as too few comments. With too many comments, the really important information can be lost in a sea of comments that just state the obvious. As we show you more Java features, we will mention likely places for comments. For now, you should normally need only two kinds of comments.

First, every program file should have an explanatory comment at the beginning of the file. This comment should give all the important information about the file: what the program does, the name of the author, how to contact the author, the date the file was last changed, and, in a course, what the assignment is. This comment should be similar to the one shown at the top of Display 2.10.

The second kind of comment you need is one to explain any nonobvious details. For example, look at the program in Display 2.10. Note the two variables named `radius` and `area`. It is obvious that these two variables will hold the values for the radius and area of a circle, respectively. It would be a mistake to include comments like the following:

```
double radius; //holds the radius of a circle.
```

However, there is something that is not obvious. What units are used for the radius? Inches? Feet? Meters? Centimeters? You should add a comment that explains the units used, as follows:

```
double radius; //in inches
double area; //in square inches
```

These two comments are also shown in Display 2.10.

Indenting

A program has a lot of structure. There are smaller parts within larger parts. For example, there is the part that starts with

```
public static void main(String[] args)
{
```

indenting

This part ends with a closing brace, }. Within the part, there are statements, such as assignment statements and `System.out.println` statements. In a simple program of the kind we have seen thus far, there are basically three levels of nested structure, as indicated by the vertical lines in Display 2.10. Each level of nesting should be indented to show the nesting more clearly. The outermost structure is not indented at all. The next level of nested structure is indented. The nested structure within that is double indented.

■ DISPLAY 2.10 **Comments and Indenting**

```
/**
 Program to determine area of a circle.
 Author: Jane Q. Programmer.
 E-mail Address: janeq@somemachine.etc.etc.
 Programming Assignment 2.
 Last Changed: October 7, 2004.
*/
public class CircleCalculation
{
    public static void main(String[] args)
    {
        double radius; //in inches
        double area; //in square inches

        System.out.println(
                "Enter the radius of a circle in inches:");
        radius = SavitchIn.readLineDouble();

        area = 3.14159 * radius * radius;

        System.out.println("A circle of radius " + radius + " inches");
        System.out.println("has an area of " + area + " square inches.");
    }
}
```

The vertical lines indicate the indenting pattern.

Later in this chapter, we will give an improved version of this program.

Sample Screen Dialog

```
Enter the radius of a circle in inches:
2.5
A circle of radius 2.5 inches
has an area of 19.6349375 square inches.
```

These levels of nesting are frequently indicated by braces, { }, but regardless of whether there are any braces, you should still indent each level of nesting.

If a statement does not fit on one line, you can write it on two or more lines. However, when you write a single statement on more than one line, indent the second and all subsequent lines more than the first line.

We prefer to indent by four spaces for each level of indenting. Indenting more than that leaves too little room on the line for the statement itself, whereas a smaller indent just does not show up well. Indenting two or three spaces is not unreasonable, but we find four spaces to be the clearest. If you are in a course, follow the rules on indenting given by your instructor. On a programming project, there is likely to be a style sheet that dictates the number of spaces you should indent. In any event, you should indent consistently within any one program.

Quick Reference: Java Comments

There are two ways to add comments to a Java program (or piece of Java code):

1. Everything after the two symbols // to the end of the line is a comment and is ignored by the compiler.
2. Anything written between the matching symbols pairs /* and */ is a comment and is ignored by the compiler.

Named Constants

Look again at the program in Display 2.10. You probably recognize the number 3.14159 as the approximate value of pi, the number that is used in many calculations involving a circle and that is often written as π. However, you might not be sure that 3.14159 is pi and not some other number, and somebody other than you might have no idea as to where the number 3.14159 came from. To avoid such confusion, you should always give a name to constants such as 3.14159 and use the name instead of writing out the number. For example, you might give the number 3.14159 the name PI. Then the assignment statement

```
area = 3.14159 * radius * radius;
```

could be written more clearly as

```
area = PI * radius * radius;
```

How do you give a number, or other constant, a name like PI? You could use a variable named PI and initialize it to the desired value, like 3.14159. But you might then inadvertently change the value of this variable. Java provides a mechanism that allows you to define and initialize a variable and moreover fix the variable's value so that it cannot be changed. The syntax is

```
public static final Type Variable = Constant;
```

For example, we can give the name PI to the constant 3.14159 as follows:

```
public static final double PI = 3.14159;
```

You can simply take this as a long, peculiarly worded way of giving a name (like PI) to a constant (like 3.14159), but we can explain most of what is on this line. The part

```
double PI = 3.14159;
```

simply declares PI as a variable and initializes it to 3.14159. The words that precede this modify the variable PI in various ways. The word public says that there are no restrictions on where you can use the name PI. The word static will have to wait until Chapter 5 for an explanation; for now, just be sure to include it. The word final means that the value 3.14159 is the final value assigned to PI or, to phrase it another way, that the program is not allowed to change the value of PI.

Quick Reference: Naming Constants

To define a name for a constant, such as a number, place the keywords public static final in front of a variable declaration that includes the constant as the initializing value. Place this declaration within the class definition, but outside of the main method and outside of any other method definitions. (See Display 2.11 for a complete example.)

Syntax:

```
public static final Type Variable = Constant;
```

Example:

```
public static final int MAX_STRIKES = 3;
public static final double MORTGAGE_INTEREST_RATE = 6.99;
public static final String MOTTO = "The customer is right!";
public static final char SCALE = 'K';
```

Although it is not required, it is the normal practice of programmers to spell named constants with all uppercase letters.

In Display 2.11, we have rewritten the program from Display 2.11 so that it uses the name PI as a defined name for the constant 3.14159. Note that the definition of PI is placed outside of the main part of the program. As indicated there, defined names for constants need not be near the beginning of a file, but it is a good practice to place them there. That way, they will be handy if you need to change the definition of a named constant. You are not likely to want to change the definition of the named constant PI, but you may want to change the definition of some other named constant in some other program. For example, suppose you have a banking program that contains the defined constant

```
public static final double MORTGAGE_INTEREST_RATE = 6.99;
```

and suppose the interest rate changes to 8.5 percent. You can simply change the defined constant to

```
public static final double MORTGAGE_INTEREST_RATE = 8.5;
```

You would then need to recompile your program, but you need not change anything else in it.

■ DISPLAY 2.11 **Naming a Constant**

```java
/**
 Program to determine area of a circle.
 Author: Jane Q. Programmer.
 E-mail Address: janeq@somemachine.etc.etc.
 Assignment Number: 2.
 Last Changed: October 7, 2001.
*/
public class CircleCalculation2
{
    public static final double PI = 3.14159;

    public static void main(String[] args)
    {
        double radius; //in inches
        double area; //in square inches

        System.out.println(
                "Enter the radius of a circle in inches:");
        radius = SavitchIn.readLineDouble();

        area = PI * radius * radius;

        System.out.println("A circle of radius "
                                    + radius + " inches");
        System.out.println("has an area of "
                                    + area + " square inches.");
    }

}
```

Although it would not be as clear, it is legal to place the definition of PI here instead.

Sample Screen Dialog

```
Enter the radius of a circle in inches:
2.5
A circle of radius 2.5 inches
has an area of 19.6349375 square inches.
```

Note that a defined constant, like MORTGAGE_INTEREST_RATE, can save you a lot of work if the constant ever needs to be changed. In order to change the mortgage interest rate from 6.99 percent to 8.5 percent, you need to change only one number. If the program did not use a defined constant, you would have to look for every occurrence of 6.99 and change it to 8.5. Moreover, even this might not be right. If some occurrences of 6.99 represented the mortgage interest rate and some of the numbers 6.99 represented another kind of interest, you would have to decide just what each 6.99 means. That would surely produce confusion and probably introduce errors.

Notice that we are spelling named constants using all uppercase letters (with the underscore symbol _ used for "punctuation"), as in the named constants PI and MORTGAGE_INTEREST_RATE. This is not required by the definition of the Java language. However, it is a custom that is almost universally followed and one that it would pay for you to adopt. Your programs will be easier to read if you can readily identify variables, constants, and so forth.

? Self-Test Questions

33. What are the two kinds of comments in Java?

34. What is the output produced by the following Java code:

```
/**
 Code for Exercise.
*/
System.out.println("One");
//System.out.println("Two");
System.out.println("And hit it!");
```

35. Although it is kind of silly, state legislatures have been known to pass laws that "change" the value of pi. Suppose you live in a state where, by law, the value of pi is exactly 3.14. How must you change the program in Display 2.11 to make it comply with the law?

36. What is the normal spelling convention for named constants?

CHAPTER SUMMARY

- A variable can be used to hold values, such as numbers. The type of the variable must match the type of the value stored in the variable.

- Variables (and all other items in a program) should be given names that indicate how the variable is used.

- All variables should be initialized before the program uses their values.

- Parentheses in arithmetic expressions indicate the order in which the operations are performed.

■ The methods in the class `SavitchIn` can be used to read keyboard input. The class `SavitchIn` is not part of the Java language, so you must have a copy of `Savitch-In` in order to use it.

■ Your program should output a prompt line when the user is expected to enter data from the keyboard.

■ You can have variables and constants of type `String`. `String` is a class type that behaves very much like a primitive type.

■ You can use the plus sign to concatenate two strings.

■ There are methods in the class `String` that can be used for string processing.

■ You should define names for number constants in a program and use these names rather than writing out the numbers within your program.

■ Programs should be self-documenting to the extent possible. However, you should also insert comments to explain any unclear points.

✔ Answers to Self-Test Questions

1. The following are all legal variable names:

   `rate1, TimeLimit, numberOfWindows`

   `TimeLimit` is a poor choice, however, since it violates the normal convention that variables should start with a lowercase letter. A better choice would be `timeLimit`.

   `1stPlayer` is illegal because it starts with a digit. `myprogram.java` is illegal because it contains an illegal character, the dot. Finally, `long` is illegal as a variable because it is a keyword.

2. Yes, a Java program can have two different variables with the names `aVariable` and `avariable`, since they use different capitalization and so are different identifiers in Java. However, it is not a good idea to use identifiers that differ only in the way they are capitalized.

3. `int count = 0;`

4. `double rate = 0.0, time = 0.0;`
   The following is also correct, because Java will automatically convert the `int` value 0 to the `double` value 0.0:

   `double rate = 0, time = 0;`

5.
   ```
   int miles = 0;
   double flowRate = 50.56;
   ```

6. `interest = 0.05 * balance;`

The following is also correct:

```
interest = balance * 0.05;
```

7. `interest = balance * rate;`
8. `count = count + 3;`
9.

```
b
c
c
```

The last output is c, because the last assignment, `a = b;`, has no quotes:
This last assignment sets the variable a equal to the value of the variable b, which is `'c'`.

10.

```
(int)symbol - (int)'0'
```

To see that this works, note that it works for `'0'`, and then see that it works for `'1'`, and then `'2'`, and so forth. You can use an actual number in place of `(int)'0'`, but `(int)'0'` is a bit easier to understand.

11. `result is 30`

12.

```
quotient = 2
remainder = 1
```

13. `(1/2) * 2 is equal to 0.0`
This is because 1/2 is integer division, which discards the part after the decimal point and produces 0 instead of 0.5.

14. The dialog would change to the following:

```
Enter a whole number from 1 to 99
I will output a combination of coins
that equals that amount of change.
87
2 cents in coins can be given as:
3 quarters
1 dimes
0 nickels and
2 pennies
```

15. `result is 5`

16.

```
n == 3
n == 2
```

17. `How do you doSeven of Nine.`
Note that there is no space in `doSeven`.

18.

```
7
b
```

19. `defg`

20.

    ```
    abc
    def
    ```

21. `abc\ndef`

22. `HELLO JOHN`

23. `End`

    Note that the strings are not equal.

24.

    ```
    Equal
    End
    ```

25.

    ```
    System.out.println("Once upon a time,");
    System.out.println("there were three little programmers.");
    ```

    Since we did not specify where the next output goes, the following is also correct:

    ```
    System.out.println("Once upon a time,");
    System.out.print("there were three little programmers.");
    ```

26. With `System.out.println`, the next output goes on the next line. (By the next output, we mean the output that is produced by the first output statement after the `System.out.println` under discussion.) With `System.out.print`, the next output goes on the same line.

27. `number = SavitchIn.readLineInt( );`

28. `amount = SavitchIn.readLineDouble( );`

29. `answer = SavitchIn.readLineNonwhiteChar( );`

30. The whitespace characters are the blank symbol, the tab symbol, and the new-line symbol, `'\n'`. At this point you are likely to be concerned mostly with the blank symbol when discussing whitespace characters.

31. The class `SavitchIn` is not part of the Java language. The programmer (like you) is supposed to define the class `SavitchIn`. To get you started, we have defined it for you, but think of it as a class that you have defined.

32.

    ```
    String line;
    System.out.println("Enter a line of input:");
    line = SavitchIn.readLine( );
    line = line.toUpperCase( );
    System.out.println("With all uppercase, that is:");
    System.out.println(line);
    ```

33. The two kinds of comments are `//` comments and `/* */` comments. Everything following a `//` on the same line is a comment. Everything between a `/*` and a matching `*/` is a comment.

34.
```
One
And hit it!
```

35. Change the line

    ```
    public static final double PI = 3.14159;
    ```

    to

    ```
    public static final double PI = 3.14;
    ```

    Since values of type `double` are stored with only a limited amount of accuracy, you could argue that this is not "exactly" 3.14, but any legislator who is stupid enough to legislate the value of pi is unlikely to be aware of this subtlety.

36. The normal practice of programmers is to spell named constants with all upper-case letters, with the underscore symbol used to separate words.

● Programming Projects

1. Write a program that reads in three whole numbers and outputs the average of the three numbers.

2. Write a program that reads in the amount of a monthly mortgage payment and the outstanding balance (i.e., the amount still owed) and then outputs the amount of the payment that goes to interest and the amount that goes to principal (i.e., the amount that goes to reducing the debt). Assume that the annual interest rate is 7.49 percent. Use a defined constant for the interest rate. Note that payments are made monthly, so the interest is only one-twelfth of the annual interest of 7.49 percent.

3. Write a program that reads in a four-digit number (such as `1998`) and outputs the number, one digit per line, like so:

    ```
    1
    9
    9
    8
    ```

    Your prompt should tell the user to enter a four-digit number and can then assume that the user follows directions. Your program will not read the number as a value of type `int`, but as four characters of type `char`.

4. Write a program that reads in a line of text and then outputs the line with the first occurrence of `"hate"` changed to `"love"`. For example, a possible sample dialog might be

    ```
    Enter a line of text.
    I hate you.
    I have rephrased that line to read:
    I love you.
    ```

    You can assume that the word `"hate"` occurs in the input. If the word `"hate"` occurs more than once in the line, your program will replace only the first occurrence of `"hate"`.

5. Write a program that will read a line of text as input and then output the line with the first word moved to the end of the line. For example, a possible sample dialog might be

```
Enter a line of text. No punctuation please.
Java is the language
I have rephrased that line to read:
Is the language Java
```

Assume that there is no space before the first word and that the end of the first word is indicated by a blank (not by a comma or other punctuation).

6. Write a program that will print out statistics for eight coin tosses. The user will input either an 'h' for heads or a 't' for tails for the eight tosses. The program will then print out the total number and percentages of heads and tails. Use the increment operator to count each 'h' and 't' that is input. For example, a possible sample dialog might be

```
For each coin toss enter either 'h' for heads
or 't' for tails.

First toss: h
Second toss: t
Third toss: t
Fourth toss: h
Fifth toss: t
Sixth toss: h
Seventh toss: t
Eighth toss: t

Number of heads: 3
Number of tails: 5
Percent heads: 37.5
Percent tails: 62.5
```

7. Write a program that asks the user to enter the first name of a friend or relative, a favorite color, a favorite food, and a favorite animal and then prints the following two lines, with the user's input replacing the items in italics:

```
I had a dream that Name ate a Color Animal
and said it tasted like Food!
```

For example, if the user entered Jake for the person's name, blue for the color, hamburger for the food, and dog for the animal, the output would be

```
I had a dream that Jake ate a blue dog
and said it tasted like hamburger!
```

Don't forget to put the exclamation mark at the end.

8. Write a program that converts degrees Celsius to Fahrenheit, using the formula

$$DegreesC = 5(DegreesF - 32)/9$$

Prompt the user to enter a temperature in degrees Fahrenheit (just a whole number of degrees, without a fractional part), and then let the program print out the equivalent Celsius temperature, including the fractional part to at least one decimal point. A possible dialog might be

```
Enter a temperature in degrees Fahrenheit: 72
72 degrees Fahrenheit = 22.2 degrees Celsius.
```

9. Write a program that determines the change to be dispensed from a vending machine. An item in the machine can cost between 25 cents and a dollar, in 5-cent increments (25, 30, 35, . . ., 90, 95, or 100), and the machine accepts only a single dollar bill to pay for the item. For example, a possible sample dialog might be

```
Enter price of item
(from 25 cents to a dollar, in 5-cent increments): 45

You bought an item for 45 cents and gave me a dollar,
so your change is
2 quarters,
0 dimes, and
1 nickel.
```

Flow of Control

"Would you tell me, please, which
way I ought to go from here?"
"That depends a good deal on where
you want to get to," said the Cat. -Lewis Carroll, *Alice in Wonderland*

flow of control

branching
statement

loop statement

Flow of control is the order in which a program performs actions. Until this chapter, that order has been simple. Actions were taken in the order in which they were written down. In this chapter, we show you how to write programs with a more complicated flow of control. Java, and most other programming languages, uses two kinds of statements to regulate flow of control: A **branching statement** chooses one action from a list of two or more possible actions. A **loop statement** repeats an action again and again until some stopping condition is met.

OBJECTIVES

Learn about Java branching statements.

Learn about loops.

Learn about the type `boolean`.

PREREQUISITES

You need to be familiar with all the material in Chapter 2 before reading this chapter.

3.1 BRANCHING STATEMENTS

When you come to a fork in the road, take it. -Attributed to Yogi Berra

We begin our discussion of branching with a kind of Java statement that chooses between two possible alternative actions.

The `if-else` Statement

In programs, as in everyday life, things can sometimes go in one of two different ways. With some checking accounts, if you have money in your checking account, the bank will pay you a little interest. On the other hand, if you have overdrawn your checking account so your account balance is negative, you will be charged a penalty that will make your balance more negative than it already is. This might be reflected in the bank's accounting program by the following Java statement, known as an `if-else` statement:

if-else

```
if (balance >= 0)
    balance = balance + (INTEREST_RATE * balance)/12;
else
    balance = balance - OVERDRAWN_PENALTY;
```

The pair of symbols >= is used to mean greater-than-or-equal-to in Java, because the symbol ≥ is not on the keyboard.

The meaning of an if-else Statement is really just the meaning it would have if read as an English sentence. When your program executes an if-else statement, it first checks the expression in parentheses after the if. This expression must be something that is either true or false. If it is true, the statement before the else is executed. If the expression is false, the statement after the else is executed. In the preceding example, if balance is positive (or zero), then the following action is taken (the division by 12 is because this is for only 1 of 12 months):

```
balance = balance + (INTEREST_RATE * balance)/12;
```

On the other hand, if the value of balance is negative, the following is done instead:

```
balance = balance - OVERDRAWN_PENALTY;
```

Display 3.1 shows this if-else statement in a complete program.

■ DISPLAY 3.1   A Program Using if-else (Part 1 of 2)

```
public class BankBalance
{
    public static final double OVERDRAWN_PENALTY = 8.00;
    public static final double INTEREST_RATE = 0.02;//2% annually

    public static void main(String[] args)
    {
        double balance;

        System.out.print("Enter your checking account balance: $");
        balance = SavitchIn.readLineDouble();
        System.out.println("Original balance $" + balance);

        if (balance >= 0)
            balance = balance + (INTEREST_RATE * balance)/12;
        else
            balance = balance - OVERDRAWN_PENALTY;

        System.out.println("After adjusting for one month");
        System.out.println("of interest and penalties,");
        System.out.println("your new balance is $" + balance);
    }
}
```

■ **DISPLAY 3.1   A Program Using** `if-else`   *(Part 2 of 2)*

Sample Screen Dialog 1

```
Enter your checking account balance: $505.67
Original balance $505.67
After adjusting for one month
of interest and penalties,
your new balance is $506.51278
```

Sample Screen Dialog 2

```
Enter your checking account balance: $–15.53
Original balance $–15.53
After adjusting for one month
of interest and penalties,
your new balance is $–23.53
```

If you want to include more than one statement in each branch, simply enclose the statements in braces, as in the following example:

```
if (balance >= 0)
{
    System.out.println("Good for you. You earned interest.");
    balance = balance + (INTEREST_RATE * balance)/12;
}
else
{
    System.out.println("You will be charged a penalty.");
    balance = balance – OVERDRAWN_PENALTY;
}
```

`else` is
optional

If you omit the `else` part, then nothing happens when the expression after the `if` is false. For example, if your bank does not charge any overdraft penalty, then the statement in its program would be like the following:

```
if (balance >= 0)
{
    System.out.println("Good for you. You earned interest.");
    balance = balance + (INTEREST_RATE * balance)/12;
}
```

To see how this statement works, let's give it a little more context by adding some additional statements, as shown on the next page:

Quick Reference: `if-else` Statements

The *Boolean_Expression* referred to in the following is an expression that is either true or false, such as `balance <= 0`.

Syntax: (Basic Form)

```
if (Boolean_Expression)
    Statement_1
else
    Statement_2
```

If the *Boolean_Expression* is true, then *Statement_1* is executed; otherwise, *Statement_2* is executed.

Example:

```
if (time < limit)
    System.out.println("You made it.");
else
    System.out.println("You missed the deadline.");
```

Syntax: (Omitting the `else` Part)

```
if (Boolean_Expression)
    Action_Statement
```

If the *Boolean_Expression* is true, then the *Action_Statement* is executed; otherwise, nothing happens and the program goes on to the next statement.

Example:

```
if (weight > ideal)
    calorieAllotment = calorieAllotment - 500;
```

Multiple Statement Alternatives:

If you want to include several statements as an alternative, group them using braces, as in the following example:

```
if (balance >= 0)
{
    System.out.println("Good for you. You earned interest.");
    balance = balance + (INTEREST_RATE * balance)/12;
}
else
{
    System.out.println("You will be charged a penalty.");
    balance = balance - OVERDRAWN_PENALTY;
}
```

```
System.out.print("Enter your balance $");
balance = SavitchIn.readLineDouble( );
if (balance >= 0)
{
    System.out.println("Good for you. You earned interest.");
    balance = balance + (INTEREST_RATE * balance)/12;
}
System.out.println("Your new balance is $" + balance);
```

Now suppose that your checking account balance is $100.00. The dialog would then be

```
Enter your balance $100.00
Good for you. You earned interest.
Your new balance is $100.16
```

The expression after the `if` is true, so you earn a little interest. (We are using an interest rate of 2 percent per year, as in Display 3.1, but all you need to note is that some interest was added. The exact amount is irrelevant to this example.)

Next, suppose that your balance is $–50.00 (that is, minus 50 dollars). The dialog would then be as follows:

```
Enter your balance $–50.00
Your new balance is $–50.00
```

In this case, the expression after the `if` is false and there is no `else` part, so nothing happens—the balance is not changed, and the program simply goes on to the next statement, which is an output statement.

Introduction to Boolean Expressions

boolean
expression

A **boolean expression** is simply an expression that is either true or false. The name *boolean* is derived from George Boole, a 19th-century English logician and mathematician whose work was related to these kinds of expressions.

We have already been using simple boolean expressions in `if-else` statements. The simplest boolean expressions are comparisons of two expressions, such as

```
time < limit
```

and

```
balance <= 0
```

Note that a boolean expression need not be enclosed in parentheses to qualify as a boolean expression. However, a boolean expression does need to be enclosed in parentheses when it is used in an `if-else` statement,

Display 3.2 shows the various Java comparison operators you can use to compare two expressions.

You can form more-complicated boolean expressions from simpler ones, by joining the expression with the Java version of "and." The Java version of "and" is spelled **&&**. For example, consider the following:

&& for "and"

```
if ((pressure > min) && (pressure < max))
    System.out.println("Pressure is OK.");
else
    System.out.println("Warning: Pressure is out of range.");
```

■ DISPLAY 3.2   **Java Comparison Operators**

Math Notation	Name	Java Notation	Java Examples
=	Equal to	==	`balance == 0` `answer == 'y'`
≠	Not equal to	!=	`income != tax` `answer != 'y'`
>	Greater than	>	`expenses > income`
≥	Greater than or equal to	>=	`points >= 60`
<	Less than	<	`pressure < max`
≤	Less than or equal to	<=	`expenses <= income`

If the value of `pressure` is greater than `min` *and* the value of `pressure` is less than `max`, then the output will be

    Pressure is OK.

Otherwise, the output is

    Warning: Pressure is out of range.

Note that you *cannot* use a string of inequalities in Java, like the following

    min < pressure < max

Instead, you must express each inequality separately and connect them with &&, as follows:

    (pressure > min) && (pressure < max)

When you form a larger boolean expression by connecting two smaller expressions with &&, the entire larger expression is true provided that both of the smaller expressions are true. If at least one of the smaller expressions is false, then the larger expression is false. For example,

    (pressure > min) && (pressure < max)

is true provided that both (pressure > min) and (pressure < max) are true; otherwise, the expression is false.

Remember: **Use && for "and"**

The symbol pair && means "and" in Java. Using &&, you can form a larger boolean expression out of two smaller boolean expressions.

Syntax:

    (*Sub_Expression_1*) && (*Sub_Expression_2*)

Example:

```java
if ((pressure > min) && (pressure < max))
    System.out.println("Pressure is OK.");
else
    System.out.println("Warning: Pressure is out of range.");
```

|| for "or"

The Java way of expressing "or" is ||, which you create by typing two vertical lines. (The symbol | prints with a break in the line on some systems.) You can form a larger boolean expression from smaller ones by using ||. The meaning is essentially the same as the English word "or." For example, consider

```java
if ((salary > expenses) || (savings > expenses))
    System.out.println("Solvent");
else
    System.out.println("Bankrupt");
```

If the value of `salary` is greater than the value of `expenses` *or* the value of `savings` is greater than the value of `expenses` (or both), then the output will be `Solvent`; otherwise, the output will be `Bankrupt`.

Remember: Use || for "or"

The symbol pair || means "or" in Java. Using ||, you can form a larger boolean expression out of two smaller boolean expressions.

Syntax:

(*Sub_Expression_1*) || (*Sub_Expression_2*)

Example:

```java
if ((salary > expenses) || (savings > expenses))
    System.out.println("Solvent");
else
    System.out.println("Bankrupt");
```

---

parentheses

As we noted earlier, the boolean expression in an `if-else` statement must be enclosed in parentheses. An `if-else` statement that uses the && operator is normally parenthesized as follows:

```java
if ((pressure > min) && (pressure < max))
    System.out.println("Pressure is OK.");
else
    System.out.println("Warning: Pressure is out of range.");
```

The parentheses in (`pressure > min`) and the parentheses in (`pressure < max`) are not required, but we will normally include them to aid readability.

Parentheses are used in expressions containing || in the same way that they are used with &&.

In Java, you can negate a boolean expression with !. For example,

```java
if (!(number >= min))
    System.out.println("Too small");
else
    System.out.println("OK");
```

This will output `Too Small` if `number` is not greater than or equal to `min`, and `OK` otherwise.

You normally can, and should, avoid using `!`. For example, the previous `if-else` statement is equivalent to

```
if (number < min)
    System.out.println("Too small");
else
    System.out.println("OK");
```

If you avoid using `!`, your programs will be easier to understand.

▲ *Gotcha*

Using == with Strings

Although `==` correctly tests two values of a primitive type, such as two numbers, to see if they are equal, it has a different meaning when applied to objects.[1] Recall that an object is something that is a member of a class, such as a string. All strings are in the class `String`, so `==` applied to two strings does not test to see whether the strings are equal. To test two strings (or any two objects) to see if they have equal values, you should use the method `equals` rather than `==`.

The program in Display 3.3 illustrates the use of the method `equals` as well as the `String` method `equalsIgnoreCase`. The notation may seem a bit awkward at first, because it is not symmetric between the two things being tested for equality. The two expressions

```
s1.equals(s2)
s2.equals(s1)
```

are equivalent.

The method `equalsIgnoreCase` behaves similarly to `equals`, except that with `equalsIgnoreCase` the uppercase and lowercase versions of the same letter are considered the same. For example, `"Hello"` and `"hello"` are not equal because their first characters, `'H'` and `'h'`, are different characters. But they would be considered equal by the method `equalsIgnoreCase`. For example, the following will output `Equal`:

```
if ("Hello".equalsIgnoreCase("hello"))
    System.out.println("Equal");
```

Notice that it is perfectly valid to use a quoted string with a `String` method, as in the preceding use of `equalsIgnoreCase`. A quoted string is an object of type `String` and has all the methods that any other object of type `String` has.

For the kinds of applications we are looking at in this chapter, you could also use `==` to test for equality of objects of type `String`, and it would deliver the correct answer. However, there are situations in which `==` does not correctly test strings for equality, so you should get in the habit of using `equals` rather than `==` to test strings. △

---

1. When applied to two strings (or any two objects), `==` tests to see if they are stored in the same memory location, but we will not discuss that until Chapter 4. For now, we need only note that `==` does something other than test for the equality of two strings.

■ DISPLAY 3.3   Testing Strings for Equality

```java
public class StringEqualityDemo
{
    public static void main(String[] args)
    {
        String s1, s2;

        System.out.println("Enter two lines of text:");
        s1 = SavitchIn.readLine( );
        s2 = SavitchIn.readLine( );

        if (s1.equals(s2))
            System.out.println("The two lines are equal.");
        else
            System.out.println("The two lines are not equal.");

        if (s2.equals(s1))
            System.out.println("The two lines are equal.");
        else
            System.out.println("The two lines are not equal.");

        if (s1.equalsIgnoreCase(s2))
            System.out.println(
                        "But the lines are equal, ignoring case.");
        else
            System.out.println(
                        "Lines are not equal, even ignoring case.");
    }
}
```

These two invocations of the method equals are equivalent.

Sample Screen Dialog

```
Enter two lines of text:
Java is not coffee.
Java is NOT COFFEE.
The two lines are not equal.
The two lines are not equal.
But the lines are equal, ignoring case.
```

Remember: **The Methods** `equals` **and** `equalsIgnoreCase`

When testing strings for equality, do not use `==`. Instead, use either `equals` or `equalsIgnore-Case`.

Syntax:

String`.equals`(*Other_String*)
String`.equalsIgnoreCase`(*Other_String*)

Example:

```
String s1;
s1 = SavitchIn.readLine( );
if ( s1.equals("Hello") )
    System.out.println("The string is Hello.");

else
    System.out.println("The string is not Hello.");
```

● Programming Tip
Alphabetical Order

Programs frequently need to compare two strings to determine which is alphabetically before the other. There is no built-in Java comparison operator for alphabetic order, but it is easy to test for alphabetic order using the two `String` methods, `compareTo` and `toUpperCase`, which we described in Display 2.6.

The method `compareTo` will test two strings to determine their lexicographic order. **Lexicographic ordering** is similar to alphabetic ordering and is sometimes, but not always, the same as alphabetic ordering. The easiest way to think about lexicographic ordering is to think of it as being the same as alphabetic ordering *but with the alphabet ordered differently*. Specifically, in lexicographic ordering, the letters and other characters are ordered as in the ASCII ordering, which is shown in Appendix 3. If you look at that appendix, you will see that *all* uppercase letters come before *all* lowercase letters. For example, `'Z'` comes before `'a'` in lexicographic order. So when comparing two strings consisting of a mix of lowercase and uppercase letters, lexicographic and alphabetic ordering are not the same. However, as shown in Appendix 3, all the lowercase letters are in alphabetic order. So for any two strings of all lowercase letters, lexicographic order is the same as ordinary alphabetic order. Similarly, in the ordering of Appendix 3, all the uppercase letters are in alphabetic order. So for any two strings of all uppercase letters, lexicographic order is the same as ordinary alphabetic order. Thus, to compare two strings of letters for (ordinary) alphabetic order, you need only convert the two strings to all uppercase letters (or to all lowercase letters) and then compare them for lexicographic ordering. Let's look at the Java details.

lexicographic
ordering

If s1 and s2 are two variables of type String that have been given String values, then

```
s1.compareTo(s2)
```

returns a negative number if s1 comes before s2 in lexicographic ordering, returns zero if the two strings are equal, and returns a positive number if s2 comes before s1. Thus,

```
s1.compareTo(s2) < 0
```

returns true if s1 comes before s2 in lexicographic order and returns false otherwise. For example, the following will produce correct output:

```
if (s1.compareTo(s2) < 0)
    System.out.println(
        s1 + " precedes " + s2 + " in lexicographic ordering");
else if (s1.compareTo(s2) > 0)
    System.out.println(
        s1 + " follows " + s2 + " in lexicographic ordering");
else //s1.compareTo(s2) == 0
    System.out.println(s1 + " equals " + s2);
```

As we mentioned previously, one way to test two strings for alphabetic ordering is to convert them each to all uppercase letters and then use compareTo to test the uppercase versions of s1 and s2 for lexicographic ordering. Thus, the following will produce correct output:

```
String upperS1 = s1.toUpperCase();
String upperS2 = s2.toUpperCase();

if (upperS1.compareTo(upperS2) < 0)
    System.out.println(
        s1 + " precedes " + s2 + " in ALPHABETIC ordering");
else if (upperS1.compareTo(upperS2) > 0)
    System.out.println(
        s1 + " follows " + s2 + " in ALPHABETIC ordering");
else //s1.compareTo(s2) == 0
    System.out.println(s1 + " equals " + s2 + " IGNORING CASE");
```

The preceding code will compile and produce results no matter what characters are in the strings s1 and s2. However, alphabetic order makes sense, and the output makes sense, only if the two strings consist entirely of letters.

? Self-Test Questions

1. Suppose goals is a variable of type int. Write an if-else statement that outputs the word Wow if the value of the variable goals is greater than 10 and outputs the words Oh Well if the value of goals is at most 10.

2. Suppose goals and errors are variables of type int. Write an if-else statement that outputs the word Wow if the value of the variable goals is greater than 10 and the value of errors is zero. Otherwise, the if-else statement outputs the words Oh Well.

3. Suppose `salary` and `deductions` are variables of type `double` that have been given values. Write an `if-else` statement that outputs `OK` and sets the variable `net` equal to `salary` minus `deductions`, provided that `salary` is at least as large as `deductions`. If, however, `salary` is less than `deductions`, the `if-else` statement simply outputs the word `Crazy` and does not change the value of any variables.

4. Suppose `speed` and `visibility` are variables of type `int`. Write an `if` statement that sets the variable `speed` equal to 25 and outputs the word `Caution`, provided the value of `speed` is greater than 25 and the value of `visibility` is under 20. There is no `else` part.

5. Suppose `salary` and `bonus` are variables of type `double`. Write an `if-else` statement that outputs the word `OK` provided that either `salary` is greater than or equal to `MIN_SALARY` or `bonus` is greater than or equal to `MIN_BONUS`. Otherwise, it outputs `Too low`. `MIN_SALARY` and `MIN_BONUS` are named constants.

6. Assume that `nextWord` is a `String` variable that has been given a `String` value consisting entirely of letters. Write some Java code that outputs the message `"First half of the alphabet"`, provided `nextWord` precedes `"N"` in alphabetic ordering. If `nextWord` does not precede `"N"` in alphabetic ordering, it outputs `"Second half of the alphabet"`. (Note that `"N"` uses double quotes to produce a `String` value, as opposed to using single quotes to produce a `char` value.)

7. Suppose `x1` and `x2` are two variables that have been given values. How do you test whether they are equal when the variables are of type `int`? How do you test whether they are equal when the variables are of type `String`?

Nested Statements and Compound Statements

Notice that an `if-else` statement contains two smaller statements within it. For example, consider the statement

```
if (balance >= 0)
    balance = balance + (INTEREST_RATE * balance)/12;
else
    balance = balance - OVERDRAWN_PENALTY;
```

This statement contains within it the following two smaller statements:

```
balance = balance + (INTEREST_RATE * balance)/12;
balance = balance - OVERDRAWN_PENALTY;
```

Note that these smaller statements are indented one more level than the `if` and the `else`.   *indenting*
    An `if-else` statement can contain any sort of statements within it. In particular, you can use one `if-else` statement within another `if-else` statement, as illustrated by the following:

```
if (balance >= 0)
    if (INTEREST_RATE >= 0)
        balance = balance + (INTEREST_RATE * balance)/12;
```

```
        else
            System.out.println("Cannot have a negative interest.");
    else
        balance = balance - OVERDRAWN_PENALTY;
```

If the value of `balance` is greater than or equal to zero, then the entire following `if-else` statement is executed:

```
if (INTEREST_RATE >= 0)
    balance = balance + (INTEREST_RATE * balance)/12;
else
    System.out.println("Cannot have a negative interest.");
```

Later in this chapter, we will discuss the most common way of using `if-else` statements nested within an `if-else` statement.

Another simple but useful way of nesting smaller statements within a larger statement is to place a list of statements in braces { }. When you enclose a list of statements within braces, they are considered to be one larger statement. So the following is one large statement that has two smaller statements inside of it:

```
{
    System.out.println("Good for you. You earned interest.");
    balance = balance + (INTEREST_RATE * balance)/12;
}
```

compound statement

These statements formed by enclosing a list of statements within braces are called **compound statements.** They are seldom used by themselves but are often used as substatements of larger statements such as `if-else` statements. The preceding compound statement might occur in an `if-else` statement such as the following:

```
if (balance >= 0)
{
    System.out.println("Good for you. You earned interest.");
    balance = balance + (INTEREST_RATE * balance)/12;
}
else
{
    System.out.println("You will be charged a penalty.");
    balance = balance - OVERDRAWN_PENALTY;
}
```

Notice that compound statements can simplify our description of an `if-else` statement. Once we know about compound statements, we can say that every `if-else` statement is of the form

```
if (Boolean_Expression)
    Statement_1
else
    Statement_2
```

If you want one branch to contain several statements instead of just one, use a compound statement. A compound statement is, technically speaking, just one statement, so each branch of the preceding `if-else` statement (the one that starts with `if (balance >= 0)`) is, technically speaking, a single statement.

■ **Java Tip**
Matching `else` and `if`

When writing nested `if-else` statements, you may sometimes become confused about which `if` goes with which `else`. To eliminate this confusion, you can use braces like parentheses to group statements.

For example, consider the following nested statement that we used earlier in this chapter:

```java
if (balance >= 0)
    if (INTEREST_RATE >= 0)
        balance = balance + (INTEREST_RATE * balance)/12;
    else
        System.out.println("Cannot have a negative interest.");
else
    balance = balance - OVERDRAWN_PENALTY;
```

This statement can be made clearer with the addition of braces, as follows:

```java
if (balance >= 0)
{
    if (INTEREST_RATE >= 0)
        balance = balance + (INTEREST_RATE * balance)/12;
    else
        System.out.println("Cannot have a negative interest.");
}
else
    balance = balance - OVERDRAWN_PENALTY;
```

In this case, the braces are an aid to clarity but are not, strictly speaking, needed. In other cases, they are needed. If we omit an `else`, things get a bit trickier. The following two statements differ only in that one has a pair of braces, but they do not have the same meaning:

```java
//First Version
if (balance >= 0)
{
    if (INTEREST_RATE >= 0)
        balance = balance + (INTEREST_RATE * balance)/12;
}
else
    balance = balance - OVERDRAWN_PENALTY;

//Second Version
if (balance >= 0)
    if (INTEREST_RATE >= 0)
        balance = balance + (INTEREST_RATE * balance)/12;
else
    balance = balance - OVERDRAWN_PENALTY;
```

In an `if-else` statement, each `else` is paired with the nearest unmatched `if`. Thus, in the second version (the one without braces), the `else` is paired with the second `if`, so the meaning is

```
//Equivalent to Second Version
if (balance >= 0)
{
    if (INTEREST_RATE >= 0)
        balance = balance + (INTEREST_RATE * balance)/12;
    else
        balance = balance - OVERDRAWN_PENALTY;
}
```

To clarify the difference a bit more, consider what happens when `balance` is greater than or equal to zero. In the first version, this causes the following action:

```
if (INTEREST_RATE >= 0)
    balance = balance + (INTEREST_RATE * balance)/12;
```

If `balance` is not greater than or equal to zero in the first version, then the following action is taken instead:

```
balance = balance - OVERDRAWN_PENALTY;
```

In the second version, if `balance` is greater than or equal to zero, the following entire `if-else` statement is executed:

```
if (INTEREST_RATE >= 0)
    balance = balance + (INTEREST_RATE * balance)/12;
else
    balance = balance - OVERDRAWN_PENALTY;
```

If `balance` is not greater than or equal to zero in the second version, no action is taken. ☐

Multibranch `if-else` Statements

If you have the ability to branch two ways, then you have the ability to branch four ways. Just branch two ways and have each of those two outcomes branch two ways. Using this trick, you can use nested `if-else` statements to produce multiway branches that branch into any number of possibilities. There is a standard way of doing this. In fact, it has become so standard that it is treated as if it were a new kind of branching statement rather than just a nested statement made up of a lot of nested `if-else` statements. Let's start with an example.

Suppose `balance` is a variable that holds your checking account balance, and you want to know whether your balance is positive, negative (overdrawn), or zero. (To avoid any questions about accuracy, let's assume that `balance` is of type `int`. To be specific, let's say `balance` is the number of dollars in your account, with the cents ignored.) To find out if your balance is positive, negative, or zero, you could use the following nested if-else statement:

```
if (balance > 0)
    System.out.println("Positive balance");
else if (balance < 0)
    System.out.println("Negative balance");
else if (balance == 0)
    System.out.println("Zero balance");
```

First, note the way we have indented this statement. This is the preferred way of indenting a multibranch if-else statement. A multibranch if-else statement is really an ordinary nested if-else statement, but the way we have indented it reflects the way we think about multibranch if-else statements.

indenting

When a multibranch if-else statement is executed, the computer tests the boolean expressions one after the other, starting from the top. When the first true boolean expression is found, the statement following that true boolean expression is executed. For example, if balance is greater than zero, the preceding code will output "Positive balance". If balance is less than zero, then "Negative balance" will be output. If balance is equal to zero, then "Zero balance" will be output. Exactly one of the three possible outputs will be produced, depending on the value of the variable balance.

In this first example, we had three possibilities, but you can have any number of possibilities; just add more else-if parts.

In this first example, the possibilities were mutually exclusive. However, you can use any boolean expressions, even if they are not mutually exclusive. If more than one boolean expression is true, then only the action associated with the first true boolean expression is executed. A multibranch if-else statement never performs more than one action.

If none of the boolean expressions is true, nothing happens. However, it is a good practice to add an else clause (without any if) at the end, so that the else clause will be executed in case none of the boolean expressions is true. In fact, we can rewrite our original example (about a checking account balance) in this way. We know that, if balance is neither positive nor negative, it must be zero. So we do not need the test

```
if (balance == 0)
```

Our preceding multibranch if-else statement is equivalent to the following:

```
if (balance > 0)
    System.out.println("Positive balance");
else if (balance < 0)
    System.out.println("Negative balance");
else
    System.out.println("Zero balance");
```

Programming Example
Assigning Letter Grades

Display 3.4 contains a program that assigns letter grades according to the traditional rule that 90 or above is an A, 80 or above (up to 90) is a B, and so forth.

Quick Reference: **Multibranch `if-else` Statement**

Syntax:

```
if (Boolean_Expression_1)
    Action_1
else if (Boolean_Expression_2)
    Action_2
      .
      .
      .
else if (Boolean_Expression_n)
    Action_n
else
    Default_Action
```

Example:

```
if (number < 10)
    System.out.println("number < 10");
else if (number < 50)
    System.out.println("number >= 10 and number < 50");
else if (number < 100)
    System.out.println("number >= 50 and number < 100");
else
    System.out.println("number >= 100.");
```

The actions are Java statements. The boolean expressions are tested one after the other, starting from the top one. When the first true boolean expression is found, the action following that true boolean expression is executed. The *Default_Action* is executed if none of the boolean expressions is true.

■ **DISPLAY 3.4**   **Multibranch `if-else` Statement** *(Part 1 of 2)*

```
public class Grader
{
    public static void main(String[] args)
    {
        int score;
        char grade;

        System.out.println("Enter your score: ");
        score = SavitchIn.readLineInt();

        if (score >= 90)
            grade = 'A';
        else if (score >= 80)
            grade = 'B';
        else if (score >= 70)
            grade = 'C';
```

■ DISPLAY 3.4   **Multibranch** `if-else` **Statement** *(Part 2 of 2)*

```
        else if (score >= 60)
            grade = 'D';
        else
            grade = 'F';

        System.out.println("Score = " + score);
        System.out.println("Grade = " + grade);
    }
}
```

Sample Screen Dialog

```
Enter your score:
85
Score = 85
Grade = B
```

Note that, as with any multibranch `if-else` statement, the boolean expressions are checked in order, so the second boolean expression is not checked unless the first boolean expression is found to be false. Thus, when and if the second boolean expression is checked, we know that the first boolean expression is false, and so we know that `score < 90`. Thus, the multibranch `if-else` statement would have the same meaning if we replaced

```
(score >= 80)
```

with

```
((score >= 80) && (score < 90))
```

Using the same sort of reasoning on each boolean expression, we see that the multibranch `if-else` statement in Display 3.4 is equivalent to the following:

```
if (score >= 90)
    grade = 'A';
else if ((score >= 80) && (score < 90))
    grade = 'B';
else if ((score >= 70) && (score < 80))
    grade = 'C';
else if ((score >= 60) && (score < 70))
    grade = 'D';
else
    grade = 'F';
```

Most programmers would use the version in Display 3.4, because it is a bit more efficient and is more elegant, but either version is acceptable. ■

? Self-Test Questions

8. What output is produced by the following code?

```
int time = 2, tide = 3;
if (time + tide > 6)
    System.out.println("Time and tide wait for no one.");
else
    System.out.println("Time and tide wait for me.");
```

9. What output is produced by the following code?

```
int time = 4, tide = 3;
if (time + tide > 6)
    System.out.println("Time and tide wait for no one.");
else
    System.out.println("Time and tide wait for me.");
```

10. What output is produced by the following code?

```
int time = 2, tide = 3;
if (time + tide > 6)
    System.out.println("Time and tide wait for no one.");
else if (time + tide > 5)
    System.out.println("Time and tide wait for some one.");
else if (time + tide > 4)
    System.out.println("Time and tide wait for every one.");
else
    System.out.println("Time and tide wait for me.");
```

11. Suppose `number` is a variable of type `int` that has been given a value. Write a multibranch `if-else` statement that outputs the word `High` if `number` is greater than 10, `Low` if `number` is less than 5, and `So-so` if `number` is anything else.

The `switch` Statement

switch statement

The `switch` **statement** is a multiway branch that makes its decision as to which way to branch based on the value of an integer or character expression. Display 3.5 shows a sample `switch` statement. The `switch` statement begins with the keyword `switch` followed by an expression in parentheses. In Display 3.5, the expression is the variable `numberOf-Babies`. This expression is called the **controlling expression.**

controlling expression

case label

Below this is a list of cases enclosed in braces, each case consisting of the keyword `case` followed by a constant, then a colon, and then a list of statements, which are the actions for that case. The constant that is placed after the word `case` is called a **case label.** When the `switch` statement is executed, the controlling expression—in this example `numberOfBabies`—is evaluated. The list of alternatives is searched until a case label that matches the controlling expression is found, and the action associated with that label is executed. You are not allowed to have repeated case labels. That would produce an ambiguous situation. If no match is found, the case labeled `default` is executed.

default case

■ DISPLAY 3.5   A `switch` **Statement** *(Part 1 of 2)*

```
public class MultipleBirths
{
    public static void main(String[] args)
    {
        int numberOfBabies;
        System.out.print("Enter number of babies: ");
        numberOfBabies = SavitchIn.readLineInt();

        switch (numberOfBabies)
        {                              ← controlling expression
            case 1:
                System.out.println("Congratulations.");
                break;
            case 2:
                System.out.println("Wow. Twins.");
                break;        ← break statement
            case 3:
                System.out.println("Wow. Triplets.");
                break;
            case 4:
            case 5:
                System.out.println("Unbelieveable.");
                System.out.println(numberOfBabies + " babies");
                break;
            default:
                System.out.println("I don't believe you.");
                break;
        }
    }
}
```

case label

Sample Screen Dialog 1

```
Enter number of babies: 1
Congratulations.
```

Sample Screen Dialog 2

```
Enter number of babies: 3
Wow. Triplets.
```

■ DISPLAY 3.5   A switch Statement *(Part 2 of 2)*

Sample Screen Dialog 3

```
Enter number of babies: 4
Unbelievable.
4 babies
```

Sample Screen Dialog 4

```
Enter number of babies: 6
I don't believe you.
```

The default case is optional. If there is no default case and no match is found to any of the cases, then no action is taken. Although the default case is optional, you are encouraged to always use it. If you think your cases cover all the possibilities without a default case, you can insert an error message as the default case. You never know when you might have missed some obscure case.

break

Notice that the action for each case in Display 3.5 ends with the word break. This is a break **statement,** and it ends the switch statement. The break statement consists of the word break followed by a semicolon. If there is no break statement, then the action just continues on into the next case until either a break statement is encountered or the end of the switch statement is reached.

Sometimes you want a case without a break statement. You cannot have multiple labels in one case, but you can list cases one after the other so they all apply to the same action. For example, in Display 3.5, both case 4 and case 5 produce the same case action, because case 4 has no break statement (and, in fact, case 4 has no action statements at all).

As another example, consider the following switch statement:

```java
switch (eggGrade)
{
    case 'A':
    case 'a':
        System.out.println("Grade A");
        break;
    case 'C':
    case 'c':
        System.out.println("Grade C");
        break;
    default:
        System.out.println("We only buy grade A and grade C.");
        break;
}
```

In this example, the variable eggGrade would be of type char.

Note that the cases need not form any sort of range; you can have `'A'` and `'C'` and no `'B'`, as in the preceding example. Similarly, in a `switch` statement with integer case labels, you could have integers 1 and 3, but no 2.

The controlling expression in a `switch` statement need not be a single variable. It can be a more complicated expression involving +, *, or other operators, but the expression must evaluate to something of an integer type, such as the type `int`, or to something of type `char`.

The Quick Reference box labeled "`switch` Statement" explains the `switch` statement syntax. Be sure to notice the colons after the case labels.

Quick Reference: `switch` Statement

Syntax:

```
switch (Controlling_Expression)
{
    case Case_Label:
        Statement;
        Statement;
        ...
        Statement;
        break;
    case Case_Label:
        Statement;
        Statement;
        ...
        Statement;
        break;
```

Each Case_Label is a constant of the same type as the Controlling_Expression. Each case must have a different Case_Label. The Controlling_Expression must be of type `char`, `int`, `short`, or `byte`.

A break may be omitted. If there is no break, execution just continues to the next case.

\<There can be any number of cases like the above. The following default case is optional:\>

```
    default:
        Statement;
        Statement;
        ...
        Statement;
        break;
}
```

Example:

```
int seatLocationCode;
...
switch (seatLocationCode)
{
    case 1:
        System.out.println("Orchestra.");
        price = 40.00;
        break;
```

```
            case 2:
                System.out.println("Mezzanine.");
                price = 30.00;
                break;
            case 3:
                System.out.println("Balcony.");
                price = 15.00;
                break;
            default:
                System.out.println("Unknown ticket code.");
                break;
        }
```

▲ *Gotcha*

Omitting a **break** Statement

If you test a program that contains a `switch` statement and it executes two cases when you expect it to execute only one case, you have probably forgotten to include a `break` statement where one is needed. △

The Conditional Operator *(Optional)*

To allow compatibility with older programming styles, Java included an operator that is a notational variant on certain forms of the `if-else` statement. For example, consider the statement

```
if (n1 > n2)
    max = n1;
else
    max = n2;
```

conditional operator

This can be expressed using the **conditional operator** as follows:

```
max = (n1 > n2) ? n1 : n2;
```

The expression on the right-hand side of the assignment statement is the conditional operator expression

```
(n1 > n2) ? n1 : n2
```

The ? and : together are known as the **conditional operator** (or **ternary operator**). A **conditional operator expression** starts with a boolean expression followed by a ? and then two expressions separated by a colon. If the boolean expression is true, then the first of the two expressions is returned; otherwise, the second of the two expressions is returned.

As illustrated here, the most common use of the conditional operator is to set a variable to one of two different values, depending on a boolean condition. Be sure to note that a conditional expression always returns a value and so is equivalent to only certain special kinds of `if-else` statements. Another example may help to illustrate the conditional operator.

Consider the following:

```
if (hoursWork <= 40)
    pay = hoursWorked*payRate;
else
    pay = hoursWorked*payRate + 1.5*(hoursWorked − 40)*payRate;
```

This says that an employee pay rate is the rate of pay multiplied by the hours worked, but if the employee works more than 40 hours, any time over 40 hours is paid at 1.5 times the usual pay rate. This can be expressed using the conditional operator, as follows:

```
pay =
    (hoursWorked <= 40) ?
       (hoursWorked*payRate) :
       (hoursWorked*payRate + 1.5*(hoursWorked − 40)*payRate);
```

? Self-Test Questions

12. What output is produced by the following code?

    ```
    int code = 2;
    switch (code)
    {
        case 1:
            System.out.println("Hello.");
        case 3:
            System.out.println("Good-bye.");
            break;
        default:
            System.out.println("Till we meet again.");
            break;
    }
    ```

13. Suppose you change the code in question 12 so that the first line is the following:

    ```
    int code = 1;
    ```

    What output would be produced?

14. What output is produced by the following code?

    ```
    char letter = 'B';
    switch (letter)
    {
        case 'A':
        case 'a':
            System.out.println("Some kind of A.");
        case 'B':
        case 'b':
            System.out.println("Some kind of B.");
            break;
        default:
            System.out.println("Something else.");
            break;
    }
    ```

15. What output is produced by the following code?

```java
int key = 1;
switch (key + 1)
{
    case 1:
        System.out.println("Cake");
        break;
    case 2:
        System.out.println("Pie");
        break;
    case 3:
        System.out.println("Ice cream");
    case 4:
        System.out.println("Cookies");
        break;
    default:
        System.out.println("Diet time");
}
```

16. Suppose you change the code in question 15 so that the first line is the following:

```java
int key = 3;
```

What output would be produced?

17. Suppose you change the code in question 15 so that the first line is the following:

```java
int key = 5;
```

What output would be produced?

3.2 JAVA LOOP STATEMENTS

One more time. -Count Basie, Recording of "April in Paris"
Play it again, Sam. -Reputed (incorrectly) to be in the movie *Casablanca,* which does contain similar phrases, such as **"Play it, Sam."**

Programs often need to repeat some action. For example, a grading program would contain some code that assigns a letter grade to a student on the basts of the student's scores on assignments and exams. To assign grades to the entire class, the program would repeat this action for each student in the class. A portion of a program that repeats a statement or group of statements is called a **loop.** The statement (or group of statements) to be repeated in a loop is called the **body** of the loop. Each repetition of the loop body is called an **iteration** of the loop.

body

iteration

When you design a loop, you need to determine what action the body of the loop will take, and you need to determine a mechanism for deciding when the loop should stop repeating the loop body.

while Statements

One way to construct a loop in Java is with a while **statement**, which is also known as a while **loop.** A while statement repeats its action again and again until a controlling bool-

while loop

ean expression becomes false. That is why it is called a while loop; the loop is repeated *while* the controlling boolean expression is true. For example, Display 3.6 contains a toy example of a while statement. The statement starts with the keyword while followed by a boolean expression in parentheses. That is the controlling boolean expression. The loop body (the repeated part) is repeated while that controlling boolean expression is true. The loop body is a statement, typically a compound statement enclosed in braces {}. The loop body normally contains some action that can change the controlling boolean expression from true to false and so end the loop. Let's step through the execution of the while loop in Display 3.6.

Consider the first sample dialog for the while statement in Display 3.6. The user enters a 2, and this 2 becomes the value of the variable number. The controlling boolean expression is

```
(count <= number)
```

■ DISPLAY 3.6 A while Loop *(Part 1 of 2)*

```java
public class WhileDemo
{
    public static void main(String[] args)
    {
        int count, number;

        System.out.println("Enter a number");
        number = SavitchIn.readLineInt();

        count = 1;
        while (count <= number)
        {
            System.out.print(count + ", ");
            count++;
        }

        System.out.println();
        System.out.println("Buckle my shoe.");
    }
}
```

■ **DISPLAY 3.6**   **A** while **Loop** *(Part 2 of 2)*

Sample Screen Dialog 1

```
Enter a number:
2
1, 2,
Buckle my shoe.
```

Sample Screen Dialog 2

```
Enter a number:
3
1, 2, 3,
Buckle my shoe.
```

Sample Screen Dialog 3

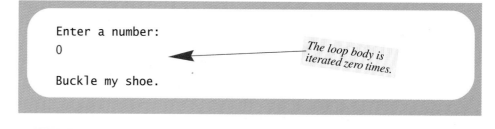

```
Enter a number:
0

Buckle my shoe.
```

The loop body is iterated zero times.

Since count is 1 and number is 2, this boolean expression is true, so the loop body, shown here, is executed:

```
{
    System.out.println(count + ", ");
    count++;
}
```

The loop body writes out the value of count to the screen and then increases the value of count by 1, so 1 is written to the screen, and the value of count becomes 2.

After one iteration of the loop body, the controlling boolean expression is checked again. Since count is 2 and number is 2, the boolean expression is still true. So the loop body executes one more time. It again writes out the value of count to the screen and again increases the value of count by 1, so 2 is written to the screen and the value of count becomes 3.

After the second iteration of the loop body, the controlling boolean expression is checked again. The value of `count` is now 3 and the value of `number` is still 2, and so the controlling boolean expression, repeated in what follows, is now false:

```
(count <= number)
```

Because the controlling boolean expression is false, the `while` loop ends and the program goes on to execute the two `System.out.println` statements that follow the `while` statement. The first `System.out.println` statement ends the line of numbers output in the `while` loop, and the second outputs `"Buckle my shoe."`

All `while` statements are formed in a way similar to the sample shown in Display 3.6. The statement has the general form

```
while (Boolean_Expression)
    Body_Statement
```

The *Body_Statement* can be a simple statement, as in the following example:

```
while (next > 0)
    next = SavitchIn.readLineInt( );
```

But it is much more likely that the *Body_Statement* is a compound statement, as in Display 3.6, and so the most common form of a `while` loop is

```
while (Boolean_Expression)
{
    First_Statement
    Second_Statement
        . . .
    Last_Statement
}
```

The semantics (meaning) of a `while` loop is described in Display 3.7.

Quick Reference: **The `while` Statement**

Syntax:

```
while (Boolean_Expression)
    Body
```

The *Body* may be either a simple statement or, more likely, a compound statement consisting of a list of statements enclosed in braces { }.

Example:

```
while (next > 0)
{
    next = SavitchIn.readLineInt( );
    total = total + next;
}
```

■ **DISPLAY 3.7**   **Semantics of the** `while` **Statement**[2]

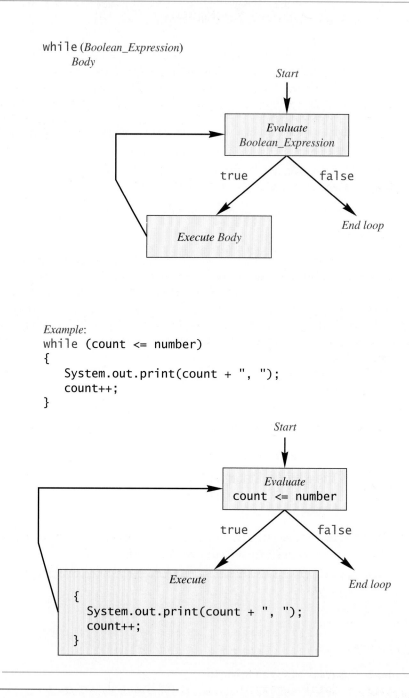

```
while (Boolean_Expression)
    Body
```

Example:
```
while (count <= number)
{
    System.out.print(count + ", ");
    count++;
}
```

2. In a later subsection we discuss the use of the `break` statement within loops. This semantics assumes that there is no `break` statement in the body of the loop.

■ **Java Tip**
A while **Loop Can Perform Zero Iterations**

The body of a while loop can be executed zero times. The first thing that happens *zero loop*
when a while loop is executed is that the controlling boolean expression is checked. *iterations*
If that boolean expression is false, then the loop body is not executed, not even one
time. This may seem strange. After all, why write a loop if the body is never executed? The answer is that you may want a loop whose body is executed zero times or
more than zero times, depending on input from the user. Perhaps the loop adds up the
sum of all your bills for the day. If there are no bills, you do not want the loop body
to be executed at all. Sample Screen Dialog 3 in Display 3.6 shows a toy example of
a while loop that iterates its loop body zero times. ■

The do-while Statement

The do-while **statement** (also called a do-while **loop**) is very similar to the while-
statement. The main difference is that, with a do-while statement, the loop body is
always executed at least once. As you will recall, the body of a while loop might be executed zero times. Display 3.8 contains a sample do-while loop that is similar (but not
identical) to the while loop in Display 3.6. Note that with the do-while loop, the loop
body is always executed at least once, even if the boolean expression starts out false, as in
Sample Screen Dialog 3.

The syntax for a do-while statement is as follows: *do-while*
statement

```
do
    Body_Statement
while (Boolean_Expression);
```

The *Body_Statement* can be a simple statement, as in the following example:

```
do
    next = SavitchIn.readLineInt();
while (next > 0);
```

However, it is much more likely that the *Body_Statement* is a compound statement, as in
Display 3.8, so the most common form of a do-while loop is

```
do
{
    First_Statement
    Second_Statement
        . . .
    Last_Statement
}while (Boolean_Expression);
```

Be sure to notice the semicolon after the *Boolean_Expression* in parentheses.

(Note that we place the ending brace } and the while on the same line. Some programmers prefer to place them on different lines. Either form is fine, but be consistent.)

■ **DISPLAY 3.8   A do-while Loop**

```java
public class DoWhileDemo
{
    public static void main(String[] args)
    {
        int count, number;

        System.out.println("Enter a number");
        number = SavitchIn.readLineInt();

        count = 1;
        do
        {
            System.out.print(count + ", ");
            count++;
        }while (count <= number);

        System.out.println();
        System.out.println("Buckle my shoe.");
    }
}
```

Sample Screen Dialog 1

```
Enter a number:
2
1, 2,
Buckle my shoe.
```

Sample Screen Dialog 2

```
Enter a number:
3
1, 2, 3,
Buckle my shoe.
```

Sample Screen Dialog 3

```
Enter a number:
0
1,
Buckle my shoe.
```

The loop body is always executed at least one time.

When a do-while loop is executed, the first thing that happens is that the loop body is executed. *After that*, a do-while loop behaves in exactly the same way as a while loop. The boolean expression is checked. If the boolean expression is true, then the loop body is executed one more time. If the boolean expression is false, the loop ends. This is done again and again as long as the boolean expression is true.

Although we do not recommend rewriting your do-while loops in this way, it may help you to understand a do-while loop if you see the following rewriting done one time. The do-while loop in Display 3.8 can be written as the following equivalent code that includes a while loop:

```
{
    System.out.print(count + ", ");
    count++;
}
while (count <= number)
{
    System.out.print(count + ", ");
    count++;
}
```

When viewed in this way, it is obvious that a do-while loop differs from a while loop in only one detail. With a do-while loop, the loop body always executes at least once; with a while loop, the loop body may execute zero times.

The semantics (meaning) of a do-while loop is shown in Display 3.9.

Quick Reference: **The do-while Statement**

With a do-while statement, the loop body is always executed at least one time.

Syntax:

```
do
      Body
while (Boolean_Expression);
```

The *Body* may be either a simple statement or, more likely, a compound statement consisting of a list of statements enclosed in braces {}. Be sure to notice the semicolon after the *Boolean_Expression* in parentheses.

Example:

```
do
{
    next = SavitchIn.readLineInt();
    total = total + next;
}while (next > 0);
```

■ DISPLAY 3.9   Semantics of the do-while Statement[3]

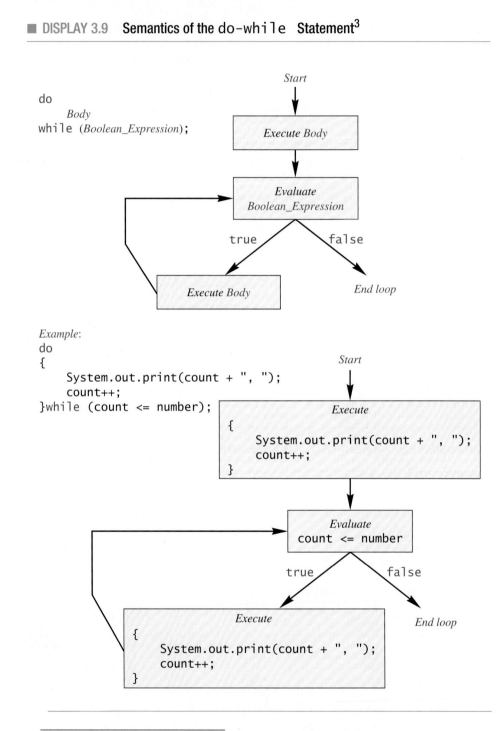

```
do
      Body
while (Boolean_Expression);
```

Example:
```
do
{
    System.out.print(count + ", ");
    count++;
}while (count <= number);
```

---

3. In a later subsection we discuss the break statement used within loops. This semantics assumes that there is no break statement in the body of the loop.

Programming Example
Bug Infestation

Your hometown has been hit with an infestation of roaches. This is not the most pleasant topic, but fortunately a local company called Debugging Experts Inc. has a treatment that can eliminate roaches from a house. As the saying goes, "It's a dirty job, but somebody has to do it." The only problem is that the town's citizens are too complacent and may not exterminate the roaches before they get out of hand. So the company has installed a computer at the local shopping mall to let people know how bad the problem could be at their particular house. The program that is run on this computer is shown in Display 3.10.

The defined constants give the basic facts about this species of roach. The population grows relatively slowly for roaches, but that is still pretty bad. Left unchecked, the population of roaches will almost double every week. If the population doubled every week, the growth rate would be 100 percent per week, but fortunately it is only 95 percent per week. These roaches are also pretty big. Expressed in cubic feet, their average size is 0.002 cubic feet (which is just a bit smaller than 0.3 cubic inches). The program does make some simplifying assumptions. It assumes that there is no furniture in the house, and it assumes that the roaches would fill the house with no space between them. The real situation would be even worse than that portrayed by this program with its simplifying assumptions.

Let's look at the `while` loop from the program in Display 3.10:

```java
while (totalBugVolume < houseVolume)
{
    population = population + (GROWTH_RATE*population);
    totalBugVolume = population*ONE_BUG_VOLUME;
    countWeeks++;
}
```

This loop simply updates the population of the roaches and the volume of roaches, using the following statements, which show how the population and volume will change in one week:

```java
population = population + (GROWTH_RATE*population);
totalBugVolume = population*ONE_BUG_VOLUME;
```

Because the growth rate and the volume of one bug are both positive, we know that the value of `population`, and hence the value of `totalBugVolume`, will increase with each loop iteration. So eventually, the value of `totalBugVolume` will exceed the value of `houseVolume` and the controlling boolean expression, reproduced here, will become false and end the `while` loop:

```java
(totalBugVolume < houseVolume)
```

The variable `countWeeks` starts out as zero and is increased by 1 on each loop iteration, so when the loop ends, the value of `countWeeks` is the total number of weeks it takes for the volume of roaches to exceed the volume of the house. ■

■ DISPLAY 3.10 **Roach Population Program** *(Part 1 of 2)*

```
/**
 Program to calculate how long it will take a population of
 roaches to completely fill a house from floor to ceiling.
*/
public class BugTrouble
{
    public static final double GROWTH_RATE = 0.95;//95% per week
    public static final double ONE_BUG_VOLUME = 0.002;//cubic feet

    public static void main(String[] args)
    {
        System.out.println("Enter the total volume of your house");
        System.out.print("in cubic feet: ");
        double houseVolume = SavitchIn.readLineDouble();

        System.out.println("Enter the estimated number of");
        System.out.print("roaches in your house:");
        int startPopulation = SavitchIn.readLineInt();
        int countWeeks = 0;
        double population = startPopulation;
        double totalBugVolume = population*ONE_BUG_VOLUME;

        while (totalBugVolume < houseVolume)
        {
            population = population + (GROWTH_RATE*population);
            totalBugVolume = population*ONE_BUG_VOLUME;
            countWeeks++;
        }

        System.out.println("Starting with a roach population of "
                                            + startPopulation);
        System.out.println("and a house with a volume of "
                                + houseVolume + " cubic feet,");
        System.out.println("after " + countWeeks + " weeks,");
        System.out.println("the house will be filled");
        System.out.println("floor to ceiling with roaches.");
        System.out.println("There will be " + (int)population
                                    + " roaches.");
        System.out.println("They will fill a volume of "
                        + (int)totalBugVolume +" cubic feet.");
        System.out.println("Better call Debugging Experts Inc.");
    }
}
```

(int) is a type cast as discussed in Chapter 2.

■ DISPLAY 3.10 **Roach Population Program** *(Part 2 of 2)*

Sample Screen Dialog

```
Enter the total volume of your house
in cubic feet: 20000
Enter the estimated number of
roaches in your house: 100
Starting with a roach population of 100
and a house with a volume of 20000.0 cubic feet,
after 18 weeks,
the house will be filled
floor to ceiling with roaches.
There will be 16619693 roaches.
They will fill a volume of 33239 cubic feet.
Better call Debugging Experts Inc.
```

▲ *Gotcha*

Infinite Loops

A common program bug is a loop that does not end, but simply repeats its loop body again and again forever. (Well, conceptually forever.) A loop that iterates its body repeatedly without ever ending is called an **infinite loop.** Normally, some statement in the body of a while loop or do-while loop will change some variables so that the controlling boolean expression becomes false. However, if the variable does not change in the right way, you could get an infinite loop. In order to provide an example of an infinite loop, we need only make a slight change to a loop you have already seen.

infinite loop

Let's consider a slight variation of the program in Display 3.10. Suppose your town is hit by an infestation of roach-eating frogs. These frogs eat roaches so quickly that the roach population actually decreases, so that the roaches have a negative growth rate. To reflect this fact, you could change the definition of one defined constant to the following and recompile the program:

`public static final double GROWTH_RATE = -0.05;//-5% per week`

If you make this change and run the program, the while loop will be an infinite loop (provided the house starts out with a relatively small number of roaches). This is because the total number of roaches, and so the volume of roaches, continually *decreases*, and hence the controlling boolean expression, shown again in what follows, is always true:

`(totalBugVolume < houseVolume)`

Therefore, the loop never ends.

Some infinite loops will not really run forever but will instead end your program in an abnormal state when some system resource is exhausted. However, some infinite loops will run forever if left alone. To be able to end a program with an infinite loop, you should learn how to force a program to stop running. The way to do this is different for different operating systems. On many systems (but not all), you can stop a program by typing Control-C, which you do by holding down the Control key while pressing the C key.

Sometimes a programmer might intentionally write an infinite loop. For example, an ATM machine would typically be controlled by a program with an infinite loop that handles deposits and withdrawals indefinitely. However, at this point in your programming, an infinite loop is likely to be an error. △

? Self-Test Questions

18. What output will be produced by the following code?

```
int count = 0;
while (count < 5)
{
    System.out.println(count);
    count++;
}
System.out.println("count after loop = " + count);
```

19. Can the body of a while loop execute zero times? Can the body of a do-while loop execute zero times?

20. What output will be produced by the following code?

```
int count = 0;
do
{
    System.out.println(count);
    count++;
}while (count < 0);
System.out.println("count after loop = " + count);
```

21. Rewrite the following do-while loop to obtain some equivalent code that does not contain a do-while loop:

```
int number;
do
{
    System.out.println("Enter a whole number:");
    number = SavitchIn.readLineInt( );
    System.out.println("You entered " + number);
}while (number > 0);
System.out.println("number after loop = " + number);
```

22. What output is produced by the following code?

```
int count = 0;
while (count < 5)
```

```
    {
        System.out.println(count);
        count--;
    }
    System.out.println("count after loop = " + count);
```

The for Statement

The `for` statement is a specialized loop statement that allows you to easily convert pseudocode such as the following into a Java loop:

for loop

> Do the following for each value of `count` from 1 to 3:
>   `System.out.println(count);`
> `System.out.println("Go");`

This particular pseudocode can be expressed in Java as the following `for` statement (followed by an output statement):

```
for (count = 1; count <= 3; count++)
    System.out.println(count);
System.out.println("Go");
```

The first two of the preceding lines are a `for` statement that causes the output

```
1
2
3
```

After the `for` statement ends, the last line outputs the word "Go".

In this first example of a `for` statement, the loop body is the statement

```
System.out.println(count);
```

The iteration of the loop body is controlled by the line

```
for (count = 1; count <= 3; count++)
```

The first of the three expressions in parentheses, `count = 1`, tells what happens before the loop body is executed for the first time. The third expression, `count++`, is executed after each iteration of the loop body. The middle expression, `count <= 3`, is a boolean expression that determines when the loop will end, and it does so in the same way as the controlling boolean expression in a `while` loop. Thus, the loop body is executed while `count <= 3` is true. To rephrase what we just said, the `for` statement

```
for (count = 1; count <= 3; count++)
    for-loop body
```

is equivalent to

```
count = 1;
while (count <= 3)
{
    for-loop body
    count++;
}
```

The syntax for a **for** statement is as follows:

```
for (Initializing_Action; Boolean_Expression; Update_Action)
        Body_Statement
```

The *Body_Statement* can be a simple statement, as in the following example:

```
for (count = 1; count <= 3; count++)
    System.out.println(count);
```

However, it is more likely that the *Body_Statement* is a compound statement, as in Display 3.11, so the more common form of a **for** loop can be described as follows:

```
for (Initializing_Action; Boolean_Expression; Update_Action)
{
    First_Statement
    Second_Statement
        .
        .
        .
    Last_Statement
}
```

When it is executed, a **for** statement of the preceding form is equivalent to the following:

```
Initializing_Action;
while (Boolean_Expression)
{
    First_Statement
    Second_Statement
        .
        .
        .
    Last_Statement
    Update_Action;
}
```

■ DISPLAY 3.11 **A for Statement** *(Part 1 of 2)*

```java
public class ForDemo
{
    public static void main(String[] args)
    {
        int countDown;

        for (countDown = 3; countDown >= 0; countDown--)
        {
            System.out.println(countDown);
            System.out.println("and counting.");
        }

        System.out.println("Blast off!");
    }
}
```

■ DISPLAY 3.11 **A** for **Statement** *(Part 2 of 2)*

Screen Output

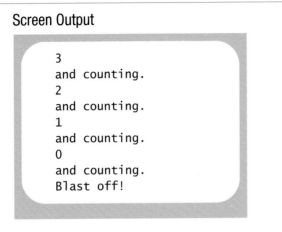

```
3
and counting.
2
and counting.
1
and counting.
0
and counting.
Blast off!
```

Notice that a for statement is basically another notation for a kind of while loop. Thus, just like a while loop, a for statement might repeat its loop body zero times.

The semantics (meaning) of the for loop is described in Display 3.12.

■ DISPLAY 3.12 **Semantics of the** for **Statement** *(Part 1 of 2)*

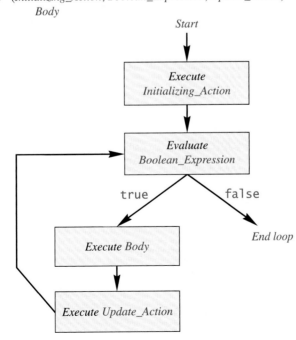

for (*Initializing_Action*; *Boolean_Expression*; *Update_Action*)
        Body

■ DISPLAY 3.12 **Semantics of the** for **Statement** *(Part 2 of 2)*

Example:

```
for (countDown = 3; countDown >= 0; countDown--)
{
    System.out.println(countDown);
    System.out.println("and counting.");
}
```

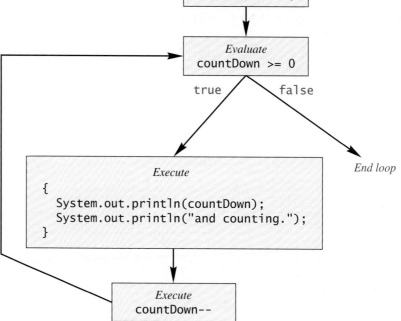
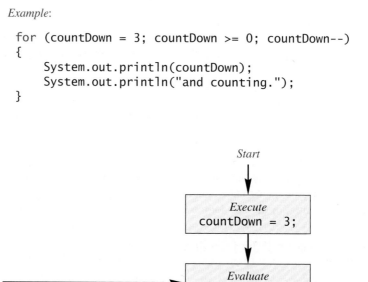

The Comma in `for` Statements *(Optional)*

A `for` loop can perform more than one initialization. To use a list of initialization actions, simply separate the actions with commas, as in the following example:

```java
for (n = 1, product = 1; n <= 10; n++)
    product = product*n;
```

This `for` loop initializes n to 1 and also initializes `product` to 1. Note that we use a comma, not a semicolon, to separate the initialization actions.

You cannot have multiple boolean expressions to test for ending a `for` loop. However, you can string together multiple tests using the `&&` operator to form one larger boolean expression.

You can have multiple update actions by stringing them together with commas. This can sometimes lead to a situation in which the `for` statement has an empty body and still does something useful. For example, the previous `for` statement can be rewritten as follows:

```java
for (n = 1, product = 1; n <= 10; product = product*n, n++);
```

In effect, we have made the loop body part of the update action. However, your code will be more readable if you use the update action only for the variables that control the loop, as in the previous version of this `for` loop. We do not advocate using `for` loops with no body, but many programmers consider them "clever." As indicated in the Gotcha section "Extra Semicolon in a Loop Statement," `for` loops with no body can also often occur as the result of a programmer error.

(If you have programmed in other programming languages that have a general-purpose comma operator, you need to be warned that, in Java, the comma operator can be used only in `for` statements.)

Quick Reference: **The `for` Statement**

Syntax:

```java
for (Initializing_Action; Boolean_Expression; Update_Action)
        Body
```

The *Body* may be either a simple statement or, more likely, a compound statement consisting of a list of statements enclosed in braces { }. Notice that the three items in parentheses are separated by two, not three, semicolons.

Our `for` loops *Update_Action* will always change only one variable. However, you are allowed to use any Java expression, and so you can use more, or fewer, than one variable in this expression, and moreover, the variables can be of any types. The *Initializing_Action* and *Boolean_Expression* also may include multiple variables.

Example:

```java
for (next = 0; next <= 10; next = next + 2)
{
    sum = sum + next;
    System.out.println("sum now is " + sum);
}
```

▲ *Gotcha*

Extra Semicolon in a Loop Statement

The following code looks quite ordinary. Moreover, it will compile and run with no error messages. It does, however, contain a mistake. See if you can find the mistake before reading on.

```
int product = 1, number;
for (number = 1; number <= 10; number++);
    product = product * number;
System.out.println(
            "Product of the numbers 1 through 10 is " + product);
```

If you include this code in a program and run the program, the output will be

```
Product of the numbers 1 through 10 is 11
```

Now can you see what is wrong? Try to explain the problem before reading on.

If you were testing the program that produced this puzzling output, it could leave you bewildered. Clearly, something is wrong with the `for` loop, but what? The `for` loop is supposed to set the value of `product` equal to

```
1 * 2 * 3 * 4 * 5 * 6 * 7 * 8 * 9 * 10
```

but instead, it sets the value of `product` equal to 11. How could that happen?

The problem is typographically very small. The `for` statement has an extra semicolon at the end of the first line:

```
for (number = 1; number <= 10; number++);
    product = product * number;
```

What does this `for` statement do? The semicolon at the end means that the body of the `for` statement is empty. A semicolon by itself is considered a statement that does nothing. (This statement that does nothing is called the **empty statement** or the **null statement**.) This `for` statement with the extra semicolon is equivalent to

empty statement

```
for (number = 1; number <= 10; number++)
{
    //Do nothing.
}
```

Thus, the body of the `for` statement is in fact executed 10 times; however, each time it executes, the loop does nothing but increment the variable `number` by 1. That leaves `number` equal to 11 when the program reaches the statement

```
product = product * number;
```

(Remember, `number` starts out equal to 1 and is increased by one 10 times, which adds 10 more to the initial 1, so the value becomes 11.)

Let's look again at the entire piece of troublesome code:

```java
int product = 1, number;
for (number = 1; number <= 10; number++);
    product = product * number;
System.out.println(
        "Product of the numbers 1 through 10 is " + product);
```

After the line that starts with `for` has executed, the value of `product` is 1 and, as we have just seen, the value of `number` is 11. Then the following assignment statement is executed:

```java
product = product * number;
```

This sets the value of `product` to 1 * 11, and so `product` ends up with the value 11, as the output says. To fix the problem, simply remove the extra semicolon at the end of the line that begins with `for`.

The same sort of problem can occur with a `while` loop. The following `while` loop has the same problem as our troublesome `for` loop, but the results are even worse:

```java
int product = 1, number = 1;
while (number <= 10);
{
    product = product * number;
    number++;
}
System.out.println(
        "Product of the numbers 1 through 10 is " + product);
```

The extra semicolon ends the `while` loop, so the body of the `while` loop is the empty statement. Because the body of the loop is the empty statement, nothing happens on each loop iteration. Therefore, the value of `number` never changes, and the condition

```java
number <= 10
```

is always `true`. So the loop is an infinite loop that does nothing and does it forever! △

? Self-Test Questions

23. What output is produced by the following code?

```java
int n;
for (n = 1; n <= 4; n++)
    System.out.println(n);
```

24. What output is produced by the following code?

```java
int n;
for (n = 1; n > 4; n++)
    System.out.println(n);
```

25. What output is produced by the following code?

```
int n;
for (n = 4; n > 0; n--)
    System.out.println(n);
```

26. What output is produced by the following code?

```
int n;
for (n = 4; n > 0; n--);
    System.out.println(n);
```

(This is not the same as the previous question. Look carefully.)

27. What output is produced by the following code?

```
double test;
for (test = 0; test < 3; test = test + 0.5)
    System.out.println(test);
```

28. Write a for statement that writes out the even numbers 2, 4, 6, 8, and 10. The output should put each number on a separate line. Declare all the variables you use.

■ **Java Tip**
Choosing a Loop Statement

Suppose you decide that your program needs a loop. How do you decide whether to use a while statement, a do-while statement, or a for statement? There are some general guidelines we can give you: You *cannot* use a do-while statement unless you are certain that, for all possible inputs to your program, the loop should be iterated at least one time. If you know that your loop will always be iterated at least one time, a do-while statement is likely to be a good choice. However, more often than you might think, a loop requires the possibility of iterating the body zero times. In those cases, you must use either a while statement or a for statement. If it is a computation that changes some numeric quantity by some equal amount on each iteration, consider a for statement. If the for statement does not work well, use a while statement. The while statement is always the safest choice. You can easily realize any sort of loop as a while statement, but sometimes one of the other alternatives is nicer. ▢

The break Statement in Loops

break

As we have presented them so far, the while, do-while, and for statements always complete their entire loop body on each iteration. Sometimes, however, you may want to end a loop in the middle of the loop body. You can do this by using the break statement. For example, the program in Display 3.13 reads a list of purchase amounts and totals them to see how much the user has spent. However, the user has a limit of $100, so as soon as the total reaches (or exceeds) $100, the program uses a break statement to end the loop immediately. When a break statement is executed, the immediately enclosing loop ends, and the remainder of the loop body is not executed. The break statement can be used with a while loop, a do-while loop, or a for loop.

This is the same break statement that we used earlier in switch statements. If the loop is contained within a larger loop (or if the loop is inside a switch statement), then the break statement ends only the innermost loop. Similarly, if the break statement is within a switch statement that is inside a loop, then the break statement ends the switch statement but not the loop. The break statement ends only the *innermost* loop or switch statement that contains the break statement.

■ DISPLAY 3.13 **Ending a Loop with a break Statement** *(Part 1 of 2)*

```java
public class BreakDemo
{
    public static void main(String[] args)
    {
        int itemNumber;
        double amount, total;

        System.out.println("You may buy ten items, but");
        System.out.println("the total price must not exceed $100.");

        total = 0;
        for (itemNumber = 1; itemNumber <= 10; itemNumber++)
        {
            System.out.print("Enter cost of item #"
                                        + itemNumber + ": $");
            amount = SavitchIn.readLineDouble();
            total = total + amount;
            if (total >= 100)
            {
                System.out.println("You spent all your money.");
                break;
            }
            System.out.println("Your total so far is $" + total);
            System.out.println("You may purchase up to "
                            + (10 - itemNumber) + " more items.");
        }
        System.out.println("You spent $" + total);
    }
}
```

■ DISPLAY 3.13 **Ending a Loop with a** break **Statement** *(Part 2 of 2)*

Sample Screen Dialog

```
You may buy ten items, but
the total price must not exceed $100.
Enter cost of item #1: $90.93
Your total so far is $90.93
You may purchase up to 9 more items.
Enter cost of item #2: $10.50
You spent all your money.
You spent $101.43
```

▲ *Gotcha*

Misuse of **break** Statements

A loop *without* a break statement has a simple, easy-to-understand structure. There is a test for ending the loop at the top (or bottom) of the loop, and every iteration will go to the end of the loop body. When you add a break statement, this can make it more difficult to understand the loop. The loop might end because of the condition given at the start (or bottom) of the loop or because of the break statement. Some loop iterations may go to the end of the loop body, but one loop iteration may end prematurely. Because of the complications they introduce, break statements in loops should be avoided. Some authorities contend that a break statement should never be used to end a loop, but virtually all programming authorities agree that they should be used at most sparingly. △

Quick Reference: **The** break **Statement in Loops**

The break statement can be used in a switch statement or in any kind of loop statement. When the break- statement is executed, the immediately enclosing loop (or switch statement) ends, and the remainder of the loop body is not executed.

The exit **Method**

Sometimes your program can encounter a situation that makes continuing with the program pointless. In such cases, you can end your program with a call to the exit method, as follows:

```
System.exit(0);
```

The preceding statement will end a Java program as soon as it is executed.

For example,

```java
if (numberOfWinners == 0)
{
    System.out.println("Error: Dividing by zero.");
    System.exit(0);
}
else
{
    oneShare = payoff/numberOfWinners;
    System.out.println("Each winner will receive $" + oneShare);
}
```

This statement will normally output the share that each winner should receive. However, if the number of winners is zero, that would produce a division by zero, which is an invalid operation. To avoid this division by zero, the program checks to see whether the number of winners is zero, and if it is zero, it ends the program with a call to the `exit` method.

The number 0 given as the argument to `System.exit` is returned to the operating system. In many situations, you can use any number and the program will behave in the same way. But most operating systems use 0 to indicate a normal termination of the program and 1 to indicate an abnormal termination of the program (just the opposite of what most people would guess). Thus, if your `System.exit` statement ends your program normally, the argument should be 0. In this case, *normal* means the program did not violate any system or other important constraints. It does not mean that the program did what you wanted it to do. So you would almost always use 0 as the argument.

Quick Reference: **The `exit` Method**

An invocation of the `exit` method ends the program. The normal form for an `exit` method invocation is

```java
System.exit(0);
```

? Self-Test Questions

29. What output is produced by the following code?

```java
int n;
for (n = 1; n <= 5; n++)
{
    if (n == 3)
        break;
    System.out.println("Hello");
}
System.out.println("After the Loop.");
```

30. What output is produced by the following code?

```java
int n;
for (n = 1; n <= 5; n++)
{
    if (n == 3)
        System.exit(0);
    System.out.println("Hello");
}
System.out.println("After the Loop.");
```

31. What output is produced by the following code?

```java
int n;
for (n = 1; n <= 3; n++)
{
    switch (n)
    {
        case 1:
            System.out.println("One.");
            break;
        case 2:
            System.out.println("Two.");
            break;
        case 3:
            System.out.println("Three.");
            break;
        default:
            System.out.println("Default case.");
            break;
    }
}
System.out.println("After the Loop.");
```

3.3 PROGRAMMING WITH LOOPS

The cautious seldom err. -Confucius

A loop is often broken into three parts: the initializing statements that must precede the loop, the loop body, and the mechanism for ending the loop. In this section we give you techniques for designing each of these loop components. Although the initializing statements come before the loop body, the loop body is naturally designed first, and so we will start our discussion with the loop body.

The Loop Body

One way to design a loop body is to write out the sequence of actions that you want your code to accomplish. For example, you might want your loop to perform the following actions:

Output instructions to the user.

Initialize variables.

Read a number into the variable next.
```
sum = sum + next;
```
Output the number and the sum so far.
Read another number into the variable next.
```
sum = sum + next;
```
Output the number and the sum so far.
Read another number into the variable next.
```
sum = sum + next;
```
Output the number and the sum so far.
Read another number into the variable next.
> and so forth.

Then look for a repeated pattern in the list of actions. In this case, we have the repeated pattern is

Read another number into the variable next.
```
sum = sum + next;
```
Output the number and the sum so far.

So the body of the loop, expressed in pseudocode, can be the preceding three actions. The entire pseudocode can be

Output instructions to the user.
Initialize variables.
Do the following for the appropriate number of times:
{
    Read a number into the variable next.
```
        sum = sum + next;
```
    Output the number and the sum so far.
}

Note that the pattern need not start with the first action. There may be some actions that need to be done before or after the loop is executed.

Quick Reference: Pseudocode

In Chapter 1, we said that algorithms are usually written in pseudocode. **Pseudocode** is a mixture of English and Java. When using pseudocode, you simply write each part the algorithm in whatever language is easiest for you. If a part is easier to express in English, you use English. If another part is easier to express in Java, you use Java. The following simple algorithm is an example of pseudocode:

Read another number into the variable next.
```
sum = sum + next;
```
Output the number and the sum so far.

Initializing Statements

Consider the pseudocode we designed in the previous subsection. Notice that the variable `sum` is expected to have a value every time the following loop body statement is executed:

```
sum = sum + next;
```

In particular, this is true the first time the loop is iterated. So `sum` must be initialized to some value before the loop starts. When trying to decide on the correct initializing value for `sum`, it helps to consider what you want to happen after one loop iteration. In the loop we are currently designing, after one loop iteration, the value of `sum` should be set to the first value of `next`. The only way that `sum + next` can evaluate to `next` is if `sum` is 0. This means that the value of `sum` must be initialized to 0. Thus, one of the variable initializations must be

```
sum = 0;
```

The only other variable used in the loop is `next`. The first statement performed with `next` is

Read a number into the variable `next`.

This statement gives `next` a value, so `next` does not need to have a value before the loop is started. Thus, the only variable that needs to be initialized is `sum`, and we can rewrite the pseudocode as follows:

```
Output instructions to the user.
sum = 0;
Do the following the appropriate number of times:
{
    Read a number into the variable next.
    sum = sum + next;
    Output the number and the sum so far.
}
```

Variables are not always initialized to zero. To see this, consider another example. Suppose your loop was computing the product of n numbers as follows:

```
for (count = 1; count <= n; count++)
{
    Read a number into the variable next.
    product = product * next;
}
```

In this case, let's say that all variables are of type `int`.

If you initialize the variable `product` to 0, then no matter how many numbers are read in and multiplied, the value of `product` will still be 0. So 0 clearly is not the correct initialization value for `product`. The correct initializing value for `product` is 1. To see that 1 is the correct initial value, notice that the first time through the loop, you want `product` to be set equal to the first number read in. Initializing `product` to 1 will make this happen. Thus, the loop, with a correct initialization statement, is

```
product = 1;
for (count = 1; count <= n; count++)
```

```
{
    Read a number into the variable next.
    product = product * next;
}
```

Ending a Loop

In this subsection, we discuss some standard techniques you can use to end a loop.

If you are lucky, your program will know exactly how many times the loop body must be repeated before the loop starts. In this simple case, you can use a `for` loop to count the number of loop body iterations. For example, suppose that `numberOfStudents` contains the number of students in a class, and you want to know the average score on an exam in the course. The following will do nicely:

```
double next, average, sum = 0;
int count;
for (count = 1; count <= numberOfStudents; count++)
{
    next = SavitchIn.readLineDouble();
    sum = sum + next;
}
if (numberOfStudents > 0)
    average = sum/numberOfStudents;
else
    System.out.println("No scores to average.");
```

Notice that the variable `count` is not used in the loop body. The `for` loop mechanism is simply being used to count from 1 to `numberOfStudents` and repeat the loop body that many times. Loops such as this one, that know the number of loop iterations before the loop starts, are called **count-controlled loops.** Count-controlled loops do not need to be implemented as `for` loops, but that is the easiest way to implement them. (Also note that we have allowed for the possibility of no students being in the class. In that case, the loop body is iterated zero times and the `if-else` statement prevents division by zero.)

count-controlled
loops

The most straightforward way of ending a loop is simply to ask the user if it is time to end the loop. This technique is called **ask-before-iterating**. It works very well in situations in which the total number of loop body iterations is expected to be fairly small. For example, the following would work nicely if each customer makes only a few purchases:

ask before iterating

```
do
{
    System.out.println("Enter price $");
    price = SavitchIn.readLineDouble();
    System.out.print("Enter number purchased: ");
    number = SavitchIn.readLineInt();
    System.out.println(number + " items at $" + price);
    System.out.println("Total cost $" + price*number);
    System.out.println("Want to make another purchase?");
    System.out.println("Enter y for yes or n for no.");
    answer = SavitchIn.readLineNonwhiteChar();
}while ((answer == 'y') || (answer == 'Y'));
```

In some situations, this is best done with a `while` loop. But if you know that each user will want at least one loop iteration, a `do-while` loop will work fine.

sentinel value   For long input lists, you can sometimes use a **sentinel value.** A sentinel value is used to signal the end of the input. It must be a value that is different from all possible real input values. For example, suppose you want some code to compute the highest and lowest scores on an exam, and suppose you know that there will be at least one exam score. If you know that nobody is ever given a negative score on the exam, then you can ask the user to mark the end of the list of scores with a negative number. The negative number is the sentinel value. It is not one of the exam scores. It is just an end marker. The code for computing the highest and lowest scores could be as follows:

```
System.out.println("Enter scores for all students.");
System.out.println("Enter a negative number after");
System.out.println("you have entered all the scores.");
double max = SavitchIn.readLineDouble();
double min = max;//The max and min so far are the first score.
double next = SavitchIn.readLineDouble();
while (next >= 0)
{
    if (next > max)
        max = next;
    if (next < min)
        min = next;
    next = SavitchIn.readLineDouble();
}
System.out.println("The highest score is " + max);
System.out.println("The lowest score is " + min);
```

Be sure to notice that the last number (the sentinel value) is not used to determine the lowest score (or to determine the highest score). Suppose the user enters the scores as follows:

```
100
90
10
-1
```

The output will be

```
The highest score is 100
The lowest score is 10
```

Be sure to note that the lowest score is 10, not −1. The −1 is just an end marker.

In Section 3.4 we will discuss another method for ending a loop, but the three methods discussed here cover most situations you are likely to encounter.

Programming Example
Nested Loops

The body of a loop can contain any sort of statements. In particular, you can have a loop statement within the body of a larger loop statement. For example, the program in Display 3.14

computes the average of a list of scores, using a `while` loop. The program asks the user to enter a list of nonnegative scores, with a negative sentinel value to mark the end of the list. This `while` loop is then placed inside a `do-while` loop, so that the user can repeat the entire process for another exam, and another, until the user wishes to end the program. ■

● Programming Tip
Avoid Declaring Variables in a Loop Body

Note that in Display 3.14, we have placed the declaration of all the variables at the beginning of the program so that they are outside of the body of the outer `do-while` loop. If we had left some of the declarations inside the `do-while` loop, those declarations would be repeated on each execution of the body of the `do-while` loop. Depending on how the compiler is written, this can be inefficient, because it may be re-creating the variables on each loop iteration. There are times when it makes sense to declare a variable in a loop body, but if the variable declaration can easily be moved outside the loop, it is usually a good idea to do so. ○

? Self-Test Questions

32. Write a Java loop statement that will output the phrase `"One more time."` to the screen four times. Also, give any declarations or initializing statements that are needed.

33. Give a Java loop statement that will set the variable `result` equal to 2^5. Do this with a loop that starts out with the value of `result` equal to 1 and multiplies the value of `result` by 2 for each of 5 loop iterations. Also, give any declarations or initializing statements that are needed.

34. What output is produced by the following code:

```java
int count, innerCount;
for (count = 0; count <= 3; count++)
    for (innerCount = 0; innerCount < count; innerCount++)
        System.out.println(innerCount);
```

35. Give a Java loop statement that will read in a list of numbers of type `double` and then output their average. The numbers are all greater than or equal to `1.0`. The list is ended with a sentinel value. You must specify the sentinel value. Also, give any declarations or initializing statements that are needed.

Loop Bugs

Programs with loops are more likely to contain mistakes than the simpler programs you saw before you started using loops. Fortunately, there is a pattern to the kinds of mistakes you are most likely to make in designing a loop, so we can tell you what to look for. Moreover, there are some standard techniques you can use to locate and fix bugs in your loops.

■ DISPLAY 3.14 **Nested Loops** *(Part 1 of 2)*

```
/**
 Determines the average of a list of (nonnegative) exam scores.
 Repeats for more exams until the user says she/he is finished.
*/
public class ExamAverager
{
    public static void main(String[] args)
    {
        System.out.println("This program computes the average of");
        System.out.println("a list of (nonnegative) exam scores.");

        double sum;
        int numberOfStudents;
        double next;
        char answer;

        do
        {
            System.out.println();
            System.out.println("Enter all the scores to be averaged.");
            System.out.println("Enter a negative number after");
            System.out.println("you have entered all the scores.");
            sum = 0;
            numberOfStudents = 0;
            next = SavitchIn.readLineDouble();
            while (next >= 0)
            {
                sum = sum + next;
                numberOfStudents++;
                next = SavitchIn.readLineDouble();
            }
            if (numberOfStudents > 0)
                System.out.println("The average is "
                                    + (sum/numberOfStudents));
            else
                System.out.println("No scores to average.");

            System.out.println("Want to average another exam?");
            System.out.println("Enter y for yes or n for no.");
            answer = SavitchIn.readLineNonwhiteChar();
        }while ((answer == 'y') || (answer == 'Y'));
    }
}
```

■ DISPLAY 3.14   **Nested Loops** *(Part 2 of 2)*

Sample Screen Dialog

```
This program computes the average of
a list of (nonnegative) exam scores.

Enter all the scores to be averaged.
Enter a negative number after
you have entered all the scores.
100
90
100
90
-1
The average is 95.0
Want to average another exam?
Enter y for yes or n for no.
y

Enter all the scores to be averaged.
Enter a negative number after
you have entered all the scores.
90
70
80
-1
The average is 80.0
Want to average another exam?
Enter y for yes or n for no.
n
```

The two most common kinds of loop errors are unintended infinite loops and off-by-one errors. Let's consider them in order.

We have already discussed infinite loops. There is, however, one subtlety about infinite loops that we need to emphasize. A loop might terminate for some input values but be an infinite loop for other values. Just because you tested your loop for some program input values and found that the loop ended, that does not mean that it will not be an infinite loop for some other input values. Let's consider an example.

infinite loops

You have a friend whose checking account balance is overdrawn. The bank charges a penalty each month that the balance is negative. Your friend wants a program that will tell him how long it will take to get a nonnegative account balance if he deposits a fixed amount each month. You design the following code:

```
count = 0;
while (balance < 0)
{
    balance = balance - penalty;
    balance = balance + deposit;
    count++;
}
System.out.println("You will have a nonnegative balance in "
                                    + count + " months.");
```

You place this code in a complete program and test the code with some reasonable values, like $15 for the penalty and $50 for the size of the deposit. The program runs fine. So you give it to your friend, who runs it and finds that it goes into an infinite loop. What happened? Your friend obviously does not have a head for numbers and has decided to make small deposits of only $10 per month. But, the bank charges a penalty of $15 per month when an account goes negative. So the account simply gets a larger negative balance every month, even though your friend makes deposits.

It may seem as though this could not happen. Your friend would not make such a stupid mistake. Don't count on it! It can happen even if your friend is not stupid. People are sometimes careless. One way to fix this bug is to add code that will test to see whether the loop is infinite or not. For example, you might change the code to the following:

```
if (payment <= penalty)
    System.out.println("payment is too small.");
else
{
    count = 0;
    while (balance < 0)
    {
        balance = balance - penalty;
        balance = balance + payment;
        count++;
    }
    System.out.println("You will have a nonnegative balance in "
                                        + count + " months.");
}
```

off-by-one error   The other common kind of loop bug is an **off-by-one error.** This means that your loop repeats the loop body one too many times or one too few times. These sorts of errors can result from carelessness in designing a controlling boolean expression. For example, if you use less-than when you should use less-than-or-equal, your loop could easily iterate the body the wrong number of times.

Another common problem with the controlling boolean expression of a loop has to do with the use of == to test for equality. This sort of equality testing works satisfactorily for integers and characters but is not reliable for floating-point numbers. This is because the floating-point numbers are approximate quantities, and == tests for exact equality. The result of such a test is unpredictable. When comparing floating-point numbers, always use something involving less-than or greater-than, such as <=; do not use == or !=. Using ==

or != to test floating-point numbers can produce an off-by-one error, an unintended infinite loop, or even some other type of error.

One big danger with off-by-one errors is that they can easily go unnoticed. If a loop is iterated one too many times, or one too few times, the results might still look reasonable but be off by enough to cause trouble later on. Always make a specific check for off-by-one errors by comparing your loop results to results you know to be true by some other means, such as a pencil-and-paper calculation of a simple case.

Remember: Always Retest

Whenever you find a bug in a program and "fix" it, always retest the program. There may be yet another bug, or your "fix" may have introduced a new bug.

Tracing Variables

If your program misbehaves but you cannot see what is wrong, your best bet is to trace some key variables. **Tracing variables** means watching the variables change value while the program is running. A program typically does not output the value of a variable every time it changes, but seeing how the variables change can help you to debug your program.

tracing variables

Many systems have a built-in utility that lets you easily trace variables without making any changes to your program. These debugging systems vary from one installation to another. If you have such a debugging facility, it is worth learning how to use it. If you do not have such a debugging facility, you can trace variables simply by inserting some extra, temporary output statements in your program. For example, suppose you want to trace the variables in the following code (which contains an error):

```
count = 0;
while (balance < 0)
{
    balance = balance + penalty;
    balance = balance - deposit;
    count++;
}
System.out.println("Nonnegative balance in "
                                + count + " months.");
```

You can trace the variables by adding the following output statements:

```
count = 0;
System.out.println("count == " + count);//trace
System.out.println("balance == " + balance);//trace
System.out.println("penalty == " + penalty);//trace
System.out.println("deposit == " + deposit);//trace
while (balance < 0)
{
    balance = balance + penalty;
    System.out.println(
            "balance + penalty == " + balance);//trace
    balance = balance - deposit;
```

```
        System.out.println(
                "balance - deposit == " + balance);//trace
        count++;
        System.out.println("count == " + count);//trace
    }
    System.out.println("Nonnegative balance in "
                                    + count + " months.");
```

After you have discovered the error and fixed the bugs in the code, you can remove the trace statements.

It may seem like a lot of bother to insert all the trace statements in the preceding example, but it is not so very much work. If you wish, you can first try tracing only some of the variables to see if that gives you enough information to find the problem. However, it is usually fastest to just trace all, or almost all, of the variables right from the start.

? Self-Test Questions

36. What is the bug in the code in the subsection "Tracing Variables"?

37. Add some suitable output statements to the following code, so that all variables are traced:

```
int n, sum = 0;
for (n = 1; n < 10; n++)
    sum = sum + n;
System.out.println("1 + 2 + ...+ 9 + 10 == " + sum);
```

38. What is the bug in the following code? What do you call this kind of loop bug?

```
int n, sum = 0;
for (n = 1; n < 10; n++)
    sum = sum + n;
System.out.println("1 + 2 + ...+ 9 + 10 == " + sum);
```

3.4 THE TYPE boolean

The truth is out there. -Included in the credits for the television program *The X Files.*
He who would distinguish the true from the false must have an adequate idea of what is true and false. -Benedict Spinoza, *Ethics*

The type boolean is a primitive type, just like the types int, double, and char. As with these other types, you can have expressions of type boolean, values of type boolean, constants of type boolean, and variables of type boolean. However, there are only two values of type boolean: true and false. You can use the two values true and false in a program, just as you use numeric constants, such as 2 and 3.45, and character constants, such as 'A'.

Boolean variables can be used, among other things, to make your program easier to read. For example, a program might contain the following statement, where `systemsAreOK` is a boolean variable that is `true` if, in fact, the launch systems are ready to go:

```
if (systemsAreOK)
    System.out.println("Initiate launch sequence.");
else
    System.out.println("Abort launching sequence.");
```

If you do not use a boolean variable, the preceding code is likely to read something like the following:

```
if ((temperature <= 100) && (thrust >= 12000)
                        && (cabinPressure > 30))
    System.out.println("Initiate launch sequence.");
else
    System.out.println("Abort launching sequence.");
```

Clearly, the first version with the boolean variable is easier for a human being to understand.

Of course, your program needs to set the value of the boolean variable `systemsAreOK` in some way. As you will see, that is easy to do.

Boolean Expressions and Boolean Variables

A boolean expression evaluates to one of the two values `true` or `false`. For example, the expression `number > 0` in the following is a boolean expression:

```
if (number > 0)
    System.out.println("The number is positive.");
else
    System.out.println("The number is negative or zero.");
```

If `number > 0` evaluates to `true`, the output is "The number is positive." If, on the other hand, `number > 0` evaluates to `false`, then the output is "The number is negative or zero." The meaning of a boolean expression like `number > 0` is a bit easier to understand within a context, such as an `if-else` statement. However, when programming with boolean variables, you need to think about a boolean expression more or less without a context. A boolean expression can be evaluated and can produce a value of `true` or `false` without reference to any `if-else` statement, `while` loop, or other context that you have seen before this section.

A boolean variable can be given the value of a boolean expression by using an assignment statement, in the same way that you use an assignment statement to set the value of an `int` variable or any other type of variable. For example, the following sets the value of the boolean variable `isPositive` to `false`.:

boolean variables in assignments

```
int number = -5;
boolean isPositive;
isPositive = (number > 0);
```

If you prefer, you can combine the last two lines as follows:

```
boolean isPositive = (number > 0);
```

The parentheses are not needed, but they do make it a bit easier to read.

Once a boolean variable has a value, you can use the boolean variable just as you would use any other boolean expression. For example,

```
boolean isPositive = (number > 0);
if (isPositive)
    System.out.println("The number is positive.");
else
    System.out.println("The number is negative or zero.");
```

is equivalent to

```
if (number > 0)
    System.out.println("The number is positive.");
else
    System.out.println("The number is negative or zero.");
```

Of course, this is just a toy example. It is unlikely that anybody would use the first of the preceding two examples, but you might use something like it if the value of `number`, and therefore the value of the boolean expression, might change, as in the following code, which could (by some stretch of the imagination) be part of a program to evaluate lottery tickets:

```
System.out.println("Enter your number:");
number = SavitchIn.readLineInt();
boolean isPositive = (number > 0);
while (number > 0);
{
    System.out.println("Wow!");
    number = number - 1000;
}
if (isPositive)
    System.out.println("Your number is positive.");
else
    System.out.println("Sorry, your number is not positive.");
System.out.println("Only positive numbers can win.");
```

More complicated boolean expressions can be used in the same way. For example, if `systemsAreOK` is a variable of type `boolean`, it can be given a value as follows:

```
systemsAreOK = (temperature <= 100) && (thrust >= 12000)
                                    && (cabinPressure > 30);
```

● **Programming Tip**

Naming Boolean Variables

When naming a boolean variable, choose a statement that will be true when the value of the boolean expression is `true`, such as `isPositive`, `systemsAreOK`, and so forth. That way you can easily understand the meaning of the boolean variable when it is used in a `while` loop, `if-else` statement, or other control statement. Avoid names that do not unambiguously describe the meaning of the value of the variable. Do not use names like `numberSign`, `systemStatus`, and so forth. ○

Precedence Rules

Java evaluates boolean expressions using the same strategy that it uses to evaluate arithmetic expressions. Let's consider an example:

```
(score >= 80) && (score < 90)
```

Suppose the value of `score` is 95. The first subexpression `(score >= 80)` evaluates to `true`. The second subexpression `(score < 90)` evaluates to `false`. So the entire expression is reduced to

```
true && false
```

The computer combines the values of `true` and `false` according to rules called **truth tables** that are given in Display 3.15. So, the preceding expression evaluates to `false`.

truth tables

■ DISPLAY 3.15   **Truth Tables for Boolean Operators** *(Part 1 of 2)*

&& (and)

Value of *A*	Value of *B*	Resulting Value of *A* **&&** *B*
true	true	true
true	false	false
false	true	false
false	false	false

|| (or)

Value of *A*	Value of *B*	Resulting Value of *A* **||** *B*
true	true	true
true	false	true
false	true	true
false	false	false

! (not)

Value of *A*	Resulting Value of **!** (*A*)
true	false
false	true

precedence rules

When writing boolean expressions or arithmetic expressions, it is usually best to indicate the order of operations with parentheses. However, if parentheses are omitted, the computer will perform the operations in the order determined by the **precedence rules** shown in Display 3.16. (Display 3.16 shows all the operators you are likely to use for some time. A more complete list of precedence rules is given in Appendix 2.) Operators listed higher on the list are said to have **higher precedence.** When the computer is deciding which of two operations to perform first and the order is not dictated by parentheses, it performs the operation with higher precedence before the operation with lower precedence. Some operators have equal precedence, and then the order of operations is determined by the left-to-right order of the operators. Binary operators of equal precedence are performed in left-to-right order. Unary operators of equal precedence are performed in right-to-left order.

higher precedence

Let's consider an example. (Recall that a unary operator has only one argument—one thing that it applies to. A binary operator has two arguments.) The following is rather poor style, but the computer has no problem with it, and evaluating it using the precedence rules will be a good exercise:

```
score < min/2 - 10 || score > 90
```

Of all the operators in the expression, the division operator has the highest precedence, and so the division operation is performed first:

```
score < (min/2) - 10 || score > 90
```

Of the remaining operators in the expression, the subtraction operator has the highest precedence, and so that operation is performed next:

```
score < ((min/2) - 10) || score > 90
```

■ DISPLAY 3.16 **Precedence Rules**

Highest Precedence

First: the unary operators +, −, ++, −−, and !

Second: the binary arithmetic operators *, /, %

Third: the binary arithmetic operators +, −

Fourth: the boolean operators <, >, <=, >=

Fifth: the boolean operators ==, !=

Sixth: the boolean operator &

Seventh: the boolean operator |

Eighth: the boolean operator &&

Ninth: the boolean operator ||

Lowest Precedence

Of the remaining operators in the expression, the > and < operators have the highest precedence, and so those operations are performed next. Because the > and < operators have
equal precedence, they are performed in left-to-right order:

```
(score < ((min/2) - 10)) || (score > 90)
```

We have produced a fully parenthesized version of the expression by using the precedence
rules. To the computer, the two expressions are equivalent.

You should include most parentheses in order to make your arithmetic and boolean
expressions easier to understand. However, one place where parentheses can safely be
omitted is a simple string of **&&**s or **||**s (but not a mixture of the two). For example, the
following is good style even though a few parentheses are omitted:

```
(temperature > 95) || (rainFall > 20) || (humidity >= 60)
```

The way Java handles **||** and **&&** is just a bit more complicated than what you have seen
so far. Consider the following boolean expression:

short-circuit
evaluation

```
(score > 90) || (assignmentsDone > 8)
```

Suppose that the value of score is 95. In this case we know that the boolean expression
evaluates to `true`, no matter what the value of `assignmentsDone` is. This is because
`true || true` and `true || false` both evaluate to `true`. So regardless of whether
`assignmentsDone > 8` evaluates to `true` or `false`, the value of the whole expression is
bound to be `true`. Java evaluates an expression connected with **||** or **&&** in just this way.
It evaluates the first subexpression, and if that is enough information to determine the
value of the whole expression, it does not evaluate the second subexpression. So, in this
example, Java never bothers to evaluate the expression `assignmentsDone > 8`. This way
of evaluating only as much of an expression as it needs is called **short-circuit evaluation**
and is the kind of evaluation that Java does with **&&** and **||**. (Short-circuit evaluation is
also sometimes called **lazy evaluation.**)

Now let's look at an example using **&&** and let's give the boolean expression some context by placing it in an `if-else` statement:

```
if ((assignmentsDone > 0)
                && ((totalScore/assignmentsDone) > 60))
    System.out.println("Good work.");
else
    System.out.println("Work harder.");
```

Suppose `assignmentsDone` has a value of 0. Then the first subexpression is `false`.
Because both `false && true` and `false && false` evaluate to `false`, the entire boolean
expression is `false`, regardless of whether the second expression is `true` or `false`.
Therefore, Java does not bother to evaluate the second subexpression:

```
(totalScore/assignmentsDone) > 60
```

In this case, not evaluating the second subexpression makes a big difference, because the
second subexpression includes a division by zero. If Java had tried to evaluate the second
subexpression, it would have produced a run-time error. By using short-circuit evaluation,
Java has prevented a run-time error.

complete
evaluation

Java also allows you to ask for **complete evaluation.** In complete evaluation, when two expressions are joined by an "and" or an "or," *both* subexpressions are *always evaluated*, and then the truth tables are used to obtain the value of the final expression. To obtain complete evaluation in Java, you use & rather than && for "and" and use | in place of || for "or."

In most situations, short-circuit evaluation and complete evaluation give the same result, but as you have just seen, there are times when short-circuit evaluation can avoid a run-time error. There are also some situations in which complete evaluation is preferred, but we will not use those techniques in this book, and so we will always use && and || to obtain short-circuit evaluation.

Input and Output of Boolean Values

The values `true` and `false` of the type `boolean` can be input and output in the same way that values of the other primitive types, such as `int` and `double`, can. For example, consider the following fragment from a Java program:

```java
boolean booleanVar = false;
System.out.println(booleanVar);
System.out.println("Enter a boolean value:");
booleanVar = SavitchIn.readLineBoolean();
System.out.println("You entered " + booleanVar);
```

This code could produce the following dialog:

```
false
Enter a boolean value:
true
You entered true
```

T and F

As you can see from this example, the class `SavitchIn` has a method named `readLineBoolean` that will read a single `boolean` value on a line by itself. For this method, you may spell `true` and `false` with either uppercase or lowercase letters; you also may use the single letter `t` or `f` (uppercase or lowercase) for `true` and `false`. These spelling variations of `true` and `false` apply only to input and only when using the method `readLineBoolean`. In a Java program, the spelling must always be either `true` or `false`, spelled out and in all lowercase.

Case Study
Using a Boolean Variable to End a Loop

In this case study, you will not solve a complete problem, but you will design a loop for a commonly occurring subtask and place it in a demonstration program. This will allow you to become familiar with one of the most common uses of boolean variables.

task
specification

The loop you will design will read in a list of numbers and compute the sum of all the numbers on the list. You know that the numbers are all nonnegative. For example, the numbers might be a list of the number of hours worked for each person on a pro-gramming team. Because nobody works a negative number of hours, you know the numbers are all nonnegative, and so you can use a negative number as a sentinel val-ue to mark the end of the list. For this task, you know the numbers will all be integers, but the same technique would work for other kinds of numbers and even for reading in nonnumeric data.

You will get a better grasp of the problem and possible solutions if you first design the loop in pseudocode. So, you design the following pseudocode:

```
int sum = 0;
Do the following for each number on the list:
        if (the number is negative)
                Make this the last loop iteration.
        else
                sum = sum + the number;
```

Because you know that there is a negative number marking the end of the list, you refine the pseudocode to the following:

```
int next, sum = 0;
while (There are numbers left to read.)
{
        next = SavitchIn.readLineInt();
        if (next < 0)
                Make this the last loop iteration.
        else
                sum = sum + next;
}
```

There are a number of different ways to finish converting this pseudocode to Java code. You have just learned about boolean variables, so let's say you decide to try them (and that will turn out to be a good decision). One nice thing about a boolean variable is that it can read just like an English sentence. So you decide to try a boolean variable named `thereAreNumbersLeftToRead`. Simply declaring this boolean variable and substituting it for the phrase "There are numbers left to read." yields the following:

```
int next, sum = 0;
boolean thereAreNumbersLeftToRead;
Initialize the variable thereAreNumbersLeftToRead.
while (thereAreNumbersLeftToRead)
{
        next = SavitchIn.readLineInt();
        if (next < 0)
                Make this the last loop iteration.
        else
                sum = sum + next;
}
```

Now it is straightforward to complete this loop to produce working Java code. The phrase "Make this the last loop iteration." can be translated in one obvious way. The loop ends when the boolean variable `thereAreNumbersLeftToRead` has a value of `false`. So the way to end the loop is to set `thereAreNumbersLeftToRead` equal to `false`. Thus, "Make this the last loop iteration." will translate into

```
thereAreNumbersLeftToRead = false;
```

All that is left to do is to determine the initial value for the boolean variable `thereAreNumbersLeftToRead`. You know that even if the list of numbers is empty, there will at least be the sentinel value to read, so you know the loop body must be iterated at least once. Thus, in order for the loop to get started, `thereAreNumbersLeftToRead` must be `true`, meaning that it must be initialized to `true`. Thus, you come up with the following code:

```
int next, sum = 0;
boolean thereAreNumbersLeftToRead = true;
while (thereAreNumbersLeftToRead)
{
    next = SavitchIn.readLineInt( );
    if (next < 0)
        thereAreNumbersLeftToRead = false;
    else
        sum = sum + next;
}
```

When the loop ends, the variable `sum` contains the sum of the numbers on the input list (not including the sentinel value).

All that is left is to put the loop into a program. You decide that the variable name `thereAreNumbersLeftToRead` is a bit too long, and so you shorten it to `numbersLeft` and produce the program shown in Display 3.17. ■

? Self-Test Questions

39. What output is produced by the following statements?

```
int number = 7;
boolean isPositive = (number > 0);
if (number > 0);
    number = -100;
if (isPositive)
    System.out.println("Positive.");
else
    System.out.println("Not positive.");
```

40. What output is produced by the following statements?

```
System.out.println(false);
System.out.println(7 < 0);
System.out.println(7 > 0);
int n = 7;
System.out.println(n > 0);
```

■ DISPLAY 3.17 **Use of a Boolean Variable to End a Loop**

```java
/**
 Illustrates the use of a boolean variable to control loop ending.
*/
public class BooleanDemo
{
    public static void main(String[] args)
    {
        System.out.println(
                    "Enter nonnegative numbers, one per line.");
        System.out.println("Place a negative number at the end");
        System.out.println("to serve as an end marker.");

        int next, sum = 0;
        boolean numbersLeft = true;
        while (numbersLeft)
        {
            next = SavitchIn.readLineInt();
            if (next < 0)
                numbersLeft = false;
            else
                sum = sum + next;
        }

        System.out.println("The sum of the numbers is " + sum);
    }
}
```

Sample Screen Dialog

```
Enter nonnegative numbers, one per line.
Place a negative number at the end
to serve as an end marker.
1
2
3
−1
The sum of the numbers is 6
```

41. What output is produced by the following statements?

```
System.out.println(true && false);
System.out.println(true || false);
System.out.println(true || (x > 0));
```

CHAPTER SUMMARY

- A statement that chooses one of a number of actions to perform is called a branch. The `if-else` and `switch` statements are branch statements.

- Java has two forms of multiway branches: the `switch` statement and the multi-branch `if-else` statement.

- A loop is a programming construct that repeats an action some number of times. The part that is repeated is called the body of the loop. Every repetition of the loop body is called a loop iteration.

- Java has three kinds of loop statements: the `while` statement, the `do-while` statement, and the `for` statement.

- One way to end an input loop is to place a sentinel value at the end of the input list and have your loop check for the sentinel value.

- The most common kinds of loop bugs are unintended infinite loops and off-by-one errors.

- Tracing a variable means that the value of the variable is output every time the variable is changed. This can be done with special debugging utilities or by inserting temporary output statements. (Sometimes you do not output every change but just selected changes.)

- The value of a boolean expression can be stored in a variable of type `boolean`. This variable of type `boolean` can then be used to control an `if-else` statement or a `while` statement and can also be used anyplace else that a boolean expression is allowed.

✔ Answers to Self-Test Questions

1.
```
if (goals > 10)
    System.out.println("Wow");
else
    System.out.println("Oh Well");
```

2.
```
if ((goals > 10) && (errors == 0))
    System.out.println("Wow");
else
    System.out.println("Oh Well");
```

3.
```
if (salary >= deductions)
{
    System.out.println("OK");
    net = salary - deductions;
}
else
{
    System.out.println("Crazy");
}
```
It is also acceptable to omit the braces in the else part.

4.
```
if ((speed > 25) && (visibility < 20))
{
    speed = 25;
    System.out.println("Caution");
}
```

5.
```
if ((salary >= MIN_SALARY) || (bonus >= MIN_BONUS))
    System.out.println("OK");
else
    System.out.println("Too low");
```

6.
```
String upperWord = nextWord.toUpperCase( );
if (upperWord.compareTo("N") < 0)
    System.out.println("First half of the alphabet");
else
    System.out.println("Second half of the alphabet");
```

7. If they are of type int, you use x1 == x2. If they are of type String, you use x1.equals(x2).

8. Time and tide wait for me.

9. Time and tide wait for no one.

10. Time and tide wait for every one.

11.
```
if (number > 10)
    System.out.println("High");
else if (number < 5)
    System.out.println("Low");
else
    System.out.println("So-so");
```

12. Till we meet again.

13.
```
Hello
Good-bye
```

14. Some kind of B.

15. Pie

16. Cookies

17. Diet time

18.
```
0
1
2
3
4
count after loop = 5
```

19. Yes, the body of a while loop can execute zero times. No, the body of a do-while loop must execute at least once.

20.
```
0
count after loop = 1
```

21.
```
int number;
{
    System.out.println("Enter a whole number:");
    number = SavitchIn.readLineInt( );
    System.out.println("You entered " + number);
}
while (number > 0)
{
    System.out.println("Enter a whole number:");
    number = SavitchIn.readLineInt( );
    System.out.println("You entered " + number);
}
System.out.println("number after loop = " + number);
```

22. This is an infinite loop. The println statement after the loop will never be executed. The output begins
```
0
−1
−2
−3
.
.
.
```

23.
```
1
2
3
4
```

24. This loop causes no output. The boolean expression n > 4 is not satisfied the first time through the loop, so the loop ends without iterating its body.

25.
```
4
3
2
1
```

26. The only output is

```
0
```

Be sure to notice the semicolon that was added at the end of the first line of the `for` loop.

27.
```
0.0
0.5
1.0
1.5
2.0
2.5
```

28.
```
int n;
for (n = 1; n <= 5; n++)
    System.out.println(2*n);
```

29.
```
Hello
Hello
After the Loop.
```

30.
```
Hello
Hello
```

Note that it does not output "After the Loop." because the program ends.

31.
```
One
Two
Three
After the Loop.
```

Note that the `break` statement ends the `switch` statement, but does not end the `for` loop.

32.
```
int time;
for (time = 1; time <= 4; time++)
    System.out.println("One more time.");
```

33.

```
int result = 1;
int count;
for (count = 1; count <= 5; count++)
    result = 2*result;
```

34.

```
0
0
1
0
1
2
```

35. You can use any number less than 1.0 as a sentinel value, but to avoid any problems with the approximate nature of double values, the number you choose should be significantly less than 1.0.

```
double sum = 0, next;
System.out.println("Enter a list of numbers. All the");
System.out.println("numbers must be 1.0 or larger");
System.out.println("Place a zero at the end");
System.out.println("to mark the end of the list.");
next = SavitchIn.readLineDouble();
int count = 0;
while (next > 0.9)
            //next >=1.0 runs a risk of being inaccurate.
{
    sum = sum + next;
    count++;
    next = SavitchIn.readLineDouble();
}
if (count > 0)
    System.out.println("Average is " + (sum/count));
else
    System.out.println("No numbers to average.");
```

36. The code contains

```
balance = balance + penalty;
balance = balance - deposit;
```

but it should contain

```
balance = balance - penalty;
balance = balance + deposit;
```

Even after it is fixed in this way, it still has the following problem: If penalty is greater than deposit, it is an infinite loop. This is discussed in the subsection "Loop Bugs."

37.

```java
int n, sum = 0;
System.out.println("sum == " + sum);
for (n = 1; n < 10; n++)
{
    sum = sum + n;
    System.out.println("n == " + n);
    System.out.println("sum == " + sum);
}
System.out.println("1 + 2 + ... + 9 + 10 == " + sum);
```

38. The boolean expression should be n <= 10, not n < 10. This is an off-by-one error.

39. `Positive`

40. The output produced is

```
false
false
true
true
```

41. The output produced is

```
false
true
true
```

Because of short-circuit evaluation, you do not need to know the value of x.

● Programming Projects

1. Write a program that takes a one-line sentence as input and then outputs the following response: If the sentence ends with a question mark `'?'` and the input contains an even number of characters, then output the word `"Yes"`. If the sentence ends with a question mark `'?'` and the input contains an odd number of characters, output the word `"No"`. If the sentence ends with an exclamation mark `'!'`, output the word `"Wow"`. In all other cases, your program will output the string `"You always say "` followed by the input string enclosed in quotes. Your output should all be on one line. Be sure to note that in the last case, your output must include quotation marks around the echoed input string. In all other cases, there are no quotes in the output. Your program should have a loop that allows the user to repeat this until the user indicates that she/he wants to end the program. Your program does not have to check the input to see that the user has entered a legitimate sentence.

2. Write a program that allows the user to convert either from degrees Celsius to Fahrenheit or from degrees Fahrenheit to Celsius. Use the following formulas:

   degreesC = 5(*degreesF* − 32)/9
   degreesF = (9(*degreesC*)/5) + 32

   Prompt the user to enter a temperature and either a `'C'` (or `'c'`) for Celsius or an `'F'` (or `'f'`) for Fahrenheit; allow either uppercase or lower case, but if anything other than `'C'`, `'c'`, `'F'`, or `'f'` is entered, print an error message and ask the user to reenter a valid selection (uppercase or lowercase `'C'` or `'F'`). Convert the temperature to Fahrenheit if Celsius is entered, or to Celsius if Fahrenheit is entered, and then ask the user to press `'Q'` or `'q'` to quit or to press any other key to repeat the loop and perform another conversion.

3. Write a program to read in a list of nonnegative integers and to output the largest integer, the smallest integer, and the average of all the integers. The end of the input is indicated by the user entering a negative sentinel value. Note that the sentinel value is not used in finding the largest, smallest, or average. It is only an end marker. The average should be a value of type `double` so that the average is computed with a fractional part.

4. Write a program to read a list of exam scores (integer percentages in the range 0 to 100) and to output the total number of grades and the number of grades in each letter-grade category (90 to 100 = A, 80 to 89 = B, 70 to 79 = C, 60 to 69 = D, and 0 to 59 = F). The end of the input is indicated by a negative score as a sentinel value. (The negative value is used only to end the loop, so do not use it in the calculations). For example, if the input is

```
98
87
86
85
85
78
73
72
72
72
70
66
63
50
-1
```

the output would be

```
Total number of grades = 14
Number of A's = 1
Number of B's = 4
Number of C's = 6
Number of D's = 2
Number of F's = 1
```

5. Combine the programs from Programming Projects 3 and 4 to read in test scores (whole-number percentages from 0 to 100) and print out the following statistics:

Total number of scores
Total number of each letter grade
Percentage of total for each letter grade
Range of scores: lowest and highest
Average score

As before, enter a negative score as a sentinel value to end the data input and print out the statistics.

6. Write a program that takes as input a bank account balance and an interest rate and outputs the value of the account in 10 years. The output should show the value of the account for three different methods of compounding interest: annually, monthly, and daily. When compounded annually, the interest is added once per year at the end of the year. When compounded monthly, the interest is added 12 times per year. When computed daily, the interest is added 365 times per year. You do not have to worry about leap years. Assume all years have 365 days. For annual interest, you can assume that the interest is posted exactly one year from the date of deposit. In other words, you do not have to worry about interest being posted on a specific day of the year, like December 31. Similarly, you can assume that monthly interest is posted exactly one month after it is deposited. Since the account earns interest on the interest, the account should have a higher balance when interest is posted more frequently. Be sure to adjust the interest rate for the time period of the interest. If the rate is 5 percent, then when posting monthly interest, you use (5/12) percent. When posting daily interest, you use (5/365) percent. Do your calculation using a loop that adds in the interest for each time period. (In other words, do not use some sort of algebraic formula.) Your program should have an outer loop that allows the user to repeat this calculation for a new balance and interest rate. The calculation is repeated until the user indicates that she/he wants to end the program.

7. Modify Programming Project 9 from Chapter 2 to include input checking. Print the change only if a valid price is entered (no less than 25 cents, no more than 100 cents, and an integer multiple of 5 cents). Otherwise, print separate error messages for any of the following invalid inputs: a cost under 25 cents, a cost that is not an integer multiple of 5, and a cost that is more than a dollar.

8. Write a program that asks the user to enter the size of triangle to print out (an integer from 1 to 50), then print the triangle by printing a series of lines consisting of asterisks. The first line will have one asterisk, the next two, and so on, with each line having one more asterisk than the previous line, up to the number entered by the user. On the next line print one less asterisk and continue by decreasing the number of asterisks by 1 for each successive line until only one asterisk is printed. Hint: Use nested `for` loops; the outside loop controls the number of lines to print, and the inside loop controls the number of asterisks to print on a line. For example, if the user enters 5, the output would be

```
*
**
***
****
*****
****
***
**
*
```

Defining Classes and Methods

class n. 1. a. A set, collection, group, or configuration containing members having or thought to have at least one attribute in common; kind; sort. . . . - The American Heritage Dictionary of the English Language, Third Edition

Recall that an object is named by a variable of a class type. Objects have data, but they also can take actions. The actions they can take are called methods. You have already been using some objects. The type `String` is a class, and values of type `String` are objects. For example, if `name` is an object of type `String`, then the method `length` can be used to determine the length of the string. The length of the string is the value returned by the expression `name.length( )`. In this chapter, we will show you how to define your own simple classes and how to use objects and methods of those classes.

OBJECTIVES

Become familiar with the concepts of a class and of an object that instantiates the class.

Learn how to define classes in Java.

Learn to define and use methods (object actions) in Java.

Learn to create objects in Java.

Find out how parameters work in Java.

Learn about information hiding and encapsulation.

Become familiar with the notion of reference so that you can understand class variables and class parameters.

PREREQUISITES

You need to be familiar with the material in Chapters 2 and 3 before reading this chapter.

4.1 CLASS AND METHOD DEFINITIONS

A Java program consists of objects, from various classes, interacting with one another. Before we go into the details of how you define and use classes and objects in Java, it will help to have a general idea of what classes and objects are all about.

object
class

Objects can represent objects in the real word, like automobiles, houses, employee records—almost anything you want. A **class** is the definition of a kind of object. It is like an outline or a plan for constructing specific objects. For example, Display 4.1 describes a class called `Automobile`. The class is a general description of what an automobile is and what it can do. Objects are particular automobiles. The figure shows three **Automobile** objects. An object that satisfies the class definition of an **Automobile** is said to **instantiate** the **Automobile** class. Thus, objects are the individual automobiles, while the **Automobile** class is a description of what an automobile is and does. This is, of course, a very simplified **Automobile** class, but it illustrates the basic idea of what a class is. Let's look at some details.

instantiate

A class specifies the kind of data the objects of that class have. The **Automobile** class definition says that an **Automobile** object has three pieces of data: a number telling how many gallons of fuel are in the fuel tank, another number telling how fast the automobile is moving, and a string that shows what is written on the license plate. The class definition has no data (that is, no numbers and no string). The individual objects have the data, but the class specifies what kind of data they have.

■ DISPLAY 4.1   **A Class as an Outline**

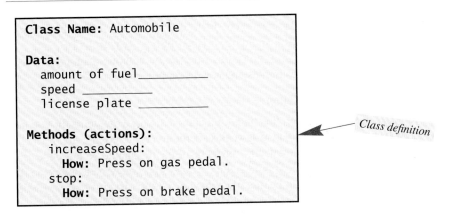

Instantiations of the Class **Automobile** :

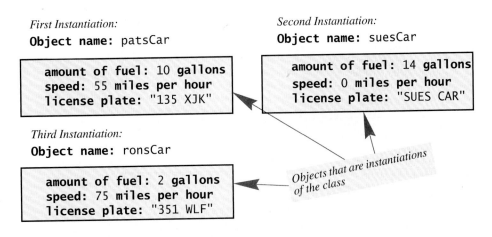

method

The class also specifies what actions the objects can take and how they accomplish those actions. The `Automobile` class specifies two actions: `increaseSpeed` and `stop`. Thus, in a program that uses the class `Automobile`, the only actions an `Automobile` object can take are `increaseSpeed` and `stop`. These actions are called **methods.** All objects of the class `Automobile` have identical methods. All objects of any one class have the same methods. As you can see in our sample `Automobile` class, the definitions of the methods (how the actions are performed) are given in the class definition. However, the methods' actions are performed by the objects.

class diagram

UML

The notation in Display 4.1 is a bit cumbersome, so programmers often use a simpler graphical notation to summarize some of the main properties of a class. This notation, illustrated in Display 4.2, is called a **UML class diagram,** or simply a **class diagram.** (UML is an acronym for Universal Modeling Language.) The class described in Display 4.2 is the same as the one described in Display 4.1. Any annotations in Display 4.2 that are new will be explained later in the chapter.

Notice a few more things about a class and the objects that instantiate the class. Each object has a name. In Display 4.1, the names are `patsCar`, `suesCar`, and `ronsCar`. Among other things, a class is a data type. In a Java program, these object names (`patsCar`, `suesCar`, and `ronsCar`) would be variables of type `Automobile`.

Before we get further into the nitty gritty of Java code by defining a simple class, we should tell you how to store classes in files and how to compile them.

Class Files and Separate Compilation

Whether you use a class taken from this book or a class that you write yourself, you need to know a few basic details about how a Java class definition is stored in a file. Each Java class definition should be in a file by itself,[1] the name of the file should be the same as the name of the class, and the file name should end in `.java`. So if you write a definition for a class called `Automobile`, it should be in a file named `Automobile.java`. If you write a definition for a class called `MyClass`, it should be in a file named `MyClass.java`.

■ DISPLAY 4.2   A Class Outline as a UML Class Diagram

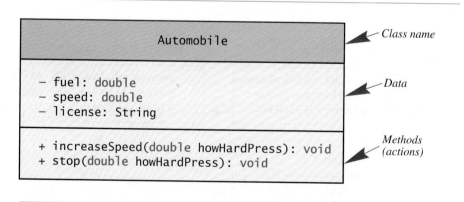

---

1. There are exceptions to this rule, but we will seldom encounter them, and we need not be concerned about them yet.

You can compile a Java class before you have a program in which to use it. The compiled byte-code for the class will be stored in a file of the same name, but ending in `.class` rather than `.java`. So compiling the file `Automobile.java` will create a file called `Automobile.class`. Later, you can compile a program file with a `main` part that uses the class `Automobile`, and you will not need to recompile the class definition for `Automobile`. This naming requirement applies to full programs as well as to classes. Notice that every program with a `main` part has a class name at the start of the file; this is the name you need to use for the file that holds the program. For example, the program in Display 4.4 should be in a file named `SpeciesFirstTryDemo.java`. As long as all the classes you use in a program are in the same directory as the program file, you need not worry about directories. In Chapter 5, we will discuss how you can place files in more than one directory.

Instance Variables

Display 4.3 contains a simple class definition. We have simplified this class to make this first example easier to explain. Later in the chapter, we will give the same example in a better style. But this example has all the essentials of a class definition.

■ DISPLAY 4.3   A Class Definition *(Part 1 of 2)*

We will give a better version of this class later in this chapter.

Later in this chapter you will see that the modifier `public` should be replaced with `private`.

```java
public class SpeciesFirstTry
{
    public String name;
    public int population;
    public double growthRate;

    public void readInput()
    {
        System.out.println("What is the species' name?");
        name = SavitchIn.readLine();
        System.out.println("What is the population of the species?");
        population = SavitchIn.readLineInt();
        while (population < 0)
        {
            System.out.println("Population cannot be negative.");
            System.out.println("Reenter population:");
            population = SavitchIn.readLineInt();
        }
        System.out.println(
                    "Enter growth rate (percent increase per year):");
        growthRate = SavitchIn.readLineDouble();
    }

    public void writeOutput()
    {
        System.out.println("Name = " + name);
        System.out.println("Population = " + population);
        System.out.println("Growth rate = " + growthRate + "%");
    }
```

■ DISPLAY 4.3   **A Class Definition** *(Part 2 of 2)*

```
public int populationIn10( )
{
    double populationAmount = population;
    int count = 10;
    while ((count > 0) && (populationAmount > 0))
    {
        populationAmount = (populationAmount +
                            (growthRate/100) * populationAmount);
        count--;
    }
    if (populationAmount > 0)
        return (int)populationAmount;
    else
        return 0;
}
}
```

(int) is a type cast, as discussed in Chapter 2.

The class name is `SpeciesFirstTry`, and the class is designed to hold records of endangered species. (It's called `FirstTry` because we will later give an improved version of this class.) Each object of this class has three pieces of data: a name, a population size, and a growth rate. The objects have three methods: `readInput`, `writeOutput`, and `populationIn10`. Both the data items and the methods are sometimes called **members** of the object because they belong to the object; they are also sometimes called **fields.** However, we will call the data items **instance variables** and we will call the methods **methods.** Let's discuss the data items (that is, the instance variables) first.

The following three lines from the start of the class definition define three instance variables (three data members):

```
public String name;
public int population;
public double growthRate;
```

The word `public` simply means that there are no restrictions on how these instance variables are used. Each of these lines declares one instance variable name. You can think of an object of the class as a complex item with instance variables inside of it. So you can think of an instance variable as a smaller variable inside each object of the class. In this case, the instance variables are called `name`, `population`, and `growthRate`. Each object of the class will have these three instance variables. Display 4.4 contains a program that demonstrates the use of this class definition. Let's see how it handles these instance variables.

The following line from Display 4.4 creates an object of type `SpeciesFirstTry` and attaches the name `speciesOfTheMonth` to this object:

```
SpeciesFirstTry speciesOfTheMonth = new SpeciesFirstTry( );
```

member

field

instance variable

■ DISPLAY 4.4   **Using Classes and Methods**

```
public class SpeciesFirstTryDemo
{
    public static void main(String[] args)
    {
        SpeciesFirstTry speciesOfTheMonth = new SpeciesFirstTry();
        int futurePopulation;

        System.out.println("Enter data on the Species of the Month:");
        speciesOfTheMonth.readInput();
        speciesOfTheMonth.writeOutput();

        futurePopulation = speciesOfTheMonth.populationIn10();
        System.out.println("In ten years the population will be "
                                            + futurePopulation);

        speciesOfTheMonth.name = "Klingon ox";
        speciesOfTheMonth.population = 10;
        speciesOfTheMonth.growthRate = 15;
        System.out.println("The new Species of the Month:");
        speciesOfTheMonth.writeOutput();
        System.out.println("In ten years the population will be "
                                + speciesOfTheMonth.populationIn10());
    }
}
```

Sample Screen Dialog

```
Enter data on the Species of the Month:
What is the species' name?
Ferengie fur ball
What is the population of the species?
1000
Enter growth rate (percent increase per year):
-20.5
Name = Ferengie fur ball
Population = 1000
Growth rate = -20.5%
In ten years the population will be 100
The new Species of the Month:
Name = Klingon ox
Population = 10
Growth rate = 15.0%
In ten years the population will be 40
```

Like all objects of type `SpeciesFirstTry`, the object `speciesOfTheMonth` has three instance variables called `name`, `population`, and `growthRate`. You can refer to one of these instance variables by writing the object name followed by a dot and then the instance variable's name. For example,

```
speciesOfTheMonth.name
```

denotes the `name` instance variable for the object `speciesOfTheMonth`. Look again at the three lines that define the instance variables (repeated here):

```
public String name;
public int population;
public double growthRate;
```

Notice that each instance variable has a type. For example, the instance variable `name` is of type `String`, and so the instance variable `speciesOfTheMonth.name` is a variable of type `String` and can be used anyplace that you can use a variable of type `String`. For example, all of the following are valid Java expressions:

```
speciesOfTheMonth.name = "Klingon ox.";
System.out.println("Save the " + speciesOfTheMonth.name);
String niceName = speciesOfTheMonth.name;
```

Each object of type `SpeciesFirstTry` has its own three instance variables. For example, suppose that your program also contained the statement

```
SpeciesFirstTry speciesOfLastMonth = new SpeciesFirstTry();
```

Then `speciesOfTheMonth.name` and `speciesOfLastMonth.name` would be two different instance variables that might have different string values.

FAQ: **Why Do We Need** new?

When `new` is used in an expression such as the following, you can think of it as creating the instance variables of the object.

```
SpeciesFirstTry speciesOfLastMonth = new SpeciesFirstTry();
```

An object of a class type, such as `speciesOfLastMonth`, can have smaller variables inside of it, namely, the instance variables of the object. The `new` places these instance variables inside of the object. We will explain this use of `new` more completely in Section 4.3.

Using Methods

invoke
call

When you use a method, you are said to **invoke** or **call** it. You have already invoked methods. For example, your programs have invoked the method `readLineInt( )` of the class `SavitchIn`. You have also invoked the method `println` with the object `System.out`, as in the following statement:

```
System.out.println("Enter data on the Species of the Month:");
```

There are two kinds of methods: (1) those that return a single value and (2) those that perform some action other than returning a single value. The method `readLineInt` is an example of a method that returns a single value. It returns a value of type int. The method println is an example of a method that performs some action other than returning a single value. These two different kinds of methods are used in slightly different ways.

Remember: **Two Kinds of Methods**

There are two kinds of methods: (1) those that return a single value and (2) those that perform some action other than return a value. Methods that perform some action other than returning a value are called void **methods.**

Let's first discuss how you invoke a method that returns a value, using the method readLineInt as an example. Suppose you have the following declaration in a program:

    int next;

The following is an example of an invocation of the method readLineInt for the class SavitchIn:

    next = SavitchIn.readLineInt();

(If you want to see this invocation in the context of a full program, refer back to Display 3.17 in Chapter 3.) Let's look at this method invocation in more detail.

A method defined in a class is usually invoked using an object of that class. This object is known as the **calling object,** and it is the first item that you give when writing a method invocation. For certain special methods, you can use the name of the class instead of using an object of the class, and our first example will use the class name SavitchIn rather than an object of that class. You invoke a method by writing the calling object name or the class name (such as SavitchIn), followed by a dot, and then the name of the method (such as readLineInt), and finally a set of parentheses that may (or may not) have information for the method. If the method is one that returns a single value, such as the method readLineInt, you can use this method invocation anyplace that it is valid to use a value of the type returned by the method. The method readLineInt returns a value of type int, and so you can use the method invocation

calling object

value returned

    SavitchIn.readLineInt()

anyplace that it is valid to use a value of type int. For example, a value of type int, such as 6, can be used in an assignment statement, like this:

    next = 6;

So, the method invocation SavitchIn.readLineInt() can be used in the same way, like so:

    next = SavitchIn.readLineInt();

When a method that returns a single value is invoked, it is as if the method invocation were replaced by the value returned. So, if SavitchIn.readLineInt() returns the value 3, then the assignment statement

    next = SavitchIn.readLineInt();

produces the same effect as

```
next = 3;
```

not returning
a value

Methods that perform some action other than returning a single value are similar, except that they are used to produce Java statements rather than Java values. For example, the following statement from the program in Display 4.4 includes an invocation of the method `println` with the calling object `System.out`:

```
System.out.println("Enter data on the Species of the Month:");
```

This method call causes the string `"Enter data on the Species of the Month:"` to be written to the screen. The method `writeOutput` for the class `SpeciesFirstTry` (used in Display 4.4) is similar, except that you do not have to tell `writeOutput` what to output by including something inside the parentheses. The method `writeOutput` gets the information to send to the screen from its calling object.

For example, the program in Display 4.4 (after doing some other things) sets the values of the instance variables of the object `speciesOfTheMonth` with the following three assignment statements:

```
speciesOfTheMonth.name = "Klingon ox";
speciesOfTheMonth.population = 10;
speciesOfTheMonth.growthRate = 15;
```

The program then uses the following statements to output these values:

```
System.out.println("The new Species of the Month:");
speciesOfTheMonth.writeOutput();
```

The second of the previous two lines of code contains an invocation of the method `writeOutput` with the calling object `speciesOfTheMonth`. This invocation produces the output

```
Name = Klingon ox
Population = 10
Growth rate = 15.0%
```

Recall that, to invoke a method for an object, you write the calling object name (such as `speciesOfTheMonth`), followed by a dot, the name of the method (such as `writeOutput`), and finally a set of parentheses that may have information for the method. If, as is true in this case, the method invocation is one that produces some action other than returning a single value, then you make it into a Java statement by placing a semicolon after the method invocation. For example, the following is an invocation of the method `writeOutput` for the object `speciesOfTheMonth`:

```
speciesOfTheMonth.writeOutput();
```

This causes the method to perform whatever action is specified in the method definition.

Quick Reference: Method Invocation (Calling a Method)

You **invoke** a method by writing the calling object followed by a dot, then the name of the method, and finally a set of parentheses that may (or may not) have information to pass to the method.

If the method invocation returns a value, then you can use the method invocation anyplace that you are allowed to write a value of the type returned by the method. For example, the following includes an invocation of the method `populationIn10` by the calling object `speciesOfTheMonth`:

```
futurePopulation = speciesOfTheMonth.populationIn10();
```

If the method invocation is one that performs some action other than returning a single value, then you place a semicolon after the method invocation, and that produces a Java statement. (These methods that perform actions are called `void` methods.) For example, the following is an invocation of the `void` method `readInput` with the calling object `speciesOfTheMonth`:

```
speciesOfTheMonth.readInput();
```

This method invocation causes the method to perform whatever action is specified in the method definition.

For certain special methods (like the methods in the class `SavitchIn`), you can use the class name rather than a calling object. These kinds of methods are discussed more fully in Chapter 5.

`void` Method Definitions

The following method invocation is from Display 4.4:

```
speciesOfTheMonth.writeOutput();
```

Let's look at the definition of the method `writeOutput` to see how method definitions are written. The definition is given in Display 4.3 and is repeated here:

Body

```
public void writeOutput()          Heading
{
    System.out.println("Name = " + name);
    System.out.println("Population = " + population);
    System.out.println("Growth rate = " + growthRate + "%");
}
```

All method definitions belong to some class, and all method definitions are given inside the definition of the class to which they belong. If you look at Display 4.3, you will see that this method definition is inside the definition of the class `SpeciesFirstTry`. This means that the method can be used only with objects of the class `SpeciesFirstTry`.

The definition of a method that does not return a value starts with the keywords `public void`, followed by the name of the method and a pair of parentheses. The word `public` indicates that there are no special restrictions on the use of the method. Later in this chapter, you will see that the word `public` can sometimes be replaced with other modifiers to restrict the use of the method. The word `void` is a rather poor choice, but it is what is used in Java and in other languages. The word `void` indicates that the method does not return a value. The parentheses enclose any extra information that the method will need. In this case, no extra information is needed, and so there is nothing inside the parentheses. Later in the chapter, you will see examples of the sorts of things that might appear inside these parentheses (for other method definitions). This first part of the method definition is called the **heading** for the method. The heading is normally written on a single line; but, if it is too long for one line, it can be broken into two (or more) lines. Because of the

void method

method heading

method
body

use of the word void in the method heading, these methods (that do not return a value) are called void **methods**.

After the heading comes the **body** of the method definition, and that completes the method definition. The body of the method definition is enclosed between braces { }. Between the braces, you can place any statement or declaration that you can place in the main part of a program. Any variable used in a method definition (other than an instance variable) should be declared within that method definition.

When a void method is invoked, it is as if the method invocation were replaced by the body of the method definition, and the statements (and declarations) within the body are executed. There are some subtleties about this replacement process, but for the simple examples we will look at now, it is like a literal replacement of the method invocation by the body of the method definition. Eventually, you'll want to learn to think of the method definition as defining an action to be taken, rather than as a list of statements to substitute for the method invocation, but this substitution idea is correct and is a good way to start understanding method invocations.

For example, the following method invocation occurs in the program in Display 4.4:

```
speciesOfTheMonth.writeOutput();
```

When this method invocation is executed, it is as if the line with the method invocation were replaced by the body of the method definition for the method writeOutput. In this case, it is as if the preceding method invocation were replaced with the following:

```
{
    System.out.println("Name = " + name);
    System.out.println("Population = " + population);
    System.out.println("Growth rate = " + growthRate + "%");
}
```

The instance variable names (name, population, and growthRate) refer to the instance variables of the calling object; in this example, they refer to the instance variables of the object speciesOfTheMonth. To be more precise, the invocation is equivalent to the following:

```
{
    System.out.println("Name = " + speciesOfTheMonth.name);
    System.out.println("Population = "
                        + speciesOfTheMonth.population);
    System.out.println("Growth rate = "
                        + speciesOfTheMonth.growthRate + "%");
}
```

To be very concrete, if speciesOfTheMonth.name has the value "Klingon ox", speciesOfTheMonth.population has the value 10, and speciesOfThe-Month.growthRate has the value 15, then the method invocation

```
speciesOfTheMonth.writeOutput();
```

will cause the following to be written to the computer screen:

```
Name = Klingon ox
Population = 10
Growth rate = 15.0%
```

If you look at the program in Display 4.4, you will see that it looks like a class definition that has no instance variables and only a single method that is named `main`. It is in fact true that `main` is a method. A program is simply a class that has a method named `main`. All the programs that we have written so far have no instance variables and no methods other than the method `main`, but a program can have other methods and can have instance variables. When you run a program, you are simply invoking the `void` method that is named `main`. Of course, this is a special kind of method invocation, but it is a method invocation nonetheless. For now, those extra words like `static` and `String[] args` will remain a bit of a mystery. Just put them in, and eventually we will explain them all.

main method

Methods That Return a Value

You define a method that returns a single value in basically the same way that you define a `void` method, with one added complication—namely, specifying the value returned. Let's consider the method `populationIn10` from the class `SpeciesFirstTry`. The method is used in the following line of the program in Display 4.4:

methods that return a value

```
futurePopulation = speciesOfTheMonth.populationIn10();
```

This sets the value of the variable `futurePopulation` equal to the value returned by the method invocation

```
speciesOfTheMonth.populationIn10()
```

The definition of the method `populationIn10` tells the computer how to compute the value returned. Let's look at that method definition, reproduced here from Display 4.3:

```java
public int populationIn10()
{
    double populationAmount = population;
    int count = 10;
    while ((count > 0) && (populationAmount > 0))
    {
        populationAmount = (populationAmount +
                        (growthRate/100) * populationAmount);
        count--;
    }
    if (populationAmount > 0)
        return (int)populationAmount;
    else
        return 0;
}
```

As was true of a `void` method definition, the definition of a method that returns a value can be divided into two parts: the method heading and the method body. The following is the method heading for the method `populationIn10`:

```java
public int populationIn10()
```

The description of a method heading for a method that returns a value is almost the same as that for the heading of a `void` method. The only difference is that a method that returns a value uses a type name instead of the keyword `void`. The heading begins with the keyword `public`, followed by a type name (rather than the word `void`), followed by the name of the method and a pair of parentheses. The parentheses enclose a description of any extra information that the method will need. In this case, no extra information is needed, and so there is nothing inside the parentheses. The keyword `public` indicates that there are no special restrictions on the use of the method. Later in this chapter, you will see that the word `public` can be replaced with other modifiers to restrict the use of the method. The important new element is the use of a type name—`int` in this example—in the method heading. Let's consider that type name.

type returned

The heading of a method that returns a value includes a type name. The type name is the type of the value returned. Each method can return values of only one type. In different situations, a method may return different values, but they must all be values of the type specified in the method heading.

return
statement

The body of a method definition that returns a value is just like the body of a `void` method definition, except that it must contain the following in one or more places:

    return *Expression*;

This is called a `return` **statement.** The *Expression* can be any expression that produces a value of the type specified in the heading of the method definition. This statement says that the value returned by the method is the value of this expression. For example, the definition of the method `populationIn10` contains two `return` statements:

    return (int)populationAmount;

and

    return 0;

When a method that returns a value is invoked, the statements in the body of the method definition are executed. For example, consider the following method invocation from Display 4.4:

    futurePopulation = speciesOfTheMonth.populationIn10( );

When this assignment statement is executed, the body of the method definition for `populationIn10` is executed. That body follows:

```
{
    double populationAmount = population;
    int count = 10;
    while ((count > 0) && (populationAmount > 0))
    {
        populationAmount = (populationAmount +
                        (growthRate/100) * populationAmount);
        count--;
    }
    if (populationAmount > 0)
        return (int)populationAmount;
    else
        return 0;
}
```

(int) is a type cast, as discussed in Chapter 2.

The instance variable `population` refers to the instance variable of the calling object, which in this case is `speciesOfTheMonth`. The value of `population` is copied into the variable `populationAmount`, and then the `while` loop is executed. Each iteration of the loop increases the value of populationAmount by the amount that the population will change in one year, and the loop is iterated 10 times. So when the while loop ends, the value of populationAmount is the projected size of the population in 10 years. At that point, populationAmount has the value that we want the method to return. For now, let's assume that that number is positive (that is, that the species is not extinct). In that case, the following return statement is executed, and it says that the value (int)populationAmount is the value computed by (returned by) the method invocation:

```
return (int)populationAmount;
```

The (int) is a type cast that changes the double value to an int value so that you do not have a fraction of an animal. (Ugh!) It is as if the method invocation were replaced by (int)populationAmount. In this case, the method invocation is in the following assignment statement:

```
futurePopulation = speciesOfTheMonth.populationIn10( );
```

Therefore, the variable futurePopulation is set to the value of (int)populationAmount.

If populationAmount happens to be zero or negative, the following return statement is executed instead:

```
return 0;
```

This is a minor detail that ensures that the projected population will not be negative. After all, in the real world, once a population reaches zero individuals, the population just stays at zero; it does not go negative.

When a return statement is executed, that statement determines the value returned by the method. When a return statement is executed, that also ends the method invocation. If there are more statements after the return statement, they are not executed.

A method that returns a value may perform some other action as well, such as reading a value from the keyboard, but it definitely must return a value.

Remember: **Naming Methods**

Java will let you use any valid (nonkeyword) identifier as the name for a method. But if you choose clear, meaningful names, your code will be easier to read. A good rule to follow when naming methods is to (usually) use verbs to name void methods and to (usually) use nouns to name methods that return a value. This is because, like a verb, a void method names an action. On the other hand, a method that returns a value can be used like a value, and a value is a thing, and nouns are used to denote things.

The normal convention when naming classes and methods is to start all method names with a lower-case letter and to start all class names with an uppercase letter.

FAQ: **What Is a Function?**

Methods that return a value are called functions in some other programming languages, and a method that returns a value does correspond to the mathematical notion of a function. However, in Java they are called methods (that return a value). They are not called functions.

■ **Java Tip**

Use of `return` in `void` Methods

A `void` method returns no value and so is not required to have any `return` statement. However, there is a kind of `return` statement that you may sometimes want to use in a `void` method. A `return` statement within a `void` method has the form

```
return;
```

It is just like the other `return` statements you have seen, except that you do not include any expression for the value returned (because no value is returned). When this `return` statement is executed, the invocation of the `void` method ends. This can be used to end a method invocation early, such as when the method discovers some sort of problem. For example, you might add the following method to the definition of the class `SpeciesFirstTry`:

```
public void showLandPortion()
{
    if (population == 0)
    {
        System.out.println("Population is zero.");
        return;//Ends here to avoid division by zero.
    }
    double fraction;
    fraction = 6.0/population;
    System.out.println("If the population were spread");
    System.out.println("over 6 continents, then each");
    System.out.println("individual would have a fraction of");
    System.out.println("its continent equal to " + fraction);
}
```

The method ends with a `return` if the rest of the method would involve a division by zero. (It's not a very likely method, but it does illustrate the point.) ■

Quick Reference: Method Definitions

Every method belongs to some class. The definition of a method is given in the definition of the class to which it belongs. The two most common forms for a method definition follow.

`void` Method Definition:

```
public void Method_Name(Parameters)
{
    Statement_1
    Statement_2
        . . .
```

Statement_Last
    }

(So far, we have not discussed *Parameters*, but we will do so shortly. If there are no *Parameters*, the parentheses are empty.)

Example:

```
public void writeOutput()
{
    System.out.println("Name = " + name);
    System.out.println("Population = " + population);
    System.out.println("Growth rate = " + growthRate + "%");
}
```

Definition of a Method That Returns a Value:

public *Type_Returned Method_Name* (*Parameters*)
    {
        <List of statements, at least one of which
                must contain a return statement.>
    }

(So far, we have not discussed *Parameters*, but we will do so shortly. If there are no *Parameters*, the parentheses are empty.)

Example: (this could be added to the class in Display 4.3):

```
public int halfThePopulation()
{
    return (population/2);
}
```

Quick Reference: `return` Statements

Every method definition for a method that returns a value must have one or more `return` statements. A `return` statement specifies the value returned by the method and ends the method invocation.

Syntax:

return *Expression*;

Example:

```
public int halfThePopulation()
{
    return (population/2);
}
```

A `void` method is not required to have a `return` statement, but it can have one if you want to end the method invocation before the end of the code. The form for a `return` statement in a `void` method is

return;

The `this` Parameter

Look back at the class definition of the class `SpeciesFirstTry` in Display 4.3, and then look at the program in Display 4.4 that uses this class. Notice that instance variables are written differently depending on whether they are within the class definition or someplace outside the class definition, such as in a program that uses the class. Outside of the class definition, you name an instance variable by giving the name of an object of the class, followed by a dot and the name of the instance variable, as in the following reference to the instance variable `name` that appears in Display 4.4:

```
speciesOfTheMonth.name = "Klingon ox";
```

However, inside the definition of a method of that same class, you can simply use the instance variable name without any object name or dot. For example, the following line occurs inside the definition of the method `readInput` of the class `SpeciesFirstTry` in Display 4.3:

```
name = SavitchIn.readLine();
```

this

As you know, every instance variable, including this instance variable `name`, is an instance variable of some object. In cases like this, the object is understood to be there, but its name usually is omitted. This understood object has the somewhat unusual name of `this`. Although `this` is usually omitted (but understood to be there), you can include it if you want. For example, the preceding assignment of the instance variable `name`, which we copied from the definition of the method `readInput` in Display 4.3, is equivalent to the following:

```
this.name = SavitchIn.readLine();
```

As another example, the following is a rewrite of the method definition for the method `writeOutput`. It is equivalent to the version used in Display 4.3.

```
public void writeOutput()
{
    System.out.println("Name = " + this.name);
    System.out.println("Population = " + this.population);
    System.out.println("Growth rate = " + this.growthRate + "%");
}
```

The keyword `this` stands for the calling object. For example, consider the following method invocation from Display 4.4:

```
speciesOfTheMonth.writeOutput();
```

The calling object is `speciesOfTheMonth`. So this invocation of the method `writeOutput` is equivalent to

```
{
    System.out.println("Name = " + speciesOfTheMonth.name);
    System.out.println("Population = "
                         + speciesOfTheMonth.population);
    System.out.println("Growth rate = " +
                         speciesOfTheMonth.growthRate + "%");
}
```

which we got by replacing `this` with `speciesOfTheMonth`.

The keyword `this` is like a blank waiting to be filled in by the object that invokes the method. Because you would be using `this` so often if it were required, Java lets you omit it and the dot that follows it, but the `this` and the dot are understood to be there implicitly. This is an abbreviation that is almost always used. Programmers seldom use the `this` parameter, but there are some situations in which it is needed.

Quick Reference: **The `this` Parameter**

When giving a method definition, you can use the keyword `this` as a name for the calling object.

? Self-Test Questions

1. Consider the program in Display 4.4. Suppose you wanted to add another species object called `speciesOfTheYear`, and suppose you wanted the user to give it data, specifically a name, population, and growth rate. What code do you need to add to the program? (*Hint:* It requires only three or four lines of code.)

2. Suppose `Employee` is a class with a `void` method named `readInput` and `dilbert` is an object of the class `Employee`. So `dilbert` was named and created by the following:

   ```
   Employee dilbert = new Employee();
   ```

   Write an invocation of the method `readInput` with `dilbert` as the calling object. The method `readInput` needs no information in parentheses.

3. Let's say you want to assign a number as well as a name to each species in the world, perhaps to make it easier to catalog them. Modify the definition of the class `SpeciesFirstTry` in Display 4.3 so that it allows for a number. The number is to be of type `int`. (*Hint:* You mostly have to just add stuff. Note that part of what you need to do is to change some methods by adding stuff.)

4. Suppose you live in an idealized world where every species has exactly the same number of male and female members in its population. Give the definition of a method, called `femalePopulation`, that you could add to the definition of the class `SpeciesFirstTry` in Display 4.3. The method `femalePopulation` returns the number of females in the population. If the population is an odd number, you have one species member left over after pairing; assume that member is a female. For example, if the population is 6, there are 3 males and 3 females. If the population is 7, there are 3 males and 4 females. Also give the definition of a method called `malePopulation` that similarly returns the number of males in the population. (*Hint:* The definitions are very short. The bodies of the two definitions are a little bit different.)

5. Rewrite the definition of the method `writeOutput` in Display 4.3, using the `this` parameter. Note that the meaning of the definition will not change at all. You

will just write it slightly differently. (*Hint:* All you need to do is add `this` and dots in certain places.)

6. Rewrite the definition of the method `readInput` in Display 4.3, using the `this` parameter.

7. Rewrite the definition of the method `PopulationIn10` in Display 4.3, using the `this` parameter.

8. What is the meaning of `(int)` that appears in the definition of the method `PopulationIn10` in Display 4.3, and why is it needed?

Local Variables

local variable

Notice the definition of the method `populationIn10` given in Display 4.3. That method definition includes the declaration of variables called `populationAmount` and `count`. A variable declared within a method is called a **local variable.** It is called local because its meaning is local to—that is, confined to—the method definition. If you have two methods and each of them declares a variable of the same name—for example, if both were named `populationAmount`—they would be two different variables that just happened to have the same name. Any change that was made to the variable named `populationAmount` within one method would have no effect upon the variable named `populationAmount` in the other method. It would be as if the two methods were executed on different computers, or as if the computer changed the name of the variable named `populationAmount` in one of the two methods to `populationAmount2`.

Since the `main` part of a program is itself a method, all variables declared in `main` are local variables for the method `main`. If one happens to have the same name as a variable declared in some other method, then they are two different variables that just happen to have the same name. For example, look at the program and class definition in Display 4.5. First consider the program, which is shown in the lower half of the display. The method `main` in the program includes the declaration of a variable named `newAmount`. Now look at the class definition in the upper half of the display. The method `showNewBalance` in the class also declares a variable named `newAmount`. These are two different variables, both of which are named `newAmount`. The variable named `newAmount` in `main` is set equal to `800.00`. After that, there is the following method invocation:

```
myAccount.showNewBalance();
```

If you look at the definition of the method `showNewBalance` and do a little arithmetic, you will see that, within this method, another variable named `newAmount` is set equal to `105.00`. Yet this variable has no effect on the other variable named `newAmount` that is in `main`. After that method invocation, the variable named `newAmount` in `main` is written out, and its value is still `800.00`. Changing the value of `newAmount` in the method `showNewBalance` had no effect on the variable named `newAmount` in `main`. In this case, the two variables with the same name are in different definitions in two different files. However, the situation would be the same if the two methods were in the same class definition and thus in the same file.

■ DISPLAY 4.5   **Local Variables**

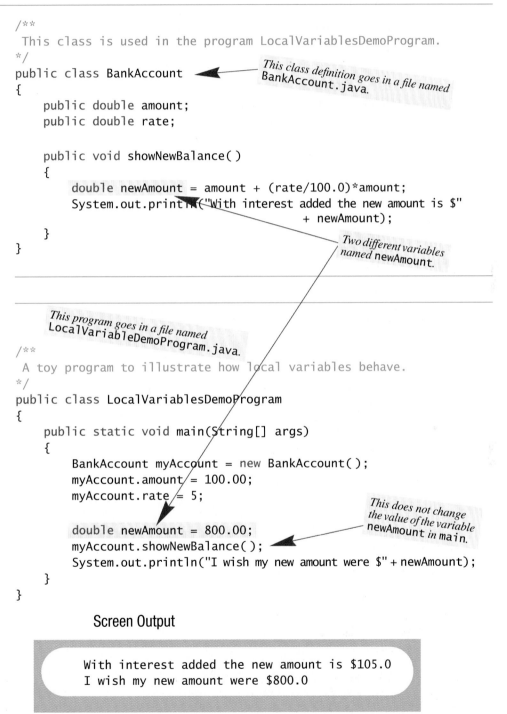

```
/**
 This class is used in the program LocalVariablesDemoProgram.
*/
public class BankAccount
{
    public double amount;
    public double rate;

    public void showNewBalance( )
    {
        double newAmount = amount + (rate/100.0)*amount;
        System.out.println("With interest added the new amount is $"
                                        + newAmount);
    }
}
```

This class definition goes in a file named `BankAccount.java`*.*

Two different variables named `newAmount`*.*

This program goes in a file named `LocalVariableDemoProgram.java`*.*

```
/**
 A toy program to illustrate how local variables behave.
*/
public class LocalVariablesDemoProgram
{
    public static void main(String[] args)
    {
        BankAccount myAccount = new BankAccount( );
        myAccount.amount = 100.00;
        myAccount.rate = 5;

        double newAmount = 800.00;
        myAccount.showNewBalance( );
        System.out.println("I wish my new amount were $" + newAmount);
    }
}
```

This does not change the value of the variable `newAmount` *in* `main`*.*

Screen Output

```
With interest added the new amount is $105.0
I wish my new amount were $800.0
```

Quick Reference: **Local Variable**

A variable declared within a method definition is called a **local variable.** If two methods each have a local variable of the same name, they are two different variables, even though they have the same name.

Quick Reference: **Global Variables**

Thus far, we have discussed two kinds of variables: instance variables, whose meaning is confined to an object of a class, and local variables, whose meaning is confined to a method definition. Some programming languages have another kind of variable, called a **global variable,** whose meaning is confined only to the program, which means that it's not confined at all. Java does not have these global variables.

Blocks

compound
statement

block

The terms **block** and **compound statement** really mean the same thing, namely, a set of Java statements enclosed in braces {}. However, the two terms tend to be used in different contexts. When you declare a variable within a compound statement, the compound statement is usually called a block.

If you declare a variable within a block (that is, within a compound statement), that variable is local to the block. This means that when the block ends, all variables declared within the block disappear. In many programming languages, you can even use that variable's name to name some other variable outside of the block. However, *in Java, you cannot have two variables with the same name inside of a single method definition.*

Local variables within blocks can sometimes be a little troublesome in Java. In Java, you cannot reuse the local variable name outside the block for another variable. Thus, it is sometimes easier to declare the variable outside the block. If you declare a variable outside of a block, you can use it both inside and outside the block, and it will have the same meaning whether it is in the block or outside the block.

Quick Reference: **Blocks**

A **block** is another name for a compound statement, that is, a list of statements enclosed in braces. Although a block and a compound statement are the same thing, we tend to use the term *block* when there is a variable declaration contained within the braces. The variables declared in a block are local to the block, and so these variables disappear when the execution of the block is completed. However, even though the variables are local to the block, their names cannot be used for anything else within the same method definition.

▲ *Gotcha*

Variables Declared in a Block

When you declare a variable within a block, that variable becomes a local variable for the block. This means that you cannot use the variable outside of the block. If you want to use a variable outside of a block, you must declare it outside of the block. Declaring the variable outside of the block will let you use the variable both outside and inside the block. △

■ **Java Tip**
Declaring Variables in a `for` Statement

You can declare a variable within the initialization part of a `for` statement, as in the following example:

```
int sum = 0;
for (int n = 1; n <= 10; n++)
    sum = sum + n*n;
```

If you do this, the variable, in this case n, will be **local to the `for` loop,** and cannot be used outside of the `for` loop. For example, the following use of n in the System.out.println statement is not allowed:

```
for (int n = 1; n <= 10; n++)
    sum = sum + n*n;
System.out.println(n);//Invalid
```

This can sometimes be more of a nuisance than a helpful feature. Moreover, variables declared in the initialization part of a `for` loop are treated differently in different programming languages and even in different versions of Java. For these reasons, we prefer not to use this feature and to instead declare our variables outside of the `for` loop. However, you should be aware of this feature, since you will see it in other programmers' code. ☐

Parameters of a Primitive Type

Consider the method `populationIn10` for the class `SpeciesFirstTry` defined in Display 4.3. It returns the projected population of a species 10 years in the future. But what if you want the projection for 5 years in the future or 50 years in the future? It would be much more useful to have a method that starts with an integer for some number of years and returns the projected population for that many years into the future. In order to do this, we need some way of leaving a blank in a method, so that each call of the method can have the blank filled in with a different value for the number of years. The things that serve as blanks in methods are called formal parameters, or simply **parameters**. They are a bit more complicated than simple blanks, but you will not go too far wrong if you think of them as blanks or placeholders to be filled in with some value when the method is invoked.

parameter

The class `SpeciesSecondTry` defined in Display 4.6 includes a method called `projectedPopulation` that has one formal parameter called `years`. When you call the method, you give the value that you want to have substituted for the parameter `years`. For example, if `speciesOfTheMonth` is declared to be of type `SpeciesSecondTry`, you can use the method `projectedPopulation` to calculate the population in 12 years as follows:

```
futurePopulation = speciesOfTheMonth.projectedPopulation(12);
```

■ DISPLAY 4.6   **A Method with a Parameter**

```
public class SpeciesSecondTry
{
    public String name;
    public int population;
    public double growthRate;

    public void readInput()
    {
        <The definition of the method readInput is the same as in Display 4.3.>
    }

    public void writeOutput()
    {
        <The definition of the method writeOutput is the same as in Display 4.3.>
    }

    /**
     Returns the projected population of the calling object
     after the specified number of years.
    */
    public int projectedPopulation(int years)
    {
        double populationAmount = population;
        int count = years;
        while ((count > 0) && (populationAmount > 0))
        {
            populationAmount = (populationAmount +
                        (growthRate/100) * populationAmount);
            count--;
        }
        if (populationAmount > 0)
            return (int)populationAmount;
        else
            return 0;
    }
}
```

Later in the chapter, you will see that the modifier public should be replaced with private.

We will give an even better version of the class later in the chapter.

In Display 4.7, we have rewritten the program from Display 4.4 so that it uses the class SpeciesSecondTry and its method projectedPopulation. With this version of the class, we could project a population any number of years into the future. We could even use a variable for the number of years, as follows:

```
int projectedYears, futurePopulation;
System.out.println("Enter the projected number of years:");
```

```
projectedYears = SavitchIn.readLineInt( );
futurePopulation =
        speciesOfTheMonth.projectedPopulation(projectedYears);
System.out.println("In " + projectedYears + " years, the");
System.out.println("population will be " + futurePopulation);
```

Let's look at the definition of the method `projectedPopulation` in more detail. The heading, shown below, has something new:

```
public int projectedPopulation(int years)
```

■ DISPLAY 4.7   Using a Method with a Parameter

```
/**
 Demonstrates the use of a parameter
 with the method projectedPopulation.
*/
public class SpeciesSecondTryDemo
{
    public static void main(String[] args)
    {
        SpeciesSecondTry speciesOfTheMonth = new SpeciesSecondTry( );
        int futurePopulation;

        System.out.println("Enter data on the Species of the Month:");
        speciesOfTheMonth.readInput( );
        speciesOfTheMonth.writeOutput( );

        futurePopulation = speciesOfTheMonth.projectedPopulation(10);
        System.out.println("In ten years the population will be " +
                                                  futurePopulation);

        speciesOfTheMonth.name = "Klingon ox";
        speciesOfTheMonth.population = 10;
        speciesOfTheMonth.growthRate = 15;
        System.out.println("The new Species of the Month:");
        speciesOfTheMonth.writeOutput( );
        System.out.println("In ten years the population will be " +
                          speciesOfTheMonth.projectedPopulation(10));
    }
}
```

Sample Screen Dialog

The dialog is exactly the same as in Display 4.4.

formal parameter

argument

The word `years` is called a **formal parameter** or simply a **parameter.** A formal parameter is used in the method definition as a stand-in for a value that will be plugged in when the method is called. The item that is plugged in is called an **argument.** (In some other books arguments are called **actual parameters.**) For example, in the following call, the value 10 is an argument:

```
futurePopulation = speciesOfTheMonth.projectedPopulation(10);
```

When you have a method invocation like the preceding, the argument (in this case 10) is plugged in for the formal parameter *everywhere that the parameter occurs in the method definition*. In this case, the argument 10 would be plugged in for the formal parameter `years` in the definition of the method `projectedPopulation` in Display 4.6. After that, the method invocation proceeds as in all previous method invocations you have seen. The statements in the body of the method definition are executed until they reach a `return` statement. At that point, the value specified by the expression in the `return` statement is returned as the value returned by the method call.

It is important to note that only the value of the argument is used in this substitution process. If the argument in a method invocation is a variable, it is the value of the variable that is plugged in, not the variable name. For example, consider the following, which might occur in some program that uses the class `SpeciesSecondTry` defined in Display 4.6:

```
SpeciesSecondTry mySpecies = new SpeciesSecondTry();
int yearCount = 12;
int futurePopulation;
futurePopulation =
        mySpecies.projectedPopulation(yearCount);
```

call-by-value

In this case, it is the value 12 that is plugged in for the formal parameter `years` in the definition of the method `projectedPopulation` (in Display 4.6). It is *not* the variable `yearCount` that is plugged in for `years`. Because only the value of the argument is used, this method of plugging in arguments for formal parameters is known as the **call-by-value** mechanism. In Java, this is the only method of substitution that is used with parameters of a primitive type, such as `int`, `double`, and `char`. As you will eventually see, parameters of a class type use a somewhat different substitution mechanism, but for now, we are concerned only with parameters and arguments of primitive types, such as `int`, `double`, and `char`.

parameters as local variables

The exact details of this method of parameter substitution are a bit more complicated than what we have said so far. Usually, you need not be concerned with this extra detail, but occasionally, you will need to know how the substitution mechanism actually works. So here are the exact technical details: *The formal parameter that occurs in the method definition is a local variable that is initialized to the value of the argument.* The argument is given in parentheses in the method invocation. For example, consider the following method call:

```
futurePopulation =
        mySpecies.projectedPopulation(yearCount);
```

The parameter `years` of the method `projectedPopulation` in Display 4.6 is a local variable of the method `projectedPopulation`, and in this method invocation, the local variable `years` is set equal to the value of the argument `yearCount`. The effect is the same as if the body of the method definition were changed to the following:

This is the effect of plugging in the argument `yearCount`.

```
{
    years = yearCount;
    double populationAmount = population;
    int count = years;
    while ((count > 0) && (populationAmount > 0))
    {
        populationAmount = (populationAmount +
                            (growthRate/100) * populationAmount);
        count--;
    }
    if (populationAmount > 0)
        return (int)populationAmount;
    else
        return 0;
}
```

Finally, notice that the formal parameter in a method heading has a type, such as the type `int` before the parameter `years`, as shown here:

parameters have a type

```
public int projectedPopulation(int years)
```

Every formal parameter has a type, and the argument that is plugged in for the parameter in a method invocation must match the type of the parameter. Thus, for the method `projectedPopulation`, the argument given in parentheses in a method invocation must be of type `int`. This rule is not as strict in practice as what we have just said. In many cases, Java will perform an automatic type conversion (type cast) if you use an argument in a method call that does not match the type of the formal parameter. For example, if the type of the argument in a method call is `int` and the type of the parameter is `double`, Java will convert the value of type `int` to the corresponding value of type `double`. The following list shows the type conversions that will be performed for you automatically. An argument in a method invocation that is of any of these types will automatically be converted to any of the types that appear to its right if that is needed to match a formal parameter:[2]

```
byte --> short --> int --> long --> float --> double
```

Note that this is exactly the same as the automatic type casting we discussed in Chapter 2 for storing values of one type in a variable of another type. Thus, we can express both the automatic type casting for arguments and the automatic type casting for variables as one more general rule: You can use a value of any of the listed types anywhere that Java expects a value of a type further down on the list.

All of our examples so far have been methods that return a value, but everything we said about formal parameters and arguments applies to `void` methods as well: `void` methods may have formal parameters, and they are handled in exactly the same way as we just described for methods that return a value.

---

2. An argument of type `char` will also be converted to a matching number type, if the formal parameter is of type `int` or any type to the right of `int` in our list of types. However, we do not advocate using this feature.

Quick Reference: **Parameters of a Primitive Type**

Formal parameters are given in parentheses after the method name at the beginning of a method definition. A formal parameter of a primitive type, such as `int`, `double`, or `char`, is a local variable. When
the method is invoked, the parameter is initialized to the value of the corresponding argument in the
method invocation. This mechanism is known as the **call-by-value** parameter mechanism. The argument in a method invocation can be a literal constant, like 2 or `'A'`; a variable; or any expression that
yields a value of the appropriate type.

Note that if you use a variable of a primitive type as an argument in a method invocation, then the
method invocation cannot change the value of this argument variable.

---

more than one
parameter

It is possible, even common, to have more than one formal parameter in a method definition. In that case, each formal parameter is listed in the method heading, and each
parameter is preceded by a type. For example, the following might be the heading of a
method definition:

```
public void doStuff(int n1, int n2, double cost, char code)
```

Note that each of the formal parameters must be preceded by a type name, even if there is
more than one parameter of the same type.

In a method invocation, there must be exactly the same number of arguments in parentheses as there are formal parameters in the method definition heading. For example, the
following might be an invocation of our hypothetical method `doStuff`:

```
anObject.doStuff(42, 100, 9.99, 'Z');
```

As suggested by this example, the correspondence is one of order. The first argument in
the method call is plugged in for the first parameter in the method definition heading, the
second argument in the method call is plugged in for the second parameter in the heading
of the method definition, and so forth. Each argument must match its corresponding
parameter in type, except for the automatic type conversions that we discussed earlier.

class
parameters

One word of warning: Parameters of a class type behave differently from parameters of
a primitive type. We will discuss parameters of a class type later in this chapter.

Quick Reference: **Correspondence Between Formal Parameters and
                   Arguments**

Formal parameters are given in parentheses after the method name at the beginning of a method definition. In a method invocation, **arguments** are given in parentheses after the method name. There must
be exactly the same number of arguments in a method invocation as there are formal parameters in the
corresponding method definition.

The arguments are plugged in for the formal parameters according to their position in the lists in
parentheses. The first argument in the method invocation is plugged in for the first parameter in the
method definition, the second argument in the method invocation is plugged in for the second parameter
in the method definition, and so forth. Arguments should be of the same types as their corresponding formal parameters, although in some cases, Java will perform an automatic type conversion when the types
do not match.

▲ *Gotcha*

Use of the Terms *Parameter* and *Argument*

The use of the terms *formal parameter* and *argument* that we follow in this book is consistent with common usage, but people also often use the terms *parameter* and *argument* interchangeably. Many people use the term *parameter* both for what we call a *formal parameter* and for what we call an *argument*. Other people use the term *argument* both for what we call a *formal parameter* and for what we call an *argument*. When you see the term *parameter* or *argument*, you must determine the exact meaning from the context. △

Summary of Class and Method Definition Syntax

In basic outline, a class definition has the following form:

```
public class Class_Name
{
        Instance_Variable_Declaration_1
        Instance_Variable_Declaration_2
            .  .  .
        Instance_Variable_Declaration_Last

        Method_Definition_1
        Method_Definition_2
            .  .  .
        Method_Definition_Last
}
```

This is the form we will use most often, but you are also allowed to intermix the method definitions and the instance variable declarations.

A method definition consist of two parts, in the following order:

Method_Heading
Method_Body

The method headings we have seen thus far are all of the form

```
public Type_Name_Or_void Method_Name(Parameter_List)
```

The *Parameter_List* consists of a list of formal parameter names, each preceded by a type. If the list has more than one entry, the entries are separated by commas. There may be no parameters at all, in which case there is nothing inside the parentheses.

Here are some sample method headings:

```
public double Total(double price, double tax)
public void setValue(int count, char rating)
public void readInput( )
public int projectedPopulation(int years)
```

The *Method_Body* consists of a list of Java statements enclosed in braces {}. If the method returns a value, the method definition must include one or more `return` statements.

To see complete examples of class definitions, see Display 4.3 and Display 4.6.

? Self-Test Questions

9. What is the difference between the unqualified term *parameter* and the term *formal parameter*?

10. Define a method called `density` that could be added to the definition of the class `SpeciesSecondTry` in Display 4.6. The method `density` has one parameter of type `double` that is named `area`. The parameter `area` gives the area occupied by the species, expressed in square miles. The method `density` returns a value of type `double` that is equal to the number of individuals per square mile of the species. You can assume that the area is always greater than zero. (*Hint:* The definition is very short.)

11. Define a method called `fixPopulation` that could be added to the definition of the class `SpeciesSecondTry` in Display 4.6. This method has one parameter of type `double` that is named `area`, which gives the area occupied by the species in square miles. The method `fixPopulation` changes the value of the instance variable `population` so that there will be one pair of individuals per square mile.

12. Define a method called `changePopulation` that could be added to the definition of the class `SpeciesSecondTry` in Display 4.6. This method has two parameters. One parameter is of type `double`, is named `area`, and gives the area occupied by the species in square miles. The other parameter is of type `int`, is named `numberPerMile`, and gives the desired number of individuals per square mile. The method `changePopulation` changes the value of the instance variable `population` so that the number of individuals per square mile is (approximately) equal to `numberPerMile`.

4.2   INFORMATION HIDING AND ENCAPSULATION

The cause is hidden, but the result is well known. -Ovid, *Metamorphoses*

Information hiding sounds as though it could be a bad thing to do. What advantage could there be to hiding information? As it turns out, the term *information hiding* as it is used in computer science does indeed refer to a genuine kind of hiding of information, but it is considered a good programming technique. The idea is that, when certain kinds of information are hidden, the programmer's job becomes simpler and the programmer's code becomes easier to understand. It is basically a way to avoid "information overload."

Information Hiding

A programmer who is using a method that you have defined does not need to know the details of the code in the body of the method definition in order to use the method. If a method (or other piece of software) is well written, a programmer who uses the method need only know *what* the method accomplishes and need not worry about *how* the method accomplishes its task. For example, you can use the method `SavitchIn.readlineInt` without even looking at the definition of that method. It is not that the code contains some secret that is forbidden to you. If you really want to see the definition, it is in Appendix 4. The point is that viewing the code will not help you use the method, but it will give you more things to keep track of, which could distract you from your programming tasks.

Designing a method so that it can be used without any need to understand the fine detail of the code is called **information hiding,** to emphasize the fact that the programmer acts as though the body of the method were hidden from view. If the term *information hiding* sounds too negative to you, you can use the term *abstraction*. The two terms *information hiding* and *abstraction* mean the same thing in this context. This use of the term *abstraction* should not be surprising. When you abstract something, you lose some of the details. For example, an abstract of a paper or a book is a brief description of the paper or book, as opposed to the entire book or paper.

information hiding

abstraction

● **Programming Tip**
Parameter Names Are Local to the Method

Methods should be self-contained units that are designed separately from the incidental details of other methods and separately from any program that uses the method. Among the incidental details are the names of the formal parameters. Fortunately, in Java you can choose the formal parameter names without any concern that the name of a formal parameter will be the same as an identifier used in some other method. This is because the formal parameters are really local variables, and so their meanings are confined to their respective method definitions. ○

Precondition and Postcondition Comments

An efficient and standard way to describe what a method does is by means of specific kinds of comments known as preconditions and postconditions. The **precondition** for a method states the conditions that must be true before the method is invoked. The method should not be used, and cannot be expected to perform correctly, unless the precondition is satisfied.

precondition

The **postcondition** describes the effect of the method call. The postcondition tells what will be true after the method is executed in a situation in which the precondition holds. For a method that returns a value, the postcondition will describe the value returned by the method. For a `void` method, the postcondition will, among other things, describe any changes to the calling object. In general, the postcondition describes all the effects produced by a method invocation.

postcondition

For example, the following shows some suitable precondition and postcondition comments for the method `writeOutput` shown in Display 4.3:

```
/**
 Precondition: The instance variables of the calling
 object have values.
 Postcondition: The data stored in (the instance variables
 of) the calling object have been written to the screen.
*/
public void writeOutput()
```

The comment for the method `projectedPopulation` in Display 4.6 can be expressed as follows:

```
/**
 Precondition: years is a nonnegative number.
 Postcondition: Returns the projected population of the
 calling object after the specified number of years.
*/
public int projectedPopulation(int years)
```

If the only postcondition is a description of the value returned, programmers usually omit the word `Postcondition`. The previous comment would typically be written in the following alternative way:

```
/**
 Precondition: years is a nonnegative number.
 Returns the projected population of the calling object
 after the specified number of years.
*/
public int projectedPopulation(int years)
```

Some design specifications may require preconditions and postconditions for all methods. Others omit explicit preconditions and postconditions from certain methods whose names make their action obvious. Names such as `readInput`, `writeOutput`, and `set` are often considered self-explanatory. However, the sound rule to follow is to adhere to whatever guidelines your instructor or supervisor gives you, and when in doubt, add preconditions and postconditions.

Some programmers prefer not to use the words *precondition* and *postcondition* in their comments. However, you should always think in terms of preconditions and postconditions when writing method comments. The really important thing is not the words *precondition* and *postcondition*, but the concepts they name.

■ Java Tip
Assertion Checks

assertion

An **assertion** is a statement that says something about the state of your program. An assertion can be either true or false and should be true if there are no mistakes in your program. Precondition and postcondition commments are examples of assertions. You can have assertion comments at other points in your program as well. For example, all the comments in the following code are assertions:

```
//n == 1
while (n < limit)
{
    n = 2*n;
}
//n >= limit
//n is the smallest power of 2 >= limit.
```

Note that while each of these assertions can be either true or false, depending on the values of n and `limit`, they all should be true if the program is performing correctly. An assertion "asserts" that something is true about your program code (when program execution reaches the location of the assertion).

In Java, you can insert a check to see if an assertion is true and to stop the program and output an error message if the assertion is not true. An **assertion check** in Java has the following form:

assertion check

```
assert Boolean_Expression;
```

assert

If you compile and run your program in the proper way, the following happens when the assertion check is executed: If the *Boolean_Expression* evaluates to `true`, nothing happens, but if the *Boolean_Expression* evaluates to `false`, the program ends and outputs an error message saying that an assertion failed.

For example, the previously displayed code can be written as follows, with two of the comments replaced by assertion checks:

```
assert n == 1;
while (n < limit)
{
    n = 2*n;
}
assert n >= limit;
//n is the smallest power of 2 >= limit.
```

Note that we translated only two of the three comments into assertion checks. Not all assertion comments lend themselves to becoming assertion checks. For example, the final comment is an assertion. It is either true or false, and if the program code is correct, it will be true. However, there is no simple way to convert this last comment into a Boolean expression. Doing so would not be impossible, but you would need to use code that would itself be more complicated than what you would be checking. Your decision as to whether to translate a comment like the last one shown here into an assertion check will depend on the details of the particular case.

You can turn assertion checking on and off. You can turn it on when debugging code so that a failed assertion will stop your program and output an error message. Once your code is debugged, you can turn assertion checking off to make your code run more efficiently.

A class containing assertions must be compiled in a different way, even if you do not intend to run it with assertion checking turned on. After all the code is compiled, you can run a program with assertion checking either turned on or turned off.

If you compile your classes using a one-line command, you would compile a class with assertion checking as follows:

```
javac -source 1.4 YourProgram.java
```

You can then run your program with assertion checking turned on or off. The normal way of running a program has assertion checking turned off. To run your program with assertion checking turned on, use the following command:

```
java -enableassertions YourProgram
```

If you are using an IDE, you should have some way to set options for assertion checking. Check the documentation for your IDE. (If you are using TextPad, one way to turn on assertion checking for compiling and running code is as follows: On the Configure menu, choose Preferences, then choose Compile Java from the Tools submenu, and select the check box for the "Prompt for parameters" option. On the same Tools submenu, you will also find the Run Java Application command, and you will need to set the "Prompt for parameters" option for it as well.[3] Then, when you compile a class, a window will appear in which you can enter arguments for the `javac` compile command (for example, `-source 1.4 "YourProgram.java"`). Similarly, when you run a program, a window will appear in which you can enter arguments for the `java` run command (for example, `-enableassertions YourProgram`). The window will already have the last argument in the correct form, such as with or without quotes and full path name or not. You just add `-source 1.4` or `-enableassertions`.) ☐

Quick Reference: **Assertion Checking**

An **assertion check** consists of the keyword `assert` followed by a Boolean expression and a semicolon. You can insert an assertion check anywhere in your code. If assertion checking is turned on and the Boolean expression in the assertion check evaluates to `false`, your program will end and output a suitable error message. If assertion checking is not turned on, then the assertion check is treated as a comment.

Syntax:

```
assert Boolean_Expression;
```

Example:

```
assert n >= limit;
```

The `public` and `private` Modifiers

It is *not* considered good programming practice to make the instance variables of a class `public`. Normally, all instance variables are given the modifier `private`. In this subsection, we explain the differences between the modifiers `public` and `private`.

`public`

As you know, the modifier `public` means that any other class or program can directly access and change the instance variable. For example, the program in Display 4.7 contains the following three lines, which set the values of the `public` instance variables for the object `speciesOfTheMonth`:

```
speciesOfTheMonth.name = "Klingon ox";
speciesOfTheMonth.population = 10;
speciesOfTheMonth.growthRate = 15;
```

The object `speciesOfTheMonth` is an object of the class `SpeciesSecondTry`, the definition for which is given in Display 4.6. As you can see by looking at that class definition, the instance variables `name`, `population`, and `growthRate` all have the modifier `public`, and so the preceding three statements are perfectly valid.

---

3. If you are running applets, you will also need to select the "Prompt for parameters" option for the Run Java Applet command on the Tools submenu.

Now suppose that we change the modifier `public` before the instance variable `name` in the definition of the class `SpeciesSecondTry` in Display 4.6 to `private` so that the class definition begins as follows:

private

```
public class SpeciesSecondTry
{
    private String name;
    public int population;
    public double growthRate;
```

With this change, it is invalid to have the following statement in the program in Display 4.7:

```
speciesOfTheMonth.name = "Klingon ox"; //Invalid when private.
```

The following two statements remain valid, because we left the modifiers of `population` and `growthRate` as `public`:

```
speciesOfTheMonth.population = 10;
speciesOfTheMonth.growthRate = 15;
```

It is considered good programming practice to make all instance variables `private`, as illustrated in Display 4.8. Whenever you place the modifier `private` before an instance variable, that instance variable's *name* is not accessible outside of the class definition. Within any method of the class definition, you can use the instance variable name in any way you wish. In particular, you can directly change the value of the instance variable. However, outside of the class definition, you cannot make any direct reference to the instance variable name.

For example, consider the class `SpeciesThirdTry`, shown in Display 4.8. Because the instance variables are all marked `private`, the last three of the following statements would be invalid in any program (or in any class method definition other than methods of the class `SpeciesThirdTry`):

```
SpeciesThirdTry secretSpecies = new SpeciesThirdTry();//Valid
secretSpecies.readInput();//Valid
secretSpecies.name = "Aardvark";//Invalid. name is private.
System.out.println(secretSpecies.population);//Invalid
                        //population is private.
System.out.println(secretSpecies.growthRate);//Invalid.
                        //growthRate is private.
```

Notice that the invocation of the method `readInput` is valid. So there is still a way to set the instance variables of an object, even though those instance variables are `private`. Making an instance variable `private` does not mean that there is no way to change it. It means only that you cannot use the *instance variable name* to refer directly to the variable (except within the class definition that includes the instance variable).

Within the definition of methods in the same class, you can access private instance variables in any way you want. Notice the definition of the method `readInput`, which is shown in Display 4.8. It sets the value of instance variables with assignment statements such as

```
name = SavitchIn.readLine();
```

and

```
population = SavitchIn.readLineInt();
```

■ DISPLAY 4.8   **A Class with Private Instance Variables**

```java
public class SpeciesThirdTry
{
    private String name;
    private int population;
    private double growthRate;

    public void readInput()
    {
        System.out.println("What is the species' name?");
        name = SavitchIn.readLine();
        System.out.println(
                    "What is the population of the species?");
        population = SavitchIn.readLineInt();
        while (population < 0)
        {
            System.out.println("Population cannot be negative.");
            System.out.println("Reenter population:");
            population = SavitchIn.readLineInt();
        }
        System.out.println(
                  "Enter growth rate (percent increase per year):");
        growthRate = SavitchIn.readLineDouble();
    }

    public void writeOutput()
```
<The definition of the method `writeOutput` is the same as in Display 4.3.>

```java
    /**
     Precondition: years is a nonnegative number.
     Returns the projected population of the calling object
     after the specified number of years.
    */
    public int projectedPopulation(int years)
```
        <The definition of the method `projectedPopulation` is the same as in Display 4.6.>
```java
}
```

We will give an even better version of this class later in the chapter.

Within any class method, you can access all the instance variables of that class in any way you want, even if the instance variables are marked `private`.

private methods

Class methods can also be `private`. If a method is marked `private`, then it cannot be invoked outside of the class definition, but it can still be invoked within the definition of any other method in that same class. Most methods are marked `public`, but if you have a method whose only purpose is to be used within the definition of other methods of that class, it makes sense to mark this "helping" method `private`.

Quick Reference: The `public` and `private` Qualifiers

Within a class definition, each instance variable declaration and each method definition can be preceded with either `public` or `private`. If an instance variable is preceded with `private`, then it cannot be referred to by name anyplace except within the definitions of methods of the same class. If it is preceded by `public`, there are no restrictions on the use of the instance variable name. If a method definition is preceded with `private`, then the method cannot be invoked outside of the class definition. If the method is preceded by `public`, there are no restrictions on the method's use.

Normally, all instance variables are marked `private` and most or all methods are marked `public`.

● **Programming Tip**
Instance Variables Should Be `private`

You should make all the instance variables in a class `private`. The reason for this is that it forces the programmer who uses the class (whether that is you or somebody else) to access the instance variables only via methods. This allows the class to control how a programmer accesses the instance variables.

Making all instance variables `private` does control access to them, but what if you have a legitimate reason to access an instance variable? For these cases, you should provide accessor methods. An **accessor method** is simply a method that allows you to read data contained in one or more instance variables. In Display 4.9, we have rewritten the class for a species yet another time. This version has accessor methods for obtaining the value of each instance variable. They are the methods that start with the word `get`, as in `getName`.

accessor method

Accessor methods allow you to read the data in a private instance variable. Other methods, known as **mutator methods**, allow you to change the data stored in private instance variables. Our class definition has a mutator method, called `set`, for setting the instance variables to new values. The program in Display 4.10 illustrates the use of the mutator method `set`. That program is similar to the one in Display 4.7, but because this version of our species class has private instance variables, we must use the mutator method `set` to reset the values of the instance variables.

mutator method

It may seem that accessor methods and mutator methods defeat the purpose of making instance variables `private`, but there is a method to this madness. (No pun intended, I think.) A mutator method can check that any change is appropriate and warn the user if there is a problem. For example, the mutator method `set` checks to see if the program inadvertently sets `population` equal to a negative number.

Quick Reference: Accessor and Mutator Methods

A public method that reads and returns data from one or more private instance variables is called an **accessor method**. The names of accessor methods typically begin with `get`.

A public method that changes the data stored in one or more private instance variables is called a **mutator method**. The names of mutator methods typically begin with `set`.

■ DISPLAY 4.9   **A Class with Accessor and Mutator Methods**

```java
public class SpeciesFourthTry
{
    private String name;
    private int population;
    private double growthRate;
```

Yes, we will define an even better version of this class later.

<The definition of the methods readInput, writeOutput, and projectedPopulation go here. They are the same as in Display 4.3 and Display 4.6.>

```java
    public void set(String newName,
                    int newPopulation, double newGrowthRate)
    {
        name = newName;
        if (newPopulation >= 0)
            population = newPopulation;
        else
        {
            System.out.println(
                    "ERROR: using a negative population.");
            System.exit(0);
        }
        growthRate = newGrowthRate;
    }

    public String getName()
    {
        return name;
    }

    public int getPopulation()
    {
        return population;
    }

    public double getGrowthRate()
    {
        return growthRate;
    }
}
```

An accessor method can check to make sure that instance variables are not set to improper values.

■ DISPLAY 4.10 Using a Mutator Method *(Part 1 of 2)*

```
/**
 Demonstrates the use of the mutator method set.
*/
public class SpeciesFourthTryDemo
{
    public static void main(String[] args)
    {
        SpeciesFourthTry speciesOfTheMonth =
                                        new SpeciesFourthTry( );
        int numberOfYears, futurePopulation;

        System.out.println("Enter number of years to project:");
        numberOfYears = SavitchIn.readLineInt( );

        System.out.println(
                    "Enter data on the Species of the Month:");
        speciesOfTheMonth.readInput( );
        speciesOfTheMonth.writeOutput( );

        futurePopulation =
            speciesOfTheMonth.projectedPopulation(numberOfYears);
        System.out.println("In " + numberOfYears
                            + " years the population will be "
                            + futurePopulation);

        speciesOfTheMonth.set("Klingon ox", 10, 15);

        System.out.println("The new Species of the Month:");
        speciesOfTheMonth.writeOutput( );
        System.out.println("In " + numberOfYears
            +" years the population will be "
            + speciesOfTheMonth.projectedPopulation(numberOfYears));
    }
}
```

■ **DISPLAY 4.10** **Using a Mutator Method** *(Part 2 of 2)*

Sample Screen Dialog

```
Enter number of years to project:
10
Enter data on the Species of the Month:
What is the species' name?
Ferengie fur ball
What is the population of the species?
1000
Enter growth rate (percent increase per year):
-20.5
Name = Ferengie fur ball
Population = 1000
Growth rate = -20.5%
In 10 years the population will be 100
The new Species of the Month:
Name = Klingon ox
Population = 10
Growth rate = 15.0%
In 10 years the population will be 40
```

? Self-Test Questions

13. In Display 4.10, we set the data for the object `speciesOfTheMonth` as follows:

    ```
    speciesOfTheMonth.set("Klingon ox", 10, 15);
    ```

    Could we have used the following code instead?

    ```
    speciesOfTheMonth.name = "Klingon ox";
    speciesOfTheMonth.population = 10;
    speciesOfTheMonth.growthRate = 15;
    ```

    If we could have used this alternative code, why didn't we? If we could not have used this alternative code, explain why we cannot use it.

14. Give preconditions and postconditions for the following method, which is intended to be added to the class `SpeciesFourthTry` in Display 4.9:

    ```
    public void updatePopulation()
    {
        population = (int)(population
                          + (growthRate/100)*population);
    }
    ```

15. What is an assertion? Give examples of assertions.

16. Suppose that you did not have assertion checking in Java. (Earlier versions of Java did not.) Write some code to simulate the following assertion check:

    ```
    assert balance > 0;
    ```

    `balance` is a variable of type `double`.

17. What is an accessor method? What is a mutator method?

18. Give the complete definition of a class called `Person` that has two instance variables, one for the person's name and the other for the person's age. Include accessor methods and mutator methods, following the model in Display 4.9. Also include methods for input and output. There are no other methods.

Programming Example
A Purchase Class

Display 4.11 contains a class for a single purchase, such as 12 apples or 2 quarts of milk. It is designed to be part of a program to be used at the checkout stand of a supermarket. Recall that supermarkets often give prices not in unit costs, that is, not as the price for one, but as the price for some number, such as 5 for $1.25 or 3 for $1.00. They hope that if they price apples at 5 for $1.25, you will buy 5 apples instead of 2. But 5 for $1.25 is really $0.25 each, and if you buy 2 apples, they charge you only $0.50.

The instance variables are as follows:

```
private String name;
private int groupCount; //Part of price,
                        //like the 2 in 2 for $1.99.
private double groupPrice; //Part of price,
                           //like the $1.99 in 2 for $1.99.
private int numberBought; //Total number being purchased.
```

It is easiest to explain the meaning of these instance variables with an example. If you buy 12 apples at 5 for $1.25, then `name` has the value `"apples"`, `groupCount` has the value `5`, `groupPrice` has the value `1.25`, and `numberBought` has the value `12`. Note that the price of 5 for $1.25 is stored in the two instance variables `groupCount` (for the 5) and `groupPrice` (for the $1.25).

Consider the method `getTotalCost`, for example. The total cost of the purchase is calculated as

```
(groupPrice/groupCount)*numberBought
```

Or, to be very specific, if this purchase is 12 apples at 5 for $1.25, the total cost is

```
(1.25 / 5) * 12
```

Also notice the methods `readInput`, `setPrice`, and `setNumberBought`. All of these methods check for negative numbers when it does not make sense to have a negative number, such as when the user enters the number purchased. A simple demonstration program that uses this class is given in Display 4.12. ∎

■ DISPLAY 4.11 Purchase Class *(Part 1 of 3)*

```java
/**
 Class for the purchase of one kind of item, such as 3 oranges.
 Prices are set supermarket style, such as 5 for $1.25.
*/
public class Purchase
{
    private String name;
    private int groupCount; //Part of price, like the 2 in 2 for $1.99.
    private double groupPrice;
                    //Part of price, like the $1.99 in 2 for $1.99.
    private int numberBought; //Total number being purchased.

    public void setName(String newName)
    {
        name = newName;
    }

    /**
     Sets price to count pieces for $costForCount.
     For example, 2 for $1.99.
    */
    public void setPrice(int count, double costForCount)
    {
        if ((count <= 0) || (costForCount <= 0))
        {
            System.out.println("Error: Bad parameter in setPrice.");
            System.exit(0);
        }
        else
        {
            groupCount = count;
            groupPrice = costForCount;
        }
    }

    public void setNumberBought(int number)
    {
        if (number <= 0)
        {
            System.out.println("Error: Bad parameter in setNumberBought.");
            System.exit(0);
        }
        else
            numberBought = number;
    }
```

DISPLAY 4.11 Purchase Class *(Part 2 of 3)*

```java
/**
 Gets price and number being purchased from keyboard.
*/
public void readInput()
{
    System.out.println("Enter name of item you are purchasing:");
    name = SavitchIn.readLine();
    System.out.println("Enter price of item on two lines.");
    System.out.println("For example, 3 for $2.99 is entered as");
    System.out.println("3");
    System.out.println("2.99");
    System.out.println("Enter price of item on two lines, now:");
    groupCount = SavitchIn.readLineInt();
    groupPrice = SavitchIn.readLineDouble();

    while ((groupCount <= 0) || (groupPrice <= 0))
    {//Try again:
        System.out.println(
                "Both numbers must be positive. Try again.");
        System.out.println("Enter price of item on two lines.");
        System.out.println(
                        "For example, 3 for $2.99 is entered as");
        System.out.println("3");
        System.out.println("2.99");
        System.out.println(
                        "Enter price of item on two lines, now:");
        groupCount = SavitchIn.readLineInt();
        groupPrice = SavitchIn.readLineDouble();
    }


    System.out.println("Enter number of items purchased:");
    numberBought = SavitchIn.readLineInt();

    while (numberBought <= 0)
    {//Try again:
        System.out.println(
                    "Number must be positive. Try again.");
        System.out.println("Enter number of items purchased:");
        numberBought = SavitchIn.readLineInt();
    }
}
```

■ DISPLAY 4.11 **Purchase** **Class** *(Part 3 of 3)*

```java
/**
 Outputs price and number being purchased to screen.
*/
public void writeOutput()
{
    System.out.println(numberBought + " " + name);
    System.out.println("at " + groupCount
                                + " for $" + groupPrice);
}

public String getName()
{
    return name;
}

public double getTotalCost()
{
    return ((groupPrice/groupCount)*numberBought);
}

public double getUnitCost()
{
    return (groupPrice/groupCount);
}

public int getNumberBought()
{
    return numberBought;
}
}
```

■ DISPLAY 4.12 **Use of the Purchase** **Class** *(Part 1 of 2)*

```java
public class PurchaseDemo
{
    public static void main(String[] args)
    {
        Purchase oneSale = new Purchase();

        oneSale.readInput();
        oneSale.writeOutput();
        System.out.println("Cost each $" + oneSale.getUnitCost());
        System.out.println("Total cost $"
                                + oneSale.getTotalCost());
    }
}
```

■ DISPLAY 4.12 **Use of the** `Purchase` **Class** *(Part 2 of 2)*

Sample Screen Dialog

```
Enter name of item you are purchasing:
grapefruit
Enter price of item on two lines.
For example, 3 for $2.99 is entered as
3
2.99
Enter price of item on two lines, now:
4
5.00
Enter number of items purchased:
0
Number must be positive. Try again.
Enter number of items purchased:
2
2 grapefruit
at 4 for $5.0
Cost each $1.25
Total cost $2.5
```

Encapsulation

In Chapter 1, we said that **encapsulation** is the process of hiding all the details of a class definition that are not necessary to understanding how objects of the class are used. For encapsulation to be useful, the class definition must be given in such a way that the programmer is spared the bother of worrying about the internal details of the class definition. We have already discussed some of the techniques for doing this under the topic of information hiding. Encapsulation is a form of information hiding. Encapsulation, when done correctly, neatly divides a class definition into two parts, which we will call the user interface[4] and the implementation. The **user interface** tells a programmer all that she or he needs to know in order to use the class. The user interface consists of the headings for the public methods and the defined constants of the class, along with comments that tell a

encapsulation

user interface

---

4. The word *interface* also has a technical meaning in the Java language. We are using the word slightly differently when we say *user interface*, although in spirit, the two uses of the word *interface* are the same.

programmer how to use these public methods and the public defined constants of the class. The user interface part of the class definition should be all you need to know in order to use the class in your program.

implementation

The **implementation** consists of all private elements of the class definition, principally the private instance variables of the class, along with the definitions of both the public and private methods. Note that the user interface and implementation of a class definition are not separated in your Java code. They are mixed together. For example, the user interface for the class `Purchase` in Display 4.11 is highlighted. Although you need the implementation in order to run a program that uses the class, you should not need to know anything about the implementation in order to write the code that uses the class.

When defining a class using the principle of encapsulation, you must define the class in such a way that the user interface and the implementation do indeed neatly separate conceptually, so that the interface is a simplified and safe description of the class. One way to think of this is to imagine that there is a wall between the implementation and the interface, with well-regulated communication across the wall. This is shown graphically in Display 4.13. When a class is defined in this way, using encapsulation to neatly separate the implementation and the user interface, we say that the class is **well encapsulated.**

well encapsulated

■ DISPLAY 4.13 **Encapsulation**

A Well-Encapsulated Class Definition

Implementation:

Private instance variables
Private constants
Private methods
Bodies of public and private
method definitions

⟷

Interface:

Comments
Headings of public methods
Public defined constants

⟷

*Programmer who
uses the class*

*A well-encapsulated class definition has
no public instance variables.*

Some of the most important guidelines for defining a well-encapsulated class are the following:

1. Place a comment before the class definition that describes how the programmer should think about the class data and methods. (Note that this need not be a list of instance variables. If the class describes an amount of money, the programmer should think in terms of dollars and cents and not in terms of an instance variable of type `double`, if that is what is used to record the amount of money, nor should the programmer think in terms of two instance variables of type `int` for dollars and cents, if that is what is used to record the amount of money. In fact, the programmer using the class should not care whether the money is represented as an instance variable of type `double` or as two instance variables of type `int`, or is represented in some other way.)

2. All the instance variables in the class should be marked `private`.

3. Provide public accessor and mutator methods to read and change the data in an object. Also, provide public methods for any other basic methods that a programmer needs in order to manipulate the data in the class; for example, you should provide input and output methods.

4. Fully specify how to use each public method with a comment placed before the method heading.

5. Make any helping methods `private`.

6. Some of the comments in a class definition are part of the user interface, describing how to use the class. These comments are usually placed before the class definition to describe general properties and before particular method definitions to explain how to use that particular method. Other comments are needed only to understand the implementation. A good rule to follow is to use the `/**/` types of comments for user-interface comments and the `//` types of comments for implementation comments. In Display 4.11, the user-interface comments are highlighted.

When you use encapsulation to define your class, you should be able to go back and change the implementation details of the class definition without requiring changes in any program that uses the class. This is a good way to test whether you have written a well-encapsulated class definition. There are often very good reasons for changing the implementation details of a class definition. For example, you may come up with a more efficient way to implement a method so that the method invocations run faster. You may even decide to change some details of what the implementation does without changing the way the methods are invoked and the basic things they do. For example, if you have a class for bank account objects, you might change the amount of the penalty charged to an account that is overdrawn.

FAQ: What Is an API?

The term **API** stands for *application programming interface*. The API for a class is essentially the same thing as the user interface for the class. You will often see the term *API* when reading the documentation for class libraries.

FAQ: What is an ADT?

The term **ADT** is short for *abstract data type*. An ADT is a data type that is written using good information hiding techniques. Thus in Java, an ADT is basically the same thing as a well-encapsulated class definition.

Quick Reference: Encapsulation

Encapsulation is a term often heard when describing modern programming techniques. **Encapsulation** means that the data and the actions are combined into a single item (in our case, a class object) and that the details of the implementation are hidden. Thus, the terms *information hiding, ADT,* and *encapsulation* all refer to basically the same general idea: In very operational terms, the idea is to spare the programmer who uses your class from needing to read the details of how your class is implemented.

Automatic Documentation with `javadoc`

If your copy of Java came from Sun Microsystems (or even from certain other places), it includes a program named `javadoc` that will automatically generate documentation for the user interfaces to your classes. This documentation tells somebody who uses your program or class what she or he needs to know in order to use it. To get a more useful `javadoc` document, you must write your comments in a particular way. All the classes in this book have been commented for use with `javadoc` (although because of space constraints, the comments are a little sparser than would be ideal). If you comment your class definition correctly, such as the way the class in Display 4.11 is commented, `javadoc` will take your class definition as input and produce a nicely formatted display of the user interface for your class. For example, if `javadoc` is run on the class definition in Display 4.11, the output will consist only of the highlighted text. (It will also adjust spacing and line breaks and such.)

You do not need to use `javadoc` in order to understand this book. Nor do you do need to use `javadoc` in order to write Java programs. Moreover, in order to read the documents produced by `javadoc`, you must use a Web browser (or other HTML viewer). However, if you are already using a Web browser, such as Netscape Navigator or Microsoft's Internet Explorer, you are likely to find `javadoc` both easy to use and very useful. Appendix 9 covers `javadoc`.

UML Class Diagrams

We gave an example of a class diagram at the start of the chapter (Display 4.2). You now know enough to understand all the notation in that diagram. However, rather than looking at that class diagram, let's look at a new one. Display 4.14 contains a UML class diagram for the class `Purchase` from Display 4.11. The details are pretty much self-explanatory, except for the plus and minus signs. A plus sign (+) before an instance variable or method means the member is public. A minus sign (−) before an instance variable or method means the member is private.

Notice that the class diagram contains more than the interface for the class and less than a full implementation. Normally, the class diagram is done before the class is defined. It is an outline of both the interface and the implementation. The class diagram is primarily for the programmer defining the class. The interface is for the programmer who will use the class when producing additional software.

■ DISPLAY 4.14 **UML Class Diagram**

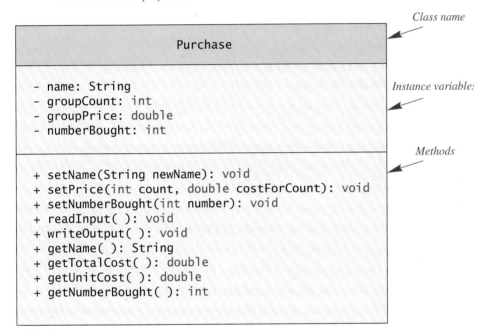

This is the class diagram for the class
    Purchase *in Display* 4.11.

Purchase
- name: String - groupCount: int - groupPrice: double - numberBought: int
+ setName(String newName): void + setPrice(int count, double costForCount): void + setNumberBought(int number): void + readInput( ): void + writeOutput( ): void + getName( ): String + getTotalCost( ): double + getUnitCost( ): double + getNumberBought( ): int

Class name

Instance variables

Methods

A minus sign (−) means the member is private.
A plus sign (+) means the member is public.

? Self-Test Questions

19. What is a well-encapsulated class definition?

20. When should an instance variable in a class definition be labeled private and when should it be labeled public?

21. Why would you ever label a method private?

22. In a class definition, is anything labeled private ever part of the user interface?

23. In a class definition, is the body of any method definition ever part of the user interface?

4.3 OBJECTS AND REFERENCE

"You are sad," the Knight said in anxious tone: "let me sing you a song to comfort you."
"Is it very long?" Alice asked, for she had heard a good deal of poetry that day.
"It's long," said the Knight, "but it's very, very beautiful. Everybody that hears me sing it—either it brings the tears into their eyes, or else—"
"Or else what?" said Alice, for the Knight had made a sudden pause.
"Or else it doesn't, you know. The name of the song is called 'Haddocks' Eyes.'"
"Oh, that's the name of the song, is it?" Alice asked, trying to feel interested.
"No, you don't understand," the Knight said, looking a little vexed. "That's what the name is called. The name really is 'The Aged Aged Man.'"
"Then I ought to have said 'That's what the song is called'?" Alice corrected herself.
"No, you oughtn't: that's quite another thing! The song is called 'Ways and Means': *but that's only what it's called, you know!"*
"Well, what is the song, then?" said Alice, who was by this time completely bewildered.
"I was coming to that," the Knight said. "The song really is 'A-sitting On A Gate': *and the tune's my own invention." -Lewis Carroll, Through the Looking-Glass*

Variables of a class type, such as the variable `oneSale` in Display 4.12, behave very differently from variables of the primitive types, such as `int`, `double`, and `char`. Variables of a class type are names for objects of their class, but the objects are not the values of the variables in the same way that, say, the number 6 can be the value of a variable of type `int`. A variable of a class type can name an object, but the naming process is a bit subtle. In this section, we discuss how a variable of a class type names objects, and we also discuss the related topic of how method parameters of a class type behave in Java.

Variables of a Class Type and Objects

Variables of a class type name objects in a way that is different from how variables of primitive types, such as `int` or `char`, store their values. Every variable, whether of a primitive type or a class type, is implemented as a memory location. (If this sounds unfamiliar, read Chapter 1.) If the variable is of a primitive type, the value of the variable is stored in the memory location assigned to the variable. However, if the variable is of a class type, then an object named by the variable is stored in some other location in memory, and the memory address of where the object is located is what is stored in the variable that names the object.

memory addresses

There is a reason why variables of a primitive type and variables of a class type name values in different ways. A value of a primitive type, such as the type `int`, always requires the same amount of memory to store one value. In Java, there is a maximum value of type `int`, and so values of type `int` have a limit on their size. However, an object of a class type, such as an object of the class `String`, might be of any size. The memory location for a variable of type `String` is of a fixed size, so it cannot store an arbitrarily long string. It can, however, store the address of any string, since there is always a last address and thus a limit on the size of an address.

reference

The memory address of where an object is stored is called a **reference** to the object, and that is why this section is named "Objects and Reference."

The fact that variables of a class type contain references can produce some surprising results. Variables of a class type behave very differently from variables of a primitive type. Consider the following lines of code that might begin the main part of a program:

```
SpeciesFourthTry klingonSpecies, earthSpecies;
klingonSpecies = new SpeciesFourthTry( );
earthSpecies = new SpeciesFourthTry( );
int n, m;
n = 42;
m = n;
```

As you would expect, there are two variables of type int: n and m. Both have a value of 42, but if you change one, the other still has a value of 42. For example, if the program continues with

```
n = 99;
System.out.println(n + " and " + m);
```

then the output produced will be

```
99 and 42
```

No surprises so far, but let's suppose the program continues as follows:

assignment
with variables
of a class type

```
klingonSpecies.set("Klingon ox", 10, 15);
earthSpecies.set("Black rhino", 11, 2);
earthSpecies = klingonSpecies;
earthSpecies.set("Elephant", 100, 12);
System.out.println("earthSpecies:");
earthSpecies.writeOutput( );
System.out.println("klingonSpecies:");
klingonSpecies.writeOutput( );
```

You might think that the klingonSpecies is the Klingon ox and the earthSpecies is the elephant, but the output produced may surprise you. It is the following:

```
earthSpecies:
Name = Elephant
Population = 100
Growth rate = 12%
klingonSpecies:
Name = Elephant
Population = 100
Growth rate = 12%
```

What has happened? You have two variables, klingonSpecies and earthSpecies, but you have only one object. Both variables contain the same reference, and so both variables name the same object. When you change klingonSpecies, you also change earthSpecies, and when you change earthSpecies, you also change klingonSpecies, because they are the same object.

Each object is stored in the computer's memory in some location, and that location has an address. The variables earthSpecies and klingonSpecies are really just ordinary variables (like the kind we use for int variables), but they store memory addresses for objects of the class SpeciesFourthTry. *When we say that a variable of a class type names an object, we mean that the variable contains the memory address of that object.* This is illustrated in Display 4.15.

■ DISPLAY 4.15 **Class Variables** *(Part 1 of 2)*

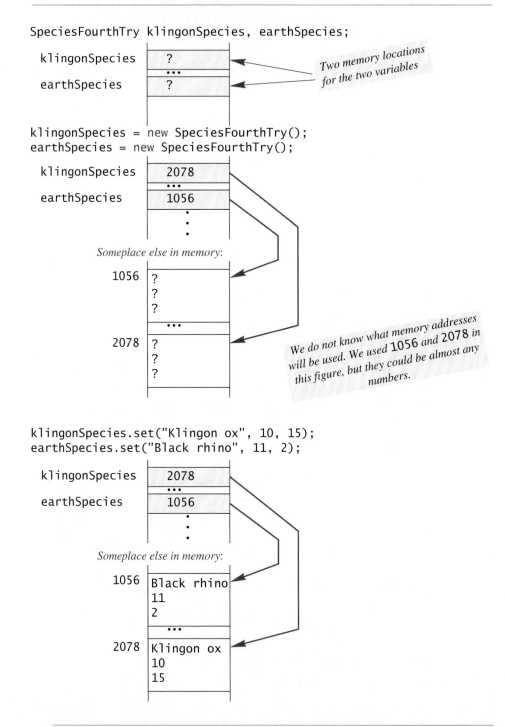

SpeciesFourthTry klingonSpecies, earthSpecies;

klingonSpecies   ?

earthSpecies   ?

Two memory locations for the two variables

klingonSpecies = new SpeciesFourthTry();
earthSpecies = new SpeciesFourthTry();

klingonSpecies   2078

earthSpecies   1056

Someplace else in memory:

1056   ?
        ?
        ?

2078   ?
        ?
        ?

We do not know what memory addresses will be used. We used 1056 and 2078 in this figure, but they could be almost any numbers.

klingonSpecies.set("Klingon ox", 10, 15);
earthSpecies.set("Black rhino", 11, 2);

klingonSpecies   2078

earthSpecies   1056

Someplace else in memory:

1056   Black rhino
        11
        2

2078   Klingon ox
        10
        15

■ DISPLAY 4.15 **Class Variables** *(Part 2 of 2)*

earthSpecies = klingonSpecies;

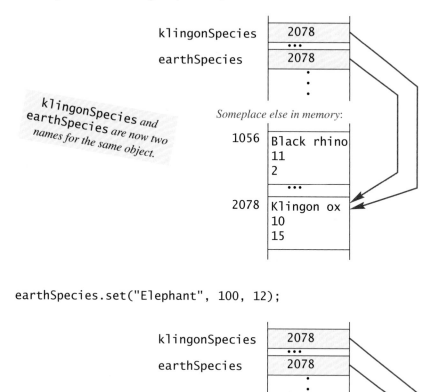

earthSpecies.set("Elephant", 100, 12);

When we have an assignment statement such as

earthSpecies = klingonSpecies;

it just copies the memory address in klingonSpecies into the variable earthSpecies, so that they both have the same memory address and so both name the same object.

One word of warning about memory addresses: A memory address is a number, but it is not the same kind of number as an `int` value. So do not try to treat it as an ordinary integer.

Remember: Variables of a Class Type Store Memory Addresses

A variable of a primitive type stores a value of that type. Variables of a class type behave differently. A variable of a class type does not store an object of that class. A variable of a class type stores the memory address of where the object is located in the computer's memory. This allows a variable of a class type to be used as a name for an object of that class. However, some operations, such as = and ==, behave quite differently for variables of a class type than they do for variables of a primitive type.

Remember: Memory Addresses Are and Are Not Numbers

A variable of a class type stores a memory address. A memory address is a number. But a variable of class type cannot be used like a variable that stores a number. This is not crazy. This is abstraction. The important property of a memory address is that it identifies a memory location. The fact that the implementors used numbers, rather than letters or colors or something else, to identify memory locations is an accidental property. Java prevents you from using this accidental property. It does so to keep you from doing things you should not do, such as obtaining access to restricted memory or otherwise screwing up the computer. It also makes your code easier to understand.

Quick Reference: Class Types and Reference Types

A variable of a class type does not actually hold an object of that class. A variable of a class type holds only the address of where that object is stored in memory. This memory address is often called a **reference** to the object in memory. For this reason, class types are often called reference types. A **reference type** is just a type whose variables hold references (that is, hold memory addresses), as opposed to actual values of objects. However, there are reference types other than class types, so we will use the term *class type* when referring to the name of a class. All class types are reference types, but as you will see in Chapter 6, there are reference types that are not class types.

FAQ: What's new ?

Variables of a class type work differently than variables of a primitive type. A variable of a primitive type holds a value of that type. A variable of a class type does not actually hold an object of that class. Instead, it holds the address of where that object is stored in memory. The declaration

```
SpeciesFourthTry s;
```

creates a variable s that can hold a memory address. At this point, your program has a place to store a memory address, but no place to store the data in the instance variables of an object of type `SpeciesFourthTry`. To get a memory location to store the values of instance variables, your program needs to use new. The following assigns a memory location to an object of type `Species-FourthTry` and places the address of that memory location in the variable s:

```
s = new SpeciesFourthTry();
```

In a very informal sense, you can think of new as creating the instance variables of the object.

▲ *Gotcha*

Use of = and == with Variables of a Class Type

==
with variables
of a class type

In the previous subsection, you saw some of the surprises you can get when using the assignment operator with variables of a class type. The test for equality also behaves in what may seem like a peculiar way. Suppose the class `SpeciesFourthTry` is defined as shown in Display 4.9, and suppose you have the following in a program:

```
SpeciesFourthTry klingonSpecies = new SpeciesFourthTry();
SpeciesFourthTry earthSpecies = new SpeciesFourthTry();
klingonSpecies.set("Klingon ox", 10, 15);
earthSpecies.set("Klingon ox", 10, 15);
if (klingonSpecies == earthSpecies)
    System.out.println("They are EQUAL.");
else
    System.out.println("They are NOT equal.");
```

This will produce the output

```
They are NOT equal.
```

Display 4.16 illustrates the execution of this code.

The problem is that, although, the two species are equal in an intuitive sense, a variable of a class type really contains only a memory address. There are two objects of type `SpeciesFourthTry` in memory. Both of them represent the same species in the real world, but they have different memory addresses, and the == operator checks only to see if the memory addresses are equal. The == operator tests for a kind of equality, but it is not the kind of equality you usually care about. When defining a class, you should normally define a method for the class that is called `equals` and that tests objects to see if they are equal. △

■ **Java Tip**

Define an `equals` Method for Your Classes

When you compare two objects using the == operator, you are checking to see whether they have the same address in memory. You are not testing for what you would intuitively call "being equal." To test for your intuitive notion of equality, you should define a method called `equals`. In Display 4.17, we have redefined our definition of a class for species one last time. This time, we have added a method called `equals`. This method `equals` is used with objects of the class `Species` in exactly the same way that we used the `String` method `equals` with objects of type `String`. The program in Display 4.18 demonstrates the use of the method `equals`.

Our definition of the method `equals` for the class `Species` uses the method `equalsIgnoreCase` of the class `String`. As we pointed out in Chapter 2, this method is automatically provided as part of the Java language. The method `equalsIgnoreCase` returns `true` if the two strings being compared are the same except that some letters might differ by being uppercase in one string and lowercase in the other string; otherwise, it returns `false`. ■

equals-
IgnoreCase

■ DISPLAY 4.16 **Dangers of == with Objects**

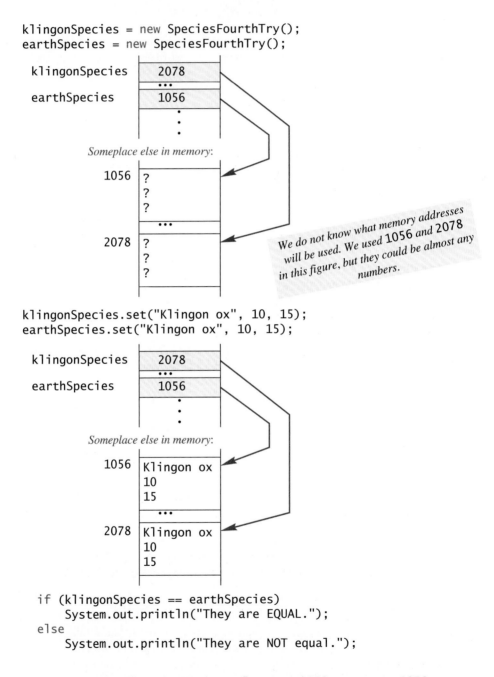

```
klingonSpecies = new SpeciesFourthTry();
earthSpecies = new SpeciesFourthTry();
```

We do not know what memory addresses will be used. We used 1056 and 2078 in this figure, but they could be almost any numbers.

```
klingonSpecies.set("Klingon ox", 10, 15);
earthSpecies.set("Klingon ox", 10, 15);
```

```
if (klingonSpecies == earthSpecies)
    System.out.println("They are EQUAL.");
else
    System.out.println("They are NOT equal.");
```

The output is They are Not equal, *because* 2078 *is not equal to* 1056.

■ DISPLAY 4.17 **Defining an** `equals` **Method**

```
public class Species
{
    private String name;
    private int population;
    private double growthRate;

        <The definition of the methods readInput, writeOutput, and projectedPopulation
                go here. They are the same as in Display 4.3 and Display 4.6.>

        <The definition of the methods set, getName, getPopulation,
                and getGrowthRate go here. They are the same as in Display 4.9.>

    public boolean equals(Species otherObject)
    {
        return ((this.name.equalsIgnoreCase(otherObject.name))
                && (this.population == otherObject.population)
                && (this.growthRate == otherObject.growthRate));
    }
}
```

equalsIgnoreCase is a method of the class String and is automatically provided as part of the Java language.

Notice that the method `equals` in Display 4.17 always returns either `true` or `false`, and so the type for the value returned is `boolean`. The `return` statement may seem a bit strange, but it is nothing other than a boolean expression of the kind you might use in an `if-else` statement. It may help you to understand things if you note that the definition of `equals` in Display 4.17 can be expressed by the following pseudocode:

returning a `boolean` *value*

```
if ((this.name.equalsIgnoreCase(otherObject.name))
            && (this.population == otherObject.population)
            && (this.growthRate == otherObject.growthRate))
then return true
otherwise return false
```

Therefore, the following (from the program in Display 4.18):

```
if (s1.equals(s2))
    System.out.println("Match with the method equals.");
else
    System.out.println("Do Not match with the method equals.");
```

■ DISPLAY 4.18 **Demonstrating an equals Method**

```
public class SpeciesEqualsDemo
{
    public static void main(String[] args)
    {
        Species s1 = new Species(), s2 = new Species();

        s1.set("Klingon Ox", 10, 15);
        s2.set("Klingon Ox", 10, 15);

        if (s1 == s2)
            System.out.println("Match with ==.");
        else
            System.out.println("Do Not match with ==.");

        if (s1.equals(s2))
            System.out.println("Match with the method equals.");
        else
            System.out.println(
                            "Do Not match with the method equals.");

        System.out.println(
                    "Now we change one Klingon Ox to all lowercase.");
        s2.set("klingon ox", 10, 15);
        if (s1.equals(s2))
            System.out.println("Still match with the method equals.");
        else
            System.out.println(
                            "Do Not match with the method equals.");
    }
}
```

Screen Output

```
Do Not match with ==.
Match with the method equals.
Now we change one Klingon Ox to all lowercase.
Still match with the method equals.
```

is equivalent to the following pseudocode:

```
if it is true that
        (s1.name.equalsIgnoreCase(s2.name))
            && (s1.population == s2.population)
            && (s1.growthRate == s2.growthRate), then
```

```
    System.out.println("Match with the method equals.");
else
    System.out.println("Do Not match with the method equals.");
```

We did not need to use the `this` parameter in the definition of `equals` in Display 4.17. The definition given there is equivalent to the following:

use of `this` is optional

```
public boolean equals(Species otherObject)
{
    return ((name.equalsIgnoreCase(otherObject.name))
            && (population == otherObject.population)
            && (growthRate == otherObject.growthRate))
}
```

The instance variable `population` by itself always means the same as `this.population`. Similarly, any other instance variable by itself is treated as though it were preceded by `this` and a dot.

We will say more about methods that return a value of type `boolean` in the subsection "Boolean-Valued Methods" a little later in the chapter.

There is no unique definition of `equals` that has been handed down by the gods for all time. The definition of `equals` that you write will depend on how you intend to use the class. The definition in Display 4.17 says that two objects of the class `Species` are equal if they represent the same records—that is, the same species name, the same population size, and the same growth rate. In some other context, you might want to define `equals` to mean that two objects are equal if they have the same species name, but possibly different populations or different growth rates. This would correspond to considering two objects to be equal if they are records for the same species, even if they are records for the same species at different times.

You should always use the identifier `equals` for the name of the method you create to test whether two objects are equal. Do not use some other identifier, such as `same`; do not even use `equal` (without an `s`). This is because certain software that is part of Java depends on your using the exact name `equals` to test for equality of objects. This software invokes a method named `equals`, so your method had better be named `equals`.

If you do not define an `equals` method for your class, Java will automatically create a default definition of `equals`, but it is unlikely to behave the way you want it to. Thus, it is best to define your own `equals` method.

Programming Example

A Species Class

The final version of our class for species objects is given in Display 4.19. It is the same definition as the one in Display 4.17, but this time we have included all of the details so that you can see a complete example. We have also written the definition of the method `equals` without using the `this` parameter, since that is the form most programmers use. The definition of `equals` in Display 4.19 is completely equivalent to the definition in Display 4.17. Display 4.20 contains the class diagram for this class `Species`. ∎

■ DISPLAY 4.19 **A Complete** Species **Class** *(Part 1 of 3)*

```
/**
 Class for data on endangered species.
*/
public class Species
{
    private String name;
    private int population;
    private double growthRate;

    public void readInput()
    {
        System.out.println("What is the species' name?");
        name = SavitchIn.readLine();
        System.out.println(
                    "What is the population of the species?");
        population = SavitchIn.readLineInt();
        while (population < 0)
        {
            System.out.println("Population cannot be negative.");
            System.out.println("Reenter population:");
            population = SavitchIn.readLineInt();
        }
        System.out.println(
                "Enter growth rate (percent increase per year):");
        growthRate = SavitchIn.readLineDouble();
    }

    public void writeOutput()
    {
        System.out.println("Name = " + name);
        System.out.println("Population = " + population);
        System.out.println("Growth rate = " + growthRate + "%");
    }

    /**
     Precondition: years is a nonnegative number.
     Returns the projected population of the calling object
     after the specified number of years.
    */
    public int projectedPopulation(int years)
    {
        double populationAmount = population;
        int count = years;
```

This is the same class definition as in Display 4.17, but with all the details shown.

<Definition of projectedPopulation continued on next page.>

■ DISPLAY 4.19 **A Complete Species Class** *(Part 2 of 3)*

```
    while ((count > 0) && (populationAmount > 0))
    {
        populationAmount = (populationAmount +
                        (growthRate/100) * populationAmount);
        count--;
    }
    if (populationAmount > 0)
        return (int)populationAmount;
    else
        return 0;
}

public void set(String newName, int newPopulation,
                                double newGrowthRate)
{
    name = newName;
    if (newPopulation >= 0)
        population = newPopulation;
    else
    {
        System.out.println("ERROR: using a negative population.");
        System.exit(0);
    }
    growthRate = newGrowthRate;
}

public String getName()
{
    return name;
}

public int getPopulation()
{
    return population;
}

public double getGrowthRate()
{
    return growthRate;
}
```

■ DISPLAY 4.19 **A Complete Species Class** *(Part 3 of 3)*

```java
public boolean equals(Species otherObject)
{
    return ((name.equalsIgnoreCase(otherObject.name))
            && (population == otherObject.population)
            && (growthRate == otherObject.growthRate));
}
```
}

This version of equals is equivalent to the version in Display 4.17. In Display 4.17, we explicitly used the this parameter. This version, omits the this parameter, but it is understood to be there implicitly.

■ DISPLAY 4.20 **Class Diagram for the Class** Species **in Display 4.19**

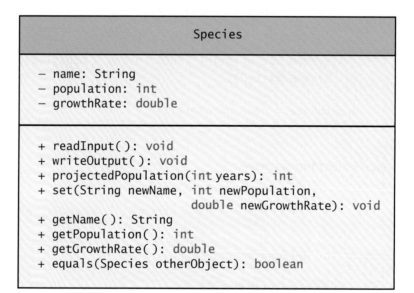

Boolean-Valued Methods

Methods can return a value of type boolean. There is really nothing new about this:
You just specify a return type of boolean and use a boolean expression in the return

statement. You have already seen one such method, namely the `equals` method for the class `Species` in Display 4.19, reproduced in what follows:

equals

```java
public boolean equals(Species otherObject)
{
    return ((name.equalsIgnoreCase(otherObject.name))
                && (population == otherObject.population)
                && (growthRate == otherObject.growthRate));
}
```

This method simply evaluates the boolean expression in the `return` statement. That boolean expression produces a value of `true` or `false`. The method `equals` returns this value.

As you have already seen, you can use an invocation of the method `equals` in an `if-else` statement, a `while` statement, or another statement that requires a boolean expression. You can also store the value returned by the method `equals`, or any other boolean-valued method, in a variable of type `boolean`. For example,

```java
Species s1 = new Species( ), s2 = new Species( );
<Some code to set the values of s1 and s2.>
boolean areEqual;
areEqual = s1.equals(s2);
<Some more code.>
if (areEqual)
    System.out.println("They are equal.");
else
    System.out.println("They are not equal.");
```

As another example of a boolean-valued method, you might add the following method to the definition of the class `Species` in Display 4.19:

examples

```java
/**
 Precondition: The calling object and the argument
 otherSpecies both have values for their population.
 Returns true if the population of the calling object
 is greater than the population of otherSpecies;
 otherwise, returns false.
*/
public boolean largerPopulationThan(Species otherSpecies)
{
    return (population > otherSpecies.population);
}
```

You can then use the method `largerPopulationThan` in the same sorts of ways that you use the method `equals`. For example, the following might appear in some program:

```java
Species s1 = new Species( ), s2 = new Species( );
<Some code to set the values of s1 and s2.>
if (s1.largerPopulationThan(s2))
    System.out.println(s1.getName( )
                            + " has the larger population.");
else
    System.out.println(s2.getName( )
                            + " has the larger population.");
```

As an additional example, you might also add the following method to the definition of the class `Species` in Display 4.19:

```
/**
 Precondition: The calling object has a value for
 its population.
 Returns true if the population of the calling object
 is zero; otherwise, returns false.
*/
public boolean isExtinct()
{
    return (population == 0);
}
```

The following sample code might then appear in a program:

```
Species s1 = new Species();
<Some code to set the value of s1.>
if (s1.isExtinct())
    System.out.println(s1.getName() + " is extinct.");
else
    System.out.println(s1.getName() + " is still with us.");
```

? Self-Test Questions

24. What is a reference type? Are class types reference types? Are primitive types (like `int`) reference types?

25. When comparing two objects of a class type to see if they are "equal" or not, should you use `==` or the method `equals`?

26. When comparing two objects of a primitive types (like `int`) to see if they are "equal" or not, should you use `==` or the method `equals`?

27. Write a method definition for a method called `largerGrowthRateThan` that could be added to the class `Species` in Display 4.19. The method `larger-GrowthRateThan` has one argument of type `Species`. The method returns `true` if the calling object has a larger growth rate than the growth rate of the one argument; otherwise, it returns `false`.

Class Parameters

Parameters of a class type are treated differently than parameters of a primitive type. In a sense, we have already discussed this difference when we discussed using the assignment operator with objects of a class type. Recall the following two points, which will help us describe how class parameters work:

1. First, recall how the assignment operator works with classes:
   When you use an assignment operator with objects of a class type, you are actually copying a memory address. Suppose that `Species` is the class defined in Display 4.19, and consider the following code:

```
Species species1 = new Species();
Species species2 = new Species();
```

```
species2.readInput( );
species1 = species2;
```

As we discussed in the previous section, species1 and species2 are now two names for the same object.

2. Now consider how parameters *of a primitive type* work. For example, consider the following call to the method projectedPopulation that we used in Display 4.10:

```
futurePopulation =
    speciesOfTheMonth.projectedPopulation(numberOfYears);
```

The method definition for projectedPopulation is in Display 4.19. The definition begins as follows:

```
public int projectedPopulation(int years)
{
    double populationAmount = population;
    int count = years;
    while ((count > 0) && (populationAmount > 0))
    {
        .
        .
        .
```

Recall that the formal parameter years is actually a local variable. When the method projectedPopulation is invoked, this local variable years is initialized to the value of the argument numberOfYears. So when the method is called, it is as if the following assignment statement were temporarily inserted into the method definition:

```
years = numberOfYears;
```

In other words, it is as if the definition of the method projectedPopulation was, for the duration of this method invocation, changed as follows:

```
public int projectedPopulation(int years)
{
    years = numberOfYears;
    double populationAmount = population;
    int count = years;
    while ((count > 0) && (populationAmount > 0))
    {
        .
        .
        .
```

Wow—that's a long preamble, but if you understand these two points, it will be very easy to explain how parameters of a class type work. Parameters of a class type work the same as described in point 2 for parameters of a primitive type, *but because the assignment operator means something different for variables of a class type, the effect is very different!* [5]

Let's go through that explanation again with slightly different words (but the same message). Consider the following call to the method `equals` that was used in Display 4.18:

```
if (s1.equals(s2))
    System.out.println("Match with the method equals.");
else
    System.out.println("Do Not match with the method equals.");
```

In this call, `s2` is an argument of the class type `Species` defined in Display 4.19. We reproduce here the definition for the method `equals`. (This version of `equals` was given in Display 4.17 and is equivalent to the version in Display 4.19):

```
public boolean equals(Species otherObject)
{
    return ((this.name.equalsIgnoreCase(otherObject.name))
            && (this.population == otherObject.population)
            && (this.growthRate == otherObject.growthRate))
}
```

When the method `equals` is called in `s1.equals(s2)`, it is as if the following assignment statement was temporarily inserted at the start of the method definition:

```
otherObject = s2;
```

In other words, the method definition, for the duration of this call to `equals`, is equivalent to

```
public boolean equals(Species otherObject)
{
    otherObject = s2;//You cannot do this, but
                     //Java acts as if you could and did do this.
    return ((this.name.equalsIgnoreCase(otherObject.name))
            && (this.population == otherObject.population)
            && (this.growthRate == otherObject.growthRate))
}
```

Recall, however, that this assignment statement merely copies the memory address of `s2` into the variable `otherObject`, so `otherObject` becomes just another name for the object named by `s2`. Thus, anything done with the object named `otherObject` will in

---

5. Some programmers refer to the parameter mechanism for class parameters as **call-by-reference** parameter passing. Others say that this terminology is incorrect. The problem is that there is more than one commonly used definition of *call-by-reference*. One point is clear, however: class parameters in Java behave a bit differently than what is known as call-by-reference parameters in other languages. So we will not use the term *call-by-reference* here. In any event, the important thing is to understand how class parameters work, no matter what you call them.

fact be done with the object named s2. Thus, it is as if the method performed the following action:

```
return ((this.name.equalsIgnoreCase(s2.name))
        && (this.population == s2.population)
        && (this.growthRate == s2.growthRate))
```

Notice that with a parameter of a class type, whatever action is taken with the formal parameter (in this example, otherObject) is actually taken with the argument used in the method call (in this case, s2). So the argument used in the method call is actually acted upon and can be changed by the method call.

In the case of the method equals, the effect of this parameter-passing mechanism for parameters of a class type is not so different from what happens with parameters of a primitive type. With some other methods, however, the difference is more dramatic. The next subsection gives a more dramatic example of how parameters of a class type differ from parameters of a primitive type.

Quick Reference: **Parameters of a Class Type**

Formal parameters are given in parentheses after the method name at the beginning of a method definition. A formal parameter of a class type is a local variable that holds the memory address of an object of that class type. When the method is invoked, the parameter is initialized to the address of the corresponding argument in the method invocation. In less technical terms, this means that the formal parameter will serve as an alternative name for the object given as the corresponding argument in a method invocation.

Note that this means that if you use an argument of a class type in a method invocation, then the method invocation can change the argument.

Comparing Class Parameters and Primitive-Type Parameters

Suppose we add a method named makeEqual to the class Species to form a new class called DemoSpecies, as shown in Display 4.21. This class is only for our demonstration, so do not worry about the rest of the class definition. Notice that the method makeEqual has parameters of type DemoSpecies, and that makeEqual changes the parameter. Let's play with this toy class.

Look at the demonstration program in Display 4.22. The call to makeEqual has an argument s2 of type DemoSpecies. Note that the change performed in the method body is actually performed on the argument s2. A method can actually change the value of an argument of a class type.

Now look at the method named tryToMakeEqual, also in Display 4.21. Notice that tryToMakeEqual has a parameter of the primitive type int and that tryToMakeEqual changes the formal parameter. The demonstration program in Display 4.22 calls tryToMakeEqual using the argument aPopulation of type int. Note that the change performed in the method body has no effect on the argument aPopulation. This is because, with arguments of a primitive type, Java uses the call-by-value parameter mechanism, and because variables of a primitive type hold actual values, not memory addresses. Thus, the parameter is a local variable that holds the value of the argument, and any changes are made to this local variable and not to the argument.

Parameters of a class type are more versatile than parameters of a primitive type. Parameters of a primitive type can be used to give values to a method, but a method cannot change the value of any primitive-type variable that is given to it as an argument. On the other hand, not only can parameters of a class type be used to give information to a method, but the method can also change the object named by an argument of a class type.

■ DISPLAY 4.21   **Just a Demonstration Class**

```
/**
 This is a version of the class Species, but is only a toy
 example designed to demonstrate the difference between
 parameters of a class type and parameters of a primitive type.
*/
public class DemoSpecies
{
    private String name;
    private int population;
    private double growthRate;

    /**
     Precondition: Calling object has been given values.
     Postcondition: otherObject has the same data as the
     calling object. The calling object is unchanged.
    */
    public void makeEqual(DemoSpecies otherObject)
    {
        otherObject.name = this.name;
        otherObject.population = this.population;
        otherObject.growthRate = this.growthRate;
    }

    /**
     Tries to set intVariable equal to the population of
     the calling object. But it cannot succeed, because
     arguments of a primitive type cannot be changed.
    */
    public void tryToMakeEqual(int intVariable)
    {
        intVariable = this.population;
    }

    public boolean equals(DemoSpecies otherObject)
    <The rest of the class definition of the method equals is the same as in Display 4.19.>


    <The rest of the class definition is the same as that of the class Species in Display 4.19.>


}
```

■ DISPLAY 4.22 Comparing Parameters of a Class Type and a Primitive Type

```
public class ParametersDemo
{
    public static void main(String[] args)
    {
        DemoSpecies s1 = new DemoSpecies(),
                    s2 = new DemoSpecies();

        s1.set("Klingon Ox", 10, 15);
        s2.set("Ferengie Fur Ball", 90, 56);
        System.out.println("Value of s2 before call to method:");
        s2.writeOutput( );
        s1.makeEqual(s2);
        System.out.println("Value of s2 after call to method:");
        s2.writeOutput( );

        int aPopulation = 42;
        System.out.println(
                    "Value of aPopulation before call to method: "
                    + aPopulation);
        s1.tryToMakeEqual(aPopulation);
        System.out.println(
                    "Value of aPopulation after call to method: "
                    + aPopulation);
    }
}
```

Screen Output

```
Value of s2 before call to method:◄━━━━━━━━━━  An argument of a class
Name = Ferengie Fur Ball                       type can change.
Population = 90
Growth Rate = 56.0%
Value of s2 after call to method:◄━━
Name = Klingon Ox
Population = 10
Growth Rate = 15.0%
Value of aPopulation before call to method: 42      An argument of
Value of aPopulation after call to method: 42 ◄━━   a primitive type
                                                    cannot change.
```

Remember: Differences Between Primitive and Class-Type Parameters

A method cannot change the value of a variable of a primitive type that is an argument to the method. On the other hand, a method can change the values of the instance variables of an argument of a class type.

? Self-Test Questions

28. What is wrong with a program that starts as follows (the class `Species` is defined in Display 4.19)?

```
public class SpeciesEqualsDemo
{
    public static void main(String[] args)
    {
        Species s1, s2;

        s1.set("Klingon Ox", 10, 15);
        s2.set("Klingon Ox", 10, 15);

        if (s1 == s2)
            System.out.println("Match with ==.");
        else
            System.out.println("Do Not match with ==.");
    }
}
```

29. What is the biggest difference between a parameter of a primitive type and a parameter of a class type?

30. What is the output produced by the following program (the class `Species` is defined in Display 4.19)?

```
public class ExerciseProgram
{
    public static void main(String[] args)
    {
        Species s1 = new Species();
        ExerciseClass mysteryMaker = new ExerciseClass();
        int n = 0;
        s1.set("Hobbit", 100, 2);
        mysteryMaker.mystery(s1, n);
        s1.writeOutput();
        System.out.println("n = " + n);
    }
}
```

The class `ExerciseClass` is as follows:

```
public class ExerciseClass
{
    public void mystery(Species s, int m)
    {
        s.set("Klingon Ox", 10, 15);
        m = 42;
    }
}
```

31. Redefine the class `Person` from Self-Test Question 18 so that it includes an `equals` method.

CHAPTER SUMMARY

- Classes have instance variables to store data and methods to perform actions.

- All instance variables in a class should be declared to be `private`. When they are declared `private`, they cannot be accessed by name except within the definition of a method of the same class.

- Encapsulation means that the data and the actions are combined into a single item (in our case, a class object) and that the *details of the implementation are hidden.* Making all instance variables `private` is part of the encapsulation process.

- A variable of a class type is a reference variable. This means that a variable of a class type holds the memory address of where the object it names is stored in memory.

- There are two kinds of methods: methods that return a value and `void` methods.

- Methods can have parameters of a primitive type or parameters of a class type, but the two types of parameters behave differently.

- A parameter of a primitive type is a local variable that is initialized to the value of the corresponding argument when the method is called. This mechanism of substituting arguments for formal parameters is known as the call-by-value mechanism.

- A parameter of a class type becomes another name for the corresponding argument in a method invocation. Thus, any change that is made to the parameter will be made to the corresponding argument.

- The operators = and ==, when used on objects of a class, do not behave the same as they do when used on primitive types.

- You usually want to define an `equals` method for the classes you define.

✔ Answers to Self-Test Questions

1.
```
SpeciesFirstTry speciesOfTheYear = new SpeciesFirstTry( );
System.out.println("Enter data for Species of the Year:");
speciesOfTheYear.readInput( );
```

2. `dilbert.readInput( );`

3.
```
public class SpeciesFirstTry
{
    public String name;
    public int number;
```

```java
public int population;
public double growthRate;
public void readInput( )
{
    System.out.println("What is the species' name?");
    name = SavitchIn.readLine( );
    System.out.println("What is the species' number?");
    number = SavitchIn.readLineInt( );
    while (number < 0)
    {
        System.out.println(
                "Number cannot be negative.");
        System.out.println("Reenter number:");
        number = SavitchIn.readLineInt( );
    }
    System.out.println(
                "What is the population of the species?");
    population = SavitchIn.readLineInt( );
    while (population < 0)
    {
        System.out.println(
                "Population cannot be negative.");
        System.out.println("Reenter population:");
        population = SavitchIn.readLineInt( );
    }
    System.out.println(
        "Enter growth rate (percent increase per year):");
    growthRate = SavitchIn.readLineDouble( );
}

public void writeOutput( )
{
    System.out.println("Name = " + name);
    System.out.println("Number = " + number);
    System.out.println("Population = " + population);
    System.out.println("Growth rate = " + growthRate + "%");
}

public int populationIn10( )
<This method does not change.>
}
```

4.

```java
public int femalePopulation( )
{
    return (population/2 + population%2);
}

public int malePopulation( )
{
    return population/2;
}
```

5.
```java
public void writeOutput()
{
    System.out.println("Name = " + this.name);
    System.out.println("Population = " + this.population);
    System.out.println("Growth rate = "
                          + this.growthRate + "%");
}
```

6.
```java
public void readInput()
{
    System.out.println("What is the species' name?");
    this.name = SavitchIn.readLine();

    System.out.println(
            "What is the population of the species?");
    this.population = SavitchIn.readLineInt();
    while (this.population < 0)
    {
        System.out.println(
                "Population cannot be negative.");
        System.out.println("Reenter population:");
        this.population = SavitchIn.readLineInt();
    }

    System.out.println(
        "Enter growth rate (percent increase per year):");
    this.growthRate = SavitchIn.readLineDouble();
}
```

7.
```java
public int populationIn10()
{
    double populationAmount = this.population;
    int count = 10;
    while ((count > 0) && (populationAmount > 0))
    {
        populationAmount = (populationAmount +
                (this.growthRate/100) * populationAmount);
        count--;
    }
    if (populationAmount > 0)
        return (int)populationAmount;
    else
        return 0;
}
```

8. The expression (int) is a type cast. It is needed because the method heading specifies that the type of the returned value is int, and so the value of populationAmount must be changed from double to int before it is returned.

9. In this book the terms *parameter* and *formal parameter* mean the exact same thing.

10.
```
public double density(double area)
{
    return population/area;
}
```

11.
```
public void fixPopulation(double area)
{
    population = (int)(2*area);
}
```

12.
```
public void changePopulation(double area,
                                     int numberPerMile)
{
    population = (int)(numberPerMile*area);
}
```

13. We cannot use the alternative code because the instance variables are labeled private in the class definition and so cannot be accessed directly except within a method definition of the class SpeciesFourthTry.

14.
```
/**
 Precondition: Calling object's population and growth
 rate have been given values.
 Postcondition: Calling object's population was updated to
 reflect one year's change.
 Other data values are unchanged.
*/
```

15. An assertion is a statement that says something about the state of your program. An assertion can be either true or false and should be true if there are no mistakes in the program. Precondition and postcondition statements are examples of assertions. The following is another example of an assertion given two times, once as a comment and once as an assertion check:
```
// (timeLeft > 30) && (points < 10)
assert (timeLeft > 30) && (points < 10);
```

16.
```
if (balance <= 0) //if (balance > 0) is false.
{
    System.out.println("Assertion (balance > 0) failed.");
    System.out.println("Aborting program.");
    System.exit(0);
}
```

17. An accessor method is a public method that reads and returns data from one or more private instance variables. (The names of accessor methods typically begin with get.) A mutator method is a public method that changes the data stored in one or more private instance variables. (The names of mutator methods typically begin with set.)

18.
```java
public class Person
{
    private String name;
    private int age;

    public void readInput()
    {
        System.out.println("What is the person's name?");
        name = SavitchIn.readLine();

        System.out.println("What is the person's age?");
        age = SavitchIn.readLineInt();
        while (age < 0)
        {
            System.out.println("Age cannot be negative.");
            System.out.println("Reenter age:");
            age = SavitchIn.readLineInt();
        }
    }

    public void writeOutput()
    {
        System.out.println("Name = " + name);
        System.out.println("Age = " + age);
    }

    public void set(String newName, int newAge)
    {
        name = newName;
        if (newAge >= 0)
            age = newAge;
        else
        {
            System.out.println("ERROR: Used a negative age.");
            System.exit(0);
        }
    }

    public String getName()
    {
        return name;
    }

    public int getAge()
    {
        return age;
    }
}
```

19. A well-encapsulated class definition is one written so that it neatly separates into user interface and implementation. A programmer who uses the class should need to know only about the user interface without being concerned with the implementation details.

20. Instance variables should always be labeled `private`.

21. If a method is a helping method that is used only in the definitions of other methods, it should be labeled `private`.

22. No, it is part of the implementation.

23. No, it is part of the implementation.

24. A reference type is a type whose variables hold references (that is, hold memory addresses), as opposed to actual values of objects. Class types are reference types. (There are reference types other than class types, but we will not see any until later in the book.) Primitive types are not reference types.

25. Normally, you use the method `equals` when testing two objects to see if they are "equal" or not. (The only time you would use `==` is if you wanted to see whether the objects were in the same place in memory, and it is unlikely that you would want to make such a test.)

26. You use `==` when comparing two objects of a primitive type (like `int`) to see if they are "equal" or not. In fact, there normally is no `equals` method for primitive types.

27.

```
/**
 Precondition: The calling object and the argument
 otherSpecies both have values for their growth rates.
 Returns true if the growth rate of the calling object is
 greater than the growth rate of otherSpecies;
 otherwise, returns false.
*/
public boolean largerGrowthRateThan(Species otherSpecies)
{
    return (growthRate > otherSpecies.growthRate);
}
```

28. The variables `s1` and `s2` are names for object of type `Species`, but this program does not create any objects for them to name. They are just names, not yet objects. The program should begin as follows:

```
public class SpeciesEqualsDemo
{
    public static void main(String[] args)
    {
        Species s1 = new Species(), s2 = new Species();
        <The rest of the code is OK.>
```

29. The biggest difference is in how a method handles arguments that correspond to the different kinds of parameters. A method cannot change the value of a variable of a primitive type that is an argument to the method. On the other hand, a method can change the values of the instance variables of an object of a class type whose name is an argument to the method.

30.

```
Name = Klingon ox
Population = 10
Growth rate = 15.0%
n = 0
```

31. The class definition is the same as before except for the addition of the method `equals`. The following are two possible definitions of `equals`. The first corresponds to saying that a person at one age is equal to the same person at another (possibly different) age. The second one corresponds to saying that a person at one age is not equal to what she or he will be at another age.

```java
public boolean equals(Person otherObject)
{
    return (this.name.equalsIgnoreCase(otherObject.name));
}
public boolean equals(Person otherObject)
{
    return ((this.name.equalsIgnoreCase(otherObject.name))
            && (this.age == otherObject.age) );
}
```

They are also correct if you omit all the occurrences of `this` and the following dot.

● Programming Projects

1. Write a program to answer questions like the following: Suppose the species Klingon ox has a population of 100 and a growth rate of 15 percent, and the species elephant has a population of 10 and a growth rate of 35 percent. How many years will it take for the elephant population to exceed the Klingon ox population? Use the class `Species` in Display 4.19. Your program will ask for the data on both species and will respond by telling how many years it will take for the populations to change so that the species that starts with the lower population outnumbers the species that starts with the higher population. The two species may be entered in any order. Note that it is possible that the species with the smaller population will never outnumber the other species. In this case, your program should output a suitable message stating this fact.

2. Define a class called `Counter`. An object of this class is used to count things, so it records a count that is a nonnegative whole number. Include methods to set the counter to 0, to increase the count by 1, and to decrease the count by 1. Be sure that no method allows the value of the counter to become negative. Also include an accessor method that returns the current count value, as well as a method that outputs the count to the screen. There will be no input method. The only method that can set the counter is the one that sets it to zero. Write a program to test your class definition. *Hint:* You need only one instance variable.

3. Write a grading program for a class with the following grading policies:

    a. There are two quizzes, each graded on the basis of 10 points.

    b. There is one midterm exam and one final exam, each graded on the basis of 100 points.

    c. The final exam counts for 50 percent of the grade, the midterm counts for 25 percent, and the two quizzes together count for a total of 25 percent. (Do not forget to normalize the quiz scores. They should be converted to percentages before they are averaged in.)

Any grade of 90 or more is an A, any grade of 80 or more (but less than 90) is a B, any grade of 70 or more (but less than 80) is a C, any grade of 60 or more (but less than 70) is a D, and any grade below 60 is an F. The program will read in the student's scores and output the student's record, which consists of two quiz scores and two exam scores as well as the student's overall numeric score for the entire course and final letter grade.

Define and use a class for the student record. The class should have instance variables for the quizzes, midterm, final, overall numeric score for the course, and final letter grade. The overall numeric score is a number in the range 0 to 100, which represents the weighted average of the student's work. The class should have input and output methods. The input method should not ask for the final numeric grade, nor should it ask for the final letter grade. The class should have methods to compute the overall numeric grade and the final letter grade. These last two methods will be `void` methods that set the appropriate instance variables. Remember, one method can call another method. If you prefer, you can define a single method that sets both the overall numeric score and the final letter grade, but if you do this, use a helping method. Your program should use all the methods we discussed. Your class should have a reasonable set of accessor and mutator methods, whether or not your program uses them. You may add other methods if you wish.

4. Add methods to the `Person` class from Self-Test Question 18 to set just the name attribute of a `Person`, to set just the age attribute of a `Person`, to test whether two `Person`s are equal (have the same name and age), to test whether two `Person`s have the same name, to test whether two `Person`s are the same age, to test whether one `Person` is older than another, and to test whether one `Person` is younger than another. Write a driver (test) program that demonstrates each method, with at least one true and one false case for each of the test methods.

5. Create a class that graphs a grade distribution (number of A's, B's, C's, D's, and F's) horizontally by printing lines with proportionate numbers of asterisks corresponding to the percentage of grades in each category. Write methods to set the number of each letter grade; read the number of each letter grade; return the total number of grades; return the percentage of each letter grade as a whole number between 0 and 100, inclusive; and draw the graph. Set it up so that 50 asterisks correspond to 100 percent (each one corresponds to 2 percent), include a scale on the horizontal axis indicating each 10 percent increment from 0 to 100 percent, and label each line with its letter grade. For example, if there are 1 A, 4 B's, 6 C's, 2 D's, and 1 F, the total number of grades is 14, the percentage of A's is 7, the percentage of B's is 29, the percentage of C's is 43, the percentage of D's is 14, and

the percentage of F's is 7. The A row would contain 4 asterisks (7 percent of 50 rounded to the nearest integer), the B row 14, the C row 21, the D row 7, and the F row 4, so the graph would look like this:

```
0    10   20   30   40   50   60   70   80   90  100%
|    |    |    |    |    |    |    |    |    |    |
*****************************************************
**** A
************** B
********************* C
******* D
**** F
```

6. Write a program that uses the Purchase class (Display 4.11) to set the following prices:
   Oranges: 10 for 2.99
   Eggs: 12 for 1.69
   Apples: 3 for 1.00
   Watermelons: 4.39 each
   Bagels: 6 for 3.50

   Then calculate the total bill and subtotals for each item for the following:
   2 dozen oranges
   3 dozen eggs
   20 apples
   2 watermelons
   1 dozen bagels

7. Write a program to answer questions like the following: Suppose the species Klingon ox has a population of 100 and a growth rate of 15 percent, and it lives in an area of 1500 square miles. How long would it take for the population density to exceed 1 per square mile? Use the class Species in Display 4.19 with the addition of the density method from Self-Test Question 10.

More About
Objects and Methods

5

A tourist stopped an elderly gentleman on the streets of New York
City and asked him,
"Please sir, could you tell me how I can get to Carnegie Hall?"
"Practice, practice, practice," the old gentleman replied. -A very old joke

In this chapter, we continue our discussion of how to define and use classes and their methods. We will discuss a technique called overloading that allows you to have two or more methods with the same name within the same class.

We will also teach you how to define static methods. You have already used static methods. They are methods that can be invoked with the class name, rather than an object. All the methods in `SavitchIn` are static methods. Now you will learn how to define such static methods.

We also introduce constructors, which are methods used to automatically initialize a new object.

Our last topic is packages. Packages are libraries of classes that you can conveniently use in other class definitions.

Along the way, we also cover a number of program design techniques that will help you to write better method definitions.

OBJECTIVES

Become familiar with more techniques for programming with classes and objects.

Learn about static methods and static variables.

Learn about overloading a method name

Learn to define constructor methods in Java.

Learn about packages and import statements in Java.

Learn to design methods using the top-down design technique.

Learn a number of techniques for testing methods, including the use of stub methods and driver programs.

PREREQUISITES

You must cover the material in Chapter 4 before reading this chapter. As we describe next, certain sections of this chapter may be postponed until after you've read some of the following chapters.

Section 5.6 discusses some subtle points about using instance variables of a class type. Strictly speaking, this section is not required for the rest of the material in this book and so can be postponed. However, Section 5.6 does discuss fundamental issues that you should read at some point.

The material on packages in Section 5.7 requires a knowledge of directories (folders) and path variables. Directories (folders) and path variables are not Java topics; they are operating system topics, and the details depend on what operating system you are using. Section 5.7 is not required for any other material in this book, so you need not cover this section until you are ready to do so.

5.1 PROGRAMMING WITH METHODS

The greatest invention of the nineteenth century was the invention of the method of invention.
-Alfred North Whitehead, *Science and the Modern World*

In this section, we describe a number of basic techniques you can use when designing and testing methods.

Methods Calling Methods

A method body may contain an invocation of another method. The situation for this sort of method call is exactly the same as it would be if the method call had occurred in the `main` part of a program. However, if all the methods are in the same class, they are typically invoked without writing any calling object, as we will explain.

Display 5.1 contains the definition of a class called `Oracle`. The method `dialog` of this class conducts a dialog with the user that answers a series of one-line questions that the user asks. Notice that within the definition of the method `dialog`, there is a call to the method `answerOne`, which is also a method in the same class `Oracle`. If you look at the definition of the method `answerOne`, you will see that it in turn includes calls to the two other methods, `seekAdvice` and `update`, both of which are also in the same class `Oracle`.

Let's first consider the invocation of the method `answerOne` within the definition of the method `dialog`. Display 5.2 contains a demonstration program that creates an object named `delphi` of the class `Oracle` and then uses this object to invoke the method `dialog`. When this invocation takes place, the method `dialog` is executed using the object `delphi`. The definition of the method `dialog` is as follows:

omitting this

```
public void dialog()
{
    do
    {
        answerOne();
        System.out.println(
                "Do you wish to ask another question? (y/n)");
        ans = SavitchIn.readLineNonwhiteChar();
    } while ((ans != 'n') && (ans != 'N'));

    System.out.println("The oracle will now rest.");
}
```

Note that the method named `answerOne` is not preceded by an object and a dot. The calling object is understood to be the calling object of the method `dialog`. In the program in Display 5.2, the method `dialog` is invoked by the object `delphi` as follows:

```
delphi.dialog();
```

■ DISPLAY 5.1   Methods Calling Other Methods

```java
public class Oracle
{
    private String oldAnswer = "The answer is in your heart.";
    private String newAnswer;
    private String question;

    public void dialog()
    {
        char ans;
        do
         {
            answerOne();
            System.out.println("Do you wish to ask another question? (y/n)");
            ans = SavitchIn.readLineNonwhiteChar();
        } while ((ans != 'n') && (ans != 'N'));

        System.out.println("The oracle will now rest.");
    }

    private void answerOne()
    {
        System.out.println("I am the oracle.");
        System.out.println("I will answer any one-line question.");
        System.out.println("What is your question?");
        question = SavitchIn.readLine();
        seekAdvice();
        System.out.println("You asked the question:");
        System.out.println(question);
        System.out.println("Now, here is my answer:");
        System.out.println(oldAnswer);
        update();
    }

    private void seekAdvice()
    {
        System.out.println("Hmm, I need some help on that.");
        System.out.println("Please give me one line of advice.");
        newAnswer = SavitchIn.readLine();
        System.out.println("Thank you. That helped a lot.");
    }

    private void update()
    {
        oldAnswer = newAnswer;
    }
}
```

■ DISPLAY 5.2 **Oracle Demonstration Program**

```java
public class OracleDemo
{
    public static void main(String[] args)
    {
        Oracle delphi = new Oracle();
        delphi.dialog();
    }
}
```

Sample Screen Dialog

```
I am the oracle.
I will answer any one-line question.
What is your question?
What time is it?
Hmm, I need some help on that.
Please give me one line of advice.
Seek and ye shall find the answer.
Thank you. That helped a lot.
You asked the question:
What time is it?
Now, here is my answer:
The answer is in your heart.
Do you wish to ask another question? (y/n)
yes
I am the oracle.
I will answer any one-line question.
What is your question?
What is the meaning of life?
Hmm, I need some help on that.
Please give me one line of advice.
Ask the car guys.
Thank you. That helped a lot.
You asked the question:
What is the meaning of life?
Now, here is my answer:
Seek and ye shall find the answer.
Do you wish to ask another question? (y/n)
no
The oracle will now rest.
```

So for this invocation of `dialog( )`, the invocation

```
answerOne( );
```

in the definition of `dialog` is understood to mean,

```
delphi.answerOne( );
```

When you write the definition of a method like `dialog`, you do not know what the name of the calling object will be. It could be different at different times, such as

```
delphi.dialog( );
```

in one program and

```
myObject.dialog( );
```

in another program. Because you do not—in fact, cannot—know the name of the calling object, you omit it. So, in the definition of the class `Oracle` in Display 5.1, when you write

```
answerOne( );
```

within the definition of the method `dialog`, it means

```
The_Calling_Object.answerOne( );
```

Because the `this` parameter just means *The_Calling_Object*, you can use the `this` parameter to name the calling object. Therefore, the following two calls to `answerOne` are equivalent:

```
answerOne( );
```

and the equivalent

```
this.answerOne( );
```

This omitting of the `this` and a dot when you refer to a method in the same class is not really new. We have already been doing the exact same thing with instance variables. This omitting of the calling object and dot works only with methods in the same class. If you call a method of one class within the definition of a method of another class, you must include an object and a dot.

Note also that this omitting of the calling object applies only if the calling object can be expressed with the `this` parameter. This is a simple and sure test for whether you can omit the calling object and dot. If the calling object is some object declared and created with `new` within a method definition, then within that method definition, you must include the object name and dot.

methods calling
methods calling
other methods

Let's continue with our discussion of method definitions in the class `Oracle`. You can have methods that call other methods that in turn call yet other methods. In the class `Oracle`, the definition of the method `answerOne` includes calls to the two methods `seekAdvice` and `update`, both of which are also in the same class `Oracle`. As we just discussed, these two methods named `seekAdvice` and `update` are not preceded by an object and a dot.

Let's consider the following invocation from the program in Display 5.2:

```
delphi.dialog( );
```

The definition of `dialog` includes the invocation

```
answerOne();
```

which is equivalent to

```
this.answerOne();
```

Because the calling object is `delphi`, this is also equivalent to the invocation

```
delphi.answerOne();
```

The definition of `answerOne` includes the invocations

```
seekAdvice();
```

and

```
update();
```

which are equivalent to

```
this.seekAdvice();
```

and

```
this.update();
```

Because the calling object again is `delphi`, these are also equivalent to

```
delphi.seekAdvice();
```

and

```
delphi.update();
```

You can have methods calling methods calling methods for any number of method calls. The details are always handled just as we've described here.

Remember: Omitting the Calling Object

When the calling object in a method invocation is the `this` parameter, you can omit the `this` and the dot.

Example:

The following are equivalent:

```
public void answerOne()
{
        .
        .
        .
    this.seekAdvice();
        .
        .
        .
    this.update();
}
```

and

```
public void answerOne( )
{
        .
        .
        .

    seekAdvice( );
        .
        .
        .

    update( );
}
```

● **Programming Tip**
Make Helping Methods Private

Look again at Display 5.1. The methods `answerOne`, `seekAdvice`, and `update` are labeled `private` rather than `public`. Recall that if a method is labeled `private`, it can be used only in the definitions of other methods of the same class. Thus, in some other class or program, the following invocation of the private method `answerOne` would be invalid and would produce a compiler error message:

```
Oracle myOracle = new Oracle( );
myOracle.answerOne( ); //Invalid: answerOne is private.
```

whereas the following call to the public method `dialog` would be perfectly valid:

```
myOracle.dialog( ); //Valid.
```

The reason we made the methods `answerOne`, `seekAdvice`, and `update` private is that they are just helping methods. A user of the class `Oracle` is not expected to use these methods. They are used only in the definition of the method `dialog`. This means that the methods `answerOne`, `seekAdvice`, and `update` are part of the class implementation and are not part of the user interface for the class. As we discussed in the subsection of Chapter 4 entitled "Encapsulation," it is good programming practice to keep the implementation portion of a class private. ○

■ **Java Tip**
Make the Compiler Happy

The compiler will try to check to make sure you have done certain necessary things, such as initializing variables and including a `return` statement in the definition of a method that returns a value. Sometimes you may find that the compiler is asking you to do one of these things, yet you are certain either that you have done it or that you do not need to do it. In such cases, it does no good to argue with the compiler. Just change something to make the compiler stop complaining. First of all, check to make sure the compiler is not correct. It usually is correct. If you cannot find a true error in your code, change your code so that it is more obvious that you have done what the compiler is asking for.

For example, if you declare a variable `line` as follows:

```
String line;
```

and the compiler insists that you must initialize the variable `line`, then you could change the declaration to

```
String line = null;
```

The constant value `null` is a special constant that can be used to give a value to any variable of any class type.

As another example, suppose that you have a method that returns a value of type `int` and the method definition ends with the following:

```
if (something > somethingElse)
    return something;
else
    return somethingElse;
```

In this case, every computation does end with a `return` statement. If the compiler nonetheless complains that you need a `return` statement, change that last `if-else` statement to the following:

```
int answer;
if (something > somethingElse)
    answer = something;
else
    answer = somethingElse;
return answer;  □
```

Quick Reference: `null`

`null` is a special constant that can be used to give a value to any variable of any class type. The constant `null` is not an object but a sort of placeholder for an object address. Because it is like an address, you use `==` and `!=` rather than the method `equals` when you test to see whether a variable is equal to `null`.

▲ Gotcha
Null Pointer Exception

If the compiler asks you to initialize a class variable, you can always initialize the variable to `null`. However, `null` is not an object, and so you cannot invoke a method using a variable that is initialized to `null`. If you try, you will get an error message that says "Null Pointer Exception." For example, the following code would produce a "Null Pointer Exception," if it was included in a program:

```
Species specialSpecies = null;
System.out.println("Enter data on special species:");
specialSpecies.readInput();
```

The class `Species` is defined in Display 4.19 in Chapter 4. However, there is no need to look at that class definition. These three lines of code will produce an error message no matter how the class `Species` is defined. The way to correct the problem is to use `new` to create an object of type `Species`, as follows:

```
Species specialSpecies = new Species()
System.out.println("Enter data on special species:");
specialSpecies.readInput();
```

Use `null` only to initialize a class variable when you know that, before the variable is used as a calling object for some method, your code will assign an object to the class variable, using `new` (or some other technique). This means that you should use `null` to initialize a class variable only when it is conceptually unnecessary. However, the compiler will sometimes insist on an initialization even when it is not needed.

As you do more programming, you will probably encounter other situations that produce a "Null Pointer Exception" message. In these cases, look for an uninitialized class variable. △

? Self-Test Questions

1. Can you invoke a method inside the definition of another method in the same class?

2. Suppose you changed the following line in the definition of the method answerOne in Display 5.1 from

   ```
   seekAdvice();
   ```

   to the following:

   ```
   this.seekAdvice();
   ```

   What effect would this have?

3. What is wrong with a program that starts as follows (the class `Species` is defined in Display 4.19 in Chapter 4)?

   ```
   public class SpeciesDemo
   {
       public static void main(String[] args)
       {
           Species s1 = null;
           Species s2 = null;

           s1.set("Klingon Ox", 10, 15);
           s2.set("Naked Mole Rat", 10000, 25);
   ```

5.2 STATIC METHODS AND STATIC VARIABLES

. . . there's no there there. -Gertrude Stein

Static methods and static variables are methods and variables that belong to a class as a whole and that do not require any object. You have already been using static methods. All the methods in the class `SavitchIn` are static methods. In this section, we show you how to define your own static methods and static variables.

Static Methods

Sometimes you need a method that does not require an object of any kind. For example, you might need a method to compute the maximum of two integers, or a method to compute the square root of a number, or a method to convert a letter character from lowercase to uppercase. None of these methods has any obvious object to which they should belong. In these cases, you can define the method as **static.** When you define a method as static, the method is still a member of a class, since you define it in a class, but the method can be invoked without using any object. Instead of using an object name, you normally use the class name when invoking a static method.

static method

For example, Display 5.3 has the definition of a class named `CircleFirstTry`, which has two static method definitions. The methods may be called as in the following example:

```
double areaOfCircle = CircleFirstTry.area(12.7);
double circumOfCircle = CircleFirstTry.circumference(12.7);
```

■ DISPLAY 5.3   **Static Methods**

```
/**
Class with static methods to perform calculations on circles.
*/
public class CircleFirstTry
{
    public static final double PI = 3.14159;

    public static double area(double radius)
    {
        return (PI*radius*radius);
    }

    public static double circumference(double radius)
    {
        return (PI*(radius + radius));
    }
}
```

Later in the chapter, we will give an alternate version of this class.

Note that with a static method the class name serves the same purpose as a calling object. (It would be valid to create an object of the class `CircleFirstTry` and use it to invoke the method `area` or the method `circumference`, but that is a confusing style, so we usually use the class name when invoking a static method.) Another sample use of these static methods is given in Display 5.4.

You define a static method in the same way that you would define any other method, but you add the keyword `static` to the heading.

In the example of the class `CircleFirstTry` in Display 5.3, the class has no instance variables, but it is perfectly valid for a class to have both instance variables and static methods (and regular, nonstatic methods).

Within the definition of a static method you cannot do anything that refers to a calling object, such as accessing an instance variable. This makes perfectly good sense, because a static method can be invoked without using any calling object and so can be invoked when there is no instance variable to refer to. This is explained more fully in the "Gotcha" section on the next page.

■ DISPLAY 5.4   **Using Static Methods**

```
public class CircleDemo
{
    public static void main(String[] args)
    {
        double radius;

        System.out.println(
            "Enter the radius of a circle in inches:");
        radius = SavitchIn.readLineDouble();

        System.out.println("A circle of radius "
                                    + radius + " inches");
        System.out.println("has an area of " +
            CircleFirstTry.area(radius) + " square inches,");
        System.out.println("and a circumference of " +
            CircleFirstTry.circumference(radius) + " inches.");
    }
}
```

Sample Screen Dialog

```
Enter the radius of a circle in inches:
2.3
A circle of radius 2.3 inches
has an area of 16.61901 square inches,
and a circumference of 14.45131 inches.
```

Remember: **The Methods in** `SavitchIn` **Are Static**

The method `readLineInt` and all of the other input methods in the class `SavitchIn` are static methods, and so they can be used with the class name in place of a calling object, as we have been doing all along. For example,

```
int n = SavitchIn.readLineInt();
```

▲ *Gotcha*

Invoking a Nonstatic Method Within a Static Method

Display 5.5 shows the definition of another class to use in circle calculations. It is designed to be simple and yet to have both static and nonstatic methods, so that you can see how the two kinds of methods can and cannot interact. The method `areaDialog` illustrates the only way that it is valid to invoke a nonstatic method from within a static method. The nonstatic methods `setDiameter` and `showArea` are invoked within the static method `areaDialog`. Let's look at the details more closely.

■ DISPLAY 5.5   **Mixing Static and Nonstatic Methods**

```
public class PlayCircle
{
    public static final double PI = 3.14159;
    private double diameter;
    public void setDiameter(double newDiameter)
    {
        diameter = newDiameter;
    }

    public static double area(double radius)
    {
        return (PI*radius*radius);
    }

    public void showArea()
    {
        System.out.println("Area is " + area(diameter/2));
    }

    public static void areaDialog()
    {
        System.out.println("Enter diameter of circle:");
        double newDiameter = SavitchIn.readLineDouble();
        PlayCircle c = new PlayCircle();
        c.setDiameter(newDiameter);
        c.showArea();
    }
}
```

A static variable (used as a constant)

An instance variable

You can invoke a nonstatic method within a static method definition only if you create a calling object, such as c, *by using* new.

Because areaDialog is a static method, it can be invoked with only the class name, and without any object, as shown in the following line from Display 5.6:

```
PlayCircle.areaDialog();
```

The method areaDialog, in this invocation, has no object associated with it. Hence, if you want to invoke the nonstaic method showArea within the definition of areaDialog, you must create an object and use that object to invoke the method showArea. This is what we did in the definition of the method areaDialog, which we reproduce here:

```
public static void areaDialog()
{
    System.out.println("Enter diameter of circle:");
    double newDiameter = SavitchIn.readLineDouble();
    PlayCircle c = new PlayCircle();
    c.setDiameter(newDiameter);
    c.showArea();
}
```

By contrast, suppose that you delete the calling object c, so that the last line of the method definition reads as follows:

```
showArea();
```

■ DISPLAY 5.6   **Using Static and Nonstatic Methods**

```
public class PlayCircleDemo
{
    public static void main(String[] args)
    {
        PlayCircle circle = new PlayCircle();
        circle.setDiameter(2);
        System.out.println("If circle has diameter 2,");
        circle.showArea();

        System.out.println("Now you choose the diameter:");
        PlayCircle.areaDialog();
    }
}
```

Sample Screen Dialog

```
If circle has diameter 2,
Area is 3.14159
Now you choose the diameter:
Enter diameter of circle:
4
Area is 12.56636
```

which looks as though it is equivalent to

```
this.showArea();
```

If you make this change to the definition of the method `areaDialog` and recompile the class definition for `PlayCircle`, you will get a compiler error. This is because any invocation of the method `showArea` must have a calling object with data for the diameter of a circle. It cannot get that diameter data in any other way. Within the definition of a static method, such as `areaDialog`, you have no instance variable available for any purpose whatsoever. Note that the problem is not that the class lacks instance variables. The class has a suitable instance variable named `diameter`. The problem is that the nonstatic method `showArea` is being invoked within the static method `areaDialog`.

You will often hear people say, "You cannot invoke a nonstatic method within the definition of a static method." This is not quite true, however. A more precise, and correct, statement is, "You cannot invoke a nonstatic method within a static method *unless you create and use a calling object for the nonstatic method*." Put another way, in the definition of a static method, you cannot use an instance variable or method that has an implicit or explicit `this` for a calling object. This is because a static method can be invoked without any calling object and so can be invoked when there is no meaning for `this`. As Gertrude Stein might have said, in a static method, "there is no `this` there." △

■ Java Tip
You Can Put a `main` in Any Class

So far, whenever we have used a class in the `main` part of a program, that `main` method was by itself in a different class definition within another file. However, sometimes it makes sense to have a `main` method within a regular class definition. The class can then be used for two purposes: It can be used to create objects in other classes, or it can be run as a program. For example, you can combine the class definition `Play-Circle` in Display 5.5 with the program in Display 5.6 by placing the `main` method shown in Display 5.6 inside the definition of the class `PlayCircle`, to obtain the class definition shown in Display 5.7. With the class `PlayCircle` redefined in this way, it can be used in another program as an ordinary class to create objects of the class `PlayCircle`, but it can also be run as a program. When it is run as a program, the `main` method is invoked and the rest of the class definition is ignored (except for its use in `main`). When it is used as an ordinary class to create objects, the `main` method is ignored.

Java requires that a program's `main` method be static. Thus, within a `main` method, you cannot invoke a nonstatic method of the same class unless you create an object of the class and use it as a calling object for the nonstatic method. Notice the `main` method in Display 5.7. It invokes the methods `showArea` and `setDiameter` by first creating an object `circle` of the class `PlayCircle` and then using `circle` as the calling object. This is necessary even though the `main` method is inside the definition of the class `PlayCircle`.

You will not want to place just any `main` method in a class definition that is to be used as a regular class to create objects. However, one handy trick is to place a small diagnostic program in a `main` method that is inside of your class definition. ■

■ DISPLAY 5.7   **Placing a main Method in a Class Definition**

```java
public class PlayCircle
{
    public static final double PI = 3.14159;

    private double diameter;

    public static void main(String[] args)
    {
        PlayCircle circle = new PlayCircle();
        circle.setDiameter(2);
        System.out.println("If circle has diameter 2,");
        circle.showArea();

        System.out.println("Now you choose the diameter:");
        PlayCircle.areaDialog();
    }

    public void setDiameter(double newDiameter)
    {
        diameter = newDiameter;
    }

    public static double area(double radius)
    {
        return (PI*radius*radius);
    }

    public void showArea()
    {
        System.out.println("Area is " + area(diameter/2));
    }

    public static void areaDialog()
    {
        System.out.println("Enter diameter of circle:");
        double newDiameter = SavitchIn.readLineDouble();
        PlayCircle c = new PlayCircle();
        c.setDiameter(newDiameter);
        c.showArea();
    }
}
```

On the CD, this is PlayCircle2.java.

Because this main is inside the definition of the class PlayCircle, you can omit this PlayCircle, if you wish.

Quick Reference: **Static Methods**

If you place the keyword `static` in the heading of the definition of a method, the method can be invoked using the class name in place of a calling object.

Since it does not need a calling object, a static method cannot refer to a (nonstatic) instance variable of the class, nor can it invoke a nonstatic method of the class (unless it creates a new object of the class and uses this object as the calling object). Another way to phrase it is that, in the definition of a static method, you cannot use an instance variable or a method that has an implicit or explicit `this` for a calling object.

Example (of invoking a static method):

```
int result = Math.max(n1, n2);
```

`Math` is a predefined class.

? Self-Test Questions

4. Is the following valid (the class `CircleFirstTry` is defined in Display 5.3)?

```
CircleFirstTry c = new CircleFirstTry();
double areaOfCircle = c.area(2.5);
```

5. Can a class contain both static and nonstatic (that is, regular) methods? Can it contain both instance variables and static methods?

6. Can you invoke a nonstatic method within a static method?

7. Can you invoke a static method within a nonstatic method?

8. Can you reference an instance variable within a static method? Why or why not?

9. Is the following valid (even though `readLineInt` is a static method and does not need a calling object)?

```
SavitchIn inputObject = new SavitchIn();
System.out.println("Enter an integer:");
int n = inputObject.readLineInt()
```

10. Is the following valid? The class `PlayCircle` is defined in Display 5.5.

```
System.out.println("Enter the diameter of a circle:");
double newDiameter = SavitchIn.readLineDouble();
PlayCircle.setDiameter(newDiameter);
```

Static Variables *(Optional)*

It is possible for a class to have variables that are static as well as methods that are static. We have already been using static variables in one special case, namely, the definition of constant values such as

```
public static final double PI = 3.14159;
```

There are also **static variables** that can change value. These are declared in the same way as defined constant values, except that you do not use the word `final`. Thus, if the following occurred in a class definition, it would define a static variable that can change value:

static variable

```
public static double PI;
```

although this might be a poor choice for a static variable name.

A static variable can be initialized or not, and can be public or private. However, like instance variables, static variables should normally be private and should be read or changed only via accessor and mutator methods. Thus, the following is a more likely example of a static (nonconstant) variable declaration:

```
private static int numberOfInvocations = 0;
```

The variable `numberOfInvocations` is initialized to 0. There is only one variable `numberOfInvocations`, and it can be accessed by every object of the class. So this static variable could allow objects to communicate or perform some joint action. For example, in the class definition in Display 5.8, this static variable is used to keep track of how many invocations have been made by all objects of the class `StaticDemo`. The program counts all invocations of the methods defined in Display 5.8, except for the method `main`.

■ DISPLAY 5.8   **A Static Variable** *(Optional) (Part 1 of 2)*

object1 and object2 use the same static variable numberOfInvocations.

```
public class StaticDemo
{
    private static int numberOfInvocations = 0;
    public static void main(String[] args)
    {
        int i;
        StaticDemo object1 = new StaticDemo( );
        for (i = 1; i <=10 ; i++)
            object1.outPutCountOfInvocations( );

        StaticDemo object2 = new StaticDemo( );
        for (i = 1; i <=10 ; i++)
            object2.justADemoMethod( );

        System.out.println("Total number of invocations = "
                           + numberSoFar( ));
    }

    public void justADemoMethod( )
    {
        numberOfInvocations++;
        //In a real example, more code would go here.
    }

    public void outPutCountOfInvocations( )
    {
        numberOfInvocations++;
        System.out.println(numberOfInvocations);
    }

    public static int numberSoFar( )
    {
        numberOfInvocations++;
        return numberOfInvocations;
    }
}
```

■ DISPLAY 5.8   **A Static Variable** *(Optional) (Part 2 of 2)*

Sample Screen Dialog

```
1
2
3
4
5
6
7
8
9
10
Total number of invocations = 21
```

There are cases in which you want to use a static variable, but they are rare. and we will not be using static variables in this text after we finish this discussion.

Static variables are also called **class variables.** Do not confuse the term *class variable* (which simply means a static variable within a class) with the notion of a variable of a class type (which means a variable whose type is a class—that is, a variable that is used to name objects of a class).

class variable

? Self-Test Questions

11. What is the difference between a static variable and an instance variable?

12. Can you reference (by name) a *static variable* (without anything like a class name and dot) in the definition of a *static method?* Can you reference (by name) an *instance variable* (without anything like an object name and dot) in the definition of a *static method?*

13. Can you reference (by name) a *static variable* (without anything like a class name and dot) in the definition of a *nonstatic method?* Can you reference (by name) an *instance variable* (without anything like an object name and dot) in the definition of a *nonstatic method?*

The Math Class

The predefined class Math provides you with a number of standard mathematical methods. This class is automatically provided when you use the Java language. Some of the

Math methods

methods in the class Math are described in Display 5.9. All of these methods are static, which means that you do not need (and in fact have no real use for) an object of the class Math. You normally call these methods by using the class name, Math, in place of a calling object. For example, the following outputs the maximum of the two numbers 2 and 3.

```
int ans;
ans = Math.max(2, 3);
System.out.println(ans);
```

It would also be valid to omit the variable ans and simply write

```
System.out.println(
            "The maximum of 2 and 3 = " + Math.max(2, 3));
```

■ DISPLAY 5.9   Static Methods in the Class Math

Name	Description	Type of Argument	Type of Value Returned	Example	Value Returned
pow	Powers	double	double	Math.pow(2.0,3.0)	8.0
abs	Absolute value	int, long, float, or double	Same as the type of the argument	Math.abs(-7) Math.abs(7) Math.abs(-3.5)	7 7 3.5
max	Maximum	int, long, float, or double	Same as the type of the arguments	Math.max(5, 6) Math.max(5.5, 5.3)	6 5.5
min	Minimum	int, long, float, or double	Same as the type of the arguments	Math.min(5, 6) Math.min(5.5, 5.3)	5 5.3
round	Rounding	float or double	int or long, respectively	Math.round(6.2) Math.round(6.8)	6 7
ceil	Ceiling	double	double	Math.ceil(3.2) Math.ceil(3.9)	4.0 4.0
floor	Floor	double	double	Math.floor(3.2) Math.floor(3.9)	3.0 3.0
sqrt	Square root	double	double	sqrt(4.0)	2.0

■ DISPLAY 5.10 **Predefined Constants**

```java
/**
 Class with static methods to perform calculations on circles.
*/
public class Circle
{
    public static double area(double radius)
    {
        return (Math.PI*radius*radius);
    }

    public static double circumference(double radius)
    {
        return (Math.PI*(radius + radius));
    }
}
```

CircleDemo2.java on the CD is a demonstration program for this class.

This class behaves the same as the class CircleFirstTry in Display 5.3. This version differs only in that it uses the predefined constant Math.PI, rather than defining PI within the class.

The class Math also has the two predefined constants E and PI. The constant PI (often written π in mathematical formulas) is used in calculations involving circles, spheres, and other geometric figures based on circles. PI is approximately 3.14159. The constant E is the base of the natural logarithm system (often written *e* in mathematical formulas) and is approximately 2.72. (We do not use the predefined constant E in this text.) The constants PI and E are defined constants, as described in Chapter 2. For example, the following computes the area of a circle, given its radius:

Math constants

```java
area = Math.PI * radius * radius;
```

Be sure to note that because the constants PI and E are defined in the class Math, they must be preceded by the class name Math and a dot. For example, you could use the constant Math.PI in the definition of the class CircleFirstTry in Display 5.3. In Display 5.10, we have rewritten the class in Display 5.3 to use Math.PI.

If you look at the methods in the table in Display 5.9, you will find three similar, but not identical, methods named round, floor, and ceil. Some of these return a value of type double, but they all return a value that is intuitively a whole number that is close to the value of their arguments. The method round rounds a number to the nearest whole number and (if the argument is a double) returns that whole number as a value of type long. If you want that whole number as a value of type int, you must use a type cast, as in the following:[1]

```
double start = 3.56;
int answer = (int)Math.round(start);
```

floor and ceil

The methods floor and ceil are similar to round, with slight differences. Neither one really rounds, although they both yield a whole number that is close to their argument. They both return a whole number as a value of type double (not of type int or long). The method floor returns the nearest whole number that is less than or equal to its argument. So Math.floor(3.9) returns 3.0, not 4.0. Math.floor(3.3) also returns 3.0.

The method ceil returns the nearest whole number that is greater than or equal to its argument. So Math.ceil(3.1) returns 4.0, not 3.0. Of course, Math.ceil(3.9) also returns 4.0. (The word ceil is short for *ceiling*.)

If you want to store the value returned by either floor or ceil in a variable of type int, you must use a type cast, as in the following example:

```
double start = 3.56;
int lowAnswer = (int)Math.floor(start);
int highAnswer = (int)Math.ceil(start);
```

In this example, Math.floor(start) returns the double value 3.0, and the variable lowAnswer receives the int value 3. Math.ceil(start) returns the double value 4.0, and the variable highAnswer receives the int value 4.

? Self-Test Questions

14. What values are returned by each of the following?

    Math.round(2.3), Math.round(2.7), Math.floor(2.3), Math.floor(2.7), Math.ceil(2.3), and Math.ceil(2.7).

15. Suppose that speed is a variable of type double and you want to assign Math.round(speed) to the variable approxSpeed, which is of type int. How do you write the assignment statement?

16. Suppose that speed is a variable of type double and you want to assign Math.round(speed) to the variable longSpeed, which is of type long. How do you write the assignment statement?

17. Suppose that n1 is of type int and n2 is of type long. What is the type of the value returned by Math.min(n1, n2)?

Integer, Double, and Other Wrapper Classes

Java makes a distinction between the primitive types, such as int, double, and char, and the class types, such as the class String and the programmer-defined classes. For example,

---

1. You cannot store a long value in a variable of type int, even if it is a value like 4, which might just as well have been an int. The value 4, for example, can have a type of either int or long, depending on how it was created.

you saw in Chapter 4 that an argument to a method is treated differently depending on whether the argument is of a primitive type or a class type. To make things uniform, it would be handy sometimes to be able to convert a value of a primitive type, such as the `int` value 42, to an object of some class type that corresponds to the primitive type `int`.

In order to convert a value of a primitive type to an "equivalent" value of a class type, Java provides **wrapper classes** for each of the primitive classes. For example, the wrapper class for the primitive type `int` is the predefined class `Integer`. If you want to convert an `int` value, such as 42, to an object of type `Integer`, you can do so as follows:

wrapper class

Integer
class

```
Integer n = new Integer(42);
```

After the preceding executes, n names an object of the class `Integer` that corresponds to the `int` value 42. (The object n does in fact have the `int` value 42 stored in an instance variable of the object n.) To convert in the reverse direction, from an object of type `Integer` to an `int` value, you can do the following:

```
int i = n.intValue();//n names an object of the class Integer.
```

The method `intValue( )` recovers the equivalent `int` value from an object of type `Integer`.

The wrapper classes for the primitive types `long`, `float`, `double`, and `char` are `Long`, `Float`, `Double`, and `Character`, respectively. And, of course, rather than the method `intValue`, the classes `Long`, `Float`, `Double`, and `Character` use the methods `longValue`, `floatValue`, `doubleValue`, and `charValue`, respectively.

other wrapper
classes

Quick Reference: **Wrapper Classes**

Every primitive type has a wrapper class. Wrapper classes allow you to have a class object that corresponds to a value of a primitive type. Wrapper classes also contain a number of useful predefined constants and static methods

---

This brief introduction to wrapper classes explains why they are called wrapper classes, but for us, the main importance of these wrapper classes is that they contain a number of useful constants and static methods.

For example, you can use the associated wrapper class to find the largest and smallest values of any of the primitive number types. The largest and smallest values of type `int` are

largest and
smallest values

```
Integer.MAX_VALUE and Integer.MIN_VALUE
```

The largest and smallest values of type `double` are

```
Double.MAX_VALUE and Double.MIN_VALUE
```

Static methods in the wrapper classes can be used to convert a string to the corresponding number of type `int`, `double`, `long`, or `float`. For example, the static method `parseDouble` of the wrapper class `Double` will convert a string to a value of type `double`. So

parseDouble

```
Double.parseDouble("199.98")
```

returns the `double` value `199.98`. Of course, you knew that the number value was `199.98`, and so it hardly seems worth all this effort. But the same technique can be used to change the value of a string variable. For example, suppose `theString` is a variable of type `String` whose value is the string representation of a number of type `double`. The following will return the `double` value corresponding to the string value of `theString`:

```
Double.parseDouble(theString)
```

If there is any possibility that the string named by `theString` has extra leading or trailing blanks, you should instead use

```
Double.parseDouble(theString.trim( ))
```

The method `trim` is a method in the class `String` that trims off leading and trailing whitespace, such as blanks.

If the string is not a correctly formed numeral, the invocation of `Double.parse-Double` will cause your program to end. The use of `trim` helps some in avoiding this problem.

This conversion of a string to a number can be done with any of the wrapper classes `Integer`, `Long`, and `Float`, as well as with the wrapper class `Double`. Just use the static method `Integer.parseInt`, `Long.parseLong`, or `Float.parseFloat` instead of `Double.parseDouble`.

parseInt
parseLong

Each of the numeric wrapper classes also has a static method called `toString` that will convert in the other direction—that is, `toString` converts from a numeric value to a string representation of the numeric value. For example,

```
Integer.toString(42)
```

returns the string value `"42"`. And

```
Double.toString(199.98)
```

returns the string value `"199.98"`.

Character

`Character` is the wrapper class for the primitive type `char`. The following piece of code illustrates some of the basic methods for this class:

```
Character c1 = new Character('a');
Character c2 = new Character('A');
if (c1.equals(c2))
    System.out.println(c1.charValue( ) +
                            " is the same as " + c2.charValue( ));
else
    System.out.println(c1.charValue( ) +
                        " is not the same as " + c2.charValue( ));
```

This outputs

```
a is not the same as A
```

The `equals` method checks for equality as characters, so uppercase and lowercase letters are considered different.

Some of the static methods in the class `Character` are listed in Display 5.11.

There is also a wrapper class `Boolean`. It has names for the two constants of type `boolean`: `Boolean.TRUE` and `Boolean.FALSE`. However, the Java keywords `true` and `false` are much easier to use.

`Boolean`

■ DISPLAY 5.11   **Static Methods in the Class** `Character`

Name	Description	Type of Arguments	Type of Value Returned	Example	Value Returned
`toUpperCase`	Convert to uppercase	`char`	`char`	`Character.toUpperCase('a')` `Character.toUpperCase('A')`	Both return `'A'`
`toLowerCase`	Convert to lowercase	`char`	`char`	`Character.toLowerCase('a')` `Character.toLowerCase('A')`	Both return `'a'`
`isUpperCase`	Test for uppercase	`char`	`boolean`	`Character.isUpperCase('A')` `Character.isUpperCase('a')`	`true` `false`
`isLowerCase`	Test for lowercase	`char`	`boolean`	`Character.isLowerCase('A')` `Character.isLowerCase('a')`	`false` `true`

`isWhitespace`	Test for whitespace	`char`	`boolean`	`Character.is-`
				`Whitespace(' ')`
				`Character.is-`
				`Whitespace('A')`
					`true`
					
					`false`

Whitespace characters are those that print as white space, such as the blank, the tab character (`'\t'`), and the line break character (`'\n'`).

Name	Description	Type of Arguments	Type of Value Returned	Example	Value Returned
`isLetter`	Test for being a letter	`char`	`boolean`	`Character.isLetter('A')` `Character.isLetter('%')`	`true` `false`
`isDigit`	Test for being a digit	`char`	`boolean`	`Character.isDigit('5')` `Character.isDigit('A')`	`true` `false`

Remember: **A Wrapper Class Has Two Personalities**

Each wrapper class has two related but distinct uses. For example, consider the wrapper class `Integer`. It can be used to produce objects of the class `Integer` that correspond to values of type `int`, as in

```
Integer n = new Integer(42);
```

The wrapper class `Integer` also serves as a library of useful static methods, such as the method `parseInt`, as in

```
String inputString = SavitchIn.readLineWord( );
int number = Integer.parseInt(inputString);
```

Any one program can use both personalities of a wrapper class, but it is perhaps more likely that any given program will use only one of these personalities.

? Self-Test Questions

18. Which of the following are valid?

    ```
    Integer n = new Integer(77);
    int m = 77;
    n = m;
    m = n;
    ```

    If any are invalid, tell how to write a valid Java statement that does what the invalid statement is trying to do.

19. Write a Java expression to convert the number in the `double` variable x to a string. The expression returns a string that is the normal way of writing the value in x.

20. Write a Java expression to convert the string in the variable s to the corresponding value of type `int`. The variable s is of type `String`. Assume that s contains a string that is the normal way of writing some integer, such as `"123"`.

21. How would you do Self-Test Question 20 if the string might contain leading or trailing blanks, such as `"   123   "`?

22. Write Java code to output the largest and smallest values of type `double` that you can have in Java.

5.3 DESIGNING METHODS

It is common sense to take a method and try it. If it fails, admit it frankly and try another. But above all, try something. -Franklin Delano Roosevelt, Address at Oglethorpe University [May 22, 1932]

In this section we discuss some basic techniques that will help you to design and test methods. We start with a case study.

Case Study
Formatting Output

If you have a variable of type `double` that stores some amount of money, you would like your programs to output the amount in a nice format. However, if you just use `System.out.println`, you are likely to get output that looks like the following:

```
Your cost, including tax, is $19.98123576432
```

You would like the output to look like the following:

```
Your cost, including tax, is $19.98
```

task specification

In this case study, you will define a class called `Dollars` with two static methods named `write` and `writeln` that can be used to produce this kind of nicely formatted output.[2] For example, if the amount of money is in a variable of type `double` that is named `amount`, then (after you finish with this case study) the output can be produced as follows:

```
System.out.print("Your cost, including tax, is ");
Dollars.writeln(amount);
```

Note that the method should add the dollar sign for you, and that it should always output exactly two digits after the decimal point. So it would output `$2.10`, not `$2.1`.

When the amount being written out has more than two digits after the decimal point, you must decide what to do with the extra digits. You decide to round the number to two digits after the decimal point, so if the value to be output is `9.128`, you would get an output of `$9.13`.

The difference between `write` and `writeln` will be the same as the difference between `print` and `println`. With `write`, the next output will go on the same line. With `writeln`, the next output will go on the next line.

In order to output an amount like `9.98`, you have little choice but to break it into the pieces 9 and 98 and then output each piece separately. So, you come up with the following pseudocode as an outline for the method `write`:

Algorithm to Output a `double` Amount as Dollars and Cents
(The amount is in a variable named `amount`.)

pseudocode

Determine the number of whole dollars in `amount` and store it in an `int` variable called `dollars`.

Determine the number of cents in `amount` and store it in an `int` variable named `cents`. Round if there are more than two digits after the decimal point.

```
System.out.print('$');
System.out.print(dollars);
System.out.print('.');
```
Output `cents` in the usual dollars and cents format.

---

2. Java has classes that allow you to output numbers in any format that you wish. However, using these classes can get quite involved. It will be instructive, and perhaps even easier, to program the details ourselves. If you want to know more about such formatting classes, look at Appendix 6, which has a brief discussion of the class `DecimalFormat`.

You now need to convert each of these pseudocode instructions to Java code. Let's take them in order.

To obtain the number of whole dollars and the number of cents as two `int` values, you need to somehow get rid of the decimal point. One way to do this is to convert the amount to all cents. To convert 10.95 in dollars and cents to all cents, you multiply by 100 to obtain 10.95*100, which is 1095.0. If there is a fraction of a penny, such as when converting 10.9567 to 1095.67 (pennies), you can use the `round` method:

```
Math.round(1095.67)
```

This returns 1096, as a value of type `long`.

Note that you want to store the result of this rounding in the `int` variable for holding the total amount expressed as all cents. However, `Math.round` returns a value of type `long`, and you cannot store a value of type `long` in a variable of type `int`, not even if it is a small integer. So you need to perform a type cast to convert this `long` value to an `int` value as follows:

```
(int)(Math.round(1096 to 1095.67))
```

This returns 1096, as an `int` value.

Thus, your code will begin with something like

```
int allCents = (int)(Math.round(amount*100));
```

Now you need to convert `allCents` to a dollar amount and a cents amount. There are 100 cents in a dollar, so you use integer division to obtain the number of dollars:

```
int dollars = allCents/100;
```

The number of cents is just the amount left over when you divide `allCents` by 100, so you can use the % operator to obtain the amount of cents:

```
int cents = allCents%100;
```

Thus, you have translated the first two steps in your pseudocode to the following Java code:

```
int allCents = (int)(Math.round(amount*100));
int dollars = allCents/100;
int cents = allCents%100;
```

The next three instructions in your pseudocode are already expressed in Java, so all that is left to do is to translate the last instruction into Java code. That last instruction is

Output `cents` in the usual dollars and cents format.

This looks pretty easy. You try the following:

```
System.out.println(cents);
```

early testing

You then test your code and see the following output:

$10.95

which looks pretty good. When you try some more examples, however, you run into a problem with amounts less than 10. For example, one output you get is

$7.5

when you were expecting

$7.05

This quick test makes you realize that you need to output a 0 before the amount of cents whenever the amount of cents is less than 10. So you change your code for outputting the number of cents to

```java
if (cents < 10)
{
    System.out.print('0');
    System.out.print(cents);
}
else
    System.out.print(cents);
```

The full definition of the class you derived is shown in Display 5.12.

■ DISPLAY 5.12 The DollarsFirstTry Class

```java
public class DollarsFirstTry
{
    /**
     Outputs amount in dollars and cents notation.
     Rounds after two decimal points.
     Does not advance to the next line after output.
    */
    public static void write(double amount)
    {
        int allCents = (int)(Math.round(amount*100));
        int dollars = allCents/100;
        int cents = allCents%100;

        System.out.print('$');
        System.out.print(dollars);
        System.out.print('.');

        if (cents < 10)
        {
            System.out.print('0');
            System.out.print(cents);
        }
        else
            System.out.print(cents);
    }
    /**
     Outputs amount in dollars and cents notation.
     Rounds after two decimal points.
     Advances to the next line after output.
    */
    public static void writeln(double amount)
    {
        write(amount);
        System.out.println();
    }
}
```

■ DISPLAY 5.13 **Testing a Method**

```
public class DollarsFirstTryDriver
{
    public static void main(String[] args)
    {
        double amount;
        char ans;

        System.out.println("Testing DollarsFirstTry.write:");
        do
        {
            System.out.println("Enter a value of type double:");
            amount = SavitchIn.readLineDouble();
            DollarsFirstTry.write(amount);
            System.out.println();
            System.out.println("Test again?(y/n)");
            ans = SavitchIn.readLineNonwhiteChar();
        }while ((ans == 'y') || (ans == 'Y'));
        System.out.println("End of test.");
    }
}
```

*This kind of testing program is often called a **driver program**.*

Sample Screen Dialog

```
Testing DollarsFirstTry.write:
Enter a value of type double:
1.2345
$1.23
Test again?(y/n)
y
Enter a value of type double:
1.235
$1.24
Test again?(y/n)
y
Enter a value of type double:
9.02
$9.02
Test again?(y/n)
y
Enter a value of type double:
−1.20
$−1.0−20          ◀—————————   OOPS. There's
Test again?(y/n)                 a problem here.
n
```

Now that you have a complete definition of the class, it is time for some serious testing. Display 5.13 shows the program you use to test the method `write`. These sorts of programs are often called **driver programs** because they do nothing but exercise ("drive") the method. Any method can be tested in a program like this.

The testing goes quite well until you decide to try a negative number. After all, there is such a thing as a negative amount of money. It's called a debt. But the amount −1.20 is output as $−1.0−20. Something is wrong with the way your method handles negative amounts.

It is easy to see what is wrong here. After outputting $−1., you want to output 20, not −20. There are a number of ways to fix this, but you hit on one clean and simple way. Since you have code that correctly outputs nonnegative numbers, you can convert any negative number to a positive number and then output the positive number and insert the minus sign. The revised version of the class is shown in Display 5.14. Notice that the new method `writePositive` (Display 5.14) has a body that is almost the same as the old method `write` (Display 5.12). The only difference is that `writePositive` does not output the dollar sign. The dollar sign is output in the new version of the method `write`.

Every time you change the definition of a class or method, you should test it. So you retest the class `Dollars` with a program similar to the one you used to test `DollarsFirstTry`. In this case, the test is successful.

A driver program for the method `write` of the class `Dollars` is in the file `DollarsDriver.java` on the accompanying CD. ▪

more testing

driver program

retest

extra code on CD

Top-Down Design

In the last case study, we used the following pseudocode for our first attempt to design the method `write` of the class `Dollars` (Display 5.14):

> Determine the number of whole dollars in `amount` and store it in an `int` variable called `dollars`.
> Determine the number of cents in `amount` and store it in an `int` variable named `cents`. Round if there are more than two digits after the decimal point.
> ```
> System.out.print('$');
> System.out.print(dollars);
> System.out.print('.');
> ```
> Output `cents` in the usual dollars and cents format.

What we have done with this pseudocode is to decompose the task for outputting an amount of money into a number of subtasks, such as

> Determine the number of whole dollars in `amount` and store it in an `int` variable called `dollars`.

We then solved each of these subtasks separately and produced code for each subtask. After that, all we had to do to produce the final definition of the method was to combine the code for the subtasks.

As it turned out, we ended up using the code derived from the preceding pseudocode for the method `writePositive`, rather than using it for the method `write`. But this was just a further illustration of using subtasks. The method `writePositive` solved a subtask that we used in the final definition of the method `write`.

■ DISPLAY 5.14 **The Corrected Class** `Dollars` *(Part 1 of 2)*

```java
public class Dollars
{
    /**
     Outputs amount in dollars and cents notation.
     Rounds after two decimal points.
     Does not advance to the next line after output.
    */
    public static void write(double amount)
    {
        if (amount >= 0)
        {
            System.out.print('$');
            writePositive(amount);
        }
        else
        {
            double positiveAmount = -amount;
            System.out.print('$');
            System.out.print('-');
            writePositive(positiveAmount);
        }
    }

    //Precondition: amount >= 0;
    //Outputs amount in dollars and cents notation. Rounds
    //after two decimal points. Omits the dollar sign.
    private static void writePositive(double amount)
    {
        int allCents = (int)(Math.round(amount*100));
        int dollars = allCents/100;
        int cents = allCents%100;

        System.out.print(dollars);
        System.out.print('.');
        if (cents < 10)
        {
            System.out.print('0');
            System.out.print(cents);
        }
        else
            System.out.print(cents);
    }
```

The case for negative amounts of money.

DollarsDriver.java on the CD is a testing and demonstration program for this class.

■ DISPLAY 5.14   **The Corrected Class** Dollars *(Part 2 of 2)*

```
    /**
     Outputs amount in dollars and cents notation.
     Rounds after two decimal points.
     Advances to the next line after output.
    */
    public static void writeln(double amount)
    {
        write(amount);
        System.out.println();
    }
}
```

Often, though not always, the solutions to subtasks are implemented as private helping methods. If a subtask is large, you use the same technique. Divide the subtask into smaller subsubtasks and solve the subsubtasks separately. These subsubtasks may be further decomposed into smaller tasks, but eventually the tasks become small enough to be easy to design and code.

This technique of dividing the task to be performed by a method into subtasks is called **top-down design** or **divide and conquer.**

Testing Methods

One way to test a method is to use a driver program like the one in Display 5.13. These driver programs are just for your use, and so they can be quite simple. They need not have any fancy output or anything else very fancy. All they have to do is to give the method some arguments and invoke the method.

driver program

Every method you write for a class should be tested. Moreover, it should be tested in a program in which it is the only method that has not yet been fully tested. In that way, if you discover that something is wrong, you know which method contains the mistake. If you test more than one method in the same program, you can easily be fooled into thinking that the mistake is in one method when in fact it is in some other method.

Remember: Test Methods Separately

Every method should be tested in a program in which it is the only untested method.

One way to test every method in a program in which it is the only untested program is a technique called **bottom-up testing.** With bottom-up testing, if method A uses method B, then method B is fully tested before you test method A.

bottom-up testing

Bottom-up testing is a good and safe method of testing, but sometimes it can become tedious, and there are other ways to find bugs quicker and less painfully. Sometimes you want to test a method before all the methods it uses are tested. However, you should still test the method in a program in which it is the only untested method. For example, you might want to test your general approach to the problem before even writing all the methods. Sometimes you will find yourself in a situation in which method A uses method B, and you want to test method A before you test method B (maybe even before you write method B). This presents a problem. If method A uses method B and method B is not yet tested, how can you test method A in a program in which it is the only untested method? The answer is to use a stub for method B.

stub

A **stub** is a simplified version of a method that is not good enough for the final class definition, but that is good enough for testing and is simple enough for you to be sure it is correct (or as sure as you can be). For example, suppose you are testing the class `Dollars` in Display 5.14 and you want to test the method `writeln` before you test the method `write`. You can use a stub for the method `write`, as follows:

```
public static void write(double amount)
{
    System.out.print("$99.12");
}
```

Now this is certainly not a correct definition of the class `write`. It always outputs `$99.12`, no matter what it gets as an argument. However, it is good enough to use in testing the method `writeln`. If you test the method `writeln` using this stub for the method `write`, and `writeln` outputs `99.12` in the correct way, then `writeln` is almost certain to be correct. Note that using this stub for `write` will let you test the method `writeln` before you even write either of the methods `write` or `writePositive`.

? Self-Test Questions

23. Design a class to output values of type `double` (not necessarily for money amounts). Call the class `OutputFormat`. It should have two static methods, `write` and `writeln`, each of which takes two arguments. The first argument gives a `double` value to be written to the screen. The second argument is an `int` value telling how many digits to show after the decimal point. Have your methods round any extra digits. This is very similar to the methods `write` and `writeln` in the class `Dollars`, and you can use the class `Dollars` as a model, but there are some differences between the methods in the two classes. As you would expect, output after `write` goes on the same line and output after `writeln` goes on the following line; otherwise, `write` and `writeln` do the same thing. The following is some sample output:

```
OutputFormat.writeln(9.1234667, 4);
OutputFormat.writeln(9.9999, 2);
OutputFormat.writeln(7.01234, 4);
```

It should produce the following output:

```
9.1235
10.00
7.0123
```

Do not forget to test your methods on numbers with zeros after the decimal point, like `1.023` and `1.0023`. *Hint:* You may find the static method `Math.pow`

(Display 5.9) helpful as part of an expression to move a decimal point. This is a fairly difficult exercise, so allow yourself some time to complete it. If you do not succeed in writing this class, be sure that you at least understand the answer given at the end of the chapter. This is a very useful class.

24. In your definition of the class `OutputFormat` in Self-Test Question 23, would it be valid to use the names `print` and `println`, rather than `write` and `writeln`, or would this produce a name conflict with `System.out.println`?

25. Consider the variable `allCents` in the method `writePositive` in Display 5.14. It holds an amount of money as if it were all cents. So for the amount $12.95, the `int` variable `allCents` would be set to `1295`. This is somewhat limiting. The largest value of type `int` is `2147483647`, meaning that the largest amount the method can handle is $21,474,836.47. That is more than $21 million, a nice large sum, but we often need to consider larger amounts, such as the national budget, a large company's budget, or even the salary for the CEO of a large company. How can you easily change the definitions of the methods in the class `Dollars` so that they handle larger amounts of money?

5.4 OVERLOADING

A good name is better than precious ointment . . . -Ecclesiastes 7:1

You have seen that two (or more) different classes can have methods with the same name. For example, many classes have a method named `readInput`. This is not so surprising. The type of the calling object allows Java to decide which definition of the method `read-Input` to use. You may be more surprised to hear that you can also have two or more methods *in the same class* that have the same method name. How is this possible? Read on.

Overloading Basics

When you give two or more definitions of the same method name *within the same class*, it is known as **overloading** the method name. In order for this to work out, you must ensure that the different definitions of the method name have something different about their parameter lists. For example, Display 5.15 contains a very simple example of overloading.

overloading

The class `Statistician` (Display 5.15) has three different methods, all named `average`. When `Statistician.average` is invoked, how does Java know which definition of `average` to use? First, let's assume that the arguments are all of type `double`. In that case, Java can tell which definition of `average` to use by the number of arguments. If there are two arguments of type `double`, it uses the first definition of `average`. If there are three arguments, it uses the second definition of `average`.

Now suppose that there is an invocation of the method `average` that has two arguments of type `char`. Java knows that it should use the third definition of `average` because of the types of the arguments. Only one of the definitions has two arguments of type `char`. (For now, don't worry about how this method averages two letters. That's a side issue that we will come back to shortly.)

■ DISPLAY 5.15 **Overloading**

```
/**
 This is just a toy class to illustrate overloading.
*/
public class Statistician
{
    public static void main(String[] args)
    {
        double average1 = Statistician.average(40.0, 50.0);
        double average2 = Statistician.average(1.0, 2.0, 3.0);
        char average3 = Statistician.average('a', 'c');

        System.out.println("average1 = " + average1);
        System.out.println("average2 = " + average2);
        System.out.println("average3 = " + average3);
    }

    public static double average(double first, double second)
    {
        return ((first + second)/2.0);
    }

    public static double average(double first,
                                    double second, double third)
    {
        return ((first + second + third)/3.0);
    }

    public static char average(char first, char second)
    {
        return (char)(((int)first + (int)second)/2);
    }
}
```

Sample Screen Dialog

```
average1 = 45.0
average2 = 2.0
average3 = b
```

Suppose you overload a method name by giving more than one definition to that method name within the same class definition. When that method name is invoked, Java determines which definition to use according to the number of arguments and the types of the arguments. If a definition of that method name has the same number of parameters as there are arguments in the invocation, and if the types also match—that is, if the first argument has the same type as the first parameter, the second argument has the same type as the second parameter, and so forth—then that is the definition of the method name that is used. If there is no such match, Java will try some simple type conversions of the kinds we discussed earlier, such as casting an `int` to a `double`, to see if that produces a match. If that fails, you will get an error message.

Now let's take a short side trip to explain how we average two characters. For this example, it does not matter whether we use a crazy way of averaging two characters, but, in fact, the technique we use in Display 5.15 is a very sensible way to average characters, or at least to average two letters. If the two letters are both lowercase, the average computed will be the lowercase letter halfway between them in alphabetical order. (If no letter is exactly halfway, it chooses one of the two that are as close to halfway as possible.) Similarly, if the two letters are both uppercase, the average computed will be the uppercase letter halfway between them in alphabetical order. This works because the letters are assigned numbers in order. The number assigned to `'b'` is one more than the number assigned to `'a'`, the number assigned to `'c'` is one more than the number assigned to `'b'`, and so forth. So if you convert two letters to numbers, average the numbers, and then convert them back to letters, you get the letter halfway in between.

averaging
characters

Overloading can be applied to any kind of method. It can be applied to `void` methods, to methods that return a value, to static methods, to nonstatic methods, or to any combination of these.

Note that you have already been using overloading, even though you may not have known the term before. In the previous section, many of the methods of the class `Math` use overloading. For example, the `max` method uses overloading based on the type of its arguments. If its two arguments are of type `int`, it returns a value of type `int`. If its two arguments are of type `double`, it returns a value of type `double`. Of course, this is not a very dramatic use of overloading, since the different definitions of `max` would be identical except for some type names. A more dramatic example is the division operator /, which we discussed in Chapter 2. If its arguments are of type `double`, it is defined to do floating-point division and so `5.0/2.0` returns `2.5`. But if both arguments are of type `int`, it is defined to perform integer division, so `5/2` is `2`.

Quick Reference: Overloading

Within one class, you can have two (or more) definitions of a single method name. This is called **overloading** the method name. When you overload a method name, any two definitions of the same method name must either have different numbers of parameters or some parameter position must be of differing types in the two definitions.

■ DISPLAY 5.16 **Class Diagram for** `Pet` **Class**

Pet
– name: String – age: int – weight: double
+ writeOutput( ): void + set(String newName): void + set(int newAge): void + set(double newWeight): void + set(String newName, int newAge, double newWeight): void + getName( ): String + getAge( ): int + getWeight( ): double

Programming Example
A Pet Class

Display 5.16 shows the class diagram for a class named `Pet`. Note that there are four methods named `set`. This is an example of overloading a method name. The various `set` methods set different instance variables. One sets all three of the instance variables `name`, `age`, and `weight`. The other three set only one instance variable each.

Display 5.17 shows the full definition of the class `Pet`. There is a `main` method with a simple demonstration program. Notice that each invocation of the method `set` has either a different number of arguments or an argument whose type is different from the other invocations of `set`. Thus, each invocation of `set` uses a different definition of `set`. ■

▲ *Gotcha*
Overloading and Automatic Type Conversion

In some situations, two friends are not better than one. Two good things can sometimes interact in a bad way. Overloading is a friend, or at least a helpful feature of the Java language. Automatic type conversion of arguments is also a helpful feature of the Java language (such as converting an `int` like 2 to a `double` like 2.0 when a method wants a `double` as an argument). But these two nice features can sometimes get in the way of each other.

■ DISPLAY 5.17 **Pet Class** *(Part 1 of 3)*

```java
/**
 Class for basic pet records: name, age, and weight.
*/
public class Pet
{
    private String name;
    private int age; //in years
    private double weight; //in pounds

    /**
     This main is just a demonstration program.
    */
    public static void main(String[] args)
    {
        Pet myDog = new Pet();
        myDog.set("Fido", 2, 5.5);
        myDog.writeOutput();
        System.out.println("Changing name.");
        myDog.set("Rex");
        myDog.writeOutput();
        System.out.println("Changing weight.");
        myDog.set(6.5);
        myDog.writeOutput();
        System.out.println("Changing age.");
        myDog.set(3);
        myDog.writeOutput();
    }

    public void writeOutput()
    {
        System.out.println("Name: " + name);
        System.out.println("Age: " + age + " years");
        System.out.println("Weight: " + weight + " pounds");
    }

    public void set(String newName)
    {
        name = newName;
        //age and weight are unchanged.
    }
```

■ DISPLAY 5.17 Pet Class *(Part 2 of 3)*

```java
public void set(int newAge)
{
    if (newAge <= 0)
    {
        System.out.println("Error: invalid age.");
        System.exit(0);
    }
    else
        age = newAge;
    //name and weight are unchanged.
}

public void set(double newWeight)
{
    if (newWeight <= 0)
    {
        System.out.println("Error: invalid weight.");
        System.exit(0);
    }
    else
        weight = newWeight;
    //name and age are unchanged.
}

public void set(String newName, int newAge, double newWeight)
{
    name = newName;
    if ((newAge <= 0) || (newWeight <= 0))
    {
        System.out.println("Error: invalid age or weight.");
        System.exit(0);
    }
    else
    {
        age = newAge;
        weight = newWeight;
    }
}

public String getName()
{
    return name;
}
```

■ DISPLAY 5.17 **Pet Class** *(Part 3 of 3)*

```
      public int getAge()
      {
          return age;
      }
      public double getWeight()
      {
          return weight;
      }
  }
```

Sample Screen Dialog

```
Name: Fido
Age: 2 years
Weight: 5.5 pounds
Changing name.
Name: Rex
Age: 2 years
Weight: 5.5 pounds
Changing weight.
Name: Rex
Age: 2 years
Weight: 6.5 pounds
Changing age.
Name: Rex
Age: 3 years
Weight: 6.5 pounds
```

For example, look at the `main` method in Display 5.17 and consider the following lines:

automatic type
conversion

```
System.out.println("Changing weight.");
myDog.set(6.5);
```

This changes the weight of `myDog` to `6.5` pounds. Suppose, however, that `myDog` does not weigh 6.5 pounds, but instead weighs only 6 pounds. In that case, we should change these two lines to

```
System.out.println("Changing weight.");
myDog.set(6.0);
```

This will change myDog's weight to 6 pounds. But suppose that we forget the decimal point and the zero and write the following:

```
System.out.println("Changing weight.");
myDog.set(6);
```

We want this to change myDog's weight to 6, but instead it will change myDog's age to 6. This is because 6 is of type int, and the definition of set that has one parameter of type int will change the instance variable age, not the instance variable weight. If Java can find a definition of set that matches the number and types of arguments, it will not do any type conversion of int to double, or any other type conversions.

In the case we just looked at, we needed a type conversion, but we did not get one. There are also cases in which you do not want a type conversion and you do get one. For example, suppose we want to set myDog's name to "Cha Cha", weight to 2, and age to 3. We might try the following:

```
myDog.set("Cha Cha", 2, 3);
```

This will set myDog's age to 2, not 3, and myDog's weight to 3.0, not 2.0. The real problem, of course, is that we have reversed the second and third arguments, but let's look at it as Java does. Given the preceding invocation, Java looks for a definition of set with a heading of the following form:

```
public void set(String Name_1, int Name_2, int Name_3)
```

There is no such definition of set, however. So there is no exact match for the invocation. Java then tries to convert an int to a double to get a match. It notices that if it converts the 3 to 3.0, it will have a match to

```
public void set(String newName, int newAge, double newWeight)
```

and so it does the type conversion.

What went wrong (besides reversing two arguments)? We should have given the weight as 2.0, not 2. If we had used 2.0, or if Java had not done any automatic type conversions for us, we would have received an error message. In this case, Java tried to help, but the help just got in the way.

There are situations in which a method invocation can be resolved in two different ways, depending on how overloading and type conversion interact. Such ambiguous method invocations are not allowed in Java and will produce a run-time error message (or sometimes even a compiler error message). For example, you can overload a method name (problemMethod) so that it has the following two method headings in a SampleClass:

```
public class SampleClass
{
    public static void problemMethod(double n1, int n2)
        .
        .
        .

    public static void problemMethod(int n1, double n2)
        .
        .
        .
```

Such method definitions will compile. However, an invocation such as the following will produce an error message, because Java cannot decide which overloaded definition of problemMethod to use:

```
SampleClass.problemMethod(5, 10);
```

Java cannot decide whether it should convert the int value 5 to a double value and use the first definition of problemMethod, or whether it should convert the int value 10 to a double value and use the second definition. In this situation, Java issues an error message indicating that the method invocation is ambiguous.

The following two method invocations are allowed:

```
SampleClass.problemMethod(5.0, 10);
SampleClass.problemMethod(5, 10.0);
```

However, such situations, while valid, are confusing and should be avoided. △

Remember: **Overloading and Automatic Type Conversion**

Java always tries to use overloading before it tries to use automatic type conversion. If Java can find a definition of a method that matches the types of the arguments, it will use that definition. Java will not do an automatic type conversion of a method's argument until after it has tried and failed to find a definition of the method name with parameter types that exactly match the arguments in the method invocation.

▲ *Gotcha*

You Cannot Overload on the Basis of the Returned Type

You cannot overload a method name by giving two definitions with headings that differ only in the type of the value returned. For example, consider the class Pet in Display 5.17. You might have wanted to add a method called getWeight, which returns a character telling whether the pet is overweight or underweight—say, '+' for overweight, '-' for underweight, and '*' for just right. This would return a value of type char. If you did add this method getWeight, you would then have two methods with the following headings:

```
/**
 Returns the weight of the pet.
*/
public double getWeight( )

/**
 Returns '+' if overweight, '-' if
 underweight and '*' if weight OK.
*/
public char getWeight( )
```

You CANNOT have both of these methods within a single class.

Unfortunately, this is invalid. In any class definition, two definitions of the same method name must have either different numbers of parameters or one or more parameters of differing types. You cannot overload on the basis of the type returned.

If you think about it, it is not even possible to write the compiler so that it overloads on the basis of the type returned. For example, suppose you have

```java
Pet myFriend = new Pet( );
       .
       .
       .
double value = myFriend.getWeight( );
```

Now suppose that, contrary to actual fact, we allowed methods with both of the above headings. Consider the job of the poor compiler in this situation. Although we have not made an issue of it, it is true that you can store a value of type char in a variable of type double. Java will perform an automatic type cast to change the char to a double. Thus, in this hypothetical scenario, the variable value is happy with either a double or a char. So there is no way to tell whether the programmer who wrote this code meant for getWeight to return a char or a double. The compiler would have to ask the programmer what she or he meant, and compilers are not allowed to ask the programmer questions. △

? Self-Test Questions

26. Would the following method invocation be valid to include in the program in Display 5.17?

    ```java
    myDog.set("Fido", 2, 7);
    ```

27. Can a class possibly contain both of the following method definitions?

    ```java
    /**
     Postcondition: Returns the number of people
     in numberOfCouples couples.
    */
    public static int howMany(int numberOfCouples)
    {
        return 2*numberOfCouples;
    }

    /**
     Postcondition: Returns the number of children,
     assuming that each couple has 2.3 children.
    */
    public static double howMany(int numberOfCouples)
    {
        return 2.3*numberOfCouples;
    }
    ```

28. Can a class possibly contain both of the following method definitions?

    ```java
    /**
     Postcondition: Returns an int value approximately
     equivalent to number.
    ```

```
    But converts all negative numbers to zero.
    */
    public static int convertedValue(double number)
    {
        if (number > 0.0)
            return (int) number;
        return 0;
    }

    /**
     Postcondition: Returns a double value approximately
     equivalent to number.
     But converts all negative numbers to zero.
     */
    public static double convertedValue(int number)
    {
        if (number > 0)
            return (double) number;
        return 0.0;
    }
```

29. Consider the class `Species` in Display 4.19 of Chapter 4. It has a method called `set` that sets the name, population, and growth rate of a species. Could this class have another method that is also named `set`, that has only one parameter for the name of the species, and that sets both the population and the growth rate to zero? If so, give the definition of this other method named `set`.

30. Again consider the class `Species` in Display 4.19 of Chapter 4. It has a method called `set` that sets the name, population, and growth rate of a species. Could this class have another method that is also named `set`, that has only one parameter for the name of the species, and that does not set any other instance variables? If so, give the definition of this other method named `set`.

31. Still considering the class `Species` in Display 4.19 of Chapter 4, could both of the methods named `set`, defined in Self-Test Questions 29 and 30, be added to the class `Species`?

Programming Example
A Class for Money

Display 5.18 contains a class, named `Money`, whose objects represent amounts of (U.S.) money, such as $9.99, $500.00, $0.50, and so forth. You may be inclined to think of money amounts as values of type `double`, but a user who does not know about programming (and many end users do not know about programming) would think of them in terms of dollars and cents. To the "person on the street," $9.99 is not a value of type `double`. It turns out that the "person on the street" is correct. Sometimes you can get away with using values of type `double` to represent amounts of money, but there is a problem with doing so. A value of type `double` is, practically speaking, an approximate quantity, and if you are writing an accounting program, approximate quantities are not always good enough. If

■ DISPLAY 5.18 **Money Class** *(Part 1 of 3)*

```java
/**
 Objects represent nonnegative amounts of money,
 such as $100, $41.99, $0.05.
*/
public class Money
{
    private long dollars;
    private long cents;
    public void set(long newDollars)
    {
        if (newDollars < 0)
        {
            System.out.println(
                "Error: Negative amounts of money are not allowed.");
            System.exit(0);
        }
        else
        {
            dollars = newDollars;
            cents = 0;
        }
    }

    public void set(double amount)
    {
        if (amount < 0)
        {
            System.out.println(
                "Error: Negative amounts of money are not allowed.");
            System.exit(0);
        }
        else
        {
            long allCents = Math.round(amount*100);
            dollars = allCents/100;
            cents = allCents%100;
        }
    }

    public void set(Money otherObject)
    {
        this.dollars = otherObject.dollars;
        this.cents = otherObject.cents;
    }
```

■ DISPLAY 5.18 Money Class *(Part 2 of 3)*

```java
/**
 Precondition: The argument is an ordinary representation
 of an amount of money, with or without a dollar sign.
 Fractions of a cent are not allowed.
*/
public void set(String amountString)
{
    String dollarsString;
    String centsString;

    //Delete '$' if any:
    if (amountString.charAt(0) == '$')
        amountString = amountString.substring(1);
    amountString = amountString.trim();

    //Locate decimal point:
    int pointLocation = amountString.indexOf(".");

    if (pointLocation < 0) //If no decimal point
    {
        cents = 0;
        dollars = Long.parseLong(amountString);
    }
    else //String has a decimal point.
    {
        dollarsString =
                amountString.substring(0, pointLocation);
        centsString =
                amountString.substring(pointLocation + 1);
        if (centsString.length() <= 1)
        //if one digit meaning tenths of a dollar
            centsString = centsString + "0";

        dollars = Long.parseLong(dollarsString);
        cents = Long.parseLong(centsString);
        if ((dollars < 0) || (cents < 0) || (cents > 99))
        {
            System.out.println(
                "Error: Illegal representation of money.");
            System.exit(0);
        }
    }
}
```

■ DISPLAY 5.18 Money Class *(Part 3 of 3)*

```java
    public void readInput( )
    {
        System.out.println("Enter amount on a line by itself:");
        String amount = SavitchIn.readLine( );
        set(amount.trim( ));
    }

    /**
     Does not go to the next line after outputting money.
    */
    public void writeOutput( )
    {
        System.out.print("$" + dollars);
        if (cents < 10)
            System.out.print(".0" + cents);
        else
            System.out.print("." + cents);
    }

    /**
     Returns n times the calling object.
    */
    public Money times(int n)
    {
        Money product = new Money( );
        product.cents = n*cents;
        long carryDollars = product.cents/100;
        product.cents = product.cents%100;
        product.dollars = n*dollars + carryDollars;
        return product;
    }

    /**
     Returns the sum of the calling object and the argument.
    */
    public Money add(Money otherAmount)
    {
        Money sum = new Money( );
        sum.cents = this.cents + otherAmount.cents;
        long carryDollars = sum.cents/100;
        sum.cents = sum.cents%100;
        sum.dollars = this.dollars
                    + otherAmount.dollars + carryDollars;
        return sum;
    }
}
```

a bank has account balances that are off by a few dollars or even a few cents, that will produce dissatisfied customers and probably some sort of legal action by either customers or the government. The class Money is meant to hold data that represent money. To the programmer who uses the class Money, or to the end user of any software product produced, the data are not thought of as values of type double or int or any other Java predefined type. They are values of type Money.[3]

Of course, to implement the class Money, we must choose some sort of data representation. We want to represent money amounts as exact quantities, so we will use an integer type. However, the type int cannot represent very large numbers and so cannot easily represent very large amounts of money. Therefore, we will use the type long. An amount of money, such as $3500.36, will be represented as two integers—in this case, 3500 and 36—stored in instance variables of type long. It certainly makes sense to have negative amounts of money, and a final professional-strength Money class would allow for negative amounts of money, but we want a fairly simple example for learning purposes, and so we will limit ourselves to nonnegative amounts of money.

negative amounts

Notice the overloaded method name set. The four methods named set allow a programmer to set an amount of money in any way that is convenient. The programmer can use a single integer value for an amount of dollars without any cents, a single value of type double, another object of type Money, or a string, such as "$9.98" or "9.98". The programmer does not, and should not, worry about what instance variables are used inside the class Money. Instead, the programmer should think in terms of money amounts, not in terms of any instance variables.

set

Let's look at some details in the definitions of the set methods. The set method with one parameter of type long is straightforward.

The set method with one parameter of type double works by converting the double value to a value that represents the amount of money as the number of pennies in the amount. This is done as follows:

double

```
long allCents = Math.round(amount*100);
```

The method Math.round eliminates any fractional part of a penny. It returns a value of type long when its argument is of type double, as it is here. The integer division operators / and % are then used to convert the pennies to dollars and cents.

The set method with one parameter of type Money is also straightforward, but you should notice one important point. The instance variables of the parameter, such as otherObject.dollars, can be directly accessed inside the class definition for the class Money. In the definition of a class, such as Money, you can directly access the instance variables of *any* object of the class.

Money

The set method with one parameter of type String is an exercise in string processing. It changes a string, such as "$12.75" or "12.75", into two integers, such as 12 and 75. The main details are highlighted and we will review these details later in our discussion. The rest of the definition has to do with special cases and checking for invalid arguments.

String

---

3. In Display 5.14 we defined a class named Dollars that is concerned with treating amounts of money as values of type double. This programming example shows another approach to handling amounts of money and is not directly related to the class Dollars.

First, there is a check to see whether there is a dollar sign as the first character in the string. This is done as follows:

```
if (amountString.charAt(0) == '$')
    amountString = amountString.substring(1);
```

charAt

The first character in the string `amountString` is returned by the string method invocation `amountString.charAt(0)`. If this character is `'$'`, then the string, which has index positions 0 through some last index, is replaced by the substring at indices 1 through the end of the string, effectively removing the first character. This is done as follows:

```
amountString = amountString.substring(1);
```

trim

There may also have been a blank (or blanks) between the character `'$'` and the dollar amount. Blanks are trimmed off with an invocation of the `String` method `trim`, as follows:

```
amountString = amountString.trim();
```

indexOf

The string is then broken into the dollars substring and the cents substring, by locating the decimal point and breaking the string at the decimal point. The decimal point position is stored in the variable `pointLocation` as follows:

```
int pointLocation = amountString.indexOf(".");
```

substring

The dollars and cents substrings are recovered as follows:

```
dollarsString =
    amountString.substring(0, pointLocation);
centsString =
    amountString.substring(pointLocation + 1);
```

You may want to review the descriptions of the `substring` methods given in Display 2.6 of Chapter 2.

Finally, the dollars and cents substrings are converted to values of type `long`, using the static method `parseLong` in the wrapper class `Long`:

parseLong

```
dollars = Long.parseLong(dollarsString);
cents = Long.parseLong(centsString);
```

If the method `parseLong` sounds unfamiliar, check the earlier subsection of this chapter entitled "`Integer`, `Double`, and Other Wrapper Classes."

times and add

The method `times` is used to multiply an amount of money by an integer. The method `add` is used to add two objects of type `Money`. For example, if `m1` and `m2` are objects of type `Money` that both represent the amount $2.00, then `m1.times(3)` returns an object of the class `Money` that represents the amount $6.00, and `m1.add(m2)` returns an object of the class `Money` that represents the amount $4.00.

To understand the definition of the methods `times` and `add`, remember that there are 100 cents in a dollar, so if `product.cents` might have a value of 100 or more, then the following will set the variable `carryDollars` equal to the number of whole dollars in that many cents.

```
long carryDollars = product.cents/100;
```

The number of cents left over after removing that many dollars is given by

```
product.cents%100
```

A demonstration program for the class Money is given in Display 5.19. ■

■ DISPLAY 5.19 Using the Money Class

```java
public class MoneyDemo
{
    public static void main(String[] args)
    {
        Money start = new Money();
        Money goal = new Money();

        System.out.println("Enter your current savings:");
        start.readInput();

        goal = start.times(2);
        System.out.print(
            "If you double that, you will have ");
        goal.writeOutput();

        System.out.println(", or better yet:");
        goal = start.add(goal);
        System.out.println(
            "If you triple that original amount, you will have:");
        goal.writeOutput();
        System.out.println();
    }
}
```

Needed to end the line, because writeOutput does not end the line.

```java
        System.out.println("Remember: A penny saved");
        System.out.println("is a penny earned.");
    }
}
```

Sample Screen Dialog

```
Enter your current savings:
Enter amount on a line by itself:
$500.99
If you double that, you will have $1001.98, or better yet:
If you triple that original amount, you will have
$1502.97
Remember: A penny saved
is a penny earned.
```

? Self-Test Questions

32. Rewrite the method add in Display 5.18 so that it does not use the this parameter.

33. In Display 5.18, the set method with a String parameter does not allow extra leading and trailing blanks in the string. Rewrite it so that it ignores leading and trailing whitespace. For example, it should allow " $5.43 " as an argument.

5.5   CONSTRUCTORS

First things first. -Common saying

When you create an object of a class, you often want certain initializing actions performed, such as giving values to the instance variables. A constructor is a special kind of method that is designed to perform such initializations. In this section, we tell you how to define and use constructors.

Defining Constructors

Until now, we have created new objects in the manner illustrated by the following example:

```
Pet goodScout = new Pet( );
```

(The definition of the class Pet is in Display 5.17, but the point is independent of the details of this particular class.) For the classes you've seen thus far, this creates an object whose instance variables have no initial values (or have some default initial value that may not be what you want as the default). You may wish to have some or all instance variables automatically initialized to your specifications when an object is created. You can do this with a special kind of method called a constructor.

constructor

A **constructor** is a method that is called when a new object is created. It can perform any action you write into its definition, but a constructor is meant to perform initializing actions, such as initializing the values of instance variables. Constructors serve very much the same purpose as the methods named set in our definition of the class Pet in Display 5.17. But unlike the set methods, the constructors are called almost automatically whenever you create an object using the new operator.

One property of constructors that may seem strange at first is that each constructor has the same name as its class. So if the class is named Pet, the constructors will be named Pet. If the class is named Species, the constructors will be named Species.

overloading constructor

As an example, in Display 5.20, we have rewritten our definition of the class for pet records so that it has constructor methods. Like our set methods, constructors are normally overloaded so that there are multiple definitions of the constructor, each with different numbers or types of parameters. Display 5.20 and Display 5.17 are similar, but most of the differences between them are important. Let's look at those differences.

1. In Display 5.20, the class name is changed from Pet to PetRecord because each class must have a different name. Also, in Display 5.20, we have deleted the method main, because it was just a demonstration program that we no longer need. These changes are rather mundane. Now on to the important differences.

■ DISPLAY 5.20 **PetRecord Class with Constructors** *(Part 1 of 3)*

```java
/**
 Class for basic pet records: name, age, and weight.
*/
public class PetRecord
{
    private String name;
    private int age;//in years
    private double weight;//in pounds

    public void writeOutput( )
    {
        System.out.println("Name: " + name);
        System.out.println("Age: " + age + " years");
        System.out.println("Weight: " + weight + " pounds");
    }

    public PetRecord(String initialName, int initialAge,
                                            double initialWeight)
    {
        name = initialName;
        if ((initialAge < 0) || (initialWeight < 0))
        {
            System.out.println("Error: Negative age or weight.");
            System.exit(0);
        }
        else
        {
            age = initialAge;
            weight = initialWeight;
        }
    }

    public void set(String newName, int newAge, double newWeight)
    {
        name = newName;
        if ((newAge < 0) || (newWeight < 0))
        {
            System.out.println("Error: Negative age or weight.");
            System.exit(0);
        }
        else
        {
            age = newAge;
            weight = newWeight;
        }
    }
```

Constructors are called only when you create an object with new. *To change an existing object, you need one or more methods like these* set *methods.*

■ DISPLAY 5.20 PetRecord Class with Constructors *(Part 2 of 3)*

```java
public PetRecord(String initialName)
{
    name = initialName;
    age = 0;
    weight = 0;
}

public void set(String newName)
{
    name = newName; //age and weight are unchanged.
}

public PetRecord(int initialAge)
{
    name = "No name yet.";
    weight = 0;
    if (initialAge < 0)
    {
        System.out.println("Error: Negative age.");
        System.exit(0);
    }
    else
        age = initialAge;
}

public void set(int newAge)
{
    if (newAge < 0)
    {
        System.out.println("Error: Negative age.");
        System.exit(0);
    }
    else
        age = newAge;
    //name and weight are unchanged.
}
```

■ DISPLAY 5.20 PetRecord Class with Constructors *(Part 3 of 3)*

```java
    public PetRecord(double initialWeight)
    {
        name = "No name yet";
        age = 0;
        if (initialWeight < 0)
        {
            System.out.println("Error: Negative weight.");
            System.exit(0);
        }
        else
            weight = initialWeight;
    }
    public void set(double newWeight)
    {
        if (newWeight < 0)
        {
            System.out.println("Error: Negative weight.");
            System.exit(0);
        }
        else
            weight = newWeight; //name and age are unchanged.
    }
    public PetRecord( )            Default constructor
    {
        name = "No name yet.";
        age = 0;
        weight = 0;
    }
    public String getName( )
    {
        return name;
    }
    public int getAge( )
    {
        return age;
    }
    public double getWeight( )
    {
        return weight;
    }
}
```

2. We have added constructor methods named `PetRecord`. Note that the headings of these constructors do not have the word `void`, as the `set` methods do. When you define a constructor, you do not specify any return type. You do not even write `void` in place of a return type. These constructors are very much like the `set` methods. However, unlike some of the `set` methods, the constructors give values to all the instance variables, even though there may not be an argument for each instance variable. The constructors would compile even if some of the instance variables were not given values, but it is normal practice to give values to all the instance variables when defining a constructor. As you will see, constructors and the `set` methods are used in related but different ways.

3. We have added a constructor named `PetRecord` that has no parameters. Whenever you define at least one constructor, you should be sure to include a constructor with zero parameters. Such a constructor is called a **default constructor.**

default constructor

new calls a
constructor

Constructors are called at the time that you use `new` to create an object. We have already been using constructors in statements such as the following, from the program in Display 5.17:

```
Pet myDog = new Pet( );
```

This line defines `myDog` to be a name for an object of the class `Pet` and then creates a new object of the class `Pet`. The part that creates the new object is

```
new Pet( )
```

The part `Pet( )` is a call to a constructor for the class `Pet`. The parentheses are empty because this constructor takes no arguments.

automatically
defined
constructor

If you look at the definition of the class `Pet` (Display 5.17), you might object that the class definition includes no constructor definitions at all. Whenever a class definition does not have a constructor definition, Java automatically creates a default constructor, that is one with zero parameters. This automatically-created constructor essentially does nothing, but it allows you to create objects of the class. However, once you add at least one constructor definition to a class, then you are in charge of all of its constructors. That is, *once you add at least one constructor to a class, no constructors are created automatically.* Thus, in Display 5.20, in the class `PetRecord` with constructors, we were careful to include a constructor with no parameters to serve as the default constructor. A complete program illustrating the use of constructors with the class `PetRecord` is given in Display 5.21.

constructor
arguments

When you create a new object with the operator `new`, you must always include a call to a constructor after the operator `new`. As with any method invocation, you list any arguments in parentheses after the constructor name (which is the same as the class name). For example, suppose you want to use `new` to create a new object of the class `PetRecord` defined in Display 5.20. You might do so as follows:

```
PetRecord fish = new PetRecord("Wanda", 2, 0.25);
```

The part `PetRecord("Wanda", 2, 0.25)` is a call to the constructor for the class `PetRecord` that takes three arguments: one of type `String`, one of type `int`, and the last of type `double`. This creates a new object to represent a pet named Wanda who is 2 years old and weighs 0.25 pound.

■ DISPLAY 5.21   **Using Constructors and** `set` **Methods**

```java
public class PetRecordDemo
{
    public static void main(String[] args)
    {
        PetRecord usersPet = new PetRecord("Jane Doe");
        System.out.println("My records on your pet are inaccurate.");
        System.out.println("Here is what they currently say:");
        usersPet.writeOutput();

        System.out.println("Please enter the correct pet name:");
        String correctName = SavitchIn.readLine();
        System.out.println("Please enter the correct pet age:");
        int correctAge = SavitchIn.readLineInt();
        System.out.println("Please enter the correct pet weight:");
        double correctWeight = SavitchIn.readLineDouble();
        usersPet.set(correctName, correctAge, correctWeight);
        System.out.println("My updated records now say:");
        usersPet.writeOutput();
    }
}
```

Sample Screen Dialog

```
My records on your pet are inaccurate.
Here is what they currently say:
Name: Jane Doe
Age: 0
Weight: 0.0 pounds
Please enter the correct pet name:
Moon Child
Please enter the correct pet age:
5
Please enter the correct pet weight:
24.5
My updated records now say:
Name: Moon Child
Age: 5
Weight: 24.5 pounds
```

Let's look at another example. Consider the following:

```
PetRecord newBorn = new PetRecord( );
```

This creates a new object of the class `PetRecord` and calls the default constructor (that is, the constructor with zero parameters). If you look at the definition of the class `PetRecord` in Display 5.20, you will see that the constructor with zero parameters gives the object the name `"No name yet"` and sets both the `age` and `weight` instance variables to 0. (A newborn pet does not weigh zero, of course. The value of 0 is just being used as a placeholder until the real weight can be determined, but anyway, that's biology, not computer science.)

resetting
object values

A constructor can be called only when you create a new object with the operator `new`. Calls such as the following to objects of the class `PetRecord` are invalid:

```
newBorn.PetRecord("Fang", 1, 150.0); //Invalid!
```

Since you cannot call a constructor for an object after it is created, you need some other way to change the values of the instance variables of an object. That is the purpose of the `set` methods in Display 5.20. Thus, instead of the preceding invalid invocation of the constructor `PetRecord`, we would call `set` as follows:

```
newBorn.set("Fang", 1, 150.0);
```

You need not name these methods `set`; you can use any method name that is convenient. For example, you might prefer to give them names like `reset` or `giveNewValues`. However, it is traditional to name these methods `set` or some name that includes "`set`".

Quick Reference: Constructor

A **constructor** is a method that is called when an object of the class is created using `new`. Constructors are used to initialize objects. A constructor must have the same name as the class to which it belongs. Arguments for a constructor are given in parentheses after the class name, as in the following examples:

Examples:

```
PetRecord myDog = new PetRecord("Fido", 2, 4.5),
         yourDog = new PetRecord("Cha Cha", 3, 2.3);
```

A constructor is defined like any other method except that it does not have a type returned and does not even include a `void` in the method heading. See Display 5.20 for examples of constructor definitions.

Remember: Constructors Return a Reference

You can think of a constructor invocation, such as `new PetRecord( )`, as returning a reference to an object—that is, as returning the memory address of an object.

Example:

If PetRecord is a class, then PetRecord is the name of a constructor for this class, and new PetRecord( ) is an invocation of the constructor for the class PetRecord. You can think of this constructor invocation as returning a reference to (returning the memory address of) an object of the class PetRecord. If pet is a variable of type PetRecord, the following assigns this reference to the variable pet:

```
pet = new PetRecord( );
```

Display 5.22 illustrates how this works.

■ DISPLAY 5.22 **Constructor Returning a Reference**

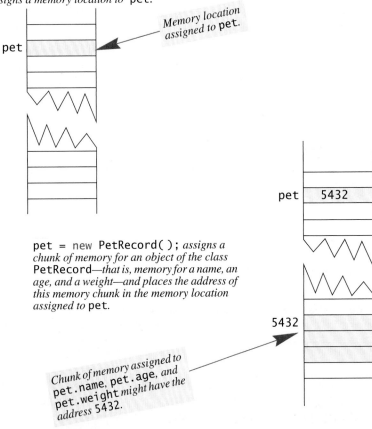

PetRecord pet;
Assigns a memory location to pet.

pet

Memory location assigned to pet.

pet   5432

pet = new PetRecord( ); *assigns a chunk of memory for an object of the class* PetRecord—*that is, memory for a name, an age, and a weight—and places the address of this memory chunk in the memory location assigned to* pet.

5432

Chunk of memory assigned to pet.name, pet.age, *and* pet.weight *might have the address 5432.*

FAQ: How Do I Write Constructors in a Class Diagram?

A class diagram need not include all the methods in a class. A class diagram is a design tool and need be only as complete as is needed for the design task at hand. Normally, constructors are not listed in a class diagram. This is because constructors are always needed and always serve the same basic function.

● **Programming Tip**
You Can Use Other Methods in a Constructor

A constructor is a method you use to create an object, and so it is the first method invoked with the object. However, this should not discourage you from using other methods of the same class in your definitions of constructors. For example, all of the constructors in the definition of the class `PetRecord` in Display 5.20 can be rewritten using the method `set`. Consider the following constructor definition from that class definition:

```
public PetRecord(String initialName, int initialAge,
                                       double initialWeight)
{
    name = Name;
    if ((initialAge < 0) || (initialWeight < 0))
    {
        System.out.println("Error: Negative age or weight.");
        System.exit(0);
    }
    else
    {
        age = initialAge;
        weight = initialWeight;
    }
}
```

If you prefer, you can use the following equivalent definition instead:

```
public PetRecord(String initialName, int initialAge,
                                       double initialWeight)
{
    set(initialName, initialAge, initialWeight);
}
```

The other constructors in that class definition can also be rewritten using the method `set`.

Many programmers would prefer the second definition using `set`. It is certainly shorter. Some programmers might prefer the first version because it avoids any confusion about the order of the arguments to `set`, and it also avoids the overhead of another method invocation. Either version is acceptable. Use whichever version your instructor or supervisor prefers. ◯

▲ *Gotcha*

Omitting the Default Constructor

Suppose we were to omit the constructor with zero parameters from the definition of the class `PetRecord` in Display 5.20; that is, suppose we omitted the following constructor definition:

```java
public PetRecord()
{
    name = "No name yet";
    age = 0;
    weight = 0;
}
```

With this constructor omitted, the following would be invalid and would produce an error message:

```java
PetRecord heinz57 = new PetRecord();
```

You might object that Java automatically provides a default constructor if none is defined, and so this should be valid. However, the situation is slightly more complicated than that. If your class definition includes no constructors whatsoever, Java will automatically provide a default constructor. However, as we mentioned previously, if your class definition contains at least one constructor definition, then Java does not provide any constructors for you. *Once you start defining constructors, you are completely in charge of constructors and no constructors are generated other than the ones that you define.*

Classes are often reused again and again, and sooner or later you will probably want to create a new object without specifying parameters, as in

```java
PetRecord heinz57 = new PetRecord();
```

You will avoid a lot of problems if you follow a policy of including a default constructor definition in every class you define. △

Quick Reference: **Default Constructor**

A constructor with no parameters is called the **default constructor.** Most of the classes you define should include a default constructor.

▲ *Gotcha*

Many Wrapper Classes Have No Default Constructor

The wrapper classes `Integer`, `Double`, `Character`, `Boolean`, `Byte`, `Short`, `Long`, and `Float` have no default constructors. When you create a new object of one of these classes, you must give an argument for an initializing value, as in the following example:

```java
Character myMark = new Character('Z');
```

(This is because the argument to the constructor is the only way to set the instance variables of these wrapper classes.) △

---

34. If a class is named `Student`, what name can you use for a constructor for this class?

35. When defining a constructor, what do you specify for the type of the value returned? A primitive type? A class type? `void`?

36. What is a default constructor?

37. Does every class in Java automatically have a default constructor? If not, when is a default constructor provided automatically by Java and when is it not provided?

5.6   INFORMATION HIDING REVISITED

The material in this section is not needed to understand most of the rest of this book. If you prefer, you can safely postpone reading this material until you are more comfortable with classes. This section discusses a subtle problem that can arise when defining certain kinds of classes. If you do not wish to read this section now but still want to avoid the problem, simply note that the problem discussed here does not apply to any class you define, provided that each instance variable in the class is either of a primitive type (such as `int`, `double`, `char`, and `boolean`) or of the type `String`. So you can define lots of classes without being concerned with this problem.

▲ *Gotcha*

Privacy Leaks

A class can have instance variables of any type, including any class type. This can sometimes be a natural and useful thing to have. However, using instance variables of a class type can introduce a problem that requires special care, The problem results from the fact that variables of a class type contain the memory address of where an object is stored in memory. For example, suppose that `goodGuy` and `badGuy` are both variables of type `PetRecord`, a class we defined in Display 5.20. Now, suppose that `goodGuy` names some object, and your program executes the following assignment statement:

```
badGuy = goodGuy;
```

After this assignment statement is executed, `badGuy` and `goodGuy` are two names for the same object. So if you change `badGuy`, you will also change `goodGuy`. (There must be a moral lesson there someplace.) Let's give this assignment statement a bit more context to see the implications of this:

```
PetRecord goodGuy = new PetRecord( );
goodGuy.set("Faithful Guard Dog", 5, 75);
PetRecord badGuy;
badGuy = goodGuy;
```

```
badGuy.set("Dominion Spy", 1200, 500);
goodGuy.writeOutput();
```

Because badGuy and goodGuy name the same object, this code will produce the following output:

```
Name: Dominion Spy
Age: 1200 years
Weight: 500.0 pounds
```

The change to badGuy also changed goodGuy because goodGuy and badGuy name the same object. The same thing can happen with instance variables and can cause some subtle problems. Let's look at an example.

Display 5.23 contains the definition of a class called CadetClass, which was written by a cadet programmer as a homework exercise. It does not have very many methods, but that is not the problem. (This is, after all, just an exercise.) The problem is that our cadet programmer mistakenly thinks that the data named by the instance variable pet cannot be changed by any program using the class PetRecord. This is an easy mistake for a cadet programmer to make. After all, our cadet made the instance variable pet private so it cannot be accessed by name. And just to be super safe, the cadet did not include any mutator methods that change the private instance variable pet. Our cadet will let anybody see the value of the object pet by using the public accessor method getPet, but our naive cadet thinks that no programmer can change the "Faithful Guard Dog". Our cadet is in for a rude awakening.

■ DISPLAY 5.23 An Insecure Class

```
/**
 Example of a class that does NOT correctly
 hide its private instance variable.
*/
public class CadetClass
{
    private PetRecord pet;

    public CadetClass()
    {
        pet =
            new PetRecord("Faithful Guard Dog", 5, 75);
    }

    public void writeOutput()
    {
        System.out.println("Here's the pet:");
        pet.writeOutput();
    }

    public PetRecord getPet()
    {
        return pet;
    }
}
```

A realistic class would have more methods, but these are all we need for our demonstration.

Look at the program in Display 5.24. That program has changed the values of the instance variables in the object named by the private instance variable `pet`! How could that be? The problem is that a variable of a class type stores a memory address, and as you saw at the beginning of this section, this means you can use the assignment operator to

■ **DISPLAY 5.24 Changing Private Data in a Poorly Defined Class**

```
/**
 Toy program to demonstrate how a programmer can access and
 change private data in an object of the class CadetClass.
*/
public class Hacker
{
    public static void main(String[] args)
    {
        CadetClass starFleetOfficer = new CadetClass();
        System.out.println("starFleetOfficer contains:");
        starFleetOfficer.writeOutput();
        PetRecord badGuy;
        badGuy = starFleetOfficer.getPet();
        badGuy.set("Dominion Spy", 1200, 500);
        System.out.println("Looks like a security breach:");
        System.out.println("starFleetOfficer now contains:");
        starFleetOfficer.writeOutput();
        System.out.println("The pet wasn't so private!");
    }
}
```

Screen Output

```
starFleetOfficer contains:
Here's the pet:
Name: Faithful Guard Dog
Age: 5 years
Weight: 75.0 pounds
Looks like a security breach:
starFleetOfficer now contains:
Here's the pet:
Name: Dominion Spy
Age: 1200 years
Weight: 500.0 pounds
The pet wasn't so private!
```

This program has changed an object named by a private instance variable of the object starFleetOfficer.

produce two names for the same object. That is what our hacker programmer who wrote the program in Display 5.24 did. Our hacker programmer had the accessor method getPet return the value of the private instance variable pet. But that value was a memory address that was stored in the variable badGuy. So badGuy is another name for pet. Our hacker cannot use the private name pet, but she or he can use the equivalent name badGuy. All that our hacker needed to do was to use the name badGuy to invoke the method set of the class PetRecord, and because badGuy is another name for the object named by pet, our hacker has changed the object named by the private instance variable pet.

How can you write your class definitions to avoid this problem? It might seem impossible to have a private instance variable of a class type that is truly secure. A hacker can always find a way to get at it, or so it would seem. There are, however, at least two ways around this problem: an easy way and a harder but better way.

The easy way around this problem is to use only instance variables of a primitive type or of the type String. The type String has no accessor methods that can change the String object's data, and so our hacker's trick will not work on them. Primitive types are not class types, and so the hacker's trick will not work on them either. This easy solution is the one we will take in this book. (You can also have private instance variables of class types other than String, provided that these class types do not have methods that can change an object. However, the only class of this kind that we will frequently encounter here is the class String.)

The harder solution is the better one, but it is beyond the scope of this book, although we can give you a hint of it. There are methods that can produce an exact copy of an object. These exact copies are called **clones.** The harder solution is never to return an object named by a private instance variable of a class type that could be insecure, but to instead return a clone of the object. That way the hacker can do whatever she or he wants with the clone and the private data will not be affected. A brief introduction to cloning is given in Appendix 8. After you become comfortable with classes, you may wish to look at that appendix.

clone

Do not get the impression that instance variables of a class type are a bad idea. They are very natural and very useful. However, dealing with them effectively requires skill and care. Think of them as you think of brain surgery: if you need it, it is very, very good, but don't try it unless you know what you are doing. △

? Self-Test Question

38. Give the definitions of three accessor methods that you can use in the definition of the class CadetClass (Display 5.23) instead of the single accessor method getPet. These new accessor methods will not produce the problem described in the Gotcha section "Privacy Leaks." They will return all of the data in an object of the class CadetClass, but will not return any object with mutator methods that can change anything. One method will return the pet's name, one will return the pet's age, and one will return the pet's weight. The previous section gave two ways to avoid the problem in the Gotcha section. This question suggests a third way to avoid the problem.

5.7   PACKAGES

From mine own library with volumes that
I prize above my dukedom. -William Shakespeare, *The Tempest*

A package is a way of grouping and naming a collection of related classes so that they can serve as a library of classes that you can use in any program without having to place all those classes in the same directory as your program. Although this is an important and useful topic, it is nevertheless true that the rest of the material in this book does not use the material on packages presented here. Therefore, you may cover this section at any time during your reading of this book.

To understand this material, you need to know about directories (which are called folders in some operating systems), you need to know about path names for directories (folders), and you need to know how your operating system uses a path (environment) variable. If you do not know about directories (folders), path names, and path (environment) variables, you may wish to skip this section until you have had some experience with these topics. These are not Java topics. They are part of your operating system, and the details depend on your particular operating system. If you can find out how to set the path variable, you will know enough about path variables to understand this section.

Packages and Importing

package

A **package** is nothing other than a collection of classes that have been grouped together into a directory and given a package name. The classes in the package are each placed in a separate file, and the file is named the same as the class, just as we have been doing all along. The only difference is that each file has the following line at the start of the file:

    package *Package_Name*;

There may be blank lines or comments before this line, but nothing else may come before it. The *Package_Name* typically consists of all lowercase letters, often punctuated with the dot symbol. For example, if `general.utilities` is the name of the package, then each of the files in the package would have the following at the start of the file:

    package general.utilities;

Any program or class definition can use all of the classes in the package by placing a suitable `import` statement at the start of the file containing the program or class definition. This is true even if the program or class definition is not in the same directory as the classes in the package. For example, if you want to use the classes in the package `general.utilities`, you would place the following at the start of the file you are writing:

import

    import general.utilities.*;

Package Names and Directories

A package name is not an arbitrary identifier. It tells the compiler where to find the classes in the package. In effect, the package name tells the compiler the path name for the directory containing the classes in the package.

In order to find the directory for a package, Java needs two things: the name of the package and the directories listed in the value of your class path variable.

The value of your **class path variable** tells Java where to begin its search for a package, so we will discuss it first. The class path variable is not a Java variable. It is a variable that is part of your operating system and that contains the path names of a list of directories. When Java is looking for a package, it begins its search in these directories. Let us call these directories the **class path base directories.** We will tell you how Java uses these class path base directories and how packages are named, and then we will give you some information on how to set the class path variable.

class path
base directory

Quick Reference: Package

A **package** is a collection of classes that have been grouped together into a directory and given a package name. The classes in the package are each placed in a separate file, and the file is given the same name as the class, just as we have been doing all along. Each file in the package must have the following as the first instruction line in the file (that is, the first line that is neither blank nor solely a comment).

Syntax:

```
package Package_Name;
```

Examples:

```
package general.utilities;
package java.io;
```

Quick Reference: `import` Statement

You can use all the classes in a package in any program or class definition by placing an `import` statement that names the package at the start of the file containing the program or class definition. The program or class need not be in the same directory as the classes in the package.

Syntax:

```
import Package_Name;
```

Examples:

```
import general.utilities.*;
import java.io.*;
```

The dot and the * at the end mean that you are importing all the classes in this package. You can also import just a single class from a package by using the class name in place of the *.

The name of a package specifies the relative path name for the directory that contains the package classes. It is a relative path name because it assumes that you start in a class path base directory and follow the path of subdirectories given by the package name. For example, suppose the following is a class path base directory (your operating system may use / instead of \):

```
\myjavastuff\libraries
```

and suppose your package classes are in the directory

```
\myjavastuff\libraries\general\utilities
```

In this case, the package *must* be named

```
general.utilities
```

Notice that the package name tells you (and Java) what subdirectories to go through in order to find the package classes, starting from the base class directory. This is depicted in Display 5.25. Notice that a package name is not arbitrary, but must be a list of directories leading from a class path base directory to the package classes. The dot in the package name means essentially the same thing as the \ or /, whichever symbol your operating system uses for directory paths.

■ DISPLAY 5.25 **A Package Name**

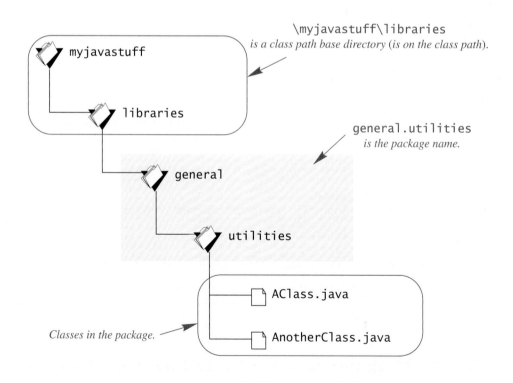

\myjavastuff\libraries
is a class path base directory (is on the class path).

general.utilities
is the package name.

Classes in the package.

You specify the class path base directories by setting the class path (environment) variable. The way you set the class path variable depends on your operating system, but we can give you some suggestions that may work. The class path variable is usually spelled as one word with all uppercase letters, as in CLASSPATH. You will probably have a plain old "path variable" that tells the operating system where to find the code for commands like javac and other commands that you can give as single-line commands. If you can find out how to set the path variable, you should be able to set the CLASSPATH variable in the same way.

class path variable

If you are on a UNIX system, you are likely to be able to set the class path with some command similar to the following:

```
export c:/myjavastuff/libraries;.
```

If you are using a Windows machine, you can set the class path variable by setting or creating an environment variable named CLASSPATH using the Control Panel.

Quick Reference: **Package Names**

A package name must be a path name for the directory that contains the classes in the package, but the package name uses dots in place of \ or / (whichever your operating system uses). When naming the package, you use a relative path name that starts from any directory named in the setting of the class path (environment) variable.

Examples:

```
general.utilities
java.io
```

▲ *Gotcha*

Not Including the Current Directory in Your Class Path

Your class path variable will allow you to list more than one base directory, typically by separating them with a semicolon. For example, the following might be a class path:

```
c:\myjavastuff\libraries;f:\yourjavastuff
```

This means that you can create package directories as either subdirectories of

```
c:\myjavastuff\libraries
```

or subdirectories of

```
f:\yourjavastuff
```

When looking for package directories, Java will first look in subdirectories of

```
c:\myjavastuff\libraries
```

If it does not find the package there, it will then look in subdirectories of

```
f:\yourjavastuff
```

current directory

Whenever you set or change the class path variable, be sure to include the current directory as one of the alternatives. The **current directory** is the directory in which your program (or other class) is located. On most systems, the current directory is indicated by a dot. So you would use the following for your class path variable:

```
c:\myjavastuff\libraries;f:\yourjavastuff;.
```

with the current directory added to the end. Then if the package is not found in either of the previous two base directories, Java will look in the subdirectories of the current directory—that is, in subdirectories of your program (or whatever class you are compiling).

If you want Java to check the current directory before the other directories on the class path, list the current directory (the dot) first.

Omitting the current directory from the class path variable not only will limit the locations you can use for your packages, but can interfere with programs that do not use packages; if you program without packages but with all classes in the same directory (as we do in the rest of this book), Java will not be able to find the classes unless the current directory is on the class path. For example, if your program uses `SavitchIn`, and the files `SavitchIn.java` and `SavitchIn.class` are in the same directory as your program, Java will probably not be able to find `SavitchIn` unless the current directory is on your class path. (This problem will not occur if you have no class path variable at all; it arises only if you decide to set the class path variable.) △

Name Clashes

Packages are a convenient way to group and use libraries of classes, but there is also another reason for using packages. They can help in dealing with name clashes; that is, they can help in handling situations in which two classes have the same name. If different programmers writing different packages have used the same name for a class, the ambiguity can be resolved by using the package name.

If a package named `mystuff` contains a class called `CoolClass` and another package named `yourstuff` also contains a class named `CoolClass`, you can use both classes named `CoolClass` in the same program by using the more complete names `mystuff.CoolClass` and `yourstuff.CoolClass`. For example,

```
mystuff.CoolClass object1 = new mystuff.CoolClass();
yourstuff.CoolClass object2 = new yourstuff.CoolClass();
```

If you list the package name along with the class name like this, you do not need to import the package, since this longer class name includes the package name.

? Self-Test Questions

39. Suppose you want to use classes in the package `mypackages.library1` in a program you write. What do you need to put near the start of the file containing your program?

40. Suppose you want to make a class a member of the package named `mypackages.library1`. What do you need to put in the file containing the class definition? Where does this statement go in the file?

41. Can a package have any name you might want, or are there restrictions on what you can use for a package name? Explain any restrictions.

42. On your system, place the class `SavitchIn` into a package so that in any Java program, you can use the class `SavitchIn` by including a suitable `import` statement and you need not move the class `SavitchIn` to the same directory (folder) as your program.

C H A P T E R   S U M M A R Y

- A method definition can include a call to another method of the same class.

- If a method definition is labeled `static`, that method can be invoked using the class name, rather than an object name. (It can also be invoked using an object name.)

- A static variable is a variable that is declared using the keyword `static`. For each static variable name, there is only one variable of that name that is shared by all the objects of the class.

- The top-down design method helps you to write method definitions by dividing the task to be accomplished by the method into subtasks.

- Every method should be tested in a program in which it is the only untested method.

- Each primitive type has a wrapper class that serves as a class version of that primitive type.

- A method name can have two different definitions within the same class, provided the two definitions have different numbers of parameters or some parameters of differing types. This is called overloading the method name.

- A constructor is a class method that is called when you create an object of the class using `new`. A constructor must have the same name as the class.

- A constructor with no parameters is called a default constructor. Class definitions typically include a default constructor.

- You can form a package of class definitions you use frequently. You can then use the classes in any program without needing to move them to the same directory (folder) as the program.

✔ Answers to Self-Test Questions

1. Yes. See Display 5.1 for an example.

2. No effect at all. The following two lines are equivalent in this context:

```
seekAdvice( );
```

and

```
this.seekAdvice( );
```

3. This will produce a "Null Pointer Exception" error message. The variables s1 and s2 do not name any objects. The lines

```
Species s1 = null;
Species s2 = null;
```

should be changed to

```
Species s1 = new Species( );
Species s2 = new Species( );
```

4. It is valid, but a more normal way of doing the same thing is

```
double areaOfCircle = CircleFirstTry.area(2.5);
```

5. Yes, you can have all these kinds of things together in one class.

6. You cannot invoke a nonstatic method within the definition of a static method unless you create an object of the class and use that object as the calling object of the nonstatic method

7. Yes, you can invoke a static method within the definition of a nonstatic method. This requires nothing special.

8. No, you cannot reference an instance variable within the definition of a static method, because a static method can be invoked with no calling object, and if there is no calling object, there are no instance variables.

9. Yes, it is valid, although it is not the normal way of invoking the method read-LineInt. A more normal way of invoking readLineInt is

```
int n = SavitchIn.readLineInt( )
```

10. No, the following is invalid, because setDiameter is not a static method:

```
PlayCircle.setDiameter(newDiameter);
```

11. An *instance variable* is declared in a class definition *without* using the keyword static. A *static variable* is declared in a class definition using the keyword static. Every object of the class has its own *instance variables*. There is only one of each *static variable* for a class, and all objects share that static variable.

12. Yes, you can reference (by name) a *static variable* (without anything like a class name and dot) in the definition of a *static method*. An example is the static variable `numberOfInvocations` in the method `justADemoMethod` in Display 5.8. No, you cannot reference (by name) an *instance variable* (without anything like an object name and dot) in the definition of a *static method*. This is because a static method can be used with the class name rather than a calling object, and with no calling object, there are no instance variables.

13. Yes, you can reference (by name) a *static variable* (without anything like a class name and dot) in the definition of a *nonstatic method*. Yes, you can reference (by name) an *instance variable* (without anything like an object name and dot) in the definition of a *nonstatic method*. Note that this means you can reference both kinds of variables in a nonstatic method.

14. `2, 3, 2.0,`
    `2.0, 3.0, 3.0.`
    Note that the first two values are of type `long`, while the last four values are of type `double`.

15. `approxSpeed = (int)Math.round(speed);`
    This is because `Math.round` returns a value of type `long`.

16. `longSpeed = Math.round(speed);`
    In other words, you need not do anything special.

17. `long`. Since one argument is of type `long`, the result is of type `long`.

18.
```
Integer n = new Integer(77); //Valid
int m = 77; //Valid
n = m; //Invalid, should be:
n = new Integer(m);
m = n; //Invalid, should be
m = n.intValue( );
```

19. `Double.toString(x)`

20. `Integer.parseInt(s)`

21. If the string might contain leading or trailing blanks, you should use `Integer.parseInt(s.trim( ))`. In fact, it is always safest to use this version. You never know when leading or trailing blanks might appear.

22.
```
System.out.println("Largest double is " + Double.MAX_VALUE);
System.out.println("Smallest double is " + Double.MIN_VALUE);
```

23. The class `OutputFormat` is in the file `OutputFormat.java` included with the software on the CD that accompanies this text. We also list it here:

```
public class OutputFormat
{
    /**
     Writes out number with digitsAfterPoint digits after
```

```
        the decimal point. Rounds any extra digits.
        Does not advance to the next line after output.
    */
    public static void write(double number,
                                       int digitsAfterPoint)
    {
        if (number >= 0)
            writePositive(number, digitsAfterPoint);
        else
        {
            double positiveNumber = -number;
            System.out.print('-');
            writePositive(positiveNumber, digitsAfterPoint);
        }
    }

    //Precondition: number >= 0
    //Writes out number with digitsAfterPoint digits after the
    //decimal point. Rounds any extra digits.
    private static void writePositive(double number,
                                              int digitsAfterPoint)
    {
        int mover = (int)(Math.pow(10, digitsAfterPoint));
                //1 followed by digitsAfterPoint zeros
        int allWhole; //number with the decimal point
                      //moved digitsAfterPoint places
        allWhole = (int)(Math.round(number*mover));
        int beforePoint = allWhole/mover;
        int afterPoint = allWhole%mover;

        System.out.print(beforePoint);
        System.out.print('.');
        writeFraction(afterPoint, digitsAfterPoint);
    }

    //Outputs the integer afterPoint with enough zeros
    //in front to make it digitsAfterPoint digits long.
    private static void writeFraction(int afterPoint,
                                             int digitsAfterPoint)
    {
        int n = 1;
        while (n < digitsAfterPoint)
        {
            if (afterPoint < Math.pow(10, n))
                System.out.print('0');
            n = n + 1;
        }
```

```
            System.out.print(afterPoint);
        }

        /**
         Writes out number with digitsAfterPoint digits after
         the decimal point. Rounds any extra digits.
         Advances to the next line after output.
        */
        public static void writeln(double number,
                                          int digitsAfterPoint)
        {
            write(number, digitsAfterPoint);
            System.out.println( );
        }
    }
```

24. Yes, you could use the names `print` and `println`, rather than `write` and `writeln`, in the class `OutputFormat`. This would produce no name confusion with `System.out.println`, because when you invoke the method in `Output-Format`, you specify the class name before the dot. (If you invoke the method with an object instead of the class name, Java still knows the class name because it knows the type of the object.) However, the methods in `OutputFormat` behave a little differently from the method `System.out.println`, so it seems that a different name would be clearer.

25. Use variables of type `long`, rather than variables of type `int`. Note that, because the method `Math.round` returns a value of type `long` in the method `writePositive`, this will even save a type cast. For example,

    ```
    int allCents = (int)(Math.round(amount*100));
    ```

    would become

    ```
    long allCents = (Math.round(amount*100));
    ```

    The variables `dollars` and `cents` should also be changed to type `long`.

26. Yes, the 7 would be converted to 7.0 by Java, so that the types match the heading of one of the definitions of `set`.

27. No, you cannot overload a method name on the basis of the type returned.

28. Yes, they differ in the type of their parameter, so this is a valid overloading of the method name `convertValue`. (Note that the fact that they return values of different types does not affect whether or not both definitions can be used. It is only the types of the parameters that count in making overloading valid.)

29. Yes, it would be valid because no other method named `set` has the same number and types of parameters. The definition follows:

    ```
    public void set(String newName)
    {
        name = newName;
    ```

```
        population = 0;
        growthRate = 0;
    }
```

30. Yes, it would be valid because no other method named `set` has the same number and types of parameters. The definition follows:

```
public void set(String newName)
{
    name = newName;
}
```

31. No, if you add both of these new methods `set`, the class will have two definitions of the method name `set` that have the same number and types of parameters.

32. Simply delete all occurrences of `this.` from the definition.

33. Simply add an invocation of the method `trim`. The rewritten version follows:

```
    public void set(String amountString)
    {
        String dollarsString;
        String centsString;

        amountString = amountString.trim( );
```

<The rest of the method definition is the same as in Display 5.18.>

34. If a class is named `Student`, then every constructor for this class must also be named `Student`.

35. You specify no type returned for a constructor, not even `void`.

36. A default constructor is a constructor with no parameters.

37. No. Here are the details: If you give no constructor definition for a class, Java will automatically provide a default constructor. If you provide one or more constructors of any sort, then Java does not provide any constructors beyond what you define. So if you define one or more constructors and none of them is a default constructor, then the class has no default constructor.

38.

```
public String getPetName( )
{
    return pet.getName( );
}

public int getPetAge( )
{
    return pet.getAge( );
}
```

```
    public double getPetWeight()
    {
        return pet.getWeight();
    }
```

39. `import mypackages.library1.*;`

40. You must make the following the first instruction line in the file:

    `package mypackages.library1;`

41. A package name must be a path name for the directory that contains the classes in the package, but the package name uses dots in place of \ or / (whichever one your operating system uses). When naming the package, you use a relative path name that starts from any directory named in the setting of the class path (environment) variable.

42. The way to do this depends a little on your operating system and on your personal preferences. Here is an outline of what you should do: Choose a package name and insert the following at the start of the file `SavitchIn.java`:

    `package` *Whatever_Package_Name_You_Choose*;

    Then compile the modified file `SavitchIn.java` and move both of the files `SavitchIn.java` and `SavitchIn.class` to the directory corresponding to *Whatever_Package_Name_You_Choose*.

● Programming Projects

1. Define a utility class for outputting values of type `double`. Call the class `Double-Out`. Include all the methods from the class `Dollars` in Display 5.14, all the methods from the class `OutputFormat` of Self-Test Question 23, and a method called `scienceWrite` that outputs a value of type `double` in the e notation, such as `2.13e-12`. (This e notation is also called scientific notation, which explains the method name.) When output in e notation, the number should always show exactly one (nonzero) digit before the decimal point (unless the number is exactly zero). The method `scienceWrite` will not advance to the next line. Also add a method called `scienceWriteln` that is the same as `scienceWrite` except that the next output goes on the next line. All but the last two method definitions can simply be copied from the text (or more easily from the files on the CD that accompanies this text). Note that you will be overloading the method names `write` and `writeln`. Write a driver program to test your method `scienceWriteln`. This driver program should use a stub for the method `scienceWrite`. (Note that this means you can write and test `scienceWriteln` before you even write `scienceWrite`.) Then write a driver program for the method `scienceWrite`. Finally, write a program that is a sort of super driver program that takes a `double` value as input and then outputs it using the two `writeln` methods and the `scienceWriteln` method. Use the number 5 for the number of digits after the decimal point when

you need to specify such a number. This super driver program should allow the user to repeat this testing with additional type `double` numbers until the user is ready to end the program.

2. Modify the definition of the class `Species` in Display 4.19 (Chapter 4) by removing the method `set` and adding the following methods: (1) five constructors: one for each instance variable, one with three parameters for the three instance variables, and a default constructor; (2) four methods named `set` that can reset values: one is the same as the method `set` in Display 4.19, and the other three each reset one of the instance variables. Be sure that each constructor sets all of the instance variables. Then write a test program to test all the methods you have added. Finally, redo (or do for the first time) Programming Project 1 in Chapter 4. Be sure to use some constructor other than the default constructor when you define new objects of the class `Species`.

3. Redo (or do for the first time) Programming Project 4 in Chapter 4. This time, be sure your class definition contains suitable constructors and reset methods. Use at least one of the methods from the class `OutputFormat` of Self-Test Question 23.

4. Redo (or do for the first time) Programming Project 4 in Chapter 4. This time, in addition to the reset and "test" methods (for the same name, same age, older, or younger), add the following four constructor methods: one for each instance variable, one with two parameters for the two instance variables, and a default constructor. Be sure that each constructor sets all of the instance variables. Write a test program to test each of the methods, including each of the four constructors and at least one true and one false case for each of the test methods.

5. Write a new class `TruncatedDollars` that is the same as the class `Dollars` from Display 5.14, except that it truncates rather than rounding to obtain two digits after the decimal point. (When truncating, all digits after the first two are discarded, so `1.229` becomes `1.22`, not `1.23`.) Use this class to redo (or to do for the first time) Programming Project 6 in Chapter 3.

6. Write a program to read in data for five pets (use the `PetRecord` class from Display 5.20) and display the following data: name of smallest pet, name of largest pet, name of oldest pet, name of youngest pet, average weight of the five pets, and average age of the five pets.

7. Write a `Temperature` class that has two parameters: a temperature value (a floating-point number) and a character for the scale, either `'C'` for Celsius or `'F'` for Fahrenheit. The class should have four constructor methods: one for each instance variable (assume zero degrees if no value is specified and Celsius if no scale is specified), one with two parameters for the two instance variables, and a default constructor (set to zero degrees Celsius). Include (1) two accessor methods to return the temperature, one to return the degrees Celsius, the other to return the degrees Fahrenheit—use the formulas from Programming Project 2 of Chapter 3 to write the two methods, and round to the nearest tenth of a degree; (2) three reset methods, one to set the value, one to set the scale (`'F'` or `'C'`), and one to set both; and (3) three comparison methods, one to test whether two temperatures are equal,

one to test whether one temperature is greater than another, and one to test whether one temperature is less than another. Then write a driver program that tests all the methods. Be sure to use each of the constructors, to include at least one true and one false case for each of the comparison methods, and to test at least the following temperature equalities: 0.0 degrees C = 32.0 degrees F, –40.0 degrees C = –40.0 degrees F, and 100.0 degrees C = 212.0 degrees F.

Chapter

6

Arrays

They stood at attention in a neat row, all with the same uniform, yet each with his own values.
-Warren Peace, *The Lieutenant's Array*

An array is a special kind of object used to store a (possibly large) collection of data. An array differs from the other objects you have seen in two ways:

1. All the data stored in an array must be of the same type. For example, you might use an array to store a list of values of type `double` that record rainfall readings in centimeters. You might use an array to store a list of objects of some class called `Species` that contain the records for various endangered species.

2. The only methods for an array object are a small number of predefined methods. Because they were used by programmers for many years before classes were invented, arrays use a special notation of their own to invoke those few predefined methods, and most people do not even call them methods.

In this chapter, we introduce you to arrays and show you how to use them in Java.

OBJECTIVES

Find out what an array is and how to use arrays in simple Java programs.

Learn how to use array parameters and how to define methods that return an array.

Learn the proper way to use an array as an instance variable in a class.

Introduce yourself to the topic of sorting an array.

Become familiar with multidimensional arrays.

PREREQUISITES

You can cover Section 6.1 with only the material in Chapters 1 through 3. You should be familiar with the material in all five previous chapters before reading the rest of this chapter (Sections 6.2, 6.3, 6.4, and 6.5).

This is the first point in this book where you have a significant choice of what to read next. If you prefer, instead of reading this chapter now, you can go on in the book and return to this chapter at a later time. If you want to delay reading this chapter, you can read as much of Chapters 7, 8, and 9 as you wish before you read this chapter.

6.1 ARRAY BASICS

And in such indexes, although small pricks
To their subsequent volumes, there is seen
The baby figure of the giant mass
Of things to come. -William Shakespeare, *Troilus and Cressida*

Suppose you want to compute the average temperature for the seven days in a week. You might use the following code:

```
int count;
double next, sum, average;
System.out.println("Enter 7 temperatures:");
sum = 0;
for (count = 0; count < 7; count++)
{
    next = SavitchIn.readLineDouble();
    sum = sum + next;
}
average = sum/7;
```

This works fine if all you want to know is the average. But let's say you also want to know which temperatures are above and which are below the average? Now you have a problem. In order to compute the average, you must read in the seven temperatures, and you must do this before comparing each temperature to the average. Thus, in order to compare each temperature to the average, you must remember the seven temperatures. How can you do this? The obvious answer is to use seven variables of type double. This is a bit awkward, because seven is a lot of variables to declare, and in other situations, the problem can be even worse. Imagine doing the same thing for each day of the year instead of just each day of the week. Writing 365 variable declarations would be absurd. Arrays provide us with an elegant way to declare a collection of related variables. An **array** is something like a list   array of variables, but it handles the naming of the variables in a nice, compact way.

Creating and Accessing Arrays

In Java, an array is a special kind of object, but it is often more useful to think of an array as a collection of variables all of the same type. For example, an array to serve as a collection of seven variables of type double can be created as follows:

```
double[] temperature = new double[7];
```

This is like declaring the following to be seven variables of type double:

```
temperature[0], temperature[1], temperature[2], temperature[3],
temperature[4], temperature[5], temperature[6]
```

Note that the numbering starts with 0, *not* 1. Each of these seven variables can be used just like any other variable of type double. For example, all of the following are allowed in Java:

```
temperature[3] = 32;
temperature[6] = temperature[3] + 5;
System.out.println(temperature[6]);
```

But these seven variables are more than just seven plain old variables of type `double`. That number in square brackets allows you to actually compute the name of one of these variables. Instead of writing an integer constant in the square brackets, you can use any expression that evaluates to an integer that is at least 0 and at most 6. So the following is allowed:

```
System.out.println("Enter day number (0-6):");
int index = SavitchIn.readLineInt( );
System.out.println("Enter temperature for day " + index);
temperature[index] = SavitchIn.readLineDouble( );
```

These variables with an integer expression in square brackets, such as `tempera-ture[0]` and `temperature[1]`, are referred to by various names. We will call them **indexed variables, or elements.** Some people call them **subscripted variables.** The integer expression within the square brackets is called an **index** (or **subscript**). When we think of these indexed variables grouped together into one collective item, we will call them an **array**. So we can refer to the array named `temperature` (without using any square brackets).

indexed variable

index

The program in Display 6.1 shows an example of using our sample array `tempera-ture` as seven indexed variables, all of type `double`.

Note that the program can compute the name of an indexed variable by using a variable as the index, as in the following `for` loop:

```
for (index = 0; index < 7; index++)
{
    temperature[index] = SavitchIn.readLineDouble( );
    sum = sum + temperature[index];
}
```

Array Details

An array is created like an object of a class type is created, but there are some small differences in the notation used. When creating an array of elements of type *Base_Type*, the syntax is as follows:

Base_Type`[]` *Array_Name* `= new` *Base_Type*`[`*Length*`];`

For example, the following creates an array named `pressure` that is equivalent to 100 variables of type `int`:

```
int[] pressure = new int[100];
```

Alternatively, the preceding can be broken down into two steps:

```
int[] pressure;
pressure = new int[100];
```

base type

length
of an array

The type for the elements, in this example `int`, is called the **base type** of the array. The number of elements in an array is called the **length** or the **size** of the array. So this sample array `pressure` has length 100, which means it has indexed variables `pressure[0]` through `pressure[99]`. Note that because the indices start at 0, an array of length 100, like `pressure`, will have *no* indexed variable `pressure[100]`.

■ DISPLAY 6.1   An Array Used in a Program *(Part 1 of 2)*

```java
public class ArrayOfTemperatures
{
    /**
     Reads in 7 temperatures and shows which are above and
     which are below the average of the 7 temperatures.
    */
    public static void main(String[] args)
    {
        double[] temperature = new double[7];

        int index;
        double sum, average;
        System.out.println("Enter 7 temperatures:");
        sum = 0;
        for (index = 0; index < 7; index++)
        {
            temperature[index] = SavitchIn.readLineDouble( );
            sum = sum + temperature[index];
        }
        average = sum/7;

        System.out.println("The average temperature is "
                                        + average);
        System.out.println("The temperatures are");
        for (index = 0; index < 7; index++)
        {
            if (temperature[index] < average)
                System.out.println(
                        temperature[index] + " below average.");
            else if (temperature[index] > average)
                System.out.println(
                        temperature[index] + " above average.");
            else //temperature[index] == average
                System.out.println(
                        temperature[index] + " the average.");
        }

        System.out.println("Have a nice week.");
    }
}
```

■ DISPLAY 6.1   **An Array Used in a Program** *(Part 2 of 2)*

A Common Way to Visualize an Array:

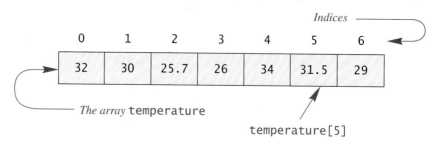

The array temperature

temperature[5]

Sample Screen Dialog

```
Enter 7 temperatures:
32
30
25.7
26
34
31.5
29
The average temperature is 29.7428
The temperatures are
32.0 above average
30.0 above average
25.7 below average
26.0 below average
34.0 above average
31.5 above average
29.0 below average
Have a nice week.
```

The base type of an array can be any type. In particular, it can be a class type. The following will create an array named entry that is equivalent to a collection of the three variables entry[0], entry[1], and entry[2], all of type Species (where Species is some class):

```
Species[] entry = new Species[3];
```

Quick Reference: Declaring and Creating an Array

You declare an array name and create an array in almost the same way that you create and name objects of classes. There is only a slight difference in the syntax.

Syntax:

Base_Type[] *Array_Name* = new *Base_Type*[*Length*] ;

Examples:

```
char[] symbol = new char[80];
double[] reading = new double[100];
Species[] specimen = new Species[80];
```

Species is a class.

Do not confuse the three ways to use the square brackets [] with an array name. First, the square brackets can be used to create a type name, such as the int[] in the following:

square brackets []

```
int[] pressure;
```

Second, the square brackets can be used with an integer value as part of the special syntax Java uses to create a new array, as in

```
pressure = new int[100];
```

The third use of square brackets is to name an indexed variable of the array, such as pressure[0] or pressure[3], as illustrated by the following two lines:

```
pressure[3] = SavitchIn.readLineInt();
System.out.println("You entered " + pressure[3]);
```

As we mentioned previously, the integer inside the square brackets can be any expression that evaluates to an integer. For example, you can read in the length of an array from the keyboard, as follows:

reading an array length

```
System.out.println("How many temperatures will there be?");
int size = SavitchIn.readLineInt();
double[] temperature = new double[size];
```

A similar remark applies to the integer inside the square brackets in other situations. The integer can be given as any expression that evaluates to an appropriate integer, as in the following examples:

```
int point = 2;
temperature[point + 3] = 32;
System.out.println(
            "Temperature 5 is " + temperature[point + 3]);
```

■ DISPLAY 6.2   **Array Terminology**

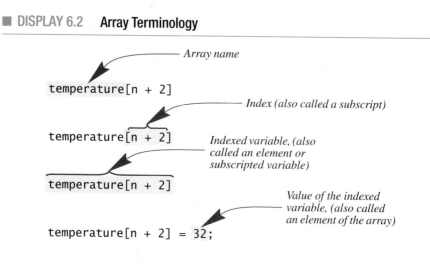

Note that, in the preceding code, `temperature[point + 3]` and `temperature[5]` are the same indexed variable, because `point + 3` evaluates to 5.

element

Display 6.2 illustrates some of the most common terms used when referring to arrays. Notice that the word **element** has two meanings. An indexed variable is sometimes called an element. The value of an indexed variable is also sometimes called an element.

● **Programming Tip**
Use Singular Array Names

If you want an array to hold entries, each of which is an object of a class called `Species`, you might be tempted to use something like the following:

```
Species[] entries = new Species[20]; //Valid but not nice.
```

Using a plural, like `entries`, seems to make sense, since the array holds more than one element. However, programmers find that their programs often read better if they use a singular form, like the following:

```
Species[] entry = new Species[20]; //Nicer.
```

The reason that the singular form works better here is that, when the array name is used in some sort of computation, the name refers to only one element. The expression `entry[2]` is a single element of the array, as in a statement such as

```
System.out.println("The entry is " + entry[2]);
```

The use of singular names for arrays is not an absolute rule. Sometimes it makes sense to use plural names. For example, if an array indexed variable contains the number of hours worked by employee number n, then the plural form `hours[n]` makes sense. The only sure test of whether to use a singular or plural name is to consider how an indexed variable would read in the context of your Java code. ⃝

The `length` Instance Variable

An array is a kind of object, and like other objects, it might have instance variables. As it turns out, an array has only one public instance variable, namely the variable `length`, which is equal to the length of the array. For example, if you create an array as follows:

```
Species[] entry = new Species[20];
```

then `entry.length` has a value of 20.

The `length` instance variable can be used to make your program clearer by replacing a constant, like 20, whose meaning may not always be obvious, with a meaningful name like `entry.length`. In Display 6.3 we have rewritten the program in Display 6.1 using the `length` instance variable.

■ **Java Tip**
Array Indices Start with Zero

In Java, the indices of an array always start with 0. They never start with 1 or any number other than 0. This means that the last index number is not the length of the array, but is one less than the length of the array.

In a situation in which you normally think in terms of some other numbering scheme, you might need to adjust your code to reconcile the array indices with the intuitive numbering. For example, you might want to think of the data stored in the array as being numbered starting with 1. If, say, your company's employees are numbered starting with 1, you might use code such as the following in a payroll program:

```
int[] hours = new int[100];
System.out.println("Enter hours worked for each employee:");
int index;
for (index = 0; index < hours.length; index++);
{
    System.out.println(
                "Enter hours for employee " + (index + 1));
    hours[index] = SavitchIn.readLineInt();
}
```

With this code, employees are numbered 1 through 100, but their hours worked are stored in elements `hours[0]` through `hours[99]`. ☐

■ DISPLAY 6.3   **The `length` Instance Variable**

```java
public class ArrayOfTemperatures2
{
    /**
     Reads in 7 temperatures and shows which are above and
     which are below the average of the 7 temperatures.
    */
    public static void main(String[] args)
    {
        double[] temperature = new double[7];
        int index;
        double sum, average;
        System.out.println("Enter " + temperature.length
                                    + " temperatures:");
        sum = 0;
        for (index = 0; index < temperature.length; index++)
        {
            temperature[index] = SavitchIn.readLineDouble( );
            sum = sum + temperature[index];
        }
        average = sum/temperature.length;
        System.out.println("The average temperature is "
                                                + average);
        System.out.println("The temperatures are");
        for (index = 0; index < temperature.length; index++)
        {
            if (temperature[index] < average)
                System.out.println(
                        temperature[index] + " below average.");
            else if (temperature[index] > average)
                System.out.println(
                        temperature[index] + " above average.");
            else //temperature[index] == average
                System.out.println(
                        temperature[index] + " the average.");
        }
        System.out.println("Have a nice week.");
    }
}
```

The dialog is the same as in Display 6.1.

The `length` instance variable cannot be changed by your program (other than by creating a new array with another use of **new**). For example, the following is invalid:

```
entry.length = 10;//Illegal!
```

● **Programming Tip**
Use a **for** Loop to Step Through an Array

The `for` statement is the perfect mechanism for stepping through the elements of an array. For example, the following `for` loop from Display 6.3 illustrates how you can step through an array:

```
for (index = 0; index < temperature.length; index++)
{
    temperature[index] = SavitchIn.readLineDouble();
    sum = sum + temperature[index];
}
```

▲ *Gotcha*
Array Index Out of Bounds

An easy mistake to make when programming with arrays is to use an indexed expression that evaluates to an invalid array index. For example, consider the following array declaration:

```
double[] entry = new double[5];
```

Every index for the array `entry` must evaluate to one of the five integers: 0, 1, 2, 3, or 4. For example, if your program contains the indexed variable `entry[n + 2]`, then the n + 2 must evaluate to one of the five integers 0, 1, 2, 3, or 4. If an index expression evaluates to some integer other than 0 through one less than the length of the array, the index is said to be **out of bounds** or **invalid.** If your program uses an index expression that is out of bounds, then your program (or class) will compile without any error message, but Java will complain when you run your program.

index out of bounds

One common way that array indices go out of bounds is when an array-processing loop is iterated one too many times. This can happen with almost any kind of loop that deals with array indices, but one very common example of this is a loop that fills an array. For example, when reading in a list of nonnegative numbers from the keyboard with a negative number as a sentinel value at the end, you might use the following:

```
System.out.println("Enter a list of nonnegative integers.");
System.out.println("Place a negative integer at the end.");
int[] a = new int[10];
```

```
int number = SavitchIn.readLineInt( );
int i = 0;
while (number >= 0)
{
    a[i] = number;
    i++;
    number = SavitchIn.readLineInt( );
}
```

If, however, the user enters more numbers than can fit in the array, this will produce an array index that is out of bounds. A better version of the preceding `while` loop is the following:

```
while ( (i < a.length) && (number >= 0) )
{
    a[i] = number;
    i++;
    number = SavitchIn.readLineInt( );
}
if (number >= 0)
{
    System.out.println("Could not read in all the numbers.");
    System.out.println("Only read in " + a.length
                                        + " numbers.");
}
```

With this `while` loop, the loop will end when the array is full.

Notice that in the second `while` loop, we tested to see that the index `i` is strictly less than `a.length`. Because indices start at 0, the last index is *not* `a.length`, but is one less than `a.length`. △

Initializing Arrays

An array can be initialized at the time that it is declared. To do this, you enclose the values for the individual indexed variables in braces and place them after the assignment operator, as in the following example:

```
double[] reading = {3.3, 15.8, 9.7};
```

The array length (size) is set to the minimum that will hold the given values. So this initializing declaration is equivalent to the following statements:

```
double[] reading = new double[3];
reading[0] = 3.3;
reading[1] = 15.8;
reading[2] = 9.7;
```

automatic
initialization

If you do not initialize the elements of an array, they may automatically be initialized to a default value for the base type. For example, if you do not initialize an array of integers, each element of the array will be initialized to 0. However, it is usually clearer to do your own explicit initialization. You can initialize either by using the braces, as we just described, or by some other method, such as the following `for` loop.

```java
int[] count = new int[100];
int i;
for (i = 0; i < count.length; i++)
    a[i] = 0;
```

? Self-Test Questions

1. What output will be produced by the following code?

```java
int i;
int[] a = new int[10];
for (i = 0; i < a.length; i++)
    a[i] = 2*i;
for (i = 0; i < a.length; i++)
    System.out.print(a[i] + " ");
System.out.println();
```

2. What output will be produced by the following code?

```java
char[] vowels = {'a', 'e', 'i', 'o', 'u'};
int index;
for (index = 0; index < vowels.length; index++)
    System.out.println(vowels[index]);
```

3. What output will be produced by the following code?

```java
double tide[] = {12.2, -7.3, 14.2, 11.3};
System.out.println("Tide 1 is " + tide[1]);
System.out.println("Tide 2 is " + tide[2]);
```

4. What is wrong with the following code to initialize an array b?

```java
int[] b = new int[10];
int i;
for (i = 1; i <= b.length; i++)
    b[i] = 5*i;
```

5. Consider the following array:

```java
int[] a = new int[10];
```

What is the last index of a? What is the value of `a.length`?

6. Write a complete Java program that will fill an array a with 20 values of type double read in from the keyboard, and that will output the numbers in the array as well as indicate how much each number differs from the last number in the input list. For example, if an array element is 2.0 and the last value in the input list is 5.0, the difference is 3.0. If an array element is 7.0 and the last value in the input list is 5.0, the difference is −2.0. Assume that the users enter 20 numbers, one per line, from the keyboard. You need not give elaborate instructions to the user.

6.2   ARRAYS IN CLASSES AND METHODS

A little more than kin, and less than kind. -William Shakespeare, *Hamlet*

Arrays can be used as instance variables in classes. Both an indexed variable of an array and an entire array can be an argument to a method. Methods can return an array value. In short, arrays can be used with classes and methods just as other objects can. We begin with a case study that uses an array as an instance variable in a class.

Case Study
Sales Report

task specification

In this case study, you will write a program to generate sales reports for a company's team of sales associates. The company wants to easily see which associate or associates have the highest sales and also wants to know how the sales of each associate compare to the average.

You know that you will need to record a name and the sales figures for each associate. So you design a class for a single sales associate that holds these two data items, does input and output, and has a reasonable complement of accessor and mutator methods. The class you design is shown in Display 6.4. This class definition is routine.

some data

Your program will use an array to keep track of the data for all sales associate. It will also need to record the average sales and the highest sales. Therefore, you know you will need the following instance variables:

```
private double highest;
private double average;
private SalesAssociate[] record;
```

some data

Your program will use an array to keep track of the data for all sales associate. It will also need to record the average sales and the highest sales. Therefore, you know you will need the following instance variables:

```
private double highest;
private double average;
private SalesAssociate[] record;
```

You realize that you need to know the number of associates. This will be the same as `record.length`, but it will be good to have a separate well-named variable for the number of associates. So you decide to also include the following instance variable:

```
private int numberOfAssociates; //Same as record.length
```

subtasks

The job of your program breaks down into three main subtasks:

Obtain the data.
Compute some figures (update the instance variables).
Display the results.

Thus, you know that your program class will look like this:

```java
public class SalesReporter
{
    private double highest;
    private double average;
    private SalesAssociate[] record;
    private int numberOfAssociates; //Same as record.length

    public static void main(String[ ] args)
    {
        SalesReporter clerk = new SalesReporter();
        clerk.getFigures();
        clerk.update();
        clerk.displayResults();
    }

            <More stuff needs to be added here.>
}
```

All that remains is to design the three methods getFigures, update, and displayResults (and to test and debug the program). You tackle the three methods in order.

■ DISPLAY 6.4   Sales Associate Record Class *(Part 1 of 2)*

```java
/**
 Class for sales associate records.
*/
public class SalesAssociate
{
    private String name;
    private double sales;

    public SalesAssociate()
    {
        name = "No record";
        sales = 0;
    }

    public SalesAssociate(String initialName,
                            double initialSales)
    {
        set(initialName, initialSales);
    }
```

■ **DISPLAY 6.4   Sales Associate Record Class** *(Part 2 of 2)*

```java
    public void set(String newName, double newSales)
    {
        name = newName;
        sales = newSales;
    }

    public void readInput()
    {
        System.out.print("Enter name of sales associate: ");
        name = SavitchIn.readLine();
        System.out.print("Enter associate's sales: $");
        sales = SavitchIn.readLineDouble();
    }

    public void writeOutput()
    {
        System.out.println("Sales associate: " + name);
        System.out.println("Sales: $" + sales);
    }

    public String getName()
    {
        return name;
    }

    public double getSales()
    {
        return sales;
    }
}
```

getFigures

The input method `getFigures` is relatively straightforward, especially since you have an input method for objects of the class `SalesAssociate`. However, there are a couple of subtle points to worry about. You design the following basic input loop:

```java
int i;
for (i = 0; i < numberOfAssociates; i++)
{
    System.out.println(
                    "Enter data for associate number " + (i + 1));
    record[i].readInput();
}
```

You handled one of the subtle points very nicely. The array indices are numbered starting with 0 but the associates are numbered starting with 1, and so you have used `record[i]` for associate (i + 1). But another problem remains.

When you test this loop, you get an error message saying something about a "null pointer." This problem is due to the fact that the base type of the array `record` is a class type. To see the problem, consider another situation first. Suppose you had the following code:

```
SalesAssociate a;
a.readInput();
```

This code would produce the same error message regarding a "null pointer." The problem is that the variable a is just a name; it does not yet name any object of the class `SalesAssociate`. The preceding code omitted the usual use of `new`. The code should be

```
SalesAssociate a;
a = new SalesAssociate();
a.readInput();
```

The indexed variable `record[i]` is also a variable of a class type, and so it is also just a name. You need to use `new` with `record[i]` before it can be used with the method `readInput` (or any other method). Your code needs the following to be added:

```
record[i] = new SalesAssociate();
```

The complete definition of the method `getFigures` with this line inserted is shown in Display 6.5.

Next you turn your attention to the method `update`. You come up with the following code:

update

```
for (i = 0; i < numberOfAssociates; i++)
{
    sum = sum + record[i].getSales();
    if (record[i].getSales() > highest)
        highest = record[i].getSales(); //highest sales figure
                                        //so far.

}
average = sum/numberOfAssociates;
```

This loop is basically OK, but you realize that the variables `sum` and `highest` must be initialized before the loop begins. You can initialize `sum` to 0, but what value do you use to initialize `highest`? Perhaps a negative number, since sales cannot be negative. Or can they? If a customer returns goods, that is considered a negative sale, so sales can indeed be negative. However, you know that the company always has at least one sales associate, and so you initialize both `sum` and `highest` to the sales for the first associate. This takes one case outside of the loop and places it before the loop as follows:

```
highest = record[0].getSales();
double sum = record[0].getSales();
for (i = 1; i < numberOfAssociates; i++)
{
    sum = sum + record[i].getSales();
    if (record[i].getSales() > highest)
        highest = record[i].getSales();//highest sales figure
                                        //so far.

}
average = sum/numberOfAssociates;
```

■ DISPLAY 6.5   **Sales Report Program** *(Part 1 of 3)*

```java
/**
 Program to generate sales report.              The main method is in
*/                                               Part 3 of the Display.
public class SalesReporter
{
    private double highest;
    private double average;
    private SalesAssociate[] record;//The array object is
                                    //created in getFigures.

    private int numberOfAssociates; //Same as record.length

    public void getFigures()
    {
        System.out.println("Enter number of sales associates:");
        numberOfAssociates = SavitchIn.readLineInt();
        record = new SalesAssociate[numberOfAssociates];
        int i;
        for (i = 0; i < numberOfAssociates; i++)        Array object
        {                                               created here.

            record[i] = new SalesAssociate();
            System.out.println("Enter data for associate " + (i + 1));
            record[i].readInput();
            System.out.println();                       SalesAssociate
        }                                               objects created here.
    }

    /**
     Computes the average and highest sales figures.
     Precondition: There is at least one salesAssociate.
    */
    public void update()
    {
        int i;
        double nextSales = record[0].getSales( );
        highest = nextSales;
        double sum = nextSales;
        for (i = 1; i < numberOfAssociates; i++)
        {                                               Already processed
            nextSales = record[i].getSales( );          record[0], so the loop
            sum = sum + nextSales;                      starts with record[1].
            if (nextSales > highest)
                highest = nextSales; //highest sales figure so far.
        }
        average = sum/numberOfAssociates;
    }
```

■ DISPLAY 6.5 **Sales Report Program** *(Part 2 of 3)*

```java
/**
 Displays sales report on console screen.
*/
public void displayResults()
{
    System.out.println("Average sales per associate is $" +
            average);
    System.out.println("The highest sales figure is $" + highest);
    System.out.println();
    int i;
    System.out.println("The following had the highest sales:");
    for (i = 0; i < numberOfAssociates; i++)
    {
        double nextSales = record[i].getSales();
        if (nextSales == highest)
        {
            record[i].writeOutput();
            System.out.println("$" + (nextSales - average)
                                    + " above the average.");
            System.out.println();
        }
    }

    System.out.println("The rest performed as follows:");
    for (i = 0; i < numberOfAssociates; i++)
    {
        double nextSales = record[i].getSales();
        if (record[i].getSales() != highest)
        {
            record[i].writeOutput();
            if (nextSales >= average)
                System.out.println("$" + (nextSales - average)
                                    + " above the average.");
            else
                System.out.println("$" + (average - nextSales)
                                    + " below the average.");
            System.out.println();
        }
    }
}
```

■ DISPLAY 6.5   **Sales Report Program** *(Part 3 of 3)*

```java
    public static void main(String[] args)
    {
        SalesReporter clerk = new SalesReporter();
        clerk.getFigures();
        clerk.update();
        clerk.displayResults();
    }
}
```

Sample Screen Dialog

```
    Enter number of sales associates:
    3
    Enter data for associate number 1
    Enter name of sales associate: Dusty Rhodes
    Enter associate's sales: $36000

    Enter data for associate number 2
    Enter name of sales associate: Natalie Dressed
    Enter associate's sales: $50000

    Enter data for associate number 3
    Enter name of sales associate: Sandy Hair
    Enter associate's sales: $10000

    Average sales per associate is $32000
    The highest sales figure is $50000

    The following had the highest sales:
    Name: Natalie Dressed
    Sales: $50000
    $18000 above the average.

    The rest performed as follows:
    Name: Dusty Rhodes
    Sales: $36000
    $4000 above the average.

    Name: Sandy Hair
    Sales: $10000
    $22000 below the average.
```

The preceding loop will work, but you realize that this code contains a repeated calculation. There are three identical method invocations of `record[i].getSales()`. You decide to only have one such invocation and store the result in a variable as follows:

```
int i;
double nextSales = record[0].getSales();
highest = nextSales;
double sum = nextSales;
for (i = 1; i < numberOfAssociates; i++)
{
    nextSales = record[i].getSales();
    sum = sum + nextSales;
    if (nextSales > highest)
        highest = nextSales;//highest sales figure so far.
}
average = sum/numberOfAssociates;
```

The complete final definition for the method `update` is given in Display 6.5.

The design of the final method `displayResults` uses only techniques that you have already seen, and so we will not go over the details. The final method definition is shown in Display 6.5. ■

7. Write some Java code that will declare an array named `entry` that has length 3, has `SalesAssociate` (Display 6.4) as its base type, and is filled with three identical records. The records use the name `"Jane Doe"` and sales of $5000. Use a `for` loop.

8. Rewrite the method `displayResults` of the program `SalesReporter` (Display 6.5) so that it uses the methods in the class `Dollars` (Display 5.14 of Chapter 5) to output the dollar amounts in the correct format for dollars and cents.

Indexed Variables as Method Arguments

An indexed variable for an array `a`, such as `a[i]`, can be used anyplace that you can use any other variable of the base type of the array. So an indexed variable can be an argument to a method in exactly the same way that any other variable of the array's base type can be an argument. For example, the program in Display 6.6 contains a program that illustrates the use of an indexed variable as an argument to a method.

Consider the method `average`, which takes two arguments of type `int`. In the program in Display 6.6, the array `nextScore` has base type `int`, and so the program can use `nextScore[i]` as an argument to the method `average`, as in the following line from that program:

```
possibleAverage = average(firstScore, nextScore[i]);
```

The variable `firstScore` is an ordinary variable of type `int`. To help drive home the point that the indexed variable `nextScore[i]` can be used just like any other variable of type `int`, note that the program in Display 6.6 would behave exactly the same if the two

■ **DISPLAY 6.6   Indexed Variables as Arguments**

```java
/**
 A program to demonstrate the use of
 indexed variables as arguments.
*/
public class ArgumentDemo
{
    public static void main(String[] args)
    {
        System.out.println("Enter your score on exam 1:");
        int firstScore = SavitchIn.readLineInt();
        int[] nextScore = new int[3];
        int i;
        double possibleAverage;
        for (i = 0; i < nextScore.length; i++)
            nextScore[i] = 80 + 10*i;
        for (i = 0; i < nextScore.length; i++)
        {
            possibleAverage = average(firstScore, nextScore[i]);
            System.out.println("If your score on exam 2 is "
                                    + nextScore[i]);
            System.out.println("your average will be "
                                    + possibleAverage);
        }
    }

    public static double average(int n1, int n2)
    {
        return (n1 + n2)/2.0;
    }
}
```

Sample Screen Dialog

```
Enter your score on exam 1:
80
If your score on exam 2 is 80
your average will be 80.0
If your score on exam 2 is 90
your average will be 85.0
If your score on exam 2 is 100
your average will be 90.0
```

arguments to the method `average` were interchanged, changing the preceding invocation of `average` to the following:

```
possibleAverage = average(nextScore[i], firstScore);
```

Also note the definition of the method `average`. That definition contains no indication that its arguments can be indexed variables for an array of `int`. The method `average` accepts arguments of type `int` and neither knows nor cares whether those `int`s came from an indexed variable, a regular `int` variable, or a constant `int` value.

There is one subtlety that applies to indexed variables used as method arguments. For example, again consider the method call:

evaluating indices

```
possibleAverage = average(firstScore, nextScore[i]);
```

If the value of `i` is 2, the argument is `nextScore[2]`. On the other hand, if the value of `i` is 0, the argument is `nextScore[0]`. The indexed expression is evaluated in order to determine exactly which indexed variable to use as the argument.

Be sure to note that an indexed variable of an array `a`, such as `a[i]`, is a variable of the base type of the array. When `a[i]` is used as an argument to a method, it is handled *in exactly the same way as any other variable of the base type of the array* `a`. In particular, if the base type of the array is a primitive type, such as `int`, `double`, or `char`, then the method cannot change the value of `a[i]`. On the other hand, if the base type of the array is a class type, then the method can change the object named by `a[i]`. This is nothing new. Just remember that an indexed variable, like `a[i]`, is a variable of the base type of the array and is handled just like any other variable of the base type of the array.

Quick Reference: Array Indexed Variables as Arguments

An array indexed variable can be used as an argument anyplace that a variable of the array base type can be used. For example, suppose you have

```
double[] a = new double[10];
```

Indexed variables such as `a[3]` and `a[index]` can then be used as arguments to any method that accepts a `double` variable as an argument.

FAQ: When Can a Method Change an Indexed Variable Argument?

Suppose `a[i]` is an indexed variable of an array `a` and `a[i]` is used as an argument in a method invocation such as

```
doStuff(a[i]);
```

Whether or not the method `doStuff` can change the array element `a[i]` depends on the base type of the array `a`. If the base type of the array `a` is a primitive type, such as `int`, `double`, or `char`, then as with any argument of a primitive type, the method `doStuff` cannot change the value of `a[i]`. However, if the base type of the array `a` is a class, the method `doStuff` can change the object named by `a[i]`. Note that there is nothing new here. The indexed variable `a[i]` is treated just like any other variable of the base type of the array. (To review the details on method arguments, see Chapter 4.)

Entire Arrays as Method Arguments

You have already seen that an indexed variable of an array can be used as an argument to a method. An entire array can also be used as a single argument to a method. The way you specify an array parameter in a method definition is similar to the way you declare an array. For example, the method `incrementArrayBy2` (which follows) will accept any array of `double` as its single argument:

```
public class SampleClass
{
    public static void incrementArrayBy2(double[] a)
    {
        int i;
        for (i = 0; i < a.length; i++)
            a[i] = a[i] + 2;
    }
    <The rest of the class definition goes here.>
}
```

To illustrate this, suppose you have the following in some method definition:

```
double[] a = new double[10];
double[] b = new double[30];
```

and suppose that the elements of the arrays a and b have been given values. Both of the following are then valid method invocations:

```
SampleClass.incrementArrayBy2(a);
SampleClass.incrementArrayBy2(b);
```

length of array
arguments

There are a few things that we need to emphasize about array arguments. First, no square brackets are used when you give an entire array as an argument to a method. Second, a method can change the values in an array. This is illustrated by the preceding method `incrementArrayBy2`. Third, the same array parameter can be replaced with array arguments of different lengths. Note that the preceding method `incrementArrayBy2` can take an array of any length as an argument. When you specify a parameter as an array parameter, you specify the base type of the array, but you do not specify the length of the array.

Arguments for the Method main

The heading for the `main` method of a program is as follows:

```
public static void main(String[] args)
```

The part `String[] args` makes it look as though `args` is a parameter for an array with base type `String`. And not only does it look that way, but it is in fact true that the method `main` takes an array of `String` values as an argument. But we have never given `main` an array argument, or any other kind of argument, when we ran any of our programs. What's the story?

As you know, an invocation of `main` is a very special sort of invocation. A default array of strings is automatically provided as a default argument to `main` when you run your program.

Quick Reference: **Array Parameters and Array Arguments**

An argument to a method may be an entire array. Array arguments are like objects of a class, in that the method can change the values in an array argument. A method with an array parameter is defined and invoked as illustrated by the following examples. (All the examples are assumed to be somewhere within a class definition.)

Examples (of array parameters):

```
public static void showArray(char[] a)
{
    int i;
    for (i = 0; i < a.length; i++)
        System.out.println(a[i]);
}
public static void reinitialize(int[] anArray)
{
    int i;
    for (i = 0; i < anArray.length; i++)
        anArray[i] = 0;
}
```

Examples (of array arguments):

```
char[] symbol = new char[10];
int[] a = new int[10];
int[] b = new int[20];

    <Some code to fill the arrays goes here.>

showArray(symbol);
reinitialize(a);
reinitialize(b);
```

Note that arrays a and b have different lengths. Also note that no square brackets are used with array arguments.

It is possible to provide additional "string arguments" when you run a program, and those "string arguments" will automatically be made elements of the array argument that is provided to main. This is normally done by running the program from the command line of the operating system, like so:

```
java TestProgram Sally Smith
```

This will set args[0] to "Sally" and args[1] to "Smith," and these two indexed variables can be used in the method main, as shown in the following sample program:

```
public class TestProgram
{
    public static void main(String[] args)
    {
        System.out.println("Hello " + args[0] + " " + args[1]);
    }
}
```

If the preceding program is compiled and then run with the one-line command

```
java TestProgram Josephine Student
```

The output produced by the program will be

```
Hello Josephine Student
```

Since the identifier `args` is a parameter, you can use any other (nonkeyword) identifier in place of `args`, and the meaning will be unchanged (as long as you change any occurrences of `args` that also occur in the body of `main`). However, it is traditional to use the identifier `args` for this parameter.

Finally, be sure to note that the argument to `main` is an array of *strings*. If you want numbers, you must convert the string representations of the numbers to values of a number type or types.

Quick Reference: **The Method `main` Has an Array Parameter**

The heading for the `main` method of a program is as follows:

```
public static void main(String[] args)
```

The identifier `args` is a parameter for an array of base type `String`. The details are explained in the text.

▲ *Gotcha*
Use of = and == with Arrays

assignment
with arrays

Arrays are objects, and so the assignment operator = and the equality operator == behave (and misbehave) the same way with arrays as they do with the kinds of objects we saw before discussing arrays. To understand how this applies to arrays, you need to know a little bit about how arrays are stored in the computer's main memory. The important point for this discussion is that the entire array contents (that is, the contents of all of the indexed variables) are stored together in one (possibly large) section of memory so that the location of the entire array contents can be specified by one memory address.

Recall that a variable for an object really contains the memory address of the object. The assignment operator copies this memory address. For example, consider the following code:

```
int[] a = new int[3];
int[] b = new int[3];
int i;
for (i = 0; i < a.length; i++)
    a[i] = i;
b = a;
System.out.println("a[2] = " + a[2] + " b[2] = " + b[2]);
a[2] = 2001;
System.out.println("a[2] = " + a[2] + " b[2] = " + b[2]);
```

This will produce the following output:

```
a[2] = 2 b[2] = 2
a[2] = 2001 b[2] = 2001
```

The assignment statement b = a; (in the preceding code) gives the array variable b the same memory address as the array variable a. So a and b are two different names for the same array. Thus, when we change the value of a[2], we are also changing the value of b[2].

Because of the complication we discussed in the previous paragraph, it is best simply not to use the assignment operator = with arrays (and similarly not to use == with arrays). If you want the arrays a and b in the preceding code to be different arrays with the same values, then instead of the assignment statement

```
b = a;
```

you must use something like the following:

```
int i;
for (i = 0; i < a.length; i++)
    b[i] = a[i];
```

Note that the preceding code assumes that the arrays a and b have the same length.

The equality operator == tests two arrays to see if they are stored in the same place in the computer's memory. For example, consider the following code:

```
== with arrays
```

```
int[] a = new int[3];
int[] b = new int[3];
int i;
for (i = 0; i < a.length; i++)
    a[i] = i;
for (i = 0; i < a.length; i++)
    b[i] = i;

if (b == a)
    System.out.println("Equal by ==");
else
    System.out.println("Not equal by ==");
```

This produces the output

```
Not equal by ==
```

This is the output despite the fact that the arrays a and b contain the same integers in the same indexed variables. This happens because the arrays a and b are stored in different places in memory, and == tests for equal memory addresses.

If you want to test two arrays to see if they contain the same elements, then you can define an equals method for the arrays, just as you defined an equals method for a class. For example, Display 6.7 contains one possible definition of equals for arrays in a small demonstration class. △

■ DISPLAY 6.7   Two Kinds of Equality *(Part 1 of 2)*

```java
/**
 This is just a demonstration program to see how
 equals and == work.
*/
public class TestEquals
{
    public static void main(String[] args)
    {
        int[] a = new int[3]; int[] b = new int[3]; int i;
        for (i = 0; i < a.length; i++)
            a[i] = i;
        for (i = 0; i < b.length; i++)
            b[i] = i;
        if (b == a)
            System.out.println("Equal by ==.");
        else
            System.out.println("Not equal by ==.");
        if (equals(b,a))
            System.out.println("Equal by the equals method.");
        else
            System.out.println("Not equal by the equals method.");
    }
    public static boolean equals(int[] a, int[] b)
    {
        boolean match;
        if (a.length != b.length)
            match = false;
        else
        {
            match = true; //tentatively
            int i = 0;
            while (match && (i < a.length))
            {
                if (a[i] != b[i])
                    match = false;
                i++;
            }
        }
        return match;
    }
}
```

The arrays a and b contain the same integers in the same order.

■ DISPLAY 6.7   **Two Kinds of Equality** *(Part 2 of 2)*

Screen Output

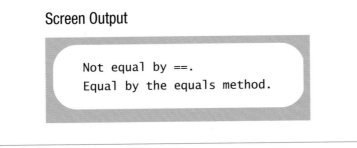

```
Not equal by ==.
Equal by the equals method.
```

Remember: Array Types Are Reference Types

A variable of an array type holds only the address of where the array is stored in memory. This memory address is often called a **reference** to the array object in memory. For this reason, array types are often called reference types. A **reference type** is any type whose variables hold references (that is, memory addresses), as opposed to the actual item named by the variable. Array types and class types are both reference types. Primitive types are not reference types.

FAQ: Are Arrays Really Objects?

Arrays do not belong to any class. There are also other features of class objects that do not apply to arrays, such as inheritance (which we will discuss in Chapter 7). So whether or not arrays should be considered objects is not 100 percent clear. However, that is primarily an academic debate. *In Java, arrays are officially objects.* Whenever Java documentation says that something applies to all objects, it also applies to arrays.

Methods That Return Arrays

In Java, a method may return an array. You specify the returned type for a method that returns an array in the same way that you specify a type for an array parameter. For example, Display 6.8 contains a slightly rewritten version of the program in Display 6.6. The program in Display 6.8 performs pretty much the same computation as the one in Display 6.6. However, in this new version, the various possible average scores are computed by the method `averageArray` and returned as an array of scores (of type `double`).

Notice that a new array is created and then it is returned, as follows:

```
double temp = new double[nextScore.length];
<Fill the array temp.>
return temp;
```

Quick Reference: Returning an Array

A method can return an array. The details are basically the same as for any other returned type.

Quick Reference continues on page 371.

■ **DISPLAY 6.8   A Method That Returns an Array**

```java
/**
 A program to demonstrate a method returning an array.
*/
public class ReturnArrayDemo
{
    public static void main(String[] args)
    {
        System.out.println("Enter your score on exam 1:");
        int firstScore = SavitchIn.readLineInt();
        int[] nextScore = new int[3];
        int i;
        for (i = 0; i < nextScore.length; i++)
            nextScore[i] = 80 + 10*i;
        double[] averageScore;
        averageScore = averageArray(firstScore, nextScore);
        for (i = 0; i < nextScore.length; i++)
        {
            System.out.println("If your score on exam 2 is "
                                    + nextScore[i]);
            System.out.println("your average will be "
                                    + averageScore[i]);
        }
    }

    public static double[] averageArray(int firstScore,
                                              int[] nextScore)
    {
        double[] temp = new double[nextScore.length];
        int i;
        for (i = 0; i < temp.length; i++)
            temp[i] = average(firstScore, nextScore[i]);
        return temp;
    }

    public static double average(int n1, int n2)
    {
        return (n1 + n2)/2.0;
    }
}
```

The sample screen dialog is the same as in Display 6.6.

Syntax (for a typical way of returning an array):

```
public static Base_Type[]  Method_Name(Parameter_List)
{
    Base_Type[] temp = new Base_Type[Array_Size]
    Statements_To_Fill_temp
    return temp;
}
```

The method need not be static and need not be public. The following are some of the other acceptable method headings:

```
public Base_Type[]  Method_Name(Parameter_List)

private static Base_Type[]  Method_Name(Parameter_List)

private Base_Type[]  Method_Name(Parameter_List)
```

Examples (assumed to be in a class definition):

```
public static char[] vowels()
{
    char[] newArray = new char[5];
    newArray[0] = 'a';
    newArray[1] = 'e';
    newArray[2] = 'i';
    newArray[3] = 'o';
    newArray[4] = 'u';
    return newArray;
}
```

Quick Reference: Array Type Names

An array type name is always of the form

```
Base_Type[]
```

This is true when declaring an array variable, specifying the type for an array parameter, or specifying an array type as the type returned by a method.

Examples:

```
int[] n = new int[10];
Species[] s = new Species[20];
public static double[] halfAll(int[] arryToBeHalved);
{
        .
        .
        .
```

9. What output will be produced by the following code?

```java
char[] a = new char[3];
char[] b;
int i;
for (i = 0; i < a.length; i++)
    a[i] = 'a';
b = a;
System.out.println("a[1] = " + a[1] + " b[1] = " + b[1]);
System.out.println("a[2] = " + a[2] + " b[2] = " + b[2]);
b[2] = 'b';
System.out.println("a[1] = " + a[1] + " b[1] = " + b[1]);
System.out.println("a[2] = " + a[2] + " b[2] = " + b[2]);
```

10. Give the definition of a method called showArray that has a single parameter for an array of base type char and that writes a line of text to the screen consisting of the characters in the array argument written in order. Make it a static method. To test it, you can add it to any class or, better yet, write a class with a test program in the method main.

11. Give the definition of a method called halfArray that has a single parameter for an array of base type double and that returns another array of base type double that has the same length and in which each element has been divided by 2.0. Make it a static method. To test it, you can add it to any class, or better yet, write a class with a test program in the method main.

12. What is wrong with the following method definition?

```java
public static void doubleSize(int[] a)
{
    a = new int[a.length * 2];
}
```

It will compile but does not work as you might hope.

6.3 PROGRAMMING WITH ARRAYS AND CLASSES

The Moving Finger writes; and, having writ,
Moves on; nor all your Piety and Wit.
Shall lure it back to cancel half a line.
Nor all your Tears wash out a Word of it. -Omar Khayyam, *The Ruba'iyat* (Fitzgerald translation)

In this section, we present some additional techniques for working with arrays. In particular, we discuss using an array variable as an instance variable in a class. We begin with a programming example that illustrates some basic techniques.

Programming Example
A Specialized List Class

One way to use an array for a special purpose is to make the array an instance variable of a class and access it only through the class methods. This allows you to define classes whose objects are something like special-purpose arrays. The array is accessed only through the class methods, and so you can add any checks and automatic processing that you want. In this programming example, we present an example of one such class.

We will define a class whose objects can be used for keeping lists of items, such as a grocery list or a list of things to do. The class will have the rather long name OneWayNoRepeatsList.[1]

The class OneWayNoRepeatsList will have a method for adding items to the list. An item on the list is a string, which in an application would say whatever you want the item to say, such as "Buy milk". This class has no method to change or delete a single item from the list. It does, however, have a method that lets you erase the entire list and start over again with a blank list. Each object of the class OneWayNoRepeatsList has a maximum number of items it can hold. At any time, the list might contain anywhere from zero to the maximum number of items.

An object of the class OneWayNoRepeatsList has an array of strings as an instance variable. This array holds the items on the list. However, you do not access the array directly. Instead, you use accessor and mutator methods. You can use int variables to hold numbers that indicate positions in the list. One of these int variables is the same thing as an index, but the positions are numbered starting with 1 rather than 0. For example, there is a method named getEntryAt that lets you recover the item at a given position. If toDoList is an object of the class OneWayNoRepeatsList, the following sets the string variable next to the entry at the second position:

```
String next = toDoList.getEntryAt(2);
```

There is no way to (directly) change an entry on the list. There is a method to add an entry to the end of the list and a method to erase the entire list, but those are the only ways that the list can be changed.

In Chapter 4 we discussed encapsulation. The class OneWayNoRepeatsList will be a good example of a well-encapsulated class. As we discussed in Chapter 4, a well-encapsulated class is defined so that the programmer who uses the class need not know the details of how the class is defined. If that is true of the class OneWayNoRepeatsList, it makes sense to tell you how to use the class OneWayNoRepeatsList *before we give the definition of that class*. So let's do that.

Display 6.9 contains a program that demonstrates how to use some of the methods for the class OneWayNoRepeatsList. Notice that there is a constructor that takes an integer argument. This integer specifies the maximum number of entries that can be placed in the list. Normally, the list will contain fewer than the maximum number of entries.

---

1. Long names are traditional in Java, but we did not choose a long name just to be traditional. All the short names, like *List*, *Table*, and so forth, already have a technical meaning in computer science, and it could be confusing to use these short names for something other than their usual meaning.

■ DISPLAY 6.9   **Using the Class** OneWayNoRepeatsList *(Part 1 of 2)*

```java
public class ListDemo
{
    public static void main(String[] args)
    {
        OneWayNoRepeatsList toDoList =
                            new OneWayNoRepeatsList(3);

        System.out.println(
                    "Enter items for the list, when prompted.");
        boolean more = true;
        String next = null;
        char ans;

        while ( more && (! toDoList.full()))
        {
            System.out.println("Input an entry:");
            next = SavitchIn.readLine();
            toDoList.addItem(next);
            if (toDoList.full())
            {
                System.out.println("List is full.");
            }
            else
            {
                System.out.print(
                            "More items for the list?(y/n): ");
                ans = SavitchIn.readLineNonwhiteChar();
                if ((ans == 'n') || (ans == 'N'))
                    more = false;
            }
        }

        System.out.println("The list contains:");
        int position = toDoList.START_POSITION;
        next = toDoList.getEntryAt(position);
        while (next != null)
        {
            System.out.println(next);
            position++;
            next = toDoList.getEntryAt(position);
        }
    }
}
```

null *indicates the end of the list.*

■ DISPLAY 6.9   **Using the Class** OneWayNoRepeatsList *(Part 2 of 2)*

Sample Screen Dialog

```
Enter items for the list, when prompted.
Input an entry:
Buy milk.
More items for the list?(y/n): y
Input an entry:
Walk dog.
More items for the list?(y/n): y
Input an entry:
Buy milk.
More items for the list?(y/n): y
Input an entry:
Write program.
The list is full.
The list contains:
Buy milk.
Walk dog.
Write program.
```

The method addItem adds a string to the list. For example, the following adds the string named by the variable next to the list toDoList.

```
toDoList.addItem(next);
```

If you look at the sample dialog, you will see that "Buy milk." is added to the list twice, but that it appears on the list only once. If the item being added is already on the list, then the method addItem has no effect. That way the list has no repeats.

You can use an int variable to step through the list from beginning to end. The technique is illustrated in Display 6.9. The following initializes an int variable to the first position on the list:

stepping through a list

```
int position = toDoList.START_POSITION;
```

The defined constant toDoList.START_POSITION is simply another name for 1, but we use it because we are thinking of this as the start of the list, not as the number 1. You can recover the item at a given position with the method getEntryAt. For example, the following sets the string variable next equal to the string at the position (at the index) given by the variable position:

```
next = toDoList.getEntryAt(position);
```

To obtain the next item on the list, the program simply increments the value of `position`. The following code, taken from Display 6.9, illustrates stepping through the list:

```
int position = toDoList.START_POSITION;
next = toDoList.getEntryAt(position);
while (next != null)
{
    System.out.println(next);
    position++;
    next = toDoList.getEntryAt(position);
}
```

Once the value of `position` is incremented beyond the last position in the list, there is no entry at the index indicated by `position`. So we need some way to conveniently indicate that the end of the list has been reached, or we might access some "garbage value" in the unused portion of the array. To take care of this problem, we will define `toDoList.getEntryAt(position)` so that it returns the value `null` when there is no entry at the given position. Note that `null` is different from any real string, and so `null` is an item that will not appear on any list. Thus, your program can test for the end of the list by checking for the value `null`. Recall that to test for equality or inequality with `null`, you use `==` or `!=`; you do not use an `equals` method.

null marks the end

The complete definition of the class `OneWayNoRepeatsList` is given in Display 6.10. The entries in a list are kept in the instance variable `entry`, which is an array of base type `String`. Thus, the maximum number of entries that the list can hold is `entry.length`. However, the list will not normally be full, but will typically contain fewer than `entry.length` entries. In order to keep track of how much of the array `entry` is currently being used, the class has an instance variable called `countOfEntries`. The entries themselves are kept in the indexed variables `entry[0]`, `entry[1]`, `entry[2]`, and so on through `entry[countOfEntries − 1]`. The values of the elements with indices `countOfEntries` or higher are just garbage values and do not represent entries on the list. Thus, when you want to step through the items on the list, you stop after `entry[countOfEntries − 1]`.

garbage values

For example, in the definition of the method `onList`, there is a `while` loop that steps through the array, checking to see if the argument is equal to any of the entries on the list. The code checks only array elements with indices less than `countOfEntries`. It does not check the entire array, because array entries at indices greater than or equal to `countOfEntries` are not "on the list." So the `while` loop that checks to see whether `item` is on the list is

```
while ((! found) && (i < countOfEntries))
{
    if (item.equalsIgnoreCase(entry[i]))
        found = true;
    else
        i++;
}
```

The class `OneWayNoRepeatsList` has a few more methods than those we used in the demonstration program in Display 6.9. These extra methods make the class more useful for a wider variety of applications.

■ DISPLAY 6.10 **An Array Wrapped in a Class** *(Part 1 of 3)*

```java
/**
 An object of this class is a special kind of list. The list can
 be written only from beginning to end. You can add to the end of
 the list, but you cannot change individual entries. You can erase
 the entire list and start over. No entry may appear more than once
 on the list. You can use int variables as position markers into
 the list. Position markers are similar to array indices,
 but are numbered starting with 1.
*/
public class OneWayNoRepeatsList
{
    public static int START_POSITION = 1;
    public static int DEFAULT_SIZE = 50;

    //entry.length is the total number of items you have room
    //for on the list. countOfEntries is the number of items
    //currently on the list.
    private int countOfEntries; //can be less than entry.length.
    private String[] entry;

    public OneWayNoRepeatsList(int maximumNumberOfEntries)
    {
        entry = new String[maximumNumberOfEntries];
        countOfEntries = 0;
    }

    /**
     Creates an empty list with a capacity of DEFAULT_SIZE.
    */
    public OneWayNoRepeatsList()
    {
        entry = new String[DEFAULT_SIZE];
        countOfEntries = 0;
    }

    public boolean full()
    {
        return (countOfEntries == entry.length);
    }

    public boolean empty()
    {
        return (countOfEntries == 0);
    }
```

■ DISPLAY 6.10 An Array Wrapped in a Class *(Part 2 of 3)*

```java
/**
 Precondition: List is not full.
 Postcondition: If item was not on the list,
 it has been added to the list.
*/
public void addItem(String item)
{
    if (! onList(item))
    {
        if (countOfEntries == entry.length)
        {
            System.out.println("Adding to a full list!");
            System.exit(0);
        }
        else

        {
            entry[countOfEntries] = item;
            countOfEntries++;
        }
    }//else do nothing. Item is already on the list.
}

/**
 If the argument indicates a position on the list,
 then the entry at that specified position is returned;
 otherwise, null is returned.
*/
public String getEntryAt(int position)
{
    if ((1 <= position) && (position <= countOfEntries))
        return entry[position - 1];
    else
        return null;
}

/**
 Returns true if position is the index of the
 last item on the list; otherwise, returns false.
*/
public boolean atLastEntry(int position)
{
    return (position == countOfEntries);
}
```

■ DISPLAY 6.10 An Array Wrapped in a Class *(Part 3 of 3)*

```java
/**
 Returns true if item is on the list;
 otherwise, returns false. Does not differentiate
 between upper- and lowercase letters.
*/
public boolean onList(String item)
{
     boolean found = false;
     int i = 0;
     while ((! found) && (i < countOfEntries))
     {
          if (item.equalsIgnoreCase(entry[i]))
              found = true;
          else
              i++;
     }
     return found;
}

public int maximumNumberOfEntries()
{
     return entry.length;
}

public int getNumberOfEntries()
{
     return countOfEntries;
}

public void eraseList()
{
     countOfEntries = 0;
}

}
```

Note that although the array entry has indices starting with 0, if you use an int variable as a position marker, such as the variable position in Display 6.9, the numbering starts at 1, not 0. The class methods automatically adjust the indices, so when you want the item at location position, it gives you entry[position − 1].

Note that the class OneWayNoRepeatsList provides three ways to detect the end of a list. First, if you move an int variable position through the list, then when position equals maximumNumberOfEntries(), it is at the last entry. Second, position is at the last entry when `atLastEntry(position)` returns `true`. Finally, when `position` is advanced beyond the last entry, `getEntryAt(position)` returns `null`.

Partially Filled Arrays

The array `entry` in the class `OneWayNoRepeatsList` in Display 6.10 is being used as a partially filled array. In some situations, you need some but not all of the indexed variables in an array, such as when the array `entry` contains the entries on a list and the list is not yet full. In these situations, you need to keep track of how much of the array has been used and how much is not currently being used. This is normally done with an `int` variable, like the instance variable `countOfEntries` in the class `OneWayNoRepeatsList` in Display 6.10. For example, the instance variable `countOfEntries` tells the methods that the list consists of the array elements with indices 0 through `countOfEntries - 1`. This is diagrammed in Display 6.11. It is very important to keep track of how much of the array is currently being used, because the other array entries contain garbage values that do not represent anything. When accessing a partially filled array, you want to access only those elements in the first part of the array that contain meaningful values, and you want to ignore the garbage values in the rest of the array. Of course, as you add or delete entries from a partially filled array, the borderline between meaningful values and garbage values can move, and this movement is recorded by changing the value of a suitable `int` variable, such as `countOfEntries`.

garbage values

Searching an Array

The method `onList` of the class `OneWayNoRepeatsList` (Display 6.10) searches the array `entry` to see if the parameter `item` is in the array `entry`. This is an example of a **sequential search** of an array. The sequential search algorithm is very simple and straightforward: Your code looks at the array elements in order from first to last to see if the sought-after item is equal to any of the array elements. (If the array is a partially filled array, the search stops when it reaches the end of the meaningful values.)

sequential search

■ DISPLAY 6.11 **A Partially Filled Array**

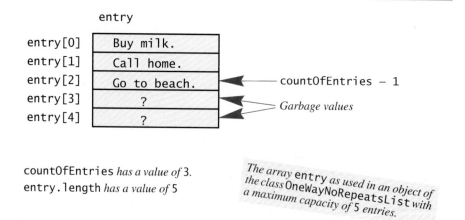

countOfEntries *has a value of* 3.
entry.length *has a value of* 5

The array entry *as used in an object of the class* OneWayNoRepeatsList *with a maximum capacity of 5 entries.*

▲ *Gotcha*

Returning an Array Instance Variable

Consider the following accessor method that somebody might want to add to the class OneWayNoRepeatsList in Display 6.10:

```
public String[] getEntryArray( )
{
    return entry;
}
```
Read the text to see what is wrong with this definition.

This definition looks innocent enough. It is pretty much like all the other accessor methods we have written for reading the data in a private instance variable. However, the fact that an array is returned, instead of a primitive type such as int or double, makes the situation very different. As you will see, the fact that this function returns an array and the fact that an array variable contains a reference (that is, a memory address) means that this method provides a way to get around the designation private. Let's look at the details of the problem.

Suppose you add the method getEntryArray to the class OneWayNoRepeatsList and you define the method as we did at the beginning of this Gotcha section. Suppose further that a programmer creates an object of type OneWayNoRepeatsList as follows:

```
OneWayNoRepeatsList myList = new OneWayNoRepeatsList( );
```

Now suppose that the programmer wants direct access to the private array instance variable entry in the object myList. The programmer should not be able to get such access. The qualifier private before the declaration of entry (in the class definition) was designed expressly to prevent such access. However, all that this sneaky (or maybe just careless) programmer needs to do to get access to the private array variable myList.entry is the following:

```
String[] a = myList.getEntryArray( );
```

After the preceding is executed, the array variable a contains the address of the array myList.entry. *So a is another name for the private array* myList.entry! Our sneaky programmer can do anything she or he wants to the private array myList.entry simply by using the array name a. For example, suppose the programmer wants to do the following:

```
myList.entry[2] = "Party tonight!";
```

Because the instance variable myList.entry is private, the programmer cannot use the name entry, and the preceding code will produce a compiler error message. But, she or he can do the following, which means the exact same thing, because a is another name for myList.entry:

```
a[2] = "Party tonight!";
```

The arrays myList.entry and a are the exact same array!

Obviously, the preceding definition of the accessor method getEntryArray is not a suitable accessor method. So what should we do about providing an accessor method to the array entry? The first answer is that you do not need any accessor (or mutator) methods beyond those already in the class. The methods getEntryAt, full, empty, and so forth allow a programmer to do anything that legitimately needs to be done with a `OneWayNoRepeatsList` object. It is, in fact, extremely unlikely that you would ever need an accessor method that returns an entire array instance variable. Unlikely, but not impossible.

Suppose that for some unusual reason you need to add the accessor method `getEntryArray` to the class `OneWayNoRepeatsList`. The correct way to define the method is as follows:

```
public String[] getEntryArray( )
{
    String[] temp = new String[entry.length];
    int i;
    for (i = 0; i < countOfEntries; i++)
        temp[i] = entry[i];
    return temp;
}
```

The array `temp` constructed in this method definition has the same entries as the array `entry`, but it is a different array. It is a copy of the array `entry`, but it is not the array `entry` itself. With this new definition of `getEntryArray`, the following is perfectly safe:

```
String[] a = myList.getEntryArray( );
```

The programmer can change the array `a`, but any changes will have no effect on the array `myList.entry`. The array `a` is an identical copy of `myList.entry` but is not the same array.[2]

If the array in question has a base type that is either a primitive type or the type `String`, this is pretty much the whole story. If the base type of the array is a class type, however, the problem does not go away that easily. If you have a private array instance variable with a class type as the base type, and you want an accessor method to return a safe copy of the array, not only must you copy the array, but you must make a copy of each array entry. However, it is unlikely that you will need an accessor method that returns an entire array copy for a private instance variable whose base type is a class (other than the class `String`, which can be treated like a primitive type for this discussion.) Therefore, we will not pursue this point any further. The problem is essentially the same as the problem we discussed in the Gotcha subsection of Chapter 5 entitled "Privacy Leaks." △

? Self-Test Questions

13. Suppose `a` is an array of values of type `double`. Write some code to display all the elements in `a` on the screen, one element per line.

14. Suppose `a` is an array of values of type `double`. It is a partially filled array that contains meaningful values in only the first `numberUsed` elements. (`numberUsed` is a variable of type `int` that contains the number of elements that contain meaningful values.) Write some code to display all the meaningful values in the array `a`.

15. Suppose `a` is a partially filled array with room for 10 elements but that contains only 3 elements. What indexed variables will contain the 3 elements?

---

2. You could argue that the arrays are not *identical* because we did not copy the garbage values at the end of the partially filled array `entry`. However, these are only garbage values. Moreover, if you really wanted to, you could also copy the garbage values, but there is no reason to do so.

16. Consider the array a from Self-Test Question 14. Write some code that will add the number 42 to this partially filled array a. (*Hint:* You must update numberUsed. You can assume the array a is not full.)

17. Redo Self-Test Question 16, but this time assume that you do not know whether the array a is full. If the array a is full, your code should output an appropriate message to the screen.

6.4 SORTING ARRAYS

A place for everything and everything in its place. -Isabella Mary Beeton, *The Book of Household Management*

Suppose you have an array of values. You might want the array values to be sorted in some way. For example, you might want to sort an array of numbers from lowest to highest or from highest to lowest, or you might want to sort an array of strings into alphabetical order. In this section, we will discuss a simple sorting algorithm and give a Java implementation of that algorithm. We will present this algorithm as a way to sort an array of values of type int. However, with only minor, obvious changes, it can be adapted to sort arrays of values of any type that can be ordered, such as an array of objects that represents employee records and that needs to be sorted by social security number.

Selection Sort

In this subsection, we discuss one of the easiest of the sorting algorithms to understand, which is known as **selection sort.**

The algorithm will be implemented as a method that has an array of int as a parameter and that sorts the array a. The method will rearrange the values in the indexed variables of the array so that

```
a[0] <= a[1] <= a[2] <= ... <= a[a.length - 1]
```

The selection sort algorithm almost follows automatically from the specification of what we want the algorithm to do. We want the algorithm to rearrange the values of the array so that a[0] is the smallest, a[1] is the next smallest, and so forth. That specification leads to the following algorithm outline:

```
for (index = 0; index < a.length; index++)
    Place the index^th smallest element in a[index].
```

(In this case, we count starting with 0, so the smallest element is the 0th smallest element, the next smallest is the 1th smallest, and so forth.)

We will implement the details of this algorithm using only the one array a. This means that we have no extra locations to store any of the array elements we are moving. The only way we can move an array element without losing any of the elements is to have the element swap places with another element of the array. Any sorting algorithm that uses this sort of swapping of values is called an **interchange sorting algorithm.** Thus, our selection sort algorithm is an interchange sorting algorithm. Let's start with an example to see how the array elements are interchanged.

interchange sorting

Display 6.12 shows how an array is sorted by interchanging values. The first array picture shows the starting values. The smallest value in the array is the 3 in a[4]. So the value in a[4] needs to be interchanged with the value in a[0]. After that interchange, the smallest value is in a[0] where it belongs. The next smallest value is the 5 in a[6]. So the value in a[6] needs to be interchanged with the value in a[1]. After that, the values in a[0] and a[1] are the smallest and next smallest values, which is what they should be in the final sorted array. The algorithm then interchanges the next smallest element with a[2] and so forth until the entire array is sorted.

■ DISPLAY 6.12   **Sorting by Swapping Values**

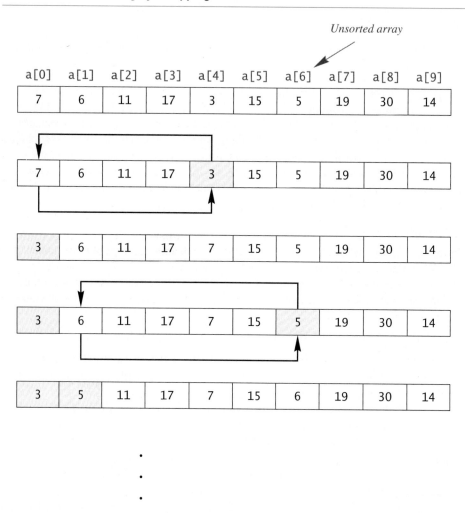

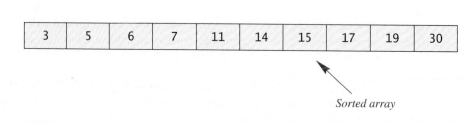

This analysis produces the following pseudocode version of the selection sort algorithm: pseudocode

Selection Sort Algorithm to Sort an Array a

```
for (index = 0; index < a.length - 1; index++)
{//Place the correct value in a[index]:
     indexOfNextSmallest = the index of the smallest value among
                    a[index], a[index+1], ..., a[a.length-1];
     Interchange the values of a[index] and a[indexOfNextSmallest].
     //a[0] <= a[1] <=...<= a[index] and these are the
     //smallest of the original array elements.
     //The remaining positions contain the rest of
     //the original array elements.
}
```

Notice that the for loop ends after correctly filling a[a.length − 2], even though the last index is a.length − 1. This is OK because when there is only one element left to be switched into position (namely, a[a.length − 1]), that element must already be in the correct place. To see this, note that when the algorithm gets all the elements except a[a.length − 1] correctly sorted, the correct value for a[a.length − 1] is the smallest value left to be moved, and the only value left to be moved is the value that is already in a[a.length − 1].

Display 6.13 contains a class with a static method named sort that implements this selection sort algorithm. The method sort uses two private helping methods named indexOfSmallest and interchange. Once you understand the methods indexOf-Smallest and interchange, it is easy to see that the definition of the method sort is a direct translation of our pseudocode into Java code. So let's discuss these two methods.

The method indexOfSmallest searches the following array elements and returns the   indexOfSmallest
index of the smallest of the following:

   a[startIndex], a[startIndex+1], ..., a[a.length-1]

It does this using the two local variables min and indexOfMin. At any point in its search, min is equal to the smallest array value found so far, and indexOfMin is the index of that value. Thus, among other things, a[indexOfMin] has the value min. Initially, min is set to a[startIndex], which is the first value considered for min, and indexOfMin is set to startIndex. Then each array element is considered in turn to see if it is a new minimum. After all of the candidate array elements have been checked, the method returns the value of indexOfMin.

The method named interchange interchanges the values of a[i] and a[j]. There is   interchange
one subtle point in this definition. If you execute the code

    a[i] = a[j];

you will lose the value originally held in a[i]. So before this is executed, the value of a[i] is saved in the local variable temp.

Display 6.14 contains a demonstration program that shows the selection sort class in action.

There are a number of well-known sorting algorithms, many of them more efficient (and more complicated) than selection sort. However, selection sort will suffice as an introduction to the general topic of sorting.

■ DISPLAY 6.13   **Selection Sort Class** *(Part 1 of 2)*

```java
/**
 Class for sorting an array of base type int from smallest to largest.
*/
public class SelectionSort
{
    /**
     Precondition: Every indexed variable of a has a value.
     Action: Sorts a so that a[0] <= a[1] <= ... <= a[a.length - 1].
    */
    public static void sort(int[] a)
    {
        int index, indexOfNextSmallest;
        for (index = 0; index < a.length - 1; index++)
        {//Place the correct value in a[index]:
            indexOfNextSmallest = indexOfSmallest(index, a);
            interchange(index,indexOfNextSmallest, a);
            //a[0] <= a[1] <=...<= a[index] and these are the smallest
            //of the original array elements. The remaining positions
            //contain the rest of the original array elements.
        }
    }

    /**
     Returns the index of the smallest value among
     a[startIndex], a[startIndex+1], ... a[a.length - 1]
    */
    private static int indexOfSmallest(int startIndex, int[] a)
    {
        int min = a[startIndex];
        int indexOfMin = startIndex;
        int index;
        for (index = startIndex + 1; index < a.length; index++)
            if (a[index] < min)
            {
                min = a[index];
                indexOfMin = index;
                //min is smallest of a[startIndex] through a[index]
            }
        return indexOfMin;
    }
```

■ DISPLAY 6.13 **Selection Sort Class** *(Part 2 of 2)*

```
/**
 Precondition: i and j are valid indices for the array a.
 Postcondition: Values of a[i] and a[j] have been interchanged.
*/
private static void interchange(int i, int j, int[] a)
{
    int temp;
    temp = a[i];
    a[i] = a[j];
    a[j] = temp; //original value of a[i]
}
}
```

■ DISPLAY 6.14 **Demonstration of the** `SelectionSort` **Class**

```
public class SelectionSortDemo
{
    public static void main(String[] args)
    {
        int[] b = {7, 5, 11, 2, 16, 4, 18, 14, 12, 30};

        System.out.println("Array values before sorting:");
        int i;
        for (i = 0; i < b.length; i++)
            System.out.print(b[i] + " ");
        System.out.println();

        SelectionSort.sort(b);

        System.out.println("Array values after sorting:");
        for (i = 0; i < b.length; i++)
            System.out.print(b[i] + " ");
        System.out.println();
    }
}
```

Screen Output

```
Array values before sorting:
7 5 11 2 16 4 18 14 12 30
Array values after sorting:
2 4 5 7 11 12 14 16 18 30
```

Other Sorting Algorithms

The selection sort algorithm is not the most efficient sorting algorithm. In fact, it is significantly less efficient than a number of well-known sorting algorithms. The selection sort is, however, much simpler than these other algorithms. A simpler algorithm is less likely to have errors creep in when you code it. So, if you need to code a sorting algorithm in a hurry, it is safer to use a selection sort (or some other simple algorithm).

On the other hand, if efficiency is a major issue, you may wish to use a more complicated and more efficient algorithm. But be aware that the more complicated algorithm will take longer to code, test, and debug. Efficiency can be a subtle topic. Remember, getting the wrong result is always inefficient, no matter how quickly your program can come up with the result.

Programming Projects 4 and 5 at the end of this chapter describe two other sorting algorithms. A more efficient sorting algorithm is described in the Programming Projects for Chapter 11 (which covers recursion).

? Self-Test Questions

18. How do you sort the following array, using the class `SelectionSort`?

    ```
    int[] myArray = {9, 22, 3, 2, 87, -17, 12, 14, 33, -2};
    ```

19. How would you need to change the class `SelectionSort` so that it can sort an array of values of type `double` (rather than of type `int`)?

20. How would you need to change the class `SelectionSort` so that it can sort an array of values of type `int` into decreasing order, instead of increasing order?

21. If an array of `int` values has a value that occurs twice (like `b[0] == 7` and `b[5] == 7`) and you sort the array using the method `SelectionSort.sort`, will there be one or two copies of the repeated value after the array is sorted?

6.5 MULTIDIMENSIONAL ARRAYS

Never trust to general impressions, my boy,
but concentrate yourself upon details. -Sir Arthur Conan Doyle, *A Case of Identity* (Sherlock Holmes)

It is sometimes useful to have an array with more than one index. For example, suppose you wanted to store the figures in Display 6.15 in some sort of array. The nonhighlighted part of the table is just labeling. The highlighted portion shows the actual entries. There are 60 entries. If you use an array with one index, the array will have length 60, and it would be almost impossible to keep track of which entry goes with which index number. On the other hand, if you allow yourself two indices, you can use one index for the row and one index for the column. This is illustrated in Display 6.16.

Note that, as was true for the simple arrays we have already seen, we begin numbering indices with 0 rather than 1. The Java notation for array elements with multiple indices is also illustrated in Display 6.16. If the array is named `table` and it has two indices, then `table[3][2]` is the entry in row number 3 and column number 2. Arrays that have exactly two entries can be displayed on paper as a two-dimensional table and are called **two-dimensional arrays.** By convention, we think of the first entry as denoting the row

two-dimensional array

■ DISPLAY 6.15 A Table of Values

Year	\multicolumn{6}{c}{Balances for Various Interest Rates Compounded Annually (Rounded to Whole Dollar Amounts)}					
	5.00%	5.50%	6.00%	6.50%	7.00%	7.50%
1	$1050	$1055	$1060	$1065	$1070	$1075
2	$1103	$1113	$1124	$1134	$1145	$1156
3	$1158	$1174	$1191	$1208	$1225	$1242
4	$1216	$1239	$1262	$1286	$1311	$1335
5	$1276	$1307	$1338	$1370	$1403	$1436
6	$1340	$1379	$1419	$1459	$1501	$1543
7	$1407	$1455	$1504	$1554	$1606	$1659
8	$1477	$1535	$1594	$1655	$1718	$1783
9	$1551	$1619	$1689	$1763	$1838	$1917
10	$1629	$1708	$1791	$1877	$1967	$2061

■ DISPLAY 6.16 Row and Column Indices for an Array Named `table`

Row index 3

Indices	0	1	2	3	4	5
0	$1050	$1055	$1060	$1065	$1070	$1075
1	$1103	$1113	$1124	$1134	$1145	$1156
2	$1158	$1174	$1191	$1208	$1225	$1242
3	$1216	$1239	$1262	$1286	$1311	$1335
4	$1276	$1307	$1338	$1370	$1403	$1436
5	$1340	$1379	$1419	$1459	$1501	$1543
6	$1407	$1455	$1504	$1554	$1606	$1659
7	$1477	$1535	$1594	$1655	$1718	$1783
8	$1551	$1619	$1689	$1763	$1838	$1917
9	$1629	$1708	$1791	$1877	$1967	$2061

`table[3][2]` *has a value of* 1262

Column index 2

n-dimensional
array

and the second as denoting the column. More generally, an array is said to be an **n-dimen-sional array** if it has n indices. Thus, the ordinary one-index arrays that we used up to now are one-dimensional arrays.

Multidimensional-Array Basics

Arrays with multiple indices are handled much like arrays with a single index. To illustrate the details, we will take you through a Java example program that displays an array like the one in Display 6.16. The program is shown in Display 6.17. The array is called `table`. The name `table` is declared, and the array is created, as follows:

declarations

```
int[][] table = new int[10][6];
```

This is equivalent to the following two steps:

```
int[][] table;
table = new int[10][6];
```

Note that this is almost identical to the syntax we used for the one-dimensional case. The only difference is that we added a second pair of square brackets in two places, and we gave a number specifying the size of the second dimension (that is, the number of indices in the second positions). You can have arrays with any number of indices. To get more indices, you just use more square brackets in the declaration.

indexed
variables

Indexed variables for multidimensional arrays are just like indexed variables for one-dimensional arrays, except that they have multiple indices, each enclosed in a pair of square brackets. This is illustrated by the following `for` loop from Display 6.17:

```
for (row = 0; row < 10; row++)
    for (column = 0; column < 6; column++)
        table[row][column] =
            balance(1000.00, row + 1, (5 + 0.5*column));
```

Note that we used two `for` loops, one nested within the other. This is a common way of stepping through all the indexed variables in a two-dimensional array. If there had been three indices, we would use three nested `for` loops, and so forth for higher numbers of indices. The illustration in Display 6.16 may help you understand the meaning of the indices in `table[row][column]` and the meaning of the nested `for` loops.

As was true of the indexed variables for one-dimensional arrays, indexed variables for multidimensional arrays are variables of the base type and can be used anyplace that a variable of the base type is allowed. For example, for the two-dimensional array `table` in Display 6.17, an indexed variable, such as `table[3][2]`, is a variable of type `int` and can be used anyplace that an ordinary `int` variable can be used.

Quick Reference: Declaring and Creating a Multidimensional Array

You declare a multidimensional-array name and create a multidimensional array in basically the same way that you create and name a one-dimensional array. You simply use as many square brackets as there are indices.

Syntax:

```
Base_Type[]...[] Array_Name = new Base_Type[Length_1]...[Length_n];
```

Quick Reference continues on p 392.

■ DISPLAY 6.17 **Using a Two-Dimensional Array** *(Part 1 of 2)*

```java
/**
 Displays a two-dimensional table showing how interest
 rates affect bank balances.
 */
public class InterestTable
{
    public static void main(String[] args)
    {
        int[][] table = new int[10][6];
        int row, column;
        for (row = 0; row < 10; row++)
            for (column = 0; column < 6; column++)
                table[row][column] =
                    balance(1000.00, row + 1, (5 + 0.5*column));
        System.out.println("Balances for Various Interest Rates");
        System.out.println("Compounded Annually");
        System.out.println("(Rounded to Whole Dollar Amounts)");
        System.out.println("Years 5.00% 5.50% 6.00% 6.50% 7.00% 7.50%");
        System.out.println();
        for (row = 0; row < 10; row++)
        {
            System.out.print((row + 1) + "      ");
            for (column = 0; column < 6; column++)
                    System.out.print("$" + table[row][column] + "  ");
            System.out.println();
        }
    }
    /**
     Returns the balance in an account that starts with startBalance
     and is left for the indicated number of years with rate as the
     interest rate. Interest is compounded annually. The balance is
     rounded to a whole number.
     */
    public static int balance(double startBalance, int years, double rate)
    {
        double runningBalance = startBalance;
        int count;
        for (count = 1; count <= years; count++)
            runningBalance = runningBalance*(1 + rate/100);
        return (int) (Math.round(runningBalance));
    }
}
```

A real application would do something more with the array table*. This is just a demonstration program.*

■ DISPLAY 6.17 **Using a Two-Dimensional Array** *(Part 2 of 2)*

Sample Screen Dialog

```
Balances for Various Interest Rates
Compounded Annually
(Rounded to Whole Dollar Amounts)
Years   5.00%   5.50%   6.00%   6.50%   7.00%   7.50%

1       $1050   $1055   $1060   $1065   $1070   $1075
2       $1103   $1113   $1124   $1134   $1145   $1156
3       $1158   $1174   $1191   $1208   $1225   $1242
4       $1216   $1239   $1262   $1286   $1311   $1335
5       $1276   $1307   $1338   $1370   $1403   $1436
6       $1340   $1379   $1419   $1459   $1501   $1543
7       $1407   $1455   $1504   $1554   $1606   $1659
8       $1477   $1535   $1594   $1655   $1718   $1783
9       $1551   $1619   $1689   $1763   $1838   $1917
10       $1629   $1708   $1791   $1877   $1967   $2061
```

The last line is out of alignment because 10 has two digits. This is easy to fix, but that would clutter the discussion of arrays with extraneous concerns.

Examples:

```
char[][] page = new char[100][80];
int[][] table = new int[10][6];
double[][][] threeDPicture = new double[10][20][30];
SomeClass[][] entry = new SomeClass[100][80];
```

SomeClass is a class.

Multidimensional-Array Parameters and Returned Values

array
arguments

Methods may have multidimensional-array parameters and may return a multidimensional array as the value returned. The situation is similar to that of the one-dimensional case, except that you use more square brackets. A two-dimensional array parameter is illustrated in Display 6.18. That program is a slight rewrite of the program in Display 6.17. Note that the type for the array parameter is int[][].

■ DISPLAY 6.18 **A Multidimensional-Array Parameter**

```
/**
 Displays a two-dimensional table showing how interest
 rates affect bank balances.
*/
public class InterestTable2
{
    public static void main(String[] args)
    {
        int[][] table = new int[10][6];
        int row, column;
        for (row = 0; row < 10; row++)
            for (column = 0; column < 6; column++)
                table[row][column] =
                    balance(1000.00, row + 1, (5 + 0.5*column));

        System.out.println("Balances for Various Interest Rates");
        System.out.println("Compounded Annually");
        System.out.println("(Rounded to Whole Dollar Amounts)");
        System.out.println("Years 5.00% 5.50% 6.00% 6.50% 7.00% 7.50%");
        System.out.println();
        showTable(table);
    }

    /**
     Precondition: The array displayArray has 10 rows and 6 columns.
     Postcondition: The array contents are displayed with dollar signs.
    */
    public static void showTable(int[][] displayArray)
    {
        int row, column;
        for (row = 0; row < 10; row++)
        {
            System.out.print((row + 1) + "        ");
            for (column = 0; column < 6; column++)
                System.out.print("$" + displayArray[row][column] + "  ");
            System.out.println();
        }
    }

    public static int balance(double startBalance, int years, double rate)
    <The rest of the definition of balance is the same as in Display 6.17.>
}
```

We will give a better definition of showTable *later in the chapter.*

The output is the same as in Display 6.17.

If you want to return a multidimensional array, you use the same sort of type specification as you use for a multidimensional-array parameter. For example, the following
method returns a two-dimensional array with base type `double`:

```
/**
 Precondition: Each dimension of startArray is at least
 the value of size.
 The array returned is the same as the size-by-size
 upper left corner of the array startArray.
*/
public static double[][] corner(double[][] startArray, int size)
{
    double[][] temp = new double[size][size];
    int row, column;
    for (row = 0; row < size; row++)
        for (column = 0; column < size; column++)
            temp[row][column] = startArray[row][column];
    return temp;
}
```

Implementation of Multidimensional Arrays

In Java, multidimensional arrays are implemented using one-dimensional arrays. For
example, consider the array

```
int[][] table = new int[10][6];
```

The array `table` is in fact a one-dimensional array of length 10, and its base type is the
type `int[]`. In other words, multidimensional arrays are arrays of arrays.

Normally, you do not need to be concerned with the fact that multidimensional arrays
are arrays of arrays. This detail is handled automatically by the compiler. However, there
are a few occasions when you can profitably use your knowledge of this detail. For example, suppose you want to write a `for` loop to fill a two-dimensional array with values. In
the program in Display 6.18, we used the constants 6 and 10 to control the `for` loops. It

would be better style, however, to use the `length` instance variable to control the `for`
loops. But when using the `length` instance variable, you need to think in terms of arrays
of arrays. For example, the following is a rewrite of the nested `for` loop in the `main`
method in Display 6.18:

```
for (row = 0; row < table.length; row++)
    for (column = 0; column < table[row].length; column++)
        table[row][column] =
                        balance(1000.00, row + 1, (5 + 0.5*column));
```

Let's analyze this nested `for` loop in a bit more detail. The array `table` is created with
the following:

```
int[][] table = new int[10][6];
```

This means that `table` is actually a one-dimensional array of length 10, and each of
the 10 indexed variables `table[0]` through `table[9]` is a one-dimensional array with
base type `int` and with a length of 6. That is why the first `for` loop is terminated using

`table.length`. For a two-dimensional array like `table`, the value of `length` is the number of first indices or, equivalently, the number of rows—in this case, `10`. Now let's consider the second `for` loop.

The 0th row in the two-dimensional array `table` is the one-dimensional array `table[0]`, and it has `table[0].length` entries. More generally, `table[row]` is a one-dimensional array of `int`s, and it has `table[row].length` entries. That is why the second `for` loop is terminated using `table[row].length`. Of course, in this case, `table[0].length, table[1].length,...table[9].length` all happen to equal 6.

You can use the fact that multidimensional arrays are arrays of arrays to rewrite the method `showTable` in Display 6.18. Notice that in Display 6.18, the method `showTable` assumes that its array argument has 10 rows and 6 columns. That is fine for this particular program, but a nicer definition of `showTable` would work for an array of any two dimensions. In Display 6.19, we have redefined the method `showTable` so that its argument can be any two-dimensional array of base type `int` with any number of rows and any number of columns.

Quick Reference: Multidimensional-Array Parameters

An argument to a method may be an entire multidimensional array. The syntax is almost identical to that of one-dimensional array parameters, except that more square brackets `[]` are used.

Examples (of multidimensional-array formal parameters):

```
public static void showOneElement(char[][] a, int row, int column)
{
    System.out.print(a[row][column]);
}

public static void reinitialize(int[][] anArray)
{
    int row, column;
    for (row = 0; row < anArray.length; row++)
        for (column = 0; column < anArray[row].length; column++)
            anArray[row][column] = 0;
}
```

`length` is explained in the subsection "Implementation of Multidimensional Arrays."

Examples (of array arguments):

```
char[][] page = new char[100][80];
int[][] a = new int[10][20];
int[][] b = new int[30][40];
   <Some code to fill the arrays goes here.>
showOneElement(page, 5, 10);
reinitialize(a);
reinitialize(b);
```

Note that the arrays a and b have different dimensions. Also note that no square brackets are used with array arguments.

(The preceding examples are in a method definition. All method definitions are assumed to be in the same class.)

■ DISPLAY 6.19 **The Method** showTable **Redefined**

```java
/**
 The array displayArray can have any dimensions.
 Postcondition: The array contents are displayed with dollar signs.
*/
public static void showTable(int[][] displayArray)
{
    int row, column;
    for (row = 0; row < displayArray.length; row++)
    {
        System.out.print((row + 1) + "       ");
        for (column = 0; column < displayArray[row].length; column++)
            System.out.print("$" + displayArray[row][column] + "  ");
        System.out.println();
    }
}
```

The program InterestTable3 *on the accompanying CD uses this method in a complete program.*

This version of showTable *will work for an array with any number of rows and any number of columns. In the program in Display 6.18, this version would behave the same as the version given in Display 6.18, but this version is more versatile and can be used in more different situations.*

Quick Reference: **Returning a Multidimensional Array**

A method can return a multidimensional array value. The syntax is almost identical to that used to return one-dimensional arrays, except that more square brackets [] are used.

Syntax:

```
public static Base_Type[]...[] Method_Name(Parameter_List)
Method_Body
```

You can use other modifiers instead of public static.

Examples (assumed to be in a class definition):

```
public static char[][] blankPage(
                    int numberOfLines, int charPerLine)
{
    char[][] newArray = new char[numberOfLines][charPerLine];
    int line, character;
    for (line = 0; line < numberOfLines; line++)
        for (character = 0; character < charPerLine; character++)
            newArray[line][character] = ' ';
    return newArray;
}
```

Ragged Arrays *(Optional)*

Since a two-dimensional array in Java is an array of arrays, there is no need for each row to have the same number of entries. To phrase it slightly differently, different rows can have different numbers of columns. These sorts of arrays are called **ragged arrays.**

To illustrate what is involved, let's start with an ordinary, nonragged two-dimensional array, created as follows:

```
int[][] a = new int[3][5];
```

This is equivalent to the following:

```
int[][] a;
a = new int[3][];
a[0] = new int[5];
a[1] = new int[5];
a[2] = new int[5];
```

The line

```
a = new int[3][];
```

makes a the name of an array of length 3, each entry of which is a name for an array of `int`s that can be of any length. The next three lines each create an array of `int`s of length 5 to be named by a[0], a[1], and a[2]. The net result is a two-dimensional array of base type `int` with three rows and five columns.

The statements

```
a[0] = new int[5];
a[1] = new int[5];
a[2] = new int[5];
```

invite the question: "Do all the lengths need to be 5?" The answer is *no*. In what follows, we define a similar (but ragged) array b in which each row has a different length:

```
int[][] b;
b = new int[3][];
b[0] = new int[5];
b[1] = new int[7];
b[2] = new int[4];
```

It is worth noting that after you fill the preceding array b with values, you can display the array using the method `showTable` as defined in Display 6.19. However, you could not display b using the method `showTable` as defined in Display 6.18.

There are situations in which you can profitably use ragged arrays, but most applications do not require them. However, if you understand ragged arrays, you will have a better understanding of how all multidimensional arrays work in Java.

Programming Example
Employee Time Records

In this programming example, a two-dimensional array named `hours` is used to store the number of hours worked by each employee of a company for each of the five days Monday through Friday. The first array index is used to designate a day of the week, and the second array index is used to designate an employee. The two-dimensional array is a private instance variable in a class named `TimeBook` in Display 6.20. The class includes a demonstration program in the method `main` that works for a small company with only three employees. The employees are numbered starting with 1, and the array indices are numbered starting with 0, so an adjustment of minus 1 is sometimes needed when specifying and employee's array index. For example, the hours worked by employee number 3 on Tuesday is recorded in `hours[1][2]`. The first index denotes the second work day of the week (Tuesday), and the second index denotes the third employee. Days are numbered 0 for Monday, 1 for Tuesday, and so forth. Employees are numbered 1, 2, and 3 but are stored in array index positions 0, 1, and 2.

The class `TimeBook` shown in Display 6.20 is not yet complete. It needs more methods to be a really useful class, but it has enough methods for the demonstration program in `main`. You can think of the definition in Display 6.20 as a first pass at writing the class definition. It even still has a stub for the definition of the method `setHours`. Recall that a stub is a definition of a method that can be used for testing, but that is not the final method definition. In one of the Programming Projects, you are asked to complete this class definition, but at this stage, it is complete enough to illustrate the use of the two-dimensional array `hours`, which is an instance variable of the class.

The class `TimeBook` uses two ordinary one-dimensional arrays as instance variables, in addition to the two-dimensional array `hours`. The array `weekHours` is used to record the total hours worked in a week for each of the employees. The method `computeWeekHours` sets `weekHours[0]` equal to the total number of hours worked by employee 1 in the week, `weekHours[1]` equal to the total number of hours worked by employee 2 in the week, and so forth.

The array `dayHours` is used to record the total number of hours worked by all the employees on each day of the week. The method `computeDayHours` sets `dayHours[0]` equal to the total number of hours worked on Monday by all of the employees combined, sets `dayHours[1]` equal to the total number of hours worked on Tuesday by all of the employees, and so forth. Display 6.21 illustrates the relationships among the arrays `hours`, `weekHours`, and `dayHours`. In that display, we have shown some sample data for the array `hours`. These data, in turn, determine the values stored in `weekHours` and in `dayHours`.

stub

weekHours

dayHours

■ DISPLAY 6.20 **Time-Keeping Program** *(Part 1 of 4)*

```java
/**
 Class for a one-week record of the time worked by
 each employee. Uses a five-day week (Mon.-Fri.).
 main has a sample application.
*/
public class TimeBook
{
    private int numberOfEmployees;
    private int[][] hours;
        //hours[i][j] has the hours for employee j on day i.
    private int[] weekHours;
        //weekHours[i] has the week's hours worked for
        //employee i+1.
    private int[] dayHours;
        //dayHours[i] has the total hours worked by all
        //employees on day i. Monday is 0, Tuesday 1, etc.

    /**
     Reads hours worked for each employee on each day of
     the week into the two-dimensional array hours. (The method
     for input is just a stub in this preliminary version.)
     Computes the total weekly hours for each employee and
     the total daily hours for all employees combined.
    */
    public static void main(String[] args)
    {
        TimeBook book = new TimeBook(3);
        book.setHours();
        book.update();
        book.showTable();
    }
```

A real class would have more methods. We have shown only the methods used in `main`

```java
    public TimeBook(int theNumberOfEmployees)
    {
        numberOfEmployees = theNumberOfEmployees;
        hours = new int[5][numberOfEmployees];
        //the 5 is for the 5 days Monday through Friday.
        weekHours = new int[numberOfEmployees];
        dayHours = new int[5];
    }
```

■ DISPLAY 6.20 **Time-Keeping Program** *(Part 2 of 4)*

```java
public void setHours( ) //This is just a stub.
{
    hours[0][0] = 8;   hours[0][1] = 0;   hours[0][2] = 9;
    hours[1][0] = 8;   hours[1][1] = 0;   hours[1][2] = 9;
    hours[2][0] = 8;   hours[2][1] = 8;   hours[2][2] = 8;
    hours[3][0] = 8;   hours[3][1] = 8;   hours[3][2] = 4;
    hours[4][0] = 8;   hours[4][1] = 8;   hours[4][2] = 8;
}

public void update( )
{
    computeWeekHours( );
    computeDayHours( );
}

private void computeWeekHours( )
{
    int dayNumber, employeeNumber, sum;

    for (employeeNumber = 1;
            employeeNumber <= numberOfEmployees; employeeNumber++)
    {//Process one employee:
        sum = 0;
        for(dayNumber = 0; dayNumber < 5; dayNumber++)
            sum = sum + hours[dayNumber][employeeNumber - 1];
            //sum contains the sum of all the hours worked
            //in one week by employee with number employeeNumber.
        weekHours[employeeNumber - 1] = sum;
    }
}

private void computeDayHours( )
{
    int dayNumber, employeeNumber, sum;

    for (dayNumber = 0; dayNumber < 5; dayNumber++)
    {//Process one day (for all employees):
        sum = 0;
        for (employeeNumber = 1;
                    employeeNumber <= numberOfEmployees;
                                employeeNumber++)
            sum = sum + hours[dayNumber][employeeNumber - 1];
            //sum contains the sum of all hours worked by all
            //employees on day dayNumber.
        dayHours[dayNumber] = sum;
    }
}
```

■ DISPLAY 6.20 **Time-Keeping Program** *(Part 3 of 4)*

```java
public void showTable()                     The method showTable can and
{                                           should be made more robust. See
    int row, column;                        Programming Project 6.
    System.out.print("Employee  ");
    for (column = 0; column < numberOfEmployees; column++)
        System.out.print((column + 1) + "    ");
    System.out.println("Totals");
    System.out.println();

    for (row = 0; row < 5; row++)
    {
        System.out.print(day(row) + " ");
        for (column = 0; column < hours[row].length; column++)
            System.out.print(hours[row][column] + "    ");
        System.out.println(dayHours[row]);
    }
    System.out.println();

    System.out.print("Total  =  ");
    for (column = 0; column < numberOfEmployees; column++)
        System.out.print(weekHours[column] + "  ");
    System.out.println();
}

//Converts 0 to "Monday", 1 to "Tuesday" etc.
//Blanks used to make all strings the same length.
private String day(int dayNumber)
{
    String dayName = null;
    switch (dayNumber)
    {
        case 0:
            dayName = "Monday   ";
            break;
        case 1:
            dayName = "Tuesday  ";
            break;
        case 2:
            dayName = "Wednesday";
            break;
```

■ DISPLAY 6.20 **Time-Keeping Program** *(Part 4 of 4)*

```
            case 3:
                dayName = "Thursday ";
                break;
            case 4:
                dayName = "Friday    ";
                break;
            default:
                System.out.println("Fatal Error.");
                System.exit(0);
                break;
        }

        return dayName;
    }
}
```

Sample Screen Dialog

```
<In the final program, the stub setHours would be replaced with a real method and
there would then be an input dialog here that obtains the numbers of hours worked by
each employee on each day.>

Employee   1   2   3    Totals

Monday     8   0   9    17
Tuesday    8   0   9    17
Wednesday  8   8   8    24
Thursday   8   8   4    20
Friday     8   8   8    24

Total  =   40  24  38
```

Be sure to notice how the method `computeWeekHours` uses the array indices of the two-dimensional array `hours`. There is a `for` loop nested inside of a `for` loop. The outer `for` loop cycles through all employees and the inner `for` loop is executed once for each day of the week. The inner `for` loop (together with an initialization of the variable `sum` and a following assignment statement) is reproduced here:

```
sum = 0;
for(dayNumber = 0; dayNumber < 5; dayNumber++)
```

```
      sum = sum + hours[dayNumber][employeeNumber - 1];
      //sum contains the sum of all the hours worked
      //in one week by the employee with number employeeNumber.
   weekHours[employeeNumber - 1] = sum;
```

Note that when computing the sum of the hours for one employee, the second index, which represents the particular employee, is held constant.

The method `computeDayHours` works in a similar way to compute the total number of hours worked by all employees on each day of the week. However, in this case, the inner `for` loop cycles through the second index while the first index is held constant. Or, to phrase it another way, the roles of the employee index and the day of the week index are interchanged.

The class `TimeBook` is not yet a finished piece of software ready to be saved and reused again and again. What we have done is correct, but it is not yet complete. The method `setHours` is just a stub and needs to be replaced by a more generally applicable method that obtains hours from the user at the keyboard. The method `showTable` will not give a display as neat as the one in Display 6.20 unless all the hours have the same number of digits. Thus, the method `showTable` needs to be made more robust so that it will neatly display any combination of hours worked. Finally, the class `TimeBook` should have more methods so that it will be useful in a wide range of situations. Programming Project 6 asks you to complete the definition of the class `TimeBook` in all of these ways. ■

completing class definition

■ DISPLAY 6.21 **Arrays for the Class** `TimeBook`

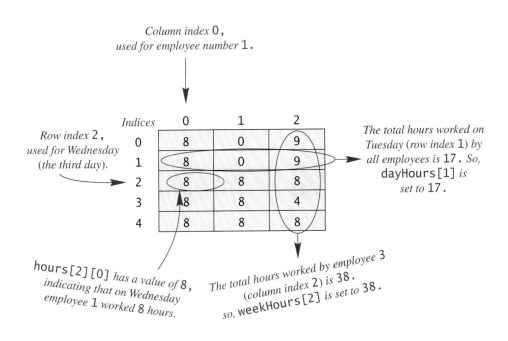

Column index 0, *used for employee number* 1.

Row index 2, *used for Wednesday (the third day).*

Indices

The total hours worked on Tuesday (row index 1*) by all employees is* 17*. So,* `dayHours[1]` *is set to* 17*.*

`hours[2][0]` *has a value of* 8, *indicating that on Wednesday employee* 1 *worked* 8 *hours.*

The total hours worked by employee 3 *(column index* 2*) is* 38*. so,* `weekHours[2]` *is set to* 38*.*

22. What is the output produced by the following code?

```java
int[][] testArray = new int[4][4];
int index1, index2;
for (index1 = 0; index1 < testArray.length; index1++)
    for (index2 = 0; index2 < testArray[index1].length; index2++)
        testArray[index1][index2] = index2;
for (index1 = 0; index1 < testArray.length; index1++)
{
    for (index2 = 0; index2 < testArray[index1].length; index2++)
        System.out.print(testArray[index1][index2] + " ");
    System.out.println();
}
```

23. Write code that will fill the array a (declared as follows) with numbers typed at the keyboard:

```java
int[][] a = new int [4][5];
```

The numbers will be input five per line, on four lines (although your solution need not depend on how the input numbers are divided into lines).

24. Write a method definition for a void method called display such that the following invocation will display the contents of the array a in Self-Test Question 23 and will display it in the same format as we specified for the input there (that is, four lines of five numbers per line):

```java
display(a);
```

Your method definition should also work for two-dimensional arrays that have sizes other than 4 by 5. Make your method a static method that can be added to a class.

CHAPTER SUMMARY

■ An array can be thought of as a collection of variables all of the same type.

■ Arrays are objects that are created with new just like the class objects we discussed before this chapter (although there is a slight difference in the syntax used).

■ Array indexed variables are numbered starting with 0 and ending with the number that is 1 less than the length of the array. If a is an array, then a[i] is an indexed variable of the array a. The index i must have a value greater than or equal to 0 and strictly less than a.length. If i has any other value, that is called an **array index out of bounds error** and will cause an error message when you run your program.

▪ When an indexed variable is used as an argument to a method, it is treated just like any other argument of the base type. In particular, if the base type is a primitive type, the method cannot change the value of the indexed variable, but if the base type is a class, the method can change the element at the indexed variable.

▪ A method may return an array as the value returned by the method.

▪ When you use only part of an array, you normally store values in an initial segment of the array and use an `int` variable to keep track of how many values are stored in the array. This is called a partially filled array.

▪ An accessor method that returns an array corresponding to a private instance variable of an array type should be careful to return a copy of the array, and not to return the private instance variable itself.

▪ The selection sort algorithm can be used to sort an array of values, such as numbers sorted into either increasing or decreasing order.

▪ You can have arrays with more than one index. These are known as multidimensional arrays.

▪ A two-dimensional array can be thought of as a two-dimensional table, with the first index giving the row and the second index giving the column.

▪ Multidimensional arrays are implemented in Java as arrays of arrays.

✔ Answers to Self-Test Questions

1. 0 2 4 6 8 10 12 14 16 18

2.
```
a
e
i
o
u
```

3.
```
Tide 1 is −7.3
Tide 2 is 14.2
```

4. The `for` loop references elements `b[1]` through `b[10]`, but there is no element indexed by 10. The array elements are `b[0]` through `b[9]`. If included in a complete class or program, the code will compile without any error messages, but when it is run, you will get an error message saying that an array index is out of bounds.

5. The last index of a is 9. The value of a.length is 10.

6.
```
public class Exercise
{
    public static void main(String[] args)
    {
        double[] a = new double[20];

        int index;
        System.out.println("Enter 20 numbers:");
        for (index = 0; index < a.length; index++)
            a[index] = SavitchIn.readLineDouble( );

        System.out.println(
            "The numbers and differences from last number are:");
        for (index = 0; index < a.length; index++)
            System.out.println(a[index]
              + " differs from last by "
              + (a[a.length - 1] - a[index]));
    }
}
```

7.
```
SalesAssociate[] entry = new SalesAssociate[3];
int i;
for (i = 0; i < entry.length; i++)
    entry[i] = new SalesAssociate("Jane Doe", 5000);
```

8. The lines that are changed are shown in color in the following code. Note that you should also change the definition of the method writeOutput in the class SalesAssociate. We have also shown this method in the following code. Remember that you must make the class Dollars available, either by placing it in the same directory or by putting it in a package and importing the package.

```
/**
 Displays sales report on console screen.
*/
public void displayResults()
{
    System.out.println("Average sales per associate is $" + average);
    System.out.println("The highest sales figure is $" + highest);
    System.out.println();
    int i;
    System.out.println("The following had the highest sales:");
    for (i = 0; i < numberOfAssociates; i++)
    {
        double nextSales = record[i].getSales();
        if (nextSales == highest)
```

```
            {
                record[i].writeOutput();
                Dollars.write(nextSales - average);
                System.out.println(" above the average.");
                System.out.println();
            }
        }

    System.out.println("The rest performed as follows:");
    for (i = 0; i < numberOfAssociates; i++)
    {
        double nextSales = record[i].getSales();
        if (record[i].getSales() != highest)
        {
            record[i].writeOutput();
            if (nextSales >= average)
            {
                Dollars.write(nextSales - average);
                System.out.println(" above the average.");
            }
            else
            {
                Dollars.write(average - nextSales);
                System.out.println(" below the average.");
            }

            System.out.println();
        }
    }
}
```

The following is the rewritten version of the method `writeOutput` of the class `SalesAssociate`, with the changes shown in color:

```
public void writeOutput()
{
    System.out.println("Sales associates: " + name);
    System.out.print("Sales: ");
    Dollars.writeln(sales);
}
```

9.

```
a[1] = a b[1] = a
a[2] = a b[2] = a
a[1] = a b[1] = a
a[2] = b b[2] = b
```

10.

```
public static void showArray(char[] a)
{
```

```
        int i;
        for (i = 0; i < a.length; i++)
            System.out.print(a[i]);
        System.out.println();//This line is optional.
    }
```

11.

```
    public static double[] halfArray(double[] a)
    {
        double[] temp = new double[a.length];
        int i;
        for (i = 0; i < a.length; i++)
            temp[i] = a[i]/2.0;
        return temp;
    }
```

12. If **b** is an array of length 10, the invocation

```
    doubleSize(b);
```

will run with no error messages, but the length of **b** will not change. In fact, nothing about **b** will change. The parameter **a** is a local variable that is initialized with a reference to **b**. The local variable **a** is changed so that it contains a reference to an array of twice the size of **b**, but that reference goes away as soon as the invocation ends.

13.

```
    int i;
    for (i = 0; i < a.length; i++)
        System.out.println(a[i]);
```

14.

```
    int i;
    for (i = 0; i < numberUsed; i++)
        System.out.println(a[i]);
```

15. `a[0]`, `a[1]`, and `a[2]`.

16.

```
    a[numberUsed] = 42;
    numberUsed++;
```

17.

```
    if (numberUsed == a.length)
        System.out.println("List is full. Cannot add 42.");
    else
    {
        a[numberUsed] = 42;
        numberUsed++;
    }
```

18.

```
SelectionSort.sort(myArray);
```

19. Just change the types for the array elements to double. You can simply replace all occurrences of int with double, *except for those occurrences of* int *that give the type of an index.* For example, you would replace

```
private static void interchange(int i, int j, int[] a)
```

with

```
private static void interchange(int i, int j, double[] a)
```

Note that i and j are indices, and so they are still of type int.

20. All you need to do to make your code work for sorting into decreasing order is to replace the < with > in the following line of the definition of indexOfSmallest:

```
if (a[index] < min)
```

However, to make your code more readable, you should rename the method indexOfSmallest to something like indexOfLargest, rename the variable min to something like max, and rename the variable indexOfMin to something like indexOfMax. You should also rewrite some of the comments.

21. If an array of base type int has a value that occurs twice, and you sort the array using the method SelectionSort.sort, there will be two copies of the repeated value after the array is sorted.

22.

```
0 1 2 3
0 1 2 3
0 1 2 3
0 1 2 3
```

23.

```
int[][] a = new int [4][5];
int row, column;

System.out.println("Enter numbers:");
for (row = 0; row < 4; row++)
    for (column = 0; column < 5; column++)
        a[row][column] = SavitchIn.readInt();
```

Alternatively, you could use

```
System.out.println("Enter numbers:");
for (row = 0; row < a.length; row++)
    for (column = 0; column < a[row].length; column++)
        a[row][column] = SavitchIn.readInt();
```

24.
```
public static void display(int[][] anArray)
{
    int row, column;
    for (row = 0; row < anArray.length; row++)
    {
        for (column = 0; column < anArray[row].length;
                                              column++)
            System.out.print(anArray[row][column] + " ");
        System.out.println();
    }
}
```

● Programming Projects

1. Write a program that reads in a list of `int` values, one per line, and outputs their sum as well as all the numbers read in, with each number annotated to say what percentage it contributes to the sum. Your program will ask the user how many integers there will be, create an array of that length, and then fill the array with the integers input. A possible dialog is

```
How many numbers will you enter?
4
Enter 4 integers, one per line:
2
1
1
2
The sum is 6.
The numbers are:
2 33.3333% of the sum.
1 16.6666% of the sum.
1 16.6666% of the sum.
2 33.3333% of the sum.
```

Use a method that takes the entire array as one argument and returns the sum of the numbers in the array.

2. Write a program that will read in a line of text and output a list of all the letters that occur in the text, along with the number of times each letter occurs. End the line with a period that serves as a sentinel value. The letters should be listed in alphabetical order when they are output. Use an array of base type `int` of length 26, so that each indexed variable contains the count of how many letters there are. Array indexed variable 0 contains the number of a's, array indexed variable 1 contains the number of b's, and so forth. Allow both uppercase and lowercase letters as input, but treat uppercase and lowercase versions of the same letter as being equal. *Hints:* You will want to use one of the functions `toUpperCase` or `toLowerCase` in the wrapper class `Character` described in Chapter 5. You will find it

helpful to define a method that takes a character as an argument and returns an `int` value that is the correct index for that character, such as `'a'` returning 0, `'b'` returning 1, and so forth. Note that you can use a type cast to change a `char` to an `int`, like `(int)letter`. Of course, this will not get the number you want, but if you subtract `(int)'a'`, you will then get the right index. Allow the user to repeat this task until the user says she or he is through.

3. A **palindrome** is a string that reads the same forward and backward, such as `"warts n straw"` or `"radar"`. Write a program that will accept a string of characters terminated by a period and will determine whether or not the string (without the period) is a palindrome. You may assume that the input contains only letters and the blank symbol. You may also assume that the input word is at most 80 characters long. Disregard blanks when deciding if a string is a palindrome, and consider uppercase and lowercase versions of the same letter to be equal, so the following will be considered a palindrome by your program:

   `"Able was I ere I saw Elba"`

   Your program need not check that the string is a correct English phrase or word. The string `"xyzczyx"` will be considered a palindrome by your program. Include a loop that allows the user to check additional strings until the she or he requests that program end. For this exercise, you should define a static method called `palindrome` that begins as follows:

   ```
   /**
    Precondition: The array a contains letters and
    blanks in positions a[0] through a[used - 1].
    Returns true if the string is a palindrome and
    false otherwise.
   */
   public static boolean palindrome(char[] a, int used)
   ```

   Your program will read the input string into an array with base type `char` and will call the preceding method with the array and one other `int` variable. The other `int` variable keeps track of how much of the array is used, as described in the subsection entitled "Partially Filled Arrays."

4. Design a class called `BubbleSort` that is similar to the class `SelectionSort` given in Display 6.13. The class `BubbleSort` will be used in exactly the same way as the class `SelectionSort`, but it will use the bubble sort algorithm.

   The bubble sort algorithm goes through all adjacent pairs of elements in the array from the beginning to the end and interchanges any two elements that are out of order. This brings the array closer to being sorted. This procedure is repeated until the array is sorted. The algorithm in pseudocode is as follows:

   ### Bubble Sort Algorithm to Sort an Array a

   Repeat the following until the array a is sorted:
   ```
   for (index = 0; index < a.length - 1; index++)
   ```

```
      if (a[index] > a[index + 1])
          Interchange the values of a[index] and a[index + 1].
```

The bubble sort algorithm is very efficient for sorting an array that is "almost sort-ed." It is not competitive with other sorting methods for most other situations.

5. Design a class called `InsertionSort` that is similar to the class `Selection-Sort` given in Display 6.13. The class `InsertionSort` will be used in exactly the same way as the class `SelectionSort`, but the class `InsertionSort` will use the insertion sort algorithm.

   The insertion sort algorithm uses an additional array and copies elements from the array to be sorted to the other array. As each element is copied, it is inserted into the correct position in the array. This will usually require moving a number of elements in the array receiving the new elements. The algorithm in pseudocode is as follows:

   ### Insertion Sort Algorithm to Sort an Array a

   ```
   for (index = 0; index < a.length; index++)
       insert the value of a[index] into the array temp so that
           all the elements copied into the array temp so far are sorted.
   Copy all the elements from temp back to a.
   ```

   The array `temp` will be a local variable in the method `sort`. The array `temp` will be a partially filled array. So, when it is only partially filled, all the values will be at the beginning of the array `temp`.

6. The class `TimeBook` in Display 6.20 is not really finished. Complete the defi-nition of this class in the way described in the text. In particular, be sure to add a default constructor, accessor methods to recover and change each of the in-stance variables, and each indexed variable of each array instance variable. Be sure you replace the stub `setHours` with a method that obtains values from the keyboard. You should also define a private method with two `int` parame-ters that will output the first `int` parameter in the number of spaces given by a second parameter. The extra spaces not filled by the first `int` parameter are to be filled with blanks. This will let you, for example, write each array in-dexed element in exactly four spaces (or however many spaces you want), and so will allow you to output neat rectangular displays of array elements. Be sure that the `main` method in Display 6.20 works correctly with these new methods. Also, write a separate test program to test all the new methods. *Hint:* To output an `int` value *n* in a fixed number of spaces, use `Integer.toString(n)` to convert the number to a string value, and then work with the string value. This is discussed in the subsection "`Integer`, `Double`, and Other Wrapper Class-es" in Chapter 5.

7. Write a class definition for a class called `TicTacToe`. An object of type `TicTac-Toe` is a single game of `TicTacToe`. Store the game board as a single two-dimen-sional array of base type `char` that has three rows and three columns. Include methods to add a move, to display the board, to tell whose turn it is (X or O), to

tell whether there is a winner, to say who the winner is, and to reinitialize the game to the beginning. Write a main method for the class that will allow users to play the game at the terminal and keyboard. Both players will sit at the keyboard and enter their moves in turn.

Inheritance

7

Like mother, like daughter. - Common saying

This chapter covers inheritance, one of the key concepts in object-oriented programming and one that is needed in order to use many of the libraries that come with the Java programming language. Inheritance will allow you to use an existing class to define new classes, making it easier to reuse software.

OBJECTIVES

Become familiar with inheritance in general.

Learn how to define and use derived classes in Java.

Learn about dynamic binding and polymorphism in general and in Java.

PREREQUISITES

You need to have read the material in Chapters 1 through 5 before you can understand this chapter. Chapter 6 is not needed for this chapter.

7.1 INHERITANCE BASICS

All men are mortal
Socrates is a man.
Therefore Socrates is mortal. -Typical syllogism

inheritance

Inheritance allows you to define a very general class and then later define more specialized classes simply by adding some new details to the older, more general class definition. This saves work, because the more specialized class *inherits* all the properties of the general class and you, the programmer, need only program the new features.

For example, you might define a class for vehicles that has instance variables to record the vehicle's number of wheels and maximum number of occupants. You might then define a class for automobiles and let the automobile class inherit all the instance variables and methods of the class for vehicles. The class for automobiles would have added instance variables for such things as the amount of fuel in the fuel tank and the license plate number, and would also have some added methods. (Some vehicles, such as a horse and wagon, have no fuel tank and normally no license plate, but an automobile is a vehicle that has these "added" items.) You would have to describe the added instance variables and added methods, but if you used Java's inheritance mechanism, you would get the instance variables and methods from the vehicle class automatically.

Before we construct an example of inheritance within Java, we first need to set the stage. We'll do so with the following Programming Example.

Programming Example
A Person Class

Display 7.1 contains a simple class called `Person`. This class is so simple that the only property it gives a person is a name. We will not have much use for the class `Person` by itself, but we will use it when defining other classes.

Most of the methods for the class `Person` are straightforward. For example, the method `sameName` is similar to the `equals` methods we've seen, but note that it considers uppercase and lowercase versions of a letter to be the same when comparing names. ■

sameName

■ DISPLAY 7.1   **A Base Class**

```java
public class Person
{
    private String name;

    public Person()
    {
        name = "No name yet.";
    }

    public Person(String initialName)
    {
        name = initialName;
    }

    public void setName(String newName)
    {
        name = newName;
    }

    public String getName()
    {
        return name;
    }

    public void writeOutput()
    {
        System.out.println("Name: " + name);
    }

    public boolean sameName(Person otherPerson)
    {
        return (this.name.equalsIgnoreCase(otherPerson.name));
    }
}
```

Derived Classes

Suppose we are designing a college record-keeping program that has records for students, faculty, and (nonteaching) staff. There is a natural hierarchy for grouping these record types: They are all records of people. Students are one subclass of people. Another subclass is employees, which includes both faculty and staff. Students divide into two smaller subclasses: undergraduate students and graduate students. These subclasses may further subdivide into still smaller subclasses.

Display 7.2 depicts a part of this hierarchical arrangement. Although your program may not need any class corresponding to people or employees, thinking in terms of such classes can be useful. For example, all people have names, and the methods of initializing, outputting, and changing a name will be the same for student, staff, and faculty records. In Java, you can define a class called `Person` that includes instance variables for the properties that belong to all subclasses of people, such as students, faculty, and staff. The class definition can also contain all the methods that manipulate the instance variables for the class `Person`. In fact, we have already defined such a `Person` class in Display 7.1.

Display 7.3 contains the definition of a class for students. A student is a person, so we
derived class   define the class `Student` to be a **derived class** of the class `Person`. A derived class is a class defined by adding instance variables and methods to an existing class. The existing
base class   class that the derived class is built upon is called the **base class.** In our example, `Person` is the base class and `Student` is the derived class. If you look at Display 7.3, you will see how we indicated that `Student` is a derived class of `Person`: We included the phrase
extends   `extends Person` on the first line of the class definition, so that the class definition of `Student` begins

```
public class Student extends Person
```

■ DISPLAY 7.2   **A Class Hierarchy**

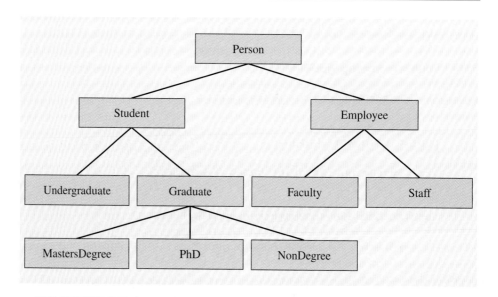

■ DISPLAY 7.3   **A Derived Class**

```java
public class Student extends Person
{
    private int studentNumber;

    public Student()
    {
        super();
        studentNumber = 0;//Indicating no number yet
    }

    public Student(String initialName, int initialStudentNumber)
    {
        super(initialName);
        studentNumber = initialStudentNumber;
    }

    public void reset(String newName, int newStudentNumber)
    {
        setName(newName);
        studentNumber = newStudentNumber;
    }

    public int getStudentNumber()
    {
        return studentNumber;
    }

    public void setStudentNumber(int newStudentNumber)
    {
        studentNumber = newStudentNumber;
    }

    public void writeOutput()
    {
        System.out.println("Name: " + getName());
        System.out.println("Student Number: " + studentNumber);
    }

    public boolean equals(Student otherStudent)
    {
        return (this.sameName(otherStudent)
            && (this.studentNumber == otherStudent.studentNumber));
    }
}
```

super is explained in a later section. Do not worry about it until you reach the discussion of it in the text.

When you define a derived class, you give only the added instance variables and the added methods. For example, the class `Student` has all the instance variables and all the methods of the class `Person`, but we do not mention them in the definition of `Student`. Every object of the class `Student` has an instance variable called `name`, but we do not specify the instance variable `name` in the definition of the class `Student`. The class `Student` (or any other derived class) is said to **inherit** the instance variables and methods of the base class that it extends.

Suppose you create a new object of the class `Student` as follows:

```
Student s = new Student( );
```

There is now an instance variable `s.name`. Because `name` is a private instance variable, it is not valid to write `s.name` (outside of the definition of the class `Person`), but the instance variable is there, and it can be accessed and changed. For example, `s.name` can be changed using the inherited public method `setName`, as in the following:

```
s.setName("Warren Peace");
```

The class `Student` inherits the method `setName` and all the other methods of the base class `Person`.

A derived class, like `Student`, can also add some instance variables or methods to those it inherits from its base class. For example, `Student` adds the instance variable `studentNumber` and the methods `reset`, `getStudentNumber`, `setStudentNumber`, `writeOutput`, and `equals`, as well as some constructors. (We will postpone the discussion of constructors until we finish explaining the other parts of these class definitions.)

Display 7.4 contains a very small demonstration program to illustrate inheritance. Notice that the object `s` of the class `Student` can invoke the method `setName`, even though this is a method of its base class `Person`. The class `Student` inherits `setName` from the class `Person`.

Quick Reference: **Derived Class**

You define a **derived class** by starting with another already defined class and adding (or changing) methods and instance variables. The class you start with is called the **base class**. The derived class inherits all of the methods and instance variables from the base class and can add more instance variables or methods.

Syntax:

```
public class Derived_Class_Name extends Base_Class_Name
{
        Declarations_of_Added_Instance_Variables
        Definitions_of_Added__And_Overridden_Methods
}
```

Syntax:

See Display 7.3.

■ DISPLAY 7.4   **Demonstrating Inheritance**

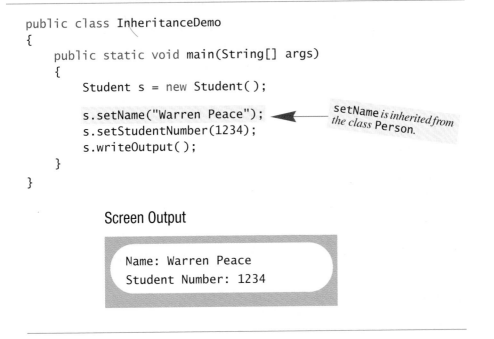

```
public class InheritanceDemo
{
    public static void main(String[] args)
    {
        Student s = new Student();

        s.setName("Warren Peace");
        s.setStudentNumber(1234);
        s.writeOutput();
    }
}
```

setName *is inherited from the class* Person.

Screen Output

```
Name: Warren Peace
Student Number: 1234
```

Overriding Method Definitions

In the definition of the class Student, we added a method called writeOutput that has no parameters (Display 7.3). But the class Person also has a method called writeOutput that has no parameters. If the class Student were to inherit the method writeOutput from the base class Person, then Student would contain two methods with the name writeOutput, both of which have no parameters. Java has a rule to avoid this problem. If a derived class defines a method with the same name as a method in the base class, and that method *also has the same number and types of parameters as in the base class*, then the definition in the derived class is said to **override** the definition in the base class. In other words, the definition in the derived class is the one that is used for objects of the derived class.

overriding a method

For example, in Display 7.4, the following invocation of the method writeOutput for the object s of the class Student will use the definition of writeOutput in the class Student, not the definition in the class Person:

```
    s.writeOutput();
```

When overriding a method, you can change the body of the method definition to anything you wish, but you cannot make any changes in the method's heading. In particular, when overriding a method definition, you cannot change the return type of the method.

Quick Reference: Overriding Method Definitions

In a derived class, if you include a method definition that has the same name and the *exact* same number and types of parameters as a method already in the base class, then *for the derived class*, this new definition replaces the old definition of the method.

In such cases, the return type for the overriding method definition must be the same as the return type for the method in the base class. That is, when overriding a method definition, you cannot change the return type of the method.

Overriding Versus Overloading

Do not confuse method *overriding* with method *overloading*. When you override a method definition, the new method definition given in the derived class has the exact same number and types of parameters. On the other hand, if the method in the derived class were to have a different number of parameters or a parameter of a different type from the method in the base class, then the derived class would have both methods. That would be overloading. For example, suppose we added the following method to the definition of the class Student (Display 7.3):

```
public String getName(String title)
{
    return (title + getName());
}
```

In this case, the class Student would have two methods named getName: It would inherit the method getName, with no parameters, from the base class Person (Display 7.1), and it would also have the method named getName, with one parameter, that we just defined. This is because these two methods called getName have different numbers of parameters, and thus the method is overloaded.

If you get overloading and overriding confused, you do have one small consolation. They are both valid.

The final Modifier

final

If you want to specify that a method definition cannot be overridden with a new definition in a derived class, you can do so by adding the final modifier to the method heading, as in the following sample heading:

```
public final void specialMethod()
{
        .
        .
        .
```

You are not very likely to need this modifier, but you are likely to see it in the specification of some methods in standard Java libraries.

If a method is declared to be final, the compiler knows more about how it will be used, and so the compiler can generate more efficient code for the method.

An entire class can be declared final, in which case you cannot use it as a base class to derive any other class.

▲ *Gotcha*

Use of Private Instance Variables from the Base Class

An object of the class `Student` (Display 7.3) inherits an instance variable called `name` from the class `Person` (Display 7.1). For example, the following would set the value of the instance variable `name` of the object `joe` to `"Josephine"`: (This also sets the instance variable `studentNumber` to 9891.)

```
Student joe = new Student("Josephine", 9891);
```

If you want to change `joe.name` (and `joe.studentNumber`), you can do so as follows:

```
joe.reset("Joesy", 9892);
```

But you must be a bit careful about how you manipulate inherited instance variables such as `name`. The instance variable `name` of the class `Student` was inherited from the class `Person`, but the instance variable `name` is a private instance variable in the definition of the class `Person`. This means that `name` can be directly accessed only within the definition of a method in the class `Person`. An instance variable (or method) that is private in a base class is not accessible *by name* in the definition of a method for *any other class, not even in a method definition of a derived class.*

For example, the following is the definition of the method `reset` from the definition of the class `Student`:

```
public void reset(String newName, int newStudentNumber)
{
    setName(newName);                          Valid definition
    studentNumber = newStudentNumber;
}
```

You might have wondered why we needed to use the method `setName` to set the value of the `name` instance variable. You might be tempted to rewrite the method definition as follows:

```
public void reset(String newName, int newStudentNumber)
{
    name = newName;//ILLEGAL!                   Illegal definition
    studentNumber = newStudentNumber;
}
```

As the comment indicates, this will not work. The instance variable `name` is a private instance variable in the class `Person`, and although a derived class like `Student` inherits the variable `name`, it cannot access that variable directly. Instead, it must use some public mutator (or accessor) method. The correct way to accomplish the definition of `reset` in the class `Student` is to use the method `setName` to set the `name` instance variable.

The fact that a private instance variable of a base class cannot be accessed in the definition of a method of a derived class often seems wrong to people. After all, students should be able to change their own names, rather than being told "Sorry, `name` is a private instance variable of the class `Person`." If you are a student, you are also a person. In Java, this is also true; an object of the class `Student` is also an object of the class `Person`.

However, the rules regarding the use of private instance variables and methods must be as we've described, or else they would be pointless. If private instance variables of a class were accessible in method definitions of a derived class, then anytime you wanted to access a private instance variable, you could simply create a derived class and access it in a method of that class. This would mean that all private instance variables would be accessible to anybody who wanted to put in a little extra effort. △

● **Programming Tip**
Assume That Your Coworkers Are Malicious

In the previous Gotcha section, we said that the reason private instance variables cannot be accessed by name in a derived class is because otherwise a (malicious) programmer could access them by using a trick. You may argue that your coworkers are not malicious. In fact, in a beginning course you may sometimes be the only programmer on an assignment, and you certainly are not trying to sabotage your own work. Those are good points. However, your coworkers (including you yourself) might inadvertently do something that, although not intended to be malicious, still creates a problem. We think in terms of a malicious programmer, not because we think our coworkers are malicious, but because that is the best way to protect against honest mistakes by well-meaning programmers (including you yourself). ○

▲ *Gotcha*

Private Methods Are Not Inherited

As we noted in the previous Gotcha section, an instance variable (or method) that is private in a base class is not directly accessible in the definition of a method for *any other class, not even in a method definition for a derived class*. Note that private methods are just like private variables in terms of not being directly available. But in the case of methods, the restriction is more dramatic. A private variable can be accessed indirectly via an accessor or mutator method. A private method is simply not available. It is just as if the private method were not inherited.

This should not be a problem. Private methods should serve only as helping methods, and so their use should be limited to the class in which they are defined. If you want a method to serve as a helping method in a number of inherited classes, then it is more than just a helping method, and you should make the method public. △

UML Inheritance Diagrams

Display 7.5 shows a portion of the hierarchy from Display 7.2, but this time we used UML notation. Note that the class diagrams are incomplete. You normally show only as much of the class diagram as you need for the design task at hand. The only significant difference between the notation in Display 7.5 and Display 7.2 is that the lines indicating inheritance

■ DISPLAY 7.5   **A Class Hierarchy in UML Notation**

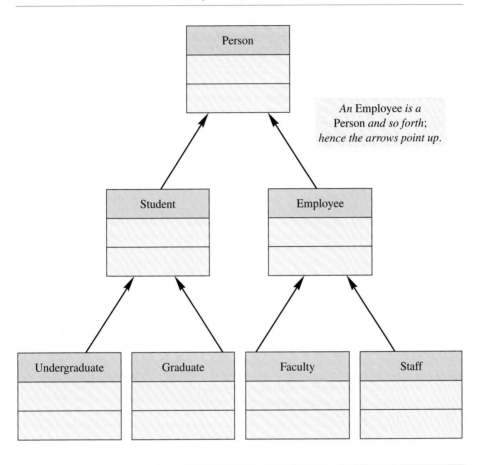

An Employee *is a* Person *and so forth;* *hence the arrows point up.*

in Display 7.5 have arrowheads. Note that the arrow heads point up from derived class to base class. This is because the arrows show the "is a" relationship. For example, a `Student` is a `Person`. In Java terms, an object of type `Student` is also of type `Person`.

"is a" relationship

The arrows also help in locating method definitions. If you are looking for a method definition for some class, the arrows show the path you (or the computer) should follow. If you are looking for the definition of a method used by an object of the class `Undergraduate`, you first look in the definition of the class `Undergraduate`; if it is not there, you look in the definition of `Student`; if it is not there, you look in the definition of the class `Person`.

Display 7.6 shows more details of the inheritance hierarchy for the two classes `Person` and one of its derived classes, `Student`. Suppose `s` is an object of the class `Student`. The diagram in Display 7.6 tells you that you can find the definition of

```
s.writeOutput();
```

and

```
s.reset("Josephine Student", 1234);
```

■ DISPLAY 7.6   Some Details of a UML Class Hierarchy

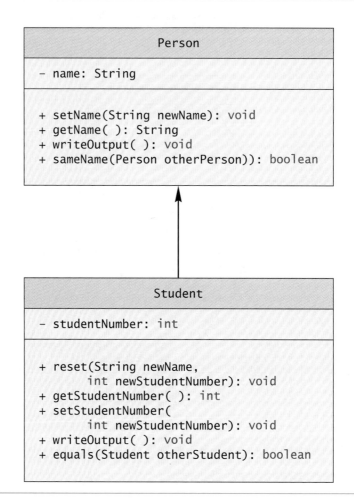

in the class Student, but that the definition of

    s.setName("Joe Student");

is found in the definition of Person.

1. Suppose the class named SportsCar is a derived class of a class called Automobile. Suppose the class Automobile has instance variables named speed, manufacturer, and numberOfCylinders. Will an object of the class SportsCar have instance variables named speed, manufacturer, and numberOfCylinders?

2. Suppose the class named `SportsCar` is a derived class of a class called `Automobile`, and suppose the class `Automobile` has public methods named `accelerate` and `addGas`. Will an object of the class `SportsCar` have methods named `accelerate` and `addGas`? If so, do these methods have to perform the exact same actions in the class `SportsCar` as in the class `Automobile`?

3. If you are defining a derived class, can you directly access a private instance variable of the base class?

4. If you are defining a derived class, can you use a private method of the base class?

5. Suppose `s` is an object of the class `Student`. Based on the inheritance diagram in Display 7.6, where will you find the definition of the method `sameName`, used in the following invocation? Explain your answer.

```
Student other = new Student("Joe Student", 7777);
if (s.sameName(other))
    System.out.println("wow");
```

6. Suppose `s` is an object of the class `Student`. Based on the inheritance diagram in Display 7.6, where will you find the definition of the method used in the following invocation? Explain your answer.

```
s.setStudentNumber(1234);
```

7.2 PROGRAMMING WITH INHERITANCE

You do not have to die in order to pass along your inheritance. -Ad for an estate planning seminar

This section presents some basic programming techniques you need when defining or using derived classes.

Constructors in Derived Classes

A derived class, such as the class `Student` in Display 7.3, has its own constructors. The base class from which it was derived, such as `Person`, also has its own constructors. When defining a constructor for the derived class, the typical first action is to call a constructor of the base class. For example, consider defining a constructor for the class `Student`. One of the things that need to be initialized is the student's name. This name initializing is normally done by the constructors for the base class `Person` (since the instance variable `name` is introduced in the definition of `Person`). For example, consider the following definition of a constructor for the derived class `Student` (from Display 7.3):

```
public Student(String initialName, int initialStudentNumber)
{
    super(initialName);
    studentNumber = initialStudentNumber;
}
```

The line

```
super(initialName);
```

is a call to a constructor for the base class—in this case, a call to a constructor for the class Person. Notice that you use the keyword super to call the constructor of the base class. You do not use the name of the constructor—that is, you do *not* use

```
Person(initialName); //ILLEGAL
```

There are some details to worry about with the use of super: It must always be the first action taken in a constructor definition. You cannot use it later in the definition. If you do not include a call to the base-class constructor, Java will automatically include a call to the default constructor of the base class as the first action of any constructor for a derived class.

Consider the following definition of a constructor for the class Student (Display 7.3):

```
public Student()
{
    super();
    studentNumber = 0;//Indicating no number yet
}
```

This definition is completely equivalent to the following:

```
public Student()
{
    studentNumber = 0;//Indicating no number yet
}
```

Quick Reference: Call to a Base-Class Constructor

When defining a constructor for a derived class, you can use super as a name for the constructor of the base class. Any call to super must be the first action taken by the constructor.

Example:

```
public Student(String initialName, int initialStudentNumber)
{
    super(initialName);
    studentNumber = initialStudentNumber;
}
```

The this Method *(Optional)*

When defining a constructor, another common action is to call one of the other constructors in the same class. You can use the keyword this in a way similar to the way you use super, but with this, the call is to a constructor of the same class, not to a constructor for the base class. For example, consider the following definition of a constructor that you might want to add to the class Student (from Display 7.3):

```
public Student(String initialName)
{
    this(initialName, 0);
}
```

The one statement in the body of this constructor definition is a call to the constructor whose definition begins

```
public Student(String initialName, int initialStudentNumber)
```

As with super, any use of this must be the first action in a constructor definition. Thus, a constructor definition cannot contain both a call using super and a call using this. What if you want to include both a call to super and a call to this? In that case, use a call with this, and have the constructor that is called with this have super as its first action.

Quick Reference: Call to Another Constructor in the Same Class *(Optional)*

When defining a constructor for a class, you can use this as a name for another constructor in the same class. Any call to this must be the first action taken by the constructor.

Example:

```
public Student(String initialName)
{
    this(initialName, 0);
}
```

Call to an Overridden Method

When you are defining a constructor for a derived class, you can use super as a name for the constructor of the base class. You can also use super to call a method of the base class that is overridden (redefined) in the derived class, but the way you do this is a bit different.

For example, consider the method writeOutput for the class Student in Display 7.3. It uses the following to output the name of the Student:

```
System.out.println("Name: " + getName());
```

Alternatively, you could output the name by calling the method writeOutput *of the class* Person (Display 7.1), since the writeOutput method for the class Person will output the person's name. The only problem is that if you use the name writeOutput for a method in the class Student, it will mean the method named writeOutput in the class Student. What you need is a way to say "writeOutput( ) as it is defined in the base class." The way you say that is `super.writeOutput( )`. So an alternative definition of the `writeOutput` method for the class `Student` is the following:

```
public void writeOutput( )
{
    super.writeOutput( );
    System.out.println("Student Number: " + studentNumber);
}
```

If you replace the definition of `writeOutput` in the definition of `Student` (Display 7.3) with the preceding, then the class `Student` will behave exactly the same as it did before.

FAQ: How Do I Call the Old Version of an Overridden Method?

Within the definition of a method of a derived class, you can call an overridden method of the base class by prefacing the method name with `super` and a dot.

Example:

```
public void writeOutput( )
{
    super.writeOutput( );
    System.out.println("Student Number: " + studentNumber);
}
```

Programming Example

Multilevel Derived Classes

You can form a derived class from a derived class. In fact, this is common. For example, in Display 7.7 we have defined the class `Undergraduate`, which is a derived class of the

■ DISPLAY 7.7   **A Derived Class of a Derived Class** *(Part 1 of 2)*

```
public class Undergraduate extends Student
{
    private int level; //1 for freshman, 2 for sophomore,
                       //3 for junior, or 4 for senior.

    public Undergraduate()
    {
        super();
        level = 1;
    }
```

■ DISPLAY 7.7   A Derived Class of a Derived Class *(Part 2 of 2)*

```
    public Undergraduate(String initialName,
                   int initialStudentNumber, int initialLevel)
    {
        super(initialName, initialStudentNumber);
        setLevel(initialLevel); //Checks 1 <= initialLevel <= 4
    }

    public void reset(String newName,
                         int newStudentNumber, int newLevel)
    {
        reset(newName, newStudentNumber);
        setLevel(newLevel); //Checks 1 <= newLevel <= 4
    }

    public int getLevel()
    {
        return level;
    }

    public void setLevel(int newLevel)
    {
        if ((1 <= newLevel) && (newLevel <= 4))
            level = newLevel;
        else
        {
            System.out.println("Illegal level!");
            System.exit(0);
        }
    }

    public void writeOutput()
    {
        super.writeOutput();
        System.out.println("Student Level: " + level);
    }

    public boolean equals(Undergraduate otherUndergraduate)
    {
        return (super.equals(otherUndergraduate)
            && (this.level == otherUndergraduate.level));
    }
}
```

class Student (Display 7.3). This means that an object of the class Undergraduate has all the methods and instance variables of the class Student. But Student is already a derived class of Person (Display 7.1). So this also means that an object of the class Undergraduate has all the methods and instance variables of the class Person. An object of the class Person has the instance variable name. An object of the class Student has the instance variables name and studentNumber. An object of the class Undergraduate has the instance variables name, studentNumber, and the added instance variable level. An object of the class Undergraduate must use accessor and mutator methods to access and change the instance variables name and studentNumber, but it definitely has these instance variables.

Display 7.8 contains a UML diagram showing the relationship among the classes Person, Student, and Undergraduate.

Note that a chain of derived classes like this can produce a good deal of efficient reusing of code. Both the classes Undergraduate and Student (as well as any other classes derived from either of them), in effect, reuse the code given in the definition of the class Person, because they inherit all the methods of the class Person.

super

Note the constructors for the class Undergraduate. They each begin with an invocation of super, which in this context stands for a constructor of the base class Student. But the constructors for the class Student also begin with an invocation of super, which in this case stands for a constructor of the base class Person. Thus, when a constructor for Undergraduate is invoked (using new), first a constructor for Person is invoked, then a constructor for Student is invoked, and then all the code following super in the constructor for Undergraduate is executed.

Notice the definition of the reset method in the class Undergraduate, which we reproduce here:

```
public void reset(String newName,
                            int newStudentNumber, int newLevel)
{
    reset(newName, newStudentNumber);
    setLevel(newLevel); //Checks 1 <= newLevel <= 4
}
```

Note that the method starts with an invocation of reset with only two arguments. This invokes the method named reset in the base class Student. In the class Undergraduate, the method named reset is overloaded because there are two definitions for the method name reset with different parameter lists. One takes two arguments, and the other takes three arguments. The one that takes two arguments is inherited from the class Student, but it is still a full-fledged method of the class Undergraduate.

In the three-argument version of reset (which is defined in the class Undergraduate and reproduced in the previous displayed code), the method resets the values of the instance variables name and studentNumber (to newName and newStudentNumber, respectively), with the following invocation:

```
reset(newName, newStudentNumber);
```

Then the new instance variable level is reset to newLevel with a call to setLevel.

■ DISPLAY 7.8   **Some More Details of a UML Class Hierarchy**

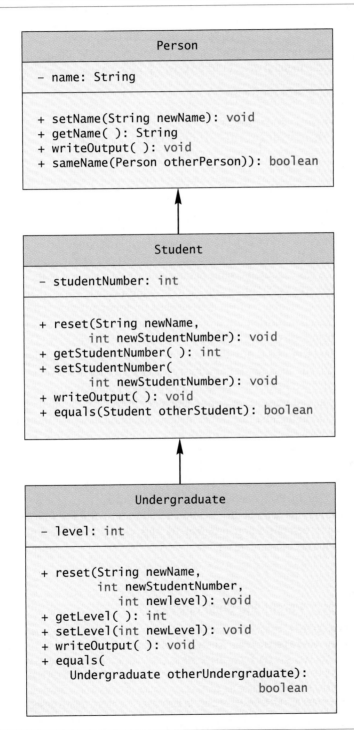

Remember that within the definition of the class `Undergraduate`, the private instance variables `name` and `studentNumber` (of base classes `Person` and `Student`, respectively) cannot be referenced by name, and so a mutator method is needed to change them. The `reset` method of the class `Student` is perfect for this purpose.

In contrast to the definition of the `reset` method in the class `Undergraduate`, notice the definition of the method `writeOutput`, which we reproduce here:

```
public void writeOutput()
{
    super.writeOutput();
    System.out.println("Student Level: " + level);
}
```

The definition of `reset` gave us an example of over*loading*. The method `writeOutput` gives us an example of over*riding*.

The version of `reset` defined in the class `Undergraduate` has a different number of parameters than the version of `reset` defined in the class `Student`. So there is no conflict in having both versions of `reset` in the derived class `Undergraduate`. This is an example of overloading. By contrast, the method `writeOutput` defined in the derived class `Undergraduate` has exactly the same parameter list as the version in the base class `Student`. Thus, when `writeOutput` is invoked, Java must decide which definition of `writeOutput` to use. For an object of the derived class `Undergraduate`, it uses the version of `writeOutput` given in the definition of the class `Undergraduate`. This is an example of overriding the definition of a method name (`writeOutput`) in a derived class. The definition of the method `writeOutput` that was given in the base class `Student` is still inherited by the derived class `Undergraduate`. But in order to invoke the version of `writeOutput` defined in the base class `Student` within the definition of the derived class `Undergraduate`, you must place `super` and a dot in front of the method name `writeOutput`, as we did in the first line of the method definition of `writeOutput` given in the definition of the derived class `Undergraduate` and displayed previously.

In Display 7.7 you can see a similar use of `super` in the method definitions of `equals`. Note that it is perfectly permissible, and indeed common, to redefine names like `writeOutput` and `equals` in a derived class. The versions in the base class are still there, and you can access them by using the prefix `super` and a dot.

extra code on CD
There is nothing unusual about how the class `Undergraduate` is used, but we have included a simple demonstration program for this class in the file `UndergraduateDemo.java` on the accompanying CD. ■

Quick Reference: **Parent and Child Classes**

parent and child

ancestor and descendant

When discussing derived classes, it is common to use terminology derived from family relationships. A base class is often called a **parent class**. A derived class is then called a **child class**. This makes the language of inheritance very smooth. For example, we can say that a child class inherits instance variables and methods from its parent class. This analogy is often carried one step further. A class that is a parent of a parent of a parent of another class (or some other number of "parent of" iterations) is often called an **ancestor class**. If class A is an ancestor of class B, then class B is often called a **descendant** of class A.

A Subtle Point About Overloading and Overriding *(Optional)*

Consider the methods named `equals` in the classes `Student` and `Undergraduate`. They have different parameter lists. The one in the class `Student` has a parameter of type `Student`, while the one in the class `Undergraduate` has a parameter of type `Undergraduate`. They have the same number of parameters—namely, one—but that one parameter is of a different type in each of the two definitions. A difference in type is enough to qualify for overloading. (As we mentioned previously, to qualify for overloading, the two method definitions need to have a different number of parameters *or* a parameter position of differing types in the two methods.) So the second definition of `equals` given in the derived class `Undergraduate` is, in some technical sense, overloading and not overriding.

Why, then, did we use `super` in the definition of `equals` within the derived class `Undergraduate`? To help us analyze the situation, we reproduce the definition (used in the derived class `Undergraduate`) below:

```
public boolean equals(Undergraduate otherUndergraduate)
{
    return (super.equals(otherUndergraduate)
            && (this.level == otherUndergraduate.level));
}
```

Since the invocation `super.equals` is invoking an overloaded version of `equals`, why do we need the `super`? To see why, try omitting it, as follows:

```
    return (equals(otherUndergraduate)
            && (this.level == otherUndergraduate.level));
```

The argument `otherUndergraduate` is of type `Undergraduate`, so Java would assume this refers to the definition of `equals` in the class `Undergraduate`. To force Java to use the definition of `equals` in the base class `Student`, we need to use the `super` and dot.

■ **Java Tip**
You Cannot Use Multiple `super`s

As we already noted, within the definition of a method of a derived class, you can call an overridden method of the base class by prefacing the method name with `super` and a dot. However, you cannot repeat the use of `super` to invoke a method from some ancestor class other than a direct parent. Suppose that the class `Student` is derived from the class `Person`, and the class `Undergraduate` is derived from the class `Student`. You might think that you can invoke a method of the class `Person` within the definition of the class `Undergraduate` by using `super.super`, as in

```
    super.super.writeOutput();//ILLEGAL!
```

However, as the comment indicates, it is illegal to have such a train of `super`s in Java. ■

parameters
types

● Programming Tip
An Object Can Have More than One Type

Consider the class Undergraduate in Display 7.7. It is a derived class of the class Student. In the real world, every undergraduate is also a student. This relationship holds true in Java as well. Every object of the class Undergraduate is also an object of the class Student. Thus, if you have a method that has a formal parameter of type Student, the argument in an invocation of this method can be an object of type Undergraduate. In this case, the method could use only those instance variables and methods that belong to the class Student, but every object of the class Undergraduate has all these instance variables and methods, so there are still lots of meaningful things that the method can do with an object of type Undergraduate.

For example, suppose that the classes Student and Undergraduate are defined as in Display 7.3 and Display 7.7, and consider the following method definition that might occur in some class:

```java
public class SomeClass
{
    public static void compareNumbers(Student s1, Student s2)
    {
        if (s1.getStudentNumber() == s2.getStudentNumber())
            System.out.println(s1.getName()
                                    + " has the same number as "
                                    + s2.getName());
        else
            System.out.println(s1.getName()
                                    + " has a different number than "
                                    + s2.getName());
    }
    ...
}
```

A program that uses this method might contain the following code:

```java
Student studentObject = new Student("Jane Doe", 1234);
System.out.println("Enter name:");
String undergradName = SavitchIn.readLine();
System.out.println("Enter student number :");
int undergradStudentNumber = SavitchIn.readLineInt();
Undergraduate undergradObject =
    new Undergraduate(undergradName, undergradStudentNumber, 1);
SomeClass.compareNumbers(studentObject, undergradObject);
```

If you look at the heading for the method compareNumbers, you will see that both parameters are of type Student. However, the invocation

```java
SomeClass.compareNumbers(studentObject, undergradObject);
```

uses one argument of type Student and one object that is of type Undergraduate. How can we use an object of type Undergraduate where an argument of type Student is required? The answer is that every object of type Undergraduate is also of type Student. To make the point a little more dramatically, notice that you can reverse the two arguments and the method invocation will still be valid, as shown below:

```
SomeClass.compareNumbers(undergradObject, studentObject);
```

Note that there is no automatic type casting here. An object of the class Undergraduate *is* a member of the class Student, and so it *is* of type Student. It need not be, and is not, type cast to an object of the class Student.

An object can actually have more than two types as a result of inheritance. Recall that the class Undergraduate (Display 7.7) is a derived class of the class Student (Display 7.3), and Student is a derived class of the class Person (Display 7.1). This means that every object of the class Undergraduate is also an object of type Student as well as an object of type Person. Thus, everything that works for objects of the class Person also works for objects of the class Undergraduate.

ancestor classes

two levels of derived classes

For example, suppose that the classes Person and Undergraduate are defined as in Displays 7.1 and 7.7, and consider the following code, which might occur in a program:

```
Person joePerson = new Person("Josephine Student");
System.out.println("Enter name:");
String newName = SavitchIn.readLine();
Undergraduate someUndergrad = new Undergraduate(newName, 222, 3);
if (joePerson.sameName(someUndergrad))
    System.out.println("Wow, same names!");
else
    System.out.println("Different names");
```

If you look at the heading for the method sameName in Display 7.1, you will see that it has one parameter, and that parameter is of type Person. However, the call

```
joePerson.sameName(someUndergrad)
```

which is used in the preceding if-else statement is perfectly valid, even though the argument someUndergrad is an object of the class Undergraduate (that is, it is of type Undergraduate) and the argument is supposed to be of type Person. This is because every object of the class Undergraduate is also an object of the class Person.

Even the following is valid:

```
someUndergrad.sameName(joePerson)
```

The method sameName requires a calling object of type Person, and someUndergrad is of type Undergraduate, but that is fine. An object of type Undergraduate is also of type Person. Everything that works for objects of an ancestor class also works for objects of any descendant class.

As you've already seen, if A is a derived class of class B, and B is a derived class of class C, then an object of class A is of type A. It is also of type B, and it is also of type C. This works for any chain of derived classes, no matter how long the chain is.

Because an object of a derived class has the types of all of its ancestor classes (as well as its "own" type), you can assign an object of a class to a variable of any ancestor type, but not the other way around. For example, if `Student` is a derived class of `Person`, and `Undergraduate` is a derived class of `Student`, the following are all valid:

```
Person p1, p2;
Student s = new Student();
Undergraduate ug = new Undergraduate();
p1 = s;
p2 = ug;
```

You can even bypass the variables s and ug and place the new objects directly into the variables p1 and p2, as follows:

```
Person p1, p2;
p1 = new Student();
p2 = new Undergraduate();
```

However, the following are all illegal:

```
Student s = new Person(); //ILLEGAL!
Undergraduate ug = new Person(); //ILLEGAL!
Undergraduate ug2 = new Student(); //ILLEGAL!
```

The following, which may look more innocent, are similarly illegal:

```
Undergraduate ug, ug2; //valid
Person p = new Person(); //valid
ug = p; //ILLEGAL!
Student s = new Student(); //valid
ug2 = s; //ILLEGAL!
```

This all makes perfectly good sense. For example, a `Student` *is a* `Person`, but a `Person` *is not necessarily* a `Student`. Some programers find the phrase "is a" to be useful in deciding what types an object can have and what assignments to variables are valid.

As another example, if `Employee` is a derived class of `Person`, then an `Employee` *is a* `Person`, so you can assign an `Employee` object to a variable of type `Person`. However, a `Person` is *not necessarily* an `Employee`, so you *cannot* assign an object created as just a plain `Person` to a variable of type `Employee`.

Remember: An Object of a Derived Class Has More than One Type

An object of a derived class has the type of the derived class, and it also has the type of the base class. More generally, a derived class has the type of every one of its ancestor classes.

Quick Reference: Assignment Compatibilities

You can assign an object of a derived class to a variable of any ancestor type, but not the other way around.

● **Programming Tip**

"Is a" and "Has a" Relations

As we noted in the previous subsection, a `Student` is a `Person`, so we made the `Student` class a derived class of the `Person` class. This is an example of the "is a" relationship between classes. It is one way to make a more complex class out of a simpler class.

Another way to make a more complex class out of a simpler class is known as the "has a" relationship. For example, if you have a class `Date` that records a date, you might add a date of enrollment to the `Student` class by adding an instance variable of type `Date` to the `Student` class. In this case we say a `Student` "has a" `Date`. As another example, if we have a class `MechanicalArm` and we are defining a class to simulate a robot, we can give the `Robot` class an instance variable of type `MechanicalArm`. In this case we say that a `Robot` "has a" `MechanicalArm`.

In most situations you can make your code work with either an "is a" relationship or a "has a" relationship. It seems silly (and it is silly) to make the `Robot` class a derived class of the `MechanicalArm` class, but it can be done and can be made to work (though perhaps with difficulty). Fortunately, the best programming technique is usually to simply follow what sounds most natural in English. It makes more sense to say "A `Robot` has a `MechanicalArm`" than it does to say "A `Robot` is a `MechanicalArm`." So it makes better programming sense to have a `MechanicalArm` as an instance variable of a `Robot` class.

You will often encounter these terms "is a" and "has a" in the literature on programming techniques. ○

"has a"
relationship

? Self-Test Questions

7. Give the complete definition of a class called `TitledPerson`. `TitledPerson` is to be a derived class of the class `Person` in Display 7.1. The class `TitledPerson` has one additional `String` instance variable for a title, such as `"Ms"`, `"Mr."`, or `"The Honorable"`. The class `TitledPerson` has two constructors, a default constructor and one that sets both the name and the title. It has a `writeOutput` method, a `reset` method, an `equals` method, an accessor method `getTitle` that returns the title, and a mutator method `setTitle` that changes the person's title. For two titled people to be equal, they must have the same name and the same title. You may want to use the class `Student` in Display 7.3 as a model.

8. Rewrite the definition of the method `writeOutput` for the class `Undergraduate` in Display 7.7, using `getName` and `getStudentNumber` instead of `super.writeOutput`. (Most programmers would use the version in Display 7.7, but you should be able to write either version.)

9. Rewrite the definition of the method `reset` for the class `Undergraduate` in Display 7.7, using `setName` and `setStudentNumber` instead of the overloaded `reset` method name. (Most programmers would use the version in Display 7.7, but you should be able to write either version.)

10. Can an object have more than one type?

11. What is the type or types of the object created in the following statement? (The definition of the class Undergraduate is given in Display 7.7.)

```
Undergraduate ug = new Undergraduate();
```

12. Describe two uses for the keyword super.

13. (Answer this question only if you read the optional section entitled "The this Method".) What is the difference between this and super when these words are used as the names of methods that are called in a constructor definition?

The Class Object

Object
class

Java has an "Eve" class—that is, a class that is an ancestor of every class. In Java, every class is a derived class of a derived class of . . . (for some number of iterations of "a derived class of") the class Object. Thus, every object of every class is of type Object, as well as being of the type of its class (and also of the types of all its ancestor classes). Even classes that you define yourself are descendant classes of the class Object. If you do not make your class a derived class of some class, then Java will automatically make it a derived class of the class Object.

Quick Reference: The Class Object

In Java, every class is a descendant of the predefined class Object. So every object of every class is of type Object, as well as being of the type of its class (and probably also of the type of other ancestor classes as well).

The class Object allows programmers to write Java code for methods with a parameter (of type Object) that can be replaced by an object of any class whatsoever. You will eventually encounter library methods that accept an argument of type Object and hence can be used with an argument that is an object of absolutely any class.

The class Object does have some methods that every Java class inherits. For example, every object inherits the methods equals and toString from some ancestor class, either directly from the class Object or from a class that ultimately inherited the methods from the class Object. However, the inherited methods equals and toString will not work correctly for almost any class you define. You need to override the inherited method definitions with new, more appropriate definitions.

(Writing a correct version of equals is a bit complicated for beginning programmers. The equals methods we present in this book will work well in most situations. If you want to read about how to write a fully complete and correct definition of equals, see the details in the optional Java Tip of this chapter entitled "A Better equals Method.")

toString

The inherited method toString takes no arguments. The method toString is supposed to return all the data in an object coded into a String. However, the inherited version of toString is almost always useless because it will not produce a nice string representation of the data. You need to override the definition of toString so it produces an appropriate String for the data in objects of the class being defined.

For example, the following definition of toString could be added to the class Student (Display 7.3):

```
public String toString()
{
    return("Name: " + getName()
                    + "\nStudent number: "
                    + studentNumber);
}
```

If this toString method were added to the class Student, it could be used, among other things, to give output in the following way:

```
Student s = new Student("Joe Student", 2001);
System.out.println(s.toString());
```

The output produced would be

```
Name: Joe Student
Student number: 2001
```

The method toString has a very special property. If you do not include it in an invocation of System.out.println, it is invoked automatically. Therefore, the following are equivalent:

```
System.out.println(s.toString());
System.out.println(s);
```

These two statements would produce the following output:

```
Name: Joe Student
Student number: 2001
Name: Joe Student
Student number: 2001
```

For this reason, it is a good idea always to define a suitable toString method for your classes.

(More details on the interaction of toString and System.out.println are given in the subsection entitled "Dynamic Binding with toString," later in the chapter.)

The version of the class Student on the accompanying CD includes this method toString, so you can easily try it out. The version of Species defined in Chapter 9 also contains a toString method. If you want to try that version, open the file Species.java, filed under Chapter 9 on the accompanying CD. Ignore or comment out the phrase "implements Serializable." That phrase will be explained in Chapter 9.

extra code on CD

Another method inherited from the class Object is the method clone. The method clone takes no arguments and returns a copy of the calling object. The returned object is supposed to have data identical to that of the calling object, but it is a different object (an identical twin or a "clone"). Like other methods inherited from the class Object, the method clone needs to be redefined (overridden) before it functions properly. However, in the case of the method clone, there are other things you must do as well. A thorough discussion of the method clone is beyond the scope of this text, but some discussion of the method clone is given in the Gotcha section "Privacy Leaks" in Chapter 5 and in Appendix 8.

? Self-Test Questions

14. Consider the code below, which was discussed in the previous subsection:

```
Student s = new Student("Joe Student", 2001);
System.out.println(s.toString());
```

Why is the output on two lines instead of being all on one line?

15. Which of the following lines are legal and which are illegal? (`Student` is a derived class of `Person`, and `Undergraduate` is a derived class of `Student`.)

```
Person p1 = new Student();
Person p2 = new Undergraduate();
Student s1 = new Person();
Student s2 = new Undergraduate();
Undergraduate ug1 = new Person();
Undergraduate ug2 = new Student();
Object ob = new Student();
Student s3 = new Object();
```

Case Study
Character Graphics

Java has classes to draw graphics on your terminal screen. In later chapters, we will discuss some of these classes. However, there are situations in which you have no graphics capability available on your screen or other output device. For example, some older terminals allow only for text output.

In this case study, you will design three simple classes to be used to produce simple graphics on a screen using only text output. These classes will produce their graphic figures by placing ordinary keyboard characters at certain places on each line, in such a way as to produce simple pictures.

task specification

Here are the exact details of what you will do in this case study: You will create two classes, one for a box and one for a triangle. You will then write a simple demonstration program that draws a pine tree using the triangle and box classes.

Each of the figures, the box and the triangle, will have an offset telling how far they are indented from the edge of the screen. Each figure will also have a size, although the size will be determined differently for a box and a triangle.

For a box, the size is given as the width and the height, *expressed in the number of characters*. Because characters are taller than they are wide, a box will look taller than you might expect when it is written on the screen. For example, a 5-by-5 box will not look square on the screen, but will look like what is shown in Display 7.9.

For a triangle, the size will be given by its base. The triangle will point up, and the base will be at the bottom. The slope of a side of the triangle is limited to what you get by indenting one character per line (if you want it to be smooth). So once the base is chosen, you have no choice regarding what the sides of the triangle will be. Display 7.9 shows a sample of both a box and a triangle.

■ DISPLAY 7.9   **Sample Box and Triangle**

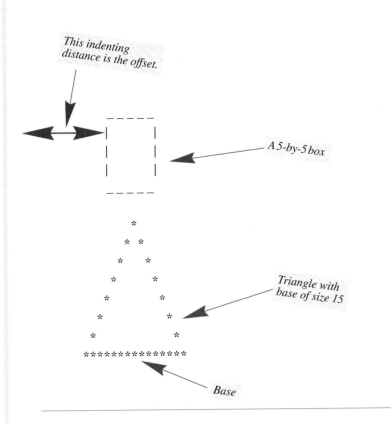

This indenting distance is the offset.

A 5-by-5 box

Triangle with base of size 15

Base

Because a box and a triangle are figures with many properties in common, you decide to design a base class named Figure. The classes Box and Triangle will then be derived classes of the class Figure. The class Figure will have instance variables for any properties that all figures have in common and will have methods for the actions that all figures have. Your analysis produces the following list of properties and actions:

base class Figure

Properties. All figures have an offset, which is the number of spaces the figure is indented, so you decide to store the offset in an instance variable of type int. All figures will have a size, but the size of some figures is described by a single number and the size of other figures is determined by two or more numbers. So you decide not to specify size as part of the class Figure. Thus, you decide that the class Figure will have only the following instance variable:

```
private int offset;
```

Actions. The only actions you need for all figures are to set the parameters for the figures and to draw the figures. Setting the parameters will be taken care of by the constructors and a setOffset method. Display 7.10 contains the definition for the class Figure that you produce.

■ **DISPLAY 7.10 The** `Figure` **Base Class** *(Part 1 of 2)*

```java
/**
 Class for simple character graphics figures to be sent to the
 screen. This class will draw an asterisk on the screen as a test.
 It is not intended to be used as a "real" figure in any graphics.
 It is intended to be used as a base class for other classes
 of figures that will be used in graphics applications.
*/
public class Figure
{
    private int offset;

    public Figure()
    {
        offset = 0;
    }

    public Figure(int theOffset)
    {
        offset = theOffset;
    }

    public void setOffset(int newOffset)
    {
        offset = newOffset;
    }

    public int getOffset()
    {
        return offset;
    }

     /**
     Draws the figure at lineNumber lines down
      from the current line.
     */
    public void drawAt(int lineNumber)
    {
        int count;
        for (count = 0; count < lineNumber; count++)
            System.out.println();
        drawHere();
    }
```

■ DISPLAY 7.10 **The** `Figure` **Base Class** *(Part 2 of 2)*

```
/**
 Draws the figure at the current line.
*/
public void drawHere()
{
    int count;
    for (count = 0; count < offset; count++)
        System.out.print(' ');
    System.out.println('*');
}
}
```

The method `drawHere` will simply indent a number of spaces on the screen equal to the offset and then write an asterisk on the screen. This is just so you can have something to test. You do not intend to use this version of `drawHere` in any application. You will override the definition of `drawHere` when you define classes for boxes and triangles.

The method `drawAt` has one parameter of type `int`. The method `drawAt` inserts a number of blank lines equal to this parameter and then draws the figure by calling `drawHere`. Of course, in this case, that does not produce very much, but when we override `drawHere`, then `drawAt` will also produce more interesting figures.

Next you turn your attention to the class for drawing a box. The class, called `Box`, will be a derived class of the class `Figure`. You need to decide what instance variables and methods to add to those in the class `Figure`. You also need to decide which method definitions in `Figure`, if any, will be overridden with a changed definition.

Box class

Properties. The class `Box` inherits the `offset` instance variables, but you need to add instance variables for the height and the width of the box, Thus, the class definition looks like the following:

```
public class Box extends Figure
{
    private int height;
    private int width;

    <Still needs method definitions.>
}
```

Note that you do not list the instance variable `offset`, which `Box` inherits from the base class `Figure`.

Actions. The class `Box` has the usual constructors and a `reset` method. It inherits both the method `drawAt` and the method `drawHere` from the class `Figure`. However, you need to override the definition of the method `drawHere` so that it does indeed draw a box. So you put `drawHere` on your list of methods to define.

Next, you consider the method `drawAt`. Does it need to be overridden? When you look at the method `drawAt` (Display 7.10), you see that, as long as `drawHere` is correctly defined, the method `drawAt` will work fine for a box or any other figure. Thus, you need not redefine the method `drawAt`. You need to redefine only the method `drawHere`. Having decided on the actions, you now must code the actions as class methods.

Let's look first at a sample constructor. You will design one of the constructors so that it sets all instance variables to values given as arguments to the constructor. But one instance variable, namely `offset`, is a private instance variable of the base class `Figure`. Thus, you cannot access it directly, but you can use a call to the base class constructor, `super`. Thus, the definition of this constructor is as follows:

```
public Box(int theOffset, int theHeight, int theWidth)
{
    super(theOffset);
    height = theHeight;
    width = theWidth;
}
```

The default constructor and `reset` method that you define are shown in Display 7.11. Note that the `reset` method needs to use an accessor method to reset the private instance variable `offset`, which is inherited from the base class `Figure`.

In your definition of the default constructor for the class `Box`, you could omit the call to the base class constructor `super()`, and it would be called automatically anyway, but you decide to leave it in for clarity.

Most of these definitions of constructors and accessor methods are similar to what they would be in any class definition. The definition of the method `drawHere`, however, depends heavily on the particulars of the figure it is drawing. You decide to define the method `drawHere` using the technique known as *top-down design*. The basic technique in top-down design is to break down the task to be performed by the method into subtasks. You decide on the following subtasks:

drawHere

subtasks

To Draw a Box

1. Draw the top line.
2. Draw the side lines.
3. Draw the bottom line.

Note that not every way of choosing subtasks will work. You might at first be tempted to have two subtasks, one for each side of the box. However, output must be produced one line after the other, and you are not allowed to back up, so you must draw the two sides together (if you want them to be side by side, as they should be). Thus, the definition of the method `drawHere` is easy:

```
public void drawHere()
{
    drawHorizontalLine();
    drawSides();
    drawHorizontalLine();
}
```

■ DISPLAY 7.11 The Box Class *(Part 1 of 2)*

```
/**
 Class for a rectangular box to be drawn on the screen.
 Because each character is higher than it is wide, these
 boxes will look higher than you might expect. Inherits
 getOffset, setOffset, and drawAt from the class Figure.
*/
public class Box extends Figure
{
    private int height;
    private int width;

    public Box()
    {
        super();
        height = 0;
        width = 0;
    }

    public Box(int theOffset, int theHeight, int theWidth)
    {
        super(theOffset);
        height = theHeight;
        width = theWidth;
    }

    public void reset(int newOffset, int newHeight, int newWidth)
    {
        setOffset(newOffset);
        height = newHeight;
        width = newWidth;
    }

    /**
     Draws the figure at the current line.
    */
    public void drawHere()
    {
        drawHorizontalLine();
        drawSides();
        drawHorizontalLine();
    }
```

■ DISPLAY 7.11 **The Box Class** *(Part 2 of 2)*

```java
    private void drawHorizontalLine( )
    {
        spaces(getOffset( ));
        int count;
        for (count = 0; count < width; count++)
            System.out.print('-');
        System.out.println( );
    }

    private void drawSides( )
    {
        int count;
        for (count = 0; count < (height - 2); count++)
            drawOneLineOfSides( );
    }

    private void drawOneLineOfSides( )
    {
        spaces(getOffset( ));
        System.out.print('|');
        spaces(width - 2);
        System.out.println('|');
    }

    //Writes the indicated number of spaces.
    private static void spaces(int number)
    {
        int count;
        for (count = 0; count < number; count++)
            System.out.print(' ');
    }
}
```

The method spaces *was made* static *because it does not need a calling object. The class would work fine if* spaces *were not made* static, *but it is clearer if you make* spaces static.

Although that was easy, it does postpone most of the work. You still need to define the methods drawHorizontalLine and drawSides. Because these are helping methods, they will be private methods.

You come up with the following pseudocode for drawHorizontalLine:

drawHori-
zontalLine

Output offset blank spaces.
Output width copies of the character '-'.
System.out.println( );

The final code for the method drawHorizontalLine is given in Display 7.11. Note that the task of writing a specified number of blanks is broken out as another helping method called spaces.

Next, you turn your attention to the method drawSides. This task is to draw a figure like the following:

drawSides

Noticing that each line is identical, you decide to break out the writing of one of these lines as a subtask. So the definition of the method drawSides is

```java
private void drawSides()
{
    int count;
    for (count = 0; count < (height - 2); count++)
        drawOneLineOfSides();
}
```

Note that you output two fewer lines than the height. The top and bottom horizontal lines account for those extra two units of height.

Just about all that is left to do is to define the helping method drawOneLineOf-Sides. You design the following pseudocode for drawOneLineOfSides:

```java
spaces(getOffset());
System.out.print('|');
spaces(width - 2);
System.out.println('|');
```

Because you already have a method for the subtask of writing spaces, the pseudocode turns out to be Java code, and so the definition of drawOneLineOf-Sides is done. The complete class definition of Box is given in Display 7.11.

Although we will not stop to describe the testing process in this case study, all the methods in the class Figure, the class Box, and the class Triangle (which we have not yet discussed) need to be tested. Remember, each method should be tested in a program in which it is the only untested method.

testing

Display 7.12 contains the definition of the class Triangle. You can design that class using the same techniques you used to design the class Box. We will discuss only one part of the method drawHere for which the technical details may not be clear at first reading. The method drawHere divides its task into two subtasks: draw the inverted V for the top of the triangle, and draw the horizontal line for the bottom of the triangle. We will discuss only the method drawTop that draws the inverted V.

Triangle class

The method drawTop draws a figure like the following:

■ DISPLAY 7.12   **The Triangle Class** *(Part 1 of 2)*

```java
/**
 Class for triangles to be drawn on the screen. For this class,
 a triangle points up and is completely determined by the size of
 its base. (Screen character spacing determines the length of the
 sides, given the base.)
 Inherits getOffset, setOffset, and drawAt from the class Figure.
*/
public class Triangle extends Figure
{
    private int base;

    public Triangle()
    {
        super();
        base = 0;
    }

    public Triangle(int theOffset, int theBase)
    {
        super(theOffset);
        base = theBase;
    }

    public void reset(int newOffset, int newBase)
    {
        setOffset(newOffset);
        base = newBase;
    }

    /**
      Draws the figure at current line.
    */
    public void drawHere()
    {
        drawTop();
        drawBase();
    }

    private void drawBase()
    {
        spaces(getOffset());
        int count;
        for (count = 0; count < base; count++)
            System.out.print('*');
        System.out.println();
    }
```

```java
    private void drawTop()
    {
        //startOfLine will be the number of spaces to the
        //first '*' on a line. Initially set to the number
        //of spaces before the top '*'.
        int startOfLine = getOffset() + (base/2);
        spaces(startOfLine);
        System.out.println('*');//top '*'
        int count;
        int lineCount = (base/2) - 1;//height above base
        //insideWidth == number of spaces between the
        //two '*'s on a line.
        int insideWidth = 1;
        for (count = 0; count < lineCount; count++)
        {
            //Down one line, so the first '*' is one more
            //space to the left.
            startOfLine--;
            spaces(startOfLine);
            System.out.print('*');
            spaces(insideWidth);
            System.out.println('*');
            //Down one line, so the inside is 2 spaces wider.
            insideWidth = insideWidth + 2;
        }
    }

    private static void spaces(int number)
    {
        int count;
        for (count = 0; count < number; count++)
            System.out.print(' ');
    }
}
```

Note that there is an offset for the entire figure. The indenting for the wide bottom of the figure is exactly this offset. But going up from bottom to top, each line has a greater indentation. Alternatively, going down (as the computer must go), each line has a slightly smaller indentation. The indentation is smaller by one character each line. So if the indentation is given by the value of the `int` variable `startOf-Line`, the indentation can be performed by

```java
spaces(startOfLine);
```

This can be made one line of a loop, and then the value of startOfLine will be decreased by 1 on each loop iteration. The size of the gap between the two asterisks on the same line increases by 2 as you go down each line. If this gap is given by the value of the int variable insideWidth, the loop for drawing all of the inverted V except for the top asterisk can be

```
for (count = 0; count < lineCount; count++)
{
    spaces(startOfLine);
    System.out.print('*');
    spaces(insideWidth);
    System.out.println('*');
    insideWidth = insideWidth + 2;
    startOfLine--;//THIS LINE WILL MOVE.
}
```

The complete definition of the method drawTop is given in Display 7.12. The preceding loop is highlighted. Also, in order to accommodate the code that comes before the loop, the line

```
startOfLine--;
```

becomes the first line of the loop instead of the last, but it is still decremented once on each loop iteration.

application program

To complete this project, you produce the sample application program shown in Display 7.13. ■

? Self-Test Question

16. Define a class called Diamond that is a derived class of the class Figure. The class Diamond is similar to the class Triangle. However, when a Diamond is drawn, it has the same sort of top half as a Triangle, but it has a bottom half that is an inverted version of its top half.

Abstract Classes

The class Figure defined in Display 7.10 was not intended to be used to create objects of the class Figure, but was designed to be used as a base class to derive other classes, such as the class Box (Display 7.11). Although, we do not really need to create objects of the class Figure, it is still valid to do so, as in the second of the following two statements:

```
Figure figureVariable;
figureVariable = new Figure();
```

In order to make this valid, however, we needed to give a definition to the method drawHere in the class Figure. The definition of the method drawHere that we gave in the class Figure is just a placeholder; all it does is draw a single asterisk, just so something would happen if you invoked it. We never intended to invoke the method drawHere with an object that is just a plain old Figure. We intended to use the method drawHere only with objects of derived classes (like the derived classes Box and Triangle).

■ DISPLAY 7.13 **Character Graphics Application**

```java
public class GraphicsDemo
{
    public static final int indent = 5;
    public static final int topWidth = 21;
    public static final int bottomWidth = 4;
    public static final int bottomHeight = 4;

    public static void main(String[] args)
    {
        System.out.println("         Save the Redwoods!");

        Triangle top = new Triangle(indent, topWidth);
        Box base = new Box(indent + (topWidth/2) - (bottomWidth/2),
                                    bottomHeight, bottomWidth);

        top.drawAt(1);
        base.drawAt(0);
    }
}
```

Screen Output

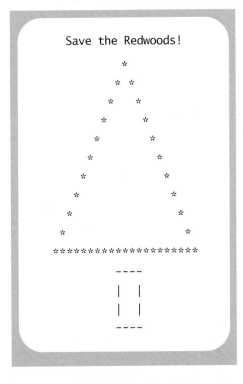

abstract
method

In cases like this, in which you have a method that you intend to be overridden in derived classes and invoked only by objects of a derived class, you can declare the method to be **abstract.** You do this as follows:

```
public abstract void drawHere();
```

Note that the keyword `abstract` is used in the method heading, that there is no method body, and that the method heading is followed by a semicolon. An abstract method is not intended to be used for anything; it must be overridden and given a "new" definition in any (nonabstract) derived class.

Java requires that, if a class has at least one abstract method, the class must be declared to be abstract. You do this by including the keyword `abstract` in the heading of the class definition, as in the following:

```
public abstract class Figure
{
    ...
```

abstract class

A class defined in this way is said to be an **abstract class.** If a class is abstract, you cannot have objects of that class (unless they are objects of a derived class). An abstract class can be used only as a base class to derive other classes.

In Display 7.14 we have redone the class `Figure` as an abstract class. If we used this abstract version of the class `Figure`, all of our derived classes would work as before, but we could not create objects that were just plain old `Figures`.

Note that even though the class `Figure` is abstract, not all of the methods are abstract. All the method definitions, except for the method `drawHere`, are exactly the same as in our original definition. They are full definitions (and do not use the keyword `abstract`). When it makes sense to give a regular method definition in an abstract class, it should be given. That way, as much detail as possible is pushed into the abstract class, so that such detail need not be repeated in each derived class.

Why have abstract classes? They simplify your thinking. We have already explained that we defined the class `Figure` so we would have to write the definitions of methods such as `drawAt` only once for every kind of figure. An abstract class makes it easier to define classes like `Figure` by relieving you of the obligation to write useless method definitions. If there is no point in defining some method, because it will always be overridden, then make it an abstract method (and so make the class abstract), and then you need not write the pointless method definition.

An abstract method serves a purpose, even though it is not given a full definition. It serves as a placeholder for a method that must be defined in all (nonabstract) derived classes. Note that in Display 7.14 the method `drawAt` includes an invocation of the method `drawHere`. If the abstract method `drawHere` were omitted, this invocation of `drawHere` would be illegal.

? Self-Test Questions

17. Is the following valid if `Figure` is defined as in Display 7.14?

```
Figure figureVariable = new Figure();
```

■ DISPLAY 7.14 **The Figure Class Redone as an Abstract Class**

```
/**
 Abstract class for simple character graphics figures to send to
 the screen. It is intended to be used as a base class for the kinds
 of figures that will be used in graphics applications.
*/
public abstract class Figure
{
    private int offset;

    public abstract void drawHere( );

        <All constructors and methods are identical to those in Display 7.10,
        except for the method drawHere. Methods other than drawHere do not use the
        keyword abstract in their headings. Below we repeat one such method definition:>

    /**
     Draws the figure at lineNumber lines down
     from the current line.
    */
    public void drawAt(int lineNumber)
    {
        int count;
        for (count = 0; count < lineNumber; count++)
            System.out.println( );
        drawHere( );
    }
}
```

18. Is the following valid if Figure is defined as in Display 7.14 and Box is as defined as in Display 7.11?

```
Figure figureVariable = new Box( );
```

Remember: **An Abstract Class Is a Type**

You cannot create an object of an abstract class, such as Figure as defined in Display 7.14. That is, with the version of Figure given in Display 7.14, the following is illegal:

```
Figure f = new Figure();
```

Nonetheless, it makes perfectly good sense to have a parameter of type Figure. Then an object of any of the descendant classes of Figure can be plugged in for the parameter.

Interfaces *(Optional)*

An **interface** is something like the extreme case of an abstract class. In fact, it is so extreme that an interface is not a class. It is, however, a type that can be satisfied by any class that *implements the interface.*

An interface specifies the headings for methods that must be defined in any class that implements the interface. For example, Display 7.15 shows an interface named `Writable`. Note that an interface contains only method headings. It contains no instance variables nor any complete method definitions. (An interface may contain defined constants, though.)

In order to **implement an interface,** a class must do two things:

1. It must include the phrase

    `implements` *Interface_Name*

    at the start of the class definition. To implement more than one interface, just list all the interface names, separated by commas, as in

    `implements MyInterface, YourInterface`

2. The class must implement all the method headings listed in the definition(s) of the interface(s).

For example, to implement the `Writable` interface, a class definition must contain the phrase `implements Writable` at the start of the method definition, as shown in the following:

```
public class WritableUndergraduate extends Student
                                    implements Writable
{
```

The class must also implement the two methods `writeOutput()` and `toString()`. The full definition of `WritableUndergraduate` is given in Display 7.16.

An interface is a type. This allows you to write a method with a parameter of an interface type, such as a parameter of type `Writable`, and that method will apply to any class you later define that implements the interface. An interface serves a function similar to a base class, but it is important to note that it is not a base class. (In fact, it is not a class of any kind.) Some programming languages allow one class to be a derived class of two different base classes. This is not allowed in Java. In Java a derived class can have only one base class. However, in addition to any base class a Java class may have, it can also implement any number of interfaces. This allows Java programs to approximate the power of multiple base classes without the complications that can arise with multiple base classes.

■ DISPLAY 7.15 **The `Writable` Interface *(Optional)***

```
public interface Writable
{
    public String toString();

    public void writeOutput();
}
```

Do not forget the semicolons at the end of the method headings.

■ DISPLAY 7.16 **Implementation of an Interface** *(Optional)*

```java
public class WritableUndergraduate extends Student
                                    implements Writable
{
    private int level; //1 for freshman, 2 for sophomore,
                       //3 for junior, or 4 for senior.

    public WritableUndergraduate( )
    {
        super( );
        level = 1;
    }

    public WritableUndergraduate(String initialName,
                    int initialStudentNumber, int initialLevel)
    {
        super(initialName, initialStudentNumber);
        setLevel(initialLevel); //Checks 1 <= initialLevel <= 4
    }

    public String toString( )
    {
        return ("Name: " + getName( ) +
                "\nStudent number: " + getStudentNumber() +
                "\nLevel: " + getLevel( ));
    }

    public void writeOutput( )
    {
        super.writeOutput( );
        System.out.println("Student Level: " + level);
    }

    public boolean equals(WritableUndergraduate other)
    {
        return (super.equals(other)
            && (this.level == other.level));
    }

    <Definitions of other methods are the same as in the class Undergraduate in Display 7.7.>

}
```

An interface definition is stored in a `.java` file and compiled just as a class definition is compiled.

7.3 DYNAMIC BINDING AND POLYMORPHISM

In this section we discuss one of the ways that different objects can have different definitions for the same method name, such as the method name `drawAt`. So if `b` is a `Box` object and `t` is a `Triangle` object, `b` and `t` use different definitions of `drawAt`, even though both `b` and `t` may be named by variables of the same type—in our example both objects will be named by variables of type `Figure`.

Dynamic Binding

Look back at the definition of the method `drawAt` in the class `Figure` (Display 7.10). It makes a call to the method `drawHere`. If the only class around were `Figure`, this would not be anything exciting. But we derived the class `Box` from the base class `Figure`. The class `Box` inherits the method `drawAt` unchanged from the class `Figure`, but the class `Box` overrides the definition of the method `drawHere`. "So what?" you may say. So plenty! Consider the poor compiler's job when it encounters the following:.

```
Box b = new Box(1, 4, 4);
b.drawAt(2);
```

The method `drawAt` was defined in the class `Figure`, but it calls the method `drawHere` that was redefined in the class `Box`. The code for `drawAt` was compiled with the class `Figure`, and that class was compiled before the class `Box` and its method `drawHere` were even written. So this compiled code for `drawAt` is using a definition of the method `drawHere` that was not even written at the time that `drawAt` was compiled. How can that be?

When the code for `drawAt` is compiled, nothing is inserted for the call to `drawHere` except for an annotation that says, "Use the currently applicable definition of `drawHere`." Then, when you invoke `b.drawAt(2)`, the compiled code for `drawAt` eventually reaches the annotation equivalent to "Use the currently applicable definition of `drawHere`." This annotation is replaced by an invocation of the version of `drawHere` that goes with `b`. If `b` is of type `Box`, the version of `drawHere` used will be the one in the definition of the class `Box`.

dynamic (late) binding

This way of handling an invocation of a method that may be overridden later is called **dynamic binding** or **late binding**, because the meaning of the method invocation is not bound to the location of the method invocation until you run the program. If Java did not use dynamic binding, then when you ran `f.drawAt( )`, you would always see what is drawn by the method `drawAt` of the class `Figure` (which happens to be a single asterisk), and this would be true even if `f` were a `Box` or a `Triangle`.

Other languages do not automatically do dynamic binding as Java does. In many other languages, you must specify in advance what methods may need dynamic binding. Java's way of doing it is less efficient but means that Java is easier to program and less prone to errors.

To see that dynamic binding really is a big deal, consider the following code, keeping in mind that drawAt includes an invocation of drawHere:

```
Figure f;
Box b = new Box(1, 4, 4);
f = b;
f.drawAt(2);
Triangle t = new Triangle(1, 21);
f = t;
f.drawAt(2);
```

The two lines shown in color are identical, and the code for the method drawAt is identical in both cases because the method definition is inherited from Figure. Yet they use different method definitions for the method drawHere, which is invoked by drawAt, and so the two invocations of drawAt produce different output. The first draws a box and the second draws a triangle. An object remembers what method definitions it had when it was created with new. Let's pursue this a bit more.

The classes Box and Triangle inherit the method drawAt from the class Figure. The method drawAt is not overridden in the definitions of either of the classes Box or Triangle. So the text of the method definition for drawAt is even the same for both Box objects and Triangle objects. It is the method drawHere, which is invoked within the definition of drawAt, that is (directly) overridden. In this situation you might say that the method name drawAt is **indirectly overridden** in the classes Box and Triangle.

indirectly
overridden

It is important to note that the decision of which method definition to use depends on the object's place in the inheritance chain. *It is not determined by the type of the variable naming the object.* For example, consider the following code:

```
Box b = new Box(1, 4, 4);
Figure f = b;
f.drawHere();
```

As we noted earlier in the chapter, it is perfectly valid to assign an object of the class Box to a variable of type Figure. However, the object still remembers that it was created as a Box. In this case, f.drawHere() will use the definition of drawHere given in Box, not the definition of drawHere given in Figure. To determine which definition of drawHere to use, Java checks which class was used when the object was created using new.[1]

---

1. Java is so good at figuring out which definition of a method to use that even a type cast will not fool it. The meaning of b.drawHere() will always have the meaning defined in the method Box, even if you use a type cast to change the type of b to the type Figure, as in the following:

```
Box b = new Box(1, 4, 4);
Figure f = (Figure)b;
f.drawHere();
```

In this case, f.drawHere() will use the definition of drawHere given in Box, not the definition of drawHere given in Figure.

Remember: Objects Know How They Are Supposed to Act

When an overridden method (or a method that uses an overridden method) is invoked, the action of that method is the one defined in the class used to create the object (with new). It is not determined by the type of the variable naming the object. A variable of any ancestor class can hold an object of a descendant class, but the object always remembers which method actions to use for every method name. The type of the variable does not matter. What matters is the class name when the object was created. This is because Java uses dynamic binding.

Type Checking and Dynamic Binding

You need to be aware of how dynamic binding interacts with the Java compiler's type checking. For example, if Employee is a derived class of the class Person, you can assign an object of type Employee to a variable of type Person, as in

```
Employee e = new Employee()
Person p;
p = e;
```

But that is not the end of the story.

Although you can assign an object of type Employee to a variable of type Person, you can invoke only a method that is in the class Person when the calling object is the variable p (of type Person). However, if the method is overridden in the definition of the class Employee and the object named by the variable p is of type Employee, then it is the version of the method defined in Employee that will be used. *So the variable determines what method names can be used, but the object determines which definition of the method name will be used.* If you want to use a method name that was first introduced in the class Employee with the object named by the variable p of type Person, you must use a type cast. Something like the following will work (assume that setEmployeeNumber was first defined in the class Employee):

```
Employee e = (Employee)p;
e.setEmployeeNumber(5678);
```

Another example may help. Recall that Student (Display 7.3) is a derived class of Person (Display 7.1). Now suppose you have the following line in a program:

```
Person p = new Student("Joe", 1234);
```

The following is then valid:

```
p.setName("Josephine");
p.writeOutput();
```

The second invocation will use the definition of writeOutput that was given in the class Student. *(The object, not the variable, determines which definition of a method name will be used.)*

On the other hand, the following is illegal, because `setStudentNumber` is not the name of a method in the class `Person`. *(The variable determines which method names can be used.)*

```
p.setStudentNumber(1234); //ILLEGAL
```

The variable p is of type `Person`, but the object in the variable p is still an object of type `Student`. Thus, although the object can still invoke the method `setStudentNumber`, the compiler does not know this! To make the invocation valid you need a type cast, such as the following:

```
Student s = (Student)p;
s.setStudentNumber(1234); //Legal
```

Remember: **The Variable Determines What Method Names Can Be Used, but the Object Determines which Definition of the Method Name Will Be Used**

When an object is created with `new` using one class, but is stored in a variable of an ancestor class, the variable determines what method names can be used with the variable name, but the class used to create the object determines which definition of the method name will be used.

You may think this is all just a silly exercise, because you would never assign an object of type `Student` to a variable of type `Person`. Not so. You may not often make such an assignment directly, but you will very often do so without realizing it. Recall that you can "plug in" an argument of type `Student` for a method parameter of type `Person`. And a parameter is a local variable that is assigned the value of the argument that is "plugged in" for it. In this case, an object of type `Student` (the argument in the method invocation) is assigned to a variable of type `Person` (the parameter in the method definition). (Yes, it is really the object reference—that is, the memory address of the object—that is assigned to the variable, but that is a side issue and is not relevant to the point at hand. Hey, this is complicated enough as is!)

Dynamic Binding with `toString`

In the subsection "The Class `Object`," we noted that, if you add an appropriate `toString` method to the class `Student`, you can send output to the screen using the `toString` method, as illustrated by the following:

```
Student s = new Student("Joe Student", 2001);
System.out.println(s.toString());
```

Thanks to dynamic binding, you do not even need to use the method `toString` in your invocation of `System.out.println`. The following will work just as well and will produce exactly the same output:

```
Student s = new Student("Joe Student", 2001);
System.out.println(s);
```

The method invocation `System.out.println(s)` is an invocation of the method `println` with the calling object `System.out`. One definition of the method `println` has a single argument of type `Object`. The definition is equivalent to the following:

```
public void println(Object theObject)
{
    System.out.println(theObject.toString( ));
}
```

(The invocation of the method `println` inside the braces is a different, overloaded definition of the method `println`. That invocation inside the braces uses a method `println` that has a parameter of type `String`, not a parameter of type `Object`.)

This definition of `println` was given before the class `Student` was defined. Yet in the invocation

```
System.out.println(s);
```

with an argument `s` of type `Student` (and hence also of type `Object`), it is the definition of `toString` in the class `Student` that is used, not the definition of `toString` in the class `Object`. Dynamic binding is what makes this work.

Polymorphism

polymorphism

Polymorphism comes from a Greek word meaning "many forms." Its original meaning (in computer science) was the ability to use different definitions of the same method name, depending on the context. With that original meaning, such things as overloading were considered polymorphism. However, the modern usage of the term is much more specific. As the word is currently used, it refers to the dynamic binding mechanism that determines which method action will be used for a (directly or indirectly) overridden method name. Thus, in current usage, *polymorphism* is basically another term to refer to dynamic binding.

So why is the title of this section "Dynamic Binding and Polymorphism"? Isn't that like saying "Dynamic Binding and Dynamic Binding"? Well, yes, but the terms still have a different feel to them. Dynamic binding is thought of as a process carried out by the computer, and polymorphism is thought of as something the objects do. (I know—the objects are really in the computer. I said they have a different *feel*, not a totally different *meaning*.)

object-oriented
programming

Polymorphism plays an important role in object-oriented programming. In fact, most authorities consider encapsulation, inheritance, and polymorphism to be the main features of object-oriented programming. So polymorphism is one of the three central features of the object-oriented programming philosophy.

Quick Reference: Polymorphism

Polymorphism means using the process of dynamic binding to allow different objects to use different method actions for the same method name.

■ **Java Tip**
A Better `equals` Method *(Optional)*

In discussing the class `Object` earlier in this chapter, we said that it has an `equals` method, and that when you define a class with an `equals` method you should override the definition of the method `equals` given in the class `Object`. However, we did not, strictly speaking, follow our own advice. The heading for the method `equals` in our definition of the class `Student` (Display 7.3) is as follows:

```
public boolean equals(Student otherStudent)
```

The heading for the method `equals` in the class `Object` is as follows:

```
public boolean equals(Object otherObject)
```

Note that the two `equals` methods have different parameter types so we have not overridden the definition of `equals`. We have merely overloaded the method `equals`. The class `Student` has both of these methods named `equals`.

For most situations, this will not matter. However, there are cases in which it does matter. Suppose we use some predefined method (or programmer-defined method) that has a parameter named `objectPar` of type `Object` and another parameter `studentPar` of type `Student`. Now suppose the code for this method includes

```
studentPar.equals(objectPar)
```

If you plug in two arguments of type `Student` for the parameters `objectPar` and `StudentPar`, Java will use the definition of `equals` defined for the class `Object`, not one defined for the class `Student`. This means that in some cases, the method `equals` will return the wrong answer.

To fix this problem, we need to change the type of the parameter for the `equals` method in the `Student` class from `Student` to `Object`. A first try might be the following:

```
public boolean equals(Object otherObject)
{
    Student otherStudent = (Student)otherObject;
    return (this.sameName(otherStudent)
        && (this.studentNumber ==
                        otherStudent.studentNumber));
}
```

Note that we need to type cast the parameter `otherObject` from type `Object` to type `Student`. If we omit the type cast, the compiler will give an error message when it sees

```
otherObject.studentNumber
```

The class `Object` does not have an instance variable named `studentNumber`. (Actually, it is likely to give an error message even before. It will probably complain about the invocation of `sameName`.)

This first try at an improved `equals` method does override the definition of `equals` given in the class `Object` and will work well in almost all cases. However, it still has a shortcoming.

Our definition of `equals` now allows an argument that can be any object at all. What happens if the method `equals` is used with an argument that is not a `Student`? The answer is that a run-time error will occur when the type cast to `Student` is executed.

We should make our definition work for any object. If the object is not a `Student`, we simply return `false`. (The calling object is a `Student`, and so if the argument is not a `Student`, they should not be considered equal.) But how can we tell when the parameter is not of type `Student`?

instanceof

The `instanceof` operator can be used to check if an object is of type `Student`. The syntax is

> *Object* `instanceof` *Class_Name*

This expression returns `true` if *Object* is of type *Class_Name*; otherwise it returns `false`. So the following will return true if `otherObject` is of type `Student`:

> `(otherObject instanceof Student)`

So the `equals` method should return `false` if the preceding boolean expression is *not* true.

Our final version of the method `equals` is shown in Display 7.17. Note that we have also taken care of one more possible case. The predefined constant `null` can be plugged in for a parameter of type `Object`. The Java documentation says that an `equals` method should return `false` when comparing an object and the value `null`. So that is what we have done. □

■ **DISPLAY 7.17 A Better `equals` Method for the Class `Student` (Optional)**

```java
public boolean equals(Object otherObject)
{
    if (otherObject == null)
        return false;
    else if (!(otherObject instanceof Student))
        return false;
    else
    {
        Student otherStudent = (Student)otherObject;
        return (this.sameName(otherStudent)
            && (this.studentNumber ==
                            otherStudent.studentNumber));
    }
}
```

19. What is the difference between overriding a method name and overloading a method name?

20. Is the definition of `drawHere` given in Display 7.11 an example of overloading or overriding?

21. Is the definition of `drawHere` given in Display 7.12 an example of overloading or overriding?

22. Are the two definitions of the constructors given in Display 7.12 an example of overloading or overriding?

23. What is polymorphism?

24. What is dynamic binding? What is late binding? Give an example of each.

25. Is overloading a method name an example of polymorphism?

26. What are the three main characteristics of object-oriented programming as described in the preceding subsection?

27. In the following code, will the two invocations of `drawAt` produce the same picture on the screen or not? (The classes are defined in the preceding section.)

```
Figure f;
f = new Box(1, 4, 4);
f.drawAt(2);
f = new Triangle(1, 21);
f.drawAt(2);
```

CHAPTER SUMMARY

■ A derived class is obtained from a base class by adding additional instance variables or additional methods. The derived class inherits all the instance variables and methods that are in the base class.

■ When defining a constructor for a derived class, your definition should first call a constructor for the base class. If you do not make an explicit call, then Java will automatically call the default constructor of the base class.

■ You can redefine a method from a base class so that it has a different definition in the derived class. This is called overriding the method definition.

■ When you override a method definition, the new method definition given in the derived class has the exact same number and types of parameters. If the method in the derived class has a different number of parameters or a parameter position of a different type from the method in the base class, that is overloading.

■ Private instance variables and private methods of a base class cannot be accessed directly in a derived class.

■ If A is a derived class of class B, then an object of class A is a member of class A (of course), but it is also a member of class B.

■ Polymorphism means using the process of dynamic binding to allow different objects to use different method actions for the same method name.

✔ Answers to Self-Test Questions

1. Yes, a derived class has all the instance variables that the base class has, and can also add more instance variables.

2. Yes, it will have the methods. A derived class has all the public methods that the base class has (and can also add more methods). If the derived class does not redefine (override) a method definition, then it performs exactly the same action in the derived class as it does in the base class. However, the derived class can contain a new definition of (an overriding definition of) the method and the new definition will replace the old definition (provided it has the same number and types of parameters).

3. No.

4. No.

5. The method `sameName` is not listed in the class diagram for `Student`. So you follow the arrow to the class diagram for `Person`. The method `sameName` with a single parameter of type `Person` is in the class diagram for `Person`. Since you know that a `Student` is a `Person`, you know that this definition works for the method `sameName` with a single parameter of type `Student`. So the definition used for the method `sameName` is in the class definition of `Person`.

6. You start at the class diagram for `Student`. The method `setStudentNumber` with a single parameter of type `int` is in the class diagram for `Student`, so you need look no further. The definition used for the method `setStudentNumber` is in the class definition of `Person`.

7.
```java
public class TitledPerson extends Person
{
    private String title;
    public TitledPerson()
    {
        super();
        title = "no title yet";
    }

    public TitledPerson(String initialName, String initialTitle)
    {
        super(initialName);
        title = initialTitle;
    }
```

```java
    public void reset(String newName, String newTitle)
    {
        setName(newName);
        title = newTitle;
    }

    public String getTitle()
    {
        return title;
    }

    public void setTitle(String newTitle)
    {
        title = newTitle;
    }

    public void writeOutput()
    {
        System.out.println("Name: " + getName());
        System.out.println("Title: " + title);
    }

    public boolean equals(TitledPerson otherPerson)
    {
        return (this.sameName(otherPerson)) &&
                (this.title.equalsIgnoreCase(otherPerson.title));
    }
}
```

8.
```java
    public void writeOutput()
    {
        System.out.println("Name: " + getName());
        System.out.println("Student Number: "
                                + getStudentNumber());
        System.out.println("Student Level: " + level);
    }
```

9.
```java
    public void reset(String newName,
                        int newStudentNumber, int newLevel)
    {
        setName(newName);
        setStudentNumber(newStudentNumber);
        level = newLevel;
    }
```

10. Yes, an object can have more than one type. If class A is derived from class B, then an object of class A is of type A and is also of type B.

11. The object has the types: Undergraduate, Student, and Person. (As you will find out soon in this chapter, it is also of type Object, a predefined Java class, that we are about to introduce).

12. It is used as the name for a constructor of the base class. (See Display 7.3.) When used as a "calling object" as in

```
super.writeOutput();
```

it is used to indicate that the method of the given name in the base class should be used. In Display 7.7, for example, this is used to indicate the method `writeOutput` of the base class `Student`, as opposed to the method `writeOutput` of the class `Undergraduate`.

13. The keyword `this`, when used as a method name, names a constructor in the same class as the one being defined. The keyword `super`, when used as a method name, names a constructor for the base class of the derived class being defined.

14. Because the value returned by `toString` includes the new-line character `'\n'`.

15.

```
Person p1 = new Student();//Valid. A Student is a Person.
Person p2 = new Undergraduate();//Valid.
                              //An Undergraduate is a Person.
Student s1 = new Person(); //ILLEGAL!
Student s2 = new Undergraduate(); //Valid.
                              //An Undergraduate is a Student.
Undergraduate ug1 = new Person(); //ILLEGAL!
Undergraduate ug2 = new Student(); //ILLEGAL!
Object ob = new Student(); //Valid.
                              //A Student is an Object.
Student s3 = new Object();//ILLEGAL!
```

16.

```
/**
 Class for diamonds to be drawn on the screen. For this class,
 a diamond is completely determined by its diameter.
 (Screen character spacing determines the rest of the figure.)
 Inherits getOffset, setOffset, and drawAt from Figure.
*/
public class Diamond extends Figure
{
    private int diameter;

    public Diamond()
      {
          super();
          diameter = 0;
      }

    public Diamond(int theOffset, int theDiameter)
      {
          super(theOffset);
          diameter = theDiameter;
      }
```

```java
public void reset(int newOffset, int newDiameter)
{
    setOffset(newOffset);
    diameter = newDiameter;
}

/**
 Draws the figure at the current line.
*/
public void drawHere()
{
    drawTop();
    drawBottom();
}

public void drawTop()
{
    int startOfLine = getOffset() + (diameter/2);
    spaces(startOfLine);
    System.out.println('*');
    int count;
    int lineCount = (diameter/2) - 1;
    int insideWidth = 1;
    for (count = 0; count < lineCount; count++)
    {
        startOfLine--;
        spaces(startOfLine);
        System.out.print('*');
        spaces(insideWidth);
        System.out.println('*');
        insideWidth = insideWidth + 2;
    }
}

public void drawBottom()
{
    int startOfLine = getOffset();
    int count;
    int lineCount = (diameter/2);
    int insideWidth = 2*lineCount - 1;
    for (count = 0; count < lineCount; count++)
    {
        spaces(startOfLine);
        System.out.print('*');
        spaces(insideWidth);
        System.out.println('*');
        insideWidth = insideWidth - 2;
        startOfLine++;
    }
}
```

```
            spaces(startOfLine);
            System.out.println('*');
        }

        private static void spaces(int number)
        {
            <This definition is identical to that of the method named
                spaces in the class Triangle (Display 7.12).>
        }
    }
```

This question points out that an alternative good way to define these character graphics classes is to have a utility class with public static methods, like the method `spaces`, and other methods that do things like draw horizontal lines, big V's, and inverted big V's.

17. It is not legal because `Figure` (as in Display 7.14) is an abstract class.

18. Yes, it is legal.

19. *Overriding* refers to redefining a base class method name so it has a different definition in a derived class. *Overloading* refers to giving a method name two definitions that are resolved by having a different parameter list. Overloading can occur in any class, whether or not you explicitly name a base class when defining the class. Here is how to tell them apart: When you *override* a method definition, the new method definition given in the derived class has the exact same number and types of parameters. On the other hand, if the method in the derived class were to have a different number of parameters or a parameter of a different type from the method in the base class, then the derived class would have both methods. That would be *overloading*. You can also overload without involving a base class, by giving two method definitions in a single class definition.

20. Overriding.

21. Overriding.

22. Overloading.

23. *Polymorphism* means using the process of dynamic binding to allow different objects to use different method actions for the same method name.

24. *Dynamic binding* and *late binding* are two terms for the same thing (so we will give only one definition and only one example). Dynamic binding (or late binding) is a way of handling an invocation of a method that may be overridden in a derived class. With dynamic binding, the meaning of the method invocation is not bound to the location of the method invocation until you run the program. Less formally, when deciding which definition of an overridden method to use, the computer uses the definition in effect *when the object was created* (with new) and does not necessarily use the definition that applies to the type of the variable naming the object. Java uses dynamic binding; an example is given in Display 7.13. If Java did not use dynamic binding, then both invocations of the method `drawAt` would use the definition of `drawHere` given in the definition

of the class `Figure` (Display 7.10), and all that would appear on the screen would be two asterisks.

25. This question may not have a definitive answer. In the original definition of *polymorphism*, overloading was considered an example of polymorphism and some books still use that old definition. In current usage, and in this book, overloading a method name is *not* an example of polymorphism.

26. Most authors list encapsulation, inheritance, and polymorphism as the main characteristics of object-oriented programming.

27. No, they will produce different pictures. The first will draw a box. The second will draw a triangle.

● Programming Projects

1. Give the definition of a class named `Employee` whose objects are records for an employee. This class will be a derived class of the class `Person` given in Display 7.1. An employee record has an employee's name (inherited from the class `Person`), an annual salary represented as a single value of type `double`, a hired date that gives the year hired as a single value of type `int`, and a social security number, which is a value of type `String`. The social security number could be stored as an integer, but it might be too large an integer. So use a string. (After all, a social security number is just an arbitrary identifier that does not use any numeric properties. Have you ever had to add two social security numbers? What could the result possibly mean?) Be sure your class has a reasonable complement of constructors, accessor methods, and mutator methods. Be sure your class has an `equals` method as well. Write a program to fully test your class definitions.

2. Define two derived classes of the class `Figure` in Display 7.10. Your two classes will be called `RightArrow` and `LeftArrow`. These classes will be like the classes `Triangle` and `Box`, but they will draw left- and right-pointing arrows that look like the following, which is a right-pointing arrow:

The size of the arrow is determined by two numbers, one for the length of the "tail," which is 12 in the preceding example, and one for the width of the base of the arrowhead, which is 7 in the preceding example. The width of the base cannot be an even number, and your constructors and mutator methods should check to make sure that it is always odd. Write a test program for each class that tests all the methods in the class. You can assume that the base of the arrowhead is 3 or more.

3. Give the definition of a class named `Doctor` whose objects are records for a clinic's doctors. This class will be a derived class of the class `Person` given in Display 7.1. A `Doctor` record has the doctor's name (inherited from the class `Person`), specialty (for example "Pediatrician," "Obstetrician," "General Practitioner," and so on, so use type `String`), and office visit fee (use type `double`). Be sure your class has a reasonable complement of constructors and accessor methods, and an `equals` method as well. Write a driver program to test all your methods.

4. Give the definition of two classes, `Patient` and `Billing`, whose objects are records for a clinic. `Patient` will be derived from the class `Person` given in Display 7.1. A `Patient` record has the patient's name (inherited from the class `Person`) and social security number (use the type `String` for the reasons described in Programming Project 1). A `Billing` object will contain a `Patient` object and a `Doctor` object (from Programming Project 3). Be sure your classes have a reasonable complement of constructors and accessor methods, and an `equals` method as well. First write a driver program to test all your methods, then write a test program that creates at least two patients, at least two doctors, and at least two `Billing` records, and then prints out the total income from the `Billing` records.

5. Create a base class called `Vehicle` that has the manufacturer's name (type `String`), number of cylinders in the engine (type `int`), and owner (type `Person` given in Display 7.1). Then create a class called `Truck` that is derived from `Vehicle` and has additional properties: the load capacity in tons (type `double`, since it may contain a fractional part) and towing capacity in pounds (type `int`). Be sure your classes have a reasonable complement of constructors and accessor methods, and an `equals` method as well. Write a driver program that tests all your methods.

6. Create the classes, `RightTriangle` and `Rectangle`, each of which is a derived class of the class `Figure` in Display 7.10. Then define a class `Square` that is a derived class of `Rectangle`. Each of these three classes will have two additional methods to calculate area and circumference, as well as the methods inherited. Do not forget to redefine the method `drawHere`. Be sure your classes have a reasonable complement of constructors and accessor methods. The `Square` class should include only one dimension, the side, and should automatically set the height and width to the length of the side. You can use the dimensions of the character width and line spacing even though they are undoubtedly unequal, so a square will not look square (just as a `Box` won't look square, as discussed in the chapter.) Note that the classes `Square` and `Box` produce the same figures, but the two classes are produced in different ways. Write a driver program that tests all your methods.

7. Create a new class called `Dog` that is derived from the `PetRecord` class given in Display 5.20. The new class has the additional attributes of `breed` (type `String`) and `boosterShot` (type `boolean`, `true` if the pet has had its booster shot, `false`

if it has not). Be sure your classes have a reasonable complement of constructors and accessor methods. Write a driver program to test all your methods, then write a program that reads in five pets of type Dog and prints out the name and breed of all dogs that are over two years old and have not had their booster shots.

Chapter

8

Exception Handling

8

It's the exception that proves the rule. -Common maxim (possibly a corruption of something like *It's the exception that tests the rule.*)

One way to write a program is first to assume that nothing unusual or incorrect will happen. For example, if the program takes an entry from a list, you might assume that the list is not empty. Once you have the program working for the core situation, in which things go as planned, you can then add code to take care of the exceptional cases. In Java, there is a way to reflect this approach in your code. Basically, you write your code as if nothing very unusual will happen. After that, you use the Java exception-handling facilities to add code for unusual cases. Exception handling allows you to divide a program or method definition into separate sections for the normal case and for the exceptional case, thereby dividing one larger programming task into two smaller and more easily doable programming tasks. This chapter introduces you to exception handling in Java.

Perhaps the most important use of exception handling is to deal with methods that have some special case that is handled differently, depending on how the method is used. Perhaps the method will be used in many programs, some of which will handle the special case in one way, while others will handle it in some other way. For example, if there is a division by zero in the method, it may turn out that, for some invocations of the method, the program should end, but for other invocations of the method, something else should happen. You will see that such a method can be defined to throw an exception if the special case occurs; this arrangement will let the special case be handled outside of the method. That way, the special case can be handled differently for different invocations of the method.

OBJECTIVES

Become familiar with the notion of exception handling.

Learn Java syntax for exception handing.

Develop the ability to use exception handling effectively in your own classes and programs.

PREREQUISITES

Except for one subsection, this chapter requires only that you have read Chapters 1 through 5 and Chapter 7. The only subsection that requires more background is entitled "ArrayIndexOutOfBoundsException *(Alternative Ordering),*" and that subsection can be considered optional. That subsection requires that you have read Chapter 6, which covers arrays.

Section 8.1 (except for the one subsection discussed in the previous paragraph) can be covered after Chapters 1 through 5. It does not require prior knowledge of the material presented in Chapters 6 and 7.

8.1 BASIC EXCEPTION HANDLING

Jack, be nimble,
Jack, be quick,
Jack, jump over the candle stick. -Anonymous

In Java, **exception handling** proceeds as follows: Either the Java language itself or your code provides a mechanism that signals when something unusual happens. This signaling process is called **throwing an exception.** At another part of your program—in a separate class or method, or just in another part of the code for your program—you place the code that deals with the exceptional case. This code performs the task of **handling the exception.** Of course, we still need to explain the details of exception handling in Java.

exception handling

Exceptions in Java

Most short programs need very little, if any, exception handling, and the exception handling they do use is often not easy to see in the code. So in order to get a simple example, we will use a toy program for our first example. First, we will write the program without using Java's exception-handling facilities, and then we will rewrite it using exception handling.

For this example, suppose that milk is such an important item in our society that people almost never allow themselves to run out of it, but still we would like our programs to accommodate the very unlikely situation of running out of milk. The basic code, which assumes that we do not run out of milk, might be as follows:

```
System.out.println("Enter number of donuts:");
donutCount = SavitchIn.readLineInt( );

System.out.println("Enter number of glasses of milk:");
milkCount = SavitchIn.readLineInt( );

donutsPerGlass = donutCount/(double)milkCount;
System.out.println(donutCount + " donuts.");
System.out.println(milkCount + " glasses of milk.");
System.out.println("You have " + donutsPerGlass
                        + " donuts for each glass of milk.");
```

If there is no milk (that is, the number of glasses of milk entered is zero), this code will produce a division by zero, which is an error. To take care of the unlikely scenario in which we run out of milk, we can add a test for this unusual situation. The complete program with this added test for the special situation is shown in Display 8.1. Now let's see how this program can be rewritten using Java's exception-handling facilities.

■ DISPLAY 8.1   **One Way to Deal with a Problem Situation**

```java
public class GotMilk
{
    public static void main(String[] args)
    {
        int donutCount, milkCount;
        double donutsPerGlass;

        System.out.println("Enter number of donuts:");
        donutCount = SavitchIn.readLineInt();

        System.out.println("Enter number of glasses of milk:");
        milkCount = SavitchIn.readLineInt();

        if (milkCount < 1)
        {
            System.out.println("No Milk!");
            System.out.println("Go buy some milk.");
        }
        else
        {
            donutsPerGlass = donutCount/(double)milkCount;
            System.out.println(donutCount + " donuts.");
            System.out.println(milkCount + " glasses of milk.");
            System.out.println("You have " + donutsPerGlass
                        + " donuts for each glass of milk.");
        }
        System.out.println("End of program.");
    }
}
```

Sample Screen Dialog

```
Enter number of donuts:
2
Enter number of glasses of milk:
0
No Milk!
Go buy some milk.
End of program.
```

In Display 8.2, we have rewritten the program from Display 8.1, using an exception. Because this example is so simple, you would probably not use an exception in this case. However, doing so enables you to learn the Java syntax for exception handling. Although the program as a whole is not made simpler by the use of an exception, the part between the words `try` and `catch` is cleaner than the code used in the other program and hints at

■ DISPLAY 8.2   **An Example of Exception Handling** *(Part 1 of 2)*

```java
public class ExceptionDemo
{
    public static void main(String[] args)
    {
        int donutCount, milkCount;
        double donutsPerGlass;

        try
        {
            System.out.println("Enter number of donuts:");
            donutCount = SavitchIn.readLineInt();

            System.out.println("Enter number of glasses of milk:");
            milkCount = SavitchIn.readLineInt();

            if (milkCount < 1)
                throw new Exception("Exception: No Milk!");

            donutsPerGlass = donutCount/(double)milkCount;
            System.out.println(donutCount + " donuts.");
            System.out.println(milkCount + " glasses of milk.");
            System.out.println("You have " + donutsPerGlass
                            + " donuts for each glass of milk.");
        }
        catch(Exception e)
        {
            System.out.println(e.getMessage());
            System.out.println("Go buy some milk.");
        }

        System.out.println("End of program.");
    }
}
```

This program is just a simple example for learning the basic syntax for exception handling.

throw statement

try *block*

catch *block*

■ **DISPLAY 8.2   An Example of Exception Handling** *(Part 2 of 2)*

Sample Screen Dialog 1

```
Enter number of donuts:
3
Enter number of glasses of milk:
2
3 donuts.
2 glasses of milk.
You have 1.5 donuts for each glass of milk.
End of program.
```

Sample Screen Dialog 2

```
Enter number of donuts:
2
Enter number of glasses of milk:
0
Exception: No Milk!
Go buy some milk.
End of program.
```

the advantage of using exceptions. Look at the code between the words `try` and `catch`. That code is basically the same as the code in Display 8.1, except that, instead of the big `if-else` statement (highlighted in Display 8.1), this program has the following smaller `if` statement:

```
if (milkCount < 1)
    throw new Exception("Exception: No Milk!");
```

This `if` statement says that, if there is no milk, the program should do something exceptional. That something exceptional is given after the word `catch`. The idea is that the normal situation is handled by the code following the word `try` and that the code following the word `catch` is used only in exceptional circumstances. Let's look at the details.

The basic way of handling exceptions in Java consists of the `try-throw-catch` threesome. A `try` **block** has the syntax

try block

```
try
{
    Code_To_Try
}
```

This `try` block contains the code for the basic algorithm that tells the computer what to do when everything goes smoothly. It is called a `try` block because you are not 100 percent sure that all will go smoothly, but you want to give it a try.

If something does go wrong, you want to throw an exception, which is a way of indicating that something went wrong. So the basic outline, when we add a `throw` statement, is as follows:

```
try
{
    Code_To_Try
    Possibly_Throw_An_Exception
    More_Code
}
```

Here is an example of a `try` block with a `throw` statement included, copied from Display 8.2:

```
try
{
    System.out.println("Enter number of donuts:");
    donutCount = SavitchIn.readLineInt();

    System.out.println("Enter number of glasses of milk:");
    milkCount = SavitchIn.readLineInt();

    if (milkCount < 1)
        throw new Exception("Exception: No Milk!");

    donutsPerGlass = donutCount/(double)milkCount;
    System.out.println(donutCount + " donuts.");
    System.out.println(milkCount + " glasses of milk.");
    System.out.println("You have " + donutsPerGlass
                        + " donuts for each glass of milk.");
}
```

`Exception` is a predefined class. The `throw` **statement,** repeated here, creates a new object of the class `Exception` and **throws** it:

throw statement

```
throw new Exception("Exception: No Milk!");
```

When an exception is thrown, the code in the surrounding `try` block stops execution, and another portion of code, known as a `catch` **block,** begins execution. Execution of the `catch` block is called **catching the exception.** When an exception is thrown, it should ultimately be caught by some `catch` block. In Display 8.2, the appropriate `catch` block immediately follows the `try` block. We repeat the `catch` block here:

catch block

```
catch(Exception e)
{
    System.out.println(e.getMessage());
    System.out.println("Go buy some milk.");
}
```

Quick Reference: `throw` Statement

Syntax:

```
throw new Exception_Class_Name(Possibly_Some_Arguments);
```

When the `throw` statement is executed, execution of the surrounding `try` block is stopped, and control typically is transferred to a `catch` block. The code in the `catch` block is executed next. See the box entitled "`try-throw-catch`" later in this chapter for more details.

Example:

```
throw new Exception("Unexpected End of Input.");
```

The `catch` block looks a little like a method definition that has a parameter of type `Exception`. Although it is *not* a method definition, a `catch` block is like a method in some ways. It is a separate piece of code that is executed when a program encounters (and executes) the following within the preceding `try` block:

```
throw new Exception(Possibly_Some_Arguments);
```

This `throw` statement is similar to a method call, but instead of calling a method, it calls the `catch` block and says to execute the code in the `catch` block.

What is that identifier `e` in the following line from a `catch` block?

```
catch(Exception e)
```

catch block
parameter

It looks like a parameter and acts very much like a parameter. So we call this `e` the **catch-block parameter**. (But remember, the `catch` block is not a method.) The `catch`-block parameter and the class name that precedes it do two things:

1. The class name preceding the `catch`-block parameter specifies what kind of exception the `catch` block can catch.
2. The `catch`-block parameter gives you a name for the exception that is caught, so that you can write code in the `catch` block in order to manipulate that exception object.

We will discuss these two functions of the `catch`-block parameter in reverse order. In this subsection, we will discuss using the `catch`-block parameter as a name for the exception object that is caught. In the subsection entitled "Multiple Throws and Catches," later in this chapter, we will discuss which exception objects go with which `catch` block. Our current example has only one `catch` block, so there is no question as to which `catch` block to use. The most common name for a `catch`-block parameter is `e`, but you can use any legal identifier in place of `e`.

throw statement

Let's see how the `catch` block in Display 8.2 works. In order to understand how it works, we also need to look at the `throw` statement in the `try` block, reproduced as follows:

```
throw new Exception("Exception: No Milk!");
```

This `throw` statement is embedded in an `if` statement, but for our purposes, we do not need to know how it comes to be executed. We only want to demonstrate what happens when it is executed. When this `throw` statement is executed, a new object of the class `Exception` is created by the code

```
new Exception("Exception: No Milk!")
```

The string `"Exception: No Milk!"` is an argument for the constructor for the class `Exception`. The `Exception` object, created with `new`, stores this string in an instance variable of the object, so that it can be recovered in the `catch` block. The word `throw` indicates that the object created with `new` is **thrown**. When an object is thrown, execution of the code in the `try` block ends, and control passes to the `catch` block (or blocks) that are placed right after the `try` block. The `catch` block from Display 8.2 is reproduced as follows:

throwing

```
catch(Exception e)
{
    System.out.println(e.getMessage());
    System.out.println("Go buy some milk.");
}
```

When an exception is thrown, it must be of type `Exception` in order for this particular `catch` block to apply; however, as you will see, all exceptions are of type `Exception`, so this `catch` block will catch any exception. The object thrown is plugged in for the `catch`-block parameter `e`, and the code in the `catch` block is executed. So in this case, you can think of `e` as being the exception thrown by the following `throw` statement:

```
throw new Exception("Exception: No Milk!");
```

Every exception has a method called `getMessage`, and unless you provide code specifying otherwise, this method retrieves the string that was given to the exception object by its constructor when the exception was thrown. In this case, `e.getMessage()` returns `"Exception: No Milk!"` Thus, when the `catch` block in Display 8.2 is executed, it causes the following to be written to the screen:

getMessage

```
Exception: No Milk!
Go buy some milk.
```

The flow of control for the program in Display 8.2 is shown in Display 8.3. Part 1 of Display 8.3 assumes that the user enters a positive number for the number of glasses of milk; as a result, *no exception is thrown* (as in the first dialog given in Display 8.2). Part 2 assumes that the user enters zero or a negative number for the number of glasses of milk; as a result, *an exception is thrown* (as shown in the second dialog given in Display 8.2).

In summary, a `try` block contains some code that we are assuming includes a `throw` statement. The `throw` statement is normally executed only in exceptional circumstances, but when it is executed, it throws an exception of some exception class. (So far, `Exception` is the only exception class we have discussed.) When an exception is thrown, execution of the `try` block ends. All the rest of the code in the `try` block is ignored, and control passes to a suitable `catch` block. A `catch` block applies only to an immediately preceding try block. If the exception is thrown, that exception object is plugged in for the catch-block parameter, and the statements in the catch block are executed. After the catch-block code is executed, the program proceeds with the code after the catch block; it does not return to the try block. So all the try-block code after the statement that threw the exception is not executed. (Later, we will discuss what happens when there is no appropriate catch block.)

■ DISPLAY 8.3   **Flow of Control with Exception Handling** *(Part 1 of 2)*

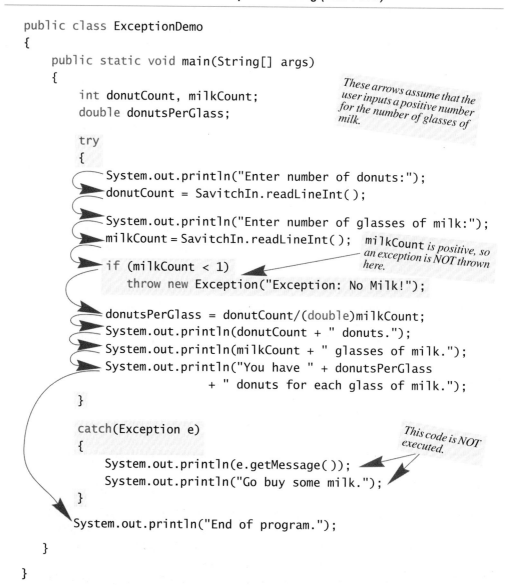

```java
public class ExceptionDemo
{
    public static void main(String[] args)
    {
        int donutCount, milkCount;
        double donutsPerGlass;

        try
        {
            System.out.println("Enter number of donuts:");
            donutCount = SavitchIn.readLineInt();

            System.out.println("Enter number of glasses of milk:");
            milkCount = SavitchIn.readLineInt();

            if (milkCount < 1)
                throw new Exception("Exception: No Milk!");

            donutsPerGlass = donutCount/(double)milkCount;
            System.out.println(donutCount + " donuts.");
            System.out.println(milkCount + " glasses of milk.");
            System.out.println("You have " + donutsPerGlass
                               + " donuts for each glass of milk.");
        }

        catch(Exception e)
        {
            System.out.println(e.getMessage());
            System.out.println("Go buy some milk.");
        }

        System.out.println("End of program.");

    }

}
```

These arrows assume that the user inputs a positive number for the number of glasses of milk.

milkCount is positive, so an exception is NOT thrown here.

This code is NOT executed.

■ DISPLAY 8.3   **Flow of Control with Exception Handling** *(Part 2 of 2)*

```
public class ExceptionDemo
{
    public static void main(String[] args)
    {
        int donutCount, milkCount;
        double donutsPerGlass;

        try
        {
            System.out.println("Enter number of donuts:");
            donutCount = SavitchIn.readLineInt();

            System.out.println("Enter number of glasses of milk:");
            milkCount = SavitchIn.readLineInt();

            if (milkCount < 1)
                throw new Exception("Exception: No Milk!");

            donutsPerGlass = donutCount/(double)milkCount;
            System.out.println(donutCount + " donuts.");
            System.out.println(milkCount + " glasses of milk.");
            System.out.println("You have " + donutsPerGlass
                            + " donuts for each glass of milk.");
        }
        catch(Exception e)
        {
            System.out.println(e.getMessage());
            System.out.println("Go buy some milk.");
        }
        System.out.println("End of program.");
    }
}
```

These arrows assume that the user inputs zero for the number of glasses of milk, and so an exception is thrown.

milkCount is zero or negative, so an exception is thrown here.

This code is NOT executed.

Now let's look at what happens when no exception is thrown in a `try` block. When the `try` block executes normally, without throwing an exception, then after the `try` block is completed, program execution continues with the code after the `catch` block. In other words, if no exception is thrown, the `catch` block is ignored.

This explanation makes it seem as though a `try-throw-catch` setup is equivalent to an `if-else` statement. They almost are equivalent, except for the message carried by the

comparison of try-
throw-catch and
if-else
thrown exception. Thus, a try-throw-catch setup is equivalent to an if-else statement *with the added ability to send a message to one of the branches*. This difference may
not seem like much, but as you will see, the ability to send a message gives the try-
throw-catch setup a lot more versatility than an if-else statement.

Quick Reference: catch-Block Parameter

The catch-block parameter is an identifier in the heading of a catch block that serves as a
placeholder for an exception that might be thrown. When a (suitable) exception is thrown in the preceding try block, that exception is plugged in for the catch-block parameter. The identifier e is
often used for catch-block parameters; however, you can use any legal (nonkeyword) identifier
instead.

Syntax:

```
catch(Exception_Class_Name  Catch_Block_Parameter)
{
    <Code to be performed if an exception of the named exception class is thrown in the
      try block.>
}
```

You may use any legal identifier for the *Catch_Block_Parameter*.

Example:

In the following code, e is the catch-block parameter:

```
catch(Exception e)
{
    System.out.println(e.getMessage());
    System.out.println("Go buy some milk.");
}
```

Quick Reference: The getMessage Method

Every exception has a String instance variable that contains some message, which typically identifies
the reason for the exception. For example, if the exception is thrown as follows, then the quoted string
given as an argument to the constructor Exception is used as the value of this String instance
variable:

```
throw new Exception(Quoted_String_Argument);
```

If the object is called e, then the method call e.getMessage() returns this string.

Example:

Suppose that the following throw statement is executed in a try block:

```
throw new Exception("Input must be positive.");
```

Also suppose that the following is a `catch` block immediately following the `try` block:

```
catch(Exception e)
{
    System.out.println(e.getMessage( ));
    System.out.println("Program aborted.");
    System.exit(0);
}
```

In this case, the method call `e.getMessage( )` returns the string
`"Input must be positive."`

Remember: **An Exception Is an Object**

The following is a `throw` statement:

```
throw new Exception("Illegal character on line 57.");
```

Such statements are typically found embedded in branching statements, but it is also legal to use
them as simple statements. A `throw` statement does not just specify some action that is taken and
forgotten. It creates an object that has a message. (In this case, the message is `"Illegal char-
acter on line 57."`) This object and its message are available to the `catch` block, and so
the effect of throwing an exception is more than just a transfer of control to the first statement of a
`catch` block.

To convince yourself that an object is really created in a `throw` statement, note that the following
statements, while unlikely to be used for anything, is legal:

```
Exception e = new Exception("Illegal character on line 57.");
```

The part `new Exception("Illegal character on line 57.")` is an invocation of a
constructor for the class `Exception`, and it creates an object of the class `Exception`. In the foregoing `throw` statement, `new Exception("Illegal character on line 57.")` is
also an invocation of a constructor for the class `Exception`, and it similarly creates an object of the
class `Exception`.

Quick Reference: **`try-throw-catch`**

When used together, the `try`, `throw`, and `catch` statements are the basic mechanism for throwing and catching exceptions. The `throw` **statement** throws the exception. The `catch` block
catches the exception. When the exception is thrown, the `try` block ends, and then the code in the
`catch` block is executed. After the `catch` block is completed, the code after the `catch` block(s)
is executed (provided that the `catch` block has not ended the program or performed some other
special action).

If no exception is thrown in the `try` block, then after the `try` block is completed, program execution continues with the code after the `catch` block(s). (In other words, if no exception is thrown, the
`catch` block(s) is (are) ignored.)

Syntax:

```
try
{
    Some_Statements
    < Either some code with a throw statement or a method invocation that might throw
      an exception.>
    Some_More_Statements
}
catch(Exception_Class_Name  Catch_Block_Parameter)
{
    < Code to be performed if an exception of the named exception class is thrown in the
      try block.>
}
```

You may use any legal identifier for the *Catch_Block_Parameter*; a common choice is e. The code in the catch block may refer to the *Catch_Block_Parameter*. If there is an explicit throw statement, it is usually embedded in an if statement or an if-else statement. There may be any number of throw statements or any number of method invocations that may throw exceptions. Each catch block can list only one exception, but there can be more than one catch block.

Example:

See Display 8.2.

? Self-Test Questions

1. What output is produced by the following code?

```
int waitTime = 46;

try
{
    System.out.println("Try block entered.");
    if (waitTime > 30)
        throw new Exception("Time Limit Exceeded.");
    System.out.println("Leaving try block.");
}
catch(Exception e)
{
    System.out.println("Exception: " + e.getMessage());
}
System.out.println("After catch block");
```

2. What output would the code in Self-Test Question 1 produce if we changed the line

```
int waitTime = 46;
```

to the following?

```
int waitTime = 12;
```

3. What kind of thing is an exception? Is it an identifier? A variable? A method? An object? A class? Something else?

4. Is the following statement legal?

```
Exception myException = new Exception("Hi Mom!");
```

5. In the code in Display 8.2, how would the program's behavior change if you were to replace

```
if (milkCount < 1)
    throw new Exception("Exception: No Milk!");
```

with the following?

```
if (milkCount < 1)
{
    Exception e = new Exception("Exception: No Milk!");
    throw e;
}
```

6. In the code given in Self-Test Question 1, what is the `throw` statement?

7. What happens when a `throw` statement is executed? Discuss what happens in general, not simply what happens in the code in Self-Test Question 1 or some other sample code.

8. In the code given in Self-Test Question 1, what is the `try` block?

9. In the code given in Self-Test Question 1, what is the `catch` block?

10. In the code given in Self-Test Question 1, what is the `catch`-block parameter?

11. Would the code given in Self-Test Question 1 perform any differently if the `catch` block were changed to the following?

```
catch(Exception messenger)
{
    System.out.println("Exception: "
                          + messenger.getMessage( ));
}
```

12. Write a statement that will throw an exception if the value of the `String` variable named `status` is `"bad"`. This statement would be inside a `try` block, but you need not write the entire `try` block. The exception is supposed to be a member of the class `Exception`, and the string recovered by `getMessage` should be `"Exception thrown: Bad Status."` You also need not write the `catch` block.

Predefined Exception Classes

When you learn about the methods of predefined classes, you will sometimes be told that they might throw certain types of exceptions. These exceptions are of predefined exception classes. If you use one of these methods, you can put the method invocation in a `try` block and follow it with a `catch` block to catch the exception. The names of predefined exceptions are designed to be self-explanatory. Some sample predefined exceptions are

```
IOException
ClassNotFoundException
FileNotFoundException
```

When you catch an exception of one of these predefined exception classes, the string returned by the getMessage method will usually provide you with enough information to identify the source of the exception. Thus, if you have a class called SampleClass, and this class has a method called doStuff, which throws exceptions of the class IOException, you might use the following code:

```
SampleClass object = new SampleClass();
try
{
    <Possibly some code>
    object.doStuff(); //may throw IOException
    <Possibly some more code>
}
catch(IOException e)
{
    <Code to handle the exception, probably including the following:>
    System.out.println(e.getMessage());
}
```

If you think the exception makes proceeding with the program infeasible, then the catch block can end the program with a call to System.exit, as follows:

```
catch(IOException e)
{
    System.out.println(e.getmessage());
    System.out.println("Program aborted");
    System.exit(0);
}
```

Exception

The predefined exception class Exception is the root class of all exceptions. Every exception class is a descendant[1] of the class Exception (that is, it is derived directly from the class Exception or from a class that is derived from the class Exception, or it arises from some longer chain of derivations ultimately starting with the class Exception). You can use the class Exception itself, just as we did in Display 8.2, but you are more likely to use it to define derived classes.

Quick Reference: **The Class Exception**

Every exception class is a descendant class of the class Exception. You can use the class Exception itself in a class or program, but you are more likely to use it to define derived classes.

ArrayIndexOutOfBoundsException *(Alternative Ordering)*

You should read some of Chapter 6, which covers arrays, before reading this short subsection. If you have already covered some of Chapter 6, you should not consider this section optional.

---

1. If you have not yet read Chapter 7, disregard all the references to descendant classes and derived classes.

If your program attempts to use an array index that is out of bounds, an `ArrayIndex-OutOfBoundsException` is thrown, and your program ends, unless the exception is caught in a `catch` block. This is a special kind of exception that need not be caught or accounted for in any way and that normally is not caught in a `catch` block. This sort of exception indicates that there is something wrong with your code and means that you need to fix your code, not catch the exception. Thus, an `ArrayIndexOutOfBoundsException` normally functions more like a run-time error announcement than a regular exception.

? Self-Test Questions

13. Is the following statement legal?

    ```
    IOException sos = new IOException("Hello Houston!");
    ```

14. Is the following statement legal?

    ```
    IOException sos = new IOException("Hello Houston!");
    throw sos;
    ```

8.2 DEFINING EXCEPTION CLASSES

I'll make an exception this time. -My mother

In this section, we show you how to define your own exception classes and describe when and how to throw and catch exceptions.

Defining Your Own Exception Classes

You can define your own exception classes, but they must be derived classes of some already defined exception class. An exception class can be a derived class of any pre-defined exception class or of any exception class that you have already successfully defined. Our examples will be derived classes of the class `Exception`.

When defining an exception class, the constructors are the most important and often the only methods, other than those inherited from the base class. For example, in Display 8.4, we've defined an exception class, called `DivideByZeroException`, whose only methods are a default constructor and a constructor with one `String` parameter. For our purposes, that is all we needed to define. However, the class does inherit all the methods of the class `Exception`.[2] In particular, the class `DivideByZeroException` inherits the

constructors

---

2. Some programmers would prefer to derive the `DivideByZeroException` class from the pre-defined class `ArithmeticException`, but that would make it a kind of exception that you are not required to catch in your code, and so you would lose the help of the compiler in keeping track of uncaught exceptions. For more details, see the subsection "Exceptions That Do Not Need To Be Caught" later in this chapter. If this footnote does not make sense to you, you can safely ignore it. It is primarily for any expert who might be looking over your, or my, shoulder.

method getMessage, which returns a string message. In the default constructor, this string message is set with the following statement, which is the first line in the default constructor definition:

```
super("Dividing by Zero!");
```

This line is a call to a constructor of the base class Exception. As we have already noted, when you pass a string to the constructor for the class Exception, it sets the value of a String instance variable that can later be recovered with a call to getMessage. The method getMessage is an ordinary accessor method of the class Exception. The class DivideByZeroException inherits this String instance variable as well as the accessor method getMessage.

For example, in Display 8.5, we give a sample program that uses this exception class. The exception is thrown using the default constructor, as follows:

```
throw new DivideByZeroException();
```

This exception is caught in the catch block shown in Display 8.5. Consider the following line from that catch block:

```
System.out.println(e.getMessage());
```

This line produces the following output to the screen in Sample Screen Dialogs 2 and 3:

```
Dividing by Zero!
```

The definition of the class DivideByZeroException in Display 8.4 has a second constructor with one parameter of type String. This constructor allows you to choose any message you like when you throw an exception. If the throw statement in Display 8.5 had instead used the string argument

```
throw new DivideByZeroException(
                        "Oops. Shouldn't Have Used Zero.");
```

■ DISPLAY 8.4   **A Programmer-Defined Exception Class**

```
public class DivideByZeroException extends Exception
{
    public DivideByZeroException()
    {
        super("Dividing by Zero!");
    }

    public DivideByZeroException(String message)
    {
        super(message);
    }
}
```

You can do more in an exception constructor, but this form is common.

super is an invocation of the constructor for the base class Exception.

```java
public class DivideByZeroExceptionDemo
{
    private int numerator;
    private int denominator;
    private double quotient;

    public static void main(String[] args)
    {
        DivideByZeroExceptionDemo oneTime =
                            new DivideByZeroExceptionDemo();
        oneTime.doIt();
    }

    public void doIt()
    {
        try
        {
            System.out.println("Enter numerator:");
            numerator = SavitchIn.readLineInt();
            System.out.println("Enter denominator:");
            denominator = SavitchIn.readLineInt();

            if (denominator == 0)
                throw new DivideByZeroException();

            quotient = numerator/(double)denominator;
            System.out.println(numerator + "/"
                                + denominator
                                + " = " + quotient);
        }
        catch(DivideByZeroException e)
        {
            System.out.println(e.getMessage());
            secondChance();
        }
        System.out.println("End of Program.");
    }
```

We will present an improved version of this program later in this chapter.

■ DISPLAY 8.5   **Using a Programmer-Defined Exception Class** *(Part 2 of 3)*

```java
public void secondChance( )
{
    System.out.println("Try again:");
    System.out.println("Enter numerator:");
    numerator = SavitchIn.readLineInt( );
    System.out.println("Enter denominator:");
    System.out.println("Be sure the denominator is not zero.");
    denominator = SavitchIn.readLineInt( );
```

Sometimes it is better to handle an exceptional case without throwing an exception.

```java
    if (denominator == 0)
    {
        System.out.println("I cannot do division by zero.");
        System.out.println("Since I cannot do what you want,");
        System.out.println("the program will now end.");
        System.exit(0);
    }

    quotient = ((double)numerator)/denominator;
    System.out.println(numerator + "/"
                                   + denominator
                                   + " = " + quotient);

    }

}
```

Sample Screen Dialog 1

```
Enter numerator:
5
Enter denominator:
10
5/10 = 0.5
End of Program.
```

■ DISPLAY 8.5   **Using a Programmer-Defined Exception Class** *(Part 3 of 3)*

Sample Screen Dialog 2

```
Enter numerator:
5
Enter denominator:
0
Dividing by Zero!
Try again.
Enter numerator:
5
Enter denominator:
Be sure the denominator is not zero.
10
5/10 = 0.5
End of Program.
```

Sample Screen Dialog 3

```
Enter numerator:
5
Enter denominator:
0
Dividing by Zero!
Try again.
Enter numerator:
5
Enter denominator:
Be sure the denominator is not zero.
0
I cannot do division by zero.
Since I cannot do what you want,
the program will now end.
```

then in Sample Screen Dialogs 2 and 3, the statement

```
System.out.println(e.getMessage( ));
```

would have produced the following output to the screen:

```
Oops. Shouldn't Have Used Zero.
```

Notice that, in Display 8.5, the `try` block is the normal part of the program. If all goes normally, that is the only code that will be executed, and the dialog will be like the one shown in Sample Screen Dialog 1. In the exceptional case, when the user enters a zero for a denominator, the exception is thrown and then is caught in the `catch` block. The `catch` block outputs the message of the exception and then calls the method `secondChance`. The method `secondChance` gives the user a second chance to enter the input correctly and then carries out the calculation. (If the user tries a second time to divide by zero, the method ends the program.) The method `secondChance` is there only for this exceptional case. So we have separated the code for the exceptional case of a division by zero into a separate method, where it will not clutter the code for the normal case.

■ Java Tip
Preserve `getMessage` When You Define Exception Classes

For all predefined exception classes, `getMessage` will return the string that is passed as an argument to the constructor (or will return a default string if no argument is used with the constructor). For example, if the exception is thrown as follows, then `"This is a big exception!"` is used as the value of the `String` instance variable:

```
throw new Exception("This is a big exception!");
```

If the object is called `e`, the method call `e.getMessage( )` returns `"This is a big exception!"`

It is a good idea to preserve this behavior of the method `getMessage` in any exception class you define. For example, suppose you define an exception class called `MySpecialException` and throw an exception as follows:

```
throw new MySpecialException("Wow, what an exception!");
```

If `e` is a name for the exception thrown, then `e.getMessage( )` should return `"Wow, what an exception!"` To ensure that the exception classes that you define behave in this way, be sure to include a constructor with a string parameter that begins with a call to `super`, as illustrated by the following constructor:

```
public MySpecialException(String message)
{
    super(message);
    //There can be more code here, but often there is none.
}
```

The call to super is a call to a constructor of the base class. If the base-class constructor handles the message correctly, then so will a class defined in this way.

You should also include a default constructor in each exception class. This default constructor should set up a default value to be retrieved by getMessage. The constructor should begin with a call to super, as illustrated by the following constructor:

```java
public MySpecialException()
{
    super("MySpecialException thrown.");
    //There can be more code here, but often there is none.
}
```

If getMessage works as we described for the base class, then this sort of default constructor will work correctly for the new exception class being defined. ☐

Remember: **Characteristics of Exception Objects**

The two most important things about an exception object are its type (the exception class) and the message that it carries in an instance variable of type String. This string can be recovered with the accessor method getMessage. The string allows your code to send a message along with an exception object, so that the catch block can use the message. (The upcoming subsections explain why the type of an exception object is important.)

● **Programming Tip**
When to Define an Exception Class

As a general rule, if you are going to insert a throw statement in your code, it is probably best to define your own exception class. That way, when your code catches an exception, your catch blocks can tell the difference between your exceptions and exceptions thrown by methods in predefined classes. For example, in Display 8.5, we used the exception class DivideByZeroException, which we defined in Display 8.4.

Although it would not be a good idea, you might be tempted to use the predefined class Exception to throw the exception in Display 8.5, as follows:

```java
throw new Exception("Dividing by Zero!");
```

You could then catch this exception with the catch block

```java
catch(Exception e)
{
    System.out.println(e.getMessage());
    secondChance();
}
```

Although this approach will work for the program in Display 8.5, it is not the best technique, because the foregoing `catch` block will catch any exception, such as an `IOException`. An `IOException`, however, might need a different action than `secondChance( )`. Rather than using the class `Exception` to catch division by zero, it is better to use the more specialized programmer-defined class `DivideByZeroException`, as we did in Display 8.5.

Quick Reference: Programmer-Defined Exception Classes

You may define your own exception classes, but every such class must be a derived class of an already existing exception class (either predefined or successfully defined by you).

Guidelines:

- If you have no compelling reason to use any other class as the base class, use the class `Exception` as the base class.

- You should define at least two constructors, as described later in this list. Your exception class inherits the method `getMessage`. Normally, you do not need to add any other methods, but it is legal to do so.

- You should start each constructor definition with a call to the constructor of the base class, such as the following:

    ```
    super("Tidal Wave Exception thrown!");
    ```

- You should include a default constructor, in which case the call to `super` should have a string argument that indicates what kind of exception it is. This string can then be recovered using the `getMessage` method.

- You should also include a constructor that takes a single string argument. In this case, the string should be an argument in the call to `super`. That way, the string can be recovered with a call to `getMessage`.

Example:

```
public class TidalWaveException extends Exception
{
    public TidalWaveException( )
    {
        super("Tidal Wave Exception thrown!");
    }

    public TidalWaveException(String message)
    {
        super(message);
    }
}
```

super is a call to the constructor for the base class Exception.

15. Define an exception class called `CoreBreachException`. The class should have a constructor with no parameters. If an exception is thrown with this zero-argument constructor, `getMessage` should return `"Core Breach! Evacuate Ship!"` The class should also have a constructor with a single parameter of type `String`. If an exception is thrown with this constructor, then `getMessage` returns the value that was used as an argument to the constructor.

16. Define an exception class called `MessageTooLongException`. The class should have a constructor with no parameters. If an exception is thrown with this zero-argument constructor, `getMessage` should return `"Message Too Long!"` The class should also have a constructor with a single parameter of type `String`. If an exception is thrown with this constructor, then `getMessage` returns the value that was used as an argument to the constructor.

17. Suppose the exception class `ExerciseException` is defined as follows:

```
public class ExerciseException extends Exception
{
    public ExerciseException()
    {
        super("Exercise Exception thrown!");
        System.out.println("Exception thrown.");
    }

    public ExerciseException(String message)
    {
        super(message);
        System.out.println(
          "ExerciseException invoked with an argument.");
    }
}
```

What output would be produced by the following code (which is just an exercise and not likely to occur in a program)?

```
ExerciseException e =
              new ExerciseException("Do Be Do");
System.out.println(e.getMessage());
```

18. Suppose the exception class `CrazyException` is defined as follows:

```
public class CrazyException extends Exception
{
    public CrazyException()
    {
        super("Crazy Exception thrown!");
        System.out.println(
                "Wow, Crazy exception thrown!!");
    }
```

```java
    public CrazyException(String message)
    {
        super(message);
        System.out.println(
         "Wow, Crazy exception thrown with an argument!");
    }

    public void crazyMethod()
    {
        System.out.println("Message is " + getMessage());
    }
}
```

What output would be produced by the following code (which is just an exercise and not likely to occur in a program)?

```java
CrazyException exceptionObject = new CrazyException();
System.out.println(exceptionObject.getMessage());
exceptionObject.crazyMethod();
```

19. Suppose the (unlikely) exception class `DoubleException` is defined as follows:

```java
public class DoubleException extends Exception
{
    public DoubleException()
    {
        super("Double Exception thrown!");
    }

    public DoubleException(String message)
    {
        super(message + message);
    }
}
```

What output would be produced by the following code (which is just an exercise and not likely to occur in a program)?

```java
int number;
try
{
    System.out.println("try block entered:");
    number = 42;
    if (number > 0)
        throw new DoubleException(
                        "Double Exception thrown!");
    System.out.println("Leaving try block.");
}

catch(DoubleException exceptionObject)
{
    System.out.println(exceptionObject.getMessage());
}
System.out.println("End of code.");
```

20. Suppose that, in Self-Test Question 19, the catch block is changed to the following:

```
catch(Exception exceptionObject)
{
    System.out.println(exceptionObject.getMessage());
}
```

(The type DoubleException is replaced with Exception.) How would this change affect the output?

21. Suppose that, in Self-Test Question 19, the line

```
number = 42;
```

were changed to

```
number = -99;
```

How would this change affect the output?

22. Although an exception class normally carries only a string message, you can define exception classes to carry a message of any type. For example, objects of the following type can also carry an int "message" (as well as a string message):

```
public class IntException extends Exception
{
    private int intMessage;
    public IntException()
    {
        super("IntException thrown!");
    }
    public IntException(String message)
    {
        super(message + message);
    }
    public IntException(int number)
    {
        super("IntException thrown!");
        intMessage = number;
    }
    public int getNumber()
    {
        return intMessage;
    }
}
```

What output would be produced by the following code (which is just an exercise and not likely to occur in a program)?

```
IntException e =
            new IntException(42);

System.out.println(e.getNumber());
System.out.println(e.getMessage());
```

23. Can you define an exception class as a derived class of the predefined class `IOException`, or must a defined exception class be derived from the class `Exception`?

8.3 USING EXCEPTION CLASSES

buck n. small object placed before the dealer in poker.
(Thus) pass the buck (means) shift responsibility (to). - The Little Oxford Dictionary of Current English, Oxford University Press, 1986
The buck stops here. -Sign on Harry S Truman's desk while he was president

In this section, we discuss techniques for using exceptions in your programs and methods.

Declaring Exceptions (Passing the Buck)

Sometimes it makes sense to delay handling of an exception. For example, you might have a method with code that throws an exception if there is an attempt to divide by zero, but you may not want to catch the exception in that method. Perhaps some programs that use the method should simply end if the exception is thrown, and other programs that use the method should do something else; as a result, you would not know what to do about the exception if you caught it inside the method. In these cases, it makes sense not to catch the exception in the method definition, but instead to have any program (or other code) that uses the method place the method invocation in a `try` block and catch the exception in a `catch` block that follows that `try` block.

If a method does not catch an exception, it must at least warn programmers that any invocation of the method might possibly throw an exception. This warning is called a throws **clause.** For example, a method that might throw a `DivideByZeroException` and that does not catch the exception would have a heading similar to the following:

```
public void sampleMethod() throws DivideByZeroException
```

The part `throws DivideByZeroException` is a `throws` clause stating that an invocation of the method `sampleMethod` might throw a `DivideByZeroException`.

Most exceptions that might be thrown when a method is invoked must be accounted for in one of two ways:

1. The possible exception can be caught in a `catch` block within the method definition.

2. The possible exception can be declared at the start of the method definition by placing the exception-class name in a `throws` clause (and letting whoever uses the method worry about how to handle the exception).

In any one method, you can mix these two alternatives, catching some exceptions and declaring others in a `throws` clause.

You already know about technique 1, handling exceptions in a `catch` block. Technique 2 is a form of "passing the buck." For example, suppose `methodA` has a `throws` clause as follows:

```
public void methodA( ) throws DivideByZeroException
```

In this case, `methodA` is absolved of the responsibility of catching any exceptions of type `DivideByZeroException` that might occur when `methodA` is executed. If, however, there is some `methodB` that includes an invocation of `methodA`, then `methodB` must handle the exception. When `methodA` adds the `throws` clause, it is "saying" to `methodB`, "If you invoke me, you must handle any `DivideByZeroException` that I throw." In effect, `methodA` has passed the responsibility ("passed the buck") for any exceptions of type `DivideByZeroException` from itself to any method that calls it.

Of course, if `methodA` passes the buck to `methodB` by including a `throws` clause such as

```
throws DivideByZeroException
```

then `methodB` may also pass the buck to whoever calls it by including the same `throws` clause in its definition. But in a well-written program, every exception that is thrown should eventually be caught by a `catch` block in some method that does not pass the buck.

Remember: Throwing an Exception Can End a Method

If a method throws an exception, and the exception is not caught inside the method, then the method invocation ends immediately after the exception is thrown.

In Display 8.6, we have rewritten the program from Display 8.5 so that the normal case is in a method called `normal`. The method `main` includes a call to the method `normal` and puts the call in a `try` block. Because the method `normal` can throw a `DivideByZeroException` that it does not catch, we need to declare this condition in a `throws` clause at the start of the definition of `normal`. If we set up our program in this way, the case in which nothing goes wrong is completely isolated and easy to read. It is not even cluttered by `try` blocks and `catch` blocks.

A `throws` clause can contain more than one exception type. In such cases, you separate the exception types with commas, as follows:

```
public int superMethod( )
                    throws IOException, DivideByZeroException
```

Quick Reference: `throws` Clause

If you define a method that might throw exceptions of some particular class, then normally either your method definition must include a `catch` block that will catch the exception or you must declare (that is, list) the exception class within a `throws` clause, as described in the rest of this box.

Quick Reference continues on page 505.

```java
public class DoDivision
{
    private int numerator;
    private int denominator;
    private double quotient;

    public static void main(String[] args)
    {
        DoDivision doIt = new DoDivision();

        try
        {
            doIt.normal();
        }
        catch(DivideByZeroException e)
        {
            System.out.println(e.getMessage());
            doIt.secondChance();
        }

        System.out.println("End of Program.");

    }

    public void normal() throws DivideByZeroException
    {
        System.out.println("Enter numerator:");
        numerator = SavitchIn.readLineInt();
        System.out.println("Enter denominator:");
        denominator = SavitchIn.readLineInt();
        if (denominator == 0)
            throw new DivideByZeroException();
        quotient = numerator/(double)denominator;
        System.out.println(numerator + "/"
                                        + denominator
                                        + " = " + quotient);
    }

    public void secondChance()
    {
        System.out.println("Try Again:");
        System.out.println("Enter numerator:");
        numerator = SavitchIn.readLineInt();
```

■ DISPLAY 8.6   Passing the Buck with a `throws` Clause *(Part 2 of 2)*

```
System.out.println("Enter denominator:");
System.out.println("Be sure the denominator is not zero.");
denominator = SavitchIn.readLineInt();

if (denominator == 0)
{
    System.out.println("I cannot do division by zero.");
    System.out.println("Since I cannot do what you want,");
    System.out.println("the program will now end.");
    System.exit(0);
}

quotient = ((double)numerator)/denominator;
System.out.println(numerator + "/"
                            + denominator
                            + " = " + quotient);
    }

}
```

Sample Screen Dialog

The input/output dialogs are identical to those for the program in Display 8.5.

Syntax (covers most common cases):

```
public Type_Or_void Method(Parameter_List) throws List_Of_Exceptions
Body_Of_Method
```

Example:

```
public void methodA(int n) throws IOException, MyException
{
    .
    .
    .
}
```

FAQ: What Happens If an Exception Is Never Caught?

If every method up to and including the `main` method simply includes a `throws` clause for a particular class of exceptions, then it may turn out that an exception of that class is thrown, but never caught. In such cases, either the program ends or its performance may become unreliable. For all the kinds of programs we have seen thus far, if an exception is thrown, but never caught, then the program ends. (For GUI programs—programs with interactive windows of the kind we will discuss in Chapter 12—when an exception is thrown, but never caught, the program will probably not end, but the program's behavior may be unreliable from then on.)

Exceptions That Do Not Need To Be Caught

Thus far, we have said that, in most cases, an exception must either be caught in a `catch` block or be declared in a `throws` clause. That is the basic rule, but there are exceptions to this rule. (An exception to a rule about exceptions! Seems reasonable enough.) There are some exceptional exceptions that you do not need to account for in this way (although you can catch them in a `catch` block if you want to). These are basically exceptions that result from errors of some sort. Normally, you do not write a `throw` statement for these exceptions. They are usually thrown by methods in predefined classes.

Exceptions that are descendants of the class `Error` or of the class `RuntimeException` do not need to be accounted for in a `catch` block or `throws` clause. One such exception is `NoSuchMethodError`. This exception occurs when your code invokes a method, but you have provided no definition for that method name. For these sorts of exceptions, you should repair your code by fixing the bug in your code, not by adding a `catch` block. Other exceptions that you do not need to catch or declare are exceptions that are more or less beyond your control. One such exception is `OutOfMemoryError`. If this exception is thrown, your program has run out of memory, which means that either you have an inefficient program or you need to buy more memory for your computer. Adding a `catch` block will not help in this case, and it is not required.[3]

How do you know if an exception is one that you must either catch or declare in a `throws` clause? If it is a predefined class, you can look up the documentation for that class. If it is a descendant of either the class `RunTimeException` or the class `Error`, then you need not account for it in a `catch` block or `throws` clause. In all other cases, you must either catch the exception in a `catch` block or list the exception in a `throws` clause. However, you normally need not go through the bother of checking the documentation.

---

3. Technically speaking, the class `Error` and its descendant classes are not considered to be exception classes, because they are not descendants of the class `Exception`. However, objects of these classes can be thrown and can be caught in a `catch` block just as real exceptions can. So to us, they look like exceptions.

In most cases, you must either catch or declare in a `throws` clause every exception that is explicitly thrown by your code, as in this example:

```
if (denominator == 0)
    throw new DivideByZeroException( );
```

Also, if a method has a `throws` clause for a type of exception, and your code includes an invocation of that method, then your code must either catch the exception or declare it in a `throws` clause.

You need not worry too much about which exceptions you do and do not need to declare in a `throws` clause. If you fail to account for some exception that Java requires you to account for, the compiler will tell you about it, and you can then either catch it or add it to a `throws` clause.

Quick Reference: Details on `throws` Clauses in Derived Classes

If you redefine a method in a derived class, then the `throws` clause for the redefined method cannot contain any exception classes that are not in the `throws` clause of the same method in the base class. In other words, you cannot add exceptions to the `throws` clause when you redefine a method. This, of course, means that you cannot throw any exceptions that are not either caught in a `catch` block or already listed in the `throws` clause of the same method in the base class. You can, however, declare fewer exceptions in the `throws` clause of the redefined method.

The `AssertionError` Class *(Optional)*

When we discussed the `assert` operator and assertion checking in Chapter 4, we said that, if your program contains an assertion check and the assertion check fails, your program will end with an error message. That statement is more or less true, but it is incomplete. What happens is that an exception of the class `AssertionError` is thrown. If it is not caught in a `catch` block, your program ends with an error message. However, if you wish, you can catch it in a `catch` block, although this is not a very common thing to do.

As the name suggests, the class `AssertionError` is derived from the class `Error`, and so you are not required to either catch it in a `catch` block or declare it in a `throws` clause.

Multiple Throws and Catches

A `try` block can potentially throw any number of exceptions, and they can be of different types. Each `catch` block can catch exceptions of only one type, but you can catch exceptions of different types by placing more than one `catch` block after a `try` block. For example, the program in Display 8.7 has two `catch` blocks after its `try` block. (The class `NegativeNumberException` is defined in Display 8.8.)

■ DISPLAY 8.7   Catching Multiple Exceptions *(Part 1 of 2)*

```
public class TwoCatchesDemo
{
    public static void main(String[] args)
    {
        try
        {
            int widgets, defective;
            double ratio;

            System.out.println("Enter number of widgets produced:");
            widgets = SavitchIn.readLineInt();
            if (widgets < 0)
                throw new NegativeNumberException("widgets");
            System.out.println("How many were defective?");
            defective = SavitchIn.readLineInt();
            if (defective < 0)
                throw new NegativeNumberException("defective widgets");

            ratio = exceptionalDivision(widgets, defective);
            System.out.println( "One in every  " + ratio
                                        + " widgets is defective.");
        }
        catch(DivideByZeroException e)
        {
            System.out.println("Congratulations! A perfect record!");
        }
        catch(NegativeNumberException e)
        {
            System.out.println("Cannot have a negative number of "
                            + e.getMessage());
        }

        System.out.println("End of program.");
    }

    public static double exceptionalDivision(double numerator,
                double denominator) throws DivideByZeroException
```

This is just a sample example for learning the basic syntax for exception handling.

■ DISPLAY 8.7   **Catching Multiple Exceptions** *(Part 2 of 2)*

```
    {
        if (denominator == 0)
            throw new DivideByZeroException();
        return (numerator/denominator);
    }
}
```

Sample Screen Dialog 1

```
Enter number of widgets produced:
1000
How many were defective?
500
One in every 2.0 widgets is defective.
End of program.
```

Sample Screen Dialog 2

```
Enter number of widgets produced:
-10
Cannot have a negative number of widgets
End of program.
```

Sample Screen Dialog 3

```
Enter number of widgets produced:
1000
How many were defective?
0
Congratulations! A perfect record!
End of program.
```

■ DISPLAY 8.8   The Class `NegativeNumberException`

```java
public class NegativeNumberException extends Exception
{
    public NegativeNumberException()
    {
        super("Negative Number Exception!");
    }
    public NegativeNumberException(String message)
    {
        super(message);
    }
}
```

■ **Java Tip**
Catch the More Specific Exception First

When catching multiple exceptions, the order of the `catch` blocks can be important. When an exception is thrown in a `try` block, the `catch` blocks are examined in order, and the first one that matches the type of the exception thrown is the one that is executed. Thus, the following ordering of `catch` blocks would not be good:

```java
catch (Exception e)
{
        .
        .
        .
}
catch(DivideByZeroExecption e)
{
        .
        .
        .
}
```

The second `catch` block can never be reached.

With this ordering, the `catch` block for `DivideByZeroException` would never be used, because all exceptions are caught by the first `catch` block. Fortunately, the compiler will probably warn you about this problem. The correct ordering is to reverse the `catch` blocks so that the more specific exception comes before its parent exception class, as shown in the following code:

```
catch(DivideByZeroException e)
{
       .
       .
       .

}
catch(Exception e)
{
       .
       .
       .

} □
```

● **Programming Tip**
Exception Handling and Information Hiding

A `throw` statement is not the only kind of statement that can throw an exception. A method invocation can also throw an exception. (Specifically, a method invocation can throw an exception that is declared in its `throws` clause). Any time an exception is thrown, regardless of the kind of statement throwing it, it is handled in the exact same way: It is either caught in a `catch` block or declared in `throws` clause. When analyzing a method invocation that might throw an exception, do not think about where in the method definition the `throw` statement is located. It does not matter how the exception is thrown. All that matters is that the method invocation might throw an exception. The exception is handled in the same way no matter what happens inside the method. ○

? Self-Test Questions

24. Correct the following method definition by adding a suitable `throws` clause:

```
public void doStuff(int n)
{
    if (n < 0)
        throw new Exception("Negative number.");
}
```

25. What happens if an exception is thrown inside a method invocation, but the exception is not caught inside the method?

26. Suppose there is an invocation of method A inside of method B, and an invocation of method B inside of method C. Invocation of method C leads to an invocation of method B, which, in turn, leads to an invocation of method A. Now suppose that method A throws an exception that it does not catch itself. Where might the exception be caught? In B? In C? Outside of C?

27. What output will be produced by the following code (the definition of the class NegativeNumberException is given in the preceding material, but you do not even need to look at those definitions in order to answer this question)?

```java
int n;
try
{
    n = 7;
    if (n > 0)
        throw new Exception();
    else if (n < 0)
        throw new NegativeNumberException();
    else
        System.out.println("Hello!");
}

catch(NegativeNumberException e)
{
    System.out.println("First catch.");
}
catch(Exception e)
{
    System.out.println("Second catch");
}
System.out.println("End of Code");
```

28. What would be the output produced by the code in Self-Test Question 27 if the line

```java
n = 7;
```

were changed to the following?

```java
n = -7;
```

29. What would be the output produced by the code in Self-Test Question 27 if the line

```java
n = 7;
```

were changed to the following?

```java
n = 0;
```

30. What is the output produced by the following program?

```java
public class CatchDemo
{
    public static void main(String[] args)
    {
        CatchDemo object = new CatchDemo();
        try
        {
            System.out.println("Trying");
            object.sampleMethod();
            System.out.println("Trying after call.");
        }
```

```java
        catch(Exception e)
        {
            System.out.println("Catching");
            System.out.println(e.getMessage( ));
        }
    }
    public void sampleMethod( ) throws Exception
    {
        System.out.println("Starting sampleMethod.");
        throw new
            Exception("From sampleMethod with love.");
    }

        <There may be more methods, and there may be instance variables,
                    but they are not needed in order to answer this question.>

}
```

▲ *Gotcha*

Overuse of Exceptions

Exceptions should be used sparingly and only in certain ways. In the next subsection, we discuss where it is good to use an exception. Another good rule is the following: If you are tempted to include a `throw` statement, think about how you might write your program or class definition without this `throw` statement. If you can think of an alternative that produces reasonable code, you probably should not include the `throw` statement. △

● **Programming Tip**

When to Throw an Exception

Thus far, we have used some very simple code to illustrate the basic concepts of exception handling. However, our examples were unrealistically simple. A more complicated, but better, guideline is to separate throwing an exception and catching the exception into separate methods. In most cases, you should include any `throw` statement within a method definition, declare the exception in a `throws` clause in that method, and place the `catch` block in *a different method*. Thus, the preferred use of the `try-throw-catch` triple is as illustrated in the following code:

```java
public void methodA( ) throws MyException
{
        .
        .
        .
    throw new MyException("Bla Bla Bla");
        .
        .
        .
}
```

Then, in *some other method* (perhaps even some other method in some other class), you have

```
public void methodB( )
{
        .
        .
        .
    try
    {
            .
            .
            .
        methodA( );
            .
            .
            .
    }
    catch(MyException e)
    {
        Handle_Exception
    }
        .
        .
        .
}
```

Moreover, even this kind of use of a `throw` statement should be reserved for cases in which it is unavoidable. If you can easily handle a problem in some other way, do not throw an exception. Reserve `throw` statements for situations in which the way the exceptional condition is handled depends on how and where the method is used. If the way that the exceptional condition is handled depends on how and where the method is invoked, then the best thing to do is to let the programmer who invokes the method handle the exception. In all other situations, it is preferable to avoid throwing exceptions.

Predefined methods often leave exception handling to the programmer invoking the method. When you learn of a predefined method, you may be told that it throws exceptions of certain kinds. You, as the programmer who uses the predefined method, are then expected to handle any exception thrown by the method.

FAQ: When Should My Code Throw an Exception?

For the most part, `throw` statements should be used within methods and declared in a `throws` clause for the method. Moreover, they should be reserved for situations in which the way the exceptional condition is handled depends on how and where the method is used. In these situations, the best thing to do is to let the programmer who invokes the method handle the exception. In all other situations, it is almost always preferable to avoid throwing an exception.

▲ *Gotcha*

Nested `try-catch` Blocks

You can place a `try` block and its subsequent `catch` blocks inside a larger `try` block or inside a larger `catch` block. In rare cases, this approach may be useful, but if you are tempted to use it, you should suspect that there is a nicer way to organize your code. It is almost always better to place the inner `try-catch` blocks inside a method definition and place an invocation of the method in the outer `try` or `catch` block (or maybe just eliminate one or more `try` blocks completely).

If you place a `try` block and its subsequent `catch` blocks inside a larger `catch` block, you will need to use different names for the `catch`-block parameters in the inner and outer blocks, respectively, because of how Java handles nested blocks of any kind. Remember, `try` blocks and `catch` blocks are blocks.

If you place a `try` block and its subsequent `catch` blocks inside a larger `try` block, and an exception is thrown in the inner `try` block, but is not caught in the inner `catch` blocks, then the exception is thrown to the outer `try` block for processing and might be caught in one of the outer `catch` blocks. △

The `finally` Block *(Optional)*

You can add a `finally` block after a `try` block and its subsequent `catch` blocks. The code in the `finally` block is executed whether or not an exception is thrown. The general syntax is as follows:

```
try
{
    ...
}
catch_Block(s)
finally
{
    < Code to be executed whether or not an exception is thrown or caught.>
}
```

To see the significance and potential usefulness of a `finally` block, suppose that the `try-catch-finally` blocks are inside a method definition. (After all, every set of `try-catch-finally` blocks is inside of some method, even if it is only the method `main`.) One of three possible outcomes will occur when the code in the `try-catch-finally` blocks is run:

1. The `try` block runs to the end, and no exception is thrown. In this situation, the `finally` block is executed after the `try` block.

2. An exception is thrown in the `try` block and is caught in a corresponding `catch` block positioned after the `try` block. In this case, the `finally` block is executed after the `catch` block is executed.

3. An exception is thrown in the `try` block, and there is no matching `catch` block in the method to catch the exception. In this case, the method invocation ends, and the

exception object is thrown to the enclosing method. In this case, the `finally` block is executed before the method ends. Note that you cannot account for this third case simply by placing code after the string of `catch` blocks.

At this stage of your programming, you may not have much need for a `finally` block, but we include a description of it for completeness. At some point, you may find it useful.

Rethrowing an Exception *(Optional)*

It is legal to throw an exception within a `catch` block. In rare cases, you may want to catch an exception and then, depending on the string produced by `getMessage` (or depending on something else), decide to throw the same or a different exception for handling further up the chain of exception-handling blocks.

? Self-Test Questions

31. Can you have a `try` block and corresponding `catch` blocks inside another, larger `try` block?

32. Can you have a `try` block and corresponding `catch` blocks inside another, larger `catch` block?

33. This question is for those who have read the optional section "The `finally` Block." What is the output produced by the given program? What would the output be if the argument to `sampleMethod` were −99 instead of 99? What would it be if the argument were 0 instead of 99?

```java
public class FinallyDemo
{
    public static void main(String[] args)
    {
        try
        {
            sampleMethod(99);
        }
        catch(Exception e)
        {
            System.out.println("Caught in main.");
        }
    }

    public static void sampleMethod(int n) throws Exception
    {
        try
        {
            if (n > 0)
                throw new Exception();
            else if (n < 0)
                throw new NegativeNumberException();
```

```
        else
            System.out.println("No Exception.");
        System.out.println("Still in sampleMethod.");
    }
    catch(NegativeNumberException e)
    {
        System.out.println("Caught in sampleMethod.");
    }
    finally
    {
        System.out.println("In finally block.");
    }
    System.out.println("After finally block.");
    }
}
```

Case Study
A Line-Oriented Calculator

You have been asked to write a program that can be used as a calculator, similar to a handheld calculator. The calculator should do addition, subtraction, multiplication, and division. This program is intended to be used with rather old equipment, so it cannot use a windowing interface, but must use simple line-by-line text input and text output (like the other programs in this chapter).

task specification

You need to specifically define the user interface. You propose that the user be instructed to enter operations and numbers such that each operation and number is typed on a line by itself, as in the following example:

specification refinement

```
+ 3.4
```

It should not matter whether there is whitespace before or after the operation, like +, or the number, like 3.4. As the user enters more operations and numbers, the program keeps track of the results of the operations performed so far, as in the following sample dialog:

```
result = 0
+ 80
result + 80 = 80
updated result = 80
−2
result − 2 = 78
updated result = 78
```

Here, the program assumes that the initial "result" is zero. The user's input is shown in color. The black text is output from the program. Notice that the input is echoed so that the user can see what the computer is doing. You further suggest that the user indicate the end of a set of calculations by entering the letter E (in either upper- or lowercase).

Your suggested interface is accepted, and you begin the project design. You decide to design a class for a calculator. The class will have a `main` method that is a complete, simple calculator program that follows the specification you have refined. Later on, you might design a more elaborate interface for the calculator. So the class will be a bit more powerful than what is needed for the method `main`.

data for class

The program keeps track of one number that serves the same purpose as the number displayed on a handheld calculator. On the screen, it is shown as, for example,

```
updated result = 80
```

The user can add, subtract, multiply, and divide with instructions such as

```
+3
```

result

The current result is kept in a private instance variable called `result`. The program always adds, subtract, multiplies, or divides the current result and the number entered. For instance, if the user enters

```
-9.5
```

and the current value of `result` is 80, then the value of `result` is changed to 70.5. When the user enters an `'e'` or an `'E'`, the program ends. If you look ahead to the sample screen dialog in Display 8.11, you can get an idea of how this calculator is used.

method actions

You decide that you need the class to have at least the following methods:

- a method named `reset` to reset the value of `result` to zero.

- a method to calculate the result of one operation. You decide to produce the result of one operation as a returned value, rather than immediately updating the instance variable `result`. This approach will make your class more versatile. You decide that the method should be approximately as follows:

```
/**
 Returns n1 op n2,
 provided op is one of '+', '-', '*',or '/'.
*/
public double evaluate(char op, double n1, double n2)
```

- an accessor method called `getResult` to recover the value of the instance variable `result`.

- a mutator method called `setResult` to reset the value of `result` to any specified value.

- a method called `doCalculation` that includes a loop to do one series of operations, producing a final result (with a call to `evaluate` on each loop iteration).

unexceptional part

You decide first to write the code as if everything will go smoothly. Perhaps you note exceptions where they might occur, but you defer writing the exception handling until after the heart of the class actions is designed. The definitions of the methods `reset`, `setResult`, and `getResult` are routine, but the methods `evaluate` and `doCalculation` require a bit of thought. Let's consider `doCalculation` first.

doCalculation

The heart of the calculator's action is performed by the method doCalculation. The basic loop sequence should repeat the following again and again until the user enters the letter 'e' or an improper operator:

```
nextOp = SavitchIn.readNonwhiteChar();
nextNumber = SavitchIn.readLineDouble();
result = evaluate(nextOp, result, nextNumber);
```

Here, nextOp is a variable of type char, nextNumber is a variable of type double, and result is the instance variable. When the user enters the letter 'e' (in lowercase or uppercase), the loop ends and the calculation ends. You convert the previous code to the following more complete Java loop:

```
boolean done = false;
while (! done)
{
    nextOp = SavitchIn.readNonwhiteChar();
    if ((nextOp == 'e') || (nextOp == 'E'))
        done = true;
    else
    {
        nextNumber = SavitchIn.readLineDouble();
        result = evaluate(nextOp, result, nextNumber);
        System.out.println("result " + nextOp + " "
                            + nextNumber + " = " + result);
        System.out.println("updated result = " + result);
    }
}
```

Note that readLineDouble reads the rest of the line after the method readNonWhiteChar has read a single character. The method readLineDouble does not have to start reading at the beginning of a line. If the user enters

```
+ 8.95
```

then the method readNonwhiteChar reads the '+', and the method readLineDouble reads the 8.95.

Next, you need to design the method evaluate, which you described as follows:

evaluate

```
/**
 Returns n1 op n2,
 provided op is one of '+', '-', '*',or '/'.
*/
public double evaluate(char op, double n1, double n2)
```

The heart of the method evaluate can be a large switch statement, something like the following:

```
switch (op)
{
    case '+':
        answer = n1 + n2;
        break;
```

```
          case '−':
              answer = n1 − n2;
              break;
          case '*':
              answer = n1 * n2;
              break;
          case '/':
              if (n2 == 0.0)
                  throw new DivideByZeroException( );
              answer = n1/n2;
              break;
    }
    return answer;
```

You decided to throw an exception if the user attempts to do a division by zero, so the preceding case for division includes the following:

```
if (n2 == 0.0)
    throw new DivideByZeroException( );
```

This approach is conceptually fine, but there is one problem: The numbers involved are of type `double`. Floating-point numbers, such as numbers of type `double`, represent only approximate quantities, so it does not make sense to use `==` to test them for exact equality. The value of n2 may be so close to zero that dividing another number by it would have the same effect as dividing by zero, yet the test would say that it is not equal to `0.0`. You therefore decide to throw a `DivideByZeroException` whenever the denominator is very close to zero. However, you are not sure of how you should define "very close to zero." You decide that any quantity that is less than one ten-thousandth will be considered very close to zero. However, since you are not sure that this value is the best choice, you decide to use an instance variable, named `precision`, that will tell how close a number must be to zero in order to be treated as if it were zero. The definition of `precision` is thus

```
private double precision = 0.0001;
```

The test for division by zero then becomes

```
if ( (−precision < n2) && (n2 < precision))
    throw new DivideByZeroException( );
```

Thus, you rewrite the `switch` statement as the following:

```
switch (op)
{
    case '+':
        answer = n1 + n2;
        break;
    case '−':
        answer = n1 − n2;
        break;
```

```
        case '*':
            answer = n1 * n2;
            break;
        case '/':
            if ( (-precision < n2) && (n2 < precision))
                throw new DivideByZeroException();
            answer = n1/n2;
            break;
    }
```

But what if the user enters some character other than '+', '−', '*', or '/' for the op? You decide that such cases will be handled by throwing an exception. So the switch statement now looks like this:

```
switch (op)
{
    case '+':
        answer = n1 + n2;
        break;
    case '-':
        answer = n1 - n2;
        break;
    case '*':
        answer = n1 * n2;
        break;
    case '/':
        if ( (-precision < n2) && (n2 < precision))
            throw new DivideByZeroException();
        answer = n1/n2;
        break;
    default:
        throw new UnknownOpException(op);
}
```

The DivideByZeroException class was defined in Display 8.4. UnknownOpException is a new exception class that you need to define. You also need to write code to catch and handle all exceptions.

The code for the UnknownOpException class is similar to that for the other exceptions we have written and is given in Display 8.9. Note that, when the user enters an unknown operator, you want to inform the user that that particular operator is unknown; thus, there is a constructor that takes an argument of type char that names the operator.

UnknownOp-
Exception

At this point, you have all of the program written except for the exception handling. You can now produce a preliminary version of your program, as shown in Display 8.10. You can use this version to test and debug the unexceptional portion of your program before you write the exception-handling portion of your program. As long as the user does not enter an unknown operator or attempt to perform a division by zero, this version will run fine.

preliminary
version

■ DISPLAY 8.9   **The** `UnknownOpException` **Class**

```java
public class UnknownOpException extends Exception
{
    public UnknownOpException()
    {
        super("UnknownOpException");
    }

    public UnknownOpException(char op)
    {
        super(op + " is an unknown operator.");
    }

    public UnknownOpException(String message)
    {
        super(message);
    }
}
```

exception
handling

Once you have debugged the preliminary version of your program, you are ready to add exception handling. The most significant exception is `UnknownOpException`, and you consider it first. You have already given the definition of the class `UnknownOpException`, but you have not yet done anything with it, other than declare it in a `throws` clause. You want to do something more serious and effective when an exception is thrown.

To make your program more robust, you use the `try-throw-catch` technique. The `UnknownOpException` will be thrown by the method `evaluate`. The method `evaluate` is invoked in the method `doCalculation`, and the method `doCalculation` is invoked in the method `main`. You have three normal ways of handling the exception:

1. Catch the exception in the method `evaluate`.

2. Declare the exception `UnknownOpException` in a `throws` clause in the method `evaluate`, and then catch the exception in the method `doCalculation`.

3. Declare the exception `UnknownOpException` in a `throws` clause in both the method `evaluate` and the method `doCalculation`, and then catch the exception in the method `main`.

The approach you choose depends on what you want to have happen when an exception is thrown. You would use method 1 or 2 if you wanted the user to reenter the operator. You would use method 3 if you wanted to restart the calculation.

■ DISPLAY 8.10 **The Unexceptional Cases** *(Part 1 of 3)*

```java
/**
 PRELIMINARY VERSION without exception handling.
 Simple line-oriented calculator program. The class
 can also be used to create other calculator programs.
*/
public class PrelimCalculator
{
    private double result;
    private double precision = 0.0001;
    //Numbers this close to zero are treated as if equal to zero.

    public static void main(String[] args)
                                    throws DivideByZeroException,
                                           UnknownOpException
    {
        PrelimCalculator clerk = new PrelimCalculator();

        System.out.println("Calculator is on.");
        System.out.print("Format of each line: ");
        System.out.println("operator number");
        System.out.println("For example: + 3");
        System.out.println("To end, enter the letter e.");
        clerk.doCalculation();

        System.out.println("The final result is "
                                + clerk.resultValue());
        System.out.println("Calculator program ending.");
    }

    public PrelimCalculator()
    {
        result = 0;
    }

    public void reset()
    {
        result = 0;
    }
```

The definition of the main method will change before this case study ends.

This version of the program does not do exception handling and thus is not yet complete. However, it does run and can be used for debugging.

■ DISPLAY 8.10 **The Unexceptional Cases** *(Part 2 of 3)*

```java
public void setResult(double newResult)
{
    result = newResult;
}

public double resultValue()
{
    return result;
}

/**
 Returns n1 op n2, provided op is one of '+', '-', '*',or '/'.
 Any other value of op throws UnknownOpException.
*/
public double evaluate(char op, double n1, double n2)
          throws DivideByZeroException, UnknownOpException
{
    double answer;
    switch (op)
    {
        case '+':
            answer = n1 + n2;
            break;
        case '-':
            answer = n1 - n2;
            break;
        case '*':
            answer = n1 * n2;
            break;
        case '/':
            if ( (-precision < n2) && (n2 < precision))
                throw new DivideByZeroException();
            answer = n1/n2;
            break;
        default:
            throw new UnknownOpException(op);
    }
    return answer;
}
```

■ DISPLAY 8.10 **The Unexceptional Cases** *(Part 3 of 3)*

```
    public void doCalculation( ) throws DivideByZeroException,
                                           UnknownOpException
    {
        char nextOp;
        double nextNumber;
        boolean done = false;
        result = 0;
        System.out.println("result = " + result);

        while (! done)
        {
            nextOp = SavitchIn.readNonwhiteChar( );
            if ((nextOp == 'e') || (nextOp == 'E'))
                done = true;
            else
            {
                nextNumber = SavitchIn.readLineDouble( );
                result = evaluate(nextOp, result, nextNumber);
                System.out.println("result " + nextOp + " "
                                      + nextNumber + " = " + result);
                System.out.println("updated result = " + result);
            }
        }
    }
}
```

Sample Screen Dialog

```
Calculator is on.
Format of each line: operator number
For example: + 3
To end, enter the letter e.
result = 0.0
+4
result + 4.0 = 4.0
updated result = 4.0
*2
result * 2.0 = 8.0
updated result = 8.0
e
The final result is 8.0
Calculator program ending.
```

You decide that the thing to do when an UnknownOpException is thrown is to restart the calculation. So you decide to use method 3, which places the try and catch blocks in the method main. This decision leads you to rewrite main, as shown in Display 8.11. In doing so, you introduce two new methods, handleUnknownOpException and handleDivideByZeroException. All that is left to do is to define these two methods for handling exceptions.

■ DISPLAY 8.11 The Complete Line-Oriented Calculator *(Part 1 of 5)*

```java
/**
 Simple line-oriented calculator program. The class
 can also be used to create other calculator programs.
*/
public class Calculator
{
    private double result;
    private double precision = 0.0001;
    //Numbers this close to zero are treated as if equal to zero.

    public static void main(String[] args)
    {
        Calculator clerk = new Calculator();

        try
        {
            System.out.println("Calculator is on.");
            System.out.print("Format of each line: ");
            System.out.println("operator number");
            System.out.println("For example: + 3");
            System.out.println("To end, enter the letter e.");
            clerk.doCalculation();
        }
        catch(UnknownOpException e)
        {
            clerk.handleUnknownOpException(e);
        }
        catch(DivideByZeroException e)
        {
            clerk.handleDivideByZeroException(e);
        }
```

```java
        System.out.println("The final result is "
                                    + clerk.resultValue());
        System.out.println("Calculator program ending.");
    }

    public Calculator()
    {
        result = 0;
    }

    public void reset()
    {
        result = 0;
    }

    public void setResult(double newResult)
    {
        result = newResult;
    }

    public double resultValue()
    {
        return result;
    }

    /**
     The heart of a calculator. This does not give
     instructions. Input errors throw exceptions.
    */
    public void doCalculation() throws DivideByZeroException,
                                       UnknownOpException
    {
        char nextOp;
        double nextNumber;
        boolean done = false;
        result = 0;
        System.out.println("result = " + result);
        while (! done)
        {
            nextOp = SavitchIn.readNonwhiteChar();
            if ((nextOp == 'e') || (nextOp == 'E'))
                done = true;
```

reset, setResult, and getResult are not used in this program, but might be needed by some other application that uses this class.

■ **DISPLAY 8.11** **The Complete Line-Oriented Calculator** *(Part 3 of 5)*

```java
            else
            {
                nextNumber = SavitchIn.readLineDouble( );
                result = evaluate(nextOp, result, nextNumber);
                System.out.println("result " + nextOp + " "
                                + nextNumber + " = " + result);
                System.out.println("updated result = " + result);
            }
        }
    }

    /**
     Returns n1 op n2,
     provided op is one of '+', '-', '*',or '/'.
     Any other value of op throws UnknownOpException.
    */
    public double evaluate(char op, double n1, double n2)
              throws DivideByZeroException, UnknownOpException
    {
        double answer;
        switch (op)
        {
            case '+':
                answer = n1 + n2;
                break;
            case '-':
                answer = n1 - n2;
                break;
            case '*':
                answer = n1 * n2;
                break;
            case '/':
                if ( (-precision < n2) && (n2 < precision))
                    throw new DivideByZeroException( );
                answer = n1/n2;
                break;
            default:
                throw new UnknownOpException(op);
        }
```

■ DISPLAY 8.11 The Complete Line-Oriented Calculator *(Part 4 of 5)*

```java
        return answer;

    }

    public void
        handleDivideByZeroException(DivideByZeroException e)
    {
        System.out.println("Dividing by zero.");
        System.out.println("Program aborted");
        System.exit(0);
    }

    public void handleUnknownOpException(UnknownOpException e)
    {
        System.out.println(e.getMessage());
        System.out.println("Try again from the beginning:");

        try
        {
            System.out.print("Format of each line: ");
            System.out.println("operator number");
            System.out.println("For example: +3");
            System.out.println("To end, enter the letter e.");
            doCalculation();
        }

        catch(UnknownOpException e2)
        {
            System.out.println(e2.getMessage());
            System.out.println("Try again at some other time.");
            System.out.println("Program ending.");
            System.exit(0);
        }


        catch(DivideByZeroException e3)
        {
            handleDivideByZeroException(e3);
        }
    }
}
```

This block is executed the first time UnknownOpException *is thrown.*

This block catches an UnknownOpException *if it is thrown a second time.*

■ **DISPLAY 8.11** **The Complete Line-Oriented Calculator** *(Part 5 of 5)*

Sample Screen Dialog

```
Calculator is on.
Format of each line: operator number
For example: + 3
To end, enter the letter e.
result = 0.0
+80
result + 80.0 = 80.0
updated result = 80.0
-2
result - 2.0 = 78.0
updated result = 78.0
%4
% is an unknown operator.
Try again from the beginning:
Format of each line is: operator number
For example: +3
To end, enter the letter e.
result = 0.0
+80
result + 80.0 = 80.0
updated result = 80.0
-2
result - 2.0 = 78.0
updated result = 78.0
* 0.04
result * 0.04 = 3.12
updated result = 3.12
e
The final result is 3.12
Calculator program ending.
```

If you look at the `catch` block in the method `main`, you will see that, when an UnknownOpException is thrown, it is handled by the method `handleUn-knownOpException`. You design the method `handleUnknownOpException` so that it gives the user a second chance to do the calculation (starting from the beginning). If the user enters an unknown operator during this second chance, then another UnknownOpException is thrown, but this time it is caught in the method `handle-UnknownOpException`. To see the code for this case, look at the `catch` block in the method `handleUnknownOpException` (Display 8.11). If UnknownOpException is thrown a second time, then the program ends. (There are other good ways to handle an UnknownOpException, but this one is satisfactory.)

handle-
UnknownOp-
Exception

Notice that, in the definition of the method `doCalculation` (Display 8.11), you needed to include a `throws` clause for the exception classes UnknownOpException and DivideByZeroException, even though the body of the method `doCalcula-tion` does not include any `throw` statements. This is because the method `doCal-culation` includes a call to the method `evaluate`, and the method `evaluate` can throw an UnknownOpException or a DivideByZeroException.

You decide that, if the user attempts to do a division by zero, you will simply end the program. (Perhaps you will do something more elaborate in a future version of this program, but this will do for now.) Thus, the method `handleDivideBy-ZeroException` is very simple. ▪

handling division
by zero

? Self-Test Questions

34. Write an accessor method called `getPrecision` that can be added to the class Calculator in Display 8.11 and that returns the value of the instance variable `precision`. Also, write a mutator method called `setPrecision` that changes the value of the instance variable `precision` to any specified value.

35. What would happen if you ran the program in Display 8.10 and the user entered an unknown operator (such as % or #) for which the program has no case to account for the operator?

CHAPTER   SUMMARY

■ An exception is an object of a class that is a descendant of the class Exception. (Descendants of the class Error are not exceptions, but they behave like them, so we are also considering them to be exceptions.)

■ Exception handling allows you to design and code the normal case for your program separately from the code that handles exceptional situations.

■ There are predefined exception classes. You can also define your own exception classes.

- Certain Java statements themselves might throw an exception. Methods from class libraries might throw exceptions. You can also explicitly throw an exception in your code by using a `throw` statement.

- An exception can be thrown in a `try` block. Alternatively, an exception can be thrown in a method definition that does not include a `try` block. In this case, an invocation of the method can be placed in a `try` block.

- When a method might throw an exception, but not catch it, the exception class usually must be listed in a `throws` clause for the method.

- An exception is caught in a `catch` block.

- A `try` block may be followed by more than one `catch` block. In this case, always list the `catch` block for a more specific exception class before the `catch` block for a more general exception class.

- Every exception has a `getMessage` method that can be used to recover a description of the caught exception.

- Do not overuse exceptions.

✔ Answers to Self-Test Questions

1.

```
Try block entered.
Exception: Time Limit Exceeded.
After catch block.
```

2.

```
Try block entered.
Leaving try block.
After catch block.
```

3. An exception is an object. For example, in the following code, `Exception` is a constructor for the class `Exception`:

```
throw new Exception("Time Limit Exceeded.");
```

The following statement creates an exception object:

```
new Exception("Time Limit Exceeded.");
```

4. Yes, it is perfectly valid, although it is unlikely that you would ever have a good reason to use it.

5. The behavior would not change. The new code is equivalent to the old code it replaces.

6.
```java
throw new Exception("Time Limit Exceeded.");
```

Note that the following is an if statement, not a throw statement, even though it contains a throw statement:

```java
if (waitTime > 30)
    throw new Exception("Time Limit Exceeded.");
```

7. When a throw statement is executed, the enclosing try block ends. No other statements in the try block are executed, and control passes to the following catch block(s). When we say that control passes to the following catch block(s), we mean that the exception object that is thrown is plugged in for the catch-block parameter and the code in the catch block is executed.

8.
```java
try
{
    System.out.println("Try block entered.");
    if (waitTime > 30)
        throw new Exception("Time Limit Exceeded.");
    System.out.println("Leaving try block.");
}
```

9.
```java
catch(Exception e)
{
    System.out.println("Exception: " + e.getMessage());
}
```

10. e is the catch-block parameter.

11. No. The catch-block parameter e is just a placeholder and can be replaced by any other (nonkeyword) identifier, like messenger.

12.
```java
if (status.equals("bad"))
    throw new Exception("Exception thrown: Bad Status.");
```

13. Yes, it is perfectly legal, although it is unlikely that you would ever have a good reason to use it.

14. Yes, it is perfectly legal, although in almost any situation, it would be preferable style to use the following instead:

```java
throw new IOException("Hello Houston!");
```

In practice, the foregoing `throw` statement would typically be included in some branching statement, such as an `if` statement.

15.

```java
public class CoreBreachException extends Exception
{
    public CoreBreachException()
    {
        super("Core Breach! Evacuate Ship!");
    }

    public CoreBreachException(String message)
    {
        super(message);
    }
}
```

16.

```java
public class MessageTooLongException extends Exception
{
    public MessageTooLongException()
    {
        super("Message Too Long!");
    }

    public MessageTooLongException(String message)
    {
        super(message);
    }
}
```

17.

```
ExerciseException invoked with an argument.
Do Be Do
```

18.

```
Wow, Crazy exception thrown!!
Crazy exception thrown!
Message is Crazy exception thrown!
```

19.

```
try block entered:
Double Exception thrown!Double Exception thrown!
End of code.
```

20. The output would not change at all. The modified program is completely equivalent to the original program.

21. The output would change to the following:
```
try block entered:
Leaving try block.
End of code.
```

22.

```
42
IntException thrown!
```

23. An exception class can be a derived class of any exception class, predefined or programmer defined. In particular, you can derive an exception class from the predefined class IOException.

24.

```
public void doStuff(int n) throws Exception
{
    if (n < 0)
        throw new Exception("Negative number.");
}
```

25. If a method throws an exception, and the exception is not caught inside the method, then the method invocation ends immediately after the exception is thrown. If the method invocation is inside a try block, then the exception is thrown to a corresponding catch block, if there is one. If there is no catch block that corresponds to the exception, then you have an uncaught exception, and the method invocation ends as soon as that exception is thrown.

26. It might be caught in method B. If it is not caught in method B, it might be caught in method C. If it is not caught in method C, it might be caught outside of method C.

27.

```
Second catch.
End of Code.
```

28.

```
First catch.
End of Code.
```

29.

```
Hello!
End of Code.
```

30.

```
Trying
Starting SampleMethod.
Catching
From sampleMethod with love.
```

31. Yes, you can have a try block and corresponding catch blocks inside another, larger try block. However, it would probably be better to place the inner try and catch blocks in a method definition and place an invocation of the method in the larger try block.

32. Yes, you can have a try block and corresponding catch blocks inside another, larger catch block. However, it would probably be better to place the inner try and catch blocks in a method definition and place an invocation of the method in the larger catch block.

33. Output for argument 99 is
```
In finally Block.
Caught in main.
```

Output for argument −99 is
```
Caught in sampleMethod.
In finally block.
After finally block.
```

Output for argument 0 is
```
No Exception.
Still in sampleMethod.
In finally block.
After finally block.
```

34.
```java
public double getPrecision()
{
    return precision;
}

public void setPrecision(double newPrecision)
{
    precision = newPrecision;
}
```

35. The program would end as soon as an UnknownOpException were thrown.

● Programming Projects

1. Write a program that converts from 24-hour time to 12-hour time. The following is a sample dialog:

```
Enter time in 24-hour notation:
13:07
That is the same as
1:07 PM
Again?(y/n)
y
Enter time in 24-hour notation:
10:15
That is the same as
10:15 AM
Again?(y/n)
y
Enter time in 24-hour notation:
10:65
There is no such time as 10:65
```

```
Try Again:
Enter time in 24-hour notation:
16:05
That is the same as
4:05 PM
Again?(y/n)
n
End of program
```

You will define an exception class called TimeFormatException. If the user enters an illegal time, like 10:65, or even gibberish, like 8&*68, your program will throw and catch a TimeFormatException.

2. Write a program that uses the class Calculator in Display 8.11 to create a more powerful calculator. This calculator will allow you to save one result in memory and call the result back. The commands the calculator takes are

 e for end
 c for clear; sets result to 0
 m for save in memory; sets memory equal to result
 r for recall memory; displays the value of memory,
   but does not change result

You should define a derived class of the class Calculator that has one more instance variable for the memory, a new main that runs the improved calculator, a redefinition of the method handleUnknownOpException, and anything else new or redefined that you need. A sample dialog is shown next. Your program need not produce an identical dialog, but it should be similar and just as clear or even clearer.

```
Calculator on:
result = 0.0
+4
result + 4.0 = 4.0
updated result = 4.0
/2
result / 2.0 = 2.0
updated result = 2.0
m
result saved in memory
c
result = 0.0
+99
result + 99.0 = 99.0
updated result = 99.0
/3
result / 3.0 = 33.0
updated result = 33.0
r
memory recall
```

```
memory value = 2.0
result = 33.0
+2
result + 2.0 = 35.0
updated result = 35.0
e
End of Program
```

3. Use the exception class `MessageTooLongException` of Self-Test Question 16 in a program that asks the user to enter a line of text with no more than 20 characters. If the user enters an acceptable number of characters, the program should print out the message, "You entered x characters, which is an acceptable length" (with the letter x replaced by the actual number of characters). Otherwise, a `MessageTooLongException` should be thrown and caught. In either case, the program should loop and ask if the user wants to enter another line or quit the program.

4. Write a program that converts dates from numerical month–day format to alphabetic month–day format (for example, 1/31 or 01/31 corresponds to January 31). The dialog should be similar to that in Programming Project 1. You will define two exception classes, one called `MonthException` and another called `DayException`. If the user enters anything other than a legal month number (integers from 1 to 12), your program will throw and catch a `MonthException`. Similarly, if the user enters anything other than a valid day number (integers from 1 to either 29, 30, or 31, depending on the month), then your program will throw and catch a `DayException`. To keep things simple, always allow 29 days for February.

5. Define an exception class called `DimensionException` to use in the driver program from Programming Project 6 in Chapter 7. Modify that driver program to throw and catch a `DimensionException` if the user enters something less than or equal to zero for a dimension.

6. Modify the driver program from Programming Project 5 in Chapter 7 to use three exception classes called `CylinderException`, `LoadException`, and `TowingException`. The number of cylinders must be an integer from 1 to 12, the load capacity must be a number from 1 to 10 (possibly with a fractional part), and the towing capacity must be an integer from 1000 to 10000. Anything other than numbers in these ranges will cause your program to throw and catch the appropriate exception. You also need to define the classes `CylinderException`, `LoadException`, and `TowingException`.

7. Write a program to enter `Employee` data, including social security number and salary, into an array. (The maximum number of employees is 100, but your program should also work for any number of employees less than 100.) Your program should use two exception classes, one called `SSNLengthException` for when the social security number entered (SSN) is not exactly nine characters and the other called `SSNCharacterException` for when any character in the social security number is not a digit. (The SSN is to be entered with just the numbers and no dashes or spaces.) When an exception is thrown, the user is reminded of what she or he entered, told why it is inappropriate, and asked to reenter the data. After all data

have been entered, your program will output the records for all employees, with an annotation stating whether the employee's salary is above or below average. You will also need to define the classes `Employee`, `SSNLengthException`, and `SSNCharacterException`. The class `Employee` will be a derived class of the class `Person` in Display 7.1 of Chapter 7. Among other things, the class `Employee` should have input and output methods, as well as constructors, accessor methods, and mutator methods. Every `Employee` object will record the employee's name, salary, and social security number (plus any other data you need or think are appropriate).

Streams and File I/O

I'll note you in my book of memory. -William Shakespeare, *Henry VI, Part II*

I/O refers to program input and output. Input can be taken from the keyboard or from a file. Similarly, output can be sent to the screen or to a file. In this chapter, we explain how you can write your programs to take input from a file and send output to a file.

Input from a file and input from the keyboard are similar. We will develop enough general material on input to enable us to explain the code for the class `SavitchIn`.

OBJECTIVES

Become familiar with the concept of an I/O stream.

Understand the difference between binary files and text files.

Learn how to save data in a file, using a Java program.

Learn how to read data from a file, using a Java program.

Learn how to use the classes `ObjectOutputStream` and `ObjectInputStream` to write and read, respectively, class objects with binary files.

PREREQUISITES

You need only to have read some of Chapter 8, on exception handling, in order to read this chapter. You do not need knowledge of Chapters 6 or 7, on arrays and inheritance, respectively, except for in the final section of this chapter (Section 9.5), which covers writing and reading of class and array objects to binary files. If you want to cover Section 9.5 before covering arrays, you can simply omit the last subsection of Section 9.5, which covers array I/O.

You may cover Section 9.3, on the `File` class, after Sections 9.4 and 9.5 if you wish. Many readers may choose to skip the coverage of binary files. Nothing in the rest of this book requires knowledge of binary files or anything else covered in this chapter.

Details on prerequisites are as follows:

Section	Prerequisite
Section 9.1	Chapters 1 through 5.
Section 9.2 Text-File I/O	Chapters 1 through 5, Section 8.1, and Section 9.1.
Section 9.3 The `File` Class	Chapters 1 through 5, Section 8.1, and Sections 9.1 and 9.2.
Section 9.4 Basic-Binary File I/O	Chapters 1 through 5, Sections 8.1 and 8.2, and Sections 9.1 and 9.2. You do not need Section 9.3.
Section 9.5 Object I/O with Object Streams	Chapters 1 through 7, Sections 8.1 and 8.2, and Sections 9.1, 9.2, and 9.4. You do not need Section 9.3.

9.1 AN OVERVIEW OF STREAMS AND FILE I/O

Fish say, they have their stream and pond,
But is there anything beyond? -Rupert Brooke, *Heaven*

In this section, we give you a general introduction to file I/O. In particular, we explain the difference between text files and binary files. The Java syntax for file I/O statements is given in subsequent sections of this chapter.

The Concept of a Stream

You are already using files to store your Java classes and programs. You can also use files to store input for a program or to hold output from a program. In Java, file I/O, as well as simple keyboard and screen I/O, is handled by **streams.** A stream is an object that either delivers data to their destination, such as a file or the screen, or takes data from a source, such as a file or the keyboard, and delivers the data to your program.

The object `System.out` is the only output stream we have used so far. The class `SavitchIn`, which we have been using for input, behaves like an input stream (and, in fact, has an input stream embedded in its definition). In this chapter, we discuss streams that connect your program to files.

file

stream

FAQ: What Is a Stream?

A **stream** is a flow of data. The data might be characters, numbers, or bytes consisting of binary digits. If the data flow *into your program*, the stream is called an **input stream.** If the data flow *out of your program*, the stream is called an **output stream.** For example, if an input stream is connected to the keyboard, the data flow from the keyboard into your program. If an input stream is connected to a file, then the data flow from the file into your program. In Java, streams are implemented as objects of special stream classes. The object `System.out` is an example of an output stream. The class `SavitchIn` is an example of an input stream.

input stream
output stream

Why Use Files for I/O?

The keyboard input and screen output we have used so far deal with temporary data. When the program ends, the data typed at the keyboard and left on the screen go away. Files provide you with a way to store data permanently. The contents of a file remain until a person or program changes the file.

An input file can be used over and over again by different programs, without the need to type in the data separately for each program. Files also provide you with a convenient way to deal with large quantities of data. When your program takes its input from a large input file, it receives a lot of data without making the user do a lot of typing.

Differences between Text Files and Binary Files

All data in any file are stored as binary digits (or bits)—that is, as a (probably long) sequence of zeros and ones. However, in many situations, we do not think of a file's

text files and
binary files

contents as a sequence of binary digits. Instead, we think of a file's contents as consisting of a sequence of characters. Files that are thought of as sequences of characters, and that have streams and methods to make the binary digits look like characters to your program and your editor, are called **text files.** Files whose contents must be handled as sequences of binary digits are called **binary files.**

Although it is not technically precise and correct, you can safely think of a text file as containing a sequence of characters, and you can think of a binary file as containing a sequence of binary digits. Your Java programs are stored in text files. Another way to understand the distinction between binary files and text files is to note that text files are designed to be read by human beings, while binary files are designed to be read only by programs.

One advantage of text files is that they usually appear the same on all computers. So you can move your text files from one computer to another with few or no problems. However, the implementation of binary files usually differs from one computer to another. So your binary data files ordinarily must be read only on the same type of computer and with the same programming language that originally created the file.

The advantage of binary files is that they are more efficient to process than text files. Unlike other programming languages, Java also gives its binary files some of the advantages of text files. In particular, the designers of Java made their binary files platform independent; that is, with Java, you can move your binary files from one type of computer to another, and your Java programs will still be able to read the binary files. This feature combines the portability of text files with the efficiency of binary files.

The one big advantage of text files is that you can read and write to them using a text editor. With binary files, all the reading and writing must normally be done by a program.

Remember: Text Files and Binary Files

Files that you write and read using an editor are called **text files**. (Text files are sometimes also called ASCII files, because they contain data encoded using a scheme known as ASCII coding.) There is another category of files called **binary files**. Binary files represent data in a way that is not convenient to read with a text editor, but can be written and read by a program very efficiently.

Remember: Input and Output Terminology

To avoid confusion, remember that the word *input* means that data move *into your program* (not into the file). The word *output* means that data move *out of your program* (not out of the file).

? Self-Test Questions

1. Why would anybody write a program that sends its output to a file instead of to the screen?
2. When we discuss input, are we referring to data moving from the program to a file or from a file to the program?
3. What is the difference between a binary file and a text file?

9.2   TEXT-FILE I/O

Proper words in proper places,
make the true definition of a style. -Jonathan Swift, letter to a young clergyman (January 9, 1720)

In this section, we give a description of the most common ways to perform text-file I/O in Java.

Text-File Output with `PrintWriter`

When you write a program that sends output to a text file, you use a method named `println`. This method behaves the same as `System.out.println`, but it is a method in the class `PrintWriter`. The class `PrintWriter` is the preferred stream class for writing to a text file. Display 9.1 contains a simple program that writes data to a text file.

Note that the program in Display 9.1 begins with the line

```
import java.io.*;
```

This statement tells the Java compiler (and linker) that you will be using the `java.io` library, which contains the definitions of the class `PrintWriter` and the other file I/O classes discussed in this chapter. Every program or class that does file I/O using any of the techniques given in this chapter must contain the preceding `import` statement near the beginning of the file.

`PrintWriter`

`import java.io.*;`

Remember: `import` Statement

Every program or class that does file I/O using any of the techniques given in this chapter must contain the following statement near the beginning of the file:

```
import java.io.*;
```

This statement tells the Java compiler (and linker) that your program will be using the `java.io` package (library), which contains the definitions of classes such as `PrintWriter` and the other file I/O classes discussed in this chapter.

The program in Display 9.1 creates a text file named `out.txt` that a person can read using an editor or that another Java program can read using the class `BufferedReader`, which we will discuss a little later. Notice how the file is opened:

```
outputStream =
            new PrintWriter(new FileOutputStream("out.txt"));
```

(The variable `outputStream` is of type `PrintWriter` and is declared outside the `try` block.) The preceding two lines of code connect the stream named `outputStream` to the file named `out.txt`. Making this connection is referred to as **opening the file.** When you connect a file to a stream in this way, your program always starts with an empty file. If the file `out.txt` already exists, the old contents of `out.txt` will be lost. If the file `out.txt` does not exist, then a new, empty file named `out.txt` will be created.

opening a file

■ DISPLAY 9.1   Sending Output to a Text File

```java
import java.io.*;

public class TextFileOutputDemo
{
    public static void main(String[] args)
    {
        PrintWriter outputStream = null;
        try
        {
            outputStream =
                new PrintWriter(new FileOutputStream("out.txt"));
        }
        catch(FileNotFoundException e)
        {
            System.out.println("Error opening the file out.txt.");
            System.exit(0);
        }

        System.out.println("Enter three lines of text:");
        String line = null;
        int count;
        for (count = 1; count <= 3; count++)
        {
            line = SavitchIn.readLine();
            outputStream.println(count + " " + line);
        }
        outputStream.close();
        System.out.println("Those lines were written to out.txt.");
    }
}
```

Creates an object of the class FileOutputStream, which is given as an argument to a constructor for the class PrintWriter.

Sample Screen Dialog

```
Enter three lines of text:
A tall tree
in a short forest is like
a big fish in a small pond.
Those lines were written to out.txt.
```

File **out.txt** (after the program is run with the given dialog)

```
1 A tall tree
2 in a short forest is like
3 a big fish in a small pond.
```

You can read this file with a text editor.

Note that the name of the file, in this case `out.txt`, is given as a `String` value and thus is given in quotes. The class `PrintWriter` has no constructor that takes a file name as its argument. So we use the class `FileOutputStream` to create a stream that can be used as an argument to a `PrintWriter` constructor. The expression

```
new FileOutputStream("out.txt")
```

creates an object of the class `FileOutputStream`, which is then used as an argument to a constructor for the class `PrintWriter` as follows:

```
new PrintWriter(new FileOutputStream("out.txt"))
```

This statement produces an object of the class `PrintWriter`, which is given the name `outputStream` by the following code (in Display 9.1):

```
outputStream =
        new PrintWriter(new FileOutputStream("out.txt"));
```

However, you can think of the entire expression

```
Output_Stream_Name =
        new PrintWriter(new FileOutputStream(File_Name));
```

as one difficult-to-spell operation that takes a file name as an argument, produces an output stream in the class `PrintWriter`, and connects the stream to the named file so that your program can send output to the file.

file name

Quick Reference: **File Names**

The rules for how you spell file names depend on your operating system, not on Java. When you give a file name to a Java constructor for a stream, you are not giving the constructor a Java identifier. You are giving the constructor a string corresponding to the file name. Most common operating systems allow you to use letters, digits, and the dot symbol when spelling file names. Many operating systems allow other characters as well, but letters, digits, and the dot symbol are enough for most purposes. A suffix, such as `.txt` in `output.txt`, has no special meaning to a Java program. We are using the suffix `.txt` to indicate a text file, but that is just a common convention. You can use any file names that are allowed by your operating system.

When you open a text file as described a little earlier, so that it is connected to a stream of type `PrintWriter`, a `FileNotFoundException` can be thrown, and any such possible exception should be caught in a `catch` block. (Actually, it is the `FileOutputStream` constructor that might throw the `FileNotFoundException`, but the net effect is the same.)

Notice that the `try` block in Display 9.1 encloses only the opening of the file. This block is the only place that an exception might be thrown. Also note that the variable `outputStream` is declared outside of the `try` block, so that the variable `outputStream` can be used outside of the `try` block. Remember. anything declared in a block (even in a `try` block) is local to the block. This concept is explained more fully in the Gotcha subsection entitled "A `try` Block Is a Block."

FAQ: Why a `FileNotFoundException`?

We said that, when you open a text file for writing output to the file, the constructor might throw a `FileNotFoundException`. But in this situation you want to create a new file for output, so why would you care that the file was not found? The answer is simply that the exception is poorly named. A `FileNotFoundException` does not mean that the file was not found. It actually means that the file could not be created. A `FileNotFoundException` is thrown if it is impossible to create the file—for example, because the file name is already used for a directory (folder) name.

A `FileNotFoundException` is a kind of `IOException`, so a `catch` block for an `IOException` would also work and would look more sensible. However, it is usually best to catch the most specific exception that you can, since that can give more information.

println

Notice that, as illustrated in Display 9.1, the method `println` of the class `PrintWriter` works the same for writing to a text file as the method `System.out.println` works for writing to the screen. The class `PrintWriter` also has the method `print`, which behaves just like `System.out.print`, except that the output goes to a text file. Display 9.2 describes some of the methods in the class `PrintWriter`.

Quick Reference: `final`[1]

The keyword `final` appears in the description of many of the methods in Display 9.2. When defining a derived class, you cannot redefine any of the methods that are marked `final`.

---

1. If you have not yet read Chapter 7, on inheritance, you can safely ignore any reference to `final`.

■ DISPLAY 9.2   **Some Methods in the Class `PrintWriter`**

`PrintWriter(OutputStream streamObject)`

This is the only constructor you are likely to need, although it can be used in a number of ways, as explained below. There is no constructor that accepts a file name as an argument. If you want to create a stream using a file name, you use

`new PrintWriter(new FileOutputStream(`*File_Name*`))`

When the constructor is used in this way, a blank file is created. If there already was a file named *File_Name*, then the old contents of the file are lost. If you want instead to append new text to the end of the old file contents, use

`new PrintWriter(new FileOutputStream(`*File_Name*`, true))`

(For an explanation of the argument `true`, read the Java Tip "Appending To a Text File .")

When used in either of these ways, the `FileOutputStream` constructor, and so the `PrintWriter` constructor invocation, can throw a `FileNotFoundException`, which is a kind of `IOException` and so can be caught in a `catch` block for `IOExceptions`.

The `File` class will be covered in Section 9.3. We include the following so you will have a more complete reference in this display, but you can ignore the rest of this entry on the constructors until after you've read Section 9.3.

If you want to create a stream using an object of the class `File`, use

`new PrintWriter(new FileOutputStream(`*File_Object*`))`

When used in this way, the `FileOutputStream` constructor, and so the `PrintWriter` constructor invocation, can throw a `FileNotFoundException`, which is a kind of `IOException`. Note that the append form with two arguments cannot be used with a `File` object.

`public final void println(`*Almost_Anything*`)`

Arguments can be strings, characters, integers, floating-point numbers, boolean values, or any combination of these, connected with + signs. The argument is output to the file connected to the stream. After the argument has been output, the line ends, and so the next output is sent to the next line. This method will also work correctly when the argument is an object of any class that has a suitable `toString( )` method.

`public final void print(`*Almost_Anything*`)`

Same as `println`, except that this method does not end the line, and so the next output will be on the same line.

`public void close( )`

Closes the stream's connection to a file. This method calls `flush` before closing the file.

`public void flush( )`

Flushes the output stream. This forces an actual physical write to the file of any data that have been buffered and not yet physically written to the file. Normally, you should not need to invoke `flush`.

closing a file

When your program is finished writing to a file, it should **close** the stream connected to that file. In Display 9.1, the stream connected to the file out.txt is closed with the statement

```
outputStream.close( );
```

The class PrintWriter, and every other class for file output or file input streams, has a method named close. When this method is invoked, the system releases any resources used to connect the stream to the file and does any other housekeeping that is needed. If your program does not close a file before the program ends, Java will close it for you when the program ends, but it is safest to close the file with an explicit call to close.

Quick Reference: Closing Text Files

When your program is finished writing to a file (or reading from a file), it should close the stream connected to that file by invoking the method close.

Syntax:

Stream_Name.close( );

Examples:

```
outputStream.close( );
inputStream.close( );
```

FAQ: Why Bother To Close a File?

If your program ends normally, but without closing a file, the system will automatically close it for you. So why should you bother to close files with an explicit call to the method close? There are at least two reasons. First, if your program ends abnormally, then Java may not be able to close the file for you, leaving the file open with no program connected to it. This condition could damage the file. The sooner you close a file, the less likely it is that damage will occur. Second, if your program writes to a file and later reads from the same file, it must close the file after it is through writing to the file and then reopen the file for reading. (Java does have a class that allows a file to be opened for both reading and writing, but we will not cover that class in this book.)

▲ *Gotcha*
A try Block Is a Block

Look again at the program in Display 9.1. It is not an accident or a minor stylistic concern that caused us to declare the variable outputStream outside of the try block. If you were to move that declaration inside the try block, you would get a compiler error message. Let's look at the details.

Suppose you replace

```
PrintWriter outputStream = null;
try
{
    outputStream =
      new PrintWriter(new FileOutputStream("out.txt"));
}
```

in Display 9.1 with the following:

```
try
{
    PrintWriter outputStream =
        new PrintWriter(new FileOutputStream("out.txt"));
}
```

This replacement looks innocent enough, but it makes the variable `outputStream` a local variable for the `try` block, which would mean that you could not use `outputStream` outside of the `try` block. If you make this change and try to compile the changed program, you will get an error message saying that `outputStream`, when used outside the `try` block, is an undefined identifier. △

▲ *Gotcha*

Overwriting a File

When you connect a stream to a text file by using the class `PrintWriter` in the following manner, you always produce an empty file:

```
PrintWriter outputStream =
        new PrintWriter(new FileOutputStream("out.txt"));
```

If there is no file named `out.txt`, this statement will create an empty file named `out.txt`. If a file named `out.txt` already exists, then this statement will eliminate that file and create a new, empty file named `out.txt`. So, if there exists a file named `out.txt` before the preceding line of code is executed, then all the data in that file will be eliminated. Section 9.3 tells you how to test for whether a file already exists, so that you can avoid accidentally overwriting a file. In the following Java Tip, we show you how to add data to a text file without losing the data that are already in the file. △

■ **Java Tip**
Appending To a Text File

The method we used in Display 9.1 to open an output file always produces an empty file. If the named file already exists, the old contents will be lost. Sometimes, that is not what you want. Sometimes, you simply want to add the program output to the end of the file. This procedure is called **appending to a file.** If you want to append program output to the file `out.txt`, you would connect the file to the stream `output-Stream` as follows:

appending

```
outputStream =
        new PrintWriter(new FileOutputStream("out.txt", true));
```

If the file `out.txt` does not already exist, Java will create an empty file of that name and append the output to the end of this empty file. (So if there is no already existing file named `out.txt`, the effect is the same as in Display 9.1.) However, if the file `out.txt` already exists, then the old contents will remain, and the program's output will be placed after those contents.

When appending to a text file in this way, you would still use the same `try` and `catch` blocks as in Display 9.1.

At this point, you're probably wondering why we use that second parameter, `true`? Why not use something like the string `"append"` instead? The reason is that this version of the constructor for the class `FileOutputStream` was designed to allow you to use a boolean variable (or expression) to decide whether to append to an existing file or to create a new file. For example, the following code might be used:

```
System.out.println("Enter A for append or N for a new file:");
char ans = SavitchIn.readLineNonwhiteChar();
boolean append = (ans == 'A' || ans == 'a');
outputStream =
        new PrintWriter(
                new FileOutputStream("out.txt", append));
```

From this point on, your program writes to the file in exactly the same way that the program in Display 9.1 does. If the user answers with `'a'` or `'A'`, then any input will be added after the old file contents. If the user answers with `'N'` (or with anything other than `'a'` or `'A'`), then any old contents of the file are lost. A version of the program in Display 9.1 that uses the foregoing way of opening the file `out.txt` is in the program `AppendTextFile.java` on the accompanying CD. ☐

extra code on CD

Quick Reference: Connecting a Text File to a Stream for Appending (Opening a Text File for Appending)

To create a stream of the class `PrintWriter` and connect it to a text file for appending text to the end of the text already in the file, proceed as follows:

Syntax:

```
PrintWriter Output_Stream_Name =
    new PrintWriter(
        new FileOutputStream(File_Name, True_Boolean_Expression));
```

Examples:

```
PrintWriter outputStream =
    new PrintWriter(
        new FileOutputStream("out.txt", true));
```

After this statement, you can use the methods `println` and `print` to write to the file, and the new text will be written after the old text in the file. (In practice, you may want to separate the declaration of the stream variable and the invocation of the constructor, as we did in Display 9.1.)

When used in this way, the `FileOutputStream` constructor, and thereby the `PrintWriter` constructor invocation, can throw a `FileNotFoundException`, which is a kind of `IOException`.

Java Tip

Use `toString` for Text-File Output

It is common to include a method `toString( )` in classes.[2] This method should produce a string value that intuitively represents the data in an object. For example, in Display 9.3, we have redefined the class `Species` from Chapter 4 so that it has a `toString( )` method. To see how `toString( )` works, consider the following code:

```
Species oneRecord =
          new Species("Calif. Condor", 27, 0.02);
outputStream.println(oneRecord.toString( ));
```

This code will produce the output

```
Name = Calif. Condor
Population = 27
Growth rate = 0.02%
```

The method `toString` has a special property. If you do not include it in an invocation of `System.out.println`, it is invoked automatically, so the following two lines are equivalent:

```
System.out.println(oneRecord.toString( ));
System.out.println(oneRecord);
```

These two statements would produce the following output:

```
Name = Calif. Condor
Population = 27
Growth rate = 0.02%
Name = Calif. Condor
Population = 27
Growth rate = 0.02%
```

The method `println` (and `print`) of the class `PrintWriter` behaves the same as `System.out.println` with regard to `toString`. This concept is illustrated in Display 9.4. ■

? Self-Test Questions

4. Write some code that will create a stream named `outStream` that is a member of the class `PrintWriter`, and that connects this stream to a text file named `sam`, so that your program can send output to the file. Do this in a way such that, if the file `sam` already exists, then *the old contents of* `sam` *will be erased*, and *the program will start with an empty file named* `sam`. (If the file `sam` does not exist, of course, the file will be created and will start off empty.)

---

2. If you have read Chapter 7, this method should sound familiar. The method `toString` is discussed there in a bit more detail than here.

■ DISPLAY 9.3   The Species Class with a toString Method

```java
/**
 Class for data on endangered species.
 */
public class Species
{
    private String name;
    private int population;
    private double growthRate;

    public Species( )
    {
        name = null;
        population = 0;
        growthRate = 0;
    }

    public Species(String initialName, int initialPopulation,
                                    double initialGrowthRate)
    {
        name = initialName;
        if (initialPopulation >= 0)
            population = initialPopulation;
        else
        {
            System.out.println("ERROR: Negative population.");
            System.exit(0);
        }
        growthRate = initialGrowthRate;
    }

    public String toString()
    {
        return ("Name = " + name + "\n"
                + "Population = " + population + "\n"
                + "Growth rate = " + growthRate + "%");
    }
```

This is a new, improved definition of the class Species and replaces the definition in Chapter 4.

        <Other methods would be the same as in Display 4.19 in Chapter 4,
                    but they are not needed for the discussion in this chapter.>

```java
}
```

■ DISPLAY 9.4   Using toString to Output an Object

```java
import java.io.*;

public class TextFileObjectOutputDemo
{
    public static void main(String[] args)
    {
        PrintWriter outputStream = null;
        try
        {
            outputStream =
                new PrintWriter(
                    new FileOutputStream("species.records"));
        }
        catch(FileNotFoundException e)
        {
            System.out.println("Error opening species.records.");
            System.exit(0);
        }

        Species oneRecord =
                    new Species("Calif. Condor", 27, 0.02);
        outputStream.println(oneRecord.toString());
        outputStream.println();
        outputStream.println(oneRecord);
        outputStream.close();
        System.out.println("End of Program.");
    }
}
```

These lines are equivalent.

File `species.records` (after the program is run)

```
Name = Calif. Condor
Population = 27
Growth rate = 0.02%

Name = Calif. Condor
Population = 27
Growth rate = 0.02%
```

The method toString is called automatically, so you get the same output if you omit it.

5. As in Self-Test Question 4, write some code that will create a stream named `out-Stream` that is a member of the class `PrintWriter`, and that connects this stream to a text file named `sam` so that your program can send output to the file. This time, however, do it in such a way that, if the file `sam` already exists, then *the old contents of `sam` will not be lost*, and *the program output will be written after the old contents of the file*. (If the file `sam` does not exist, of course, the file will be created and will start off empty.)

6. What kind of exception might be thrown by the following code, and what would be indicated if this exception were thrown?

```
PrintWriter outputStream =
        new PrintWriter(new FileOutputStream("out.txt"));
```

7. Does the class `PrintWriter` have a constructor that accepts a string (for a file name) as an argument, so that the following code would be legal?

```
PrintWriter outputStream =
        new PrintWriter("myFile.txt");
```

Text-File Input with `BufferedReader`

Display 9.5 contains a simple program that reads data from a text file and writes them back to the screen. The file `data.txt` is a text file that a person could have created with a text editor or a Java program could have created using the class `PrintWriter`.

Notice how the file is opened:

BufferedReader

```
BufferedReader inputStream =
                new BufferedReader(new FileReader("data.txt"));
```

The class `BufferedReader` is the preferred stream class for reading from a text file.

As was true of the class `PrintWriter`, the class `BufferedReader` has no constructor that takes a file name as its argument, so we need to use another class—in this case, the class `FileReader`—to help with opening of the file. The class `FileReader` will accept a file name as a constructor argument and will produce a stream that is a `Reader` object. The constructor for `BufferedReader` will accept a `Reader` object as an argument. `Reader` is an abstract class that includes all the streams with "Reader" in their name. However, rather than keep track of this rather complicated explanation, you can simply think of the following as one long, peculiarly worded expression for connecting a text file to a stream of the class `BufferedReader` so that your program can read from the file:

```
BufferedReader Stream_Name =
                new BufferedReader(new FileReader(File_Name));
```

Notice that the program in Display 9.5 catches two kinds of exceptions: `FileNotFoundException` and `IOException`. An attempt to open the file may throw a `FileNotFoundException`, and any of the invocations of `inputStream.readLine( )` may throw an `IOException`. Because `FileNotFoundException` is a kind of `IOException`, you could use only the `catch` block for `IOException`. However, if you do so, then you will get less information if an exception is thrown. If you use only one `catch` block and an exception is thrown, then you will not know whether the problem occurred when opening the file or when reading from the file after it was opened.

■ **DISPLAY 9.5** **Getting Input from a Text File** *(Part 1 of 2)*

```java
import java.io.*;
public class TextFileInputDemo
{
    public static void main(String[] args)
    {
        try
        {
            BufferedReader inputStream =
                new BufferedReader(new FileReader("data.txt"));

            String line = null;
            line = inputStream.readLine();
            System.out.println("The first line in data.txt is:");
            System.out.println(line);

            line = inputStream.readLine();
            System.out.println("The second line in data.txt is:");
            System.out.println(line);
            inputStream.close();
        }
        catch(FileNotFoundException e)
        {
            System.out.println("File data.txt was not found");
            System.out.println("or could not be opened.");
        }
        catch(IOException e)
        {
            System.out.println("Error reading from file data.txt.");
        }
    }
}
```

File **data.txt**

```
1 2
buckle my shoe.
3 4
shut the door.
```

This file could have been made with a text editor or by another Java program.

■ DISPLAY 9.5   **Getting Input from a Text File** *(Part 2 of 2)*

Screen Output

```
The first line in data.txt is:
1 2
The second line in data.txt is:
buckle my shoe.
```

Quick Reference: **Connecting a Text File to a Stream for Reading**
                    (Opening a Text File for Reading)

You create a stream of the class `BufferedReader` and connect it to a text file for reading as follows:

Syntax:

```
BufferedReader Stream_Name =
            new BufferedReader(new FileReader(File_Name));
```

Example:

```
BufferedReader inputStream =
            new BufferedReader(new FileReader("data.txt"));
```

After this statement, you can use the methods `readLine` and `read` to read from the file.
    When used in this way, the `FileReader` constructor, and thus the `BufferedReader` constructor invocation, can throw a `FileNotFoundException`, which is a kind of `IOException`.

Quick Reference: **The `FileNotFoundException` Class**

If your program attempts to open a file for reading, but there is no such file, then a `FileNotFound-Exception` is thrown. As you saw earlier in this chapter, a `FileNotFoundException` is also thrown in certain other situations.

readLine

        Notice that the method `readLine` of the class `BufferedReader` reads from a text file in the same way that the method `readLine` of the class `SavitchIn` reads a line of text from the keyboard. However, the class `BufferedReader` does not have any of the other read methods that are in `SavitchIn`, such as `readLineInt`, `readLineDouble`, and `readLineNonwhiteChar`. Display 9.6 describes some of the methods in the class `BufferedReader`.

■ DISPLAY 9.6   **Some Methods in the Class** `BufferedReader`

`BufferedReader(Reader readerObject)`

This is the only constructor you are likely to need. There is no constructor that accepts a file name as an argument. If you want to create a stream using a file name, you write

`new BufferedReader(new FileReader(`*File_Name*`))`

When used in this way, the `FileReader` constructor, and thus the `BufferedReader` constructor invocation, can throw a `FileNotFoundException`, which is a kind of `IOException`.

The `File` class will be covered in Section 9.3. We include the rest of the material here so that you will have a more complete reference in this display, but you can ignore the rest of this entry on the constructors until after you've read Section 9.3.

If you want to create a stream by using an object of the class `File`, you write

`new BufferedReader(new FileReader(`*File_Object*`))`

When used in this way, the `FileReader` constructor, and thus the `BufferedReader` constructor invocation, can throw a `FileNotFoundException`, which is a kind of `IOException`.

`public String readLine() throws IOException`

Reads a line of input from the input stream and returns that line. If the read operation goes beyond the end of the file, `null` is returned. (Note that an `EOFException` is not thrown at the end of a file. The end of a file is signaled by returning `null`.)

`public int read() throws IOException`

Reads a single character from the input stream and returns that character as an `int` value. If the read operation goes beyond the end of the file, then −1 is returned. Note that the value is returned as an `int`. To obtain a `char`, you must perform a type cast on the value returned. The end of a file is signaled by returning −1. (All of the "real" characters return a positive integer.)

`public void close() throws IOException`

Closes the stream's connection to a file.

Because `BufferedReader` has no methods that, like `readInt`, can read a number, the only way that you can use the class `BufferedReader` to read a number from a text file is to read it as a string and then convert the string to a number. Some techniques for converting strings to numbers are discussed in the subsection "The `StringTokenizer` Class," a little later in this chapter.

reading numbers

The class `BufferedReader` does have a method, named simply `read`, that will read a single character. This method `read` is similar to the method `readChar` in the class `SavitchIn`. There is, however, one complication: The method `read` returns a value of type

read method

`int` that corresponds to the character read; it does not return the character itself. Thus, to get the character, you should use a type cast, as in

```
char next = (char)(inputStream.read( ));
```

If `inputStream` is in the class `BufferedReader` and is connected to a text file, this statement will set `next` equal to the first character in the file that has not yet been read.

? Self-Test Questions

8. Write some code that will create a stream named `textStream` that is a member of the class `PrintWriter`, and that connects the stream to a text file named dobedo so that your program can send output to the text file dobedo.

9. Suppose you run a program that writes to the text file dobedo, using the stream defined in Self-Test Question 8. Write some code that will create a stream named `inputStream` that can be used to read from the text file dobedo in the ways we discussed in this section.

10. `BufferedReader` has a method named `readLine` that is essentially the same as the method `readLine` in the class `SavitchIn`, except that the former takes its input from a text file. Does `BufferedReader` have any methods like `readInt`, `readDouble`, `readWord`, or `readChar`?

11. Might the methods `read` and `readLine` in the class `BufferedReader` throw an exception? If so, what type of exception?

12. Notice one difference between the `try` blocks in Displays 9.1 and 9.7: The `try` block in Display 9.1 encloses only the opening of the file, while the `try` block in Display 9.7 encloses most of the action in the program. Why is the `try` block in Display 9.7 larger than the one in Display 9.1?

13. What is the type of a value returned by the method `readLine` in the class `BufferedReader`? What is the type of a value returned by the method `read` in the class `BufferedReader`?

Programming Example
Reading a File Name from the Keyboard

Thus far, we have used a quoted string as the file name in our programs. However, you may not know what the file name will be when you write a program, so you may want to have the user enter the file name at the keyboard when the program is run. This task is easy to do. Simply have the program read the file name into a variable of type `String`, and use that `String` variable in place of the file name. This technique is illustrated in Display 9.7.

Notice that the program in Display 9.7 reads input from two different places. The class `SavitchIn` is used to read the file name from the keyboard. The stream named `inputStream` is connected to the file `data.txt` and reads its input from that file. ■

■ DISPLAY 9.7   Reading a File Name *(Part 1 of 2)*

```java
import java.io.*;

public class TextFileInputDemo2
{
    public static void main(String[] args)
    {
        System.out.println("Enter file name:");
        String fileName = SavitchIn.readLineWord();

        try
        {
            BufferedReader inputStream =
                new BufferedReader(new FileReader(fileName));

            String line = null;
            line = inputStream.readLine();
            System.out.println("The first line in "
                                + fileName + " is:");
            System.out.println(line);

            line = inputStream.readLine();
            System.out.println("The second line in "
                                + fileName + " is:");
            System.out.println(line);

            inputStream.close();
        }
        catch(FileNotFoundException e)
        {
            System.out.println("File " + fileName + " not found.");
        }
        catch(IOException e)
        {
            System.out.println("Error reading from file " + fileName);
        }
    }
}
```

File **data.txt**

```
1 2
buckle my shoe.
3 4
shut the door.
```

This file could have been made with a text editor or by another Java program.

■ DISPLAY 9.7   **Reading a File Name** *(Part 2 of 2)*

Sample Screen Dialog

```
Enter file name:
data.txt
The first line in data.txt is:
1 2
The second line in data.txt is:
buckle my shoe.
```

■ **Java Tip**
Using Path Names

path names

When giving a file name as an argument to a constructor for opening a file in any of the ways we have discussed, you may use a simple file name, in which case it is assumed that the file is in the same directory (folder) as the one in which the program is run. You can also use a full or relative path name. A **path name** not only gives the name of the file, but also tells what directory (folder) the file is in. A **full path name,** as the name suggests, gives a complete path name, starting from the root directory. A **relative path name** gives the path to the file, starting with the directory that your program is in. The way that you specify path names depends on your particular operating system, and we will discuss only some of the details here.

A typical UNIX path name is

```
/user/smith/home.work1/data.txt
```

To create an input stream connected to this file, you use

```
BufferedReader inputStream =
        new BufferedReader(
            new FileReader("/user/smith/home.work1/data.txt"));
```

Windows uses \ instead of / in path names. A typical Windows path name is

```
D:\homework\hw1\data.txt
```

To create an input stream connected to this file, you use

```
BufferedReader inputStream =
        new BufferedReader(
            new FileReader("D:\\homework\\hw1\\data.txt"));
```

using \,
\\, or /

Note that you need to use \\ in place of \, as Java will otherwise interpret a backslash paired with a character, such as \h, as an escape character. Although you must normally be carefyl about using a backslash in a quoted string, this problem does not occur with names read in from the keyboard. Suppose you run a program like the one in Display 9.7, and suppose part of the dialog is as follows, where the second line is input typed by the user:

```
Enter file name:
D:\homework\hw1\data.txt
```

This path name will be understood. The user need not type in

```
D:\\homework\\hw1\\data.txt
```

and, in fact, the use of \\ in input might produce an incorrect reading of the file name, although not necessarily. When the user enters input at the keyboard, Java "knows" that \h must be the backslash character followed by an h and not an escape character. It "knows" this because everything the user types consists of characters.

One way to avoid these escape-character problems altogether is always to use UNIX conventions when writing path names. A Java program will accept a path name written in either Windows or UNIX format, even if it is run on a computer with an operating system that does not match the syntax. Thus, an alternative way to create an input stream connected to the Windows file

```
D:\homework\hw1\data.txt
```

is the following:

```
BufferedReader inputStream =
        new BufferedReader(
            new FileReader("D:/homework/hw1/data.txt"));  □
```

The StringTokenizer Class

When using the class BufferedReader to read input from a text file, you can read either entire lines or single characters. Often, you would like to read words, but BufferedReader has no method that reads a single word. However, you can usually do something roughly equivalent by reading an entire line of text and then using the predefined class StringTokenizer to break the line into individual words.

The following example illustrates a simple, but typical, way that the class StringTokenizer is used:

```
StringTokenizer wordFinder =
                new StringTokenizer("We love you madly.");
while (wordFinder.hasMoreTokens())
{
    System.out.println(wordFinder.nextToken());
}
```

This code will produce the following output:

```
We
love
you
madly.
```

The constructor (the part after the new) produces a new object of the class StringTokenizer. This object can produce the individual words in the string used as the argument to the constructor. These individual words are called **tokens.**

tokens

The method nextToken returns the first token (word) when it is invoked for the first time, returns the second token when it is invoked for the second time, and so forth. The method `hasMoreTokens` returns `true` as long as `nextToken` has not yet returned all the tokens in the string, and it returns `false` after the method `nextToken` has returned all the tokens in the string.

The class `StringTokenizer` is in the `java.util` (short for "utility") package. So any class or program that uses the class `StringTokenizer` must contain the following line at the start of the file:

```
import java.util.*;
```

When the constructor for `StringTokenizer` is used with a single argument, as in the preceding example, the tokens are substrings of nonwhitespace characters, and the whitespace characters are used as the separators for the tokens. Any string of one or more whitespace characters is considered a separator. (Recall that whitespace characters are the blank, new-line, and other symbols that print as whitespace on paper.) Thus, in the preceding example, the last word is `"madly."`, including the period. The period is included because it is not a whitespace character and thus is not a separator.

If you want to specify your own set of separator characters, rather than simply accepting the default set consisting of the whitespace characters, then you give a second argument to the constructor when you set up the string tokenizer via `new`. The second argument is a string consisting of all the separator characters. Thus, if you want your separators to consist of the blank, new-line character, period, and comma, you could proceed as in the following example:

```
StringTokenizer secondWordFinder =
            new StringTokenizer("Love you, madly.", " \n.,");
while (secondWordFinder.hasMoreTokens())
{
    System.out.println(secondWordFinder.nextToken());
}
```

This code will produce the output

```
Love
you
madly
```

Be sure to notice that the period and comma are not part of the tokens produced, because they are now token separators. Also note that the string of token separators is the second argument to the constructor.

You can see another example of the use of the `StringTokenizer` class in the definition of the method `readLineWord` in the class `SavitchIn`, given in Appendix 4. Some of the methods for the class `StringTokenizer` are summarized in Display 9.8.

■ DISPLAY 9.8   **Some Methods in the Class `StringTokenizer` (Part 1 of 2)**

`public StringTokenizer(String theString)`
Constructor for a tokenizer that will use whitespace characters to find tokens in `theString`.

`public StringTokenizer(String theString, String delimiters)`
Constructor for a tokenizer that will use the characters in the string `delimiters` as separators to find tokens in `theString`.

■ DISPLAY 9.8   **Some Methods in the Class** `StringTokenizer` *(Part 2 of 2)*

`public boolean hasMoreTokens( )`

Tests whether there are more tokens available from this tokenizer's string. When used in conjunction with `nextToken`, it returns `true` as long as `nextToken` has not yet returned all the tokens in the string; otherwise, it returns `false`.

`public String nextToken( )`

Returns the next token from this string tokenizer. (Throws a `NoSuchElementException` if there are no more tokens to return.)

`public int countTokens( )`

Returns the number of tokens remaining to be returned by `nextToken`.

■ **Java Tip**
Testing for the End of a Text File

When using the class `BufferedReader`, if your program tries to read beyond the end of the file with either of the methods `readLine` or `read`, then the method returns a special value to signal that the end of the file has been reached. When `readLine` tries to read beyond the end of a file, it returns the value `null`. Thus, your program can test for the end of the file by testing for whether `readLine` returns `null`. This technique is illustrated in Display 9.9. When the method `read` tries to read beyond the end of a file, it returns the value −1. Because the `int` value corresponding to each ordinary character is positive, this condition can be used to test for the end of a file. □

Quick Reference: **Checking for the End of a Text File**

The method `readLine` of the class `BufferedReader` returns `null` when it tries to read beyond the end of a text file. The method `read` of the class `BufferedReader` returns −1 when it tries to read beyond the end of a text file. (Neither of these methods would throw an `EOFException`.)

? Self-Test Questions

14. What happens when the method `readLine` in the class `BufferedReader` attempts to read beyond the end of a file? How can you use this condition to test for the end of a file?

15. What is the type of the value returned by the method `read` in the class `BufferedReader`?

16. What happens when the method `read` in the class `BufferedReader` attempts to read beyond the end of a file? How can you use this condition to test for the end of a file?

■ DISPLAY 9.9   Checking for the End of a Text File *(Part 1 of 2)*

```java
import java.io.*;
/**
 Makes storylines.txt the same as story.txt,
 but with each line numbered.
*/
public class TextEOFDemo
{
    public static void main(String[] args)
    {
        try
        {
            BufferedReader inputStream =
                    new BufferedReader(new FileReader("story.txt"));
            PrintWriter outputStream =
                    new PrintWriter(
                        new FileOutputStream("storylines.txt"));

            int count = 0;
            String line = inputStream.readLine();
            while (line != null)
            {
                count++;
                outputStream.println(count + " " + line);
                line = inputStream.readLine();
            }
            System.out.println(count
                            + " lines written to storylines.txt.");

            inputStream.close();
            outputStream.close();
        }
        catch(FileNotFoundException e)
        {
            System.out.println("File opening problem.");
        }
        catch(IOException e)
        {
            System.out.println("Error reading from file story.txt.");
        }
    }
}
```

■ **DISPLAY 9.9   Checking for the End of a Text File** *(Part 2 of 2)*

File `story.txt`

```
Once upon a time
there were three little
auto mechanics: Click,
Clack, and Joe.
```

story.txt could have been made with a text editor or by another Java program.

File `storylines.txt` (after the program is run)

```
1 Once upon a time
2 there were three little
3 auto mechanics: Click,
4 Clack, and Joe.
```

Do not be concerned if your version of storylines.txt has numbered blank lines after 4. That just means you had blank lines at the end of story.txt.

The Classes `FileReader` and `FileOutputStream`

We have used the stream class `FileReader` or `FileOutputStream` whenever we created a stream of the class `BufferedReader` or `PrintWriter`, respectively. For example, the following lines were used in Display 9.9:

```
BufferedReader inputStream =
          new BufferedReader(new FileReader("story.txt"));
PrintWriter outputStream =
      new PrintWriter(new FileOutputStream("storylines.txt"));
```

We used the classes `FileReader` and `FileOutputStream` because they accept a file name as a constructor argument, such as the arguments `"story.txt"` and `"storylines.txt"` in the preceding examples. As we explained previously, neither `BufferedReader` nor `PrintWriter` accepts a file name as an argument. Thus, when you connect a `BufferedReader` object to a file by using a string name, you must do so in two steps. First, you create an object of the class `FileReader` with, for example, `new FileReader("story.txt")`, and then you use this object of the class `FileReader` to create an object of the class `BufferedReader` with

```
BufferedReader inputStream =
          new BufferedReader(new FileReader("story.txt"));
```

It may help you to understand how this process works if we point out that this way of connecting `inputStream` to the file `story.txt` is equivalent to

```
FileReader aFileReaderObject = new FileReader("story.txt");
BufferedReader inputStream =
          new BufferedReader(aFileReaderObject);
```

Similarly, we produce a `PrintWriter` output stream from a file name in two steps, using `FileOutputStream`.

Since new FileReader("story.txt") produces an input stream connected to the file named by the string "story.txt", why didn't we just use that stream instead of going on to create a BufferedReader object? The reason is that the class FileReader does not have the nice input methods we want to use, like read and readLine. To get the nice methods in the class BufferedReader, we need to convert the FileReader object to a BufferedReader object. Whenever you chain streams together in this way, the resulting stream always has the methods of the last (that is, the leftmost) stream named. For example, in

```
BufferedReader inputStream =
          new BufferedReader(new FileReader("story.txt"));
```

the stream inputStream is an object of the class BufferedReader and thus has all the methods of the class BufferedReader, but does not have the methods of the class FileReader.

Similar remarks apply to the reason that we do not simply use the stream produced by the FileOutputStream constructor, but instead go on to form a PrintWriter stream.

Since we will use the classes FileReader and FileOutputStream only in arguments to constructors for stream classes such as BufferedReader and PrintWriter, we do not really care what methods the classes FileReader and FileOutputStream may or may not have, except for their constructor methods. We do care about what constructors these classes have because it is the constructors that we use with new in the preceding examples and similar cases. In particular, you need to know that the classes FileReader and FileOutputStream each have a constructor that accepts a file name.

Quick Reference: FileReader **and** FileOutputStream

In this book, we will use the classes FileReader and FileOutputStream for their constructors and nothing else. Each of these two classes has a constructor that takes a file name as an argument. We use these constructors to produce arguments for the constructors for stream classes such as BufferedReader and PrintWriter, whose constructors do not take a file name as an argument. The following are examples of this use of FileReader and FileOutputStream:

```
PrintWriter outputStream =
        new PrintWriter(new FileOutputStream("stuff.txt"));

BufferedReader inputStream =
                new BufferedReader(new FileReader("story.txt"));
```

The constructors for FileReader and FileOutputStream can throw an exception in the class FileNotFoundException, which is a kind of IOException.

? Self-Test Questions

17. Which of the following classes have a constructor that accepts a file name as an argument? PrintWriter; BufferedReader; FileReader; FileOutputStream.

18. Is the following code legal?

```
FileReader readerObject =
            new FileReader("myFile.txt");

BufferedReader inputStream =
            new BufferedReader(readerObject);
```

Unwrapping the Class SavitchIn

The class SavitchIn reads from the keyboard. It does not read from a text file. However, keyboard input is processed in the same way as text-file input. You do not need to read the definition of the class SavitchIn in order to be able to read the rest of this book or to be able to learn the Java language. However, if you have read up to this point in the book, you know enough to understand the definition of the class SavitchIn. This definition is given in Appendix 4. In this subsection, we point out a few things that will make it easier for you to understand the code given there.

The class SavitchIn uses System.in.read to define the method readChar. System.in.read behaves the same as the method read in the class BufferedReader, except that System.in.read reads from the keyboard rather than from a text file. The code for the method readChar in SavitchIn is repeated as follows:

readChar

```
public static char readChar()
{
    int charAsInt = -1; //To keep the compiler happy
    try
    {
        charAsInt = System.in.read();
    }
    catch(IOException e)
    {
        System.out.println(e.getMessage());
        System.out.println("Fatal error. Ending Program.");
        System.exit(0);
    }

    return (char)charAsInt;
}
```

Note that System.in.read returns an int, not a char. To obtain a char value, you must do a type cast, as shown in the preceding code.

The class SavitchIn uses the method readChar in the definition of the method readLine. The method readLine in SavitchIn behaves very much like the method readLine in the class BufferedReader. The code for the method readLine in SavitchIn is repeated as follows:

readLine

```
public static String readLine()
{
    char nextChar;
    String result = "";
    boolean done = false;
```

```
        while (!done)
        {
            nextChar = readChar();
            if (nextChar == '\n')
                done = true;
            else if (nextChar == '\r')
            {
                //Do nothing.
                //Next loop iteration will detect '\n'
            }
            else
                result = result + nextChar;
        }

        return result;
    }
```

The symbol `'\r'` is a special character called the **carriage-return symbol.** You should already know about the next-line symbol, `'\n'`. Some systems simply use `'\n'` to denote the end of a line. Other systems use `'\r'` followed by `'\n'` to denote the end of a line. The method `readLine` checks for both possibilities.

The remaining methods use `readLine`, `readChar`, or both to do their reading from the keyboard. To understand these other methods, you should know how to convert strings to numbers, as discussed in the subsection "`Integer`, `Double`, and Other Wrapper Classes" in Chapter 5. You should also know about the `StringTokenizer` class, as described in the subsection "The `StringTokenizer` Class" earlier in this chapter. You also need to know the basics of exception handling covered in Chapter 8. The exception class `Number-FormatException` is thrown when one of the methods for converting a string to a number fails because the string is not a correctly written numeral.

9.3   THE `File` CLASS

An ounce of prevention is worth a pound of cure. -Common saying

In this section, we describe the class `File`, which is not an I/O stream class, but is very useful when doing file I/O.

Using the `File` Class

You can use methods of the class named `File` to check properties of files. You can check things like whether or nor there is a file with a specified name and whether or not the file is readable. Display 9.10 gives a sample program that uses the class `File` when reading a text file. (The class `File` works the same with binary files as it does with text files.)

The `File` class is like a wrapper class for file names. A string like `"treasure.txt"` may be a file name, but it has only string properties, and Java does not recognize it as a file name. On the other hand, the object

```
    new File("treasure.txt")
```

is not simply a string. It is an object that "knows" it is supposed to name a file.

■ DISPLAY 9.10 Using the File Class When Handling Text Files

```java
/**
 Demonstrates use of the class File with text files.
*/
import java.io.*;
public class FileClassDemo
{
    public static void main(String[] args)
    {
        String name = null;

        System.out.println("I will show you the first line");
        System.out.println("in a text file you name.");
        System.out.println("The file must contain one or more lines.");

        System.out.println("Enter file name:");
        name = SavitchIn.readLineWord();
        File fileObject = new File(name);
        while (( ! fileObject.exists())
                        || ( ! fileObject.canRead()))
        {
            if ( ! fileObject.exists())
                System.out.println("No such file");
            else if ( ! fileObject.canRead())
                System.out.println("That file is not readable.");
            System.out.println("Enter file name again:");
            name = SavitchIn.readLineWord();
            fileObject = new File(name);
        }
        try
        {
            BufferedReader fileInput =
                    new BufferedReader(new FileReader(name));
            System.out.println("The first line in the file is:");
            String firstLine = fileInput.readLine();
            System.out.println(firstLine);
            fileInput.close();
        }
        catch(IOException e)
        {
            System.out.println("Problem reading from file.");
        }
    }
}
```

If you wish, you can use fileObject instead of name as the argument to FileReader.

Suppose you create a `File` object and name it `fileObject` with the following code:

```
File fileObject = new File("treasure.txt");
```

exists

You can then use the method named `exists`, of the class `File`, to test whether there is any file with the name `treasure.txt`. For example, you can write

```
if ( ! fileObject.exists())
    System.out.println("No file by that name.");
```

canRead

If there is a file with that name, you can use the method `canRead` to determine whether the operating system will let you read from the file. For example, you can write

```
if ( ! fileObject.canRead())
    System.out.println("Not allowed to read from that file.");
```

Most operating systems let you designate some files as not readable or as readable only by certain users. Method `canRead` is a good way to check whether you or somebody else has inadvertently (or intentionally) made a file nonreadable.

The method `canWrite` is similar to `canRead`, except that the former checks to see whether the operating system will allow you to write to the file. Most operating systems let you designate some files as not writable or as writable only by certain users.

Notice the annotation in Display 9.10. It says that you can use the `File` object as an argument for the `FileReader` constructor in place of a file-name argument. You can usually (but not always) use an object of type `File` as an argument for a stream constructor whenever you can use a file name as the argument. In particular, the classes `FileReader`, `FileOutputStream`, and `FileInputStream` each accept a `File` object as an argument. (The class `FileInputStream` is used with binary files and will be discussed in Section 9.4.) Thus, you can use an object of the class `File` in place of a file name in our usual code for opening a file, with one important exception: When appending to a file, you must open the file by using the file name; you cannot substitute a `File` object for the file name.

Display 9.11 lists some of the methods in the class `File`.

Quick Reference: The `File` Class

The `File` class is like a wrapper class for file names. The constructor for the class `File` takes a string as an argument and produces an object that can be thought of as the file with that name. You can use the `File` object and methods of the class `File` to answer questions such as the following: Does the file exist? Does your program have permission to read the file? Does your program have permission to write to the file? Display 9.11 has a summary of some of the methods for the class `File`.

Example:

```
File fileObject = new File("stuff.txt");
if ( ! fileObject.exists())
    System.out.println("There is no file named stuff.txt.");
else if ( ! fileObject.canRead())
    System.out.println("File stuff.txt is not readable.");
```

■ DISPLAY 9.11 **Some Methods in the Class** `File`

```
public boolean exists()
```
Tests whether there is a file with the name that was used as an argument to the constructor when the `File` object was created.

```
public boolean canRead()
```
Tests whether the program can read from the file.

```
public boolean canWrite()
```
Tests whether the program can write to the file.

```
public boolean delete()
```
Tries to delete the file. Returns `true` if it was able to delete the file. Returns `false` if it was unable to delete the file.

```
public long length()
```
Returns the length of the file, in bytes.

```
public String getName()
```
Returns the name of the file. (Note that this name is not a path name, just a simple file name.)

```
public String getPath()
```
Returns the path name of the file.

? Self-Test Questions

19. Write a complete Java program that asks the user for a file name; tests for whether the file exists; and, if the file does exist, asks the user if it should be deleted or not and then does as the user requests.

9.4 BASIC BINARY-FILE I/O

The White Rabbit put on his spectacles. "Where shall I begin, please your Majesty?" he asked. "Begin at the beginning," the King said, very gravely, "And go on till you come to the end: then stop." -Lewis Carroll, Alice in Wonderland

Binary files store data in the same format that is used in the computer's main memory (which we described in Chapter 1). Each data item, such as an integer, is stored as a sequence of bytes. Your Java program reads these bytes in very much the same way that it reads a data item, such as an integer, from the computer's main memory. The fact that binary files store data in the same format as that used in the computer's main memory is the reason that binary files can be handled so efficiently.

Binary files created by a Java program can be moved from one computer to another and still be read by a Java program—but only by a Java program. They cannot normally be read with a text editor, nor can they normally be read by a program written in any programming language other than Java.

The preferred stream classes for processing binary files are `ObjectInputStream` and `ObjectOutputStream`. Each has methods to read or write data one byte at a time. These streams can also automatically convert numbers and characters to bytes that can be stored in a binary file. They allow your program to be written as if the data placed in the file, or read from the file, are not just bytes, but are strings or items of any of Java's primitive data types, such as `int`, `char`, and `double`, or even objects of classes you define. If you do not need to access your files via an editor, then the easiest and most efficient way to read data from and write data to files is to use `ObjectOutputStream` to write to a binary file and `ObjectInputStream` to read from the binary file.

In this section, we cover binary-file I/O for the type `String` and the primitive types. In Section 9.5, we cover binary-file I/O for objects of a class type.

Remember: `import` Statement

Binary-file I/O, as discussed here, requires the same `import` statement as text-file I/O, namely,

```
import java.io.*;
```

Output to Binary Files, Using `ObjectOutputStream`

connecting a stream to a file

Display 9.12 shows a program that writes integers to a binary file. Let's look at the details shown in that program.

Note that the substance of what is going on in the program is in a `try` block. Any code that does binary-file I/O in the ways we are describing can throw an `IOException`. Your programs can catch any `IOException` in a `catch` block, so that, if an `IOException` is thrown, you get an error message, and the program ends normally.

The output stream for writing to the file `numbers.dat` is created and named with the following code:

```
ObjectOutputStream outputStream =
    new ObjectOutputStream(new FileOutputStream("numbers.dat"));
```

opening a file

As with text files, this process is called **opening** the (binary) file. If the file `numbers.dat` does not already exist, this statement will create an empty file named `numbers.dat`. If the file `numbers.dat` already exists, this statement will erase the contents of the file, so that the file starts out empty. The situation is basically the same as what you learned for text files, except that we're using a different class here.

The class `ObjectOutputStream` does not have a method named `println`, as we had with text-file and screen output. However, as shown in Display 9.12, an object of the class `ObjectOutputStream` does have a method named `writeInt` that can write a single `int` value to a file, and it also has other output methods that we will discuss shortly.

■ DISPLAY 9.12 Using ObjectOutputStream to Write to a File *(Part 1 of 2)*

```java
import java.io.*;
public class BinaryOutputDemo
{
    public static void main(String[] args)
    {
        try
        {
            ObjectOutputStream outputStream =
                new ObjectOutputStream(new FileOutputStream("numbers.dat"));
            int n;
            System.out.println("Enter nonnegative integers, one per line.");
            System.out.println("Place a negative number at the end.");

            do
            {
                n = SavitchIn.readLineInt();
                outputStream.writeInt(n);
            }while (n >= 0);

            System.out.println("Numbers and sentinel value");
            System.out.println("written to the file numbers.dat.");
            outputStream.close();
        }
        catch(IOException e)
        {
            System.out.println("Problem with output to file numbers.dat.");
        }
    }
}
```

A binary file is closed in the same way as a text file.

Sample Screen Dialog

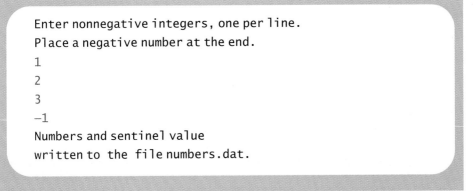

```
Enter nonnegative integers, one per line.
Place a negative number at the end.
1
2
3
−1
Numbers and sentinel value
written to the file numbers.dat.
```

File **numbers.dat** (after the program is run)

```
1
2
3
-1
```

Notice that the −1 is in the file. It does not have to be in the file, but in this program, we want it there as a sentinel value.

This file is a binary file. You cannot read this file with your text editor.

---

writeInt

Once a stream in the class `ObjectOutputStream` is connected to a file, you can write integers to the file with the method `writeInt`, as in the following line from Display 9.12:

```
outputStream.writeInt(n);
```

In Display 9.12, the preceding line writes the value of the `int` variable `n` to the file `numbers.dat`. If you look at Display 9.13, you will see that there are similar methods `writeLong`, `writeDouble`, and `writeFloat` that write numbers of other types to a file. Also note that all of these methods can throw an `IOException`.

writeDouble

In Display 9.12, we made it look as though the numbers in the file `numbers.dat` were written one per line in a human-readable form. That is not what happens, however. There are no lines or other separators between the numbers. Instead, the numbers are written in the file one immediately after the other, and they are encoded as a sequence of bytes in the same way that the numbers would be encoded in the computer's main memory. These coded `int` values cannot be read using your editor. Realistically, they can be read only by another Java program.

Display 9.13 contains a list of some of the methods in the class `ObjectOutputStream`.

Quick Reference: **Connecting a Binary File to a Stream for Writing (Opening an Output File)**

You create a stream of the class `ObjectOutputStream` and connect it to a binary file as follows:

Syntax:

```
ObjectOutputStream Output_Stream_Name =
        new ObjectOutputStream(new FileOutputStream(File_Name));
```

The constructor for `FileOutputStream` may throw a `FileNotFoundException`, which is a kind of `IOException`. If the `FileOutputStream` constructor succeeds, then the constructor for `ObjectOutputStream` may throw a different `IOException`. A single `catch` block for `IOException` would cover all cases.

Examples:

```
ObjectOutputStream myOutputStream =
                    new ObjectOutputStream(
                        new FileOutputStream("myfile.dat"));
```

After opening the file, you can use the methods of the class `ObjectOutputStream` (Display 9.13) to write to the file.

■ DISPLAY 9.13 **Some Methods in the Class** `ObjectOutputStream` *(Part 1 of 2)*

`public ObjectOutputStream(OutputStream streamObject)`

There is no constructor that takes a file name as an argument. If you want to create a stream by using a file name, you write

`new ObjectOutputStream(new FileOutputStream(`*File_Name*`))`

This statement creates a blank file. If there already is a file named *File_Name*, then the old contents of the file are lost.

If you want to create a stream by using an object of the class `File`, you use

`new ObjectOutputStream(new FileOutputStream(`*File_Object*`))`

The constructor for `FileOutputStream` may throw a `FileNotFoundException`, which is a kind of `IOException`. If the `FileOutputStream` constructor succeeds, then the constructor for `ObjectOutputStream` may throw a different `IOException`.

`public void writeInt(int n) throws IOException`

Writes the `int` value n to the output stream.

`public void writeLong(long n) throws IOException`

Writes the `long` value n to the output stream.

`public void writeDouble(double x) throws IOException`

Writes the `double` value x to the output stream.

`public void writeFloat(float x) throws IOException`

Writes the `float` value x to the output stream.

`public void writeChar(int n) throws IOException`

Writes the `char` value n to the output stream. Note that it expects its argument to be an `int` value. You can use a type cast in order to convert a `char` value to an `int` value. For example, you can write

`outputStream.writeChar((int)'A');`

In actuality, you do not need the type cast to an `int`, because Java will automatically convert a `char` value to an `int` value for you. So the following is equivalent to the foregoing invocation of `writeChar`:

`outputStream.writeChar('A');`

■ **DISPLAY 9.13** **Some Methods in the Class** `ObjectOutputStream` *(Part 2 of 2)*

```
public void writeBoolean(boolean b) throws IOException
```
Writes the `boolean` value b to the output stream.

```
public void writeUTF(String aString) throws IOException
```
Writes the `String` value `aString` to the output stream. UTF refers to a particular method of encoding the string. To read the string back from the file, you should use the method `readUTF` of the class `ObjectInputStream`.

```
public void writeObject(Object anObject) throws IOException,
        NotSerializableException, InvalidClassException
```
Writes its argument to the output stream. The object argument should be an object of a serializable class, a concept discussed later in this chapter. Throws a `NotSerializableException` if the class of `anObject` is not serializable. Throws an `InvalidClassException` if there is something wrong with the serialization. The method `writeObject` is covered in Section 9.5.

```
public void close() throws IOException
```
Closes the stream's connection to a file. This method calls `flush` before closing the file.

```
public void flush() throws IOException
```
Flushes the output stream. This method forces an actual physical write to the file of any data that have been buffered and not yet physically written to the file. Normally, you should not need to invoke `flush`.

This ends our description of the sample program in Display 9.12, but we still have not discussed all the methods of `ObjectOutputStream` listed in Display 9.13.

You can use a stream from the class `ObjectOutputStream` to output values of any primitive type and to write data of the type `String`. Each primitive data type has a corresponding write method in the class `ObjectOutputStream`. We have already mentioned the write methods for outputting numbers. The method `writeChar` can be used to output a single character. The method `writeBoolean` can be used to output a single boolean value. For example, the following would output the character `'A'` followed by the boolean value `false` to the file connected to the stream named `outputStream`:

writeChar

writeBoolean

```
outputStream.writeChar((int)'A');
outputStream.writeBoolean(false);
```

The method `writeChar` has one possibly surprising property: It expects its argument to be of type `int`. So if you start with a value of type `char`, the `char` value can be type cast to an `int` before it is given to the method `writeChar`. For example, to output the contents of a `char` variable named `symbol`, you can use

```
outputStream.writeChar((int)symbol);
```

In actuality, you do not need to write in the type cast to an `int`, because Java will automatically convert a `char` value to an `int` value for you, and this is one area where it may make sense to take advantage of that automatic type casting. So the following is equivalent to the foregoing invocation of `writeChar`:

```
outputStream.writeChar(symbol);
```

That takes care of outputting the primitive types. To output a value of type `String`, you use the method `writeUTF`. For example, if `outputStream` is a stream of type `ObjectOutputStream`, the following will write the string `"Hi Mom"` to the file connected to that stream:

writeUTF
for strings

```
outputStream.writeUTF("Hi Mom");
```

Of course, with `writeUTF` or any of the write methods, you can use a variable of the appropriate type (in this case, the type `String`) as an argument to the method.

You may write output of different types to the same file. So you may write a combination of, for example, `int`, `double`, and `String` values. However, mixing types in a file does require special care in order to make it possible to read the types back out of the file. To read them back, you need to know the order in which the various types appear in the file, because, as you will see, a program that reads from the file will use a different method to read data of each different type.

FAQ: What Does UTF Stand for?

To write an `int` (when using the class `ObjectOutputStream`), you use `writeInt`; to write a `double`, you use `writeDouble`; and so forth. However, to write a string, you do *not* use `write-String`. You use `writeUTF`. There is no method called `writeString` in `ObjectOutput-Stream`. Why this funny name `writeUTF`? UTF stands for Unicode Text Format. That is not a very descriptive name. Here is the full story:

Recall that Java uses the Unicode character set, which includes many characters used in Asian languages and other languages whose character sets are very different from that of English. Most editors and operating systems use the ASCII character set, which is the character set normally used for English and for typical Java programs. The ASCII character set is a subset of the Unicode character set, so the Unicode character set has a lot of characters you do not need. There is a standard way of encoding all the Unicode characters, but for English-speaking countries, it is not a very efficient coding scheme. The UTF coding scheme is an alternative scheme that still codes all Unicode characters, but that favors the ASCII character set. The UTF coding method gives short, efficient codes for ASCII characters. The price is that it gives long, inefficient codes for the other Unicode characters. However, because you probably will not use the other Unicode characters, this is a good deal.

Some Details about `writeUTF` *(Optional)*

The method `writeInt` writes integers into a file, using the same number of bytes—that is, the same number of zeros and ones—to store any integer. Similarly, the method `writeLong` uses the same number of bytes to store each value of type `long`. (But the methods `writeInt` and `writeLong` use a different number of bytes from each other.)

The situation is the same for all the other write methods that write primitive types to binary files. However, the method writeUTF uses differing numbers of bytes to store different strings in a file. Longer strings require more bytes than shorter strings. This condition can present a problem to Java, because there are no separators between data items in a binary file. The way that Java manages to make this method work is by writing some extra information at the start of each string. This extra information tells how many bytes are used to write the string, so that readUTF knows how many bytes to read and convert. (The method readUTF will be discussed a little later in this chapter, but as you may have already guessed, it reads a String value.)

The situation with writeUTF is even a little more complicated than what we discussed in the previous paragraph. Notice that we said that the information at the start of the string code in the file tells how many *bytes* to read, *not how many characters are in the string*. These two figures are not the same. With the UTF way of encoding, different characters are encoded in different numbers of bytes. However, all the ASCII characters are stored in just one byte, and you are undoubtedly using only ASCII characters, so this difference is more theoretical than real to you now. The box entitled "What Does UTF Stand for?" has some additional discussion of this variable-length coding.

? Self-Test Questions

20. How do you create an output stream of type ObjectOutputStream that is named toFile and is connected to a binary file named stuff.data?

21. Give three statements that will write the values of the three double variables x1, x2, and x3 to the file stuff.data. Use the stream toFile that you created as the answer to Self-Test Question 20.

22. Give a statement that will close the stream toFile created as the answer to Self-Test Question 20.

23. What import statement do you use when doing I/O as described in this section?

Reading Input from a Binary File, Using ObjectInputStream

If you write to a file by using ObjectOutputStream, you can read from that binary file by using the stream class ObjectInputStream. Display 9.14 gives some of the most commonly used methods for this class. If you compare those methods with the methods for ObjectOutputStream given in Display 9.13, you will see that each output method in ObjectOutputStream has a corresponding input method in ObjectInputStream. For example, if you write an integer to a file by using the method writeInt of ObjectOutputStream, then you can read that integer back with the method readInt of ObjectInputStream. If you write a number to a file by using the method writeDouble of ObjectOutputStream, then you can read that number back with the method readDouble of ObjectInputStream, and so forth. Display 9.15 gives an example of this use of readInt.

■ **DISPLAY 9.14   Some Methods in the Class** `ObjectInputStream` *(Part 1 of 2)*

`ObjectInputStream(InputStream streamObject)`

There is no constructor that takes a file name as an argument. If you want to create a stream by using a file name, you use

`new ObjectInputStream(new FileInputStream(`*File_Name*`))`

If you want to create a stream by using an object of the class `File`, you use

`new ObjectInputStream(new FileInputStream(`*File_Object*`))`

The constructor for `FileInputStream` may throw a `FileNotFoundException`, which is a kind of `IOException`. If the `FileInputStream` constructor succeeds, then the constructor for `ObjectInputStream` may throw a different `IOException`.

`public int readInt() throws IOException`

Reads an `int` value from the input stream and returns that `int` value. If `readInt` tries to read a value from the file, but that value was not written using the method `writeInt` of the class `ObjectOutputStream` (or written in some equivalent way), then problems will occur. If the read goes beyond the end of the file, an `EOFException` is thrown.

`public long readLong() throws IOException`

Reads a `long` value from the input stream and returns that `long` value. If `readLong` tries to read a value from the file, but that value was not written using the method `writeLong` of the class `ObjectOutputStream` (or written in some equivalent way), then problems will occur. If the read goes beyond the end of the file, an `EOFException` is thrown.

Note that it is not acceptable to write an integer with `writeLong` and later read the same integer with `readInt`, or to write an integer with `writeInt` and later read it with `readLong`.

`public double readDouble() throws IOException`

Reads a `double` value from the input stream and returns that `double` value. If `readDouble` tries to read a value from the file, but that value was not written using the method `writeDouble` of the class `ObjectOutputStream` (or written in some equivalent way), then problems will occur. If the read goes beyond the end of the file, an `EOFException` is thrown.

`public float readFloat() throws IOException`

Reads a `float` value from the input stream and returns that `float` value. If `readFloat` tries to read a value from the file, but that value was not written using the method `writeFloat` of the class `ObjectOutputStream` (or written in some equivalent way), then problems will occur. If the read goes beyond the end of the file, an `EOFException` is thrown.

Note that it is not acceptable to write a floating-point number with `writeDouble` and later read the same number with `readFloat`, or to write a floating-point number with `writeFloat` and later read it with `readDouble`. Other type mismatches, such as writing with `writeInt` and reading with `readFloat` or `readDouble`, are also not acceptable.

`public char readChar() throws IOException`

Reads a `char` value from the input stream and returns that `char` value. If `readChar` tries to read a value from the file, but that value was not written using the method `writeChar` of the class `ObjectOutputStream` (or written in some equivalent way), then problems will occur. If the read goes beyond the end of the file, an `EOFException` is thrown.

■ **DISPLAY 9.14   Some Methods in the Class** `ObjectInputStream` *(Part 2 of 2)*

`public boolean readBoolean( ) throws IOException`

Reads a `boolean` value from the input stream and returns that `boolean` value. If read-Boolean tries to read a value from the file, but that value was not written using the method `writeBoolean` of the class `ObjectOutputStream` (or written in some equivalent way), then problems will occur. If the read goes beyond the end of the file, an `EOFException` is thrown.

`public String readUTF( ) throws IOException`

Reads a `String` value from the input stream and returns that `String` value. If `readUTF` tries to read a value from the file, but that value was not written using the method `writeUTF` of the class `ObjectOutputStream` (or written in some equivalent way), then problems will occur. If the read goes beyond the end of the file, an `EOFException` is thrown.

`Object readObject( ) throws ClassNotFoundException,`
`        InvalidClassException, OptionalDataException, IOException`

Reads an object from the input stream. Throws a `ClassNotFoundException` if the class of a serialized object cannot be found. Throws an `InvalidClassException` if something is wrong with the serializable class. Throws an `OptionalDataException` if a primitive data item was found in the stream instead of an object. Throws an `IOException` if there is some other I/O problem. The method `readObject` is covered in Section 9.5.

`public void close( ) throws IOException`

Closes the stream's connection to a file.

A binary file is opened for reading with `ObjectInputStream` in a manner similar to what you have already seen for `ObjectOutputStream`. In Display 9.15, the file `numbers.dat` is opened and connected to a stream named `inputStream` as follows:

```
ObjectInputStream inputStream =
    new ObjectInputStream(new FileInputStream("numbers.dat"));
```

Note that this statement is identical to how we used `ObjectOutputStream` in Display 9.12, except that here, we've used the classes `ObjectInputStream` and `FileInputStream` instead of `ObjectOutputStream` and `FileOutputStream`, respectively. The reason that we use `FileInputStream` is the same as the reason we used `FileOutputStream` with `ObjectOutputStream`.

reading multiple types

`ObjectInputStream` allows you to read input of different types from the same file. So you may read a combination of, for example, `int` values, `double` values, and `String` values. However, if the next data item in the file is not of the type expected by the reading method, the result is likely to be a mess. For example, if your program writes an integer using `writeInt`, then any program that reads that integer should read it using `readInt`. If you instead use `readLong` or `readDouble`, your program will misbehave.

■ DISPLAY 9.15 **Using `ObjectInputStream` to Read from a File**

```java
import java.io.*;
public class BinaryInputDemo
{
    public static void main(String[] args)
    {
        try
        {
            ObjectInputStream inputStream =
                new ObjectInputStream(new FileInputStream("numbers.dat"));
            int n;
            System.out.println("Reading the nonnegative integers");
            System.out.println("in the file numbers.dat.");
            n = inputStream.readInt();
            while (n >= 0)
            {
                System.out.println(n);
                n = inputStream.readInt();
            }
            System.out.println("End of reading from file.");
            inputStream.close();
        }
        catch(FileNotFoundException e)
        {
            System.out.println("Cannot find file numbers.dat.");
        }
        catch(IOException e)
        {
            System.out.println("Problem with input from file numbers.dat.");
        }
    }
}
```

Screen Output

```
Reading the nonnegative integers
in the file numbers.dat.
1
2
3
End of reading from file.
```

Assumes the program in Display 9.12 was already run with the dialog shown there.

Notice that the sentinel value −1 is read from the file but is not output to the screen.

Quick Reference: **Connecting a Binary File to a Stream for Reading (Opening an Input File)**

You create a stream of the class `ObjectInputStream` and connect it to a binary file as follows:

Syntax:

```
ObjectInputStream Input_Stream_Name =
        new ObjectInputStream(new FileInputStream(File_Name));
```

The constructor for `FileInputStream` may throw a `FileNotFoundException`, which is a kind of `IOException`. If the `FileInputStream` constructor succeeds, then the constructor for `ObjectInputStream` may throw a different `IOException`.

Examples:

```
ObjectInputStream myInputStream =
                    new ObjectInputStream(
                        new FileInputStream("myfile.dat"));
```

After this code, you can use the methods of the class `ObjectInputStream` (Display 9.14) to read from the file.

▲ *Gotcha*

Using `ObjectInputStream` with a Text File

Binary files and text files encode their data in different ways. Thus, a stream that expects to read a binary file, such as a stream in the class `ObjectInputStream`, will have problems reading a text file. If you attempt to read a text file with a stream in the class `ObjectInputStream`, your program will either read "garbage values" or encounter some other error condition. Similarly, if you attempt to read a binary file as if it were a text file (using `BufferedReader`), you will also get into trouble. △

? Self-Test Questions

24. How do you create an input stream of type `ObjectInputStream` that is named `fromFile` and is connected to a file named `stuff.data`?

25. Give three statements that will read three `double` numbers from the file `stuff.data`. Use the stream `fromFile` that you created in Self-Test Question 24. Declare three variables to hold the three numbers.

26. Give a statement that will close the stream `fromFile` created in Self-Test Question 24.

27. Can one program write a number to a file via `writeInt` and then have another program read that number via `readLong`? Can a program read that number via `readDouble`?

28. Can you use `readUTF` to read a string from a text file?

▲ *Gotcha*

Defining a Method to Open a Stream

The following looks like a fairly reasonable method to include in some class, but it has a problem:

```
//This method does do not what we want it to do.
public static void openFile(ObjectOutputStream streamName)
                                            throws IOException
{
    System.out.println("Enter file name:");
    String fileName = SavitchIn.readLineWord();
    streamName =
          new ObjectOutputStream(
                  new FileOutputStream(fileName));
}
```

The method will compile properly and can be invoked, but it will not perform as you might hope. For example, consider the following (recall that `null` is a value that can be assigned to any variable of a class type, although the exact details of what `null` is do not matter here):

```
ObjectOutputStream outputStream = null;
openFile(outputStream);
```

After this code is executed, the value of `outputStream` is still `null`. The file that was opened in the method `openFile` went away when the method was over. The problem is a bit subtle and is unlikely to arise in very many situations, but this is one of those situations.

The problem has to do with how Java handles arguments of a class type. These arguments are passed to the method as a *memory address that cannot be changed*. The memory address normally names something that can be changed, but the memory address itself cannot be changed. An equivalent way to think about this concept is to recall that an object variable, like the preceding `outputStream`, is a name. A method can change the contents of the file named by `outputStream`. For example, it can send output to the stream and thereby change the file connected to the stream. However, a method cannot change the stream name so that it names a different file. When you use `new`, you are changing `outputStream` so that it names a different file, and that is not allowed.

Be sure to note that this is a narrow restriction that applies only in very limited circumstances. Once a stream is connected to a file, you can pass the stream name as an argument to a method, and the method can change the file.

The best way to avoid this condition problem is to use a method that returns the stream object after the stream object is connected to the file. The following method has no problems:

```
public static ObjectOutputStream openFile() throws IOException
{
    ObjectOutputStream tempStreamName;
    System.out.println("Enter file name:");
    String fileName = SavitchIn.readLineWord();
    tempStreamName =
        new ObjectOutputStream(new FileOutputStream(fileName));
    return tempStreamName;
}
```

extra code
on CD

A simple program demonstrating the use of this method is in the file `OpenFile-Demo.java` on the accompanying CD. △

? Self-Test Questions

29. Write some Java code to create a stream of type `ObjectOutputStream`. Name the stream `writer`, and connect it to the binary file whose name is stored in the `String` variable `theFile`.

30. Write some Java code to create a stream of type `ObjectInputStream`. Name the stream `reader`, and connect it to the file whose name is stored in the `String` variable named `theFile`.

31. Write a complete Java program that asks the user for a binary file name and outputs the first data item in that file to the screen. Assume that the first data item is a string that was written to the file with the method `writeUTF`.

The `EOFException` Class

EOFException

All the methods we have discussed that read from a binary file will throw an `EOFException` when they try to read beyond the end of a file. More specifically, all of the `ObjectInputStream` methods shown in Display 9.14 throw an `EOFException` if they try to read beyond the end of a file.

As illustrated in Display 9.16, the class `EOFException` can be used to test for the end of a file when you are using `ObjectInputStream`. In that sample program, the reading is placed in an "infinite loop" through the use of `true` as the boolean expression in the `while` loop. The loop is not really infinite, because when the end of the file is reached, an exception is thrown, and that ends the entire `try` block and passes control to the `catch` block.

It is instructive to compare the program in Display 9.16 with the similar program in Display 9.15. The one in Display 9.15 tests for the end of a file by testing for a negative number. This approach is fine, but it means that you cannot store negative numbers in the file (except as a sentinel value). The program in Display 9.16 uses `EOFException` to test for the end of a file; thus, it can handle files that store any kind of integers, including negative integers.

■ DISPLAY 9.16 Using EOFException *(Part 1 of 2)*

```java
import java.io.*;
public class EOFExceptionDemo
{
    public static void main(String[] args)
    {
        try
        {
            ObjectInputStream inputStream =
             new ObjectInputStream(new FileInputStream("numbers.dat"));
            int n;
            System.out.println("Reading ALL the integers");
            System.out.println("in the file numbers.dat.");
            try
            {
                while (true)
                {
                    n = inputStream.readInt();
                    System.out.println(n);
                }
            }
            catch(EOFException e)
            {
                System.out.println("End of reading from file.");
            }
            inputStream.close();
        }
        catch(FileNotFoundException e)
        {
            System.out.println("Cannot find file numbers.dat.");
        }
        catch(IOException e)
        {
            System.out.println("Problem with input from file numbers.dat.");
        }
    }
}
```

The loop ends when an exception is thrown.

■ DISPLAY 9.16 **Using EOFException** *(Part 2 of 2)*

Screen Output
(Assuming that the program in Display 9.12 was run with the dialog shown there)

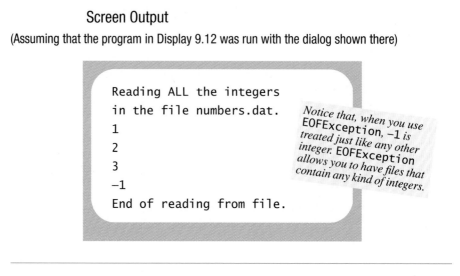

```
Reading ALL the integers
in the file numbers.dat.
1
2
3
-1
End of reading from file.
```

Notice that, when you use EOFException, −1 is treated just like any other integer. EOFException allows you to have files that contain any kind of integers.

Quick Reference: **The EOFException Class**

If your program is reading from a binary file using any of the methods listed in Display 9.14 for the class ObjectInputStream, and your program attempts to read beyond the end of the file, then an EOFException is thrown. This exception can be used to end a loop that reads all the data in a file.

Not all methods in all classes will throw an EOFException when they try to read beyond the end of a file. For the classes discussed in this book, the rule is as follows: If your program is reading from a binary file, your program will throw an EOFException when it tries to read beyond the end of a file. If, however, your program is reading from a text file, then it will not throw an EOFException (or any exception) when the program attempts to read beyond the end of the file.

The class EOFException is a derived class of the class IOException. So every exception of type EOFException is also of type IOException.

▲ *Gotcha*
Forgetting to Check for the End of a File

If your program makes no provisions for detecting the end of a file, then when the end of a file is reached, what happens will depend on the details of your program—but whatever happens, it will not be good. If your program tries to read beyond the end of a file, it may enter an infinite loop or end abnormally. Always be sure that your program checks for the end of a file and does something appropriate when it reaches the end of the file. Even if you think your program will not read past the end of the file, you should provide for this eventuality just in case things do not go exactly as you planned. △

▲ *Gotcha*

Checking for the End of a File in the Wrong Way

Different file-reading methods (usually in different classes) check for the end of a file in different ways. Some throw an exception in the class `EOFException` when they try to read beyond the end of a file. Others return a special value, such as `null`. When reading from a file, you must be careful to test for the end of a file in the correct way for the method you are using. If you test for the end of a file in the wrong way, one of two things will probably happen: Either your program will go into an unintended infinite loop or your program will terminate abnormally.

For the classes discussed in this book, the following rules apply: If your program is reading from a binary file, then an `EOFException` will be thrown when the reading goes beyond the end of the file. If your program is reading from a text file, then some special value, such as `null`, will be returned when your program attempts to read beyond the end of the file, and no `EOFException` will be thrown. △

The Classes `FileInputStream` and `FileOutputStream`

We have used the stream class `FileInputStream` or `FileOutputStream` whenever we have created a stream of the class `ObjectInputStream` or `ObjectOutputStream`, respectively. For example, we used the following statements in Display 9.12 and Display 9.16, respectively:

```
ObjectOutputStream outputStream =
                new ObjectOutputStream(
                    new FileOutputStream("numbers.dat"));

ObjectInputStream inputStream =
                new ObjectInputStream(
                    new FileInputStream("numbers.dat"));
```

We used the classes `FileOutputStream` and `FileInputStream` because they accept a file name as a constructor argument, such as the argument `"numbers.dat"` in the preceding examples. Neither `ObjectInputStream` nor `ObjectOutputStream` accepts a file name as an argument. Thus, when you connect an `ObjectInputStream` to a file by using a string name, you must do so in two steps. First, you create an object of the class `FileOutputStream` with, for example, `new FileOutputStream("numbers.dat")`. Then you use this object of the class `FileOutputStream` to create an object of the class `ObjectOutputStream` with

```
ObjectOutputStream outputStream =
                new ObjectOutputStream(
                    new FileOutputStream("numbers.dat"));
```

Similarly, you produce an `ObjectInputStream` object from a file name in two steps, using `FileInputStream`.

Quick Reference: `FileInputStream` **and** `FileOutputStream`

In this book, we use the classes `FileInputStream` and `FileOutputStream` for their constructors and nothing else. Each of these two classes has a constructor that takes a file name as an argument. We use these constructors to produce arguments for the constructors for stream classes, such as `ObjectInputStream` and `ObjectOutputStream`, that do not take a file name as an argument. Below are examples of using `FileInputStream` and `FileOutputStream`:

```
ObjectOutputStream fileOutput =
                  new ObjectOutputStream(
                        new FileOutputStream("nicestuff.dat"));

ObjectInputStream fileInput =
                  new ObjectInputStream(
                        new FileInputStream("rawstuff.dat"));
```

The constructors for `FileInputStream` and `FileOutputStream` can throw an exception in the class `FileNotFoundException`. A `FileNotFoundException` is a kind of `IOException`.

Programming Example
Processing a File of Binary Data

Display 9.17 contains a program that does some simple processing of data. It asks the user for two file names and then copies all the numbers in one file into the other file, but multiplies each number by two so that the numbers in the output file are all double the values in the input file. This programming task is not very complicated, but it does employ a lot of standard programming techniques for handling file I/O. In particular, note that the variables for stream objects connected to the files are instance variables, and note that the task is broken down into subtasks assigned to various methods.

Note that we have made the `try` blocks small, so that, when an exception is thrown, it is caught in a nearby `catch` block. If we had fewer `try` blocks, it would have been harder to decide what part of the code had thrown an exception. ∎

? Self-Test Questions

32. Suppose that you want to create an input stream and connect it to the binary file named `mydata.dat`. Will the given code work? If not, how can you write something similar that does work?

```
ObjectInputStream inputStream =
                  new ObjectInputStream("mydata.dat");
```

33. Does the class `FileInputStream` have a method named `readInt`? Does it have one named `readDouble`? Does it have one named `readUTF`?

34. Does the class `FileOutputStream` have a constructor that accepts a file name as an argument?

Exercises continue on page 593.

■ DISPLAY 9.17 **Processing a File of Binary Data** *(Part 1 of 3)*

```java
import java.io.*;
public class Doubler
{
    private ObjectInputStream inputStream = null;
    private ObjectOutputStream outputStream = null;

    /**
     Doubles the integers in one file and puts them in another file.
    */
    public static void main(String[] args)
    {
        Doubler twoTimer = new Doubler();
        twoTimer.connectToInputFile();
        twoTimer.connectToOutputFile();
        twoTimer.timesTwo();
        twoTimer.closeFiles();
        System.out.println("Numbers from input file");
        System.out.println("doubled and copied to output file.");
    }

    public void connectToOutputFile()
    {
        String outputFileName =
                    getFileName("Enter output file name:");
        try
        {
            outputStream = new ObjectOutputStream(
                            new FileOutputStream(outputFileName));
        }
        catch(IOException e)
        {
            System.out.println("Error opening output file "
                                            + outputFileName);
            System.out.println(e.getMessage());
            System.exit(0);
        }
    }
}
```

■ DISPLAY 9.17 Processing a File of Binary Data *(Part 2 of 3)*

```java
public void connectToInputFile()
{
    String inputFileName =
                    getFileName("Enter input file name:");

    try
    {
        inputStream =
          new ObjectInputStream(
                        new FileInputStream(inputFileName));
    }
    catch(FileNotFoundException e)
    {
        System.out.println("File " + inputFileName
                                    + " not found.");
        System.exit(0);
    }
    catch(IOException e)
    {
        System.out.println("Error opening input file "
                                        + inputFileName);
        System.exit(0);
    }
}

private String getFileName(String prompt)
{
    String fileName = null;
    System.out.println(prompt);
    fileName = SavitchIn.readLineWord();

    return fileName;
}

public void timesTwo()
{
    int next;
    try
    {
        while (true)
        {
            next = inputStream.readInt();
            outputStream.writeInt(2*next);
        }
    }
```

A class used in a real-life application might also have other methods that take data from the input file, transform the data in some way, and write the changed data to the output file.

```
        catch(EOFException e)
        {
            //Do nothing. This just ends the loop.
        }
        catch(IOException e)
        {
            System.out.println(
                    "Error: reading or writing files.");
            System.out.println(e.getMessage());
            System.exit(0);
        }
    }

    public void closeFiles()
    {
        try
        {
            inputStream.close();
            outputStream.close();
        }
        catch(IOException e)
        {
            System.out.println("Error closing files "
                                    + e.getMessage());
            System.exit(0);
        }
    }
}
```

35. Does the class `ObjectOutputStream` have a constructor that accepts a file name as an argument?

36. When opening a binary file for output in the ways discussed in this chapter, might an exception be thrown? What kind of exception? When opening a binary file for input in the ways discussed in this chapter, might an exception be thrown? What kind of exception?

37. Suppose that a binary file contains three numbers written to the file with the method `writeDouble` of the class `ObjectOutputStream`. Suppose further that your program reads all three numbers with three invocations of the method `readDouble` of the class `ObjectInputStream`. If your program invokes `readDouble` to try to read a fourth number from the file, what will happen?

38. The following code appears in the program in Display 9.16:

```
try
{
    while (true)
    {
        n = inputStream.readInt();
        System.out.println(n);
    }
}
catch(EOFException e)
{
    System.out.println("End of reading from file.");
}
```

Why doesn't this code cause an infinite loop to occur?

39. Write a complete Java program that will read all the numbers in a binary file named `temperatures` and write the numbers to the screen, one per line. Assume that the file consists entirely of numbers written to it with the method `writeDouble`.

9.5 OBJECT I/O WITH OBJECT STREAMS

In this section, we cover binary-file I/O for class and array objects using `ObjectInputStream` and `ObjectOutputStream`.

Binary I/O of Class Objects

You can output class objects to a binary file by using the method `writeObject` of the class `ObjectOutputStream` and then read objects from the file by using the method `readObject` of the class `ObjectInputStream`. For you to be able to do so, however, the class that your code is writing and reading must be **serializable.** It is very easy to make a class serializable. All you need to do is add the two words `implements Serializable` to the heading of the class definition, as in the following example:

serializable

```
public class Species implements Serializable
{
```

Also, to make the `Serializable` interface available to your code, you need to use the following `import` statement:

```
import java.io.*;
```

In Display 9.18, we have added these items to the class `Species`, which we used earlier in this chapter. We will return to discuss the meaning of serialization in a later subsection, but now let's use the class `Species` to illustrate the reading and writing of objects to a binary file.

■ DISPLAY 9.18 Species Class Serialized for Binary-File I/O

```java
import java.io.*;                          ← ────── Needed for Serializable.
/**
 Class for data on endangered species. This class is serialized.

 */
public class Species implements Serializable
{
    private String name;
    private int population;
    private double growthRate;

    public Species( )
    {
        name = null;
        population = 0;
        growthRate = 0;
    }

    public Species(String initialName, int initialPopulation,
                                    double initialGrowthRate)

    {
        name = initialName;
        if (initialPopulation >= 0)
            population = initialPopulation;
        else
        {
            System.out.println("ERROR: Negative population.");
            System.exit(0);
        }
        growthRate = initialGrowthRate;
    }

    public String toString()
    {
        return ("Name = " + name + "\n"
                + "Population = " + population + "\n"
                + "Growth rate = " + growthRate + "%");
    }
    <Other methods would be the same as in Display 4.19 in Chapter 4,
                        but they are not needed for the discussion in this chapter.>


}
```

Except for these two words and the import statement, this definition is the same as the one in Display 9.3.

This code is a new, improved definition of the class Species and replaces the definition in Display 9.3.

writeObject

Display 9.19 illustrates how class objects can be written to and read from a binary file. To write an object of the class `Species` to a binary file, you simply use the method `writeObject` of the class `ObjectOutputStream`. You use `writeObject` in the same way that you use the other methods of the class `ObjectOutputStream`, such as `writeInt`, but you use an object as the argument, as in

■ DISPLAY 9.19 **File I/O of Class Objects** *(Part 1 of 3)*

```java
import java.io.*;

public class ClassIODemo
{
    public static void main(String[] args)
    {
        ObjectOutputStream outputStream = null;

        try
        {
            outputStream =
                    new ObjectOutputStream(
                        new FileOutputStream("species.records"));
        }
        catch(IOException e)
        {
            System.out.println(
                    "Error opening file species.records.");
            System.out.println("for writing.");
            System.exit(0);
        }

        Species oneRecord =
                    new Species("Calif. Condor", 27, 0.02);
        Species secondRecord =
                    new Species("Black Rhino", 100, 1.0);

        try
        {
            outputStream.writeObject(oneRecord);
            outputStream.writeObject(secondRecord);
            outputStream.close();
        }
        catch(IOException e)
        {
            System.out.println(
                    "Error writing to file species.records.");
            System.exit(0);
        }

        System.out.println(
                    "Records sent to file species.record.");
```

■ DISPLAY 9.19 File I/O of Class Objects *(Part 2 of 3)*

```
System.out.println(
        "Now let's reopen the file and echo the records.");

ObjectInputStream inputStream = null;

try
{
    inputStream =
        new ObjectInputStream(
            new FileInputStream("species.records"));
}
catch(IOException e)
{
    System.out.println(
            "Error opening file species.records.");
    System.out.println("for reading.");
    System.exit(0);
}

Species readOne = null, readTwo = null;

try
{
    readOne = (Species)inputStream.readObject();
    readTwo = (Species)inputStream.readObject();
    inputStream.close();
}
catch(Exception e)
{
    System.out.println(
            "Error reading from file species.records.");
    System.exit(0);
}

System.out.println("The following were read\n"
                    + "from the file species.record:");
System.out.println(readOne);
System.out.println();
System.out.println(readTwo);

System.out.println("End of program.");
    }
}
```

Notice the type casts.

It would be better to have a separate **catch** *block for each type of exception. We have only one* **catch** *block here in order to save space.*

■ DISPLAY 9.19 **File I/O of Class Objects** *(Part 3 of 3)*

Sample Screen Dialog

```
Records sent to file species.record.
Now let's reopen the file and echo the records.
The following were read
from the file species.record:
Name = Calif. Condor
Population = 27
Growth rate = 0.02%

Name = Black Rhino
Population = 100
Growth rate = 1.0%
End of program.
```

```
outputStream.writeObject(oneRecord);
```

where `outputStream` is a stream of type `ObjectOutputStream` and `oneRecord` is of type `Species`.

Remember, the class must be serialized in order for it to be written it to a file in this way. When checking the documentation for predefined classes, you should look for documentation which says that the class implements `Serializable`.

readObject   Reading the object back into a record can be done by using the method `readObject` of the stream class `ObjectInputStream`, as illustrated by the following example taken from Display 9.19:

```
readOne = (Species)inputStream.readObject();
```

Here, `inputStream` is a stream of type `ObjectInputStream` that has been connected to a file previously filled with `Species` records, using `writeObject` of the class `ObjectOutoutStream`. The variable `readOne` is of type `Species`.

Note that `readObject` returns its value as an object of type `Object`. If you want to use it as an object of type `Species`, you must do a type cast to the type `Species`.

Before we leave this example, let's clarify a potential misconception. The class `Species` has a method `toString`. This `toString` method is needed to make output to the screen, using `System.out.println`, perform correctly and to make output to a text file, using `println`, perform correctly. However, the method `toString` has nothing to do with object I/O to a binary file. Object I/O to a binary file would work fine even if there were no `toString` method in the definition of the class `Species`.

▲ *Gotcha*

Exceptions, Exceptions, Exceptions

Many situations that do not throw exceptions with text-file I/O do throw exceptions with binary-file I/O. So you will need to do more exception handling when working with binary files than you will when working with text files. For example, closing a text file connected to a stream of type `PrintWriter` does not cause an exception to be thrown. However, closing a binary-file stream of the types we have been discussing can cause an `IOException` to be thrown. When doing binary I/O as we have described it, almost anything can cause an exception to be thrown. Also, there is a long list of exceptions that can be thrown by the methods `writeObject` and `readObject`, which you can see by checking Displays 9.13 and 9.14. △

The `Serializable` Interface

What is the effect of making a class serializable, as we did, for example, with the class `Species` in Display 9.18? In a sense, there is no direct effect on the class, but there is an effect on how Java performs file I/O with objects of the class. If a class is serializable, Java assigns a serial number to each object of the class that it writes to a stream of type `ObjectOutputStream`. If the same object is written to the stream more than once, then after the first time, Java writes only the serial number for the object and not a full description of the object's data. This feature makes file I/O more efficient and makes the files smaller. When read back out with a stream of type `ObjectInputStream`, duplicate serial numbers are returned as references to the same object. Note that this condition means that, if two variables contain references to the same object, and you write the objects to the file and later read them from the file, then the two objects that are read will again be references to the same object. So nothing in the structure of your object data is lost when you write the objects to the file and later read them back.

When a serializable class has instance variables of a class type, then the class for the instance variables should also be serializable, and so on for all levels of class instance variables within classes.

Serializability sounds great. So why aren't all classes made serializable? For security reasons. The serial-number system makes it easier for programmers to get access to the object data written to secondary storage. Also, for some classes, it may not make sense to write objects to secondary storage, since they would be meaningless when read out again later. For example, if the object contains system-dependent data, the data may be meaningless when later read out.

▲ *Gotcha*

Mixing Class Types in the Same File

The best way to write and read objects using `ObjectOutputStream` and `ObjectInput-Stream` is to store only data of one class type in any one file. If you store objects of multiple class types, or even objects of only one class type mixed in with primitive-type data, it has been our experience that the system can get confused, and you could lose your data. △

Array Objects in Binary Files

Entire arrays can be saved to a binary file by using `objectWrite` and later read by using `objectRead`. When doing so, if the array has a base type that is a class, the class should be serializable. This means that, if you store all your data for one serializable class in a single array, then you can output all your data to a binary file with one invocation of `objectWrite`.

This way of storing an array in a binary file is illustrated in Display 9.20. Note that the base-class type, `Species`, is serializable. Note also the type cast that uses the array type `Species[]`. Since `readObject` returns its value as an object of type `Object`, it must be type cast to the correct array type.

■ DISPLAY 9.20   **File I/O of an Array Object** *(Part 1 of 2)*

```java
import java.io.*;

public class ArrayIODemo
{

    public static void main(String[] args)
    {
        Species[] oneArray = new Species[2];
        oneArray[0] =
                    new Species("Calif. Condor", 27, 0.02);
        oneArray[1] =
                    new Species("Black Rhino", 100, 1.0);

        try
        {
            ObjectOutputStream outputStream =
                    new ObjectOutputStream(
                        new FileOutputStream("array.file"));
            outputStream.writeObject(oneArray);
            outputStream.close();
        }
        catch(IOException e)
        {
            System.out.println(
                    "Error writing to file array.file.");
            System.exit(0);
        }

        System.out.println(
                    "Array sent to file array.file.");

        System.out.println(
                "Now let's reopen the file and echo the array.");

        Species[] anotherArray = new Species[2];
```

■ DISPLAY 9.20 **File I/O of an Array Object** *(Part 2 of 2)*

```
        try
        {
            ObjectInputStream inputStream =
                new ObjectInputStream(
                    new FileInputStream("array.file"));
            anotherArray = (Species[])inputStream.readObject();
            inputStream.close();
        }
        catch(Exception e)
        {
            System.out.println(
                "Error reading file array.file.");
            System.exit(0);
        }

        System.out.println("The following were read\n"
                        + "from the file array.file:");
        int i;
        for (i = 0; i < anotherArray.length; i++)
        {
            System.out.println(anotherArray[i]);
            System.out.println();
        }
        System.out.println("End of program.");
    }
}
```

Notice the type casts.

It would be better to have a separate catch block for each type of exception. We have only one catch block in order to save space.

Sample Screen Dialog

```
    Records sent to file array.file.
    Now let's reopen the file and echo the records.
    The following were read
    from the file array.file:
    Name = Calif. Condor
    Population = 27
    Growth rate = 0.02%

    Name = Black Rhino
    Population = 100
    Growth rate = 1.0%

    End of program.
```

? Self-Test Questions

40. How do you make a class serializable?

41. What is the return type for the method `readObject` of the class `ObjectInput-Stream`?

42. What exception might be thrown by the method `writeObject` of the class `ObjectOutputStream`?

43. What exception might be thrown by the method `readObject` of the class `ObjectInputStream`?

CHAPTER SUMMARY

■ Files that are considered to be strings of characters and that look like characters to your program and your editor are called text files. Files whose contents must be handled as strings of binary digits are called binary files.

■ Your program can use the class `PrintWriter` to write to a text file and can use the class `BufferedReader` to read from a text file.

■ When reading from a file, you should always check for the end of a file and do something appropriate if the end of the file is reached. The way that you test for the end of a file depends on whether your program is reading from a text file or a binary file.

■ You can read a file name from the keyboard into a variable of type `String` and use that variable in place of a file name.

■ The class `File` can be used to determine whether there is a file with a given name. It can also be used to determine whether your program is allowed to read the file or write to the file.

■ Your program can use the class `ObjectOutputStream` to write to a binary file and can use the class `ObjectInputStream` to read from a binary file.

■ Your program can use the method `writeObject` of the class `ObjectOutputStream` to easily write class objects to a binary file. The objects can be read back with the method `readObject` of the class `ObjectInputStream`.

■ In order to use the methods `writeObject` of the class `ObjectOutputStream` and `readObject` of the class `ObjectInputStream`, the class whose objects are written to a file must implement the `Serializable` interface.

✔ Answers to Self-Test Questions

1. If a program sends its output to the screen, the output goes away when (or soon after) the program ends. A program that sends its output to a file has made a (more or less) permanent copy of its output. Files provide you with a way to store data permanently. The contents of a file remain until a person or program changes the file. If your program sends its output to a file, the output file will remain after the program has finished running.

2. From a file to the program.

3. Text files are files you can write to and read using an editor. They can be thought of as containing characters. Binary files represent data in a way that is not convenient to read with a text editor, but binary files can be written to and read from a program in a very efficient way. Binary files represent data through the same format as the one used to store the data in the computer's main memory.

4.
```
PrintWriter outStream =
      new PrintWriter(new FileOutputStream("sam"));
```

5.
```
PrintWriter outStream =
      new PrintWriter(new FileOutputStream("sam", true));
```

6. A `FileNotFoundException` would be thrown if the file could not be opened because, for example, there is already a directory (folder) named `out.txt`. Note that, if the file does not exist, but can be created, then no exception is thrown. If you answered `IOException`, you are not wrong, because a `FileNotFoundException` is an `IOException`. However, the better answer is the more specific exception class, namely, `FileNotFoundException`.

7. No. That is why we use an object of the class `FileOutputStream` as an argument. The correct way to express the code displayed in the question is as follows:
```
PrintWriter outputStream =
      new PrintWriter(new FileOutputStream("myFile.txt"));
```

8.
```
PrintWriter textStream =
          new PrintWriter(new FileOutputStream("dobedo"));
```

9.
```
BufferedReader inputStream =
          new BufferedReader(new FileReader("dobedo"));
```

10. No, but the method `read` in the class `BufferedReader` can be used to read a single character and thus is approximately equivalent to the method `readChar` in the class `SavitchIn`. However, the method `read` in the class `BufferedReader` returns its character as an `int` value and needs a type cast in order to make it into a `char` value.

11. Both `read` and `readLine` in the class `BufferedReader` might throw an `IOException`.

12. The `try` block in Display 9.7 is larger so that it includes the invocations of the method `readLine`, which might throw an `IOException`. The method `println` in Display 9.1 does not throw any exceptions.

13. The method `readLine` returns a value of type `String`. The method `read` reads a single *character*, but it returns it as a value of type `int`. To get the value to be of type `char`, you need to do a type cast.

14. When the method `readLine` tries to read beyond the end of a file, it returns the value `null`. Thus, you can test for the end of a file by testing for `null`.

15. The method `read` reads a single *character*, but it returns it as a value of type `int`. To get the value to be of type `char`, you need to do a type cast.

16. When the method `read` tries to read beyond the end of a file, it returns the value −1. Thus, you can test for the end of a file by testing for the value −1. This technique works because all true characters return a positive `int` value.

17. The classes `FileReader` and `FileOutputStream` have constructors that take a file name as an argument. The classes `PrintWriter` and `BufferedReader` do not have constructors that take a file name as an argument.

18. Yes, it is equivalent to the following (except that, in the following, the object `readerObject` is not given a name):

```
BufferedReader inputStream =
        new BufferedReader(new FileReader("myFile.txt"));
```

19. The code for the following program is included on the CD that accompanies this book:

```
import java.io.*;

public class FileClassExercise
{
    public static void main(String[] args)
    {
        String name = null;
        File fileObject = null;

        System.out.print("Enter a file name and I will ");
        System.out.println("tell you if it exists.");
        name = SavitchIn.readLineWord();
        fileObject = new File(name);

        if (fileObject.exists())
        {
            System.out.println("I found the file " + name);
            System.out.println("Delete the file? (y/n)");
            char ans = SavitchIn.readLineNonwhiteChar();

            if ((ans == 'y') || (ans == 'Y'))
            {
                System.out.println(
                            "If you delete the file " + name);
                System.out.println(
                            "all data in the file will");
```

```
                    System.out.println("be lost. Delete? (y/n)");
                    ans = SavitchIn.readLineNonwhiteChar();

                    if ((ans == 'y') || (ans == 'Y'))
                    {
                        if (fileObject.delete())
                            System.out.println("File deleted.");
                        else
                            System.out.println(
                                        "Cannot delete file.");
                    }
                    else
                        System.out.println("File not deleted.");
                }
                else
                    System.out.println("File not deleted.");
            }
            else
                System.out.println("I cannot find " + name);
        }
}
```

20.
```
    ObjectOutputStream toFile =
                    new ObjectOutputStream(
                        new FileOutputStream("stuff.data"));
```

21.
```
    toFile.writeDouble(x1);
    toFile.writeDouble(x2);
    toFile.writeDouble(x3);
```

22. `toFile.close();`

23. `import java.io.*;`

24.
```
    ObjectInputStream fromFile =
                    new ObjectInputStream(
                        new FileInputStream("stuff.data"));
```

25.
```
    double x1, x2, x3;
    x1 = fromFile.readDouble();
    x2 = fromFile.readDouble();
    x3 = fromFile.readDouble();
```

26. `fromFile.close();`

27. If a number is written to a file using `writeInt`, it should be read only with `read-Int`. If you use `readLong` or `readDouble` to read the number, something will go wrong.

28. You should not use `readUTF` to read a string from a text file. You should use `readUTF` only to read a string from a binary file. Moreover, the string should have been written to that file using `writeUTF`.

29.
```
ObjectOutputStream writer =
    new ObjectOutputStream(new FileOutputStream(theFile));
```

30.
```
ObjectInputStream reader =
    new ObjectInputStream(new FileInputStream(theFile));
```

31. The following program is on the CD that accompanies this book:

```
import java.io.*;

public class FileNameExercise
{
    public static void main(String[] args)
    {
        String fileName = null;//to use fileName in catch block,
                               //must declare it outside of try block.
        try
        {
            System.out.println("Enter file name:");
            fileName = SavitchIn.readLineWord();
            ObjectInputStream inputStream =
                        new ObjectInputStream(
                                new FileInputStream(fileName));

            System.out.println("The first thing in the file");
            System.out.println(fileName + " is");
            String first = inputStream.readUTF();
            System.out.println(first);
            inputStream.close();
        }
        catch(IOException e)
        {
            System.out.println("Problem with input from file "
                                        + fileName);
        }
    }
}
```

32. It will not work, because `ObjectInputStream` does not have a constructor with a parameter of type `String`. The correct way to accomplish the desired effect is by using

```
ObjectInputStream inputStream =
                new ObjectInputStream(
                        new FileInputStream("mydata.dat"));
```

33. The class `FileInputStream` does not have any of the methods `readInt`, `readDouble`, or `readUTF`.

34. Yes.

35. No.

36. When opening a binary file for either output or input in the ways discussed in this chapter, a `FileNotFoundException` and other `IOExceptions` may be thrown.

37. An EOFException will be thrown.

38. Because when the end of the file is reached, an exception will be thrown, and that will end the entire try block.

39. The following program is on the CD that accompanies this book:

```java
import java.io.*;
public class TemperatureShow
{
    public static void main(String[] args)
    {
        try
        {
            ObjectInputStream inputStream =
                    new ObjectInputStream(new FileInputStream(
                                              "temperatures"));
            double t;
            System.out.println(
                        "Numbers from the file temperatures:");

            try
            {
                while (true)
                {
                    t = inputStream.readDouble();
                    System.out.println(t);
                }
            }
            catch(EOFException e)
            {
                //Do nothing
            }

            System.out.println("End of reading from file.");
            inputStream.close();
        }
        catch(IOException e)
        {
            System.out.println("Problem reading from file.");
        }
    }
}
```

40. You add the two words implements Serializable to the beginning of the class definition.

41. The return type is Object, which means that the returned value usually needs to be type cast to its "true" class.

42. IOException, NotSerializableException, and InvalidClassException.

43. ClassNotFoundException, InvalidClassException, OptionalDataException, and IOException.

● **Programming Projects**

1. Write a program that searches a file of numbers and outputs the largest number in the file, the smallest number in the file, and the average of all the numbers in the file. The output should go to the screen. Do not assume that the numbers in the file are in any special order. Your program should obtain the file name from the user. You can do this project with either a text file or a binary file. For the text-file version, the file should be a text file with one number per line. For the binary-file version, the file should be a binary file that consists entirely of numbers of type `double` that were written using `writeDouble`.

2. Write a program that reads a file of numbers of type `int` and outputs all the numbers to another file, but without any duplicate numbers. Assume that the input file is sorted from smallest first to largest last. After the program is run, the new file will contain all the numbers in the original file, but no number will appear more than once in the file. The numbers in the output file should also be sorted from smallest to largest. Your program should obtain both file names from the user. For the text-file version, the file should be a text file with one number per line. For the binary-file version, the file should be a binary file that consists entirely of numbers of type `int` that were written using `writeInt`.

3. Write a program that will check a text file for a number of formatting and punctuation matters. The program will ask for an input-file name and an output-file name and will then copy all the text from the input file to the output file, but with the following two changes: (1) Any string of two or more blank symbols is replaced by a single blank; (2) all sentences start with an uppercase letter. Define a sentence as beginning after a period, question mark, or exclamation mark followed by one or more whitespace characters.

4. Write a program similar to Display 9.19 that allows you to write an arbitrary number of records on endangered species to a file. The file name and the data for the records, each of which contains information on a single endangered species, are to be read from the keyboard. Then write another program that can search a file created by your first program and show the user any requested record. The user gives the file name and then enters the name of the species. The program displays the entire record for that species or else gives a message saying that it has no record for that species. Allow the user to enter additional species names until the user indicates that she or he is finished.

5. Write a program that reads from a file created by the program in Programming Project 4 and outputs the following information to the screen: the record of the species with the smallest population and the record of the species with the largest population. Do not assume that the records in the file are in any particular order. The user gives the file name.

6. Programming Project 4 asks you, among other things, to write a program that creates a file of objects of the class `Species`. Write a program that reads from a file created by that program and outputs the records to another file. However, the records in the output file should not show the same population figure as in the input file, but should instead give the population as it would be in 100 years given that

species' growth rate. You will want to use the method `projectedPopulation` of the class `Species`.

7. Write a program that allows you to write and read records of type `PetRecord` (Display 5.20 in Chapter 5) to a file. The program asks the user if she or he wants to write to a file or read from a file. In either case, the program next asks for the file name. If the user asked to write to a file, she or he is then allowed to enter as many records as desired. If the user asked to read from a file, she or he is shown all of the records in the file. Be sure that the records do not scroll by so quickly that the user cannot read them. Redefine the class `PetRecord` so that it is serializable.

8. Write a program that reads records of type `PetRecord` from a file (created by the program you wrote in Programming Project 7) and outputs the following information to the screen: the name and weight of the largest pet, the name and weight of smallest pet, the name and age of the youngest pet, and the name and age of the oldest pet.

Dynamic Data Structures

10

All is in flux, nothing stays still. -Heraclitus

A **data structure** is a construct used to organize data in a specific way. For example, an array is a kind of data structure. Each data structure organizes data in its own particular way. In this chapter, we discuss two kinds of data structures that can grow (and shrink) in size while your program is running: vectors and linked data structures. Vectors are similar to arrays, but offer more flexibility in some situations.

Linked data structures are a general group of data structures that can grow and shrink in a wide variety of ways. Although there are many different kinds of linked data structures, we will emphasize one simple, but useful, linked data structure known as a linked list. In the process of covering linked lists, we will introduce inner classes, a kind of class definition within another class definition.

OBJECTIVES

Become familiar with vectors and how they are used in Java.

Learn what a linked data structure is and how it can be realized in Java.

Find out how to manipulate linked lists.

Learn to use inner classes in defining linked data structures.

Learn what iterators are and how to create and use them.

PREREQUISITES

Sections 10.1, on vectors, and 10.2, on linked data structures, may be read in either order.

You need to read Chapters 2 through 6 in order to fully understand this chapter. You also need some familiarity with basic inheritance and basic exception handling. The details are as follows:

Section	Prerequisite
Section 10.1 Vectors	Chapters 1 through 6, Section 7.1, the subsection "The Class Object" in Section 7.2, and Section 8.1.
Section 10.2 Linked Data Structures (excluding the subsection "Exception Handling with Linked Lists")	Chapters 1 through 6.

Section	Prerequisite
The subsection of Section 10.2 entitled "Exception Handling with Linked Lists"	Chapters 1 through 6 and Chapter 8.

10.1 VECTORS

"Well, I'll eat it," said Alice, "and if it makes me grow larger, I can reach the key; and if it makes me grow smaller, I can creep under the door; so either way I'll get into the garden. . . ." -Lewis Carroll, Alice's Adventures in Wonderland

Vectors can be thought of as arrays that can grow (and shrink) in length while your program is running. In Java, you can read in the length of an array when the program is running, but once your program creates an array of that length, it cannot change the length of the array. For example, suppose you write a program to record customer orders for a mail-order house, and suppose you store all the orders for one customer in an array of objects of some class called `OrderItem`. You could ask the user how many items she or he will order, store the number in a variable called `numberOfItems`, and then create the array `item` with the following statement:

comparison of vectors arrays

```
OrderItem[] item = new OrderItem[numberOfItems];
```

But suppose the customer enters `numberOfItems` items and then decides to order another item? There is no way to increase the size of the array `item`. There are ways around this problem with arrays, but they are all rather complicated and require the creation of a new array. Vectors serve the same purpose as arrays, except that vectors can change length while the program is running. So a vector could handle the customer's extra order without any problems.

If vectors are like arrays, but have the nice added feature of being able to change length, then why don't we just always use vectors instead of arrays? It often seems that every silver lining has a cloud, and that is true of vectors as well. There are two main problems with vectors: (1) They are less efficient than arrays, and (2) the elements in a vector must be objects—that is, they cannot be values of a primitive type, such as `int`, `double`, or `char`. For example, if you want a vector of `int` values, you must simulate this structure with a vector of `Integer` values, where `Integer` is the wrapper class whose objects simulate `int` values. Thus, it is best to use arrays whenever you know that the length of the array does not need to change, and to use vectors when the capacity of the vector will change often and by unpredictable amounts.

which to use?

Using Vectors

Vectors are used in much the same way as arrays, but there are some important differences. First, the definition of the class `Vector` is not provided automatically. The definition is in

`java.util.*`

the package `java.util`, and any code that uses the class `Vector` must contain the following, normally at the start of the file:

```
import java.util.*;
```

A vector is created and named in the same way as objects of any class. For example, you could write

```
Vector v = new Vector(20);
```

capacity

This statement makes v the name of a vector that has an *initial* **capacity** of 20 items. When we say that a vector has a certain capacity, we mean that it has been allocated memory for that many items, but if it needs to hold more items, the system will automatically allocate more memory. By carefully choosing the initial capacity of a vector, you can often make your code more efficient, but this capacity has no effect on how many items the vector can hold. If you choose your capacity to be large enough, then the system will not need to reallocate memory too often, and as a result, your program should run faster. On the other hand, if you make your capacity too large, you will waste storage space. However, no matter what capacity you choose, you can still do anything you want with the vector.

Quick Reference: **Creating and Naming a Vector**

An object of the class `Vector` is created and named in the same way as any other object.

Examples:

```
Vector v = new Vector( );
Vector v2 = new Vector(30);
```

When a number is given as an argument to the constructor, that number determines the initial capacity of the vector.

---

no square
brackets

Vectors can be used like arrays, but they do not have the array square-bracket notation. If you would use

```
a[index] = "Hi Mom!";
```

for an array of strings a, then the analogous statement for a vector v would be

setElementAt

```
v.setElementAt("Hi Mom!", index);
```

If you would use

```
String temp = a[index];
```

for an array of strings a, then the analogous statement for a vector v would be

```
String temp = (String)v.elementAt(index);
```

The type cast (`String`) is needed because the base type of all vectors is `Object`. This point is discussed in more detail later in this chapter. The two methods `setElementAt` and `elementAt` give vectors approximately the same functionality that square brackets give to arrays. However, you need to be aware of one important point: The method invocation

```
v.setElementAt("Hi Mom!", index);
```

is *not* always completely analogous to

```
a[index] = "Hi Mom!";
```

The method `setElementAt` can replace any existing element, but you cannot use `set-ElementAt` to put an element at just any index, as you would with an array. The method `setElementAt` is used to change the value of elements, not to set them for the first time. To set an element for the first time, you usually use the method `addElement`. The method `addElement` adds elements at index position 0, position 1, position 2, and so forth in that order. This means that vectors must always be filled in this order. But your code can then go back and change any individual element, just as it can in an array.

> setElementAt restrictions

> addElement

You can find out how many indices already have elements by using the method `size`. If `v` is a vector, `v.size( )` returns the **size** of the vector, which is the number of elements stored in it. The indices of these elements go from 0 to one less than `v.size( )`.

> size

Quick Reference: **addElement**

Elements can be added to a vector by using the method `addElement`. The elements are added to index position 0, then 1, then 2, and so forth.

Examples:

```
v.addElement("Zero");
v.addElement("One");
v.addElement("Two");
```

The object `v` is a vector.

Quick Reference: **Accessing at an Index**

If `v` is a vector, its elements can be accessed as follows:

Examples:

```
v.setElementAt("Here", index); //Sets the element
                               //at index to "Here".
String temp = (String)v.elementAt(index); //The expression
     //v.elementAt(index) returns the element at position index.
```

The `index` must be greater than or equal to 0 and less than the current size of the vector `v`.

The method invocation `elementAt(index)` always returns a value of type `Object` and thus typically needs a type cast.

Quick Reference: **The Method size**

The method `size` returns the number of elements in a vector.

Example:

```
for (index = 0; index < v.size( ); index++)
    System.out.println(v.elementAt(index));
```

`v` is a vector, and `index` is of type `int`.

With arrays, the square brackets and the instance variable `length` are the only tools automatically provided for you, the programmer. If you want to use arrays for other things, you must write code to manipulate the arrays. Vectors, on the other hand, come with a large selection of powerful methods that can do many of the things for which you would need to write code in order to do with arrays. For example, the class `Vector` has a method that inserts a new element between two elements in the vector. Most of these methods are described in Display 10.1.

■ DISPLAY 10.1 **Some Methods in the Class** `Vector` *(Part 1 of 4)*

Constructors

```
public Vector(int initialCapacity, int capacityIncrement)
```

Constructs an empty vector with the specified initial capacity and capacity increment. When the vector needs to grow, it will add room for `capacityIncrement` more items.

```
public Vector(int initialCapacity)
```

Creates an empty vector with the specified initial capacity. When the vector needs to increase its capacity, the capacity doubles.

```
public Vector( )
```

Creates an empty vector with an initial capacity of 10. When the vector needs to increase its capacity, the capacity doubles.

Arraylike Methods

```
public void setElementAt(Object newElement, int index)
```

Sets the element at the specified `index` to `newElement`. The element previously at that position is discarded. If you draw an analogy between the vector and an array `a`, this statement is analogous to setting `a[index]` to the value `newElement`. The `index` must be a value greater than or equal to 0 and less than the current size of the vector. Throws `ArrayIndexOutOf-BoundsException` if the `index` is not in this range.

■ DISPLAY 10.1 **Some Methods in the Class** Vector *(Part 2 of 4)*

```
public Object elementAt(int index)
```

Returns the element at the specified index. This statement is analogous to returning a[index] for an array a. The index must be a value greater than or equal to 0 and less than the current size of the vector. Throws ArrayIndexOutOfBoundsException if the index is not in this range.

Methods to Add Elements

```
public void addElement(Object newElement)
```

Adds the specified element to the end of the calling vector and increases the vector's size by one. The capacity of the vector is increased if that is required.

```
public void insertElementAt(Object newElement, int index)
```

Inserts newElement as an element in the calling vector at the specified index. Each element in the vector with an index greater or equal to index is shifted upward to have an index that is one greater than the value it had previously. The index must be a value greater than or equal to 0 and less than or *equal* to the current size of the vector. Throws ArrayIndexOutOfBoundsException if the index is not in this range. Note that you can use this method to add an element after the last current element. The capacity of the vector is increased if that is required.

Methods to Remove Elements

```
public void removeElementAt(int index)
```

Deletes the element at the specified index. Each element in the vector with an index greater than index is decreased to have an index that is one less than the value it had previously. The index must be a value greater than or equal to 0 and less than the current size of the vector. Throws ArrayIndexOutOfBoundsException if the index is not in this range.

```
public boolean removeElement(Object theElement)
```

Removes the first occurrence of theElement from the calling vector. If theElement is found in the vector, then each element in the vector with an index greater than theElement's index is decreased to have an index that is one less than the value it had previously. Returns true if theElement was found (and removed). Returns false if theElement was not found in the calling vector.

```
public void removeAllElements()
```

Removes all elements from the calling vector and sets the vector's size to zero.

Search Methods

```
public boolean contains(Object target)
```

Returns true if target is an element of the calling vector; otherwise, returns false.

■ **DISPLAY 10.1** **Some Methods in the Class** `Vector` *(Part 3 of 4)*

```
public int indexOf(Object target)
```

Returns the index of the first element that is equal to `target`. Uses the method `equals` of the object `target` to test for equality. Returns −1 if `target` is not found.

```
public int indexOf(Object target, int startIndex)
```

Returns the index of the first element that is equal to `target`, but considers only indices that are greater than or equal to `startIndex`. Uses the method `equals` of the object `target` to test for equality. Returns −1 if `target` is not found.

```
public int lastIndexOf(Object target)
```

Returns the index of the last element that is equal to `target`. Uses the method `equals` of the object `target` to test for equality. Returns −1 if `target` is not found.

```
public Object firstElement()
```

Returns the first element of the calling vector. Throws `NoSuchElementException` if the vector is empty.

```
public Object lastElement()
```

Returns the last element of the calling vector. Throws `NoSuchElementException` if the vector is empty.

Memory Management (Size and Capacity)

```
public boolean isEmpty()
```

Returns `true` if the calling vector is empty (that is, has size 0); otherwise, returns `false`.

```
public int size()
```

Returns the number of elements in the calling vector.

```
public int capacity()
```

Returns the current capacity of the calling vector.

```
public void ensureCapacity(int newCapacity)
```

Increases the capacity of the calling vector in order to ensure that the vector can hold at least `newCapacity` elements. Using `ensureCapacity` can sometimes increase efficiency, but its use is not needed for any other reason.

```
public void trimToSize()
```

Trims the capacity of the calling vector to the vector's current size. This method is used to save storage space.

■ DISPLAY 10.1 **Some Methods in the Class** Vector *(Part 4 of 4)*

```
public void setSize(int newSize)
```

Sets the size of the calling vector to newSize. If newSize is greater than the current size, the new elements receive the value null. If newSize is less than the current size, all elements at index newSize and greater are discarded. Throws an ArrayIndexOutOfBoundsException if newSize is negative.

Make a Copy

```
public Object clone()
```

Returns a clone of the calling vector. The clone is an identical copy of the calling vector.

The base type of an array can be any type whatsoever. On the other hand, all vectors have the base type: Object. So, in order to store an item in a vector, the item must be of type Object. As you will recall, every class is a descendant class of the class Object. Thus, every object of every class type is also of type Object. So you can add elements of any class type to a vector. In fact, you can even add elements of different class types to the same vector, but this can be a dangerous thing to do. On the other hand, you cannot add elements of any primitive type, such as int, double, or char, to a vector.

base type

If you want the equivalent of a vector of elements of some primitive type, such as the type int, you must use the corresponding wrapper class — in this case, Integer. You can have a vector of elements that are of type Integer. Wrapper classes are discussed in Chapter 5.

primitive types

● **Programming Tip**

Adding to a Vector

To place an element in a vector position (at a vector index) for the first time, you usually use the method addElement. The method addElement adds elements at index positions 0, 1, 2, and so forth, in that order. Your code can then go back and change any individual element, using setElementAt. However, set-ElementAt can reset only the element at an index that already has an element. You cannot use setElementAt to add an element to a vector at a previously unused index position.

You can also add elements to a vector by using insertElementAt. For example, to insert the string "Do Be Do" at index position 3 of a vector named v, you can use the following:

```
v.insertElementAt("Do Be Do", 3);
```

If 3 is greater than `v.size( )`, then when this code is run, you will get an error message indicating an `ArrayIndexOutOfBoundsException`. The error message (exception) mentions arrays, but in this case, it applies to vectors. Note that this is a run-time error message and not a compiler error message.

More generally, in order for the following to be valid, the value of `index` must be less than or equal to `v.size( )`:

```
v.insertElementAt(elementToInsert, index);
```

Since the last index position used is `v.size( )` − 1, this stipulation means that you can insert an element at the first unused index position (as well as at any used index position), but you cannot insert an element at any higher index position. This restriction ensures that the elements in a vector are always in positions 0, 1, and so forth, to some last index, with no gaps.

When you use the method `insertElementAt` to insert a new element at an index position, all the elements that were at that index position or higher have their index increased by one, so that there is room to insert the new element without losing any of the older elements. Unlike the procedure for inserting into an array, this process happens automatically, and you need not write any extra code to move elements.

▲ *Gotcha*

Vector Elements Are of Type `Object`

The fact that an element added to a vector must be an `Object` has more consequences than you might at first think. Consider the following code:

```
Vector v = new Vector( );
String greeting = "Hi Mom!";
v.addElement(greeting);
System.out.println("Length is " + (v.elementAt(0)).length( ));
```

Read the text to see what is wrong with this code.

Although this code may look fine, it will produce an error message telling you that the class `Object` does not have a method named `length`.

You might protest that `v.elementAt(0)` is of type `String`, and thus it does have a method named `length`. You would be right, but Java acts as if it does not "know" that `v.elementAt(0)` is of type `String`. It "knows" only that it is an element of a vector, and all Java "knows" about elements of a vector is that they are of type `Object`. You need to tell Java that `v.elementAt(0)` is of type `String` by using a type cast as follows:

```
(String)(v.elementAt(0))
```

So the troublesome output statement needs to be rewritten to the following, which will work fine:

```
System.out.println("Length is " +
                    ((String)(v.elementAt(0))).length( )); △
```

> **Remember:** **The Base Type of a Vector Is** `Object`
>
> All vectors have base type `Object`, but all classes are descendant classes of the class `Object`. This means that an element of a vector can be an object of any class, but you cannot have vector elements of a primitive type such as `int`, `double`, or `char`.

? Self-Test Questions

1. Suppose `v` is a vector. How do you add the string `"Hello"` to the vector `v`?

2. Suppose `instruction` is a vector with the string `"Stop"` at index position 5. How do you change the string at index position 5 to `"Go"`?

3. Can you use the method `setElementAt` to place an element in a vector at any index you want?

4. Can you use the method `insertElementAt` to place an element in a vector at any index you want? Can you use the method `insertElementAt` to insert an element at any position (any index) for which you cannot use `setElementAt`?

5. If you create a vector with the following statement, can the vector contain more than 20 elements?

   ```
   Vector v = new Vector(20);
   ```

6. Give code that will output all the elements in a vector `v` to the screen. Assume that the elements are of type `String`.

7. Write a class for sorting strings into lexicographic order that follows the outline of the class `SelectionSort` in Display 6.13 of Chapter 6. Your definition, however, will use a vector of elements (all of which happen to be strings), rather than an array of elements of type `int`. For words, lexicographic order reduces to alphabetic order if all the words are in either lowercase or uppercase letters. You can compare two strings to see which is lexicographically first by using the `String` method `compareTo`. For strings `s1` and `s2`, `s1.compareTo(s2)` returns a negative number if `s1` is lexicographically before `s2`, returns 0 if `s1` equals `s2`, and returns a positive number if `s1` is lexicographically after `s2`. Call your class `StringSelectionSort`. *Hint:* Vector elements are of type `Object`, so if you want to use a `String` method, such as `compareTo`, with an element of the vector, you will need to do a type cast to a `String`. A test program you can use to test your class follows (the program is on the CD that accompanies this book):

```java
import java.util.*;

public class StringSelectionSortDemo
{
    public static void main(String[] args)
    {
        Vector b = new Vector();
        b.addElement("time");
        b.addElement("tide");
```

```
            b.addElement("clouds");
            b.addElement("rain");

            System.out.println("Vector values before sorting:");
            int i;
            for (i = 0; i < b.size(); i++)
                System.out.print(b.elementAt(i) + " ");
            System.out.println();

            StringSelectionSort.sort(b);
            System.out.println("Vector values after sorting:");
            for (i = 0; i < b.size(); i++)
                System.out.print(b.elementAt(i) + " ");
            System.out.println();
    }
}
```

Comparing Vectors and Arrays

Vectors are used for the same sorts of applications as arrays. So how do you decide whether to use a vector or an array? Each has its advantages and disadvantages. An advantage of vectors is that they have many built-in features. For example, a vector is automatically a partially filled vector. The method size keeps track of how much of the vector is filled with meaningful elements. This feature is illustrated in the sample program in Display 10.2. Vectors also have built-in methods to accomplish many of the common tasks that would require you to design your own code if you were using arrays. For example, with vectors, you have a method that inserts an element at any specified point in the vector, a method that deletes an element from any place in the vector, and a method that tests whether an element is in the vector or not.

Perhaps the biggest advantage of vectors over arrays is that vectors automatically increase their capacity should your program need room for more elements. Your program can determine the size of an array when the program is run, but once the array is created, the size cannot be changed.

Some advantages of arrays are that they are more efficient, they have a very nice notation that uses the square brackets, and, perhaps most importantly, the base type of an array can be any type. The base type of a vector is always the type Object. This aspect is not a disadvantage if you want to store objects of some class in a vector, but if you want to store values of a primitive type in a vector, you need to use the wrapper class corresponding to the primitive type. With an array, you can simply make the primitive type the base type of the array.

▲ *Gotcha*

Using `capacity` Instead of `size`

In Display 10.2, we use the following code to print out a list of all strings in the vector toDoList:

```
int vectorSize = toDoList.size();
```

```
for (position = 0; position < vectorSize; position++)
    System.out.println(
                    (String)(toDoList.elementAt(position)));
```

If we had mistakenly used the method `capacity` instead of `size`, we would be trying to write out garbage values. In this case, we would be likely to find the error, because if we had used `capacity` instead of `size`, then the program would have ended with a message saying that it has thrown an `ArrayIndexOutOfBoundsException` (unless, by coincidence, the size and the capacity were equal). △

■ DISPLAY 10.2   **A Vector Demonstration** *(Part 1 of 2)*

```
import java.util.*;

public class VectorDemo
{
    public static void main(String[] args)
    {
        Vector toDoList = new Vector(10);

        System.out.println(
                        "Enter items for the list, when prompted.");

        boolean done = false;
        String next = null;
        char ans;
        while (! done)
        {
            System.out.println("Input an entry:");
            next = SavitchIn.readLine();
            toDoList.addElement(next);
            System.out.print("More items for the list?(y/n): ");
            ans = SavitchIn.readLineNonwhiteChar();
            if ((ans == 'n') || (ans == 'N'))
                    done = true;
        }

        System.out.println("The list contains:");
        int position;
        int vectorSize = toDoList.size();
        for (position = 0; position < vectorSize; position++)
        System.out.println(
                        (String)(toDoList.elementAt(position)));
    }
}
```

■ DISPLAY 10.2 **A Vector Demonstration** *(Part 2 of 2)*

Sample Screen Dialog

```
Enter items for the list, when prompted.
Input an entry
Buy milk.
More items for the list?(y/n): y
Input an entry
Wash car.
More items for the list?(y/n): y
Input an entry
Do assignment.
More items for the list?(y/n): n
The list contains:
Buy milk.
Wash car.
Do assignment.
```

■ **Java Tip**
   Use trimToSize to Save Memory

Vectors automatically increase their capacity when your program needs them to have additional capacity. However, the capacity may increase beyond what your program requires. Also, when your program needs less capacity in a vector, the vector does not automatically shrink. If your vector has a large amount of excess capacity, you can save memory by using the methods setSize and trimToSize to shrink the capacity of a vector. If v is a vector, an invocation of v.setSize(n) will set the size of v to n and discard any elements in positions n or higher. The invocation v.trimToSize( ) will shrink the capacity of the vector v down to the size of v, so that there is no unused capacity in v. Normally, you should use trimToSize only when you know that the vector will not later need its extra capacity. ■

▲ *Gotcha*

Using the Method `clone`

As was true of objects for other classes, as well as for arrays, you cannot make a copy of a vector by using the assignment statement. For example, consider the following code:

```
Vector v = new Vector(10);
<Some code to fill the vector v.>
Vector otherV;
otherV = v;
```

This code simply makes `otherV` another name for the vector `v`, so that you have two names, but only one vector. If you want to make `otherV` an identical, but different, copy of `v`, then you use the method `clone` as follows:

```
Vector otherV = (Vector)v.clone();
```

Be sure to notice the type cast to the type `Vector` in the preceding line of code. That type cast is needed. Because the method `clone` returns a value of type `Object`, the following line will produce an error message:

```
Vector otherV = v.clone(); //Incorrect form
```

The reason that `clone` returns a value of type `Object` has to do with language features other than vectors and is a bit too complicated to explain here, but the way to cope with this inconvenience is clear and simple: Just insert a type cast as shown in the preceding example.

A class can have a private instance variable of type `Vector`. However, private instance variables of type `Vector` have complications similar to those we discussed for private instance variables of an array type. Suppose you have a class with a private instance variable of an array type. In the Gotcha section "Returning an Array Instance Variable" in Chapter 6, we noted that, in order to keep programmers from having direct access to the private array instance variables, your accessor methods should return a copy of the array. The exact same lesson applies to private instance variables of type `Vector`. An accessor method should not return the private instance vector itself, but should return a copy of the vector. To produce a copy of a vector, you can use the `Vector` method `clone` to produce a clone (a copy) of the private instance vector and return the clone.

Using the method `clone`, however, can be a bit complicated and produces a few pitfalls. First of all, the return type of the method `clone` is `Object`; it is not `Vector`. To see the problems that this condition can produce, suppose that you have a private instance variable named `v` declared as follows:

```
public class SampleClass
{
    private Vector v;
        .
        .
        .
}
```

The following accessor method will produce a compiler error message when added to the class `SampleClass`:

```java
public Vector getVector( )
{
    return v.clone( );
}
```

The problem is that `v.clone` is of type `Object` and needs a type cast in order to make it match the specified return value of `Vector`. One way to avoid the compiler error message is to write this accessor method as follows:

```java
public Vector getVector( )
{
    return (Vector)v.clone( );
}
```

One other problem is a general problem frequently encountered with the use of the method `clone` with most classes, not just with the class `Vector`. If the objects stored in the vector do not themselves have a well-behaved `clone` methods, then the clone of the vector will simply copy the memory addresses of the elements in the vector and not make copies of the actual elements in the vector. This can still allow for access of private data. Even if the other classes being used all have well-behaved `clone` methods, you may still need to do some extra work in order to get the accessor method in `SampleClass` to work correctly. The exact details are beyond the scope of this book, but you have at least been warned of the potential problems. △

■ **Java Tip**
Newer Collection Classes *(Optional)*

Java has added a new group of classes known as **collection classes** (because they implement the `Collection` interface). If you go on to study and use the collection classes, you can continue to use the class `Vector`. The `Vector` class in recent versions of Java has been retrofitted to be a collection. At this stage of your learning about Java, this change is of no consequence. But if you go on to read more about Java, you will be happy to know that your knowledge of vectors still applies in this new framework. ☐

? Self-Test Questions

8. What is the base type of a vector?

9. Can you store a value of type `int` in a vector?

10. Suppose `v` is a vector. What is the difference between `v.capacity( )` and `v.size( )`?

11. Suppose v is a vector and `v.size()` returns 10. Now suppose that your program has the following invocation:

```
v.setSize(20);
```

What will be the values of the new elements at indices 10 through 19? (Garbage values? Some default value? What default value? Something else?)

10.2 LINKED DATA STRUCTURES

Do not mistake the pointing finger for the moon. -Zen saying

A **linked data structure** is a collection of objects (known as **nodes**), each of which contains data and a reference to another node. We will confine most of our discussion of linked data structures to a simple (but widely used) kind known as a linked list.

linked data structure node

Linked Lists

A predefined `LinkedList` class comes with Java as part of the `java.util` package. It makes sense to use this predefined class, since it was defined by experts, is well tested, and will save you a lot of work. However, it will not teach you how to implement linked data structures in Java. To do that, you need to see a simple example of building at least one linked data structure. A linked list is both a simple and a typical linked data structure. So we will construct our own simplified example of a linked list in order to let you see how linked data structures work.

A **linked list** is shown in diagrammatic form in Display 10.3. Like all linked data structures, a linked list consists of objects known as nodes. In the display, the nodes are the boxes that are divided in half by a horizontal line. Each node has a place for some data and a place to hold a link to another node. The **links** are shown as arrows that point to the node they "link" to. In Java, the links are implemented as references to a node, and in practice they are instance variables of the node type. However, for your first look at a linked list, you can simply think of the links as arrows. In a linked list, each node contains only one link, and the nodes are arranged one after the other so as to form a list, as in Display 10.3. In an intuitive sense, you, or, more properly, your code, moves from node to node, following the links. The link marked `head` is not on the list of nodes; in fact, it is not even a node, but is a link that gets you to the first node. (In implementations, `head` will contain a reference to a node. So, in practice, `head` is a variable of the node type.) Your program can easily move through the list in order, from the first node to the last node, by following the "arrows." Now let's see exactly how we can realize a linked list in Java.

linked list

link

Quick Reference: Linked List

A **linked list** is a data structure consisting of objects known as **nodes.** Each node can contain both data and a reference to one other node so that the nodes link together to form a list, as illustrated in Display 10.3. The first node in the list is known as the **head node.**

■ DISPLAY 10.3   **A Linked List**

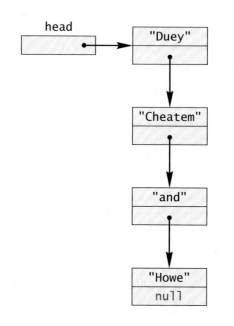

In Java, each node is an object of a class that has two instance variables, one for the data and one for the link. Display 10.4 gives the definition of a Java class that can serve as the node class for linked lists like the one shown in Display 10.3. In this case, the data in each node consists of a single `String` value.[1] (As noted in Display 10.4, we will later give a better definition of this node class and its accompanying linked-list class. But many programmers use this first version just as is, and it is sufficient for learning the basic techniques you need for linked data structures.)

links

ListNode

Notice that the `link` instance variable of the class `ListNode` in Display 10.4 is of type `ListNode`. This relationship sounds circular, and in a sense, it is circular. However, this kind of class definition is perfectly legal in Java. Recall that a variable of a class type holds a reference to an object of that class. So the `link` instance variable of an object of the `ListNode` class will contain a reference to another object of the class `ListNode`. Thus, the arrows shown in the diagram in Display 10.3 are realized as references in Java. Each node object of a linked list contains (in its `link` instance variable) a reference to another object of the class `ListNode`, and this other object contains a reference to another object of the class `ListNode`, and so on, until the end of the linked list.

When dealing with a linked list, your code needs to be able to "get to" the first node, and you need some way to detect when the last node is reached. To get your code to the

---

1. Technically speaking, the node does not contain the string, but only a reference to the string, as would be true of any variable of type `String`. However, for our purposes, we can think of the node as containing the string, since we never use this string reference as an "arrow."

first node, you use a variable of type ListNode that contains a reference to the first node. In Display 10.3, the variable with a reference to the first node is named head and is represented by the box labeled head. The first node in a linked list is called the **head node,** and it is common to use the name head for a variable that contains a reference to this first node.

head node

■ DISPLAY 10.4 **A Node Class**

```java
public class ListNode
{
    private String data;
    private ListNode link;

    public ListNode()
    {
        link = null;
        data = null;
    }

    public ListNode(String newData, ListNode linkValue)
    {
        data = newData;
        link = linkValue;
    }

    public void setData(String newData)
    {
        data = newData;
    }

    public String getData()
    {
        return data;
    }

    public void setLink(ListNode newLink)
    {
        link = newLink;
    }

    public ListNode getLink()
    {
        return link;
    }
}
```

We will give a better definition of this class later in this chapter.

This method works, but has a problem. We will discuss the problem later and provide a better alternative.

In Java, you indicate the end of a linked list by setting the `link` instance variable of a node object to `null`, as shown in Display 10.3. That way your code can test whether a node is the last node in a linked list by testing whether the node's `link` instance variable contains `null`. In Display 10.3 and in the Java node definition in Display 10.4, the `data` instance variable is of type `String`, and you normally check two such `String` instance variables for equality by using the `equals` method. However, remember that you check for a `link` being "equal" to `null` by using `==`.

Remember: **Most Nodes Have No Name**

The variable `head` contains a reference to the first node in a linked list. So `head` can be used as a name for the first node. However, the other nodes in the linked list have no named variable that contains a reference to any of them, so the rest of the nodes in the linked list are nameless. The only way to name one of them is via some indirect reference, like `head.link.link`, or by using another variable of type `ListNode`, such as the local variable `position` in the method `showList` (Display 10.5).

Display 10.5 contains a definition of a linked-list class that uses the node class definition given in Display 10.4. Note that there is only one instance variable, and it is named `head`. This `head` instance variable contains a reference to the first node in the linked list, or it contains `null` if the linked list is empty (that is, if the linked list contains no nodes). The one constructor sets this `head` instance variable to `null`, indicating an empty list.

empty list

Remember: **Use `null` for the Empty List**

Let's say the variable `head` is supposed to contain a reference to the first node in a linked list. Linked lists usually start out empty. What value do you give `head` until the first node is added? You give `head` the value `null` in order to indicate an empty list. This technique is traditional and works out nicely for many linked-list manipulation algorithms.

---

stepping through a list

Before we go on to discuss how nodes are added and removed from a linked list, let's suppose that a linked list already has a few nodes and that you want to write out the contents of all the nodes to the screen. You can do so with the method `showList` (Display 10.5), whose body is reproduced as follows:

```
ListNode position;
position = head;
while (position != null)
{
    System.out.println(position.getData());
    position = position.getLink();
}
```

■ DISPLAY 10.5 A Linked List Class *(Part 1 of 2)*

```java
public class StringLinkedList
{
    private ListNode head;

    public StringLinkedList()
    {
        head = null;
    }

    /**
     Returns the number of nodes in the list.
    */
    public int length()
    {
        int count = 0;
        ListNode position = head;
        while (position != null)
        {
            count++;
            position = position.getLink();
        }
        return count;
    }

    /**
     Adds a node at the start of the list. The added node has addData
     as its data. The added node will be the first node in the list.
    */
    public void addANodeToStart(String addData)
    {
        head = new ListNode(addData, head);
    }

    public void deleteHeadNode()
    {
        if (head != null)
        {
            head = head.getLink();
        }
        else
        {
            System.out.println("Deleting from an empty list.");
            System.exit(0);
        }
    }
}
```

We will give a better definition of this class later in this chapter.

■ DISPLAY 10.5 **A Linked List Class** *(Part 2 of 2)*

```java
public boolean onList(String target)
{
    return (Find(target) != null);
}

/**
 Finds the first node containing the target data and
 returns a reference to that node.
 If target is not in the list, null is returned.
*/
private ListNode Find(String target)
{
    ListNode position;
    position = head;
    String dataAtPosition;
    while (position != null)
    {
        dataAtPosition = position.getData();
        if (dataAtPosition.equals(target))
            return position;
        position = position.getLink();
    }
    //target was not found
    return null;
}

public void showList()
{
    ListNode position;
    position = head;
    while (position != null)
    {
        System.out.println(position.getData());
        position = position.getLink();
    }
}
}
```

The method uses a local instance variable named `position` that contains a reference to one node. The variable `position` starts out with the same reference as the `head` instance variable; thus, it starts out positioned at the first node. The `position` variable then has its position moved from one node to the next via the assignment

```
position = position.getLink();
```

This process is illustrated in Display 10.6. To see that this assignment "moves" the `position` variable to the next node, note that the `position` variable contains a reference to the node pointed to by the `position` arrow in Display 10.6. So `position` is a name for that node, and `position.link` is a name for the `link` to the next node. The value of `link` is produced with the accessor method `getLink`. Thus, a reference to the next node in the linked list is `position.getLink()`. You "move" the `position` variable by giving it the value of `position.getLink()`.

The method `showList` continues to move the `position` variable down the linked list and outputs the data in each node as it goes along. When `position` reaches the last node, it outputs the data in that node and again executes

```
position = position.getLink();
```

If you study Display 10.6, you will see that, when `position` leaves the last node, its value is set to `null`. At that point, we want to stop the loop, so we iterate the loop `while (position != null)`.

■ DISPLAY 10.6 **Moving Down a Linked List**

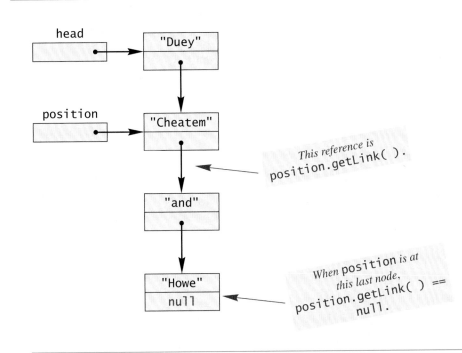

Next, let's consider how the method addANodeToStart adds a node to the start of the linked list, so that the new node becomes the first node in the list. It does this operation with the single statement

```
head = new ListNode(addData, head );
```

The new node is created with new ListNode(addData, head), which returns a reference to this new node. In other words, the variable head is set equal to a reference to this new node, making the new node the first node in the linked list. To link this new node to the rest of the list, we need only to set the link instance variable of the new node equal to a reference to the *old first node*. But we have already done that: head used to point to the old first node, so if we use the name head on the *right-hand side of an assignment operator*, head will denote a reference to the old first node. Therefore, the new node produced by new ListNode(addData, head) points to the old first node. So everything works out as it should. This process is illustrated in Display 10.7.

■ DISPLAY 10.7 **Adding a Node at the Start**

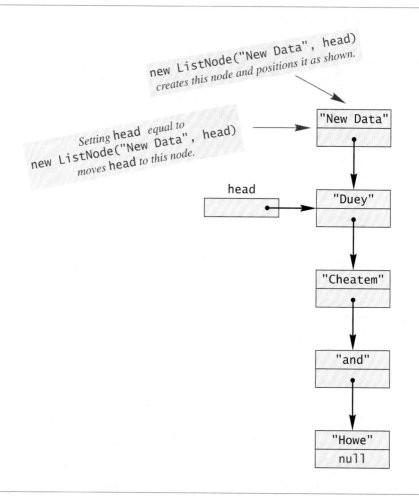

new ListNode("New Data", head)
creates this node and positions it as shown.

Setting head *equal to*
new ListNode("New Data", head)
moves head *to this node.*

"New Data"

head

"Duey"

"Cheatem"

"and"

"Howe"
null

Note that we always add a node at the start of the linked list. Later, we will discuss adding nodes at other places in a linked list, but the easiest place to add a node is at the start of the list. Similarly, the easiest place to delete a node is at the start of the linked list.

The method `deleteHeadNode` removes the first node from the linked list and leaves the `head` variable pointing to (that is, containing a reference to) the old second node (which is now the first node) in the linked list. We will leave it to you to figure out that the following assignment correctly accomplishes this deletion:

removing a node

```
head = head.getLink();
```

It is easy to see that this operation removes the first node from the linked list and leaves the linked list one node shorter, but you may wonder what happens to the deleted node. At some point, Java will automatically collect it, along with any other nodes that are no longer accessible, and recycle the memory they occupy. This process is known as **automatic garbage collection.**

garbage collection

Display 10.8 contains a simple program that demonstrates how some of the methods in the class `StringLinkedList` behave.

■ DISPLAY 10.8 **A Linked List Demonstration** *(Part 1 of 2)*

```java
public class LinkedListDemo
{
    public static void main(String[] args)
    {
        StringLinkedList list = new StringLinkedList();
        list.addANodeToStart("One");
        list.addANodeToStart("Two");
        list.addANodeToStart("Three");
        System.out.println("List has " + list.length()
                                    + " entries.");
        list.showList();

        if (list.onList("Three"))
            System.out.println("Three is on list.");
        else
            System.out.println("Three is NOT on list.");

        list.deleteHeadNode();

        if (list.onList("Three"))
            System.out.println("Three is on list.");
        else
            System.out.println("Three is NOT on list.");

        list.deleteHeadNode();
        list.deleteHeadNode();
        System.out.println("Start of list:");
        list.showList();
        System.out.println("End of list.");
    }
}
```

■ DISPLAY 10.8 **A Linked List Demonstration** *(Part 2 of 2)*

Screen Output

```
List has 3 entries.
Three
Two
One
Three is on list.
Three is NOT on list.
Start of list:
End of list.
```

▲ *Gotcha*

Null Pointer Exception

You have undoubtedly received the message NullPointerException at some time when you have run a program. (If you have not received the message, congratulations! You are an exceptionally careful programmer.) The message NullPointerException indicates that your code tried to access some member of a class variable (some instance variable, method, or such), but the class variable names no object, that is, does not contain a reference to any object. This message may seem more sensible to you now. In our nodes, we used null to indicate that a link instance variable contains no reference. So a value of null indicates no object reference, and that is why the exception is called NullPointerException.

A NullPointerException is one of the exceptions that do not need to be either caught in a catch block or declared in a throws clause. It indicates that you need to fix your code, not add a catch block. △

? Self-Test Questions

12. How do you mark the end of a linked list?

13. Assume that the variable **head** is supposed to contain a reference to the first node in a linked list and that the linked list is empty. What value should **head** have?

14. Define a method named `empty` that can be added to the class `String-LinkedList` (Display 10.5). The method `empty` returns a `boolean` value. It returns `true` if the list is empty (no nodes) and `false` if the list has at least one node in it.

15. What output is produced by the following code?

```
StringLinkedList list = new StringLinkedList();
list.addANodeToStart("A");
list.addANodeToStart("B");
list.addANodeToStart("C");
list.showList();
```

▲ Gotcha
Privacy Leaks

The point made in this section is important, but a bit subtle. It would help you to understand this section if you first review the Gotcha section of the same name in Chapter 5.

Consider the method `getLink` in the class `ListNode` (Display 10.4). It returns a value of type `ListNode`. That is, it returns a reference to a `ListNode`. In Chapter 5, we said that, if a method (such as `getLink`) returns a reference to an instance variable of a class type, then (except for certain classes such as `String`) the `private` restriction on the instance variable can easily be defeated. The privacy leak results from the fact that getting a reference to an object may allow a programmer to change the private instance variables of the object. There are a number of ways to fix this, problem; the most straightforward is to make the class `ListNode` a private inner class in the method `StringLinkedList`, as discussed in the next two subsections, "Inner Classes" and "Node Inner Classes." (Another, and similar, solution is to place both of the classes `ListNode` and `String-LinkedList` into a package; change the private instance variable restriction to the package restriction as discussed in Appendix 5; and omit the accessor method `getLink`. Of course, this method requires that you read Appendix 5.)

Note that this privacy problem can arise in any situation in which a method returns a reference to a private instance variable of a class type. The method `getData()` of the class `ListNode` comes very close to having this problem. In this case, the method `getData` causes no privacy leak, but only because the class `String` has no methods that will allow the user to change the value of the string (without changing the reference). The class `String` is a special case. If the data were of almost any other class type, you would get a problem like the one described in the Gotcha section on privacy leaks in Chapter 5.

Suppose that the type for the data in our linked lists were some class type other than `String`. Then `getData()` could produce a privacy leak. In this particular case, the privacy leak is not a problem, provided that the class `ListNode` is used only in the definition of the class `StringLinkedList` (and very similar classes). This is because no public method in the class `StringLinkedList` returns a reference to a node. Note that the method `Find` returns a reference to a `ListNode`; however, it is a private method. If the method `Find` were public, a privacy leak would result. Therefore, note that `private` in the definition of the method `Find` is not simply a minor stylistic point.

Although there is no problem with the class definition of `ListNode` when it is used in a class definition like `StringLinkedList`, there is no way to guarantee that the class `ListNode` will be used only in this way, unless you do something similar to making the class `ListNode` a private inner class in the class `StringLinkedList`. (See the next two subsections for details.) △

Inner Classes

inner class

Inner classes are classes defined within other classes. A full description of inner classes is beyond the scope of this book. However, some simple uses of inner classes can be both easy to understand and helpful. In this section, we describe inner classes in general and describe how we will use them. In the next subsection, we give an example of an inner class; more specifically, we give an example of a linked-list class whose node class is in an inner class defined within the linked-list class. That node inner class will be a solution to the privacy leak discussed in the previous subsection.

Defining an inner class is straightforward; simply include the definition of the inner class within another class, as follows:

```
public class OuterClass
{
        Declarations_of_OuterClass_Instance_Variables
        Definitions_of_OuterClass_Methods

        private class InnerClass
        {
                Declarations_of_InnerClass_Instance_Variables
                Definitions_of_InnerClass_Methods
        }
}
```

outer class

As this outline suggests, the class that includes the inner class is called an **outer class.** The definition of the inner class need not be the last item of the outer class, but it is good to place it either last or first so that it is easy to find. The inner class need not be private, but that is the only case we will consider in this book.

An inner-class definition is local to the outer-class definition. So you may reuse the name of the inner class for something else outside the definition of the outer class. If the inner class is private, as ours will always be, then the inner class cannot be used outside the definition of the inner class.

The inner-class definition can be used anywhere within the definition of the outer class, and it has a special property in order to facilitate this use: The inner and outer classes' methods have access to each other's methods and instance variables, even if they are private. As long as you are within the definition of the inner or outer classes, the modifiers `public` and `private` (used within the inner and outer classes) are equivalent. Although some details of inner-class usage can be tricky, we will consider only simple cases similar to the one in the next subsection.

We will revisit inner classes in Chapter 14.

Node Inner Classes

You can make data structures like `StringLinkedList` self-contained by making the node class an inner class. In particular, you can make the class `StringLinkedList` more self-contained by making `ListNode` an inner class of the class `StringLinkedList`, as follows:

```
public class StringLinkedList
{
    private ListNode head;
      <The methods in Display 10.5 are inserted here.>

    private class ListNode
    {
        <The rest of the definition of ListNode is the same as in Display 10.4.>
    }
}
```

Note that we've made the class `ListNode` a private inner class. If an inner class is not intended to be used elsewhere, it should be made private.

Making `ListNode` a private inner class is also safer, because it hides the method `getLink` from the world outside the `StringLinkedList` definition. As we noted in the Gotcha subsection entitled "Privacy Leaks" in this chapter, it can be dangerous for a publicly available method to return a reference to a class instance variable.

If you are going to make the class `ListNode` a private inner class in the definition of `StringLinkedList`, then you can safely simplify the definition of `ListNode` by eliminating the accessor and mutator methods (the `set` and `get` methods) and just allowing direct access to the instance variables (`data` and `link`). In Display 10.9, we have rewritten the class `StringLinkedList` in this way. This version, named `StringLinkedListSelfcontained`, is equivalent to the class `StringLinkedList` in Display 10.3 in that it has the same methods that perform the same actions. In fact, if you run the program `LinkedListDemo` in Display 10.8, replacing the class `StringLinkedList` with `StringLinkedListSelfcontained`, then the sample dialog will not change. (The program `StringLinkedListSelfcontainedDemo` on the accompanying CD does just that.)

extra code on CD

Remember: Node Inner Class

You can make a linked list (or other linked data structure) self-contained by making the node class an inner class of the linked-list class.

Iterators

When you have a collection of objects, such as the nodes of a linked list, you often need to step through all the objects in the collection and perform some action on each object, such as writing it out to the screen or in some way editing the data in each object. An **iterator** is any object that allows you to step through the list in this way.

iterator

■ DISPLAY 10.9   A Linked List with a Node Class as an Inner Class *(Part 1 of 3)*

```java
public class StringLinkedListSelfcontained
{
    private ListNode head;
    public StringLinkedListSelfcontained( )
    {
        head = null;
    }
    /**
     Returns the number of nodes in the list.
    */
    public int length( )
    {
        int count = 0;
        ListNode position = head;
        while (position != null)
        {
            count++;
            position = position.link;
        }
        return count;
    }
    /**
     Adds a node at the start of the list. The added node has
     addData as its data. The added node will be the first
     node in the list.
    */
    public void addANodeToStart(String addData)
    {
        head = new ListNode(addData, head);
    }
    public void deleteHeadNode( )
    {
        if (head != null)
            head = head.link;
        else
        {
            System.out.println("Deleting from an empty list.");
            System.exit(0);
        }
    }
}
```

Note that the outer class has direct access to the inner class instance variables, such as link.

■ DISPLAY 10.9 A Linked List with a Node Class as an Inner Class *(Part 2 of 3)*

```java
    public boolean onList(String target)
    {
        return (Find(target) != null);
    }

    /**
     Finds the first node containing the target data
     and returns a reference to that node. If target is not
     in the list, null is returned.
    */
    private ListNode Find(String target)
    {
        ListNode position;
        position = head;
        String dataAtPosition;
        while (position != null)
        {
            dataAtPosition = position.data;
            if (dataAtPosition.equals(target))
                return position;
            position = position.link;
        }
        //target was not found
        return null;
    }

    public void showList()
    {
        ListNode position;
        position = head;
        while (position != null)
        {
            System.out.println(position.data);
            position = position.link;
        }
    }
```

■ DISPLAY 10.9 **A Linked List with a Node Class as an Inner Class** *(Part 3 of 3)*

```
private class ListNode
{
    private String data;                    ←—an inner class
    private ListNode link;

    public ListNode()
    {
        link = null;
        data = null;
    }

    public ListNode(String newData, ListNode linkValue)
    {
        data = newData;
        link = linkValue;
    }
}
```

end of outer-class definition

```
} //end of StringLinkedListSelfcontained
```

An array is a collection of objects (or values of a primitive type). An iterator for an array is an `int` variable. If the array is named `a` and the `int` variable is named `index`, you can step through all the objects in the array as follows:

```
for (index = 0; index < a.length; index++)
    process a[index];
```

to iterate

The `int` variable `index` is the iterator. You can **iterate**—that is, go to the next object—with the action `index++`.

If you place all the data objects in a linked list into an array, you can iterate through the array. That process is equivalent to iterating through the linked list, provided that you do not want to change the data in the linked list, but want only to look at them. For this reason, it is common to have a method in a list class that places all the data in the linked list into an array. Such a method is shown in Display 10.10. This method, named `arrayCopy`, can be added to the linked list in Display 10.9. (This step has been done in the file `String-LinkedListSelfcontained.java` on the accompanying CD.)

extra code on CD

Quick Reference: **Iterators**

Suppose you have a collection of data items, such as an array or a linked list. Any object that allows you to step through the collection one item at a time in a reasonable way is called an **iterator**. By "a reasonable way," we mean that each item is visited exactly once in one full cycle of iterations and that each item can have its data read and, if the data items allow it, can have the data changed.

For example, an `int` variable that holds an index value can serve as an iterator for an array. To go to the next item in the collection (in the array), your code need only increase the value of the `int` variable by one.

■ DISPLAY 10.10 **Placing the Linked-List Data into an Array**

```
public String[] arrayCopy()
{
    String[] a = new String[length()];

    ListNode position;
    position = head;
    int i = 0;
    while (position != null)
    {
        a[i] = position.data;
        i++;
        position = position.link;
    }

    return a;
}
```

This method can be added to the linked-list class in Display 10.9.

If you want an iterator that will move through the linked list and allow you to perform operations, such as change the data at a node or even insert or delete a node, then an array that contains the linked-list data will not suffice. However, you can take a hint from the idea of an iterator for an array. Just as an index specifies an array element, a reference for a node specifies a node. Thus, if you add an instance variable, perhaps named `current`, to the linked-list class `StringLinkedListSelfcontained` given in Display 10.9, you can use this instance variable as an iterator. We have done so in Display 10.11 and have renamed the class `StringLinkedListWithIterator`. As you can see, we have added a number of methods to manipulate the instance variable `current`. The instance variable `current` is the iterator, but because it is marked `private`, we need methods in order to manipulate it. We have also added methods for adding and deleting a node any place in the linked list. The iterator makes it easier to express these methods for adding and deleting nodes, because the iterator gives us a way to name an arbitrary node. Let's go over the details.

In addition to the instance variables `head` and `current`, we have added an instance variable named `previous`. The idea is that, as the reference `current` moves down the linked list, the reference `previous` follows behind by one node. This setup gives us a way to refer to the node before the node named by `current`. Since the links in the linked list all move in one direction, we need the node `previous` in order to do something equivalent to backing up one node.

previous

The method `resetIteration` starts `current` at the beginning of the linked list by giving it a reference to the first (head) node, as follows:

resetIteration

```
current = head;
```

Because the instance variable `previous` has no previous node to reference, it is simply given the value `null` by the `resetIteration` method.

■ DISPLAY 10.11   **A Linked List with an Iterator** *(Part 1 of 4)*

```
/**
 Linked list with a notion of "current node." The current node
 can be changed to the next node with the method goToNext. At any
 time after the iteration is initialized, one node is the current
 node, until the iteration has moved beyond the end of the list.
*/
public class StringLinkedListWithIterator
{
    private ListNode head;
    private ListNode current;
    private ListNode previous;

    public StringLinkedListWithIterator()
    {
        head = null;
        current = null;
        previous = null;
    }

    /**
     Returns the number of nodes in the list.
    */
    public int length()
    <The rest of the definition is the same as in Display 10.9.>

    public void addANodeToStart(String addData)
    {
        head = new ListNode(addData, head);
        if (current == head.link && current != null)
        //if current is at old start node
            previous = head;
    }

    public boolean onList(String target)
    <The rest of the definition is the same as in Display 10.9.>

    /**
     Returns a reference to the first node containing the target
     data. If target is not in the list, null is returned.
    */
    private ListNode Find(String target)
    <The rest of the definition is the same as in Display 10.9.>

    public void showList()
    <The rest of the definition is the same as in Display 10.9.>
```

■ DISPLAY 10.11 A Linked List with an Iterator *(Part 2 of 4)*

```java
public String[] arrayCopy()
  <The rest of the definition is the same as in Display 10.10.>

public void resetIteration()
{
    current = head;
    previous = null;
}

public void goToNext()
{
    if (current != null)
    {
        previous = current;
        current = current.link;
    }
    else if (head != null)
    {
        System.out.println(
            "Iterated too many times or uninitialized iteration.");
        System.exit(0);
    }
    else
    {
        System.out.println("Iterating with an empty list.");
        System.exit(0);
    }
}

public boolean moreToIterate()
{
    return (current != null);
}

public String getDataAtCurrent()
{
    if (current != null)
        return (current.data);
    else
    {
        System.out.println(
                "Getting data when current is not at any node.");
        System.exit(0);
    }
    return null;//to keep the compiler happy
}
```

■ DISPLAY 10.11 **A Linked List with an Iterator** *(Part 3 of 4)*

```java
public void resetDataAtCurrent(String newData)
{
    if (current != null)
    {
        current.data = newData;
    }
    else
    {
        System.out.println(
            "Setting data when current is not at any node.");
        System.exit(0);
    }
}
/**
 Inserts node with newData after the current node. The current
 node is the same after invocation as it is before invocation.
 Should not be used with an empty list. Should not be
 used when the current node has iterated past the entire list.
*/
public void insertNodeAfterCurrent(String newData)
{
    ListNode newNode = new ListNode();
    newNode.data = newData;
    if (current != null)
    {
        newNode.link = current.link;
        current.link = newNode;
    }
    else if (head != null)
    {
        System.out.println(
                "Inserting when iterator is past all "
              + "nodes or uninitialized iterator.");
        System.exit(0);
    }
    else
    {
        System.out.println(
            "Using insertNodeAfterCurrent with empty list.");
        System.exit(0);
    }
}
```

DISPLAY 10.11 A Linked List with an Iterator *(Part 4 of 4)*

```java
/**
 Deletes the current node. After the invocation,
 the current node is the node after the
 deleted node or null if there is no next node.
*/
public void deleteCurrentNode()
{
    if ((current != null) && (previous != null))
    {
        previous.link = current.link;
        current = current.link;
    }
    else if( (current != null) && (previous == null))
    {//At head node
        head = current.link;
        current = head;
    }
    else //current == null
    {
        System.out.println(
          "Deleting with uninitialized current or an empty list.");
        System.exit(0);
    }
}

private class ListNode
{
    private String data;
    private ListNode link;

    public ListNode()
    {
        link = null;
        data = null;
    }

    public ListNode(String newData, ListNode linkValue)
    {
        data = newData;
        link = linkValue;
    }
}
}
```

deleteHeadNode is no longer needed, since you have deleteCurrentNode, but if you want to retain deleteHeadNode, it must be redefined to account for current and previous.

goToNext

The method **goToNext** moves the iterator to the next node, as follows:

```
previous = current;
current = current.link;
```

This process is illustrated in Display 10.12. In the **goToNext** method, the last two clauses of the multibranch **if-else** statement simply produce an error message when the method **goToNext** is used in a situation where it does not make sense to use it.

■ DISPLAY 10.12 **goToNext**

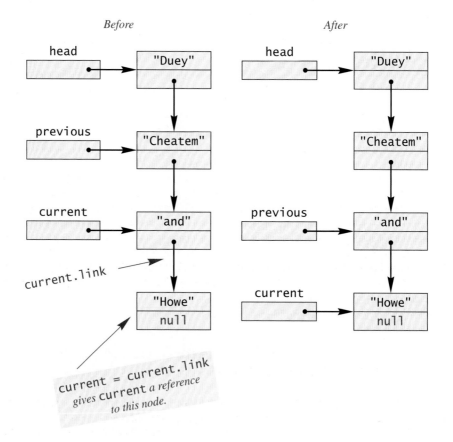

list.gotoNext( );
(*list names the linked list.*)

The method `moreToIterate` returns `true` as long as `current` is not equal to `null`, that is, as long as `current` contains a reference to some node. This approach makes obvious sense most of the time, but you may wonder why the method returns `true` when `current` contains a reference to the last node. When `current` contains a reference to the last node, your program does not "know" that `current` is at the last node. It cannot tell that `current` is at the last node until it invokes `goToNext` one more time. If you study Display 10.12 or the definition of `goToNext`, you will realize that, if your program invokes `goToNext` when the iterator contains a reference to the last node, then `current` will be set to `null`, indicating that the entire list has been iterated through. So, when `current` is equal to `null`, `moreToIterate` returns `false`.

moreToIterate

Now that your linked list has an iterator, your code has a way to refer to any node in the linked list. The `current` instance variable can hold a reference to (an "arrow" pointing to) any one node; that one node is known as the node **at the iterator.** The method `insertAfterIterator` inserts a new node after the node at the iterator (at `current`). This process is illustrated in Display 10.13. The method `deleteCurrentNode` deletes the node at the iterator. This process is illustrated in Display 10.14.

inserting and deleting inside a list

The other methods in the class `StringLinkedListWithIterator` (Display 10.11) are fairly straightforward, and we will leave it up to you to read their definitions and see how they work.

FAQ: What Happens to a Deleted Node?

When your code deletes a node from a linked list (as in Display 10.14), it removes the linked list's reference to that node. So as far as the linked list is concerned, the node is no longer in the linked list. But you gave no command to destroy the node, so it must be someplace in the computer's memory. If there is no other reference to the deleted node, then the storage that it occupies should be made available for other uses. In many programming languages, you, the programmer, must keep track of items such as deleted nodes and must give explicit commands to return their memory for recycling to other uses. This process is called **garbage collecting**. In Java, this task is done for you automatically, or, as it is ordinarily phrased, Java has **automatic garbage collection.**

Remember: A Linked List Can Be Its Own Iterator

For the linked-list class in Display 10.11, we said that the instance variable `current` was the iterator for the linked list. That statement is fine if you are speaking informally, but often you want the iterator for a linked list to be an object of some sort. If you want the iterator to be an object, you can use the same linked-list object as both the linked list and the iterator.

■ **DISPLAY 10.13   Adding a Node**

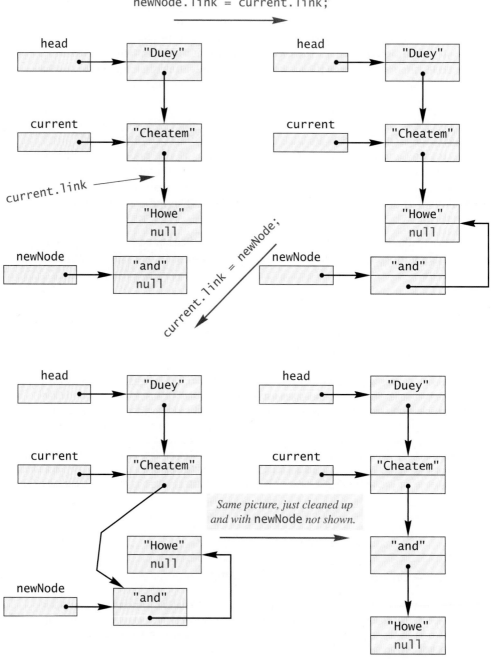

■ DISPLAY 10.14   Deleting a Node

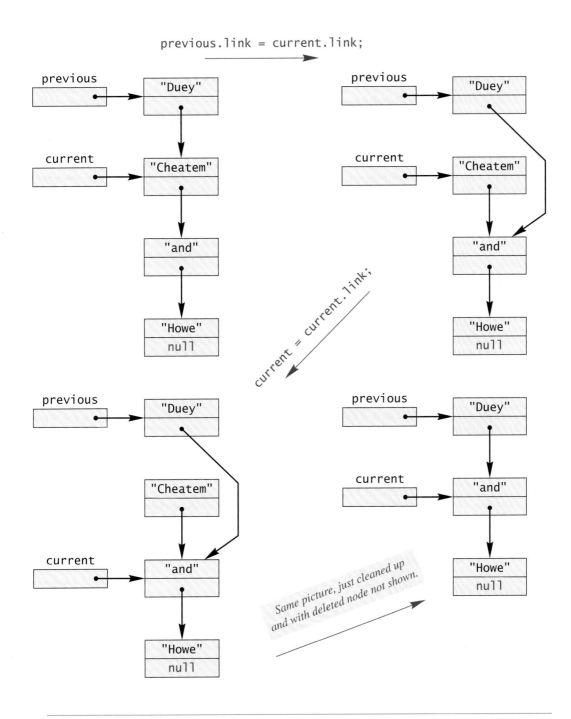

● **Programming Tip**

Internal and External Iterators

The class `StringLinkedListWithIterator` (Display 10.11) used an instance variable of type `ListNode` (named `current`) as an iterator in order to step through the linked list one node after the other. An iterator defined within the linked-list class in this way is known as an **internal iterator.**

If you write out the values in a linked list to an array via the method `copyToArray`, you can use a variable of type `int` as an iterator on the array (and hence on the linked list, provided that it does not change). The `int` variable holds one index of the array and thus specifies one element of the array (and thus one data item of the linked list). If the `int` variable is named `position` and the array is named `a`, the iterator `position` specifies the element `a[position]`. To move to the next item, simply increase the value of `position` by 1 (for example, with `position++;`). An iterator that is defined outside of the linked list, such as the `int`

variable `position`, is known as an **external iterator** (for the linked list or the array). Note that the important thing is not that the array is outside of the linked list, but that the `int` variable `position`, which is the iterator, is outside the linked list. To better understand this point, note that the `int` variable `position` is also an external iterator for the array. You can define external iterators that work directly with the linked list, rather than ones that work with an array of the linked-list data. However, that technique is a bit more complicated, and we will not go into it in this text. ○

? Self-Test Questions

16. What is an inner class?

17. Why does the definition of the inner class `ListNode` in Display 10.9 not have the accessor and mutator methods `getLink`, `setLink`, `getData`, and `setData`, as the class definition `ListNode` in Display 10.4 does?

18. What is an iterator for a collection of items, such as an array or a linked list?

Exception Handling with Linked Lists

As you may have guessed, you need to have read Chapter 8, on exception handling, before reading this subsection.

Consider the class `StringLinkedListWithIterator` in Display 10.11. We defined the methods for that class such that whenever something went wrong, the method sent an error message to the screen and ended the program. However, it may not always be necessary to end the program when something unusual happens. To allow the programmer to provide an action in these unusual situations, it would make more sense to throw an exception and let the programmer decide how to handle the situation. The programmer can still decide to end the program, but she or he also has the option of doing something else. For example, you could rewrite the method gotoNext as follows:

```
public void goToNext( ) throws LinkedListException
{
    if (current != null)
    {
        previous = current;
        current = current.link;
    }
    else if (head != null)
        throw new LinkedListException("Iterated too many times"
                          + " or uninitialized iteration.");
    else
        throw new LinkedListException(
                          "Iterating with an empty list.");
}
```

In this version, we have replaced each of the branches that end the program with a branch that throws an exception. The exception class LinkedListException can be a routine exception class, as shown in Display 10.15.

Suppose that the version of StringLinkedListWithIterator that throws exceptions (as we showed for goToNext) is named StringLinkedListWithIterator2. A programmer who uses this revised class StringLinkedListWithIterator2 could use the thrown exception for a number of different purposes. One possibility is to use the

■ DISPLAY 10.15 The LinkedListException Class

```
public class LinkedListException extends Exception
{
    public LinkedListException()
    {
        super("Linked List Exception");
    }

    public LinkedListException(String message)
    {
        super(message);
    }
}
```

exception to check for the end of a linked list. For example, the following code removes all nodes that contain a specified `BadString` from the linked list:

```
StringLinkedListWithIterator2 list =
            new StringLinkedListWithIterator2( );
String BadString;
<Some code to fill the linked list and set the variable BadString.>
list.resetIteration( );
try
{
    while (list.length( ) >= 0)
    {
        if (BadString.equals(list.getDataAtCurrent( )))
            list.deleteCurrentNode( );
        else
            list.goToNext( );
    }
}
catch(LinkedListException e)
{
    if(e.getMessage( ).equals("Iterating with an empty list."))
    {//This should never happen, but
     //the catch block is compulsory.
        System.out.println("Fatal Error.");
        System.exit(0);
    }
}
System.out.println("List cleaned of bad strings.");
```

This use of an exception to test for the end of a list may seem a bit strange at first, but Java requires something like this when checking for the end of a binary file. So similar uses of exceptions do occur in Java programming, and of course there are many other uses for the `LinkedListException` class.

The self-test questions that follow ask you to rewrite more of the methods in `String-LinkedListWithIterator` so that they throw exceptions in unusual or error situations.

Quick Reference: **The Java `Iterator` Interface**

Java has an interface named `Iterator` that specifies how Java would like an iterator to behave. It is in the package `java.util` (and thus requires that you import this package). Our iterators do not satisfy this interface, but it is easy to define classes that use our iterators and that do satisfy this interface. The `Iterator` interface uses exception handling, but is not difficult to understand. In Self-Test Question 23, you are asked to define a linked-list class that satisfies the `Iterator` interface. (The `Iterator` interface is given in Appendix 7).

? Self-Test Questions

19. Redefine the method `getDataAtCurrent` in `StringLinkedListWithItera-tor` (Display 10.11) so that it throws an exception instead of ending the program when something unusual happens (that is, when the definition in Display 10.11 would end the program).

20. Redefine the method `resetDataAtCurrent` in `StringLinkedListWithIt-erator` (Display 10.11) so that it throws an exception instead of ending the program when something unusual happens (that is, when the definition in Display 10.11 would end the program).

21. Redefine the method `insertNodeAfterCurrent` in `StringLinkedList-WithIterator` (Display 10.11) so that it throws an exception instead of ending the program when something unusual happens (that is, when the definition in Display 10.11 would end the program).

22. Redefine the method `deleteCurrentNode` in `StringLinkedListWithIter-ator` (Display 10.11) so that it throws an exception instead of ending the program when something unusual happens (that is, when the definition in Display 10.11 would end the program).

23. The class `StringLinkedListWithIterator` (Display 10.11) is its own iterator, but it does not quite implement the Java `Iterator` interface. (If you follow the instructions in this question carefully, you do not need to know what an interface is, although knowing what one is may make you feel more comfortable. Interfaces are covered in an optional section of Chapter 7.) The `Iterator` interface requires methods `next`, `remove`, and `hasNext`, as described in the second set of code in this question. Redefine the class `StringLinkedListWithIterator` so that it implements the Java `Iterator` interface. To do so, you begin the class definition with

```java
import java.util.*;

public class StringLinkedListWithIterator2 implements Iterator
{
    private ListNode head;
    private ListNode current;
    private ListNode previous; //follows current
    private ListNode twoBack; //follows previous
    private boolean removeSinceNext;//true if removed has been
                      //called since the last invocation of next.
                   //Also true if next has not been called at all.

    public StringLinkedListWithIterator2()
    {
        head = null;
        current = null;
        previous = null;
        twoBack = null;
        removeSinceNext = true;
    }
```

656 Chapter 10 Dynamic Data Structures

The rest of the definition is the same as in Display 10.11, except that you add the method definitions given in the upcoming code and delete the methods `delete-CurrentNode`, `deleteHeadNode`, `goToNext`, and `moreToIterate`, which become redundant. There is also a small change to the method `resetIterator` so that `twoBack` is reset. The method definitions to add are as follows:

```
/**
   Returns the next element (String) in the list.
   Throws a NoSuchElementException if there is
   no next element to return.
*/
public Object next( ) throws NoSuchElementException

/**
   Removes the last element that was returned by next.
   Throws an IllegalStateException if the next method has
   not yet been called or if the remove method has already
   been called after the last call to the next method.
*/
public void remove( ) throws IllegalStateException

/**
   Returns true if there is at least one more element
   for next to return. Otherwise, returns false.
*/
public boolean hasNext( )
```

Hints:

1. Despite its pretentious-sounding details, this exercise is fairly easy. The three method definitions you need to add are very easy to implement using the methods we have.

2. Note that the method `hasNext` and the method `moreToIterate` in Display 10.11 are not exactly the same.

3. The exception classes mentioned are all predefined, and you should not define them. All the exception classes are of the kind that do not require exceptions to be caught or declared in a `throws` clause. (The `Iterator` interface says that the method `remove` throws an `UnsupportedOperationException` if the `remove` method is not supported. However, your method `remove` has no need ever to throw this exception.)

Variations on a Linked List

tail

Sometimes it is handy to have a reference to the last node in a linked list. This last node is often called the **tail** of the list, so the linked-list definition might begin as follows:

```
public class StringLinkedListWithTail
{
    private ListNode head;
```

```
    private ListNode tail;
    private ListNode current;
    private ListNode previous;
```

The constructors and methods must be modified to accommodate the new reference `tail`, but the details of doing so are routine.

You can have a linked list of any kind of data. Just replace the type `String` in the definition of the node class (and other corresponding places) with the data type you want to use. You can even have a linked list of objects of different kinds by replacing the type `String` in the node definition (and other corresponding places) with the type `Object`, as shown in the following code:

other kinds of data

```
    private class ListNode
    {
        private Object data;
        private ListNode link;

        public ListNode()
        {
            link = null;
            data = null;
        }
        public ListNode(Object newData, ListNode linkValue)
        {
            data = newData;
            link = linkValue;
        }
    }
```

Because an object of any class type is also of type `Object`, you can store any kinds of objects in a linked list with nodes of this kind. (If you have read Section 10.1, on vectors, you will realize that this technique is similar to how vectors can store data of multiple types.)

An ordinary linked list allows you to move down the list in only one direction (following the links). A **doubly linked list** has one link that has a reference to the next node and one that has a reference to the previous node. Diagrammatically, a doubly linked list looks like the following:

doubly linked list

The node class for a doubly linked list can begin as follows:

```
    private class ListNode
    {
        private Object data;
        private ListNode next;
        private ListNode previous;
```

The constructors and some of the methods in the doubly linked-list class will have changes (from the singly linked case) in their definitions in order to accommodate the extra link.

Other Linked Data Structures

We have discussed a few linked lists as examples of linked data structures. The study of data structures is a large topic, with many good books on the subject. In this book, we want to introduce you to all aspects of programming and cannot go into any one topic in exhaustive detail. So we will not present any more linked data structures in detail, but will give you just an informal introduction to a few more important linked data structures.

stack

A **stack** is not necessarily a linked data structure, but it can be implemented as a linked list. A stack is a data structure that removes items in the reverse of the order in which they were inserted. So if you insert `"one"`, then `"two"`, and then `"three"` into a stack and then remove them, they will come out in the order `"three"`, then `"two"`, and finally `"one"`. Stacks are discussed in more detail in Chapter 11. A linked list that inserts and deletes only at the head of the list (such as the one in Display 10.5) is, in fact, a stack.

tree

A very common and powerful data structure is a **tree.** In a tree, each node leads to multiple other nodes. The most common form of tree is a **binary tree,** in which each node has

binary tree

links to at most two other nodes. A binary tree has the same kind of nodes as a doubly linked list, but they are used in a very different way. A binary tree can be represented diagramatically as follows:

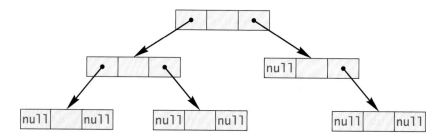

It is not an accident that we have no references leading back up the tree in our diagram of a binary tree. In a tree, the nodes must be arranged without any loops, as in the diagram just shown.

root node

The top node in a binary tree (where the top is as shown in our diagram) is known as the **root node,** and there is normally a reference to this root node, just as there is a reference to the head (start) node in a linked list. Every node can be reached from the root node by following suitable links.

CHAPTER SUMMARY

- Vectors can be thought of as arrays that can grow in length.

- The base type of all vectors is `Object`. Thus, the elements of a vector may be of any class type, but they cannot be of a primitive type.

■ A linked list is a data structure consisting of objects known as nodes, such that each node can contain data and such that each node has a reference to one other node so that the nodes link together to form a list.

■ You can make a linked list (or other linked data structure) self-contained by making the node class an inner class of the linked-list class.

■ You can use an iterator to step through the elements of a collection, such as the elements in a linked list.

✔ Answers to Self-Test Questions

1. `v.addElement("Hello");`

2. `v.setElementAt("Go", 5);`

3. No. The index for `setElementAt` must be greater than or equal to 0 and less than the size of the vector. Thus, you can replace any existing element, but you cannot place the element at any higher index. This configuration is unlike that of an array. If an array is partially filled to index 10, you can add an element at index 20, as long as the array is that large. With a vector, you cannot add an element beyond the last-used index.

4. No. The index for `insertElementAt` must be greater than or equal to 0 and less than or equal to the size of the vector. Thus, you can insert at any index that is currently holding an element, but you cannot insert an element at any higher index, except that you can insert an element in the first available unfilled position. Note that, if the vector is named `v`, you can use `insertElementAt` to insert an element at any index position that is less than or equal to `v.size()`: however, with `setElementAt`, the index position must be less than or equal to `v.size() - 1`.

5. Yes. The vector can contain more than 20 elements. The number 20 used as an argument to the constructor merely gives the initial memory allocation for the vector. More memory is automatically allocated when it is needed.

6.
```
    int index;
    for (index = 0; index < v.size(); index++)
        System.out.println(v.elementAt(index));
```

7.
```
import java.util.*;

/**
 Class for sorting a vector of Strings lexicographically
 (approximately alphabetically).
*/
```

```java
public class StringSelectionSort
{
    /**
     Sorts the vector a so that a.elementAt(0), a.elementAt(1),...,
     a.elementAt(a.size( ) - 1) are in lexicographic order.
    */
    public static void sort(Vector a)
    {
        int index, indexOfNextSmallest;
        for (index = 0; index < a.size() - 1; index++)
        {//Place the correct value in position index:
            indexOfNextSmallest =
                             indexOfSmallest(index, a);
            interchange(index,indexOfNextSmallest, a);
            //a.elementAt(0), a.elementAt(1),...,
            //a.elementAt(index) are sorted. The rest of
            //the elements are in the remaining positions.
        }
    }

    /**
      Precondition: i and j are legal indices for the vector a.
      Postcondition: The values of a.elementAt(i) and
      a.elementAt(j) have been interchanged.
    */
    private static void interchange(int i, int j, Vector a)
    {
        Object temp;
        temp = a.elementAt(i);
        a.setElementAt(a.elementAt(j), i);
        a.setElementAt(temp, j);
    }

    /**
     Returns the index of the lexicographically first value among
     a.elementAt(startIndex), a.elementAt(startIndex+1),...,
     a.elementAt(a.size( ) - 1)
    */
    private static int indexOfSmallest(int startIndex, Vector a)
    {
        String min = (String)a.elementAt(startIndex);
        int indexOfMin = startIndex;
        int index;
        for (index = startIndex + 1; index < a.size(); index++)
        if (((String)(a.elementAt(index))).compareTo(min) < 0)
        {
            min = (String)a.elementAt(index);
```

```
            indexOfMin = index;
        }
        return indexOfMin;
    }
}
```

8. `Object`. (Every object of every class is of type `Object`.)

9. No. You can store only objects of a class type in a vector. You cannot store values of any primitive type.

10. The method invocation `v.size( )` returns the number of elements in the vector `v`. The method invocation `v.capacity( )` returns the number of elements for which the vector currently has memory allocated.

11. The new elements at indices `10` through `19` will have `null` for their values.

12. You indicate the end of a linked list by setting the `link` instance variable of the last node to `null`.

13. `head` should have the value `null`.

14.
```
    public boolean empty( )
    {
        return (length( ) == 0);
    }
```

15.
```
    C
    B
    A
```

16. An inner class is a class defined within the definition of another class.

17. They are not needed, because the methods in the linked-list class have access to the instance variables `data` and `link` of the nodes. This feature is one of the advantages of using an inner class.

18. Any object that allows you to step through the collection one item at a time in a reasonable way is called an iterator. By "a reasonable way," we mean that each item is visited exactly once in one full iteration cycle and that each item can have its data read and, if the data items allow it, can have the data changed. For example, an `int` variable that holds an index value can serve as an iterator for an array. To go to the next item in the collection (in the array), your code needs only to increase the value of the `int` variable by one. An iterator can be a different object than the collection object, or the collection object can serve as its own iterator.

19.
```
public String getDataAtCurrent( )
                            throws LinkedListException
{
    if (current != null)
```

```
                return (current.data);
        else
            throw new LinkedListException(
                "Getting data when current is not at any node.");
    }


20.
    public void resetDataAtCurrent(String newData)
                                throws LinkedListException
    {
        if (current != null)
            current.data = newData;
        else
            throw new LinkedListException(
                "Setting data when current is not at any node.");
    }


21.
    /**
     Inserts node with newData after the current node. The current
     node is the same after invocation as it is before invocation.
     Should not be used with an empty list. Should not be
     used when the current node has iterated past the entire list.
    */
    public void insertNodeAfterCurrent(String newData)
                                    throws LinkedListException
    {
        ListNode newNode = new ListNode();
        newNode.data = newData;
        if (current != null)
        {
            newNode.link = current.link;
            current.link = newNode;
        }
        else if (head != null)
        {
            throw new LinkedListException(
                        "Inserting when iterator is past all"
                    + " nodes or uninitialized iterator.");
        }
        else
        {
            throw new LinkedListException(
                "Using insertNodeAfterCurrent with empty list.");
        }
    }
```

22.
```java
/**
 Deletes current node. After the invocation,
 the current node is the node after the
 deleted node, or null if there is no next node.
*/
public void deleteCurrentNode() throws LinkedListException
{
    if ((current != null) && (previous != null))
    {
        previous.link = current.link;
        current = current.link;
    }
    else if( (current != null) && (previous == null))
    {//At head node
        head = current.link;
        current = head;
    }
    else //current == null
    {
        throw new LinkedListException(
                    "Deleting with uninitialized current"
                + " or an empty list.");
    }
}
```

23.
```java
import java.util.*;

public class StringLinkedListWithIterator2 implements Iterator
{
    private ListNode head;
    private ListNode current;
    private ListNode previous; //follows current
    private ListNode twoBack; //follows previous
    private boolean removeSinceNext;//true if removed has been
                    //called since the last invocation of next.
                //Also true if next has not been called at all.

    public StringLinkedListWithIterator2()
    {
        head = null;
        current = null;
        previous = null;
        twoBack = null;
        removeSinceNext = true;
    }
```

```
/**
 Returns the next element (String) in the list.
 Throws a NoSuchElementException if there is
 no next element to return. You should invoke
 resetIteration before the first invocation of next().
*/
public Object next()
{
    if (current != null)
    {
        twoBack = previous;
        previous = current;
        current = current.link;
        removeSinceNext = false;
        return (previous.data);
    }
    else
    {
        throw new NoSuchElementException();
    }
}

/**
 Removes the last element that was returned by next.
 Throws an IllegalStateException if the next method has
 not yet been called or if the remove method has already
 been called after the last call to the next method.
*/
public void remove()
{
    if ((previous != null) && (twoBack != null)
        && (!removeSinceNext))
    {//remove node at previous
        twoBack.link = previous.link;
        previous = twoBack;
        removeSinceNext = true;
      //twoBack not updated until next invocation of next()
    }
    else if( (previous != null) && (twoBack == null)
        && (!removeSinceNext))
    {//previous at head node and current
      //at head node after deletion
        head = current;
        previous = null;
        twoBack = null;
        removeSinceNext = true;
    }
```

```
        else
        {
            throw new IllegalStateException( );
        }
    }

    /**
     Returns true if there is at least one more element
     for next to return. Otherwise, returns false.
    */
    public boolean hasNext( )
    {
        return (current != null);
    }

    public void resetIteration( )
    {
        current = head;
        previous = null;
        twoBack = null;
        removeSinceNext = true;
    }
```

<The rest of the definition is the same as in Display 10.11, except for the deleted methods. The complete definition is given in the file `StringLinkedListWithIterator2.java` on the accompanying CD. That class also includes the methods from Self-Test Questions 19 through 22.>

extra code
on CD

● Programming Projects

1. Do Programming Project 4 in Chapter 6, except that, in this exercise, the class should sort a vector rather than an array. Assume that the elements in the vector are all `String` values. (*Hint:* Check out Self-Test Question 7.)

2. Do Programming Project 5 in Chapter 6, except that, in this exercise, the class should sort a vector rather than an array. Assume that the elements in the vector are all `String` values. (*Hint:* Check out Self-Test Question 7.)

3. Write a program that reads a list of `PetRecords` from the keyboard into a vector, sorts the vector into alphabetic order by pet name, and finally writes the records from the vector to the screen. Be sure that the screen output does not go by too quickly for the user to see the records. The class `PetRecord` is given in Chapter 5, Display 5.20.

4. Write a program that reads `Species` records from a file into a vector, sorts the vector alphabetically by `Species` name, and then writes the sorted records to both the screen and a file. All file names are to be provided by the user. Be sure that the screen output does not go by too quickly for the user to see the records.

The class `Species` is given in chapter 4, Display 4.19. You can use the program in Display 9.19 to create a file of `Species` records. (If you have not yet covered the sections on binary files in Chapter 9, then read the `Species` records from the keyboard and send output only to the keyboard.)

5. Write a program that reads a list of `PetRecords` from the keyboard into a vector; sorts the records in the vector by pet weight; and finally writes the records from the vector to the screen (sorted by pet weight), followed by the number and percentage of pets under 5 pounds, the number and percentage of pets that are 5 to 10 pounds, and the number and percentage of pets over 10 pounds. Be sure that the screen output does not go by too quickly for the user to see the records. The class `PetRecord` is given in Chapter 5, Display 5.20. (If you have covered some of Chapter 9, take the input from a file, and send the output to another file. If you have covered binary files, use binary files; otherwise, use text files. The file names are obtained from the user.)

6. Define a variation on `StringLinkedListSelfcontained` from Display 10.9 that stores objects of type `Species`, rather than of type `String`. Write a program that uses that linked-list class to create a linked list of `Species` objects, asks the user to enter a `Species` name, and then searches the linked list and displays one of the following messages, depending on whether the name is or is not on the list:

Species *Species_Name* is one of the
number_of_Species_names_on_list species on the list.
The data on *Species_Name* are as follows:
Output_of_Species_Name_Data

or

There are *number_of_Species_names_on_list* species on
the list, but *Species_Name* is not one of them.

The user is allowed to enter more `Species` names until the user indicates that she or he wants to end the program. Of course, the appropriate `Species` name and number of names on the list should be inserted in place of *Species_Name* and *number_of_Species_names_on_list*, respectively.

The class `Species` is given in Chapter 4, Display 4.19.

If you have covered some of Chapter 9, then read the `Species` records from a file. If you have not covered any of Chapter 9, read the `Species` records from the keyboard.

7. Define a variation on `StringLinkedListSelfcontained` from Display 10.9 that stores objects of type `Employee`, rather than objects of type `Strings`. Write a program that uses that linked-list class to create a linked list of `Employee`'s, asks the user to enter an `Employee`'s social security number, and then searches the linked list and displays the employee record with that social security number, provided that there is such a record; otherwise, it displays a message saying that it could not find the requested social security number.

The user is allowed to enter more social security numbers until the user indicates that she or he wants to end the program.

The class Employee was defined as part of Programming Project 7 of Chapter 8. If you have not already done that project, then you will need to define the class Employee, as described there.

If you have covered some of Chapter 9, then read the Employee records from a file. If you have not covered any of Chapter 9, read the Employee records from the keyboard.

Chapter

11

Recursion

There are two kinds of people in the world: those who divide the world into two kinds of people and those who do not. -Anonymous

Many people believe that you should never define anything in terms of itself. That would be a kind of circularity, they say. However, there are situations in which it is both possible and useful to define a method in terms of itself. If you do it correctly, it need not even be circular (although that may take a little explaining).

Java permits you to, in some sense, define a method in terms of itself. More precisely, a Java method definition may contain an invocation of the very method being defined. When a method definition contains an invocation of itself, the method is said to be **recursive,** and the general topic of these recursive methods is called **recursion.** This chapter covers recursion.

OBJECTIVES

Become familiar with the idea of recursion.

Learn to use recursion as a programming tool.

Become familiar with the binary search algorithm as an example of recursion.

Become familiar with the merge sort algorithm as an example of recursion.

PREREQUISITES

The bulk of this chapter requires only Chapters 1 through 5. Only the last two subsections of the chapter—the case study "Binary Search" and the programming example "Merge Sort—A Recursive Sorting Method" require knowledge of any additional material. Those two subsections require that you know about arrays, which are covered in Chapter 6. In addition, Self-Test Question 7 uses exception handing, but you can skip that one question if you have not yet covered exception handling (Chapter 8).

11.1 THE BASICS OF RECURSION

This statement is false. -Paraphrase of an ancient paradox

It often turns out that a natural way to design an algorithm involves using the same algorithm on one or more subcases. For example, the following is an outline of an algorithm for searching for a name in a phone book: Open the phone book to the middle of the book. If the name is on that page, you are done. If the name is alphabetically before that page, search the first half of the book. If the name is alphabetically after that page, search the second half of the book. Searching half of the phone book is a smaller version of the original task of searching the entire phone book.

As you will see, this sort of algorithm can be realized as a recursive Java method. More generally, whenever an algorithm has one subtask that is a smaller version of the entire algorithm's task, you can realize the algorithm as a recursive method in Java. Of course, you must do this in the right way, or your Java code will produce problems, but the goal of this chapter is to show you that right way. We begin with a simple example that illustrates recursion in Java.

Quick Reference: **Recursive Call**

If a method definition contains an invocation of the very method being defined, that invocation is called a **recursive call,** or **recursive invocation.**

Case Study
Digits to Words

In this case study, you will write the definition of a method that takes a single integer as an argument and writes out the digits of that integer as words. For example, if the argument is the number 223, the method should output

```
two two three
```

The heading of your method will be

```
/**
 Precondition: number >= 0
 Action: The digits in number are written out in words.
*/
public static void inWords(int number)
```

If the number is only a single digit, then you can use a long `switch` statement to decide which word to use for a given digit. The method `digitWord` in Display 11.1 uses just such a `switch` statement, so that `digitWord(0)` returns `"zero"`, `digitWord(1)` returns `"one"`, and so forth.

algorithm design

We now consider a number with more than one digit. There are lots of different ways to break this task down into subtasks. Some of them lend themselves to a solution that uses recursion, and some do not. One good way to decompose this task into two subtasks, so that you can immediately solve one of the subtasks, and so that the other lends itself to the use of recursion, is as follows:

Output all but the last digit as words.
Output the word for the last digit.

■ DISPLAY 11.1 **Demonstrating Recursion** *(Part 1 of 3)*

```java
public class RecursionDemo
{
    public static void main(String[] args)
    {
        System.out.println("Enter an integer:");
        int number = SavitchIn.readLineInt();
        System.out.println("The digits in that number are:");
        inWords(number);
        System.out.println();

        System.out.println("If you add ten to that number, ");
        System.out.println("the digits in the new number are:");
        number = number + 10;
        inWords(number);
        System.out.println();
    }

    /**
     Precondition: number >= 0
     Action: The digits in number are written out in words.
    */
    public static void inWords(int number)
    {
        if (number < 10)
            System.out.print(digitWord(number) + " ");
        else //number has two or more digits
        {
            inWords(number/10);                          Recursive call
            System.out.print(digitWord(number%10) + " ");
        }
    }

    /**
     Precondition: 0 <= digit <= 9
     Returns the word for the argument digit.
    */
    private static String digitWord(int digit)
    {
        String result = null;

        switch (digit)
        {
```

■ DISPLAY 11.1 Demonstrating Recursion *(Part 2 of 3)*

```
            case 0:
                result = "zero";
                break;
            case 1:
                result = "one";
                break;
            case 2:
                result = "two";
                break;
            case 3:
                result = "three";
                break;
            case 4:
                result = "four";
                break;
            case 5:
                result = "five";
                break;
            case 6:
                result = "six";
                break;
            case 7:
                result = "seven";
                break;
            case 8:
                result = "eight";
                break;
            case 9:
                result = "nine";
                break;
            default:
                System.out.println("Fatal Error.");
                System.exit(0);
                break;
        }
        return result;
    }
}
```

■ DISPLAY 11.1 **Demonstrating Recursion** *(Part 3 of 3)*

Sample Screen Dialog

```
Enter an integer:
987
The digits in that number are:
nine eight seven
If you add ten to that number,
the digits in the new number are:
nine nine seven
```

The second subtask can be accomplished with a call to the method `digitWord`. The first subtask is a smaller version of the original problem. It is, in fact, the exact same problem as the one we started with, except that the number in question is smaller. That means that the first subtask can be accomplished by a recursive call to the very method we are defining. This scenario leads you to the following outline for an algorithm to use for the method `inWords`:

Algorithm for `inWords(number)`

recursive subtasks

```
inWords(number with the last digit deleted);
System.out.print(digitWord(last digit of number) + " ");
```

Now consider a number with more than one digit, like 534. You want to divide 534 into the two numbers 53 and 4. As it turns out, you can accomplish this task by doing integer division by 10. For example, 534/10 is 53, and 534%10 is 4. So you can refine your algorithm to the following Java code:

```
inWords(number/10);
System.out.print(digitWord(number%10) + " ");
```

You plug this code into the method, producing the following definition, and it looks as though you are done:

```java
public static void inWords(int number)//Not quite right
{
    inWords(number/10);
    System.out.print(digitWord(number%10) + " ");
}
```

As the comment indicates, however, this method will not quite work. It includes the right basic idea, but it has one big problem: The preceding definition assumes that the argument `number` is more than one digit long. You need to make a special case for numbers that are only one digit long. As you will see, unless this simple case is made to work correctly, no other case will work correctly. This condition leads you to rewrite the method definition as follows:

```java
public static void inWords(int number)
{
    if (number < 10)
        System.out.print(digitWord(number) + " ");
    else //number has two or more digits
    {
        inWords(number/10);
        System.out.print(digitWord(number%10) + " ");
    }
}
```

The definition of the method inWords is now complete. Display 11.1 shows the method embedded in a demonstration program. However, before we leave this case study, let's discuss the method inWords a bit more.

The following recursive call of the method inWords occurs in the definition of the method inWords:

```java
inWords(number/10);
```

Note that the argument number/10 used in the recursive call is smaller than the parameter number that is used for the entire method definition. It is important that the problem solved by the recursive call be a "smaller" version of the original problem (in some intuitive notion of "smaller," which we will make clearer before the end of this chapter.)

As you will see in the next subsection, the successful execution of a recursively defined method, such as inWords, requires that the simplest case be handled in a way that does not involve a recursive call. In the definition of inWords, this simplest case is handled as follows:

```java
if (number < 10)
    System.out.print(digitWord(number) + " ");
```

Note that if the argument number is only one digit in length, then no recursive call is used. ■

How Recursion Works

Exactly how does the computer handle a recursive call? To see the details, consider the following invocation of the method inWords from Display 11.1:

```java
inWords(987);
```

Although the definition of inWords contains a recursive call, the computer does nothing special to handle this or any other invocation of inWords. The computer plugs the argument 987 into the method definition and executes the resulting code. Plugging in 987 for the parameter number in the method definition produces code equivalent to the following:

```java
{//Code for invocation of inWords(987)
    if (987 < 10)
        System.out.print(digitWord(987) + " ");
```

```
        else //987 has two or more digits
        {
            inWords(987/10);
            System.out.print(digitWord(987%10) + " ");
        }
    }
```

When executing this code, the computer first checks the boolean expression after the `if`. The boolean expression evaluates to `false`, because 987 is not less than 10. Because the boolean expression evaluates to `false`, the compound statement after the `else` is executed. This compound statement starts with the following recursive call:

```
    inWords(987/10);
```

The rest of the computation cannot proceed until this recursive call is completed. The computer must stop what it is doing and make a side excursion to handle this new recursive call. So the execution of the code for `inWords(987);` is suspended, and the computer works on the new recursive call `inWords(987/10);`. After the computer completes the recursive call `inWords(987/10);`, it will return to complete the interrupted computation of `inWords(987);`.

The new recursive invocation, `inWords(987/10);`, is handled just like any other method invocation: The argument 987/10 is plugged in for the parameter `number` in the method definition, and the resulting code is executed. Since 987/10 evaluates to 98, the computer plugs in 98 for the parameter `number`, resulting in code equivalent to the following:

```
    {//Code for invocation of inWords(98)
        if (98 < 10)
            System.out.print(digitWord(98) + " ");
        else //98 has two or more digits
        {
            inWords(98/10);
            System.out.print(digitWord(98%10) + " ");
        }
    }
```

While executing this new code, the computer once again encounters a recursive call, namely, the recursive call `inWords(98/10);`. At that point, the preceding computation is suspended, and the computer proceeds to the recursive call `inWords(98/10);`. Since 98/10 is equal to 9, 9 is plugged in for the parameter `number` in the definition of `inWords`, and the following code is executed:

```
    {//Code for invocation of inWords(9)
        if (9 < 10)
            System.out.print(digitWord(9) + " ");
        else //9 has two or more digits
        {
            inWords(9/10);
            System.out.print(digitWord(9%10) + " ");
        }
    }
```

Because 9 is indeed less than 10, the first part of the `if-else` statement is executed. Therefore, only the following code is executed:

```
System.out.print(digitWord(9) + " ");
```

This case is called a **stopping case**—that is, a case with no recursive calls. A quick look at the definition of the method `digitWord` shows that the preceding `System.out.println` causes the string `"nine "` to be written to the screen. The invocation of `inWords(98/10)` is now complete. At this point, the suspended computation, shown in the code that follows, can resume:

stopping case

```
{//Code for invocation of inWords(98)
    if (98 < 10)
        System.out.print(digitWord(98) + " ");
    else //98 has two or more digits
    {
        inWords(98/10);  ◄─────────────
        System.out.print(digitWord(98%10) + " ");
    }
}
```

The computation resumes after the position indicated by the arrow, so the following code is executed:

```
System.out.print(digitWord(98%10) + " ");
```

This statement causes the string `"eight "` to be output to the screen, ending the invocation of the recursive call `inWords(98);`.

Stay with us, dear reader! The process is almost over. Once the invocation of `inWords(98);` is complete, there is one more suspended computation waiting to be completed, and it is shown in the code that follows:

```
{//Code for invocation of inWords(987)
    if (987 < 10)
        System.out.print(digitWord(987) + " ");
    else //987 has two or more digits
    {
        inWords(987/10);  ◄─────────────
        System.out.print(digitWord(987%10) + " ");
    }
}
```

The computation resumes after the position indicated by the arrow, and the following code executes:

```
System.out.print(digitWord(987%10) + " ");
```

This statement causes `"seven "` to be written to the screen, and the entire process ends. The sequence of recursive calls is illustrated in Display 11.2.

Note that the computer does nothing special when it encounters a recursive method call. It simply plugs in arguments for parameters and executes the code in the method definition, just as it does with any method invocation.

■ DISPLAY 11.2 **What Happens with a Recursive Call**

`inWords(987);` is equivalent to executing:

```
{//Code for invocation of inWords(987)
    if (987 < 10)
        System.out.print(digitWord(987) + " ");
    else //987 has two or more digits
    {
        inWords(987/10);
        System.out.print(digitWord(987%10) + " ");
    }
}
```

Computation waits here for the completion of the recursive call.

`inWords(987/10);` is equivalent to `inWords(98);`, which is equivalent to executing:

```
{//Code for invocation of inWords(98)
    if (98 < 10)
        System.out.print(digitWord(98) + " ");
    else //98 has two or more digits
    {
        inWords(98/10);
        System.out.print(digitWord(98%10) + " ");
    }
}
```

Computation waits here for the completion of the recursive call.

`inWords(98/10);` is equivalent to `inWords(9);`, which is equivalent to executing:

```
{//Code for invocation of inWords(9)
    if (9 < 10)
        System.out.print(digitWord(9) + " ");
    else //9 has two or more digits
    {
        inWords(9/10);
        System.out.print(digitWord(9%10) + " ");
    }
}
```

This invocation does not cause another recursive call to be executed.

Remember: **Key to Successful Recursion**

A definition of a method that includes a recursive invocation of the method itself will not behave correctly unless you follow some specific design guidelines. The following rules apply to most cases that involve recursion:

- The heart of the method definition can be an if-else statement or some other branching statement that leads to different cases, depending on some property of a parameter to the method being defined.

- One or more of the branches should include a recursive invocation of the method. These recursive invocations should, in some sense, use "smaller" arguments or solve "smaller" versions of the task performed by the method.

- One or more branches should include no recursive invocations. These branches are the **stopping cases** (also known as the **base cases**).

▲ *Gotcha*

Infinite Recursion

Consider the method inWords defined in Display 11.1. Suppose we had been careless and had defined it as follows:

```
public static void inWords(int number)//Not quite right
{
    inWords(number/10);
    System.out.print(digitWord(number%10) + " ");
}
```

In fact, we almost did define it this way, until we noticed an omitted case. Suppose, however, that we did not notice the omitted case and used this shorter definition. If you go through the recursive call inWords(987); as we did in the previous subsection, you will see that the process never ends. Let's quickly trace the computation of this incorrect recursive method definition.

Among other things, the method invocation inWords(987); produces the recursive call inWords(987/10);, which is equivalent to inWords(98);. The invocation of inWords(98); produces the recursive call inWords(98/10);, which is equivalent to inWords(9);. Because our incorrect version of inWords has no special case for one-digit numbers, the invocation of inWords(9); produces the recursive call inWords(9/10);, which is equivalent to inWords(0);. Now the problem becomes apparent. The invocation of inWords(0); produces the recursive call inWords(0/10);, which is equivalent to inWords(0);. So the invocation of inWords(0); produces another invocation of inWords(0);, which produces yet another invocation of inWords(0);, and so forth forever (or until your computer runs out of resources). This situation is called **infinite recursion.**

infinite recursion

The preceding shorter and incorrect definition of inWords is incorrect only in the sense that it performs the wrong computation. It is not illegal. The Java compiler will accept this definition of inWords (and any similar recursive method definition that does not have a case to stop the series of recursive calls). However, unless your recursive defini-tion is defined in such a way as to ensure that you do not get an unending chain of recur-sive calls, then when the method is invoked, you will get an infinite chain of recursive calls, causing your program either to run forever or to end abnormally.

In order for a recursive method definition to work correctly and not produce an infinite chain of recursive calls, there must be one or more cases that, for certain values of the parameter(s), will end without producing any recursive call. As stated previously, these cases are called **base cases,** or **stopping cases.** The correct definition of inWords, given in Display 11.1, has one stopping case, which is highlighted in the following code:

stopping case
base case

```java
public static void inWords(int number)
{
    if (number < 10)
        System.out.print(digitWord(number) + " ");
    else //number has two or more digits
    {
        inWords(number/10);
        System.out.print(digitWord(number%10) + " ");
    }
}
```
Stopping case

Stopping cases must be designed so that they terminate every chain of recursive calls. A method invocation can produce a recursive invocation of the same method, and that invo-cation may produce another recursive invocation, and so forth for some number of recur-sive calls, but every such chain must eventually lead to a stopping case that ends with no recursive invocation. Otherwise, an invocation of the method might never end (or might not end until the computer runs out of resources).

A typical recursive method definition includes an if-else statement or other branch-ing statement that chooses between one or more cases that each include a recursive call of the method and one or more cases that each end the method invocation without any recur-sive invocation. Every chain of recursive calls must eventually lead to one of those stop-ping cases, which do not involve any recursive calls.

The most common way to ensure that a stopping case is always reached is to make all the recursive invocations of the method use a "smaller" argument (in some intuitive sense of "smaller"). For example, consider the correct definition of inWords given in Display 11.1 and reproduced a few paragraphs back. The parameter to inWords is number. The parame-ter to the recursive invocation of inWords is the smaller value number/10. In this way, the recursive invocations in a chain of recursive calls each have a smaller argument. Because the correct definition of inWords has a stopping case for all "small" arguments, we know that, eventually, a stopping case is always reached. △

Quick Reference: Stack Overflow

When a method invocation leads to infinite recursion, your program is likely to end with an error mes-sage that refers to a "stack overflow." The term **stack** refers to a data structure that is used to keep track of recursive calls (and other things as well). You can think of a record of each recursive call as being stored on something analogous to a piece of paper. These "pieces of paper" are "stacked" one on top of the other. When this "stack" becomes too large for the computer to handle, a **stack overflow** occurs.

? Self-Test Questions

1. What is the output produced by the following program?

```java
public class RecursionExercise
{
    public static void main(String[] args)
    {
        methodA(3);
    }

    public static void methodA(int n)
    {
        if (n < 1)
            System.out.println('B');
        else
        {
            methodA(n - 1);
            System.out.println('R');
        }
    }
}
```

2. What is the output produced by the following program?

```java
public class RecursionExercise2
{
    public static void main(String[] args)
    {
        methodB(3);
    }

    public static void methodB(int n)
    {
        if (n < 1)
            System.out.println('B');
        else
        {
            //The following two lines are the reverse of
            //what they are in Self-Test Question 1.
            System.out.println('R');
            methodB(n - 1);
        }
    }
}
```

3. Write a recursive method definition for the following method:

```
/**
 Precondition: n >= 1.
 Action: Writes out n of the symbol '#' on one line
 and advances to the next line.
*/
public static void sharp(int n)
```

Note that the output advances to the next line after the last `'#'` has been output. So

```
sharp(3);
```

is equivalent to

```
System.out.println("###");
```

If you have trouble with this exercise, first do it so that the output does not advance to the next line. For that simpler case, you need not worry about the distinction between `print` and `println`. In the simpler case, you use only `print`, never `println`. After doing the simpler case, try to do the exercise as stated.

Recursive versus Iterative Definitions

Any method definition that includes a recursive call can be rewritten so that it accomplishes the same task without using recursion. For example, Display 11.3 contains a rewritten version of the program in Display 11.1, but the definition of `inWords` in this version does not use recursion. Both versions of `inWords` perform the exact same action—that is, they write the same output to the screen. As is the case here, the nonrecursive version of a method definition typically involves a loop in place of recursion and hence is called an **iterative version.**

iterative
version

A recursive version of a method definition is usually less efficient (that is, runs slower or uses more storage space) than an iterative definition of the same method, because of the overhead to the computer that results from keeping track of the recursive calls and suspended computations. Hence, you should confine your use of recursion to cases in which it makes your code easier to understand. And there are indeed times when recursion can be a big aid in terms of program clarity.

Recursive Methods That Return a Value

Any kind of method may involve recursion. A recursive method can be a `void` method, or it can be a method that returns a value. You design a recursive method that returns a value in basically the same way that you design a recursive `void` method. The basic technique for defining a well-behaved recursive method definition that returns a value is as follows:

■ The heart of the method definition can be an `if-else` statement or some other branching statement that leads to different cases, depending on some property of a parameter to the method being defined.

■ One or more of the branches lead to cases in which the value returned is computed in terms of calls to the same method (that is, using recursive calls). The arguments for the recursive calls should intuitively get "smaller" with each recursion.

■ DISPLAY 11.3 **Iterative Version of** `inWords`

```java
public class IterativeDemo
{
    public static void main(String[] args)
    <The rest of main is the same as in Display 11.1.>

    /**
     Precondition: number >= 0
     Action: The digits in number are written out in words.
    */
    public static void inWords(int number)
    {
        int divisor = powerOfTen(number);
        int next = number;
        while (divisor >= 10)
        {
            System.out.print(digitWord(next/divisor) + " ");
            next = next%divisor;
            divisor = divisor/10;
        }

        System.out.print(digitWord(next/divisor) + " ");

    }

    /**
     Precondition: n >= 0. Returns the number in the form "one
     followed by all zeros that is the same length as n."
    */
    private static int powerOfTen(int n)
    {
        int result = 1;
        while(n >= 10)
        {
            result = result*10;
            n = n/10;
        }

        return result;

    }

    private static String digitWord(int digit)
    <The rest of digitWord is the same as in Display 11.1.>
}
```

The dialog is exactly the same as in Display 11.1.

■ One or more of the branches lead to cases in which the value returned is computed without the use of any recursive calls. These cases are called **base cases**, or **stopping cases**. (Every chain of recursive calls should always end in a stopping case.)

This technique is illustrated by the method `numberOfZeros` defined in Display 11.4. This method takes a single `int` argument and returns the number of zeros in the number (when written in the usual way). For example, `numberOfZeros(2030)` returns 2, because 2030 contains two zero digits. Let's look at how the method `numberOfZeros` works.

■ DISPLAY 11.4 **A Recursive Method That Returns a Value**

```
public class RecursionDemo2
{
    public static void main(String[] args)
    {
        System.out.println("Enter a nonnegative number:");
        int number = SavitchIn.readLineInt( );
        System.out.println(number + " contains "
                              + numberOfZeros(number) + " zeros.");
    }

    /**
     Precondition: n >= 0
     Returns the number of zero digits in n.
    */
    public static int numberOfZeros(int n)
    {
        if (n == 0)
            return 1;
        else if (n < 10)//and not 0
            return 0;//0 for no zeros
        else if (n%10 == 0)
            return(numberOfZeros(n/10) + 1);
        else //n%10 != 0
            return(numberOfZeros(n/10));
    }
}
```

Sample Screen Dialog

```
Enter a nonnegative number:
2005
2005 contains 2 zeros.
```

The definition of the method `numberOfZeros` uses the following simple fact:

If n is two or more digits long, then the number of zero digits in n is (the number of zeros in n with the last digit removed) plus an additional one if that last digit is zero.

For example, the number of zeros in 20030 is the number of zeros in 2003 plus one for the last zero. The number of zeros in 20031 is the number of zeros in 2003 without adding anything, because the extra digit is not zero. With this definition in mind, let's go through a simple computation using `numberOfZeros`.

First, consider the simple expression

    numberOfZeros(0)

which might occur as the right-hand side of some assignment statement. When the method is called, the value of the parameter n is set equal to 0, and the code in the body of the method definition is executed. Because the value of n is equal to 0, the first case of the multiway `if-else` statement applies, and the value returned is 1.

Next, consider another simple expression:

    numberOfZeros(5)

When the method is called, the value of the parameter n is set equal to 5, and the code in the body of the method definition is executed. Since the value of n is not equal to 0, the first case of the multiway `if-else` statement does not apply. The value of n is, however, less than 10, so the second branch of the multiway `if-else` statement applies, and the value returned is 0. As you can see, these two simple cases work out correctly.

Now let's look at an example that involves a recursive call. Consider the expression

    numberOfZeros(50)

When the method is called, the value of n is set equal to 50, and the code in the body of the method definition is executed. Since this value of n is not equal to 0 and is not less than 10, neither of the first two branches of the multiway `if-else` statement applies. However, n%10 (that is, 50%10) is 0, so the third branch applies. Thus, the value returned is

    numberOfZeros(n/10) + 1

which in this case is equivalent to

    numberOfZeros(50/10) + 1

which, in turn, is equivalent to

    numberOfZeros(5) + 1

We've already decided that `numberOfZeros(5)` returns 0, so the value returned by `numberOfZeros(50)` is

    0 + 1

(which is 1, the correct value).

Larger numbers will produce longer chains of recursive calls. For example, consider the expression

    numberOfZeros(2005)

The value of this expression is calculated as follows:

> `numberOfZeros(2005)` is `numberOfZeros(200)` plus nothing
> `numberOfZeros(200)` is `numberOfZeros(20)` + 1
> `numberOfZeros(20)` is `numberOfZeros(2)` + 1
> `numberOfZeros(2)` is 0 (a stopping case)

When the computer reaches the stopping case, `numberOfZeros(2)`, there are three suspended computations. After calculating the value returned for the stopping case, it resumes the most recently suspended computation, which determines the value of `numberOfZeros(20)`. After that, the computer completes each of the other suspended computations, plugging each value computed into another suspended computation, until it reaches and completes the computation for the original invocation, `numberOfZeros(2005)`. The suspended computations are completed as follows (a process that basically evaluates the preceding list of suspended computation from *bottom to top*):

> `numberOfZeros(2)` is 0 (a stopping case)
> `numberOfZeros(20)` is `numberOfZeros(2)` + 1, which is 0 + 1 == 1
> `numberOfZeros(200)` is `numberOfZeros(20)` + 1, which is 1 + 1 == 2
> `numberOfZeros(2005)` is `numberOfZeros(200)` plus nothing,
> which is 2 plus nothing == 2

Thus, the final value returned by the invocation `numberOfZeros(2005)` is 2, which is correct, because 2005 has two zero digits.

Remember: Do Not Confuse Recursion and Overloading

Do not confuse recursion and overloading. When you overload a method name, you are giving two different methods the same name. If the definition of one of these two methods includes a call to the other, that is not recursion. In a recursive method definition, the definition of the method includes a call to the exact same method with the exact same definition, including the same number and types of parameters.

? Self-Test Questions

4. What is the output of the following program?

```java
public class RecursionExercise4
{
    public static void main(String[] args)
    {
        System.out.println(mysteryValue(3));
    }

    public static int mysteryValue(int n)
    {
```

```
            if (n <= 1)
                return 1;
            else
                return (mysteryValue(n - 1) + n);
        }
}
```

5. Complete the definition of the given method. Your definition should be recursive. *Hint*: 10^n is $10^{n-1} * 10$ for $n > 1$.

```
/**
 Precondition: n >= 0.
 Returns 10 to the power n.
*/
public static int tenToThe(int n)
```

6. Complete the given method definition. Your definition should be recursive. It should use the same technique you used for Self-Test Question 5, but should have one more recursive case for negative exponents. *Hints*: 10^n is $1/10^{-n}$ for negative values of *n*. Also, if *n* is negative, then $-n$ is positive. This exercise differs from Self-Test Question 5 in that it also allows negative numbers as arguments.

```
/**
 Precondition: n can be any int.
 Returns 10 to the power n.
*/
public static double tenToThe(int n)
```

11.2 PROGRAMMING WITH RECURSION

All short statements about programming techniques are false. -Anonymous

In this section, we present some programs that illustrate ways to use recursion.

● Programming Tip
Ask Until the User Gets It Right

The program in Display 11.5 simply requests a positive number and then does a countdown to zero from that number. The number is entered using the method getCount.

Notice that if the user enters a nonpositive number, the method getCount makes a recursive call to itself. This call starts the input process all over again from the beginning. If the user enters another incorrect input, there will be another recursive call, and the input process will start yet again. This procedure is repeated until the user enters a positive integer. Of course, in practice, a recursive call would seldom take place, but it will take place as often as is needed. ◯

■ DISPLAY 11.5 Recursion for Starting Over

```java
public class CountDown
{
    private int count;

    public static void main(String[] args)
    {
        CountDown countDowner = new CountDown();
        countDowner.getCount();
        countDowner.showCountDown();
    }

    public void getCount()
    {
        System.out.println("Enter a positive number:");
        count = SavitchIn.readLineInt();
        if (count <= 0)
        {
            System.out.println("Input must be positive.");
            System.out.println("Try again.");
            getCount();//start over
        }
    }

    public void showCountDown()
    {
        int left;
        System.out.println("Counting down:");
        for (left = count; left >= 0; left--)
            System.out.print(left + ", ");
        System.out.println("Blast Off!");
    }
}
```

Sample Screen Dialog

```
Enter a positive number:
0
Input must be positive.
Try again.
Enter a positive number:
3
Counting down:
3, 2, 1, 0, Blast Off!
```

7. (To answer this question, you need to know about exception handling, which is covered in Chapter 8. If you have not yet read Chapter 8, you should skip this question.) Sometimes a recursive call is not signaled by the boolean expression of an if statement, but by throwing an exception. Look at the code for the method readLineInt of the class SavitchIn (in Appendix 4 and on the CD that accompanies this book). It uses a loop to do something similar to what we did in Display 11.5. Rewrite the method readLineInt so that it uses recursion instead of a loop. (One reason we did not make the original definition of readLineInt recursive was that we wanted the code to be understood by students who had not yet covered recursion.) *Hint*: The recursive call should be in a catch block for the exception class NumberFormatException.

Case Study
Binary Search

This case study assumes that you have already covered the basics about arrays given in Chapter 6.

In this case study, you will design a recursive method that tells you whether a given number is or is not in an array of integers. If the sought-after number is in the array, the method will also tell you the index of the number's position in the array. For example, the array may contain a list of winning lottery tickets, and you might want to search the list to see if you are a winner. In Chapter 6, we discussed a method for searching an array simply by checking every array position. (See the subsection "Searching an Array" in Chapter 6.) The method you develop in this case study will be much faster than that simple serial search. However, for this faster method to work, the array must be sorted.

We will assume that the array is sorted and completely filled. So if the array is named a, we know that

task
specification

```
a[0] <= a[1] <= a[2] <= ... <= a[a.length − 1]
```

Often, you want to know more than just whether an element is or is not in an array. If the element is in the array, you typically also want to know where it is in the array. For example, if you are searching for a winning lottery number, the array index may serve as a record number. Another array indexed by these same indices may hold phone numbers to call to claim your winnings. Hence, if the sought-after value is in the array, you will want your method to tell where it is in the array. Thus, you design your method to return an integer that gives the index of the sought-after number. If the number is not in the array, the method will return −1. Before you worry about the exact setup of the class and methods and about connecting the method to an array, you first design some pseudocode to solve the search problem.

algorithm
design

The algorithm you design will make use of the fact that the numbers in the array are sorted. Notice that, because the array is sorted, you can sometimes rule out whole sections of the array that could not possibly contain the number you are looking for. For example, if you are looking for the number 7 and you know that a[5] is equal to 9, then you know, of course, that 7 is not equal to a[5], but you also know much more: You know that 7 is not equal to a[i] for any value of i that is greater than or equal to 5. Because the array is sorted, you know that

```
7 < a[5] <= a[i]
```

whenever i is greater than or equal to 5. So all the elements a[i] for i greater than or equal to 5 need not be searched. You know that the sought-after value 7 is not among them without needing to check them.

Similarly, if the sought-after number 7 were instead greater than a[5] (for example, if a[5] were 3 instead of 9), then you could rule out all the elements a[i] for i less than or equal to 5.

Replacing 5 (in the preceding examples) with whatever index is in the middle of the array leads you to your first draft of an algorithm:

```
mid = approximate midpoint between 0 and (a.length − 1);
if (target == a[mid])
        return mid;
else if (target < a[mid])
        return the result of searching a[0] through a[mid − 1].
else if (target > a[mid])
        return the result of searching a[mid + 1] through a[a.length − 1].
```

Notice that searching a subsegment of the array (as in each of the two else if cases) is a smaller version of the very task you are designing. Thus, the subsegments of the array can be searched with recursive calls to the algorithm itself.

The two pieces of pseudocode that correspond to recursive calls are

return the result of searching a[0] through a[mid − 1].

and

return the result of searching a[mid + 1] through a[a.length − 1]

There is, however, one complication. (Isn't there always?) In order to implement these recursive calls, you need more parameters. These recursive calls specify that a subrange of the array is to be searched. In the first case, it is the elements indexed by 0 through mid − 1. In the second case, it is the elements indexed by mid + 1 through a.length − 1. Thus, you need two extra parameters to specify the first and last indices of the subrange of the array to be searched. You call these extra parameters first and last, respectively. Using these parameters to specify the subrange to be searched, you can express the pseudocode more precisely as follows:

preliminary
pseudocode

Algorithm to Search a[first] Through a[last]

mid = approximate midpoint between first and last;
if (target == a[mid])

```
    return mid;
else if (target < a[mid])
  return the result of searching a[first] through a[mid - 1].
else if (target > a[mid])
  return the result of searching a[mid + 1] through a[last].
```

If you want to search the entire array, you set `first` equal to 0 and `last` equal to `a.length` − 1. Each recursive call will use some other values for `first` and `last`. For example, the first recursive call would set `first` equal to 0 and `last` equal to `mid` − 1.

You should always check that any recursive algorithm you write will not produce infinite recursion. Let's check whether every possible invocation of the algorithm will lead to a stopping case. Consider the three cases in the nested `if-else` statement. In the first case, the sought-after number is found in the list, and there is no recursive call, so the process terminates. In each of the other two cases, a smaller subrange of the array is searched by a recursive call. If the sought-after number is in the array, the algorithm will narrow the range down more and more until it finds the number. But what if the number is not anywhere in the array? Will the resulting series of recursive calls eventually lead to a stopping case if the number is not in the array? Unfortunately not, but that problem is not hard to fix.

Note that in each recursive call, the value of `first` is increased or the value of `last` is decreased. If they ever pass each other and `first` actually becomes larger than `last`, then we will know that there are no more indices left to check and that the number `target` is not in the array. If we add this test to our pseudocode, we get the following, more complete, pseudocode:

Algorithm to Search a[first] Through a[last]

complete
pseudocode

```
mid = approximate midpoint between first and last;
if (first > last)
  return -1;
else if (target == a[mid])
  return mid;
else if (target < a[mid])
  return the result of searching a[first] through a[mid - 1].
else if (target > a[mid])
  return the result of searching a[mid + 1] through a[last].
```

Next, you need to translate this pseudocode algorithm into Java code. You decide that the method will be called `search` and that it will be in a class called `Array-Searcher`. The class will have an instance variable to name the array, and the array to be searched will be given that name by the constructor. The final code is shown in Display 11.6. A diagram of how the method performs on a sample array is given in Display 11.7.

coding

■ DISPLAY 11.6 A Binary Search Class *(Part 1 of 2)*

```java
/**
 Class for searching an already sorted array of ints.
 To search the sorted and completely filled array b,
 use the following:
 ArraySearcher bSearcher = new ArraySearcher(b);
 int index = bSearcher.find(target);
 index will be given an index of where target is located.
 index will be set to -1 if target is not in the array.
*/
public class ArraySearcher
{
    private int[] a;

    /**
     Precondition: theArray is full and is sorted
     from lowest to highest.
    */
    public ArraySearcher(int[] theArray)
    {
        a = theArray;//a is now another name for theArray.
    }

    /**
     If target is in the array, returns the index of an occurrence
     of target. Returns -1 if target is not in the array.
    */
    public int find(int target)
    {
        return search(target, 0, a.length - 1);
    }

    //Uses binary search to search for target in a[first] through
    //a[last] inclusive. Returns the index of target if target
    //is found. Returns -1 if target is not found.
    private int search(int target, int first, int last)
    {
        int result = -1;//to keep the compiler happy.
        int mid;
        if (first > last)
            result = -1;
        else
```

■ DISPLAY 11.6 **A Binary Search Class** *(Part 2 of 2)*

```
            {
                mid = (first + last)/2;

                if (target == a[mid])
                    result = mid;
                else if (target < a[mid])
                    result = search(target, first, mid - 1);
                else //(target > a[mid])
                    result = search(target, mid + 1, last);
            }

            return result;
        }
    }
```

You realize that the method search has extra parameters that the user would always have to set equal to 0 and a.length − 1 in order to specify that the entire array be searched. You do not want the user to worry about this detail, so you add the method find, which allows the user simply to specify the target value and not worry about indices. The method find simply calls the method search, but this step saves the user a lot of bother. Since the method search is now just a helping method, you make it a private method.

find versus search

A simple program that demonstrates how the class ArraySearcher works is given in Display 11.8.

The binary search algorithm, which is what we have used in this case study, is extremely fast. In the binary search algorithm, you eliminate about half the array from consideration right at the start. You then eliminate another quarter of the array, then another eighth, and so forth. This set of eliminations means that most of the array need not be searched at all, saving a lot of time. For example, for an array with 1000 elements, the binary search will need to compare only about 10 array elements with the target value. By comparison, a simple serial search could compare as many as all 1000 array elements with the target value; on average, it will compare about 500 array elements to the target value. ■

efficiency

● **Programming Tip**
  Generalize the Problem

When designing a recursive algorithm, you often need to solve a more general problem than the one you set out to solve. For example, consider the method search, which you designed to search an entire array in the previous case study. You needed to design it so that it could search not only the entire array, but also any subrange of the array. This design was necessary in order to be able to express the recursive subcases. It is very often true that, when you are designing a recursive algorithm, you must make the problem a bit more general so that you can easily express the recursive subcases. ○

■ DISPLAY 11.7 **A Binary Search Example**

`target` is 33

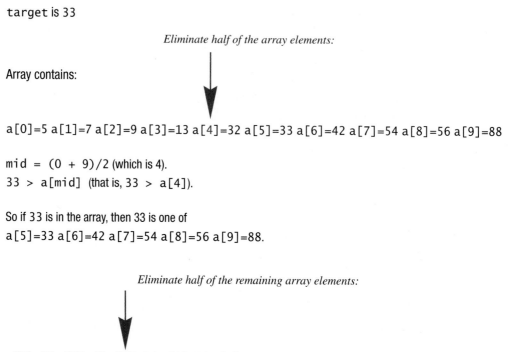

Eliminate half of the array elements:

Array contains:

`a[0]=5 a[1]=7 a[2]=9 a[3]=13 a[4]=32 a[5]=33 a[6]=42 a[7]=54 a[8]=56 a[9]=88`

`mid = (0 + 9)/2` (which is 4).
`33 > a[mid]` (that is, `33 > a[4]`).

So if 33 is in the array, then 33 is one of
`a[5]=33 a[6]=42 a[7]=54 a[8]=56 a[9]=88`.

Eliminate half of the remaining array elements:

`a[5]=33 a[6]=42 a[7]=54 a[8]=56 a[9]=88`

`mid = (5 + 9)/2` (which is 7).
`33 < a[mid]` (that is, `33 < a[7]`).

So if 33 is in the array, then 33 is one of
`a[5]=33 a[6]=42`.

Eliminate half of the remaining array elements:

`a[5]=33 a[6]=42`

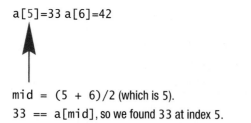

`mid = (5 + 6)/2` (which is 5).
`33 == a[mid]`, so we found 33 at index 5.

33 *found in* `a[5]`.

■ DISPLAY 11.8 A Binary Search Demonstration *(Part 1 of 2)*

```java
public class ArraySearcherDemo
{
    public static void main(String[] args)
    {
        int [] a = new int[10];
        System.out.println("Enter 10 integers in increasing order.");
        System.out.println("One per line.");
        int i;
        for (i = 0; i < 10; i++)
            a[i] = SavitchIn.readLineInt( );

        System.out.println( );
        for (i = 0; i < 10; i++)
            System.out.print("a[" + i + "]=" + a[i] + " ");
        System.out.println( );
        System.out.println( );

        ArraySearcher finder = new ArraySearcher(a);

        char ans;
        do
        {
            System.out.println("Enter a value to search for:");
            int target = SavitchIn.readLineInt( );
            int result = finder.find(target);

            if (result < 0)
                System.out.println(
                            target + " is not in the array.");
            else
                System.out.println(
                            target + " is at index " + result);

            System.out.println("Again?(y/n)");
            ans = SavitchIn.readLineNonwhiteChar( );
        }while ((ans == 'y') || (ans == 'Y'));

        System.out.println(
                    "May you find what you're searching for.");
    }
}
```

■ DISPLAY 11.8 **A Binary Search Demonstration** *(Part 2 of 2)*

Sample Screen Dialog

```
Enter 10 integers in increasing order.
One per line.
0
2
4
6
8
10
12
14
16
18
a[0]=0 a[1]=2 a[2]=4 a[3]=6 a[4]=8 a[5]=10 a[6]=12 a[7]=14 a[8]=16 a[9]=18
Enter a value to search for:
14
14 is at index 7
Again?(y/n)
y
Enter a value to search for:
0
0 is at index 0
Again?(y/n)
y
Enter a value to search for:
2
2 is at index 1
Again?(y/n)
y
Enter a value to search for:
13
13 is not in the array.
Again?(y/n)
n
May you find what you're searching for.
```

? Self-Test Questions

8. Will the binary search algorithm work if the array is not sorted?

9. Do all of the values in the array used with the constructor for `ArraySearcher` have to be different, or is it OK to have repeated values?

10. Suppose you want the class `ArraySearcher` to work for arrays whose values are sorted from largest down to smallest instead of from smallest up to largest. How do you need to change the definition of `ArraySearcher`?

Programming Example
Merge Sort—A Recursive Sorting Method

A number of the most efficient sorting algorithms are easiest to state as recursive algorithms. One such example is the merge sort algorithm for sorting an array. In this example, we present a method that implements the merge sort algorithm to sort an array of `int` values from smallest to largest. With minor changes, you can obtain a method to sort an array of items of any type that can be ordered. Some examples of these changes are discussed in the self-test questions.

Merge sort is an example of a divide-and-conquer algorithm. The array to be sorted is divided in half, and the two halves of the array are sorted by recursive calls. That process produces two smaller sorted arrays. The two sorted arrays are then merged to form a single sorted array with all the elements from the two smaller arrays. In outline form, the algorithm is as follows:

Merge Sort Algorithm to Sort the Array a: algorithm

If the array a has only one element, do nothing (stopping case).

Otherwise, do the following (recursive case):

    Copy the first half of the elements in a to a smaller array named `front`.

    Copy the rest of the elements in the array a to another smaller array named `tail`.

    Sort the array `front` with a recursive call.

    Sort the array `tail` with a recursive call.

    Merge the elements in the arrays `front` and `tail` into the array a.

It is straightforward to implement most of the details of this algorithm as Java code. However, the merging of the two arrays `front` and `tail` into a single sorted array a does require some explanation.

The basic idea of the merging algorithm is as follows: The arrays `front` and `tail` are both sorted from smallest to largest. So the smallest element in the array `front` is `front[0]`, and the smallest element in the array `tail` is `tail[0]`. Therefore, the smallest of all the elements in both arrays is the smaller of `front[0]` and `tail[0]`. Move that smallest element to `a[0]`.

For example, let's say that the smaller element is `tail[0]`, so that element gets moved to `a[0]`. The smallest of the elements left to move over to a is the smaller of `front[0]` and `tail[1]`. Move that element to `a[1]`, and continue with this process.

The Java code for the merging process will look something like the following:

```
int frontIndex = 0, tailIndex = 0, aIndex = 0;
while (some condition)
{
    if (front[frontIndex] < tail[tailIndex])
    {
        a[aIndex] = front[frontIndex];
        aIndex++;
        frontIndex++;
    }
    else
    {
        a[aIndex] = tail[tailIndex];
        aIndex++;
        tailIndex++;
    }
}
```

Now, what is the boolean condition for the `while` loop? Note that the loop does not make sense unless both of the arrays `front` and `tail` have elements left to move. So rather than looping until the array a is full, we must loop until all the elements in one of the arrays `front` or `tail` have been completely moved over to a. Hence, the `while` loop condition can be

```
while ((frontIndex < front.length)
                    && (tailIndex < tail.length))
```

When this `while` loop ends, one of the arrays `front` or `tail` may have (in fact, probably will have) elements left to move to the array a. These elements are sorted and are all larger than the elements already moved to a. So all we need do is move all the elements remaining in the array that has elements left (either `front` or `tail`) over to the array a. The complete code is given as the method `merge` shown in part 2 of Display 11.9.

Display 11.9 gives the complete Java implementation of the merge sort algorithm. Display 11.10 shows a demonstration program that uses the `MergeSort` class from Display 11.9.

efficiency   The merge sort algorithm is much more efficient than the selection sort algorithm we presented in Chapter 6. In fact, there is no sorting algorithm that is "orders of magnitude" more efficient than the merge sort algorithm. The details of what is meant by "orders of magnitude" is beyond the scope of this book, but we can hint at its meaning.

There are algorithms that, in practice, are more efficient than the merge sort algorithm. However, for very large arrays, any of these algorithms (including the merge sort algorithm) are so much faster than the selection sort algorithm that the improvement over selection sort is more dramatic than the differences between these various faster algorithms. ■

■ DISPLAY 11.9 The MergeSort Class *(Part 1 of 2)*

```java
/**
 Class for sorting an array of ints from smallest to largest,
 using the merge sort algorithm.
*/
public class MergeSort
{
    /**
     Precondition: Every indexed variable of a has a value.
     Action: Sorts a so that a[0] <= a[1] <= ... <= a[a.length - 1].
    */
    public static void sort(int[] a)
    {
        if (a.length >= 2)
        {
            int halfLength = a.length/2;
            int[] front = new int[halfLength];
            int[] tail = new int[a.length - halfLength];

            divide(a, front, tail);
            sort(front);
            sort(tail);
            merge(a, front, tail);
        }
        //else do nothing. a.length == 1, so a is sorted.
    }

    /**
     Precondition: a.length = front.length + tail.length.
     Postcondition: All the elements of a are divided
     between the arrays front and tail.
    */
    private static void divide(int[] a, int[] front, int[] tail)
    {
        int i;
        for (i = 0; i < front.length; i++)
            front[i] = a[i];

        for (i = 0; i < tail.length; i++)
            tail[i] = a[front.length + i];
    }
```

■ DISPLAY 11.9 The MergeSort Class *(Part 2 of 2)*

```java
/**
 Precondition: Arrays front and tail are sorted from smallest
 to largest, and a.length = front.length + tail.length.
 Postcondition: a contains all the values from front and tail,
 and a is sorted from smallest to largest.
*/
private static void merge(int[] a, int[] front, int[] tail)
{
    int frontIndex = 0, tailIndex = 0, aIndex = 0;
    while ((frontIndex < front.length)
                      && (tailIndex < tail.length))
    {
        if (front[frontIndex] < tail[tailIndex])
        {
            a[aIndex] = front[frontIndex];
            aIndex++;
            frontIndex++;
        }
        else
        {
            a[aIndex] = tail[tailIndex];
            aIndex++;
            tailIndex++;
        }
    }
    //At least one of front and tail have been
    //completely copied to a.

    while (frontIndex < front.length)//Copy rest of front,
                                     //if any.
    {
        a[aIndex] = front[frontIndex];
        aIndex++;
        frontIndex++;
    }

    while (tailIndex < tail.length)//Copy rest of tail, if any.
    {
        a[aIndex] = tail[tailIndex];
        aIndex++;
        tailIndex++;
    }
}
}
```

■ DISPLAY 11.10 Demonstration of the MergeSort Class

```java
public class MergeSortDemo
{
    public static void main(String[] args)
    {
        int[] b = {7, 5, 11, 2, 16, 4, 18, 14, 12, 30};

        System.out.println("Array values before sorting:");
        int i;
        for (i = 0; i < b.length; i++)
            System.out.print(b[i] + " ");
        System.out.println();

        MergeSort.sort(b);

        System.out.println("Array values after sorting:");
        for (i = 0; i < b.length; i++)
            System.out.print(b[i] + " ");
        System.out.println();
    }
}
```

Screen Output

```
Array values before sorting:
7 5 11 2 16 4 18 14 12 30
Array values after sorting:
2 4 5 7 11 12 14 16 18 30
```

? Self-Test Questions

11. How do you sort the following array, using the class MergeSort?

    ```java
    int[] myArray = {9, 22, 3, 2, 87, −17, 12, 14, 33, −2};
    ```

12. How would you need to change the class MergeSort so that it can sort an array of values of type double (rather than of type int)?

13. How would you need to change the class MergeSort so that it can sort an array of values of type int into decreasing order, instead of increasing order?

14. If a value in an array of base type `int` occurs twice (like `b[0] == 7` and `b[5] == 7`) and you sort the array by using the method `MergeSort.sort`, will there be one or two copies of the repeated value after the array is sorted?

C H A P T E R   S U M M A R Y

■ If a method definition includes an invocation of the method itself, that invocation is known as a recursive call. Recursive calls are legal in Java and can sometimes make a method definition clearer.

■ Whenever an algorithm has one subtask that is a smaller version of the entire algorithm's task, you can realize the algorithm as a Java recursive method.

■ To avoid infinite recursion, a recursive method definition should contain two kinds of cases: one or more cases that include a recursive call and one or more stopping cases that do not involve any recursive calls.

■ Two good examples of recursive algorithms are the binary search algorithm and the merge sort algorithm.

✔ Answers to Self-Test Questions

1.
```
B
R
R
R
```
Note that the `'B'` is the first output, not the last output.

2.
```
R
R
R
B
```
Note that the `'B'` is the last output.

3.
```
/**
 Precondition: n >= 1.
 Action: Writes out n of the symbol '#' on one line
 and advances to the next line.
*/
public static void sharp(int n)
{
    if (n <= 1)
        System.out.println('#');
```

```
        else
        {
            System.out.print('#');
            sharp(n - 1);
        }
    }
}
```

4. 6

5.
```
    /**
     Precondition: n >= 0
     Returns 10 to the power n.
    */
    public static int tenToThe(int n)
    {
        if (n <= 0)
            return 1;
        else
            return ( tenToThe(n - 1)*10 );
    }
```

6.
```
    /**
     Precondition: n can be any int.
     Returns 10 to the power n.
    */
    public static double tenToThe(int n)
    {
        if (n == 0)
            return 1;
        else if (n > 0)
            return (tenToThe(n - 1)*10 );
        else //n < 0
            return (1/tenToThe(-n));
    }
```

7.
```
/**
 Precondition: The user has entered a whole number of type int on
 a line by itself, except that there may be whitespace before and/or
 after the number.
 Action: Reads and returns the number as a value of type int.
 The rest of the line is discarded. If the input is not entered
 correctly, then in most cases, the user will be asked to reenter
 the input. In particular, this applies to incorrect number
 formats and blank lines.
*/
public static int readLineInt()
{
    String inputString = null;
    int number = 0;//To keep the compiler happy.
```

```
        try
        {
            inputString = readLine();
            inputString = inputString.trim();
            number = Integer.parseInt(inputString);
        }
        catch (NumberFormatException e)
        {
            System.out.println(
                "Your input number is not correct. Your input number must be");
            System.out.println(
                 "a whole number written as an ordinary numeral, such as 42");
            System.out.println(
                    "Please, try again. Enter a whole number:");
            number = readLineInt();
        }

        return number;
    }
```

8. No.

9. It is OK to have repeated values, as long as the array is sorted.

10. The multiway if-else statement in the method search needs to have two comparison operators changed so that it reads as follows:

```
if (target == a[mid])
    result = mid;
else if (target > a[mid])//Changed from < to >
    result = search(target, first, mid - 1);
else if (target < a[mid])//Changed from > to <
    result = search(target, mid + 1, last);
```

No other changes are needed, but the comments should be revised to reflect the fact that the array is sorted from largest to smallest.

11.
```
    MergeSort.sort(myArray);
```

12. Just change the types for the array elements to double. For example, you would replace

```
private static void divide(int[] a,
                              int[] front, int[] tail)
```

with

```
private static void divide(double[] a,
                              double[] front, double[] tail)
```

13. All you need to do to make your code work for sorting into decreasing order is to replace the < with > in the following line of the definition of merge:

```
if (front[frontIndex] < tail[tailIndex])
```

14. If an array of base type `int` has a value that occurs twice, and you sort the array by using the method `MergeSort.sort`, then there will be two copies of the repeated value after the array is sorted.

● Programming Projects

1. Write a static recursive method definition for a method that has one argument of type `int` and returns the length of its argument (when written in the usual way). This method should be a static method. You must allow for both positive and negative arguments. For negative arguments, the sign does not count as part of the length. So, −123 has length 3. Embed the method in a program, and test it.

2. Write a static recursive method definition for a method that has one parameter for an array of `int` values and that returns the sum of the elements in the array (that is, the sum of the integers in the array). You can assume that every indexed variable of the array has a value. Embed the method in a test program.

3. One of the most common examples of recursion is an algorithm to calculate the **factorial** of an integer. The notation $n!$ is used for the factorial of the integer n and is defined as follows:

```
0! is equal to 1
1! is equal to 1
2! is equal to 2*1 = 2
3! is equal to 3*2*1 = 6
4! is equal to 4*3*2*1 = 24
        .
        .
        .
n! is equal to n*(n–1)*(n–2)*...*3*2*1
```

An alternative way to describe the calculation of $n!$ is the recursive formula $n*(n-1)!$, plus a stopping case of 0! being defined as 1. Write a static method that implements this recursive formula for factorials. Place the method in a test program that allows the user to compute $n!$ (with an invocation of your static method), where the user inputs the value of n. Your program should allow the user to enter another value for n and repeat the calculation until he or she wants to end the program.

4. A common example of a recursive formula is one to compute the sum of the first n integers, $1 + 2 + 3 + ... + n$. The recursive formula can be expressed as

$$1 + 2 + 3 + ... + n = n + (1 + 2 + 3 + ... + (n - 1))$$

Write a static method that implements this recursive formula to compute the sum of the first n integers. Place the method in a test program that allows the user to compute the sum of the first n integers (with an invocation of your static method), where the user inputs the value of n. Your program should allow the user to enter another value for n and repeat the calculation until he or she wants to end the program. *Note*: Your method definition should not use a loop to add the first n integers.

Such a method would not be a recursive method, or at least not a nice recursive method.

5. Write a static recursive method definition for a method that takes one parameter of type `String` and returns a `boolean` value. The method returns `true` if the argument is a palindrome and `false` otherwise. A **palindrome** is a string that reads the same forward and backward, such as `"radar"`. Disregard spaces and punctuation marks, and consider upper- and lowercase versions of the same letter to be equal. For example, the following would be considered a palindrome by your method:

   `"Straw? No, too stupid a fad, I put soot on warts."`

   Your method need not check that the string is a correct English phrase or word. The string `"xyzczyx"` will be considered a palindrome by your method. Embed the method in a program, and test it.

6. Two common progressions are the **geometric progression,** defined as the product of the first n integers, and the **harmonic progression,** defined as the product of the inverses of the first n integers. The mathematical notation for a geometric progression is

$$\texttt{Geometric}(n) \text{ is equal to } \prod_{i=1}^{n} i,$$

where this notation means to multiply the integers from 1 to n.
The mathematical notation for harmonic progression is as follows:

$$\texttt{Harmonic}(n) \text{ is equal to } \prod_{i=1}^{n} \frac{1}{i}$$

Both types of progression have an equivalent recursive definition:

$$\prod_{i=1}^{n} i == n \times \prod_{i=1}^{n-1} i \text{ for a geometric progression;}$$

$$\prod_{i=1}^{n} \frac{1}{i} == \frac{1}{n} \times \prod_{i=1}^{n-1} \frac{1}{i} \text{ for a harmonic progression.}$$

Write static methods that implement these recursive formulas to compute `Geometric(n)` and `Harmonic(n)`. Do not forget to include a stopping case, which is not given in the formulas we just gave, but which you must determine. Place the methods in a test program that allows the user to compute both `Geometric(n)` and `Harmonic(n)` for an input integer n (with invocations of your static methods). Your program should allow the user to enter another value for n and repeat the calculation until he or she wants to end the program. *Note:* Neither of your methods should use a loop to multiply n numbers. Such a method would not be a recursive method, or at least not a nice recursive method.

7. The **Fibonacci** series occurs frequently in nature as the growth rate for certain idealized animal populations. The series begins with 0 and 1, and each successive Fibonacci number is the sum of the two previous Fibonacci numbers. Hence, the third number in the series is 0 + 1, which is 1; the fourth number is 1 + 1, which is 2; the fifth number is 1 + 2, which is 3; and so on. Continuing in a similar way, the first 10 Fibonacci numbers are 0, 1, 1, 2, 3, 5, 8, 13, 21, and 34. This series occurs in nature in many contexts besides population growth (for example, the series can be used to describe the form of a spiral), and the ratio of the last number to the next-to-last number in the series converges to a constant, approximately 1.618, which is called the "golden mean." Humans find the ratio so aesthetically pleasing that it is often used for such things as the length and width ratios of rooms and postcards.

Use a recursive formula to define a static method to compute the nth Fibonacci number, given n as an argument. (Your method should not use a loop to compute all the Fibonacci numbers up to the desired one, but should be a nice, simple recursive method.) Place this static recursive method in a program that demonstrates how the ratio of Fibonacci numbers converges. Your program will ask the user to specify the number of Fibonacci numbers to calculate and then display the Fibonacci numbers, one per line. After the first two lines, it will also display the ratio of the current and previous Fibonacci numbers on each line. (The ratio does not make sense for the first two lines of Fibonacci numbers.) The output should look something like the following if the user enters 5:

```
Fibonacci #1 = 0
Fibonacci #2 = 1
Fibonacci #3 = 1 and ratio = 1/1 = 1
Fibonacci #4 = 2 and ratio = 2/1 = 2
Fibonacci #5 = 3 and ratio = 3/2 = 1.5
```

Chapter

12

Window Interfaces Using Swing

"What is the use of a book," thought Alice,
"without pictures or conversations?" -Lewis Carroll, *Alice's Adventures in Wonderland*

So far, almost all your programs have used the simplest form of input. The user enters simple text at the keyboard, and simple, unadorned text is sent to the screen as output. Modern programs do not use such simple input and output.

Modern programs use window interfaces with such features as menus and buttons that allow the user to make choices by using a mouse. In this chapter and in Chapter 14, you will learn how to write Java programs that create such modern window interfaces for input and output, using a special library of classes called **Swing.** Swing is a standard Java library that comes with Java. Entire books can and have been written on Swing, so we will not have room to give you a complete description of Swing in just two chapters. However, we will teach you enough to allow you to write simple window interfaces.

Swing

There is another, older library of classes for writing window interfaces. This older library is known as the **Abstract Windows Toolkit,** or **AWT** for short. Swing can be viewed as an improved version of the AWT. However, Swing did not replace the AWT. Instead, it adds to the AWT to produce a richer collection of classes, and the AWT remains as a necessary complement to the Swing library. We will use classes from both Swing and the AWT.

AWT

OBJECTIVES

Learn the basics of event-driven programming.

Learn to design and code a simple GUI that includes buttons and text. (Menus are covered in Chapter 14.)

Learn about the Swing (or Swing-related) classes `BorderLayout`, `Color`, `Container`, `FlowLayout`, `GridLayout`, `JButton`, `JComponent`, `JFrame`, `JLabel`, `JPanel`, `JTextArea`, `JTextField`, `WindowAdapter`, and others.

PREREQUISITES

Before covering this chapter (and the next two chapters, on applets and more Swing), you need to have covered Chapters 1 through 5 and Chapter 7, which covers inheritance. Except for one subsection at the end of this chapter, you need not have read any of the other chapters that precede this chapter in order to understand the material presented.

In order to understand the last subsection, which is entitled "Catching a `Number-FormatException`," you first need to read Chapter 8. If you have not yet read Chapter 8, you can skip that section.

12.1 BACKGROUND

event n. 1. An occurrence, incident, or experience, especially one of some significance. - The American Heritage Dictionary of the English Language, First Edition

Let's begin with some general background about the elements in any window interface and about a programming technique known as event-driven programming, which is used when writing window interfaces.

GUIs—Graphical User Interfaces

Windowing systems that interact with the user are often called GUIs. **GUI** is pronounced "gooey" and stands for **graphical user interface.** The words are pretty much self-explanatory. It's called *graphical* because it uses graphical elements such as windows, buttons, and menus. It's called a *user interface* because it is the part of a program that interfaces with (that is, interacts with) the user. A GUI obtains information from the user and gives it to the program for processing. When the program is finished processing the information, the GUI gives the results to the user, usually in some sort of window.

GUI

Let's briefly list the terms used for some basic elements that make up a GUI. Although you have undoubtedly used all these elements before, you may not have given them the same names we will use. A **window** is a portion of the user's screen that serves as a smaller screen within the screen. A window usually has a border defining its outside edges and a title of some sort that gives the window a name. Inside a window may be smaller windowlike objects. Some of these smaller window-like objects are menus. A **menu** is a list of alternatives offered to the user, usually in the form of a list of names. The user chooses one of these alternatives, usually by clicking a mouse button when the mouse cursor is positioned over the menu item (a process typically referred as clicking the menu item). A **button** is very similar to an item in a menu. A button looks like a button that one would push and typically has a label. To "push" the button, you use your mouse to click on the button. These elements will have more precise definitions within Swing.

window

menu

button

Quick Reference: GUI

Windowing systems that interact with the user are often called **GUI**s. *GUI* is pronounced "gooey" and stands for **graphical user interface.**

Event-Driven Programming

Swing programs and most other GUI programs use events and event handlers. An **event** in a graphical user interface is an object that represents some action such as clicking a mouse button, dragging the mouse, pressing a key on the keyboard, clicking

event

the close-window button on a window, or any other action that is expected to elicit a response. In many contexts, an event is more general than just an action in a graphical user interface. For example, a message from a printer to the operating system saying that the printer is ready to print another document can be considered an event. However, in this chapter, the only events that we will be concerned with are those generated within a graphical user interface.

fire an event

listener object

When an object generates an event, it is said to **fire** the event. In Swing, every object that can fire events, such as a button that might be clicked, can have one or more **listener objects**. You, the programmer, specify what objects are the listener objects for any given object that might fire an event. For example, if you click a button that fires an event, and if the button has a listener object associated with it, then the event is automatically sent to the listener object. A listener object has methods that specify what will happen when events of various kinds are sent to the listener. These methods that handle events are called **event handlers.** You, the programmer, will define (or redefine) these event-handler methods. The relationship between an event-firing object, such as a button, and its event-handling listener is shown diagrammatically in Display 12.1.

event handler

Notice that event-driven programming is very different from the sort of programming you've seen up to this point. All our previous programs consisted of a list of statements executed in some order. There were some variations on this theme of performing a list of statements: Loops repeat statements, branches choose one of a list of statements to execute next, and a method invocation brings in a different list of statements to be executed. However, at some level, all the programs you have seen so far were designed to be performed by one agent (the computer) following a simple set of instructions of the form "first do this, then do that, then do something else," and so forth.

■ DISPLAY 12.1 **Event Firing and an Event Listener**

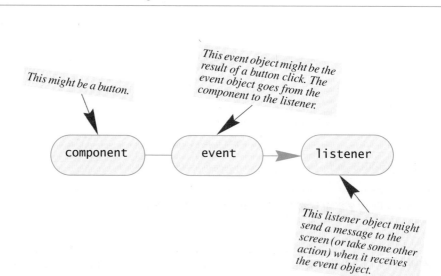

Event-driven programming is a very different game. In event-driven programming, you create objects that can fire events, and you create listener objects to react to the events. For the most part, your program does not determine the order in which things happen. The events determine that order. When an event-driven program is running, the next thing that happens depends on the next event.

Listener objects are almost like people sitting around a room waiting for phone calls. Each person has her or his own phone. When a phone rings, the person with that phone answers and does whatever the phone call says to do. Maybe the message says, "Joe, this is your mother calling. I want you to close the window in your room." Joe then goes home and closes the window in her or his room. In a graphical user interface, the message is something like "Close the window," "The 'A' key has been pressed," or "The mouse was dragged from someplace to someplace else." The message is the event. When an event is fired, it is automatically sent to the listener object(s) for the particular object that fired the event. The listener object then calls the appropriate event-handling method to handle the event.

If you have never done event-driven programming before, one aspect of it may seem strange to you: *You will be writing definitions for methods that you will never invoke in any program*. This may seem strange, because a method is of no value unless it is invoked. So somebody or something other than you the programmer must be invoking these methods. That is exactly what does happen. The Swing system automatically invokes certain methods when an event signals that the method needs to be called.

The event-driven programming that we will be doing with the Swing library makes extensive use of inheritance. The classes that we define will be derived classes of some basic predefined classes that are in the Swing library. These derived classes will inherit methods from their parent class (base class). Some of these inherited methods will work fine just as they were written for the parent class. However, often it will be necessary to override a method definition in order to provide a new definition that is appropriate to the derived class.

? Self-Test Questions

1. How does event-driven programming differ from the sort of programming we did in previous chapters?
2. How is "GUI" pronounced? What do the letters stand for?

12.2 BASIC SWING DETAILS

It Don't Mean a Thing (If It Ain't Got That Swing) -Song title, Duke Ellington

As we mentioned previously, a **window** is a portion of the user's screen that serves as a smaller screen within the screen. In this section, we will tell you how to create simple windows, using Swing.

There are lots of things you can put in a window when designing a GUI. We will start with some simple, but very useful, elements and show you how to build windows with these elements. The window elements we will introduce in this section provide a way to close (that is, end) the window, a way to put text in the window, a way to color the window, and way to put a title on the window. This set of features may not sound like much, but it will introduce you to the basic methods for doing all kinds of programming with Swing.

This section has essentially one demonstration program, although we give two versions of it. In this section, we are interested primarily in introducing you to some details of Swing, so when we first present the program, we deliberately oversimplify it. At the end of this section, we rewrite the program in the style that you should follow when writing Swing programs.

▲ *Gotcha*

Save All Your Work before Running a Swing Program

Programs that use Swing can take control of your computer screen, mouse, and keyboard. If things go awry, and they often do, the usual ways of communicating with the computer may be shut down. On a PC, this situation may require that you reboot your computer. On any system, it may require that you, in some sense, "restart the whole thing." Before running any Swing program that you have not yet fully debugged, be sure to close any files that you have open. If the Swing program causes you to restart your computer, any open files may be damaged. △

Programming Example
A Simple Window

Display 12.2 contains a Java program that produces a simple window, using Swing. After the code for the program is a picture of what the screen will look like when you run this program. This window does not do very much. It simply appears on the screen and displays the text `"Please don't click that button!"` Just about the only other thing it can do is disappear. If you click the close-window button, the program will end, and the window will disappear. The picture shown is a typical example of the kind of window this program produces. The window may look slightly different on your system. Let's look at the code for this first GUI program.

close-window button

The first line, repeated as follows, says that the program uses the Swing library:

javax.swing.*

```
import javax.swing.*;
```

A file containing any program using the Swing library should begin with this line (possibly along with other `import` statements).

The rest of the program is a simple class definition with only a `main` method. Let's look at the code in this `main` method. The first line creates an object of the class `JFrame`. That line is reproduced as follows:

```
JFrame myWindow = new JFrame();
```

■ DISPLAY 12.2 A Very Simple Swing Demonstration Program

```java
import javax.swing.*;

/**
 A simple demonstration of a window constructed with Swing.
*/
public class FirstSwingDemo
{
    public static final int WIDTH = 300;
    public static final int HEIGHT = 200;

    public static void main(String[] args)
    {
        JFrame myWindow = new JFrame();
        myWindow.setSize(WIDTH, HEIGHT);
        JLabel myLabel =
                new JLabel("Please don't click that button!");
        myWindow.getContentPane().add(myLabel);

        WindowDestroyer myListener = new WindowDestroyer();
        myWindow.addWindowListener(myListener);

        myWindow.setVisible(true);
    }
}
```

This is just a simple demo program and is not typical of the style we will use in Swing programs.

Resulting GUI

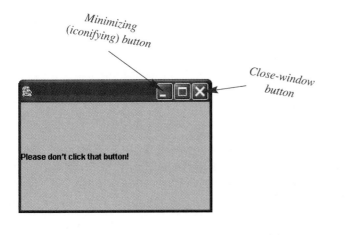

Minimizing (iconifying) button

Close-window button

Please don't click that button!

JFrame

The name myWindow is chosen by you, the programmer. The object myWindow is an object of the class JFrame. A JFrame in Swing is what you probably think of as a window. A JFrame is a very simple window, but it does have, among other things, a border, a place for a title (no title is used in this program), and the close-window button that you expect to find on any window. Soon you will see that we do not normally use simple JFrame objects, but instead define a derived class of the class JFrame and use objects of that derived class. However, for this very first demonstration program, we will use JFrame directly.

The next line, reproduced as follows, sets the size of the JFrame window:

setSize

```
myWindow.setSize(WIDTH, HEIGHT);
```

The method setSize is a method of the class JFrame and sets the size of the window.

Swing size units are discussed in a later subsection of this chapter. For now, simply note that this line says that the window is WIDTH units wide and HEIGHT units tall; do not yet worry about what those units are.

The next line creates an object of the class JLabel and names the object myLabel:

JLabel

```
JLabel myLabel = new JLabel("Please don't click that button!");
```

label

The name myLabel is chosen by you, the programmer. An object of the class JLabel is usually called simply a **label** and is a special kind of text that can be added to a JFrame (or to any of a number of other kinds of objects). The string for the label is given as an argument to the constructor for the JLabel class, so in this case the string of text for the label is "Please don't click that button!".

The next line of the program, given as follows, adds the label myLabel to the JFrame named myWindow:

getContentPane

```
myWindow.getContentPane().add(myLabel);
```

content pane

This line requires a bit of explanation. Let's take this expression apart. The method get-ContentPane is a method of the class JFrame that produces the **content pane** of the JFrame. Every JFrame has a content pane. You do not add things directly to the JFrame. Instead, you add them to its content pane. You can think of the content pane as being the "inside" of the JFrame. So, myWindow.getContentPane() is the content pane of myWindow (the "inside" of myWindow). The label myLabel is added to myWindow.get-

add

ContentPane() (that is, to the content pane of myWindow), using the method add. Every

---

Quick Reference: **The JLabel Class**

An object of the class JLabel is little more than one line of text that can be added to a JFrame (or to certain other objects).

Example:

```
JFrame myWindow = new JFrame();
JLabel myLabel = new JLabel("Please don't click that button!");
myWindow.getContentPane().add(myLabel);
```

Note that you use getContentPane().add to add a JLabel to a JFrame, as illustrated in the foregoing example.

JFrame content pane has a method named add. The method add is already defined for you; you do not define it.

You close this window by clicking the close-window button. When you click that button, the window fires an event and sends it to a listener object. The listener object closes the window. In this program, the listener object is named myListener, which is a member of the class WindowDestroyer. The following line from the program creates a new object of the class WindowDestroyer and names it myListener:

Window-
Destroyer

```
WindowDestroyer myListener = new WindowDestroyer( );
```

You, the programmer, choose the name myListener. The next line, shown as follows, associates the object myListener with the object (the window) myWindow, so that myListener will receive any event fired by the object myWindow:

```
myWindow.addWindowListener(myListener);
```

An object, like myListener, that receives events from another object is called a listener. A listener that listens to events from a window, such as a click on the close-window button, is known as a **window listener.** Associating a listener with the object to which it listens is called **registering the listener.**

registering a
listener

An object of the class WindowDestroyer will close the window myWindow when myWindow fires an appropriate event. We need to define the class WindowDestroyer, but let's postpone that for a bit. For now, just assume that the class WindowDestroyer has been defined so that, when the user clicks the close-window button of myWindow, the object myListener will close myWindow and end the program.

The last statement in main is a call to the method setVisible:

set-
Visible

```
myWindow.setVisible(true);
```

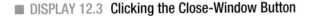 **DISPLAY 12.3 Clicking the Close-Window Button**

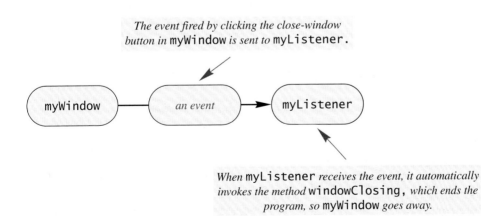

The event fired by clicking the close-window button in myWindow *is sent to* myListener.

myWindow — *an event* → myListener

When myListener *receives the event, it automatically invokes the method* windowClosing, *which ends the program, so* myWindow *goes away.*

This call to `setVisible` makes the window named `myWindow` visible on the screen. The method `setVisible` is a method of the class `JFrame` (as well as a method in many other Swing classes). With the argument `true`, as in Display 12.2, the object is displayed. If the argument `false` were to be used instead, the object would not be shown.

That's the end of the code for `main`, but it's not the end of the program. The window just sits on the screen looking pretty until the user clicks the close-window button. At that point, an event `e` is fired by the object `myWindow`. The event `e` is sent to the listener object called `myListener`. The object `myListener` recognizes `e` as an event signaling that the object `myWindow` should be closed, and `myListener` then closes the window and ends the program. This event handling is diagrammed in Display 12.3.

The object `myListener` is a member of the class `WindowDestroyer`. We have been assuming that the class `WindowDestroyer` has already been defined, but you need to define it and compile it before you can really run the program in Display 12.2. Let's do that now.

The listener class `WindowDestroyer` is defined in Display 12.4. A window listener class for a GUI that involves windows (more precisely, that involves an object of the class `JFrame`) will often be a derived class of the class `WindowAdapter`. This condition is indicated by the phrase `extends WindowAdapter` on the first line of the class definition. A derived class of the class `WindowAdapter`, such as our class `WindowDestroyer`, inherits all its methods from `WindowAdapter`. Each of these methods automatically responds to a different kind of event. Normally, no new methods are added, because there already is a method for each kind of event. However, the way the event is handled is up to you and will depend on the window you are defining. Normally, you would redefine (override) one or more of the method definitions that your class inherits from `WindowAdapter`.

WindowAdapter

■ DISPLAY 12.4 **A Listener Class for Window Events**

```java
import java.awt.*;
import java.awt.event.*;

/**
 If you register an object of this class as a listener to any
 object of the class JFrame, then if the user clicks the
 close-window button in the JFrame, the object of this class
 will end the program and close the JFrame.
*/
public class WindowDestroyer extends WindowAdapter
{
    public void windowClosing(WindowEvent e)
    {
        System.exit(0);
    }
}
```

The class `WindowDestroyer` is not defined for you in Java. This is a class that you, the programmer, must define.

You need to define (actually, redefine) only those methods that your window will use. For this application, the only kind of event that we need our listener class to respond to is one which signals that the window should close. The method that handles those events is named `windowClosing`. So we have redefined only the method `windowClosing`. The method definition is very simple; it simply executes the one command

```
System.exit(0);
```

As we explain in the upcoming Java tip, this command ends the program and thus closes the window.

To run the program in Display 12.2, you must define and compile both the class `FirstSwingDemo` in Display 12.2 and the class `WindowDestroyer` in Display 12.4. Note that the class `WindowDestroyer` is not a Swing class. It is a class that you, the programmer, must define. In this case, we have defined it for you, but you should think of it as a class that you define.

Note that the `import` statements required for the class `WindowDestroyer` are as follows:

```
import java.awt.*;
import java.awt.event.*;
```

These import statements simply tell the compiler where the definitions for `WindowAdapter` and for event handling are located. (You may recall that we said earlier that the AWT was a precursor of the Swing library. The class `WindowAdapter` and the event-handling model are in the AWT, and that is why you see the name `awt` in the `import` statements.) ■

FAQ: How Do the Other Built-In `JFrame` Buttons Work?

The close-window button in a `JFrame` is one of a group of three buttons. The other two buttons work acceptably without your needing to program them. The minimize (iconify) button, shown in Display 12.2, reduces the window to just an icon, typically at the bottom of your screen. The other button allows you to switch the size of the window (`JFrame`) back and forth from full screen to a smaller window.

■ **Java Tip**
Ending a Swing Program

A GUI program is normally based on a kind of infinite loop. There may or may not be a Java loop statement in a GUI program, but nonetheless the GUI program need not ever end. The windowing system normally stays on the screen until the user indicates that it should go away (for example, by clicking the close-window button). If the user never asks the windowing system to go away, it will never go away. Therefore, when you write a GUI program (using Swing), you need some way to say "End the program now." The `exit` method, which was introduced in Chapter 3, will end a Java program as soon as it is executed. The following invocation of the `exit` method is used in Display 12.4:

```
System.exit(0);
```

`System.exit`

As we said in Chapter 3, the number 0 given as the argument to `System.exit` is returned to the operating system. In many situations, you can use any number, and the program will behave in the same way. But most operating systems use 0 to indicate a normal termination of the program and 1 to indicate an abnormal termination of the program. □

▲ Gotcha
Forgetting to Program the Close-Window Button

The following lines from Display 12.2 ensure that when the user clicks the close-window button, the program will end and the window will go away:

```
WindowDestroyer myListener = new WindowDestroyer( );
myWindow.addWindowListener(myListener);
```

You need not use these exact lines to program the action of the close-window button. For example, you may define a class of your own in place of `WindowDestroyer`. However, you do need to do some programming to ensure that when the user clicks the close-window button, the GUI will do what you want it to. If you do not program the close-window button, then when the user clicks this button, the window will disappear, but the program will not end. If your GUI has only one window, this condition will mean that you have no easy way to end the program. There is also the added confusion that, even though the program is still running, it looks as though it has ended, because the window has disappeared. △

▲ Gotcha
Forgetting to Use `getContentPane`

Recall that in Display 12.2, we added the label `myLabel` to the `JFrame` named `myWindow` as follows:

```
myWindow.getContentPane( ).add(myLabel);
```

Because you are "adding `myLabel` to `myWindow`," you might be tempted to use the following instead:

```
myWindow.add(myLabel);
```

However, if you omit `getContentPane( )`, your program will not work correctly. Moreover, the compiler will probably not warn you about this mistake, so you must be very careful to avoid it. △

More about Window Listeners

WindowAdapter

Like our window listener class named `WindowDestroyer` in Display 12.4, any window listener class is typically a derived class of the class `WindowAdapter`. The class

WindowAdapter has a number of different methods, each of which is automatically invoked when the listener object is sent an event that matches that method. The methods and corresponding events are given in the table in Display 12.5. When you define a derived class of the class WindowAdapter, you define only those methods that you need. The only task of the class WindowDestroyer is to close windows, so when we defined WindowDestroyer, we defined only the method windowClosing. (We will not need any of these methods, except windowClosing, but, for completeness, Display 12.5 lists all the methods.)

■ DISPLAY 12.5 **Methods in the Class WindowAdapter**

public void windowOpened(WindowEvent e)
Invoked when a window has been opened.

public void windowClosing(WindowEvent e)
Invoked when a window is in the process of being closed. Clicking the close-window button causes an invocation of this method.

public void windowClosed(WindowEvent e)
Invoked when a window has been closed.

public void windowIconified(WindowEvent e)
Invoked when a window is iconified. When you click the minimize button in a JFrame, the window is iconified. See Display 12.2 for the location of the minimizing (iconifying) button.

public void windowDeiconified(WindowEvent e)
Invoked when a window is deiconified. When you activate a minimized window, it is deiconified.

public void windowActivated(WindowEvent e)
Invoked when a window is activated. When you click in a window, it becomes the activated window. Other actions can also activate a window.

public void windowDeactivated(WindowEvent e)
Invoked when a window is deactivated. When any window is activated, all other windows are deactivated. Other actions can also deactivate a window.

public void windowGainedFocus(WindowEvent e)
Invoked when a window gains focus. (Focus is not discussed in this text.)

public void windowLostFocus(WindowEvent e)
Invoked when a window loses focus. (Focus is not discussed in this text.)

public void windowStateChanged(WindowEvent e)
Invoked when a window changes state.

In discussing our definition of the class `WindowDestroyer` in Display 12.4, it would have been more proper for us to say that we *redefined* the method `windowClosing` rather than saying that we *defined* it. This is because we are changing the definition of `window-Closing`. If, in the definition of a class derived from the class `WindowAdapter`, you give no definition for a method from Display 12.5, then the class inherits the definition from the class `WindowAdapter`. However, when a method is inherited without being redefined, it seldom does what you want. The methods are useful only if they are overridden in some derived class, such as the class `WindowDestroyer`.

abstract class

The class `WindowAdapter` is an abstract class, which means that you cannot create an object of this class by using `new WindowAdapter( )`. You can use `WindowAdapter` only as a base class when defining other classes. Abstract classes were discussed in Chapter 7.

You will find more discussion of `WindowAdapter` and related topics in Chapter 14.

Size Units for Screen Objects

pixel

In Swing, the size of an object on the screen is measured in pixels. A **pixel** is the smallest unit of space on which your screen can write. Think of a pixel as a small rectangle that can have one of a small fixed number of colors, and think of your screen as being paved with these little pixels. (It may help to think in terms of a simple black-and-white screen on which a pixel is either black or white, even though screens now offer more colors than just black and white.) The more pixels you have on your screen, the greater the screen's resolution. That is, the more pixels you have, the more fine detail you can see.

The size of a pixel depends on the size of your screen and the resolution of your screen. Although Swing uses pixels as if they were units of length, they do not actually represent any fixed length. The length of a pixel will vary from one screen to another. On a screen with high resolution (lots of pixels), an object of size 300 by 200 will look very small. On a screen with low resolution (not many pixels), an object of size 300 by 200 will look very large. For example, consider the following statement from Display 12.2:

```
myWindow.setSize(WIDTH, HEIGHT);
```

This statement is equivalent to

```
myWindow.setSize(300, 200);
```

It says that the object `myWindow` (which happens to be a kind of window) will be 300 pixels wide and 200 pixels high, but the actual size will depend on the resolution of the screen you are using when you run the program.

Notice that, although Java and Swing are portable and the code you write with Swing will run on any system that supports Java, the exact size of what you produce on the screen will vary from one screen to another. This is one feature of Java that is not as portable as would be ideal. To get the desired size for a window, you may need to change the dimensions to suit your particular screen size and screen resolution. However, it is only the absolute size that will vary. At least the relative size of things will be the same no matter where you run your Swing application. Moreover, for most windowlike objects on most systems, after the window is displayed, the user can resize the window, using the mouse.

FAQ: **What Is a Pixel?**

A **pixel** is the smallest unit of space on which your screen can write. With Swing, both the size and the position of objects on the screen are measured in pixels. The more pixels you have on a screen, the greater the screen resolution. Thus, a screen object will look smaller on a screen with high resolution and larger on a screen with low resolution.

Remember: **Resolution's Relationship to Size**

The relationship between resolution and size can seem confusing at first. A high-resolution screen is a screen of better quality than a low-resolution screen, so why does an object look smaller on a high-resolution screen? Isn't bigger better? It's not quite that simple. You have to think of counting pixels if you want a complete explanation, but here's one way to make it seem more sensible: If a screen has low resolution, you cannot see smaller things. Thus, when a screen has low resolution, the only way it can display a small object is to make it larger.

More on `setVisible`

Consider the method `setVisible`, which is called in the program in Display 12.2. The particular line from Display 12.2 containing this method call is as follows:

```
myWindow.setVisible(true);
```

`setVisible`

Many classes of Swing objects have a `setVisible` method.

The method `setVisible` takes one argument of type `boolean`. In other words, the argument to `setVisible` is either `true` or `false`. If w is an object, such as a window that can be displayed on the screen, then the call

```
w.setVisible(true);
```

will make w visible, and the call

```
w.setVisible(false);
```

will make w invisible.

You might think that displaying an object on the screen should happen automatically. After all, why would you define a windowing object unless you want it to be displayed on the screen? The answer is that you may not want it to be displayed at all times. You have undoubtedly worked with windowing systems in which some windows come and go, either because they are no longer needed (like a pull-down menu after you make a choice) or because the window is covered by other windows. Swing cannot read the programmer's mind to determine when the window (or other GUI object) should be displayed, so the programmer must tell the system when to display the window. The programmer does this by inserting a call to the method `setVisible`.

If you rerun the program from Display 12.2, but omit the invocation of `setVisible`, then you will see nothing on the screen. The window will be constructed, but it will not be displayed. (But be warned: Because the window won't be displayed, the close-window button won't be displayed either, so there will be no way to end the program!)

Quick Reference: The `setVisible` Method

Many classes of Swing objects have a `setVisible` method. The `setVisible` method takes one argument of type `boolean`. If w is an object, such as a window, that can be displayed on the screen, then the call

```
w.setVisible(true);
```

will make w visible. The call

```
w.setVisible(false);
```

will hide w, that is, will make w invisible.

Syntax (for an invocation of the `setVisible` method):

Object_For_Screen`.setVisible(`*Boolean_Expression*`);`

Example (from Display 12.2):

```
public static void main(String[] args)
{
    JFrame myWindow = new JFrame( );
        .
        .
        .
    myWindow.setVisible(true);
}
```

? Self-Test Questions

3. How would you change the program in Display 12.2 so that the text in the window reads "I love you!" instead of "Please don't click that button!"?

4. What units of measure are used in the following call to `setSize` that appeared in the `main` method of the program in Display 12.2?

   ```
   myWindow.setSize(WIDTH, HEIGHT);
   ```

   In the program, this line is equivalent to

   ```
   myWindow.setSize(300, 200);
   ```

   In other words, 300 what? Inches? Feet? Centimeters? And similarly, 200 what?

5. What Swing class do you normally use to define a window? Any window class that you define would normally be an object of this class.

6. Give a Java statement that, when executed, will immediately end the program.

7. Give a Java statement that will add the label `superLabel` to the `JFrame` named `myGUI`.

8. Suppose `messageWindow` is a `JFrame` and n is an `int` variable with some value. Give a Java statement that will make `messageWindow` visible if n is positive and invisible otherwise.

9. What happens when you click the minimizing (iconifying) button of the `JFrame` shown in Display 12.2?

10. Suppose that `messageWindow` is a `JFrame` and `warningLabel` is a `JLabel`. What is wrong with the following statement?

```
messageWindow.add(warningLabel):
```

Programming Example
A Better Version of Our First Swing Program

Displays 12.6 and 12.7 together are a rewrite of the demonstration program in Display 12.2. This new version does essentially the same thing as the program in Display 12.2, except that the new version shows two windows rather than just one. However, the new version is done in the style you should follow in writing your own GUIs. Notice that the definition of the window (Display 12.6) is in a class by itself (no pun intended). The window is then displayed in a program that uses the class (Display 12.7). A window class like `FirstWindow` in Display 12.6 is typically a class for an input/output interface that can be used in any of a number of programs. Let's look more carefully at this class.

■ DISPLAY 12.6 **A Swing Window Class**

```java
import javax.swing.*;

/**
 A simple window class.
*/
public class FirstWindow extends JFrame
{
    public static final int WIDTH = 300;
    public static final int HEIGHT = 200;

    public FirstWindow()
    {
        super();

        setSize(WIDTH, HEIGHT);
        JLabel myLabel = new JLabel("Please don't click that button!");
        getContentPane().add(myLabel);

        WindowDestroyer listener = new WindowDestroyer();
        addWindowListener(listener);
    }
}
```

derived class

Observe that `FirstWindow` is a derived class of the class `JFrame`. This approach is the normal way to define a window interface. The base class `JFrame` gives some basic window facilities, and then the derived class adds whatever additional features you want in your window interface.

■ **DISPLAY 12.7 A Program That Uses the Class `FirstWindow`**

```java
import javax.swing.*;

/**
 A simple demonstration of the use of a window class. To see
 both windows, you will probably have to move the top window.
*/
public class FirstWindowDemo
{
    public static void main(String[] args)
    {
        FirstWindow window1 = new FirstWindow();
        window1.setVisible(true);

        FirstWindow window2 = new FirstWindow();
        window2.setVisible(true);
    }
}
```

Resulting GUI

If it looks as though you have only one window when you run this program, move the window. The windows may be one on top of the other.

Note that the constructor in Display 12.6 starts by calling the constructor for the parent class JFrame with the line

```
super();
```

As we noted in Chapter 7, this statement ensures that any initialization that is normally done for all objects of type JFrame will, in fact, be done. If the base-class constructor you call has no arguments, then it will be called automatically, whether you include super(); or not, so we could have omitted the invocation of super() in Display 12.6. However, if the base-class constructor needs an argument, as it may in some other situations, then you must include a call to the base-class constructor, super.

Note that almost all the initializing for the window FirstWindow in Display 12.6 is placed in the constructor for the class. That is as it should be. The initializations, such as setting the initial window size, should be part of the class definition, not actions performed by objects of the class (as they were in Display 12.2). All the initializing methods, such as setSize, getContentPane, and addWindowListener, are inherited from the class JFrame. Because they are invoked in the constructor for the window, the window itself is the calling object. In other words, a method invocation such as

constructor

```
setSize(WIDTH, HEIGHT);
```

is equivalent to

```
this.setSize(WIDTH, HEIGHT);
```

Similarly, the method invocation

```
getContentPane().add(myLabel);
```

Quick Reference: Adding Items to a JFrame

You can add a JLabel to a JFrame as follows (later you will see that you can add other items in the same way):

Syntax (inside of a constructor):

```
getContentPane().add(JLabel);
```

Example (within a constructor for a class called FirstWindow):

```
public FirstWindow()
{
        .
        .
        .
    JLabel myLabel =
            new JLabel("Please don't click that button!");
    getContentPane().add(myLabel);
        .
        .
        .
}
```

---

is equivalent to

```
this.getContentPane( ).add(myLabel);
```

Aside from the fact that they are taken care of in the constructor for a derived class, the details in the definition of FirstWindow in Display 12.6 are essentially the same as those in Display 12.2.

Let's next consider the program in Display 12.7, which uses the class FirstWindow. All this program does is display two (identical) objects of the class FirstWindow. These two windows will probably be placed one exactly on top of the other. So when you run the program, it may look as though only one window is displayed. However, if you use your mouse to move the top window, you will see a second window underneath it.

Note that almost all of the initializations for the windows in Display 12.7 have been moved to the constructor for the class FirstWindow. However, we have placed the invocations of the method setVisible in the application program that uses the window class FirstWindow. We could have placed an invocation of setVisible in the constructor for FirstWindow and omitted the invocation of setVisible from the application program (Display 12.7); if we had, we would have gotten the same results when we ran the application program. However, in normal situations, the application program "knows" when the window should be displayed, so it is normal to put the invocation of the method setVisible in the application program. The programmer writing the class FirstWindow cannot anticipate when a programmer who uses the window will want to make it visible (or invisible). ■

Quick Reference: JFrame Classes

When we say that a class is a JFrame class, we mean that the class is a descendant class of the class JFrame. For example, the class FirstWindow in Display 12.6 is a JFrame class.

Programming Example
A Window with Color

Display 12.8 contains a slight variant of the class shown in Display 12.6. This version has two constructors. The default constructor is the same as that in Display 12.6, but with four new elements added. The new elements are the title "Second Window", a local variable named contentPane to hold the content pane of the JFrame, a background color (blue), and a new way to add the window listener. Let's consider these four new elements one at a time. For the moment, we are considering only the default constructor (the one with no arguments).

We have given the window a title with the following method invocation:

setTitle

```
setTitle("Second Window");
```

■ DISPLAY 12.8 Another Simple Window Constructed with Swing

```java
import javax.swing.*;
import java.awt.*; //needed for the Color class

public class SecondWindow extends JFrame
{
    public static final int WIDTH = 200;
    public static final int HEIGHT = 200;

    public SecondWindow()
    {
        super();

        setSize(WIDTH, HEIGHT);

        Container contentPane = getContentPane();
        JLabel label = new JLabel("Now available in color!");
        contentPane.add(label);

        setTitle("Second Window");
        contentPane.setBackground(Color.BLUE);

        addWindowListener(new WindowDestroyer());
    }

    public SecondWindow(Color customColor)
    {
        super();

        setSize(WIDTH, HEIGHT);

        Container contentPane = getContentPane();
        JLabel label = new JLabel("Now available in color!");
        contentPane.add(label);

        setTitle("Second Window");
        contentPane.setBackground(customColor);

        addWindowListener(new WindowDestroyer());
    }
}
```

If you prefer, you can omit this call to super. Because it is the default constructor, it will be called automatically anyway.

If you prefer, you can omit this call to super.

The method `setTitle` is inherited from the class `JFrame`. The method `setTitle` takes one string argument and writes that string in the title bar of the window. There is no calling object for this invocation, because it is in a constructor, and the calling object is an implicit `this`. The preceding invocation is equivalent to

```
this.setTitle("Second Window");
```

Other method invocations in the constructor also have an implicit `this`.

Note the following line from the first constructor in Display 12.8:

```
Container contentPane = getContentPane( );
```

This line gives us a name, `contentPane`, for the content pane of the `JFrame` windowing GUI we are defining. Thus, an invocation of the method `add` can be written in the simpler form

```
contentPane.add(label);
```

instead of the slightly more complex (and slightly less efficient) expression

```
getContentPane( ).add(label);
```

The important thing to note here is that the method `getContentPane` produces an object of type `Container`. We will say a bit more about the class `Container` later in this chapter. For now, all you need to know about this class is that it is the type to use for the object returned by the method `getContentPane` (that is, for the content pane of the `JFrame`).

FAQ: Why Does a `JFrame` Have a Content Pane?

Unfortunately, the question of why a `JFrame` has a content pane does not have an easy answer. It has to do with ways of using a `JFrame` object that we will not go into in this book. If it seems to you that there is no need for a content pane, take comfort in the fact that your observation is well taken. It is not needed for what we are doing in this book. In fact, the precursor class of the class `JFrame` (in an older library of classes) did not have a content pane. However, a `JFrame` object does have a content pane, and you must deal with the content pane or else your programs will not work correctly.

In Display 12.8, we have also given the window a background color with the method call

```
contentPane.setBackground(Color.BLUE);
```

set-
Background

The method `setBackground` is another method that is inherited from the class `JFrame`. The method `setBackground` takes one argument, which is a color. The class `Color` contains constants for many of the common colors. `Color.BLUE` is a predefined constant that stands for the color blue. The color constants you have available are listed in Display 12.9. To see what each of these colors looks like, replace the constant `Color.BLUE` in Display 12.8 with the color you want to see and then compile and run the modified program. You can also define your own colors with the class `Color`, but we will not go into that topic in this book. Because the `Color` class is in the AWT package (library), the following import statement is needed when a class or program uses the `Color` class:

```
import java.awt.*; //needed for the Color class
```

■ DISPLAY 12.9 **The Color Constants**

```
Color.BLACK            Color.MAGENTA
Color.BLUE             Color.ORANGE
Color.CYAN             Color.PINK
Color.DARK_GRAY        Color.RED
Color.GRAY             Color.WHITE
Color.GREEN            Color.YELLOW
Color.LIGHT_GRAY
```

The class `Color` is in the AWT package (library). So when using these colors, you need the following `import` statement:

```
import java.awt.*;
```

FAQ: **What Kind of Color is Cyan?**

You might wonder why the designers of the Java libraries chose to have defined constants for some of the colors in Display 12.9. Certainly colors like black, white, red, green, and most of the others are common colors, but why did they pick the colors cyan and magenta? The answer is that one of the common ways of making colors is to mix the four colors black, yellow, cyan, and magenta. So cyan and magenta are indeed "basic colors" in some sense of the phrase.

Cyan is a very light blue. Magenta is a kind of purple. The other common way of mixing colors is to mix red, green, and blue. Your TV uses red, green, and blue. Books printed in color use black, yellow, cyan, and magenta.

At the end of the first constructor definition, we added a listener for our window with the following invocation of the method `addWindowListener`:

new in
arguments

```
addWindowListener(new WindowDestroyer());
```

Certain methods, such as `addWindowListener`, need objects as arguments, but once the object is given as an argument to the method, you never need to refer to it again in your programming. This means that you do not need a name for the argument. An argument such as `new WindowDestroyer()` in the preceding invocation of the method `addWindowListener` is a way to create an object and pass it as an argument to the method `addWindowListener` and yet not have to give the argument a name. The invocation

```
addWindowListener(new WindowDestroyer());
```

is equivalent to the following code:

```
WindowDestroyer listener = new WindowDestroyer();
addWindowListener(listener):
```

The only difference between the preceding two ways of adding a window listener is that in the first form, we do not bother to use a name for the object of type `WindowDestroyer`, while in the second, two-line version, we give the listener object the name `listener`.

Remember: **Using `new` as Part of a Method Argument**

You can create an object and pass it as an argument to a method without bothering to give the object a name. You do this by using `new` and the class name as the argument. In these cases, the class name is being used as the name of the constructor for the class.

Syntax:

Method_Name(new *Class_Name_As_Constructor*(*Possibly_Parameters*));

Example:

```
addWindowListener(new WindowDestroyer( ));
```

anonymous
object

The argument `new WindowDestroyer( )` is often called an **anonymous object,** because it has no name.

Now let's consider the second constructor. It is almost the same as the default constructor, except for how it handles the background color. This second constructor has one parameter of type `Color` and sets the background color to the color specified by this one parameter. You can easily see the difference between these two constructors by looking at the demonstration program in Display 12.10. The two windows produced are identical except that one has a blue background and one has a pink background. (As with the previous example, when you run the program in Display 12.10, one window will probably be on top of the other, so that it looks as if you have only one window. Just use your mouse to move the top window, and you will see the other window.) ■

Some Methods of the Class `JFrame`

Display 12.11 contains some of the methods for the class `JFrame`. Recall that `JFrame` is the basic class out of which you normally build windows. A window class is normally a derived class of the class `JFrame`, so the window class inherits all these methods.

Remember: **What `import` Statements to Use**

It is rather difficult to keep track of which `import` statement you need for a Swing class definition or Swing program. The following `import` statements will suffice for most Swing window interfaces:

```
import javax.swing.*;
import java.awt.*;
import java.awt.event.*;
```

The loss of efficiency for including an extra `import` statement is minimal, so there is no need to be obsessive about keeping them to a minimum. However, the class definitions in this text use only those `import` statement that are needed.

■ DISPLAY 12.10 **A Demonstration Program for** `SecondWindow`

```java
import java.awt.*; //for the class Color used in an argument.

public class SecondWindowDemo
{
    /**
     Creates and displays two windows of the class SecondWindow.
    */
    public static void main(String[] args)
    {
        SecondWindow window1 = new SecondWindow();
        window1.setVisible(true);

        SecondWindow window2 = new SecondWindow(Color.PINK);
        window2.setVisible(true);
    }
}
```

Resulting GUI

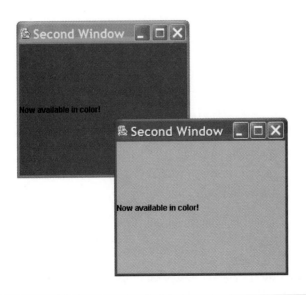

■ DISPLAY 12.11 **Some Methods in the Class JFrame**

Method	Description
JFrame()	Constructor for creating a new JFrame.
JFrame(String title)	Constructor for creating a new JFrame with the specified title.
add	JFrame has a method add, but it should not be used. (It is basically a useless inheritance from an ancestor class). To add something to a JFrame, use getContentPane().add(*Item_Added*)
void addWindowListener(WindowListener ear)	Registers ear as a listener for events fired by the JFrame.
Container getContentPane()	Returns the content-pane object of the JFrame. Note that the content pane that is returned is of type Container.
void setBackground(Color c)	Sets the background color to c.
void setForeground(Color c)	Sets the foreground color to c.
void setSize(int width, int height)	Resizes the window to the specified width and height.
void setTitle(String title)	Displays the title on the title bar of the window.
void setVisible(boolean b)	Makes the window visible if the argument is true. Makes it invisible if the argument is false.

? Self-Test Questions

11. How would you modify the class definition in Display 12.8 so that the window produced by the default constructor is yellow instead of blue?

12. How do you set the title of a window you create with Swing?

13. Suppose you declared and created a window object of the class MyWindowClass with the following code:

    ```
    MyWindowClass gui = new MyWindowClass();
    ```

    The window gui is not yet visible on the screen. Give a program statement that will make it visible.

14. Rewrite the following code without using a name for the object `listener`:

    ```
    WindowDestroyer listener = new WindowDestroyer( );
    addWindowListener(listener);
    ```

15. Suppose w is an object of the class `JFrame`. Give a Java statement that will de-clare a variable named `contentPane` and set it so that it names the content pane of w.

16. What `import` statement do you need to be able to use the type `Container`?

Layout Managers

You have seen that you can add a `JLabel` to a `JFrame` by using the method `getContentPane` to get the content pane of the `JFrame` and then using the method `add` to add the `JLabel` to the content pane. For an example, look at Display 12.8. If you add only one label, it seems that there is no question of where the label goes, but what if you add two or more labels? How are they arranged? One on top of the other? One next to the other? Which is first, which is second, and so forth? That arranging is done by a special kind of object known as a **layout manager.** The layout manager arranges the items you add, according to certain rules. Different layout managers follow different rules. The next example adds three labels to a `JFrame` and uses a layout manager to arrange the three labels.

layout manager

Display 12.12 contains an example of a class used to create a window with three labels. A layout manager is used to place the labels one below the other on three lines, rather than in some other arrangement such as all on one line. Let's look at the details.

First, note one minor point that we have not seen before in our discussion of Swing (although we have seen it in other kinds of classes—for example, in Display 5.7 in Chapter 5). We have placed a demonstration `main` method in the class definition. Normally, a Swing GUI class is used to create and display a GUI in a `main` method (or other method) in some class other than the class for the Swing GUI. However, it is perfectly legal and sometimes convenient to place a `main` method in the GUI class definition so that it is easy to display a sample of the GUI. Note that the `main` method that is given in the class itself is written in the same way as a `main` method that is in some other class. In particular, you need to construct an object of the class, as in the following line from the `main` method in Display 12.12:

```
BorderLayoutDemo gui = new BorderLayoutDemo( );
```

Now let's move on to the things that are truly new in Display 12.12.

A layout manager is added to the GUI in Display 12.12 with the following line:

```
content.setLayout(new BorderLayout( ));
```

setLayout

`BorderLayout` is a layout-manager class, so `new BorderLayout( )` produces a new object of the class `BorderLayout`. This `BorderLayout` object is given the task of arranging components (in this case, labels) that are added to the GUI. It may help to note that the foregoing invocation of `setLayout` is equivalent to the following two lines:

```
BorderLayout manager = new BorderLayout( );
content.setLayout(manager);
```

■ DISPLAY 12.12 **Using the BorderLayout Manager** *(Part 1 of 2)*

```java
import javax.swing.*;
import java.awt.*;

/**
 Simple demonstration of the use of a layout manager
 to arrange labels.
*/
public class BorderLayoutDemo extends JFrame
{
    public static final int WIDTH = 300;
    public static final int HEIGHT = 200;

    /**
     Creates and displays a window of the class BorderLayoutDemo.
    */
    public static void main(String[] args)
    {
        BorderLayoutDemo gui = new BorderLayoutDemo();
        gui.setVisible(true);
    }

    public BorderLayoutDemo()
    {
        setSize(WIDTH, HEIGHT);
        addWindowListener(new WindowDestroyer());
        setTitle("Layout Demonstration");
        Container content = getContentPane();

        content.setLayout(new BorderLayout());

        JLabel label1 = new JLabel("First label here.");
        content.add(label1, BorderLayout.NORTH);

        JLabel label2 = new JLabel("Second label there.");
        content.add(label2, BorderLayout.SOUTH);

        JLabel label3 = new JLabel("Third label anywhere.");
        content.add(label3, BorderLayout.CENTER);
    }
}
```

■ DISPLAY 12.12 **Using the** `BorderLayout` **Manager** *(Part 2 of 2)*

Resulting GUI

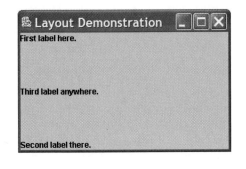

Note that the method `setLayout` is invoked not by the `JFrame` itself, but by the content pane of the `JFrame`, which in this case is named `content`. This is because we actually add the labels to the content pane and not (directly) to the `JFrame`. In general, you should invoke `setLayout` with the same object that you use to invoke `add` (and so far that has always been the content pane of a `JFrame`).

A `BorderLayout` manager places labels (or other components) into the five regions `BorderLayout.NORTH`, `BorderLayout.SOUTH`, `BorderLayout.EAST`, `BorderLayout.WEST`, and `BorderLayout.CENTER`. These five regions are arranged as follows:

`BorderLayout`

BorderLayout.NORTH		
BorderLayout. WEST	BorderLayout.CENTER	BorderLayout. EAST
BorderLayout.SOUTH		

In the foregoing diagram, the outside box represents the content pane (or other container to which you will add things). The five regions are divided by finer lines on the inside of the diagram. The fine lines will not be visible unless you do something to make them visible. We drew them in to show you where each region is located. Let's look at our example from Display 12.12. We added labels as follows:

```
JLabel label1 = new JLabel("First label here.");
content.add(label1, BorderLayout.NORTH);

JLabel label2 = new JLabel("Second label there.");
content.add(label2, BorderLayout.SOUTH);
```

```
JLabel label3 = new JLabel("Third label anywhere.");
content.add(label3, BorderLayout.CENTER);
```

BorderLayout.NORTH, BorderLayout.SOUTH, BorderLayout.EAST, Border-Layout.WEST, and BorderLayout.CENTER are five constants defined in the class Bor-derLayout, although you do not have to think of them as anything more than the five regions for a BorderLayout manager. Note that, when you use a BorderLayout man-ager, you give the region as a second argument to the method add, as in the following statement:

```
content.add(label1, BorderLayout.NORTH);
```

Note that the labels (or other components to be added) need not be added in any partic-ular order, because the second argument completely specifies where the label is placed.

That concludes our discussion of Display 12.12, except for one point. What became of the regions BorderLayout.EAST and BorderLayout.WEST? The answer is simple: They were not used. You need not use all five regions. If some regions are not used, any extra space is given to the BorderLayout.CENTER region.

Quick Reference: Layout Managers

The objects that you add to a container class are arranged by an object known as a **layout manager**. You add a layout manager with the method setLayout, which is a method of every container class, such as the content pane of a JFrame or an object of any of the other container classes that we will intro-duce later in this chapter. If you do not add a layout manager, a default layout manager will be provided for you.

Syntax:

```
Container_Object.setLayout(new Layout_Manager_Class( ));
```

Example (within a constructor for a class called FlowLayoutDemo):

```
public FlowLayoutDemo( )
{
    ...
    Container contentPane = getContentPane( );
    contentPane.setLayout(new FlowLayout( ));

    JLabel label1 = new JLabel("Labels are good.");
    contentPane.add(label1);
    ...
}
```

Quick Reference: Specifying the BorderLayout Region

We have specified the region in which to place a button (or other component) by using the five constants BorderLayout.NORTH, BorderLayout.SOUTH, BorderLayout.EAST, Border-Layout.WEST, and BorderLayout.CENTER. If you prefer, you can instead use the five strings

"North", "South", "East", "West", and "Center". The following example rewrites some code from Display 12.12, using these strings:

Example:

```
JLabel label1 = new JLabel("First label here.");
content.add(label1, "North");

JLabel label2 = new JLabel("Second label there.");
content.add(label2, "South");

JLabel label3 = new JLabel("Third label anywhere.");
content.add(label3, "Center");
```

Using the strings "North", "South", and so forth, saves typing. However, a region is not a string, so some programmers prefer to use the constants, such as BorderLayout.NORTH, for philosophical and stylistic reasons. Either approach is reasonable.

From this discussion, it sounds as though you can place only one item in each region, but later in this chapter you will see that there is a way to group items so that more than one item can (in effect) be placed in each region.

There are some standard predefined layout managers, and you can also define your own layout managers. However, for most purposes, the predefined layout managers are all that you need, and we will not discuss how you can create your own layout-manager classes. In this chapter we describe the three most commonly used predefined layout managers: the BorderLayout manager, which you have already seen, and the two layout managers we discuss next. (One additional layout manager called the BoxLayout manager will be introduced in Chapter 14.)

The simplest layout manager is the **FlowLayout manager.** An object of the class   FlowLayout
FlowLayout is a layout manager that arranges the components you add to a class in the most obvious way: The components are arranged one after the other, going from left to right, in the order in which you add them to the class, using the method **add**. For example, if the class in Display 12.12 had used the FlowLayout manager, it would have employed the following code:

```
content.setLayout(new FlowLayout( ));

JLabel label1 = new JLabel("First label here.");
content.add(label1);

JLabel label2 = new JLabel("Second label there.");
content.add(label2);

JLabel label3 = new JLabel("Third label anywhere.");
content.add(label3);
```

Note that if we had used the FlowLayout manager, as in the foregoing code, then the **add** method would have had only one argument. Also note that, with a FlowLayout manager, the items are displayed in the order they are added, so that the labels in the foregoing would be displayed all on one line as follows:

```
First label here.Second label there.Third label anywhere.
```

GridLayout

(If you want to see the full program, look at the file FlowLayoutDemo.java on the accompanying CD.) You will see a number of examples of GUIs that use the FlowLayout manager class later in this chapter.

A **GridLayout manager** arranges components in rows and columns, with each entry being the same size. For example, the following statement says to use a GridLayout manager with aContainer (which can be a content pane or other container):

```
aContainer.setLayout(new GridLayout(2, 3));
```

The two numbers given as arguments to the constructor GridLayout specify the number of rows and columns. The foregoing statement would produce the following sort of layout:

The lines will not be visible unless you do something special to make them visible. They are just to show you the region boundaries.

Although you specify a number of columns when you create a GridLayout manager, the number of columns will actually be determined by the number of items added to the container. If you add six items, the grid will be as shown. If you add seven or eight items, a fourth column is automatically added, and so forth. (If you add fewer than six components, there will be two rows and a reduced number of columns.)

When using the GridLayout class, the method add has only one argument. The items are placed in the grid from left to right, first filling the top row, then the second row, and so forth. You are not allowed to skip any grid position (although you will later see that you can add something that does not show and thereby gives the illusion of skipping a grid position).

If you want to see the class GridLayout in action, look at the classes GridLayoutDemo1.java and GridLayoutDemo2.java on the accompanying CD.

Descriptions of the three layout managers are summarized in Display 12.13. More information on layout managers will be given in Chapter 14.

■ DISPLAY 12.13 **Some Layout Managers**

Layout Manager	Description
FlowLayout	Displays components from left to right in the same fashion that you normally write things on a piece of paper.
BorderLayout	Displays the components in five areas: north, south, east, west, and center. You specify which area a component goes into in a second argument of the add method.
GridLayout	Lays components out in a grid, with each component stretched to fill its box in the grid.

Quick Reference: Default Layout Managers

If you do not add a layout manager, then a default layout manager will be provided for you. For example, in Display 12.8, we did not specify any layout manager, but we could still add a label, because a default layout manager was provided automatically. The default layout-manager class for the content pane of a `JFrame` is the `BorderLayout` class. (If you are using the `BorderLayout` class and use add with no second argument, it is the same as if you gave `BorderLayout.CENTER` as a second argument. We relied on this detail for our first few programs, but now that we know about layout managers, we will always use a second argument when adding to a container with a `BorderLayout` manager.)

Until we learned about layout managers, we simply left things to the default layout manager. However, it is preferable always to specify a layout manager. This approach makes your code clearer and more likely to survive any future changes to new versions of the Swing classes. From now on, we will always use an explicit layout manager.

? Self-Test Questions

17. How would you modify the class definition in Display 12.12 so that the three labels are displayed as follows?

    ```
    First label here.
    Second label there.
    Third label anywhere.
    ```

    (There may be space between each pair of lines.)

18. How would you modify the class definition in Display 12.12 so that the three labels are displayed as follows?

    ```
    First label here.
                                    Second label there.
    Third label anywhere.
    ```

    (There may be space between each pair of lines.)

19. The following line occurs in the definition of the constructor in Display 12.12:

    ```
    content.setLayout(new BorderLayout( ));
    ```

    What is the meaning of `new`? What kind of argument is being used?

20. Suppose you are defining a windowing GUI class in the usual way, as a derived class of the class `JFrame`, and suppose that the constructor obtains the content pane as follows:

    ```
    contentPane = getContentPane( );
    ```

    Now suppose you want to specify a layout manager for `contentPane` so as to produce the following sort of layout:

    What should the argument to `setLayout` be?

21. Suppose the situation is as described in Self-Test Question 20, except that you want the following sort of layout:

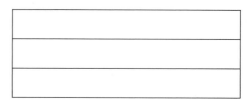

What should the argument to `setLayout` be?

12.3 BUTTONS AND ACTION LISTENERS

I claim not to have controlled events, but confess plainly
that events have controlled me. -Abraham Lincoln, letter to A. G. Hodges (April 4, 1864)

So far, the GUIs we have produced using Swing have included almost no actions. They just sat there and displayed some text. The only action they took was to go away when the user clicked the close-window button. In this section, we start to show you how to design GUIs that do things, like changing color, changing text, or performing some more complicated actions. In our first examples, the actions will be taken in response to the user clicking a button.

A button is simply a component in a GUI that looks like a button and that does something when you click on it, using your mouse. You create buttons in a way that is very similar to how you create labels. You add buttons to a `JFrame` in the same way that you add labels to a `JFrame`, but there is also something very new about buttons: You can associate an action with the button, so that when the user clicks the button, using the mouse, the GUI performs some action. An example should make the details clear.

Programming Example
Adding Buttons

Display 12.14 contains a program that creates a window with two buttons, labeled `"Red"` and `"Green"`. When the program is run, the window shown in Display 12.14 is displayed. If you click the button marked `"Red"`, using your mouse, the color of the window changes from blue (or whatever color it is) to red. If you click the button labeled `"Green"`, the color of the window changes to green. That is all the program does (but as you can see, you are gradually learning to build more complicated window interfaces). To end the program and make the window disappear, you click the close-window button.

Much of what appears in Display 12.14 is already familiar to you. The class `Button-Demo` is derived from the class `JFrame`, so it is a window interface similar to the ones you have already seen in this chapter. A window listener of the class `WindowDestroyer` is added with the method `addWindowListener`, as in previous examples. The size is set, and the content pane is obtained, with `getContentPane`, as in earlier examples. We use a layout manager as we did in the previous example (Display 12.12), although this time we use the `FlowLayout` manager class.

■ DISPLAY 12.14 **A GUI with Buttons Added** *(Part 1 of 2)*

```java
import javax.swing.*;
import java.awt.*;
import java.awt.event.*;

/**
 Simple demonstration of putting buttons in a JFrame.
*/
public class ButtonDemo extends JFrame implements ActionListener
{
    public static final int WIDTH = 300;
    public static final int HEIGHT = 200;

    /**
     Creates and displays a window of the class ButtonDemo.
    */
    public static void main(String[] args)
    {
        ButtonDemo buttonGui = new ButtonDemo();
        buttonGui.setVisible(true);
    }

    public ButtonDemo()
    {
        setSize(WIDTH, HEIGHT);

        addWindowListener(new WindowDestroyer());
        setTitle("Button Demo");
        Container contentPane = getContentPane();
        contentPane.setBackground(Color.BLUE);

        contentPane.setLayout(new FlowLayout());

        JButton stopButton = new JButton("Red");
        stopButton.addActionListener(this);
        contentPane.add(stopButton);

        JButton goButton = new JButton("Green");
        goButton.addActionListener(this);
        contentPane.add(goButton);
    }
```

It will take more than one subsection to fully explain this program. The explanation does not end until the end of the subsection entitled "Action Listeners and Action Events."

■ DISPLAY 12.14 **A GUI with Buttons Added** *(Part 2 of 2)*

```java
    public void actionPerformed(ActionEvent e)
    {
        Container contentPane = getContentPane( );

        if (e.getActionCommand( ).equals("Red"))
            contentPane.setBackground(Color.RED);
        else if (e.getActionCommand( ).equals("Green"))
            contentPane.setBackground(Color.GREEN);
        else
            System.out.println("Error in button interface.");
    }
}
```

Resulting GUI

What is new in Display 12.14 is the use of button objects of the class `JButton` and a new kind of listener class. We discuss buttons and the new listener class in the next few subsections. ■

Buttons

In this subsection, we tell you how to add buttons to your GUI. In the next subsection, we tell you how to specify what happens when a button is clicked.

adding buttons

A button object is created in the same way that any other object is created, but you use the class `JButton`. For example, the following line from Display 12.14 creates a button:

```java
JButton stopButton = new JButton("Red");
```

The argument to the construct, in this case `"Red"`, is a string that will be written on the button when the button is displayed. If you look at the GUI in Display 12.14, you will see that the two buttons are labeled `"Red"` and `"Green"`.

The button is added to the content pane with the following line of code:

```
contentPane.add(stopButton);
```

There is no second argument to the method add, because we are using a FlowLayout manager. If we had instead used the BorderLayout manager class, we would have used some second argument, such as BorderLayout.NORTH.

In the next subsection, we explain the lines from Display 12.14 involving the method addActionListener.

Quick Reference: **The JButton Class**

An object of the class JButton is displayed in a GUI as a component that looks like a button. You click the button, using your mouse, to simulate pushing it. When using new to create an object of the class JButton, you can give a string argument to the constructor, and the string will be displayed on the button.

You can add objects of the class JButton to the content pane of a JFrame by using the method add. You will later see that you can also add buttons to other GUI objects in a similar way.

Example (within a constructor for a class called ButtonDemo):

```
public ButtonDemo( )
{
        .
        .
        .
    Container contentPane = getContentPane( );
        .
        .
        .
    contentPane.setLayout(new FlowLayout( ));
        .
        .
        .
    JButton stopButton = new JButton("Red");
        .
        .
        .
    contentPane.add(stopButton);
        .
        .
        .
}
```

Remember: **The Close-Window Button Is Not in the Class JButton**

The buttons that you add to a GUI are all objects of the class JButton. The close-window button (which you get automatically in any derived class of the class JFrame) is not an object of the class JButton. It is part of the JFrame object.

FAQ: Why Do So Many Class Names Start with "J"?

"J" for "Java." Right? Well, yes, but that is not the whole story. Why not name the classes `Frame`, `Label`, `Button`, and so forth, instead of names like `JFrame`, `JLabel`, and `JButton`, respectively? The answer is that the AWT, the precursor of Swing, already has classes named `Frame`, `Label`, `Button`, and so forth. Since Swing does not completely replace the AWT library, you must use the AWT together with Swing, and thus Swing class names should be different from AWT class names. Therefore, in Swing, the corresponding classes are named `JFrame`, `JLabel`, `JButton`, and so forth.

Action Listeners and Action Events

Clicking a button by using your mouse (or activating certain other items in a GUI) creates an object known as an event and sends the object to another object (or objects) known as the listener(s). This procedure is called firing the event. The listener then performs some action. When we say that the event is "sent" to the listener object, what we really mean is that some method in the listener object is invoked with the event object as the argument. This invocation happens automatically. Your Swing GUI class definition will not normally contain an invocation of this method. However, your Swing GUI class definition does need to do two things: First, for each button, it needs to specify what object(s) are listeners that will respond to events fired by that button; this step is called **registering** the listener. Second, it must define the method(s) that will be invoked when the event is sent to the listener. Note that these methods will be defined by you, but in normal circumstances, you will never write an invocation of these methods. The invocations will take place automatically.

registering a listener

The following line from Display 12.14 registers `this` as a listener to receive events from the button named `stopButton`:

addAction-Listener

```
stopButton.addActionListener(this);
```

A similar statement also registers `this` as a listener to receive events from the button named `goButton`. Because the argument is `this`, the statement means that `this` (the class `ButtonDemo` itself) is the listener class. Recall that, within the definition of a class, an object of that class is called `this`. Thus, the class `ButtonDemo` is itself the listener class for the buttons inside of `ButtonDemo`. (To be a bit more precise, each object of the class `ButtonDemo` is the listener for the buttons in that object.) Next, we explain how to make a class, such as `ButtonDemo`, into a listener class for events fired by buttons.

*action event
action listener*

Different kinds of components require different kinds of listener classes to handle the events they fire. A button fires events known as **action events,** which are handled by listeners known as **action listeners.**

Action-Listener

An action listener is an object of type `ActionListener`. `ActionListener` is not a class, but is a property that you can give to any class you define. (These properties, such as `ActionListener`, are known as interfaces and are discussed in more detail later in this chapter.)[1] To make a class into an `ActionListener`, you need to do two things:

---

1. Interfaces were also discussed in an optional section of Chapter 7. You do not need to have read that optional section in order to understand this chapter.

1. add the phrase `implements ActionListener` to the beginning of the class definition, normally at the end of the first line;

2. define a method named `actionPerformed`.

In Display 12.14, we made the `JFrame` class named `ButtonDemo` into an `Action-Listener` in just this way. We reproduce an outline of the definition of the class `Button-Demo` as follows (with the omitted sections indicated by three dots):

```
public class ButtonDemo extends JFrame implements ActionListener
{
      .
      .
      .
    public void actionPerformed(ActionEvent e)
    {
          .
          .
          .
    }
      .
      .
      .
}
```

We could have defined a separate class that did nothing but handle button events, but it's more convenient to make the window class `ButtonDemo` into the `ActionListener` that will handle button events. This approach is convenient because the button events are supposed to change the window, and the easiest way to change a window is by using a method within the window itself.

Suppose that we create an object, `buttonGui`, of the class `ButtonDemo` as follows:

```
ButtonDemo buttonGui = new ButtonDemo( );
```

■ DISPLAY 12.15 **Buttons and an Action Listener**

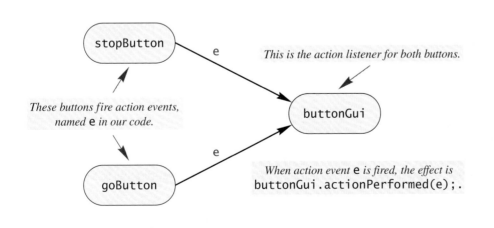

Now the `this` parameter in the definition of the class `ButtonDemo` refers to `buttonGui`. So `buttonGui` is the action listener for the two buttons inside of `buttonGui`. When a button is clicked, the method `actionPerformed` will automatically be invoked with the event fired by the button as the argument to `actionPerformed`. All that is left to explain is how the method `actionPerformed` works. The interaction of buttons and the listener is diagrammed in Display 12.15. Let's continue with the explanation of our object `buttonGui` of the class `ButtonDemo`.

If you click one of the buttons inside of `buttonGui`, using your mouse, an action event is sent to the action listener for that button. But `buttonGui` is the action listener for the buttons in `buttonGui`, so the action event goes to `buttonGui`. When an action listener receives an action event, the event is automatically passed to the method `actionPerformed`. The method `actionPerformed` is typically a branching statement that determines what kind of action event was fired and then performs some appropriate action. Let's look at the code for the method `actionPerformed` in the class `ButtonDemo` in Display 12.14. For convenience, we reproduce the definition as follows:

```
public void actionPerformed(ActionEvent e)
{
    Container contentPane = getContentPane( );

    if (e.getActionCommand( ).equals("Red"))
        contentPane.setBackground(Color.RED);
    else if (e.getActionCommand( ).equals("Green"))
        contentPane.setBackground(Color.GREEN);
    else
        System.out.println("Error in button interface.");
}
```

In this case, the method `actionPerformed` needs to know whether the action event came from the button labeled `"Red"` or the button labeled `"Green"`. If `e` is an action event that was fired by clicking a button, then `e.getActionCommand( )` returns the string written on the button; in this case, it returns either `"Red"` or `"Green"`. So all that the method `actionPerformed` needs to do is to see whether `e.getActionCommand( )` is `"Red"` or `"Green"` and perform the appropriate action for that button. Note that `e.getActionCommand( )` is an object of the class `String`. The class `String` has a method `equals` that can be used to check whether `e.getActionCommand( )` is equal to `"Red"` or `"Green"` (or any other string). The method invocation

getAction-
Command

```
e.getActionCommand( ).equals(String_Argument)
```

This text continues after the Quick Reference.

Quick Reference: **Action Events and Action Listeners**

Buttons, and certain other components, fire events in the class `ActionEvent`. These events are known as **action events** and must be handled by an action listener. Any class can be an action-listener class. The details in outline form are as follows:

1. Make some class (maybe a window class) into an action listener by adding the phrase

```
implements ActionListener
```

to the heading of the class definition and adding a definition for a method named action-Performed. The action listener can be any class. In particular, the class may serve some other function besides being an action listener.

2. Register the ActionListener object with the button (or other component that will fire the action event). To do this step, you use the method addActionListener. A button or other component may register more than (or fewer than) one listener.

Example (The complete details are in Display 12.14):

```java
public class ButtonDemo extends JFrame implements ActionListener
{
            .
            .
            .
    public ButtonDemo( )
    {
            .
            .
            .
        Container contentPane = getContentPane( );
            .
            .
            .
        JButton stopButton = new JButton("Red");
        stopButton.addActionListener(this);
        contentPane.add(stopButton);
            .
            .
            .
    }
    public void actionPerformed(ActionEvent e)
    {
            .
            .
            .
    }
}
```

Continuation of text from page 748

returns true if e.getActionCommand( ) is equal to the *String_Argument* and false otherwise. Thus, the following code tests to see whether e.getActionCommand( ) is equal to "Red" or "Green" and changes the color of the GUI accordingly:

```java
if (e.getActionCommand( ).equals("Red"))
    contentPane.setBackground(Color.RED);
else if (e.getActionCommand( ).equals("Green"))
    contentPane.setBackground(Color.GREEN);
else
    System.out.println("Error in button interface.");
```

The final `else` clause should never need to be executed. It is just there so that we would get a warning if we made some unnoticed mistake in the code.

Quick Reference: **The `actionPerformed` Method**

In order to be an action listener, a class must, among other things, have a method named `action-Performed` that has one parameter of type `ActionEvent`. This is the only method required by the `ActionListener` interface.

Syntax:

```
public void actionPerformed(ActionEvent e)
{
    Code_for_Actions_Performed
}
```

The *Code_for_Actions_Performed* is typically a branching statement that depends on some property of e. Often, the branching statement depends on `e.getActionCommand( )`. If e is an event fired by clicking a button, then `e.getActionCommand( )` is a string known as the **action command**. The action command is the string written on the button, unless you specify a different action command.

(You can specify a different action command with the method `setActionCommand`. For details, see the Java Tip entitled "Use the Method `setActionCommand`," later in this chapter.)

Example:

```
public void actionPerformed(ActionEvent e)
{
    Container contentPane = getContentPane( );

    if (e.getActionCommand( ).equals("Red"))
        contentPane.setBackground(Color.RED);
    else if (e.getActionCommand( ).equals("Green"))
        contentPane.setBackground(Color.GREEN);
    else
        System.out.println("Error in button interface.");
}
```

▲ *Gotcha*

Changing the Parameter List for `actionPerformed`

When you make a class into an action listener, the header for the method `actionPer-formed` is determined for you. It must have exactly one parameter, and that parameter must be of type `ActionEvent`, as in the following line:

```
public void actionPerformed(ActionEvent e)
```

If you change the type of the parameter or if you add (or subtract) a parameter, you will not have given a correct definition of an action listener.[2] The only thing you can change is the name of the parameter e, since it is just a placeholder. So the following change is acceptable:

```
public void actionPerformed(ActionEvent theEvent)
```

Of course, if you make this change, then inside the body of the method actionPerformed, you will use the identifier theEvent in place of the identifier e. △

Interfaces

Look again at Display 12.14. We want the class ButtonDemo to be both a JFrame and an ActionListener. But ButtonDemo can be derived from only one base class, so we made it a derived class of the class JFrame. This means that ActionListener must serve a similar, but not identical, function to that of the base class JFrame. ActionListener is not a class, but an interface. An **interface** is a property of a class that states what methods the class must have. A class such as ButtonDemo that satisfies an interface is said to **implement the interface.**

We discussed interfaces in the optional section of Chapter 7 entitled "Interfaces." Since the material is now no longer optional, we will present some of it a gain here.

Although an interface is not a class, it is a type. For example, a method can have a parameter of type ActionListener. Then, any class that implements the ActionListener interface can be an argument to that method.

In order to implement an interface, a class must do two things:

1. It must include the phrase

   ```
   implements Interface_Name
   ```

   at the start of the class definition. To implement more than one interface, just list all the interface names, separated by commas, as in

   ```
   implements MyInterface, YourInterface
   ```

2. The class must implement all the method headings listed in the definition(s) of the interface(s).

To implement the ActionListener interface, a class definition must contain the phrase implements ActionListener at the start of the method definition—for example,

```
public class ButtonDemo extends JFrame
                        implements ActionListener
{
```

---

2. Although it would be rather questionable style, you can overload the method name actionPerformed so you have multiple versions of the method actionPerformed, each with a different parameter list. But only the foregoing version of actionPerformed has anything to do with making a class into an action listener.

The class must also implement a method with the heading

```
public void actionPerformed(ActionEvent e)
```

For a complete example of the implementing on of an interface, see Display 12.14.

You can define your own interfaces. We will have no need to do so in this text, but if you want to see how it is done, read the optional section "Interfaces" in Chapter 7.

■ **Java Tip**
Code a GUI's Look and Actions Separately

You can simplify writing the code for a Swing GUI by dividing the work into two major parts: coding what the GUI looks like on the screen and coding the actions of the GUI. For example, consider the program in Display 12.14. Your first version of this program might use the following definition of the method `actionPerformed`:

```
public void actionPerformed(ActionEvent e)
{}
```

With this "do nothing" version of the method `actionPerformed`, your program will run and will display a window on the screen, just as shown in Display 12.14. If you click either of the two color-change buttons, nothing will happen, but you can use this phase of coding to adjust details, such as which button is listed first. (Note, however, that the close-window button does work.) After you get the GUI to look the way you want it to look, you can define the action parts of the GUI, typically the method `actionPerformed`. As stated previously, this approach breaks the task of coding the Swing GUI into two smaller tasks: coding its appearance and coding its actions. In this case, that may not seem like a big deal, but on a complicated Swing GUI, each of these two tasks can be formidable, but reasonable, while coding the entire GUI as one piece can be maddeningly difficult. In such cases, dividing the work into two parts can be a great help.

If you include the phrase `implements ActionListener` at the start of your `JFrame` definition, then you must include some definition of the method `action-Performed`. A "do nothing" or "do little" method definition, such as

```
public void actionPerformed(ActionEvent e)
{}
```

stub

is often called a **stub.** Using stubs is a good programming technique in many contexts, not just in Swing programs.

Alternatively, when writing your first version of a Swing GUI like the one in Display 12.14, you could omit the definition of the method `actionPerformed` completely, *provided that you also omit the phrase* `implements ActionListener` *and omit the invocations of* `addActionListener`. ■

The Model–View–Controller Pattern

The technique we advocated in the previous Java Tip is an example of a general technique known as the **Model–View–Controller** pattern. Display 12.16 gives a diagram of this pattern. The Model part of the pattern performs the heart of the application. The View part is the output part; it displays a picture of the Model's state. The Controller is the input part; it relays commands from the user to the Model. Each of the three interacting parts is realized as an object with responsibility for its own tasks. In a simple task such as implementing the JFrame in Display 12.14, you can have a single object with different methods in order to realize each of the roles Model, View, and Controller.

We have presented the Model–View–Controller pattern as if the user interacts directly with the Controller. That was done primarily to simplify the discussion. The Controller need not be under the direct control of the user, but could be controlled by some kind of software or hardware component. In a Swing GUI, the View and Controller parts might be separate classes combined into one larger class that displays a single window which allows both parts to interact with the user.

■ **Java Tip**

Use the Method `setActionCommand`

As we mentioned previously, clicking a button by using your mouse causes an event e, known as an action event, to be fired. This event e normally goes to the method `actionPerformed` of the action listener(s) for that button. The method `action-Performed` needs to find out what button was clicked when it gets the event e. When discussing the class `ButtonDemo` in Display 12.14, we said that the method invocation `e.getActionCommand( )` returns the string written on the button. That was a slightly simplified explanation. In reality, the invocation `e.getActionCommand( )` returns a string known as the **action command** for the button. The default action command is the string written on the button, but if you want to, you can specify that a different string be the action command for a button.

action command

For example, in Display 12.14, we created the `stopButton` as follows:

```java
JButton stopButton = new JButton("Red");
```

If we do nothing more, the action command for the `stopButton` will be `"Red"`. However, if you want, you can change the action command to some other string, such as `"Stop"` You would do so as follows:

setAction-Command

```java
stopButton.setActionCommand("Stop");
```

The method `actionPerformed` would then check for the string `"Stop"` rather than the string `"Red"`. A rewritten version of the class `ButtonDemo` that uses `setActionCommand` can be found in the file `SetActionCommandDemo.java` on the accompanying CD.

Extra code on CD

You may eventually find yourself in a situation in which you want the same string written on two different buttons. In such a case, you can distinguish the two buttons by using `setActionCommand` to give them different action commands. ■

■ DISPLAY 12.16 **The Model-View-Controller Pattern**

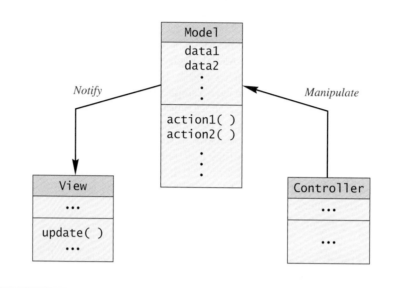

Quick Reference: `setActionCommand` and `getActionCommand`

Every button (and every other object that fires action events) has a string associated with it that is known as the **action command** for that button. When the button is clicked, it fires an action event e. The following invocation returns the action command for the button that fired e:

```
e.getActionCommand( )
```

The method `actionPerformed` typically uses this action-command string to decide which button was clicked.

The default action command for a button is the string written on the button, but if you want, you can change the action command with an invocation of the method `setActionCommand`. For example, the following code will write the string `"Red"` on the JButton named `stopButton`, but will make the string `"Stop"` the action command for the button `stopButton`:

Example:

```
JButton stopButton = new JButton("Red");
stopButton.setActionCommand("Stop");
```

FAQ: Where Is the Action Command Stored?

The action command for a button is stored in a private instance variable of the button and in a private instance variable of any event the button fires. So the methods `getActionCommand` and `setActionCommand` are accessor and mutator methods, respectively.

? Self-Test Questions

22. What kind of listener do you need for a button component? How do you create such a listener?

23. Consider the following code from Display 12.14:

```
contentPane.setLayout(new FlowLayout( ));

JButton stopButton = new JButton("Red");
stopButton.addActionListener(this);
contentPane.add(stopButton);

JButton goButton = new JButton("Green");
goButton.addActionListener(this);
contentPane.add(goButton);
```

Can you replace this code with the following without changing the meaning?

```
contentPane.setLayout(new FlowLayout( ));

JButton b = new JButton("Red");
b.addActionListener(this);
contentPane.add(b);

b = new JButton("Green");
b.addActionListener(this);
contentPane.add(b);
```

In other words, can you use only the one name, b, even though there are two buttons?

24. The method `actionPerformed` in Display 12.14 contains the following line:

```
Container contentPane = getContentPane( );
```

Does the content pane have to be named `contentPane`, or could it be named something else, as in the following:

```
Container insideOfJFrame = getContentPane( );
```

25. What does it mean when we say that an event is "sent" to a listener object?

26. What would the effect be on the program in Display 12.14 if we replaced the e with the identifier `buttonEvent` as follows?

```
public void actionPerformed(ActionEvent buttonEvent)
{
    Container contentPane = getContentPane( );

    if (buttonEvent.getActionCommand( ).equals("Red"))
        contentPane.setBackground(Color.RED);
    else if (buttonEvent.getActionCommand( ).equals("Green"))
        contentPane.setBackground(Color.GREEN);
```

```
                        else
                            System.out.println("Error in button interface.");
        }
```

12.4 CONTAINER CLASSES

Fill all the glasses there, for why
Should every creature drink but I,
Why, man of mortals, tell me why? -Abraham Cowley, *Anacreon*

When you use Swing to make a GUI such as the windows we have been defining, you build new classes for the GUI out of already existing classes. There are two principal ways to build new GUI classes out of old classes. One way is to use inheritance. For example, to build a window interface, you normally use the Swing class `JFrame` and make your window a derived class of `JFrame`. The second way to make new classes out of old classes is to use one of the Swing classes as a **container** and to place components in the container. For example, in the class `ButtonDemo` (Display 12.14), we added a button to the window as follows:

container

```
        JButton stopButton = new JButton("Red");
            ...
        contentPane.add(stopButton);
```

You do not choose between these two ways of building a GUI. In almost all cases, you use both techniques when you define a GUI class.

In this section, we will look at the class `JPanel`, which is often used to define subparts of a window. We then go on to discuss the general properties of all container classes, such as `JPanel` and the content pane of `JFrame`.

The `JPanel` Class

A GUI is often organized in a hierarchical fashion, with windowlike containers inside of other windowlike containers. In this section, we introduce a new class that facilitates this organization. The class `JPanel` is a very simple container class that does little more than group objects. It is one of the simplest container classes, but one that you will use frequently. A `JPanel` object is analogous to the braces used to combine a number of simpler Java statements into a single larger Java statement. It groups smaller objects, such as buttons and labels, into a larger component (the `JPanel`). You can then put the `JPanel` object in the content pane of a `JFrame`. Thus, one of the main functions of `JPanel` objects is to subdivide a `JFrame` into different areas. These `JPanel` objects are often simply called **panels**.

panel

The judicious use of panels can affect the arrangement of components in a window as much as the choice of a layout manager can. For example, when you use a `BorderLayout` manager, you can place components in each of the five locations `BorderLayout.NORTH`, `BorderLayout.SOUTH`, `BorderLayout.EAST`, `BorderLayout.WEST`, and `BorderLayout.CENTER`. But what if you want to put two components at the bottom of the screen, in the `BorderLayout.SOUTH` position? To do this, you would put the two components in a panel and then place the panel in the `BorderLayout.SOUTH` position.

JPanel

■ DISPLAY 12.17 Putting the Buttons in a Panel *(Part 1 of 2)*

```java
import javax.swing.*;
import java.awt.*;
import java.awt.event.*;

/**
 Simple demonstration of putting buttons in a panel.
*/
public class PanelDemo extends JFrame implements ActionListener
{
    public static final int WIDTH = 300;
    public static final int HEIGHT = 200;

    public static void main(String[] args)
    {
        PanelDemo guiWithPanel = new PanelDemo( );
        guiWithPanel.setVisible(true);
    }

    public PanelDemo( )
    {
        setSize(WIDTH, HEIGHT);
        addWindowListener(new WindowDestroyer( ));
        setTitle("Panel Demonstration");
        Container contentPane = getContentPane( );
        contentPane.setBackground(Color.BLUE);
        contentPane.setLayout(new BorderLayout( ));

        JPanel buttonPanel = new JPanel( );
        buttonPanel.setBackground(Color.WHITE);

        buttonPanel.setLayout(new FlowLayout( ));

        JButton stopButton = new JButton("Red");
        stopButton.setBackground(Color.RED);
        stopButton.addActionListener(this);
        buttonPanel.add(stopButton);

        JButton goButton = new JButton("Green");
        goButton.setBackground(Color.GREEN);
        goButton.addActionListener(this);
        buttonPanel.add(goButton);

        contentPane.add(buttonPanel, BorderLayout.SOUTH);
    }
```

■ DISPLAY 12.17   **Putting the Buttons in a Panel** *(Part 2 of 2)*

```
public void actionPerformed(ActionEvent e)
{
    Container contentPane = getContentPane( );

    if (e.getActionCommand( ).equals("Red"))
        contentPane.setBackground(Color.RED);
    else if (e.getActionCommand( ).equals("Green"))
        contentPane.setBackground(Color.GREEN);
    else
        System.out.println("Error in button interface.");
}
}
```

Resulting GUI

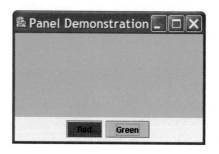

Display 12.17 contains a slight variation of the program in Display 12.14. In Display 12.17, we have placed the buttons in a panel, called `buttonPanel`, so that the portion of the window with the buttons does not change color when the rest of the window changes color. As was true for the program in Display 12.14, when you click the `"Red"` button in the GUI in Display 12.17, the window's color changes to red, and similarly, the color changes to green when you click the `"Green"` button. But here the buttons are in a separate panel that is white and that does not change color. As you can see, you use a layout manager and the method `add` with a `JPanel` object in exactly the same way that you use them with the content pane of a `JFrame`. First, you use `add` to place the buttons in the panel, as in the following example:

```
buttonPanel.add(stopButton);
```

Then you use `add` to place the `JPanel` in the `JFrame` as follows:

```
contentPane.add(buttonPanel, BorderLayout.SOUTH);
```

Note that the content pane (contentPane) and the panel (buttonPanel) each have their own layout manager.

Be sure to notice that you add things to a JFrame and to a JPanel in slightly different ways. With a JFrame, you first get the content pane with getContentPane, and then you use the method add with the content pane. With a JPanel, you use the method add directly with the JPanel object. There is no content pane to worry about with a JPanel.

Notice how the action listeners are set up. Each button registers the this parameter as a listener, as in the following line:

```
stopButton.addActionListener(this);
```

Because this line appears inside of the constructor for the class PanelDemo, the this parameter refers to PanelDemo, which is the entire window interface. Thus, the entire window container is the listener, not the JPanel. (Remember that PanelDemo is the window with the JPanel. It is not the JPanel itself.) So when you click the button labeled "Red", it is the background of the bigger window that turns red. The panel with the buttons always stays white.

Note that, because it is the PanelDemo class that is the listener for button-clicking events, it is PanelDemo that implements ActionListener and has the method actionPerformed.

Display 12.17 also introduces one other small, but new, technique. In addition to giving colors to the panel and the content pane, we also gave each button a color. We did this with the method setBackground, using basically the same technique that we used in previous examples. You can give a button or almost any other item a color by using setBackground.

You can use the method add to add one JPanel to another JPanel, and each JPanel can have a different layout manager. By building a a hierarchy of panels in this way, you can create almost any arrangement of components inside of a GUI.

hierarchies of panels

Quick Reference: The JPanel Class

A JPanel object groups smaller objects, such as buttons and labels, into a larger component (the JPanel). The JPanel object is then typically added to the content pane of a JFrame (or to another JPanel). Thus, one of the main functions of JPanel objects is to subdivide a JFrame into different areas.

The Container Class

There is a predefined class called Container. Any descendant class of the class Container can have components added to it (or, more precisely, can have components added to objects of the class). The class JFrame is a descendant class of the class Container, so any descendant class of the class JFrame can serve as a container to hold labels, buttons, panels, or other components.

Container

Similarly, the class JPanel is a descendant of the class Container, and any object of the class JPanel can serve as a container to hold labels, buttons, other panels, or other components. Display 12.18 shows a portion of the Swing hierarchy as well as some of the classes in the AWT library. Note that the Container class is in the AWT library, not in the Swing library. This is not a major issue, but it does mean that you need to import the AWT package when using the Container class. So any class definition that contains a reference to the class Container must contain the following import statement:

```
import java.awt.*;
```

container-class
component

A **container class** is any descendant class of the class Container. The class JComponent serves a similar role for components. Any descendant class of the class JComponent is called a JComponent, or, sometimes more simply, a **component.** (See Display 12.18.) You can add any JComponent object to any container-class object.

Note that the class JComponent is derived from the class Container, so you can add a JComponent to another JComponent. Sometimes, this will turn out to be a good idea, and sometimes it is something to avoid. We will discuss the different cases as we go along. The classes Component, Frame, and Window are AWT classes that some readers may have heard of. We include them in Display 12.18 for reference value, but we will have no need for these classes. We will eventually discuss all the other classes shown in Display 12.18.

Quick Reference: Container Classes

A **container class** is any descendant class of the class Container. In particular, any descendant class of the classes JFrame or JPanel is a container class, because these two classes are descendants of the class Container. Every container class can have items added to it, such as labels, buttons, panels, and so forth. The items are added in one of two ways, depending on the particular container class:

1. For a JFrame object, you add items by using the method getContentPane to obtain the content pane and then using add with the content pane as the calling object.

2. For all other container classes discussed in this book, you add items simply by using the add method directly with an object of the container class.

Quick Reference: The add Method

Every Swing container class has a method called add. You can use the method add to add any JComponent object, whether predefined or defined by you, to the container class. In the case of a JFrame, you must first use the method getContentPane to obtain the content pane and then use the method add with the content pane as the calling object.

Remember: Abstract Classes

If you look at Display 12.18, you will see that some of the classes are abstract classes. An **abstract class** is a kind of class that is used solely to simplify your thinking. You do not—in fact, you cannot—directly create objects of an abstract class. You can only derive new classes, using the abstract class as the base class. Abstract classes are discussed in Chapter 7.

■ DISPLAY 12.18 **Hierarchy of Swing Classes**

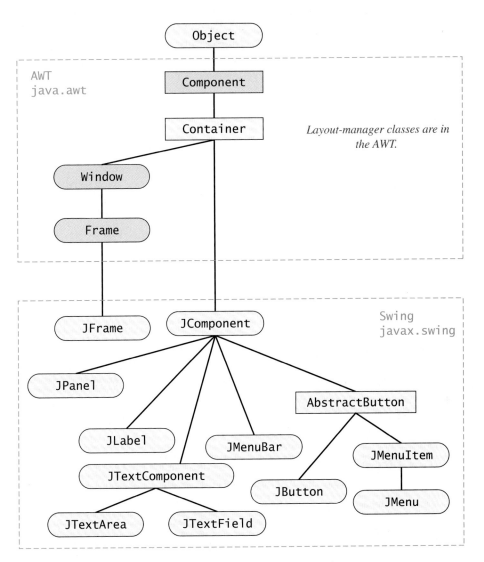

If there is a line between two classes, then the lower class is a derived class of the higher class.

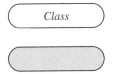 *Class* | *Abstract Class*

This color shading indicates a class that is not used in this text, but is included here for reference. If you have not heard of any of the shaded classes, you can safely ignore them.

layout
manager

When you are dealing with a Swing container class, you have three kinds of objects to deal with: the container class itself (probably some sort of panel or windowlike object); the components you add to the container (like labels, buttons, and panels); and a layout manager, which positions the components inside the container. You have seen examples of these three kinds of objects in almost every JFrame class we have defined. Almost every complete GUI interface you build, and many subparts of the GUIs you build, will be made up of these three kinds of objects.

■ **Java Tip**
Guide for Creating Simple Window Interfaces

Most simple windowing GUIs follow a pattern that is easy to learn and that will get you started with Swing. Here is an outline of some of the main points you've seen so far:

1. A typical GUI consists of some windowing object that is derived from the class JFrame and that contains a number of components, such as labels and buttons.

2. When the user clicks the close-window button, the window should close, but this will not happen correctly unless your program registers a window listener to close the window. One way to accomplish this task is to add the following line to the GUI class definition within a constructor definition:

   ```
   addWindowListener(new WindowDestroyer());
   ```

   You can use the definition of WindowDestroyer given in Display 12.4.

3. You can group components together by placing the components in a JPanel and adding the JPanel to the GUI.

4. The GUI (that is, the JFrame) and each JPanel in the GUI should be given a layout manager, using the method setLayout.

5. If any of the components, such as a button, generate action events, you need to make the GUI (or some other class) an action listener. Every component that generates an action event should have an action listener registered with it. You register an action listener with the method addActionListener.

6. To make your windowing GUI (or other class) into an action listener, you need to add the following line to the beginning of the class definition:

   ```
   implements ActionListener
   ```

   You also need to add a definition of the method actionPerformed to the class.

Following these guidelines is not the only way to create a GUI window class, but it is a simple and common way to do it, and it is basically the only way you've learned so far. ■

FAQ: **When Do You Need to Use** `getContentPane?`

You add items to a `JFrame` by using a combination of `getContentPane` and `add`, as in the following code:

```
Container contentPane = getContentPane( );
JLabel label = new JLabel("Please don't click that button!");
contentPane.add(label);
```

However, with a `JPanel`, you do not use `getContentPane`, but instead use the method `add` directly with the `JPanel` object, as illustrated in the following code:

```
JPanel buttonPanel = new JPanel( );
    . . .
JButton stopButton = new JButton("Red");
    . . .
buttonPanel.add(stopButton);
```

With `JFrame` objects (and certain other objects not discussed in this text), you need to use the method `getContentPane` to get the content pane of the `JFrame` object and then use the method `add` with the content pane as the calling object. With all other container classes discussed in this text, you use the method `add` directly with an object of the container class and do not use a content pane.

? Self-Test Questions

27. When adding components to a `JFrame`, do you need to use `getContentPane`? When adding components to a `JPanel`, do you need to use `getContentPane`?

28. What kind of listener do you need for a `JButton` component? How do you create such a listener?

29. What do the classes `WindowDestroyer` (Display 12.4) and `ButtonDemo` (Display 12.14) have in common?

30. What is the type for the object returned when you invoke `getContentPane` with a `JFrame` object, and what `import` statement do you need in order to use this type name?

31. What `import` statement do you need in order to use the layout-manager classes?

32. Is an object of the class `JPanel` a container class? Is it a component class?

33. How does a `FlowLayout` manager arrange components in a container?

34. How does a `BorderLayout` manager arrange components in a container?

35. Suppose you are using a `BorderLayout` manager, and you want to put two buttons in the region `BorderLayout.NORTH`. How do you do this?

36. How does a `GridLayout` manager arrange components in a container?

37. Suppose you give `aContainer` a layout manager as follows:

    ```
    aContainer.setLayout(new GridLayout(2, 3));
    ```

    How many components can you add to `aContainer`? (Count adding a `JPanel` as adding just one object, even if the `JPanel` contains multiple components.)

38. With a `GridLayout` manager, you cannot leave any grid element empty, but you can do something that will make a grid element look empty to the user. What can you do?

39. You are used to defining derived classes of the Swing class `JFrame`. You can also define derived classes of other Swing classes. Define a derived class of the class `JPanel` that is called `PinkJPanel`. An object of the class `PinkJPanel` can be used just as we use objects of the class `JPanel`, but an object of the class `PinkJPanel` is pink in color (unless you explicitly change its color). The class `PinkJPanel` will have only one constructor, namely the default constructor. (*Hint*: This exercise is very easy.)

12.5 TEXT I/O FOR GUIS

Polonius: *What do you read my lord?*
Hamlet: *Words, words, words.* -William Shakespeare, *Hamlet*

In this section, we show you how to add text input and text output to your Swing GUIs.

Text Areas and Text Fields

The GUI in Display 12.12 has some text in the window, but it is static text. Neither the user nor the program can change the text. Display 12.19 contains a program that produces a GUI with a text area in which the user can type any text she or he wishes. That text is then saved as a memo that can be recalled later. In this simple example, the user is allowed only two memos, but that is good enough to illustrate how a text area is created and used. The area in the center, colored white, is an object of the class `JTextArea`. The user can type any sort of text into this `JTextArea`. If the user clicks the `"Save Memo 1"` button, the text is saved as memo 1. If the user clicks the `"Save Memo 2"` button, the text is saved as memo 2. Either memo can be called back to the `JTextArea` by clicking one of the buttons `"Get Memo 1"` or `"Get Memo 2"`, respectively. The `JTextArea` can be cleared by clicking the `"Clear"` button. Let's look at how the program implements this functionality.

The buttons created in Display 12.19 are put in a `JPanel`, and then that `JPanel` is put in the `JFrame`, just as in Display 12.17. The `JTextArea` is set up using the following code, which appears in the constructor definition in Display 12.19:

JTextArea

```
JPanel textPanel = new JPanel();
textPanel.setBackground(Color.BLUE);
theText = new JTextArea(LINES, CHAR_PER_LINE);
theText.setBackground(Color.WHITE);
textPanel.add(theText);
contentPane.add(textPanel, BorderLayout.CENTER);
```

■ DISPLAY 12.19 A GUI with a Text Area *(Part 1 of 2)*

There is a demonstration main in part 2 of this display.

```java
import javax.swing.*;
import java.awt.*;
import java.awt.event.*;

public class MemoSaver extends JFrame implements ActionListener
{
    public static final int WIDTH = 600;
    public static final int HEIGHT = 300;
    public static final int LINES = 10;
    public static final int CHAR_PER_LINE = 40;

    private JTextArea theText;
    private String memo1 = "No Memo 1.";
    private String memo2 = "No Memo 2.";

    public MemoSaver()
    {
        setSize(WIDTH, HEIGHT);
        addWindowListener(new WindowDestroyer());
        setTitle("Memo Saver");
        Container contentPane = getContentPane();
        contentPane.setLayout(new BorderLayout());

        JPanel buttonPanel = new JPanel();
        buttonPanel.setBackground(Color.WHITE);
        buttonPanel.setLayout(new FlowLayout());
        JButton memo1Button = new JButton("Save Memo 1");
        memo1Button.addActionListener(this);
        buttonPanel.add(memo1Button);
        JButton memo2Button = new JButton("Save Memo 2");
        memo2Button.addActionListener(this);
        buttonPanel.add(memo2Button);
        JButton clearButton = new JButton("Clear");
        clearButton.addActionListener(this);
        buttonPanel.add(clearButton);
        JButton get1Button = new JButton("Get Memo 1");
        get1Button.addActionListener(this);
        buttonPanel.add(get1Button);
        JButton get2Button = new JButton("Get Memo 2");
        get2Button.addActionListener(this);
        buttonPanel.add(get2Button);
        contentPane.add(buttonPanel, BorderLayout.SOUTH);

        JPanel textPanel = new JPanel();
        textPanel.setBackground(Color.BLUE);
```

If you get memo 1 before you set memo 1, you get the message "No Memo 1."

■ DISPLAY 12.19 **A GUI with a Text Area** *(Part 2 of 2)*

```java
            theText = new JTextArea(LINES, CHAR_PER_LINE);
            theText.setBackground(Color.WHITE);
            textPanel.add(theText);
            contentPane.add(textPanel, BorderLayout.CENTER);
        }
        public void actionPerformed(ActionEvent e)
        {
            String actionCommand = e.getActionCommand();
            if (actionCommand.equals("Save Memo 1"))
                memo1 = theText.getText();
            else if (actionCommand.equals("Save Memo 2"))
                memo2 = theText.getText();
            else if (actionCommand.equals("Clear"))
                theText.setText("");
            else if (actionCommand.equals("Get Memo 1"))
                theText.setText(memo1);
            else if (actionCommand.equals("Get Memo 2"))
                theText.setText(memo2);
            else
                theText.setText("Error in memo interface");
        }

    public static void main(String[] args)
    {
        MemoSaver guiMemo = new MemoSaver();
        guiMemo.setVisible(true);
    }
}
```

theText is an instance variable.

Resulting GUI

The object `theText` is a member of the class `JTextArea`. Note the arguments in the constructor for `JTextArea`. The arguments LINES, which is a defined constant for 10, and CHAR_PER_LINE, which is a defined constant for 40, say that the text area will be 10 lines from top to bottom and will allow at least 40 characters per line. If you type in more text than will fit in a text area of the size specified by the two arguments to the constructor, the results can be unpredictable. So it is best to make these numbers large enough to accommodate the largest expected amount of text. (Problems concerning too much text can be handled by using the method `setLineWrap`, as described in the box at the end of this section, or by using scroll bars, as described in Chapter 14.)

We are using a `BorderLayout` manager. The `textPanel` is added to the `JFrame` in the `BorderLayout.CENTER` position. The `BorderLayout.CENTER` position always takes up all the `JFrame` room that is left. This much of our program sets up the look of the GUI, but we still need to discuss how the GUI handles writing in the text area.

The two memos are stored in the two instance variables `memo1` and `memo2`, both of type `String`. When the user clicks the "Save Memo 1" button, the text in the text area is saved as the value of the instance variable `memo1`. This task is done by the following code, which is the first three lines in the definition of the `actionPerformed` method:

getText

```
String actionCommand = e.getActionCommand( );
if (actionCommand.equals("Save Memo 1"))
    memo1 = theText.getText( );
```

Recall that the `getActionCommand` method returns the label of the button that is clicked. So this code says that if the button with the label "Save Memo 1" is clicked, the following code is executed:

```
memo1 = theText.getText( );
```

The method `getText( )` returns the text that is written in the object `theText` of the class `JTextArea`. In other words, it returns what the user typed into the text area. If you read further in the definition of the method `actionPerformed`, you will see that the second memo is stored in a similar way.

The memos are displayed in the text area, and the text area is cleared with the following clauses from the definition of the method `actionPerformed`:

setText

```
else if (actionCommand.equals("Clear"))
    theText.setText("");
else if (actionCommand.equals("Get Memo 1"))
    theText.setText(memo1);
else if (actionCommand.equals("Get Memo 2"))
    theText.setText(memo2);
```

The method `setText` of the class `JTextArea` changes the text in the text area into what is given as the argument to `setText`. Two quotes with nothing in between are given as the argument to `setText` in the second line of the preceding code. These two quotes denote the empty string and thereby produce a blank text area.

empty string

JTextField

The class JTextField (which is not used in Display 12.19) is very similar to the class JTextArea, except that the former displays only one line of text. It is useful for interfaces in which the user gives only a few characters of text, like a single number, the name of a file, or the name of a person. The constructor for JTextField takes one argument, which is the number of characters visible in the text field. The user can enter more characters, but only the specified number will be shown. So be sure to make the text field one or two characters longer than the longest string you expect to have entered into it.

initializing text

Both the classes JTextArea and JTextField can have some initial text contents specified when you use new to create an object. The initial text is a string given as the first argument to the constructor—for example,

```
JTextField inputOutputField = new JTextField("Hello User.", 20);
```

The text field inputOutputField will have room for 20 visible characters and will start out containing the text "Hello User."

Both of the classes JTextArea and JTextField have a constructor with no argument that sets the various parameters to some default values.

Quick Reference: **The Classes JTextArea and JTextField**

The classes JTextArea and JTextField can be used to add areas for changeable text to a GUI. An object of the class JTextArea has a size consisting of a specified number of lines and a specified number of characters per line. An object of the class JTextField has only one line that contains some specified number of characters. More text can be typed into a JTextArea or JTextField than is specified in its size, but the extra text is not visible.

Example (using JTextArea):

```
JPanel aPanel = new JPanel();
JTextArea someText = new JTextArea(10, 30);
aPanel.add(someText);
```

Example (using JTextField):

```
JPanel anotherPanel = new JPanel();
JTextField name = new JTextField(30);
anotherPanel.add(name);
```

Quick Reference: **Size of JTextField and JTextArea**

When you create an object of either of the classes JTextArea or JTextField, you specify the number of characters per line that will be displayed, as in the following examples, both of which specify 40 characters per line:

```
JTextField someText = new JTextField(40);
JTextArea someMoreText = new JTextArea(10, 40);
```

The number 40, in both of the foregoing lines, is not the size of just any 40 characters. That 40 represents 40 em spaces. An **em space** is the space need to hold one letter "m," which is the widest letter in the alphabet. So a line that is 40 wide, as in the foregoing examples, will always be able to hold at least 40 characters and, depending on the particular characters, may be able to hold more than 40 characters. (The 10 in the foregoing examples represents 10 lines. There is nothing more to explain about that number.)

Quick Reference: `getText` and `setText`

The classes `JTextArea` and `JTextField` both contain methods called `getText` and `setText`. The method `getText` can be used to retrieve the text written in the text area or text field. The method `setText` can be used to change the text written in the text area or text field.

Example (`theText` can be an object of the class `JTextArea` or an object of the class `JTextField`):

```
memo1 = theText.getText( );
theText.setText("Memo 1 saved.");
```

Quick Reference: Line Wrapping in Text Areas

You can set the line-wrapping policy for a `JTextArea` by using the method `setLineWrap`. The method takes one argument of type `boolean`. If the argument is `true`, then at the end of a line, any additional characters for that line will appear on the following line of the text area. If the argument is `false`, the extra characters will be on the same line and will not be visible.

Example:

If you add the following invocation of `setLineWrap` to the constructor in Display 12.19, then when the user types in more characters than can fit on a line, the extra characters will appear on the following line:

```
public MemoSaver( )
{
    ...
    theText.setLineWrap(true);
```

Quick Reference: Read-Only Text Components

You can specify that a `JTextField` or `JTextArea` cannot be written in by the user. To do so, use the method `setEditable`, which is a method in both the `JTextField` and `JTextArea` classes. If `theText` names an object in either of the classes `JTextField` or `JTextArea`, then

```
theText.setEditable(false);
```

will set `theText` so that only your GUI program can change the text in the text component `theText`; the user cannot change the text. After this invocation of `setEditable`, if the user clicks in the text component `theText` and then types at the keyboard, the text in `theText` will not change.

To reverse things and configure theText so that the user can edit the text in the text component, use true in place of false, as follows:

```
theText.setEditable(true);
```

If no invocation of setEditable is made, then the user *can* change the text in the text component.

Programming Example
Labeling a Text Field

Sometimes you want a label for a text field. For example, suppose the GUI asks for a name and an identification number and expects the user to enter this information in two text fields. In this case, the GUI needs to label the two text fields so that the user knows in which field to type the name and in which field to type the number. You can use an object of the class JLabel to label a text field or any other component in a Swing GUI.

Display 12.20 contains a program that shows how you can attach a label to a text field (or to any other component). You put both the text field and the label in a panel. You can then add the entire panel to a container. In Display 12.20, the highlighted code does just that.

The program in Display 12.20 is just a demonstration program and therefore does not do very much. If the user enters a name in the text field and clicks the "Test" button, the GUI gives an evaluation of the name. However, all names receive the same evaluation, namely, "A very good name!" So if the user enters a name and then clicks the "Test" button, the display will look like the GUI shown in Display 12.20. ∎

? Self-Test Questions

40. What is the difference between an object of the class JTextArea and an object of the class JTextField?

41. How would you change the program in Display 12.19 so that the buttons appear above the text area instead of below the text area?

42. Write a statement that will create a text field called name that has room for 30 visible characters and that starts out with the text "Your name here."

43. Change the definition of the method actionPerformed in Display 12.19 so that when the user saves the text as memo 1, the text area changes so that it says "Memo 1 saved.", and so that when memo 2 is saved, the text area changes to display "Memo 2 saved."

44. In Display 12.19, the instance variables memo1 and memo2 are of type String. An object of type String is a single string of characters. But the user can enter text that consists of multiple lines. Is something wrong? How can you get multiple lines in one String object?

■ DISPLAY 12.20   Labeling a Text Field *(Part 1 of 2)*

```java
import javax.swing.*;
import java.awt.*;
import java.awt.event.*;
/**
 Class to demonstrate placing a label on a text field.
*/
public class LabelDemo extends JFrame implements ActionListener
{
    public static final int WIDTH = 300;
    public static final int HEIGHT = 200;

    private JTextField name;

    public LabelDemo()
    {
        setTitle("Name Tester");
        setSize(WIDTH, HEIGHT);
        addWindowListener(new WindowDestroyer());
        Container content = getContentPane();
        content.setLayout(new GridLayout(2, 1));

        JPanel namePanel = new JPanel();
        namePanel.setLayout(new BorderLayout());
        namePanel.setBackground(Color.LIGHT_GRAY);

        name = new JTextField(20);
        namePanel.add(name, BorderLayout.SOUTH);
        JLabel nameLabel = new JLabel("Enter your name here:");
        namePanel.add(nameLabel, BorderLayout.CENTER);

        content.add(namePanel);

        JPanel buttonPanel = new JPanel();
        buttonPanel.setLayout(new FlowLayout());
        JButton b = new JButton("Test");
        b.addActionListener(this);
        buttonPanel.add(b);
        b = new JButton("Clear");
        b.addActionListener(this);
        buttonPanel.add(b);

        content.add(buttonPanel);
    }
```

■ DISPLAY 12.20 **Labeling a Text Field** *(Part 2 of 2)*

```java
    public void actionPerformed(ActionEvent e)
    {
        if (e.getActionCommand().equals("Test"))
            name.setText("A very good name!");
        else if (e.getActionCommand().equals("Clear"))
            name.setText("");
        else
            name.setText("Error in window interface.");
    }

    public static void main(String[] args)
    {
        LabelDemo w = new LabelDemo();
        w.setVisible(true);
    }
}
```

Resulting GUI

A label.

Inputting and Outputting Numbers

inputting
numbers

When you want to use a GUI constructed with Swing to input numbers, your GUI must convert input text to numbers. For example, when you input the number 42 in a `JTextArea` or `JTextField`, your program will receive the string `"42"`, not the number 42. Your program must convert the input string value `"42"` to the integer value 42. When you want to use a GUI constructed with Swing to output numbers, you must convert the numbers to a string and then output that string. For example, if you want to output the number 43, your program would convert the integer value 43 to the string value `"43"`. With Swing, all input typed by the user is string input, and all displayed output is string output.

Let's consider the input of numbers. Your program will need to convert a string, such as "42", to a number. The static method `parseInt` in the class `Integer` can accomplish the conversion. For example,

```
Integer.parseInt("42")
```

returns the integer 42. If these details do not make sense to you, you should review the subsection "`Integer`, `Double`, and Other Wrapper Classes" in Chapter 5.

Your GUI program can recover the input string with the method `getText`. So, for example, if the number is written in a `JTextField` named `inputOutputField`, then `inputOutputField.getText( )` would produce the input string. To change the input string to a number, you can use the following expression:

```
Integer.parseInt(inputOutputField.getText( ))
```

If there is any chance that the user might add extra whitespace before or after the input, you should add an invocation of the method `trim` to the string object `inputOutput-Field.getText( )`. Thus, a more robust way to obtain the number that was input would be the following (which adds an invocation of the method `trim`):

```
Integer.parseInt(inputOutputField.getText( ).trim( ))
```

trim

Once your program has this number, it can use it just as it can any other number. For example, to store this number in an `int` variable named n, the following assignment statement will work fine:

```
int n = Integer.parseInt(inputOutputField.getText( ).trim( ));
```

If you want to input numbers of type `double`, just use the class `Double` in place of the class `Integer`, and the method `parseDouble` in place of the method `parseInt`. For example, to store the number in `inputOutputField` in a `double` variable named x, the following assignment statement will work fine:

```
double x =
       Double.parseDouble(inputOutputField.getText( ).trim( ));
```

You can also do the analogous conversion with the classes `Long` and `Float`.

You should be able to understand and even write long expressions like

```
Integer.parseInt(stringObject.trim( ))
```

However, your code will be easier to read and write if you define a method to express this statement as a simple method invocation. The following is one such method:

```
private static int stringToInt(String stringObject)
{
    return Integer.parseInt(stringObject.trim( ));
}
```

stringTo-
Int method

Then an expression like

```
n = Integer.parseInt(inputOutputField.getText( ).trim( ));
```

can be expressed more clearly as

```
n = stringToInt(inputOutputField.getText( ));
```

If the method is to be merely a tool in some GUI class, it should be declared as private, because it has no use outside of the class. Alternatively, it could be part of a utility class with a number of different useful functions. In that case, it would make more sense to make it public.

outputting
numbers

To send an output number to a `JTextField` or `JTextArea` of a GUI, you use the static method `toString`. For example, suppose you have the number 43 stored in the `int` variable `sum`. You can convert this 43 to the string `"43"` as follows:

```
Integer.toString(sum)
```

We used the class `Integer` when invoking `toString` because we were dealing with integers. If, on the other hand, you have a variable `total` of type `double` and you want to convert the number in `total` to a string, you would use

```
Double.toString(total)
```

If you want the number in the `int` variable `sum` to appear in the `JTextField` named `inputOutputField`, you use `setText` as follows:

```
inputOutputField.setText(Integer.toString(sum));
```

These techniques for inputting and outputting numbers are illustrated in the next Programming Example.

Quick Reference: Inputting Numbers with a GUI

You can use Swing to design a GUI so that input can consist of a number typed into a text field (or text area). The following will return the number of type `int` that is typed into the text field (assuming that nothing other than the number and whitespace are typed into the text fields):

Syntax:

```
Integer.parseInt(Name_Of_Text_Field.getText( ).trim( ))
```

Example (that stores an `int` value in a variable n):

```
int n =
  Integer.parseInt(inputOutputField.getText( ).trim( ));
```

You can do the same thing for numbers of the types `double`, `float`, and `long`. Just use the class `Double`, `Float`, or `Long` in place of the class `Integer`, and use the method `parseDouble`, `parseFloat`, or `parseLong`, respectively, in place of the method `parseInt`.

Example (that stores a `double` value in a variable x):

```
double x =
  Double.parseDouble(inputOutputField.getText( ).trim( ));
```

Example:

You can also package these sorts of long formulas into methods, such as

```
private static double stringToDouble(String stringObject)
{
    return Double.parseDouble(stringObject.trim( ));
}
```

(Depending on where this method is defined and used, it might be either `public` or `private`.) You can use this method to shorten the previous example to

```
double x =
  stringToDouble(inputOutputField.getText());
```

Quick Reference: **Outputting Numbers with a GUI**

You can use Swing to design a GUI so that output consisting of a number (or numbers) is displayed in a text field (or text area). The following syntax will take a number in a variable and display the number in the text field the details are the same if you are working with a `JTextArea` rather than a `JTextField`:

Syntax:

> *Name_Of_Text_Field*.setText(*Wrapper_Class*.toString(*Variable*));

Examples:

```
inputOutputField.setText(Integer.toString(sum));
inputOutputField.setText(Double.toString(area));
```

You can do the same thing for numbers of the types `float` and `long`. Just use the class `Float` or `Long` in place of the class `Integer` or `Double`.

? Self-Test Questions

45. Write an expression to convert the `double` value `7.77` to the string `"7.77"`. Include it in an assignment statement that stores that string in the variable `s` of type `String`. (Use the techniques presented in the preceding subsection.)

46. Write an expression to convert the string `"3.14159"` to the `double` value `3.14159`. Include it in an assignment statement that stores that value in the variable `x` of type `double`. (Use the techniques presented in the preceding subsection.)

47. Suppose the `String` object `s` has the value `"   3.14159   "`. Write an expression that starts with the `String` object `s` and returns the `double` value `3.14159`. Include it in an assignment statement that stores that value in the variable `x` of type `double`. (Use the techniques presented in the preceding subsection.)

Programming Example
A GUI Adding Machine

Display 12.21 shows a program for a GUI adding machine. The resulting GUI is shown at the end of the display. The white text field initially contains the text `"Numbers   go` here." The user can enter a number by dragging the mouse cursor over the text in the white text field and then typing in the number, so that the number typed in becomes the contents of the text field. When the user clicks the "Add" button, the number is added to a running total, and the new total is displayed in the text field. The user can continue to add more numbers to the total for as long as she or he wants. To start over, the user clicks the "Reset" button, which makes the running total equal to zero.

Note that the window itself (the JFrame named Adder) is the listener that responds to button clicks. This configuration requires that the class definition implements Action-Listener. So, the class definition starts with

```
public class Adder extends JFrame implements ActionListener
```

Since we want the class itself to be the listener for buttons, such as the "Add" button, we register this as a listener to each button—for example,

```
JButton addButton = new JButton("Add");
addButton.addActionListener(this);
```

action-Performed

Since the GUI class Adder is the ActionListener, it must have an actionPerformed method that describes how the GUI responds to button clicks. The method actionPerformed is in Part 2 of Display 12.21. As usual, the heart of the definition is a multiway if-else branch that performs different actions, depending on what button is clicked. The expression e.getActionCommand( ) returns the string written on the button, and that string determines which branch of the multiway if-else statement is executed. The heart of the multiway if-else statement is highlighted in Display 12.21.

The tasks of placing components in containers and initializing the components, colors, and such are similar to other examples we have seen before. ∎

? Self-Test Questions

48. What would happen if the user running the GUI in Display 12.21 were to type the number 10 into the text field and then click the "Add" button three times? Explain your answer.

49. In the GUI in Display 12.21, why did we make the text field inputOutput-Field an instance variable, but did not make either of the buttons (addButton and resetButton) instance variables?

50. Suppose you change the main method in Display 12.21 to the following:

```
public static void main(String[] args)
{
    Adder guiAdder1 = new Adder();
    guiAdder1.setVisible(true);

    Adder guiAdder2 = new Adder();
    guiAdder2.setVisible(true);
}
```

```java
import javax.swing.*;
import java.awt.*;
import java.awt.event.*;
/**
 GUI for totaling a series of numbers.
*/
public class Adder extends JFrame implements ActionListener
{
    public static final int WIDTH = 400;
    public static final int HEIGHT = 200;

    private JTextField inputOutputField;
    private double sum = 0;

    public static void main(String[] args)
    {
        Adder guiAdder = new Adder();
        guiAdder.setVisible(true);
    }

    public Adder()
    {
        setTitle("Adding Machine");
        addWindowListener(new WindowDestroyer());
        setSize(WIDTH, HEIGHT);
        Container contentPane = getContentPane();
        contentPane.setLayout(new BorderLayout());

        JPanel buttonPanel = new JPanel();
        buttonPanel.setBackground(Color.GRAY);
        buttonPanel.setLayout(new FlowLayout());
        JButton addButton = new JButton("Add");
        addButton.addActionListener(this);
        buttonPanel.add(addButton);
        JButton resetButton = new JButton("Reset");
        resetButton.addActionListener(this);
        buttonPanel.add(resetButton);
        contentPane.add(buttonPanel, BorderLayout.SOUTH);

        JPanel textPanel = new JPanel();
        textPanel.setBackground(Color.BLUE);
        textPanel.setLayout(new FlowLayout());
```

```java
        inputOutputField = new JTextField("Numbers go here.", 30);
        inputOutputField.setBackground(Color.WHITE);
        textPanel.add(inputOutputField);
        contentPane.add(textPanel, BorderLayout.CENTER);
    }

    public void actionPerformed(ActionEvent e)
    {
        if (e.getActionCommand().equals("Add"))
        {
            sum = sum +
                stringToDouble(inputOutputField.getText());
            inputOutputField.setText(Double.toString(sum));
        }
        else if (e.getActionCommand().equals("Reset"))
        {
            sum = 0;
            inputOutputField.setText("0.0");
        }
        else
            inputOutputField.setText("Error in adder code.");
    }

    private static double stringToDouble(String stringObject)
    {
        return Double.parseDouble(stringObject.trim());
    }
}
```

Resulting GUI

This change will cause two adder windows to be displayed. (If one is on top of the other, you can use your mouse to move the top one.) If you add numbers in one of the adders, will anything change in the other adder? The best thing to do is to try it out, but the answer is at the end of the chapter if you are still unsure after trying it.

51. Suppose you change the `main` method in Display 12.21 as we described in Self-Test Question 50. This change will cause two adder windows to be displayed. If you click the close-window button in one of the windows, will one window go away or will both windows go away?

52. Suppose that, in the GUI of Display 12.21, you want to add a third button that will clear the text field, but will *not* reset the running total. The button should have `"Clear"` written on it. For example, if the running sum is 10 and you click the `"Clear"` button, the text field becomes blank. If you then type in the number 5 and click the `"Add"` button, the running sum is changed to 15, and `"15"` is displayed in the text field. How do you need to change the definition of the class `Adder` to accomplish this task?

Catching a `NumberFormatException`

This subsection builds on material from Chapter 8, on exception handling. If you have not yet covered exception handling, you should skip this subsection until after you cover Chapter 8. If you have already covered some of Chapter 8, this subsection is not especially difficult, and there is no need to skip it.

The GUI in Display 12.21 serves as an adding machine, with the user entering numbers and adding them to keep a running total. There is, however, one problem with that GUI. If the user enters a number in an incorrect format, such as placing a comma in a number, then one of the methods throws a `NumberFormatException`. In a Swing program, throwing an uncaught exception does not end the GUI, but it does leave it in an unpredictable state. On some systems, the user might be able to reenter the number, but you cannot count on that, and even if it were possible, the user may not know that she or he should and could reenter the last number. Display 12.22 contains a slight modification of the GUI class given in Display 12.21. When the user enters an incorrectly formatted number, a `NumberFormatException` is thrown, but in this version, the exception is caught, and the user is asked to reenter the number (as shown in the GUI display in Display 12.22).

When the user clicks one of the buttons in the GUI in Display 12.22, an action event `e` is fired. The method `actionPerformed` is then automatically invoked with this action event `e` as the argument. The method `actionPerformed` invokes the method `tryingCorrectNumberFormats`, using the action event `e` as an argument. The method `tryingCorrectNumberFormats` then processes the event just as it was processed in the previous version of the program (Display 12.21). If the user enters all numbers in the correct format, everything behaves as it did in the previous version (Display 12.21). But if the user enters an incorrectly formatted number, then something different happens.

■ DISPLAY 12.22 **A GUI with Exception Handling** *(Part 1 of 2)*

```java
import javax.swing.*;
import java.awt.*;
import java.awt.event.*;

/**
 GUI for totaling a series of numbers. If the user
 enters a number in an incorrect format, such as
 2,000 with a comma, then an error message is generated
 and the user can restart the computation.
*/
public class ImprovedAdder extends JFrame
                              implements ActionListener
{
    public static final int WIDTH = 400;
    public static final int HEIGHT = 200;

    private JTextField inputOutputField;
    private double sum = 0;

    public static void main(String[] args)
    {
        ImprovedAdder guiAdder = new ImprovedAdder();
        guiAdder.setVisible(true);
    }

    public ImprovedAdder()
        <The rest of the definition is the same as the constructor
                        Adder in Display 12.21 .>

    public void actionPerformed(ActionEvent e)
    {
        try
        {
            tryingCorrectNumberFormats(e);
        }
        catch (NumberFormatException e2)
        {
            inputOutputField.setText("Error: Reenter Number.");
        }
    }
```

This class is identical to the class Adder *in Display 12.21, except that the name of the class is changed and the method* actionPerformed *is changed.*

■ DISPLAY 12.22 A GUI with Exception Handling *(Part 2 of 2)*

> *NumberFormatExceptions do not need to be declared in a throws clause, but they can be caught like other exceptions.*

```java
//This method can throw a NumberFormatException.
public void tryingCorrectNumberFormats(ActionEvent e)
{
    if (e.getActionCommand( ).equals("Add"))
    {
        sum = sum +
              stringToDouble(inputOutputField.getText( ));
        inputOutputField.setText(Double.toString(sum));
    }
    else if (e.getActionCommand( ).equals("Reset"))
    {
        sum = 0;
        inputOutputField.setText("0.0");
    }
    else
        inputOutputField.setText("Error in adder code.");
}
//This method can throw a NumberFormatException.
private static double stringToDouble(String stringObject)
{
    return Double.parseDouble(stringObject.trim( ));
}
}
```

Resulting GUI

> *As long as the user enters correctly formatted numbers, this GUI behaves exactly the same as the one in Display 12.21.*

> *If the user enters a number in an incorrect format, such as a number with a comma, the GUI looks like this.*

For example, when the user enters 2,000, with a comma, instead of 2000, the method tryingCorrectNumberFormats invokes the method stringToDouble with the alleged number string "2,000" as an argument. Then stringToDouble calls Double.parse-Double, but Double.parseDouble cannot convert "2,000" to a number, because no Java number string can contain a comma. So the method Double.parseDouble throws a NumberFormatException. Since this situation happens within an invocation of stringToDouble, stringToDouble in turn throws a NumberFormatException. The invocation of stringToDouble takes place inside the invocation of tryingCorrect-NumberFormats, so tryingCorrectNumberFormats throws the NumberFormatEx-ception that it received from the invocation of stringToDouble. However, the invocation of tryingCorrectNumberFormats is inside a try-catch block (highlighted in Display 12.22). The exception is caught in the catch block. At that point, the JText-Field (named inputOutputField) is set to the error message "Error: Reenter Num-ber.", so that the GUI looks like the one shown in Display 12.22.

Whenever you have numeric input in a Swing GUI, your code must convert string input, like "2000", to a number, like 2000. If the user enters a string that is not in the correct format for a number of the appropriate type, a NumberFormatException will be thrown. It is a good idea to catch any such NumberFormatException so that the GUI can do something graceful, such as giving an error message, instead of entering some unfortunate state.

Notice that if a NumberFormatException is thrown, the value of the instance variable sum is not changed. A NumberFormatException can be thrown by an invo-cation of stringToDouble in the following line of code from the method tryingCorrectNumberFormats:

```
sum = sum +
      stringToDouble(inputOutputField.getText( ));
```

If the exception is thrown, execution of the method ends immediately. Because the excep-tion is thrown by the method stringToDouble, the exception is thrown before the fore-going addition operation is performed. Thus, if an exception is thrown, the addition operation that would change the value of sum is not performed. So sum is unchanged, and the user can reenter the last number and proceed with the GUI as if that incorrect number were never entered.

Notice that none of the methods in Display 12.22 has a throws clause of the form

```
throws NumberFormatException
```

That is because NumberFormatException is a descendant of the class RuntimeExcep-tion, and Java does not require you to declare a RuntimeException in a throws clause. However, you can still catch a NumberFormatException, just as you can catch any of the other exceptions you have seen.

CHAPTER   SUMMARY

■ GUIs (graphical user interfaces) are programmed using event-driven programming. In event-driven programming, a user action, like a mouse-button click, generates an event, and that event is automatically passed to an event-handling method that per-forms the appropriate action.

■ There are two main ways of building up a GUI, using Swing. You can use inheritance to create a derived class of one of the predefined Swing classes, or you can build a GUI by adding components to a container class. You usually use both of these methods when defining a class.

■ The class `JFrame` is the Swing class that you use to create a windowing GUI. A windowing GUI is defined as a derived class of the class `JFrame`.

■ A label is an object of the class `JLabel`. You can use a label to add a string of text to a GUI.

■ A button is an object of the class `JButton`. Clicking a button fires an action event that is handled by an action listener. An action listener is any class that implements the `ActionListener` interface.

■ When adding components to an object of a container class, such as adding a button to a window, you use the method `add`. The components in a container are arranged by an object called a layout manager.

■ For an object of the class `JFrame`, you do not use the method `add` with the object. Instead, you use the method `getContentPane` to produce the content pane of the object, and you then use the `add` method with the content pane.

■ A panel is a container object that is used to group components inside of a larger container. Panels are objects in the class `JPanel`.

■ Text fields (objects of the class `JTextField`) and text areas (objects of the class `JTextArea`) are used for text input and output in a GUI constructed with Swing.

✔ Answers to Self-Test Questions

1. All the programs we have seen before this chapter were designed to be performed by one agent (the computer) following a simple set of instructions of the form "first do this, then do that, then do something else," and so forth. In event-driven programming, you create a number of objects and let them interact via events. Each object simply waits around for some event to happen and then, if appropriate, reacts to it. So the next thing that happens depends on the next event.

2. GUI is pronounced "gooey" and stands for *graphical user interface*.

3. Change the line that creates the label from

```
JLabel myLabel = new JLabel("Please don't click that button!");
```

to the following:

```
JLabel myLabel = new JLabel("I love you");
```

4. Sizes in Swing are measured in pixels.

5. The JFrame class.

6. `System.exit(0);`

7. `myGUI.getContentPane().add(superLabel);`

8.

```
messageWindow.setVisible(n > 0);
```

The following also works, but is not good style:

```
if (n > 0)
    messageWindow.setVisible(true);
else
    messageWindow.setVisible(false);
```

9. When you click the minimizing (iconifying) button, the JFrame is reduced to an icon, usually at the bottom of your monitor screen.

10. You need to invoke getContentPane, as follows:

```
messageWindow.getContentPane().add(warningLabel);
```

11. Change the line

```
setBackground(Color.BLUE);
```

in the constructor in Display 12.8 to

```
setBackground(Color.YELLOW);
```

12. You use the setTitle method, which is inherited from the class JFrame. For example, the following line from the constructor in Display 12.8 sets the window title to "Second Window":

```
setTitle("Second Window");
```

13. Use the setVisible method, which is inherited from the class JFrame. The following line will display the window:

```
gui.setVisible(true);
```

To make the window invisible, you use

```
gui.setVisible(false);
```

14. `addWindowListener(new WindowDestroyer());`

15. `Container contentPane = w.getContentPane();`

16. You need the following `import` statement for the type `Container`:

    ```
    import java.awt.*;
    ```

17. You need to change the `add` statements, as in the following rewritten section of code:

    ```
    JLabel label1 = new JLabel("First label here.");
    content.add(label1, BorderLayout.NORTH);

    JLabel label2 = new JLabel("Second label there.");
    content.add(label2, BorderLayout.CENTER);

    JLabel label3 = new JLabel("Third label anywhere.");
    content.add(label3, BorderLayout.SOUTH);
    ```

18. You need to change the `add` statements, as in the following rewritten section of code:

    ```
    JLabel label1 = new JLabel("First label here.");
    content.add(label1, BorderLayout.NORTH);

    JLabel label2 = new JLabel("Second label there.");
    content.add(label2, BorderLayout.EAST);

    JLabel label3 = new JLabel("Third label anywhere.");
    content.add(label3, BorderLayout.SOUTH);
    ```

19. The argument `new BorderLayout( )` creates a new object of the class `BorderLayout` and passes this argument to the method `setLayout`. This use of `new` is a way to create an argument without having to give the argument a name.

20. `setLayout(new GridLayout(1, 3));`
    It is also possible to do something similar with `BorderLayout` or `FlowLayout`, but a `GridLayout` manager will work nicer here.

21. `setLayout(new GridLayout(3, 1));`
    It is also possible to do something similar with `BorderLayout`, but a `GridLayout` manager will work nicer here.

22. You need an action listener. You make a class into an action listener by adding `implements ActionListener` at the end of the class heading (after `extends JFrame` if the class is a window object). You also must add a definition of the method `actionPerformed` to the class. Every component that generates an action event normally should have one or more action listeners registered with it. You register action listeners with the method `addActionListener`.

23. Yes. The two pieces of code are equivalent. Some people think each button must have its own name, but that is not needed in this case. In the alternative piece of code, the name b is used for one button, and then, *after* the button has been set up and added to the GUI, the name b is reused for the second button. This second

way of writing the code is, in fact, the way most experienced programmers would write it, but we used the first way, with two names, to avoid confusion, and that is also OK.

24. You may name the content pane anything you wish (other than a keyword). So the following is perfectly legal:

```
Container insideOfJFrame = getContentPane( );
```

(Of course, if you make this change, then `contentPane` will need to be replaced by `insideOfJFrame` wherever else it occurs in the method `actionPerformed`.)

25. When we say that an event is "sent" to a listener object, what we really mean is that some method in the listener object is invoked with the event object as the argument. This invocation happens automatically. Your Swing GUI class definition will not normally contain an invocation of this method.

26. It would have no effect on the program. The `e` is a parameter for the method `actionPerformed`, and we can use any (non-reserved-word) identifier as the parameter.

27. When adding components to a `JFrame`, you need to use `getContentPane` to get the content pane, and then you need to add components to the content pane. When adding components to a `JPanel`, there is no content pane and no need to use `getContentPane`.

28. Events from a `JButton` go to action listeners. Buttons, and certain other components, fire events in the class `ActionEvent`. These events are known as action events and must be handled by an action listener. Any class can be an action-listener class. The details in outline form are as follows:

1. Make some class (maybe a window class) into an action listener by adding the phrase

```
implements ActionListener
```

to the heading of the class definition and adding a definition for a method named `actionPerformed`. The action listener can be any class. In particular, the class may serve some other function besides being an action listener.

2. Register the `ActionListener` object with the button (or other component) that will fire the action event. To do this task, you use the method `addActionListener`. A button or other component may register more than (or less than) one listener.

29. They have a number of trivial things in common, but the commonality we were looking for in this question is that they are both listener classes. `WindowDestroyer` is a window-listener class, and `ButtonDemo` is an action-listener class.

30. The type is `Container`. To use `Container`, you need the following line:

```
import java.awt.*;
```

(You'll also probably need other `import` statements, but this is the one you need in order to use the type (class) `Container`.)

31. `import java.awt.*;`
    (You'll also probably need other `import` statements, but this is the one you need in order to account for the layout-manager classes.)

32. Yes to both. An object of the class `JPanel` is both a container class and a component class.

33. A `FlowLayout` manager arranges the components you add to a container one after the other, going from left to right. The components are laid out in the order in which you add them to the container.

34. A `BorderLayout` manager places components into the five regions `BorderLayout.NORTH`, `BorderLayout.SOUTH`, `BorderLayout.EAST`, `BorderLayout.WEST`, and `BorderLayout.CENTER`. The five regions are arranged as follows:

BorderLayout.NORTH		
BorderLayout. WEST	BorderLayout.CENTER	BorderLayout. EAST
BorderLayout.SOUTH		

35. Put the two buttons in a `JPanel` object, and add the `JPanel` object to the region `BorderLayout.NORTH`.

36. A `GridLayout` manager arranges components in rows and columns, with each entry being the same size. For example, the following line states that a `GridLayout` manager should be used with `aContainer` (which can be a content pane or other container):

    ```
    aContainer.setLayout(new GridLayout(2, 3));
    ```

    The two numbers given as arguments to the constructor `GridLayout` specify the number of rows and columns, respectively. This line of code would produce the following sort of layout:

When using the `GridLayout` class, the method `add` has only one argument. The items are placed in the grid from left to right, first filling the top row, then the second row, and so forth. You are not allowed to skip any grid position.

37. This line of code indicates a layout manager with two rows and three columns. So it seems to indicate a maximum of six components. However, you can add any number of components. If you add more than six components, more columns will be added.

38. To make it look as though you have an empty grid element, add an empty panel to the grid element.

39.

```java
import javax.swing.*;
import java.awt.*;

public class PinkJPanel extends JPanel
{
    public PinkJPanel()
    {
        setBackground(Color.PINK);
    }
}
```

Extra code on CD

Look at the program `PinkJPanelDemo.java` on the accompanying CD to see that you use a `PinkJPanel` in the same way that you use an ordinary `JPanel`.

40. A text field (`JTextField`) displays only a single line. A text area (`JTextArea`) can display more than one line of text.

41. Change the line

```java
contentPane.add(buttonPanel, BorderLayout.SOUTH);
```

in the constructor to

```java
contentPane.add(buttonPanel, BorderLayout.NORTH);
```

42. `JTextField name = new JTextField("Your name here.", 30);`

43. The portions of the following code in color are changed from Display 12.19:

```java
public void actionPerformed(ActionEvent e)
{
    String actionCommand = e.getActionCommand();
    if (actionCommand.equals("Save Memo 1"))
    {
        memo1 = theText.getText();
        theText.setText("Memo 1 saved.");
    }
    else if (actionCommand.equals("Save Memo 2"))
    {
        memo2 = theText.getText();
        theText.setText("Memo 2 saved.");
    }
```

```
        else if (actionCommand.equals("Clear"))
            theText.setText("");
        else if (actionCommand.equals("Get Memo 1"))
            theText.setText(memo1);
        else if (actionCommand.equals("Get Memo 2"))
            theText.setText(memo2);
        else
            theText.setText("Error in memo interface");
    }
```

44. To get multiple lines in one `String` object, just insert the character `'\n'` at the line breaks. This happens automatically when `getText` returns the text in the `JTextArea`.

45. `String s = Double.toString(7.77);`

46. `double x = Double.parseDouble("3.14159");`
    Alternatively, you could add the method `stringToDouble` (see the Quick Reference box entitled "Inputting Numbers with a GUI") to the class and use

    `double x = stringToDouble("3.14159");`

47. `double x = Double.parseDouble(s.trim());`
    Alternatively, you could add the method `stringToDouble` (see the Quick Reference box entitled "Inputting Numbers with a GUI") to the class and use

    `double x = stringToDouble(s);`

    (The `trim` is in the method `stringToDouble`.)

48. Every time the user clicks the `"Add"` button, the following clause from the method `actionPerformed` applies:

    ```
    if (e.getActionCommand().equals("Add"))
    {
        sum = sum +
                stringToDouble(inputOutputField.getText());
        inputOutputField.setText(Double.toString(sum));
    }
    ```

    The assignment to `sum` takes place every time the `"Add"` button event is generated. So the number in the text field is added to the total as many times as the user clicks the `"Add"` button. Moreover, the value in the text field is the running total, and so the running total is added to itself. If the user clicks the `"Add"` button three times, the number *in the text field* will be added to the total three times.

    Let's say that the user starts the GUI, types in 10, and clicks the `"Add"` button. That adds 10 to `sum`, so the value of `sum` is 10, and 10 is displayed. Now the user clicks the `"Add"` button again. That adds 10 to `sum` again, so the value of sum is 20, and 20 is displayed. Now the user clicks the `"Add"` button a third time. This time, 20 is in the text field, so it is added to `sum`, which is 20. Thus, the value of sum is now 40, and 40 is displayed. Note that it is always the number in the text field that is added to sum.

49. We made the text field an instance variable because we needed to refer to it in the definition of the method actionPerformed, as in the following line:

```
sum = sum
      + stringToDouble(inputOutputField.getText( ));
```

On the other hand, the only direct reference we had to the buttons was in the constructor. So we need names for the buttons only in the constructor definition. (An object need not be named by an instance variable in order to be part of a Swing object, or of any kind of object, for that matter. Objects do not go away as long as they are being used, and the buttons are being used by the object of the class Adder, so they stay around whether or not you have a permanent name for them.)

50. The two adder windows are completely independent in terms of numbers. The sum or the number added to one adder has no effect on the other adder.

51. If you click the close-window button in either adder window, the entire program ends, because of the invocation System.exit(0);, so both windows go away.

52. You need to add the "Clear" button by adding the following code to the constructor:

```
JButton clearButton = new JButton("Clear");
clearButton.addActionListener(this);
buttonPanel.add(clearButton);
```

You also need to change the method actionPerformed to the following (the additions are shown in color):

```
public void actionPerformed(ActionEvent e)
{
    if (e.getActionCommand( ).equals("Add"))
    {
        sum = sum +
            stringToDouble(inputOutputField.getText( ));
        inputOutputField.setText(Double.toString(sum));
    }
    else if (e.getActionCommand( ).equals("Reset"))
    {
        sum = 0;
        inputOutputField.setText("0.0");
    }
    else if (e.getActionCommand( ).equals("Clear"))
        inputOutputField.setText("");
        //Note that sum is not changed.
```

```
        else
            inputOutputField.setText("Error in adder code.");
}
```

It would be a good idea to try making these modifications and then run the changed program.

● Programming Projects

1. Rewrite the program in Display 12.17 so that the panel with the buttons changes to pink when the larger panel turns red, and the panel with the buttons changes to blue when the larger panel turns green. Also, add a label to the larger panel that says "Watch this panel!", and add a button to the button panel that is labeled "Change". When the "Change" button is clicked, the colors change (from pink and red to blue and green, respectively, or vice versa). The "Change" button has no effect on the initial configuration, in which the big panel is blue and the button panel is gray.

2. Rewrite the program in Display 12.19 so that it has all of the following changes:

   i. The class name is MemoSaver2.

   ii. There are six buttons instead of five, and they are arranged as follows:

Save Memo 1	Save Memo 2	Clear
Get Memo 1	Get Memo 1	Exit

   The buttons are still at the bottom of the GUI, with the text area above them. (*Hint*: Use a GridLayout manager on the button panel.)

   iii. When the user saves the text as memo 1, the text area changes so that it says "Memo 1 saved.", and when memo 2 is saved, the text area changes to say "Memo 2 saved." (See Self-Test Question 43 for a hint.)

   iv. When the "Exit" button is clicked, the program ends, and the window goes away. The close-window button also ends the program. So the "Exit" button and the close-window button perform the same action.

   v. In addition to the default constructor, there is a constructor of the following form:

   ```
   public MemoSaver2(int lineCount, int charCount)
   ```

   When this constructor is used, it produces the same display, except that the text area has dimensions of lineCount number of lines and charCount number of characters per line.

   vi. The text area has line wrap, so that if more characters are entered than will fit on the line, the extra characters automatically go on the next line.

vii. The method `main` constructs two windows, one using the default constructor and one using the constructor in item v. with parameters 5 and 60, in that order.

3. (You should do Programming Project 2 before doing this one.) Write a GUI, using Swing, that behaves as follows: When the program is run, a window appears and asks the user how many lines and how many characters per line she or he wants for a memo saver. If the user clicks the close-window button, the program ends. More typically, the user enters these two numbers in two text fields. There is a button with the string `"Continue"` on it. If the user clicks the `"Continue"` button, the window disappears, and another window appears. This second window is just like the memo saver in Programming Project 2, except that the text area has the number of lines and characters per line specified by the user in the previous window.

4. (The Swing part of this project is quite straightforward, but you do need to know a little about how to convert numbers from one base to another.) Write a program that converts numbers from base-10 (ordinary decimal) notation to base-2 notation. The program uses Swing to perform input and output via a window interface. The user enters a base-10 numeral in one text field and clicks a button with `"Convert"` written on it; the equivalent base-2 numeral then appears in another text field. Be sure that the two text fields are labeled. Include a `"Clear"` button that clears both text fields when clicked. Also, be sure that the close-window button works correctly.

5. (It would probably help to do Programming Project 4 before doing this one.) Write a program that converts numbers from base-2 notation to base-10 (ordinary decimal) notation. The program uses Swing to perform input and output via a window interface. The user enters a base-2 numeral in one text field and clicks a button with `"Convert"` written on it; the equivalent base-10 numeral then appears in another text field. Be sure that the two text fields are labeled. Include a `"Clear"` button that clears both text fields when clicked. Also, be sure that the close-window button works correctly. (*Hint*: Include a private method that converts the string for a base-2 numeral to an equivalent `int` value.)

6. (It would help to do Programming Projects 4 and 5 before doing this one.) Write a program that converts numbers from base-2 notation to base-10 (ordinary decimal) notation and vice versa. The program uses Swing to perform input and output via a window interface. There are two text fields, one for base-2 numerals and one for base-10 numerals. There are three buttons with the strings `"To Base 10"`, `"To Base 2"`, and `"Clear"`, respectively. If the user enters a base-2 numeral in the base-2 text field and clicks the button with `"To Base 10"` written on it, then the equivalent base-10 numeral appears in the base 10 text field. Similarly, if the user enters a base-10 numeral in the base 10 text field and clicks the button with `"To Base 2"` written on it, then the equivalent base-2 numeral appears in the base-2 text field. Be sure that the two text fields are labeled. Include a `"Clear"` button that clears both text fields when clicked. Also, be sure that the close-window button works correctly.

7. Write a program that produces a GUI with the functionality and look of a hand-held calculator. Your calculator should allow for addition, subtraction, multiplication,

and division. It should allow you to save and later recall two different values. Use the program in Display 12.22 as a model. If you have not covered Display 12.22, use Display 12.21 as a model.

8. Do Programming Project 4 of Chapter 9, but write the program as a Swing GUI.

9. Do Programming Project 7 of Chapter 9, but write the program as a Swing GUI.

Chapter

13

Applets and HTML

13

Visit our Web site. -Common advertisement copy

All that has come before this chapter is important in learning how to program and in learning the Java language. However, we have not yet touched on what initially made Java famous. Java became famous due in large part to its connection to the Internet.

In this chapter, we describe a version of Java programs that can be run across the Internet. The World Wide Web (the Web, for short) is the collection of locations on the Internet that you can view with a Web browser. Applets are simply Java programs that are designed to run from a document (page) on the Web. HTML is a language used to create Web documents. Although Java applets were designed to run from within HTML documents, you can run an applet as a stand-alone program without any reference to HTML or the Internet. So we will discuss applets first and then discuss HTML.

OBJECTIVES

Find out how to write applets.

Learn to write a simple HTML document.

Learn how to embed an applet in an HTML document.

PREREQUISITES

Section	Prerequisite
Section 13.1 Writing applets	Chapter 12 (and its prerequisites)
Section 13.2 Introduction to HTML	None, not even Section 13.1
Section 13.3 Applets in HTML	Sections 13.1 and 13.2

If you wish to skip or delay reading this chapter, you can. Chapter 14 does not use any material from this chapter.

If you want to learn only how to write applets, and you will not be running them from an HTML document (a Web page), then Section 13.1 will give you all the information you need.

If you already know HTML, but do not know about applets, you can skip Section 13.2 and go from Section 13.1 to Section 13.3.

To really get much benefit from Sections 13.2 and 13.3, you should know how to use a Web browser such as the Netscape Navigator or Microsoft's Internet Explorer. All the constructs discussed in this chapter produce things to be viewed via a Web browser. We will assume that you have used a Web browser to read something on the Web, but we will not assume that you know how to create things to be viewed on the Web. Most readers could get sufficient experience simply by playing with a Web browser without any instruction or

Web browser

reading. To get the full benefit of this chapter, you should also understand how path names are used on your operating system, so that you can name a file that is contained in a different directory (different folder).

13.1 APPLETS

An applet a day keeps the doctor away. -Anonymous

The word *applet* sounds as though it might refer to a small apple, but it is supposed to sound like a small application. Thus, applets are just "little Java programs," in some sense of the word *little*. However, the character of applets comes not from their size, but from how and where they are run. Applets are Java programs that can be displayed on a Web site and viewed over the Internet. They can also be run on your local computer, without any connection to the Internet. In this section, we will describe how you write applets and how to view them without any connection to the Internet. In Section 13.3, we will describe one simple way to view an applet over the Internet.

An applet is very much like a Swing GUI, and if you understand some details about Swing, then you will find it very easy to write applets. In this section, we will assume that you are already familiar with the Swing material given in Chapter 12. We will show you how to write simple applets that do the same thing as the windowing systems we covered there. If you go on to learn more about Swing, you can use almost all of your new Swing techniques in your applets.

Applet Basics

An applet is a derived class of the class `JApplet` (actually, of any descendant class, but typically it is a directly derived class). The class `JApplet` is a class in the Swing library, so you need the following `import` statement when using the class `JApplet`:

```
import javax.swing.*;
```

import

When you are writing an applet, you may also need the AWT library, so your full list of `import` statements is likely to be the following:

```
import javax.swing.*;
import java.awt.*;
import java.awt.event.*;
```

Display 13.1, shows a part of the class hierarchy to help you put the class `JApplet` in context. Note that a `JApplet` is a `Container`. Thus, you can add things to an applet. You add components to an applet in the same way that you add components to a `JFrame`.

In Display 13.1, you might notice the class `Applet`. This class is an older version of the class `JApplet`. The `Applet` class was used to create applets before the introduction of `JApplet`.

You can design an applet class in much the same way that you design a windowing system, using Swing, as in Chapter 12. The main difference is that you derive an applet class from the class `JApplet` instead of the class `JFrame`. Other differences between an applet class and a regular Swing windowing class consist mostly of things that are omitted from the definition of the applet class.

■ DISPLAY 13.1 **Placing Applets in the Class Hierarchy**

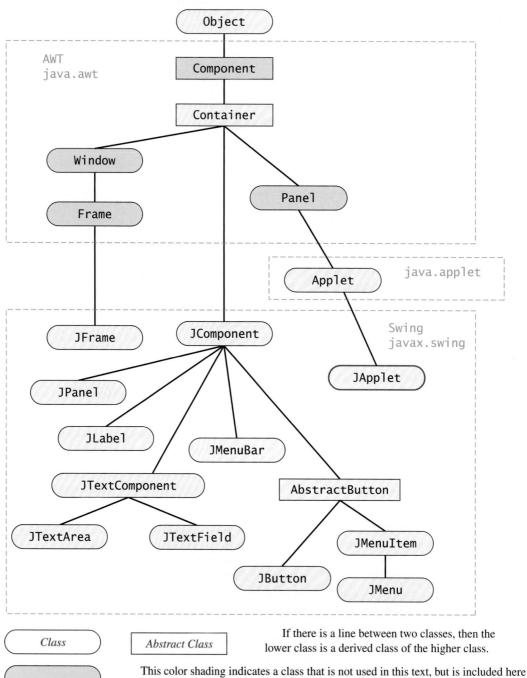

Class

Abstract Class

If there is a line between two classes, then the lower class is a derived class of the higher class.

This color shading indicates a class that is not used in this text, but is included here for reference. If you have not heard of any of these classes, you can safely ignore them.

Applets do not use the `setVisible` method. Applets are displayed automatically. For this reason, an applet also normally does not have a `main` method. A very simple applet is shown in Display 13.2. When this applet is viewed, it will simply display the text

    Hello out there!

Note that a `JApplet` has a content pane, just as a `JFrame` does, and you add components to the content pane of the `JApplet`, rather than adding them directly to the `JApplet`. As illustrated in Display 13.2, you add a `JLabel` (or other component) to a `JApplet` just as you would add one to a `JFrame`.

JLabel

Applets do not have titles, so there is no need to use the `setTitle` method in an applet. This is because applets normally are part of a Web-site display, and the display can add any title. As you will see in Section 13.3, the Web display document also takes care of sizing the applet, so you do not give any size instructions for an applet.

■ DISPLAY 13.2 **A Trivial Applet**

```
import javax.swing.*;
import java.awt.*;//For Container class
public class HelloApplet extends JApplet
{
    public void init( )
    {
        Container contentPane = getContentPane( );
        contentPane.setLayout(new FlowLayout( ));
        JLabel friendlyLabel = new JLabel("Hello out there!");
        contentPane.add(friendlyLabel);
    }
}
```

Resulting GUI (Using an Applet Viewer)

init

Applets do not normally use constructors, but they do use a method named `init` that serves a similar purpose. When defining an applet, you place all the initializing actions—such as setting colors, adding buttons, and adding text fields—in the method named `init`. The `init` method has no parameters.

Applets do not need to be closed with listeners, so they do not include an invocation of `addWindowListener` in their `init` methods. When the Web document is closed, the applet will automatically close.

(Other very simple examples of applets are given in Chapter 1. In Chapter 1, the applets have no layout manager specified. If a `JApplet` has no layout manager specified, it has the `BorderLayout` manager by default. If a component is added without specifying a region, it goes in the region `BorderLayout.CENTER`. In Chapter 1, we did not use any layout manager, in order to keep the examples simple, but now that you understand layout managers, we suggest that you always use an explicit layout manager.)

Quick Reference: The `JApplet` Class

The `JApplet` class is the class normally used to create an applet. This class is in the Swing library, so when using this class, you use the following `import` statement:

```
import javax.swing.*;
```

Running an Applet

applet viewer

You compile an applet in the same way that you compile all of the other Java classes you have seen. However, you run an applet differently from other Java programs. The normal way to run an applet is as part of a Web-site document. The applet is then viewed through a Web browser. We will discuss this means of viewing an applet in Section 13.3. However, applets can also be viewed using an **applet viewer,** a program designed to run applets as stand-alone programs. If you are using an integrated environment that has a menu command called Run Applet, Run, Execute, or something similar, you can probably use one of these commands to run an applet just as you run an ordinary Java application program. (In the TextPad environment, which comes on the CD included with this book, the command is Run Java Applet on the Tools menu. This environment command will automatically invoke an applet viewer. If a window pops up asking you to choose a file, answer "No.") If this approach does not work, you will need to check with a local expert or else read Section 13.3 for more details on viewing applets.

If you run the applet shown in Display 13.3 in an applet viewer, the result will look similar to the GUI shown in that display.

Programming Example
An Adder Applet

Display 13.3 contains an applet that will produce an adding-machine window that is essentially the same as the one we produced in Chapter 12. The details are almost identical to those in the Swing class we defined in Display 12.21. To obtain this adder applet from that Swing class, we simply did the following:

- replaced extends JFrame with extends JApplet;
- deleted the main method;
- replaced the constructor heading with the init method heading;
- deleted some lines not needed for an applet. ■

■ DISPLAY 13.3 **An Applet Adding Machine** *(Part 1 of 2)*

```java
import javax.swing.*;
import java.awt.*;
import java.awt.event.*;

public class AdderApplet extends JApplet
                         implements ActionListener
{
    private JTextField inputOutputField;
    private double sum = 0;

    public void init()
    {
        Container contentPane = getContentPane();
        contentPane.setLayout(new BorderLayout());

        JPanel buttonPanel = new JPanel();
        buttonPanel.setBackground(Color.GRAY);
        buttonPanel.setLayout(new FlowLayout());
        JButton addButton = new JButton("Add");
        addButton.addActionListener(this);
        buttonPanel.add(addButton);
        JButton resetButton = new JButton("Reset");
        resetButton.addActionListener(this);
        buttonPanel.add(resetButton);
        contentPane.add(buttonPanel, BorderLayout.SOUTH);

        JPanel textPanel = new JPanel();
        textPanel.setBackground(Color.BLUE);
        textPanel.setLayout(new FlowLayout());
        inputOutputField =
                    new JTextField("Numbers go here.", 30);
        inputOutputField.setBackground(Color.WHITE);
        textPanel.add(inputOutputField);
        contentPane.add(textPanel, BorderLayout.CENTER);
    }
```

■ DISPLAY 13.3 **An Applet Adding Machine** *(Part 2 of 2)*

```java
    public void actionPerformed(ActionEvent e)
    {
        if (e.getActionCommand().equals("Add"))
        {
            sum = sum +
                stringToDouble(inputOutputField.getText());
            inputOutputField.setText(Double.toString(sum));
        }
        else if (e.getActionCommand().equals("Reset"))
        {
            sum = 0;
            inputOutputField.setText("0.0");
        }
        else
            inputOutputField.setText("Error in adder code.");
    }

    private static double stringToDouble(String stringObject)
    {
        return Double.parseDouble(stringObject.trim());
    }
}
```

Resulting GUI (Using an Applet Viewer)

■ **Java Tip**
Converting a Swing Application to an Applet

It is easy to convert a Swing application to an applet. In most cases, you simply follow these instructions:

1. Derive the class from the class `JApplet` instead of from the class `JFrame`. That is, replace `extends JFrame` with `extends JApplet` on the first line of the class definition.

2. Remove the `main` method. An applet does not need the things that are typically placed in `main`. An applet is automatically made visible, and its size is determined by the applet viewer or by the Web page it is embedded in.

3. Replace the constructor with a method named `init`. The body of the `init` method can be the same as the body of the deleted constructor, but with some items removed, as described in steps 4–6.

4. Delete any invocation of `addWindowListener`. (The applet viewer or the Web page containing the applet will take care of ending the applet. So you do not need any window-listener object, such as an object of the class `WindowDe-stroyer` given in Chapter 12.)

5. Delete any invocation of `setTitle`. (Applets have no titles.)

6. Delete any invocation of `setSize`. (Sizing is done by the applet viewer or by the Web page in which the applet is embedded.)

For example, we obtained the applet in Display 13.3 from the Swing application in Display 12.21 by following these rules. □

? Self-Test Questions

1. Do you normally include constructors in an applet-class definition?

2. Is it normal for an applet class to have a `main` method?

3. Which of the following methods might you use in an applet? `addWindowListener`; `getContentPane`; `setTitle`; `setSize`.

Adding Icons to an Applet

Display 13.4 illustrates one way to add a picture to an applet. A simplified version of that applet was given in Chapter 1, but we can provide a more complete description of it now that you know more about applets. An icon is simply a picture. It is normally, but not always, a small picture. The easiest way to display an icon in an applet is to place the icon in a `JLabel`. In the applet in Display 13.4, the picture in the file `duke_waving.gif` is displayed as an icon that is part of the `JLabel` named `niceLabel`. The two lines that add the icon are reproduced as follows:

```
ImageIcon dukeIcon = new ImageIcon("duke_waving.gif");
niceLabel.setIcon(dukeIcon);
```

ImageIcon

■ DISPLAY 13.4 **An Applet with an Icon**

```java
import javax.swing.*;
import java.awt.*;

public class DukeApplet extends JApplet
{
    public void init()
    {
        Container contentPane = getContentPane();
        contentPane.setLayout(new BorderLayout());

        JLabel spacer = new JLabel("            ");
        contentPane.add(spacer, "West");
        JLabel niceLabel = new JLabel("Java is fun!");
        ImageIcon dukeIcon = new ImageIcon("duke_waving.gif");
        niceLabel.setIcon(dukeIcon);
        contentPane.add(niceLabel, BorderLayout.CENTER);
    }
}
```

Resulting GUI[1]

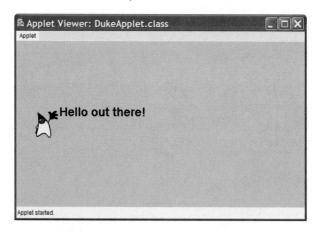

---

1. Java, Duke, and all Java-based trademarks and logos are trademarks or registered trademarks of Sun Microsystems, Inc., in the United States and other countries.

ImageIcon is a class in the Swing library. The label niceLabel is created in the normal way that we described in Chapter 12:

```
JLabel niceLabel = new JLabel("Java is fun!");
```

The icon picture is a digital picture in one of the standard formats. The picture—in this case, duke_waving.gif—must be converted to an ImageIcon before it can be added to a label. This task is done as follows: new ImageIcon("duke_waving.gif"). So the following code creates an ImageIcon based on the picture duke_waving.gif and stores a reference to the icon in the variable dukeIcon:

```
ImageIcon dukeIcon = new ImageIcon("duke_waving.gif");
```

The method setIcon adds an icon to a label, as in the following statement:

```
niceLabel.setIcon(dukeIcon);
```

If you want the label to have only the icon and no text, then simply use the default constructor when you create the JLabel. For example, if we had used

```
JLabel niceLabel = new JLabel();
```

in Display 13.4 instead of

```
JLabel niceLabel = new JLabel("Java is fun!");
```

then the string "Java is fun!" would not have appeared in the applet; only the icon would have been displayed.

Chapter 14 contains more material on icons.

Quick Reference: Icons and the Class ImageIcon

An **icon** is simply a small picture, although it is not really required to be small. The class ImageIcon is used to convert a picture file to a Swing icon.

Syntax:

```
ImageIcon Name_Of_ImageIcon =
        new ImageIcon(Picture_File_Name);
```

The *Picture_File_Name* is a string giving either a relative or an absolute path name to the picture file. (So if the picture file is in the same directory as your applet, you need give only the name of the picture file.)

Example:

```
ImageIcon SmileyFaceIcon =
        new ImageIcon("smiley.gif");
```

FAQ: Who Is Duke?

Duke is the character shown in the applet in Display 13.4. He has become a mascot for the Java language. The Duke icon is used here with permission from Sun Microsystems, Inc.

4. How do you add an icon based on the digital picture file `smiley.gif` to an applet?

5. When you specify the file for a digital picture, such as `smiley.gif`, as an argument to the `ImageIcon` constructor, can you use a path name?

13.2 INTRODUCTION TO HTML

You shall see them on a beautiful quarto page, where a neat rivulet of text shall meander through a meadow of margin. -Richard Brinsley Sheridan, *The School for Scandal*

Documents designed to be read on the Web, or through a Web browser regardless of whether they are on the Web, are typically expressed in a language called **HTML.** HTML stands for **Hypertext Markup Language. Hypertext** is simply text that contains items which you can click, using your mouse, to go to another document. These connections from document to document are called **links,** or **hyperlinks.** The documents themselves are often called **pages,** which is why a person's or a company's main location on the Web is called a **home page.** The terms **HTML document** and **HTML page** mean the same thing and simply refer to a hypertext document created with the HTML language.

HTML is not a full-blown programming language like Java. It is just a collection of simple commands that you can insert into a page of text in order to convert it to something that can be viewed with a Web browser. The commands allow you to insert pictures and hyperlinks into the page. They also allow you to write editing commands that specify a main heading, a subheading, a paragraph beginning, and so forth. In short, most of HTML is simply a language for formatting a manuscript so it can be viewed on the Web.

This is not a book on HTML programming, so we will give you only a small taste of the language. This introduction will allow you to design some very simple documents for the Web (or just for your browser). If you want to become an expert in HTML, you should eventually go on to a book dedicated entirely to that subject.

hypertext

home page

HTML Basics

Most HTML commands are of the form

```
<Command>
Some text
</Command>
```

For example, the following commands make the phrase "My Home Page" a level 1 heading, which is the largest standard heading:

<h1>

```
<h1>
My Home Page
</h1>
```

Notice that the notation `</Command>`—in this example, `</h1>`—is used to mark the end of the text to which the command applies.

<h2>

You can have smaller heads, called level 2 heads (command `h2`); even smaller heads, called level 3 heads (command `h3`); and so forth.

Remember: HTML Is Not Case Sensitive

We will write our HTML commands in lowercase letters. However, unlike Java, HTML does not distinguish between uppercase and lowercase letters in commands, so the commands, would behave the same if they were expressed in uppercase letters. (Any text to be displayed as text to be read by the person viewing the document will, of course, display uppercase letters in uppercase and lowercase letters in lowercase.)

Some commands do not need to be closed with a command of the form </*Command*>. One such command is

```
<br>
```

`<br>`

This command begins a new line. Another is

```
<p>
```

`<p>`

which is a command to begin a new paragraph.

Commands in HTML are not absolute commands that determine the exact size of a portion of text, or even the exact line breaks. When you give a command for a level 1 head, you can reasonably assume that it will be bigger than a level 2 head, but the browser will determine the exact size of the text. You can force a line break by inserting the **break command:**   break

```
<br>
```

If you write a large piece of text (or even sometimes a small amount of text), the browser will insert line breaks where necessary in order to fit the text on the screen, using rules that help it determine where such breaks "look good," and it will ignore your line breaks unless they are indicated with the `<br>` command.

You can make some layout specifications. For example, anything between the commands `<center>` and `</center>` will be centered on the page when it is displayed. The   `<center>` following commands will center the level 1 head we discussed earlier:

```
<h1>
<center>
My Home Page
</center>
</h1>
```

Or, if you prefer, this code can also be written as follows:

```
<center>
<h1>
My Home Page
</h1>
</center>
```

Remember: HTML File Names

An HTML file is a regular text file that you create and edit with a text editor, in the same way that you write a Java program. HTML files should end with .html, but otherwise they can be named using the same rules you use to name other files on your system.

---

comments

● Programming Tip
A Simple HTML-Document Outline

Display 13.5 contains an outline for a simple HTML document. That display also illustrates how you write comments in HTML. For example,

```
<!--Beginning of HTML document-->
```

is a comment. A comment begins with `<!--` and ends with `-->`. We have used comments to explain the new HTML commands, but a real document would not have this many comments, nor would it explain basic HTML commands, as we have done here.

<html>

    The entire document should be enclosed in the pair `<html>` and `</html>`, the first tag at the beginning and the second tag at the end. The head of the document is en-

<head>

closed in `<head>` and `</head>`. The head is not displayed when the document is viewed, but it does record information that is used by a browser. In our document, it

<title>

consists only of a title (enclosed in `<title>` and `</title>`). The title is used as a name for the document. For example, a browser will let users set a bookmark at a document so they can return to it at a later time. The bookmark will have the name given in this title. (Some browsers call bookmarks "Favorites.")

    The part of the document that is displayed on the screen is divided into two parts.

<body>
<address>

The **body** (enclosed in `<body>` and `</body>`) is the real content of the document. The other displayed part is enclosed in `<address>` and `</address>`, and it is optional. It is used to give an e-mail address for contacting the document's owner and usually includes the date that the document was last modified.

    Display 13.6 shows a very simple HTML document, and Display 13.7 shows how this document would appear when viewed in a browser. Remember that the exact line breaks, size of letters, and other layout details are determined by the particular browser, so it might look a little different on your browser. The portion that discusses the Sun Microsystems Web site is explained in the next subsection. ○

Inserting Hyperlinks

Well this is all nice, but it would hardly be worth the effort if an HTML document did not also contain some active elements. The key active element is a link that the person viewing the document can click to view another HTML document. The other document may be on the same computer or on a computer thousands of miles away. These links are called

hyperlink

hyperlinks, or simply **links.**

    The syntax for hyperlinks is as follows:

```
<a href="Path_To_Document">
Displayed_Text_To_Click
</a>
```

For example, the following code creates a link to the author's home page:

```
<a href="http://www-cse.ucsd.edu/users/savitch">
Walter Savitch
</a>
```

■ DISPLAY 13.5 **Outline of a Simple HTML Document**

```
<html> <!--Beginning of HTML document-->
<head> <!--Begin the document head-->
<title> <!--Begin document title. Used for browser "bookmarks"-->
```
Title of document.
```
</title> <!--End document title-->
</head> <!--End the document head-->
<body> <!--Stuff to appear on screen begins here-->
<h1>
```
First main heading.
```
</h1>
```
Maybe some text.
```
<h2>
```
First subheading.
```
</h2>
```
Probably some text.
```
<h2>
```
Second subheading.
```
</h2>
```
Probably some text.
```
<h1>
```
Second main heading.
```
</h1>
```
And then more of the same.

      ...
```
</body> <!--Regular stuff ends here, but address is displayed-->
<address> <!--Optional, but normally used-->
```
The e-mail address of the person maintaining the page.
Also, the date of the last time the page was changed.
(You can actually put in whatever you want here, but the
e-mail address and date are what people expect.)
```
</address>
</html> <!--End of HTML document-->
```

A real HTML document should not have this many comments.

■ DISPLAY 13.6 **A Very Simple HTML Document**

```
<html>
<head>
<title>
Java Club Home Page
</title>
</head>
<body>
<h1>
<center>
Java Club
</center>
</h1>

<h2>
Club Purpose
</h2>
<p>
A major goal of the club is to encourage
its members to become good programmers.
<p>
The club provides a setting where people who
like to program in the Java language can meet
and talk with other like-minded programmers.

<h2>
Meeting Times
</h2>
The first Wednesday of each month at 7 PM.
<h2>
Sun Microsystems Java Website
</h2>
<a href="http://java.sun.com">
Click here for the website
</a>
<p>
</body>

<address>
javaclub.somemachine@someschool.edu
<br>
January 1, 2004
</address>
</html>
```

Blank lines are ignored when the document is displayed, but they can make your HTML code easier to read.

Text may have different line breaks when displayed on your browser.

A new paragraph will always produce a line break and some separation.

This code is explained in the subsection entitled "Inserting Hyperlinks."

■ DISPLAY 13.7   **Browser View of Display 13.6**

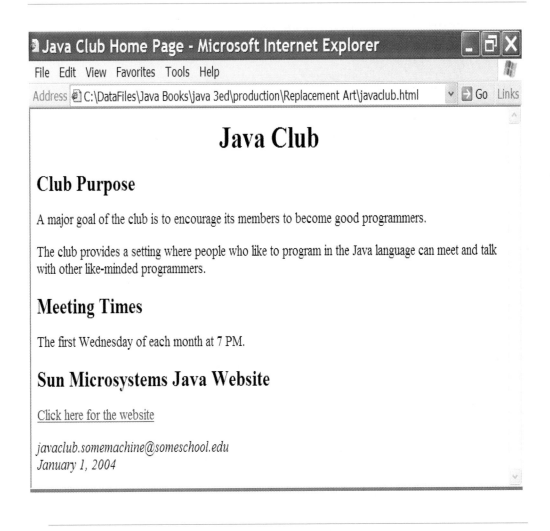

Be sure to include the quotation marks as shown. The *Displayed_Text_To_Click* will be displayed and underlined (or otherwise highlighted) by the browser. In this example, if the person viewing the document clicks the text `Walter Savitch`, then the browser will display the author's home page. You can insert this code in any document in any part of the world, and it will take you to La Jolla, California, with a click of your mouse button.

The HTML document in Display 13.6 includes a link to the Java Web site of Sun Microsystems. If you view this HTML document with a browser, it will look approximately like Display 13.7. If the user clicks the text that is underlined, the browser will display Sun Microsystems' Java Web site. (That is, it will display the HTML document on the company's computer that gives information about Java.)

Quick Reference: **Inserting a Hyperlink**

The command for inserting a hyperlink is as follows:

Syntax:

```
<a href="Path_To_Document">
Displayed_Text_To_Click
</a>
```

It may appear inside any text.

Example:

```
<a href="http://java.sun.com">
Sun Microsystems Java website
</a>
```

The *Path_To_Document* can be either a full or relative path name to an HTML file or a URL to any place on the Web. If the person viewing the document clicks the *Displayed_Text_To_Click*, the document indicated by *Path_To_Document* will be displayed.

FAQ: **What Is a URL?**

URL

The name of an HTML document on the Web is called a **URL,** which is an abbreviation for **Uniform Resource Locator.** The name is a kind of path name for the World Wide Web, a system that covers the entire globe. The hyperlinks we described in this section are all URLs, such as

```
http://java.sun.com
```

URLs are absolute path names to documents that can be anywhere in the world. You can also use relative path names for links to HTML documents on your own computer.

URLs often begin with `http`, which is the name of the protocol used to transfer and interpret the HTML document (but now we are getting beyond the scope of this book). Most browsers will allow you to omit the `http://` and will fill it in for you.

▲ *Gotcha*
Not Using Your Reload (Refresh) Button

Most browsers keep copies of the most recently used HTML pages. That way, if you want to go back to one of those pages, the browser can recover the pages very quickly. Usually, this is a good thing, since it makes your browser run faster. However, when you are designing and debugging an HTML page, it can be a problem.

Suppose you test an HTML page with your browser and notice something that needs to be fixed. If you change the HTML page to fix the problem and then look again at the page with your browser, you will probably see no change. This situation can occur even if you exit your browser; reenter the browser, starting with some other page; and then jump to the page being fixed. The problem is that, as we said, most browsers keep copies of the most recent pages that were displayed. The browser then reuses those copies instead of loading new versions of the pages.

To ensure that your browser is displaying the most current version of a page, click the button labeled Reload, Refresh, or something similar. This action will cause the browser to reload the page and thereby give you the latest version. △

Remember: Automatic Documentation with `javadoc`

The Java language comes with a program named `javadoc` that can automatically generate documentation for your Java classes. The documentation that is produced by `javadoc` is an HTML document that you read with a browser, just as you do any other HTML document. The program `javadoc` is described in Appendix 9.

Displaying a Picture

We do not need pictures for what we are doing with HTML in this chapter, but you might want to put a picture in your HTML document. The command to insert a picture is as follows:

```
<img src="File_With_Picture">
```

For example, suppose you have a digital version of a picture in the subdirectory `images`. To be specific, suppose the picture file `mypicture.gif` is in the directory `images`, and `images` is a subdirectory of the directory where the HTML page is. You could add the picture to your HTML document by inserting the following code:

```
<img src="images/mypicture.gif">
```

The picture can be in any directory, but you must give a path that will lead to the picture file. You can use either a full path name or a relative path name (that is, relative to the directory containing the HTML document) to indicate the location of the file with the encoded picture. Most commonly used picture-encoding formats are accepted.

? Self-Test Questions

6. What is the difference between the commands `<h2>` and `<H2>`?

7. How do you insert a link to the following home page?

    ```
    http://www.fool.com/
    ```

8. How will the following be displayed by a browser?

    ```
    <p>
    A major goal of the club is to encourage
    its members to become good programmers.
    <p>
    The club provides a setting where people who
    like to program in the Java language can meet
    and talk with other like-minded programmers.
    ```

    (Where would the line breaks be? Where would the browser add space?)

> ● **Programming Tip**
> ## HTML Is a Low-Level Language
>
> HTML is a low-level language. HTML for a Web browser is analogous to assembly language for a computer. Most Web-page designers now use a high-level design language that translates into HTML. If you plan to do a lot of Web-page design, you should consider learning one of these languages. Three examples of such languages are Dreamweaver (Macromedia, Inc.), FrontPage (Microsoft Corporation), and GoLive (Adobe Systems Inc.). ○

13.3 APPLETS IN HTML

*Write it here; run it there! -*Sounds like somebody's ad copy[2]

In this section, we tell you how to embed an applet in an HTML document so that the document and the applet can be viewed by a Web browser, possibly one halfway around the world.

Placing an Applet in an HTML Document

If you place the following command in an HTML document, the document will display the adder window created by the applet in Display 13.3:

```
<applet code="AdderApplet.class" width=400 height=200>
</applet>
```

This command assumes that the HTML file and the file `AdderApplet.class` are in the same directory (same folder). If they are not in the same directory, then you would use an absolute or relative path name for the file `AdderApplet.class`. An expression such as

applet tag

the one previously displayed is often called an **applet tag.**

For example, Display 13.8 contains a sample HTML document that includes the applet given in Display 13.3. When displayed with a browser, this HTML document would look approximately as shown in Display 13.9.

sizing an applet

Notice that when you place an applet in an HTML document, you give the name of the byte-code file that ends in `.class`, rather than the `.java` file or some other file name. Also notice that you specify the width and height of the applet in this command, not within the applet-class definition. The width and height are given in pixels.

Quick Reference: **Applets in HTML Documents**

You place an applet in an HTML document as shown in the given code. You use the byte-code (`.class`) file of the applet. If the file is not in the same directory (same folder) as the HTML document, you can use either a full or a relative path name to the applet file. The width and height are given in pixels.

---

2. But I just made it up.

Syntax:

```
<applet code="Name_Of_.class_File" width=Integer height=Integer>
</applet>
```

Example:

```
<applet code="AdderApplet.class" width=400 height=200>
</applet>
```

■ DISPLAY 13.8 **An HTML Document with an Applet**

```
<html>
<head>
<title>
Budget Help
</title>
</head>

<body>
<h1>
The Budget Help Home Page
<br>
Helpful Hints for a Balanced Budget
</h1>

<h2>
Pay off your credit cards every month.
</h2>

<h2>
Do not spend more than you earn.
</h2>

<h2>
Here is an adder to help you plan your budget:
</h2>
<applet code="AdderApplet.class" width=400 height=200>
</applet>
<p>
</body>

<p>
<address>
budgethelp@fleeceyou.com
<br>
December 31, 2004
</address>
</html>
```

■ DISPLAY 13.9   **Browser View of Display 13.8**

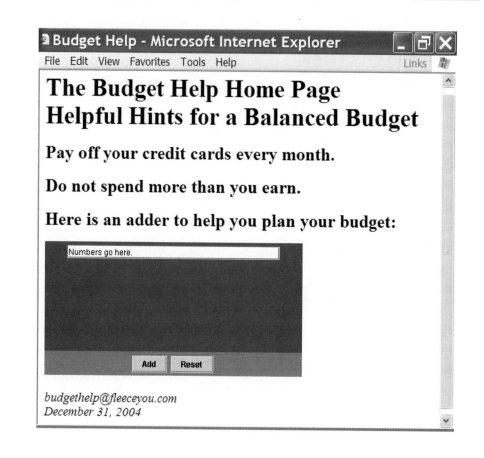

■ **Java Tip**
Applet Viewer Revisited

Even if you have not been able to run an applet viewer from an environment, you can undoubtedly run an applet viewer via a one-line command. For example, you would run the applet in Display 13.3 as follows:

```
appletviewer AdderApplet.html
```

However, if you run an applet via a one-line command in this way, you may need to create an HTML document yourself (named `AdderApplet.html` in this example) and place the applet tag in the HTML document. ■

9. When you list an applet in an HTML document, do you list the `.java` file or the `.class` file?

10. Give the HTML code to insert the applet named `HelloApplet` into an HTML document.

▲ *Gotcha*

Using an Old Web Browser

Your Web browser must be set up to run applets. Web browsers do not use the same Java interpreter that is used to run regular Java applications. If you have an old Web browser that is not set up for applets or that is set up only for applets created using an earlier version of Java, you may not be able to run applets from an HTML document. This can be the case even if Java applications run fine on your system. In such cases, all you can do is obtain a new browser.

Unfortunately, even obtaining a new browser does not always help, because the Java updates for browsers are typically made much later than the updates for the core Java language. Moreover, if you place an applet in an HTML document and expect other people to view the applet over the Web, then the applet's `.class` file will be sent to other people's computers and run on their browsers. And, of course, you cannot reasonably expect all those other people to have the most recent browser.

If you expect an applet to be widely viewed over the Web, you should test it on a number of different browsers. Testing your applet on Netscape Navigator and Microsoft's Internet Explorer should be sufficient, but you should test it on older versions of these browsers as well as the latest release. If you have trouble getting your applet to work on older browsers, consider using the older `Applet` class as described in the optional subsection "The Older `Applet` Class."

Although you may have problems running your applets on a browser, you should have no such problem running them from the applet viewer, as long as you have a recent version of Java. So you should be able to run and test your applets, even if you cannot run them from an HTML page. However, if they are not ultimately placed in HTML documents, you may as well use regular Swing GUIs derived from `JFrame`. △

applet viewer

The Older `Applet` Class *(Optional)*

If you find that your applet does not work on a wide enough array of browsers, try using the older `Applet` class instead of the `JApplet` class. You can usually do this simply by deleting all the Js, replacing `JApplet` with `Applet`, `JButton` with `Button`, `JLabel` with `Label`, and so forth. This approach will require the following `import` statements:

`Applet`

```
import java.awt.*;
import Java.awt.event.*;
import java.applet.*;
```

And you may as well delete the following `import` statement:

```
import javax.swing.*;
```

You also need to make another, slightly more complicated alteration. Unlike a `JApplet`, an `Applet` has no content pane. So you use `add` with the applet itself rather than using a content pane, and in general, whatever you did to the content pane of a `JApplet`, you need to do directly to the `Applet`. For example, if the method `init` contains the line

```
getContentPane( ).add(friendlyLabel);
```

in the `JApplet`, then to convert it to an `Applet`, you need to replace this statement with

```
add(friendlyLabel);
```

For most simple applets, these changes will produce an applet that will run on older as well as newer browsers. However, there are things you can do with a `JApplet` that you cannot do with the older `Applet` class. For example, the class `Applet` cannot easily accommodate icons, so your applets should not contain icons when you use the `Applet` class. In Chapter 14, we discuss menus. You can use menus with a `JApplet`, but not with an `Applet`, so you must use buttons instead.

Extra code on CD We have followed these rules to produce applets based on the `Applet` class instead of the `JApplet` class for the applets in Displays 13.2 and 13.3. The results are in the files `OlderHelloApplet.java` and `OlderAdderApplet.java` on the accompanying CD.

Quick Reference: **The `Applet` Class** *(Optional)*

The class `Applet` is an older applet class that was used to produce applets before the `JApplet` class came on the scene. Applets produced using the class `Applet` cannot have as many features as those produced with the class `JApplet`. However, they will work on a wider range of browsers. So if you expect your applets to be viewed by a wide array of users, it might be prudent to use the class `Applet`, rather than the class `JApplet`. For very simple applets, it is easy to convert a `JApplet` to an `Applet`. The details are given in the optional subsection "The Older `Applet` Class." The `Applet` class requires the following `import` statement:

```
import java.applet.*;
```

Applets and Security

Suppose somebody on the Web reads your HTML page and that HTML page contains an applet. That applet's byte-code is run on the reader's browser, which is on the reader's computer. So your applet can be a program that runs on other people's computers. More frightening, other people's applets can run on your computer. Moreover, you do not know that an HTML page contains an applet until you load it into your browser, and then it is too late to reject the applet. At that point, it is already stored on your computer.

Whenever somebody else's program runs on your computer, there are serious security concerns. Will the program leave a virus on your computer? Will it read confidential information from your files? Will it change and thus corrupt your operating system? Applets are designed so that they cannot (or at least cannot easily) do any of these things. Applets cannot run any of your programs, and they cannot read or write to files on your computer (unless the applet originated on your computer). But be warned: There are programs other than applets that can be run through your browser and that can gain access to things on your computer—things that you may have thought were private. Commercially available antivirus and other protection software can help to guard your computer against such invasive programs.

11. For the subsection "The Older `Applet` Class *(Optional)*": A `JApplet` has an `init` method. Does an `Applet` have an `init` method?

12. For the subsection "The Older `Applet` Class *(Optional)*": A `JApplet` has a content pane. Does an `Applet` have a content pane?

CHAPTER SUMMARY

- Applets are Java programs designed to be placed in and run from a Web-site document.

- Applets are similar to Swing GUIs derived from the class `JFrame`.

- An applet is normally a derived class of the class `JApplet`.

- An applet normally has no `main` method and no constructors. However, the method `init` serves the same purpose as a constructor for an applet.

- An applet's `init` method does not include any invocations of `addWindowListener`, `setTitle`, or `setSize`.

- Documents designed to be read across the World Wide Web or through a Web browser are typically written in a language called HTML. HTML stands for Hypertext Markup Language. Applets can be embedded in and run from HTML documents.

✔ Answers to Self-Test Questions

1. Applet classes do not usually use constructors. However, they do use a method named `init` that serves a similar purpose.

2. Applet classes do not normally have a `main` method.

3. You are very likely to use `getContentPane` when defining an applet. You would not normally use `addWindowListener`, `setTitle`, or `setSize`, because an applet does not have a title, and its size and closing are handled by the applet viewer or the Web document in which the applet is embedded. (It is possible to use them in certain kinds of components that might be added to an applet, but that is not what we are emphasizing in this question.)

4. You create a label (with or without text) by using a constructor for the class `JLabel`. You create the icon from `smiley.gif` by using a constructor for the

class `ImageIcon`. You add the icon to the label with the method `setIcon`. For example, the following code might be used in the `init` method of an applet:

```
JLabel niceLabel = new JLabel();
ImageIcon smileyFaceIcon = new ImageIcon("smiley.gif");
niceLabel.setIcon(smileyFaceIcon);
getContentPane().add(niceLabel);
```

5. You may use a relative or absolute path name when specifying the digital picture file.

6. None. HTML is not case sensitive.

7.

```
<a href="http://www.fool.com/">
Anything you want to say goes here.
</a>
```

8. A line break and some extra space will be added at each `<p>`. The line breaks in the text will be ignored, and the browser will insert line breaks where necessary to fit the text in the browser window.

9. The `.class` file.

10.

```
<applet code="HelloApplet.class" width=400 height=200>
</applet>
```

The width and height can, of course, be set to values other than 400 and 200, respectively.

11. An `Applet` has an `init` method just as a `JApplet` does.

12. An `Applet` does not have a content pane.

● Programming Projects

1. Design an HTML home page for yourself. Use your imagination to put in whatever you would like people to know about you or that you think they should know about you. Some possibilities are your name, your occupation or class schedule, where you go to school or work, your hobbies, your favorite quotation, how to reach you by e-mail, or anything else you want to say. Note that your home page, like any home page, will consist of several files, each of which contains HTML documents. The hyperlinks allow the person viewing the document to move from one HTML document to another by clicking a mouse button. *Variation*: If you are in a class, ask your instructor if you need to include an applet on your home page.

Remember, anything you place on your home page can be viewed by anybody in the world. Include only information that you do not mind being made public.

2. Convert the Swing application in Display 12.19 to an applet, and place it in an HTML document.

3. Every first-year electrical engineering student learns that two resistors (a resistor is a common type of electrical component) can be connected in either of two configurations, series or parallel, and that there are simple formulas to calculate the

equivalent resistance of both configurations (the value of a single resistor that can replace the two). If $R1$ and $R2$ are the two resistor values, then

$$\text{Series resistance} = R1 + R2, \text{ and}$$
$$\text{Parallel resistance} = (R1 * R2) / (R1 + R2).$$

Write an applet that provides a windowing interface to let a user enter two resistor values and choose which configuration to calculate. Include two text fields (label them "Resistor 1" and "Resistor 2") to read in the two values, two buttons (label them "Series" and "Parallel") to select the configuration, and another text field (label it "Equivalent Resistance") to display the calculated value and indicate which configuration was selected. For example, if the user enters 100 for $R1$ and 50 for $R2$ and clicks the "Series" button, then the message would read "Series Equivalent = 150". If the user enters the same values and clicks the "Parallel" button, then the message would read "Parallel Equivalent = 33.3". Put the applet in a Web page that explains the calculations.

4. Modify the GUI calculator program from Programming Project 7 in Chapter 12 to run as an applet. If you have not already done this project as a GUI, do it now, but do it as an applet.

5. (The Swing part of this exercise is quite straightforward, but you do need to know a little about how to convert numbers from one base to another.) Write an applet that converts numbers from base-10 (ordinary decimal) notation to hexadecimal (base-16) notation. The program uses Swing to do input and output via an applet interface. The user enters a base-10 integer numeral in one text field and clicks a button labeled "Convert". The equivalent hexadecimal numeral then appears in another text field. Be sure that the two fields are labeled. Include a "Clear" button that clears both text fields.

6. Rewrite the program in Display 12.19 so that it is an applet and so that it has all of the following changes:

i. The class name is MemoApplet.

ii. There are six buttons instead of five, and they are arranged as follows:

Save Memo 1	Save Memo 2	Clear
Get Memo 1	Get Memo 1	Exit

The buttons are still at the bottom of the GUI (applet), with the text area above them. (*Hint*: Use a GridLayout manager on the button panel.)

iii. When the user saves the text as memo 1, the text area changes so that it says "Memo 1 saved.", and when the user saves the text as memo 2, the text area changes to "Memo 2 saved." (See Self-Test Exercise 43 of Chapter 12 for a hint.)

iv. The text area has line wrap, so that if more characters are entered than will fit on the line, the extra characters automatically go on the next line.

7. Do Programming Project 4 of Chapter 9, but write it as an applet.

8. Do Programming Project 7 of Chapter 9, but write it as an applet.

More Swing

The more the merrier. -John Heywood, *Proverbs* (1546)

In this chapter, we give you some additional information about Swing, so that you can create more professional-looking GUIs. Among other topics, we will cover menus, scroll bars, icons, and inner classes.

Along the way, you will learn about the following Swing (or Swing-related) classes: `AbstractButton`, `Box`, `BoxLayout`, `BevelBorder`, `Dimension`, `EmptyBorder`, `EtchedBorder`, `ImageIcon`, `Inset`, `JMenu`, `JMenuBar`, `JMenuItem`, `JScrollPane`, `LineBorder`, `MatteBorder`, and others.

OBJECTIVES

Learn to add menus, icons, borders, and scroll bars to your GUIs.

Understand the `BoxLayout` manager and the `Box` class.

Understand some uses and advantages of inner classes.

Learn about the `WindowListener` interface.

Find out how to create GUIs with components that change from visible to invisible and vice versa.

PREREQUISITES

Before reading this chapter, you need to have covered Chapter 12, which introduces you to Swing. You do not need to have covered Chapter 13 ("Applets and HTML").

Section 14.2 uses material from Section 14.1. Aside from that one dependency, Sections 14.1, 14.2, 14.3, and 14.4 are independent of one another. You can cover them in any order so long as you cover Section 14.1 before Section 14.2.

Section 14.5 uses material presented in Section 14.4. Section 14.6 uses material presented in Sections 14.1 and 14.2.

14.1 MENUS

You pays your money and you takes your choice. -*Punch* (1846)

Swing GUIs can have menus, and you have already learned most of what you need to know about menus in Swing. You learned it when you learned about buttons in Chapter 12. Menu items behave in the same way as buttons. An example will make this clear.

Programming Example
A GUI with a Menu

Display 14.1 contains a program that constructs a GUI with a menu. This GUI does the same thing as the GUI in Display 12.19. The user types memos in the text area, and when memos are recalled, they appear in the text area, just as in Display 12.19. But the GUI in Display 14.1 does not have any buttons. Instead, it has a menu bar at the top of the window. The menu bar lists the names of all the pull-down menus. This GUI has only one pull-down menu, which is named "Memos". However, there could be more pull-down menus in the same menu bar.

The user can pull down a menu by clicking its name in the menu bar. Display 14.1 contains two pictures of the GUI. The first is what you see when the GUI first appears. In that picture, the menu name "Memos" can be seen in the menu bar, but you cannot see the menu. If you click the word "Memos", using your mouse, the menu drops down, as shown in the second picture of the GUI. If you click "Save Memo 1", the text in the text area is saved. The other menu choices behave similarly to the buttons in Display 12.19.

There is one new choice on this menu, namely, Exit. When the user clicks the entry Exit, the program ends, and the window disappears. The exact same thing happens if the user clicks the close-window button. So there are two ways that a user can end this GUI.

In the next few sections, we go over the details of the program in Display 14.1. ∎

Menu Bars, Menus, and Menu Items

When adding menus as we did in Display 14.1, you use the three Swing classes JMenuBar, JMenu, and JMenuItem. Entries on a menu are objects of the class JMenu-Item. These JMenuItems are placed in JMenus, and then the JMenus are typically placed in a JMenuBar. Let's look at the details.

An object of the class JMenuItem is one of the choices on a menu. It is identified by the string that labels it, such as "Save Memo 1". An object of the class JMenu is a menu such as the one shown in the GUI in Display 14.1. You can add as many JMenuItems as you wish to a menu. The menu lists the items in the order in which they are added. The following code, taken from the constructor in Display 14.1, creates a new JMenu object named memoMenu and then adds a JMenuItem labeled "Save Memo 1".

JMenuItem

JMenu

```java
JMenu memoMenu = new JMenu("Memos");
JMenuItem m;

m = new JMenuItem("Save Memo 1");
m.addActionListener(this);
memoMenu.add(m);
```

Other menu items are added in a similar way.

Note that, just as we did for buttons, we have registered the this parameter as an action listener. Defining action listeners and registering listeners for menu items are done in the exact same way as for buttons. In fact, the syntax is even the same. If you compare Display 12.19 and Display 14.1, you will see that the method actionPerformed is defined in the same way in both cases. The only difference is that, in Display 14.1, the method has one additional case, for the new entry labeled "Exit".

■ DISPLAY 14.1 **A GUI with a Menu** *(Part 1 of 3)*

```java
import javax.swing.*;
import java.awt.*;
import java.awt.event.*;

public class MemoGUI extends JFrame implements ActionListener
{
    public static final int WIDTH = 600;
    public static final int HEIGHT = 300;
    public static final int LINES = 10;
    public static final int CHAR_PER_LINE = 40;

    private JTextArea theText;
    private String memo1 = "No Memo 1.";
    private String memo2 = "No Memo 2.";

    public MemoGUI()
    {
        setSize(WIDTH, HEIGHT);
        addWindowListener(new WindowDestroyer());
        setTitle("Memo Saver");
        Container contentPane = getContentPane();
        contentPane.setLayout(new BorderLayout());

        JMenu memoMenu = new JMenu("Memos");
        JMenuItem m;

        m = new JMenuItem("Save Memo 1");
        m.addActionListener(this);
        memoMenu.add(m);

        m = new JMenuItem("Save Memo 2");
        m.addActionListener(this);
        memoMenu.add(m);

        m = new JMenuItem("Get Memo 1");
        m.addActionListener(this);
        memoMenu.add(m);

        m = new JMenuItem("Get Memo 2");
        m.addActionListener(this);
        memoMenu.add(m);

        m = new JMenuItem("Clear");
        m.addActionListener(this);
        memoMenu.add(m);
```

The class `WindowDestroyer` *is defined and discussed in Chapter 12.*

<Constructor MemoGUI continued in next part of display.>

■ DISPLAY 14.1 A GUI with a Menu *(Part 2 of 3)*

<Constructor MemoGUI continued.>

```java
        m = new JMenuItem("Exit");
        m.addActionListener(this);
        memoMenu.add(m);

        JMenuBar mBar = new JMenuBar();
        mBar.add(memoMenu);
        setJMenuBar(mBar);

        JPanel textPanel = new JPanel();
        textPanel.setBackground(Color.BLUE);
        theText = new JTextArea(LINES, CHAR_PER_LINE);
        theText.setBackground(Color.WHITE);
        textPanel.add(theText);
        contentPane.add(textPanel, BorderLayout.CENTER);
    }
    public void actionPerformed(ActionEvent e)
    {
        String actionCommand = e.getActionCommand();
        if (actionCommand.equals("Save Memo 1"))
            memo1 = theText.getText();
        else if (actionCommand.equals("Save Memo 2"))
            memo2 = theText.getText();
        else if (actionCommand.equals("Clear"))
            theText.setText("");
        else if (actionCommand.equals("Get Memo 1"))
            theText.setText(memo1);
        else if (actionCommand.equals("Get Memo 2"))
            theText.setText(memo2);
        else if (actionCommand.equals("Exit"))
            System.exit(0);
        else
            theText.setText("Error in memo interface");
    }
    public static void main(String[] args)
    {
        MemoGUI gui = new MemoGUI();
        gui.setVisible(true);
    }
}
```

■ DISPLAY 14.1 **A GUI with a Menu** *(Part 3 of 3)*

Resulting GUI

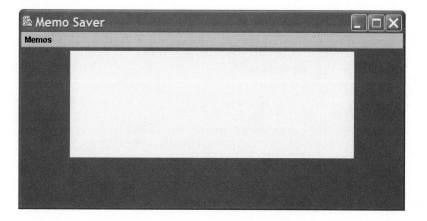

Resulting GUI (after clicking Memos in the menu bar)

You add a `JMenuItem` to an object of the class `JMenu` by using the method `add` in exactly the same way that you add a component, such as a button, to a container object. Moreover, if you look at the preceding code, you will see that you specify a string for a `JMenuItem` in the same way that you specify a string label for a button. So the syntax for adding menu items to a menu is really nothing new.

menu bar
      A **menu bar** is a container for menus, typically placed near the top of a windowing interface. You add a menu to a menu bar by using the method `add` in the same way that

you add menu items to a menu. The following code from the constructor in Display 14.1 creates a new menu bar named mBar and then adds the menu named memoMenu to this menu bar:

JMenuBar

```
JMenuBar mBar = new JMenuBar( );
mBar.add(memoMenu);
```

There are two different ways to add a menu bar to a JFrame. First, you can use the method setJMenuBar, as shown in the following code from Display 14.1:

```
setJMenuBar(mBar);
```

This code sets an instance variable of type JMenuBar so that it names the menu bar mBar. Saying it less formally, this code adds the menu bar mBar to the JFrame and places the menu bar at the top of the JFrame.

Alternatively, you can add a menu bar to the content pane of a JFrame (or to any other container). You do so in the same way that you add any other component, such as labels or buttons. An example of using add to add a JMenuBar to the content pane of a JFrame is given in the file MenuAdd.java on the accompanying CD.

extra code on CD

Quick Reference: Menus and Menu Bars

A menu item is an object of the class JMenuItem, a menu is an object of the class JMenu, and a menu bar is an object of the class JMenuBar. You add a menu item to a menu by using the method add. You also add a menu to a menu bar by using the method add. A menu bar can be added to a JFrame in two different ways. You can add a JMenuBar to the content pane of a JFrame (or to any other container, for that matter) by using the method add and any layout manager you wish. Alternatively, and perhaps more typically, you can add a menu bar to a JFrame by using the method setJMenuBar.

Events and listeners for menu items are handled in exactly the same way as they are for buttons.

Quick Reference: Setting the Action Command for a Menu Item

Like the text for a button, the text for a JMenuItem is the default action command for the menu item. And, as you can for a button, you can set the action command for a menu item to some other string by using the method setActionCommand.

Syntax:

Menu_Item_Object.setActionCommand(*Action_Command_String*);

Example:

```
JMenuItem item = new JMenuItem("Click me!");
item.setActionCommand("From the click me item with love.");
```

Nested Menus

The class JMenu is a descendant of the JMenuItem class. So every JMenu object is also a JMenuItem object. Thus, a JMenu can be a menu item in another menu. This means that you can nest menus. For example, the outer menu might give you a list of menus. You can display one of the menus on that list by clicking the name of the desired menu. You can then choose an item from that menu by using your mouse again. There is nothing new you need to know in order to create these nested menus. You simply add menus to menus just as you add other menu items. There is an example of nested menus in the file Nested-Menus.java on the accompanying CD.

extra code
on CD

Quick Reference: Adding Menus to a JFrame

In this box, we assume that all additions take place inside a constructor for a (derived class of) JFrame. Otherwise, most method invocations would require an object name and dot before them. To see the given examples put together to produce a complete GUI, see the constructor in Display 14.1.

Creating Menu Items

A menu item is an object of the class JMenuItem. You create a new menu item in the usual way, as illustrated by the following example:

```
JMenuItem m;
m = new JMenuItem("Save Memo 1");
```

The string in the argument position is the label of the menu item.

Adding Menu-Item Listeners

Events and listeners for menu items are handled in the same way as they are for buttons: Menu items fire action events that are received by objects of type ActionListener.

Syntax:

```
JMenu_Item_Name.addActionListener(Action_Listener);
```

Example:

```
m.addActionListener(this);
```

Adding Menu Items to a Menu

A menu is an object of the class JMenu. You use the method add to add menu items to a menu.

Syntax:

```
JMenu_Name.add(JMenu_Item);
```

Example (memoMenu is an object of the class JMenu):

```
memoMenu.add(m);
```

Adding a Menu to a Menu Bar

A menu bar is an object of the class JMenuBar. You add a menu to a menu bar as follows:

Syntax:

JMenu_Bar_Name.add(*JMenu_Name*);

Example (mBar is an object of the class JMenuBar):

mBar.add(memoMenu);

Adding a Menu Bar to a Frame

There are two different ways to add a menu bar to a JFrame. First, you can use the method add to add the menu bar to the content pane of the JFrame (or to any other container). Or you can use the pre-defined method setJMenuBar as follows:

Syntax:

setJMenuBar(*JMenu_Bar_Name*);

Example:

setJMenuBar(mBar);

? Self-Test Questions

1. What kind of event is fired when you click a JMenuItem? How does it differ from the kind of event fired when you click a JButton?

2. If you want to change the action command for a JButton, you use the method setActionCommand. What method do you use to change the action command for a JMenuItem?

3. Is the following code legal in Java?

   ```
   JMenu myMenu = new JMenu();
       ...
   JMenu mySubMenu = new JMenu();
       ...
   myMenu.add(mySubMenu);
   ```

4. How many JMenuBar objects can you have in a JFrame?

5. A JFrame has a private instance variable of type JMenuBar. What is the name of the mutator method to change ("set") this instance variable?

6. Write code to create a new menu item named mItem that has the label "Choose Me!"

7. Suppose you build a GUI interface, using Swing. If the user clicks a menu item, an event is fired. What kind of listener receives the event?

8. Suppose you are defining a class called MenusGalore that is a derived class of the class JFrame. Write code to add the menu item mItem to the menu m. Then add m to the menu bar mBar, and then add the menu bar to the JFrame MenusGalore. Assume that this all takes place inside a constructor for MenusGalore. Also

assume that everything has already been constructed with new and that all necessary listeners are registered. You just need to do the addition of menu features.

14.2   MAKING GUIs PRETTY (AND MORE FUNCTIONAL)

In matters of grave importance,
style, not sincerity, is the vital thing. -Oscar Wilde, *The Importance of Being Earnest*

In this section, we describe a number of Swing facilities that can make your GUIs more attractive and professional looking. Many of the enhancements are as utilitarian as they are esthetic. Topics include icons, scroll bars, and borders.

Adding Icons

icon

With Swing, labels, buttons, and menu items can have icons. An **icon** is simply a small picture, although it is not required to be small. The picture can be of anything. Pictures are produced in a number of formats that can be displayed on a computer screen (such as GIF and JPEG). A picture in almost any standard format can be used as the basis for an icon. Swing will make the picture into an icon, and you can then add the icon to a label, button, or other component. The label or button may have just a string displayed on it, just an icon, or both (or it can have nothing at all on it, for that matter).

ImageIcon

The class `ImageIcon` is used to convert a picture file to a Swing icon. For example, if you have a picture in a file named `duke_waving.gif`, the following code will produce an icon named `dukeWavingIcon` for the picture `duke_waving.gif`:

```
ImageIcon dukeWavingIcon =
        new ImageIcon("duke_waving.gif");
```

The file `duke_waving.gif` should be in the same directory as the class in which this code appears. Alternatively, you can use a complete or relative path name to specify the picture file. The pictures file name is given as the argument to the constructor `Image-Icon`. Because the picture file is given as a string, you should have quotes around the name or use a variable or expression of type `String`. The file `duke_waving.gif` and other picture files we will use in this chapter are all provided on the CD that accompanies this text.

You can add this icon to a label by giving it as an argument to the `JLabel` constructor, as follows:

```
JLabel dukePicture = new JLabel(dukeWavingIcon);
```

You can then add the label `dukePicture` to a `JFrame`, `JPanel`, or other container, and the label will display a picture instead of a string of text.

button with
only an icon

You can also produce a button with (just) an icon on it. This task is done in a similar way:

```
JButton dukeButton = new JButton(dukeWavingIcon);
```

If you create a button in this way, you should use `setActionCommand` to explicitly give the button an action command, since there is no string on the button. (See the box entitled "setActionCommand and `getActionCommand`" in Chapter 12 if this operation sounds unfamiliar to you.)

Quick Reference: Icons and the Class `ImageIcon`

An **icon** is simply a small picture, although it is not really required to be small. The class `ImageIcon` is used to convert a picture file to a Swing icon.

Syntax:

```
ImageIcon Name_Of_ImageIcon =
        new ImageIcon(Picture_File_Name);
```

The *Picture_File_Name* is a string giving either a relative or an absolute path name to the picture file. (So if the picture file is in the same directory as your program, you need give only the name of the picture file.)

Example:

```
ImageIcon smileyIcon =
        new ImageIcon("smiley.gif");
```

So far in this chapter, we have put icons on labels and buttons, and in Chapter 12, we put strings on labels and buttons. If you want, and you often will want to do this, you can place both an icon and a string on a label or button. One way to do this is to make the string the argument to the constructor for the label or button, and to add the icon with the method `setIcon`. This procedure is illustrated in the following code:

setIcon

```
JButton helloButton = new JButton("Hello");
ImageIcon dukeWavingIcon = new ImageIcon("duke_waving.gif");
helloButton.setIcon(dukeWavingIcon);
```

You can add both a string and an icon to a `JLabel` in the same way.

Display 14.2 contains a program that illustrates the use of icons with labels and buttons. The text field is initially blank. When the user clicks the "Hello" button, the phrase

```
"Glad to meet you!"
```

appears in the text field, as shown in Display 14.2. When the user clicks the "Good bye" button, the phrase

```
"OK, click the upper right button. I'll miss you."
```

appears in the text field. The program ends when the user clicks the close-window button.

Note that when a button is created using code such as

```
JButton helloButton = new JButton("Hello");
```

■ DISPLAY 14.2 **Using Icons** *(Part 1 of 2)*

```java
import javax.swing.*;
import java.awt.*;
import java.awt.event.*;
/**
 Simple demonstration of putting icons in buttons and labels.
*/
public class IconDemo extends JFrame implements ActionListener
{
    public static final int WIDTH = 400;
    public static final int HEIGHT = 200;

    private JTextField message;

    public IconDemo( )
    {
        setSize(WIDTH, HEIGHT);
        addWindowListener(new WindowDestroyer( ));
        setTitle("Icon Demonstration");
        Container content = getContentPane( );
        content.setBackground(Color.WHITE);
        content.setLayout(new BorderLayout( ));

        JLabel niceLabel = new JLabel("Nice day!");
        ImageIcon smileyIcon = new ImageIcon("smiley.gif");
        niceLabel.setIcon(smileyIcon);
        content.add(niceLabel, BorderLayout.NORTH);

        JPanel buttonPanel = new JPanel( );
        buttonPanel.setLayout(new FlowLayout( ));
        JButton helloButton = new JButton("Hello");
        ImageIcon dukeWavingIcon = new ImageIcon("duke_waving.gif");
        helloButton.setIcon(dukeWavingIcon);
        helloButton.addActionListener(this);
        buttonPanel.add(helloButton);
        JButton byeButton = new JButton("Good bye");
        ImageIcon dukeStandingIcon =
                    new ImageIcon("duke_standing.gif");
        byeButton.setIcon(dukeStandingIcon);
        byeButton.addActionListener(this);
        buttonPanel.add(byeButton);
        content.add(buttonPanel, BorderLayout.SOUTH);

        message = new JTextField(30);
        content.add(message, BorderLayout.CENTER);
    }
```

■ DISPLAY 14.2 **Using Icons** *(Part 2 of 2)*

```java
public void actionPerformed(ActionEvent e)
{
    if (e.getActionCommand().equals("Hello"))
        message.setText("Glad to meet you!");
    else if (e.getActionCommand().equals("Good bye"))
        message.setText(
            "OK, click the upper right button. I'll miss you.");
    else
        System.out.println("Error in button interface.");
}

/**
 Creates and displays a window of the class IconDemo.
 */
public static void main(String[] args)
{
    IconDemo iconGui = new IconDemo();
    iconGui.setVisible(true);
}
}
```

Resulting GUI[1]

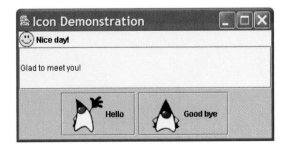

---

1. Java, Duke, and all Java-based trademarks and logos are trademarks or registered trademarks of Sun Microsystems, Inc., in the United States and other countries.

the action command is the string on the button—in this case, "Hello"—even though you may also add an icon to the button, as in the following code from Display 14.2:

```
helloButton.setIcon(dukeWavingIcon);
```

Aside from the addition of icons, there is nothing new in Display 14.2.

Both of the classes `JButton` and `JLabel` have constructors that let you specify text and an icon to appear on the button or label. The constructor can specify no text or icon, text only, icon only, or both text and icon. When you specify both text and an icon, the text is the first argument and the icon is the second argument; also, the constructor for a `JLabel` requires a third argument, as described in Display 14.3. If you omit either text or an icon (or both) from the constructor, you can add them later with the methods `setText` and `setIcon`, respectively. Some of these methods for the classes `JButton` and `Jlabel` are given in Display 14.3.

setText

Quick Reference: `setIcon` and `setText`

The method `setIcon` can be used to add an icon to a `JButton`, `JLabel`, or certain other components. The argument to `setIcon` must be an `ImageIcon` object.

Syntax:

Component.`setIcon`(*ImageIcon_Object*);

The *Component* can be a `JButton`, `JLabel`, or certain other components.

Example:

```
JLabel helloLabel = new JLabel("Hello");
ImageIcon dukeWavingIcon = new ImageIcon("duke_waving.gif");
helloLabel.setIcon(dukeWavingIcon);
```

The method `setText` can be used to add text to a `JButton`, `JLabel`, or certain other components.

Syntax:

Component.`setText`(*Text_String*);

The *Component* can be a `JButton`, `JLabel`, or certain other components.

Example:

```
ImageIcon dukeWavingIcon = new ImageIcon("duke_waving.gif");
JLabel helloLabel = new JLabel(dukeWavingIcon);
helloLabel.setText("Hello");
```

The two examples are equivalent.

■ DISPLAY 14.3 **Some Methods in the Classes** JButton **and** JLabel *(Part 1 of 2)*

```
public JButton( )
public JLabel( )
```

Creates a button or label with no text or icon on it. (Typically, you will later use setText or setIcon with the button or menu item.)

```
public JButton(String text)
public JLabel(String text)
```

Creates a button or label with the text on it.

```
public JButton(ImageIcon picture)
public JLabel(ImageIcon picture)
```

Creates a button or label with the icon picture on it.

```
public JButton(String text, ImageIcon picture)
public JLabel(
        String text, ImageIcon picture, int horizontalAlignment)
```

Creates a button or label with both the text and the icon picture on it. horizontalAlignment is one of the constants SwingConstants.LEFT, SwingConstants.CENTER, SwingConstants.RIGHT, SwingConstants.LEADING, or SwingConstants.TRAILING.

```
public void setText(String text)
```

Makes text the only text on the button or label.

```
public void setIcon(ImageIcon picture)
```

Makes picture the only icon on the button or label.

```
public void setMargin(Insets margin)
JButton has the method setMargin, but JLabel does not.
```

The method setMargin sets the size of the margin around the text and icon in the button. The following special case will work for most simple situations, where the int values give the number of pixels from the edge of the button to the text or icon:

```
public void setMargin(new Insets(
                int top, int left, int bottom, int right))
```

```
public void setPreferredSize(Dimension preferredSize)
```

Sets the preferred size of the button or label. Note that this size is only a suggestion to the layout manager. The layout manager is not required to use the preferred size. The following special case will work for most simple situations, where the int values give the width and height in pixels:

```
public void setPreferredSize(
                new Dimension(int width, int height))
```

■ DISPLAY 14.3 **Some Methods in the Classes** `JButton` **and** `JLabel` *(Part 2 of 2)*

```
public void setMaximumSize(Dimension maximumSize)
```

Sets the maximum size of the button or label. Note that this size is only a suggestion to the layout manager. The layout manager is not required to respect this maximum size. The following special case will work for most simple situations, where the `int` values give the width and height in pixels:

```
public void setMaximumSize(
                      new Dimension(int width, int height))
```

```
public void setMinimumSize(Dimension minimumSize)
```

Sets the minimum size of the button or label. Note that this size is only a suggestion to the layout manager. The layout manager is not required to respect this minimum size. The following special case will work for most simple situations, where the `int` values give the width and height in pixels:

```
public void setMinimumSize(
                      new Dimension(int width, int height))
```

```
public void setVerticalTextPosition(int textPosition)
```

Sets the vertical position of the text relative to the icon. The `textPosition` should be one of the constants `SwingConstants.TOP`, `SwingConstants.CENTER` (the default position), or `SwingConstants.BOTTOM`.

```
public void setHorizontalTextPosition(int textPosition)
```

Sets the horizontal position of the text relative to the icon. The `textPosition` should be one of the constants `SwingConstants.RIGHT`, `SwingConstants.LEFT`, `SwingConstants.CENTER`, `SwingConstants.LEADING`, or `SwingConstants.TRAILING`.

▲ *Gotcha*

Resizing Buttons

If you look at the button methods described in Display 14.3, you will see that you can change the size of a button. The methods for setting the preferred, maximum, and minimum size are a bit troublesome. They are only recommendations to the layout manager. There is no guarantee that your sizing instructions will be followed.

Changing the size of a button can change other things in the button, such as how the text in the button is displayed. Sometimes, this problem can be fixed by setting the size of the margin between the contents of the button and the edge of the button. For example, if you want no margin in a button b, you would use the following code:

```
b.setMargin(new Insets(0, 0, 0, 0));
```

Yet another problem with button sizes is that the image may be clipped if the icon is too big to fit on the button. When resizing buttons, you can expect to do a lot of tuning to get the GUI to look good. △

Adding Icons to Menu Items

You can use the method `setIcon` to add an icon to a `JMenuItem` in the exact same way that you add an icon to a `JButton`. An example is given in the file `MemoIconDemo.java` on the accompanying CD.

extra code on CD

Quick Reference: The Classes `Dimension` and `Inset`

Objects of the classes `Dimension` and `Inset` are used with buttons, labels, and other objects to specify a size. The parameters in the following constructors are in pixels:

Constructors:

```
Insets(int top, int left, int bottom, int right)
Dimension(int width, int height)
```

Examples:

```
aButton.setMargin(new Insets(10, 20, 10, 20));
aLabel.setPreferredSize(new Dimension(20, 50));
```

? Self-Test Questions

9. Suppose you want to create a button that has on it both the text `"Push Me"` and the picture in the file `alice.gif`. How would you do it?

10. How would you add the picture in the file `alice.gif` to the `JPanel` named `picturePanel`? Assume that `picturePanel` has a `FlowLayout` manager.

11. Suppose you want to create a button that has the picture in the file `alice.gif` on it and no text. Suppose further that you want the button to have the action command `"Curiouser and curiouser!"`. How would you create the button and set up the action command?

12. Suppose b is a `JButton`. Will the following line guarantee that the button's size is at least 10 pixels by 10 pixels?

```
b.setMinimumSize(new Dimension(10, 10));
```

The `JScrollPane` Class for Scroll Bars

When you create a text area, you specify the number of lines that are visible and the number of characters per line, as in the following example:

```
JTextArea theText = new JTextArea(10, 40);
```

The text area `theText` will have room for is 10 lines of text long, and each line will have room for at least 40 characters. However, it would be better not to have a firm limit on the number of lines or the number of characters per line that the user can type in and can see in some convenient way.

In professionally produced GUIs you have worked with, you have undoubtedly seen text areas where you can type any amount of text and then view the text in a "window" or **view port** that shows only part of the text at a time. You can view a different part of the text by using the scroll bars that are placed along the sides of the view port. In these professionally produced GUIs, it is as if the text were written on an unbounded sheet of paper, but the paper is covered by another piece of paper with a rectangular cutout that lets you see a portion of the text. The cutout is the view port. This concept is illustrated in Display 14.4. You then use the scroll bars to move the view port so that different portions of the text can be seen through the cut-out view port. (You may prefer to think of the view port as fixed and the text as moving. These two ways of thinking are equivalent.) Swing allows you to add scroll bars to your text areas. You provide the scroll bars by using the class `JScrollPane`.

view port

■ DISPLAY 14.4　**View Port for a Text Area**

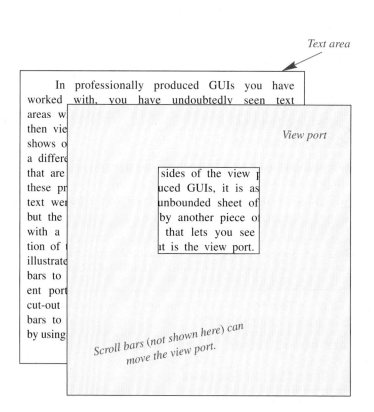

Text area

View port

Scroll bars (not shown here) can move the view port.

■ DISPLAY 14.5 **A Text Area with Scroll Bars** *(Part 1 of 2)*

```java
import javax.swing.*;
import java.awt.*;
import java.awt.event.*;

public class ScrollBarDemo extends JFrame implements ActionListener
{
    public static final int WIDTH = 600;
    public static final int HEIGHT = 300;
    public static final int LINES = 10;
    public static final int CHAR_PER_LINE = 40;

    private JTextArea theText;
    private String memo1 = "No Memo 1.";
    private String memo2 = "No Memo 2.";

    public ScrollBarDemo()
    {
        setSize(WIDTH, HEIGHT);
        addWindowListener(new WindowDestroyer());
        setTitle("Scrolling Memo Saver");
        Container contentPane = getContentPane();

                .
                .
                .

        JPanel textPanel = new JPanel();
        textPanel.setBackground(Color.BLUE);
        theText = new JTextArea(LINES, CHAR_PER_LINE);
        theText.setBackground(Color.WHITE);
        JScrollPane scrolledText = new JScrollPane(theText);
        scrolledText.setHorizontalScrollBarPolicy(
                    JScrollPane.HORIZONTAL_SCROLLBAR_ALWAYS);
        scrolledText.setVerticalScrollBarPolicy(
                    JScrollPane.VERTICAL_SCROLLBAR_ALWAYS);
        textPanel.add(scrolledText);
        contentPane.add(textPanel, BorderLayout.CENTER);
    }
```

The omitted statements are the same as in Display 14.1. In fact, this constructor is the same as that in Display 14.1, except that the name of the class and the title of the JFrame are changed, and the forgoing four highlighted statement replace a single statement in Display 14.1. All other methods are the same as in Display 14.1.

■ DISPLAY 14.5 **A Text Area with Scroll Bars** *(Part 2 of 2)*

```
    public void actionPerformed(ActionEvent e)
    {
        <This method is identical to the one in Display 14.1.>
    }

    public static void main(String[] args)
    {
        ScrollBarDemo guiMemo = new ScrollBarDemo( );
        guiMemo.setVisible(true);
    }
}
```

Resulting GUI

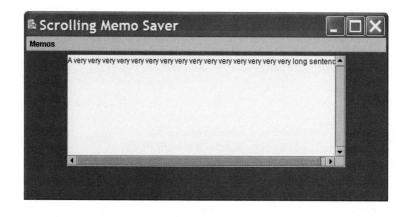

JScroll-Pane

An object of the class JScrollPane is essentially a view port with scroll bars. When you create a JScrollPane, you give the text area as an argument to the JScrollPane constructor. For example, if theText is an object of the class JTextArea (as created in the line of code at the start of this subsection), you can place theText in a JScrollPane as follows:

```
    JScrollPane scrolledText = new JScrollPane(theText);
```

The JScrollPane can then be added to a container, such as a JPanel or JFrame, as follows:

```
    textPanel.add(scrolledText);
```

This procedure is illustrated by the program in Display 14.5, which is the same as the one in Display 14.1, except that the version in Display 14.5 has scroll bars.

Note the following two lines in the constructor definition in Display 14.5:

```
scrolledText.setHorizontalScrollBarPolicy(
            JScrollPane.HORIZONTAL_SCROLLBAR_ALWAYS);
scrolledText.setVerticalScrollBarPolicy(
            JScrollPane.VERTICAL_SCROLLBAR_ALWAYS);
```

setting scroll-bar policies

Despite the imposing length of these two method invocations, they perform a very simple task. The first merely specifies that the horizontal scroll bar will always be present. The second specifies that the vertical scroll bar will always be present.

If you omit the invocation of the two methods `setHorizontalScrollBarPolicy` and `setVerticalScrollBarPolicy`, then the scroll bars will be visible only when you need them. In other words, if you omit these two method invocations and all the text fits in the view port, then no scroll bars will be visible. When you add enough text to need scroll bars, the needed scroll bars will appear automatically. Thus, you do not absolutely need the methods `setHorizontalScrollBarPolicy` and `setVerticalScrollBarPol-icy`, but they are sometimes nice to have. In some situations, the user may find it reassuring to always see the scroll bars.

Display 14.6 summarizes what we have said about the class `JScrollPane`. We are interested in using `JScrollPane` only with text areas. However, as we note in Display 14.6, `JScrollPane` can be used with almost any sort of component.

Quick Reference: `JScrollPane`

The class `JScrollPane` is used to add scroll bars to a `JTextArea` (and certain other components). The `JTextArea` object is given as an argument to the constructor that creates the `JScrollPane`.

Syntax:

```
JScrollPane Identifier = new JScrollPane(Text_Area_Object);
```

Examples:

```
JTextArea theText = new JTextArea(LINES, CHAR_PER_LINE);
JScrollPane scrolledText = new JScrollPane(theText);
textPanel.add(scrolledText);
contentPane.add(textPanel, BorderLayout.CENTER);
```

FAQ: Why Does Java Use Such Long Names?

It is part of the culture of the Java language that programmers use long, clear identifiers and do not use abbreviations for identifier names. However, some may think the following is getting a bit too long:

```
JScrollPane.HORIZONTAL_SCROLLBAR_AS_NEEDED
```

Whether you like these long names or not, you must admit that they are easy to understand and easy to remember, even if a bit of a bother to type. Most programmers eventually get used to the long, clear names and even come to prefer them.

■ DISPLAY 14.6 **Some Methods and Constants in the Class** `JScrollPane`

`public JScrollPane(Component objectToBeScrolled)`

Creates a new `JScrollPane` for the `objectToBeScrolled`. Note that the `object-ToBeScrolled` need not be a `JTextArea`, although that is the only type of argument considered in this text.

`public void setHorizontalScrollBarPolicy(int policy)`

Sets the policy for showing the horizontal scroll bar. The `policy` should be one of

`JScrollPane.HORIZONTAL_SCROLLBAR_ALWAYS`
`JScrollPane.HORIZONTAL_SCROLLBAR_NEVER`
`JScrollPane.HORIZONTAL_SCROLLBAR_AS_NEEDED`

(As indicated, these constants are defined in the class `JScrollPane`. You should not need even to be aware of the fact that they have `int` values. Think of them as policies, not as `int` values.)

`public void setVerticalScrollBarPolicy(int policy)`

Sets the policy for showing the vertical scroll bar. The `policy` should be one of

`JScrollPane.VERTICAL_SCROLLBAR_ALWAYS`
`JScrollPane.VERTICAL_SCROLLBAR_NEVER`
`JScrollPane.VERTICAL_SCROLLBAR_AS_NEEDED`

(As indicated, these constants are defined in the class `JScrollPane`. You should not need even to be aware of the fact that they have `int` values. Think of them as policies, not as `int` values.)

`JScrollPane.HORIZONTAL_SCROLLBAR_AS_NEEDED`
`JScrollPane.VERTICAL_SCROLLBAR_AS_NEEDED`

Constants in the class `JScrollPane`. The phrase "AS_NEEDED" means that the scroll bar is shown only when it is needed. This concept is explained more fully in the text. The meanings of the other policy constants are obvious from their names.

? Self-Test Questions

13. When setting up a `JScrollPane`, do you have to invoke both of the methods `setHorizontalScrollBarPolicy` and `setVerticalScrollBarPolicy`?

14. In Display 14.6, we listed the constructor for `JScrollPane` as follows:

    `public JScrollPane(Component objectToBeScrolled)`

This line indicates that the argument to the constructor must be of type `Compo-`
`nent`. But we used the constructor with an argument of type `JTextArea`. Isn't
this some sort of type violation?

15. When you want to add a `JScrollPane` to a `JTextArea`, do you "add" the
`JScrollPane` to the `JTextArea` or "add" the `JTextArea` to the `JScrollPane`?

Adding Borders

You can add a border to any `JComponent`. A **border** is simply an area around the component that frames the component. As you will see, a border can have a variety of different
appearances. A border can serve two purposes. First, it can make the component more
attractive. Second, it can provide a way to separate the component from other components;
in other words, it can add space around the component.

border

If your program uses the border classes, you need to include the following `import`
statement:

```
import javax.swing.border.*;
```

import

Display 14.7 contains a program that does little more than display some borders. In
terms of content and functionality, the GUI produced is identical to the GUI produced by
the program in Display 12.20. However, the two GUIs look quite different esthetically.
The one produced by the program in Display 14.7 may not look all that good to you,
because it is a hodgepodge of different border styles. However, it does give you samples of
the kinds of borders you can produce. These borders can be used with more restraint and a
little artistic flair to improve the look of your Swing GUIs.

You use the method `setBorder` to add a border to a component. For example, consider
the following code from Display 14.7:

setBorder

```
JButton testButton = new JButton("Test");
testButton.addActionListener(this);
testButton.setBorder(new BevelBorder(BevelBorder.LOWERED));
```

The last line gives the button `testButton` a `BevelBorder`. The general syntax is

JComponent`.setBorder(`*Border_Object*`);`

You can place a border around any `JComponent`, such as a `JButton`, `JLabel`, `JPanel`,
or `JTextField`. The exact look of the border will depend on the *Border_Object* used as an
argument to the method `setBorder`.

Each of the various border-classes produces a different looking border. Also, each border-
class constructor takes some arguments that make small adjustments to this look. For example, the `BevelBorder` class produces a border that makes the component seem either to
stand out from the plane of the GUI or to be recessed into the plane of the GUI. The argument `BevelBorder.RAISED` gives the component a raised look, and the argument `Bevel-`
`Border.LOWERED` gives it a recessed look. The `BevelBorder` class can be very effective
when used with buttons. However, any border class can be used with any `JComponent`. So
you could have a `BevelBorder` around a `JPanel` or any other `JComponent`.

*Bevel-
Border*

It is very common to use an anonymous argument for a border object, as in

```
testButton.setBorder(new BevelBorder(BevelBorder.LOWERED));
```

■ DISPLAY 14.7 **Demonstration of Different Borders** *(Part 1 of 2)*

```java
import javax.swing.*;
import java.awt.*;
import java.awt.event.*;
import javax.swing.border.*;
/**
 Class to demonstrate adding borders to components.
*/
public class BorderDemo extends JFrame implements ActionListener
{
    public static final int WIDTH = 400;
    public static final int HEIGHT = 300;

    private JTextField name;

    public BorderDemo()
    {
        setTitle("Name Tester with Borders");
        setSize(WIDTH, HEIGHT);
        addWindowListener(new WindowDestroyer());
        Container content = getContentPane();
        content.setLayout(new GridLayout(2, 1));

        JPanel namePanel = new JPanel();
        namePanel.setLayout(new BorderLayout());
        namePanel.setBackground(Color.WHITE);

        name = new JTextField(20);
        //The following border is not as dramatic as others,
        //but look closely and you will see it.
        name.setBorder(new EtchedBorder(Color.GREEN, Color.BLUE));
        namePanel.add(name, BorderLayout.SOUTH);
        JLabel nameLabel = new JLabel("Enter your name here:");
        //The following border inserts space around the label.
        //To see the difference, comment out the following line:
        nameLabel.setBorder(new EmptyBorder(20, 10, 0, 0));
        namePanel.add(nameLabel, BorderLayout.CENTER);

        namePanel.setBorder(new LineBorder(Color.BLACK, 10));
        content.add(namePanel);

        JPanel buttonPanel = new JPanel();
        buttonPanel.setLayout(new FlowLayout());
        JButton testButton = new JButton("Test");
        testButton.addActionListener(this);
        testButton.setBorder(new BevelBorder(BevelBorder.LOWERED));
        buttonPanel.add(testButton);
```

■ DISPLAY 14.7   **Demonstration of Different Borders** *(Part 2 of 2)*

```java
        JButton clearButton = new JButton("Clear");
        clearButton.addActionListener(this);
        clearButton.setBorder(new BevelBorder(BevelBorder.RAISED));
        buttonPanel.add(clearButton);

        buttonPanel.setBorder(
                new MatteBorder(60, 40, 30, 20, Color.PINK));
        content.add(buttonPanel);
    }

    public void actionPerformed(ActionEvent e)
    {
        if (e.getActionCommand().equals("Test"))
            name.setText("A very good name!");
        else if (e.getActionCommand().equals("Clear"))
            name.setText("");
        else
            name.setText("Error in window interface.");
    }

    public static void main(String[] args)
    {
        BorderDemo w = new BorderDemo();
        w.setVisible(true);
    }
}
```

Resulting GUI

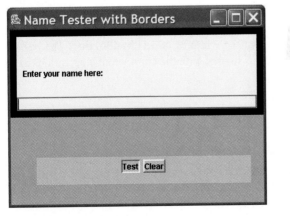

To get a really clear view of these borders, run the program.

However, if you prefer, you can give a name to the border object. The previous line of code is equivalent to the following:

```
BevelBorder myBorder = new BevelBorder(BevelBorder.LOWERED);
testButton.setBorder(myBorder);
```

Display 14.8 summarizes some border classes and their possible arguments. The best way to learn about borders is to try out each of the border classes to see what kind of borders it produces.

An `EmptyBorder` object simply inserts space around the component. You can specify the amount of space (in pixels) for each of the four borders, as in the following lines from our sample program in Display 14.7:

```
JLabel nameLabel = new JLabel("Enter your name here:");
//The following border inserts space around the label.
//To see the difference, comment out the following line:
nameLabel.setBorder(new EmptyBorder(20, 10, 0, 0));
```

Empty-
Border

The border in the preceding code adds 20 pixels of space above the label, 10 pixels of space to the left of the label, 0 pixels of space below the label, and 0 pixels of space after the label. Of course, the GUI itself may have extra space, so there may actually be some space after the label even if you don't add any. A similar remark applies to the other border classes.

Line-
Border

The class `LineBorder` inserts a colored border of a specified size around the component, as in the following example from Display 14.7 that adds a black border which is 10 pixels wide all around the outside of a `JPanel` named `namePanel`:

```
namePanel.setBorder(new LineBorder(Color.BLACK, 10));
```

Matte-
Border

A `MatteBorder` is similar to a `LineBorder`, but you can specify the size, in pixels, of each of the four borders separately. The following example from Display 14.7 places a pink border around the `buttonPanel`:

```
buttonPanel.setBorder(
            new MatteBorder(60, 40, 30, 20, Color.PINK));
```

The border will be 60 pixels wide on top, 40 pixels wide on the left side, 30 pixels wide on the bottom, and 20 pixels wide on the right side.

Etched-
Border

An `EtchedBorder` is similar to a `BevelBorder`, but it is always narrow and shows some colored shadows. You cannot set the width of an `EtchedBorder`. The best way to learn what an `EtchedBorder` is like is to play with the class, producing various examples and comparing them.

Quick Reference: The setBorder Method

You can use the `setBorder` method to add a border to any `JComponent`.

Syntax:

JComponent`.setBorder(`*Border_Object*`);`

The *JComponent* can be any `JComponent` object, such as a `JButton`, `JLabel`, `JPanel`, or other `JComponent`. The *Border_Object* can be an object of any of the border classes given in Display 14.8.

Example:

```
namePanel.setBorder(new LineBorder(Color.BLACK, 10));
```

■ DISPLAY 14.8 **Some Border Classes**

`public BevelBorder(int bevelType)`

Constructor for creating a new `BevelBorder` object. The argument `bevelType` should be one of the constants `BevelBorder.RAISED` or `BevelBorder.LOWERED`.

`public EtchedBorder(int etchType, Color highlight, Color shadow)`

Constructor for creating a new `EtchedBorder` object. An etched border is similar to a `BevelBorder`, except that you cannot set its size, and it has colored shadow properties with the specified highlight and shadow colors. The argument `etchType` should be one of the constants `EtchedBorder.RAISED` or `EtchedBorder.LOWERED`.

`public EtchedBorder(Color highlight, Color shadow)`

Constructor for creating a new lowered `EtchedBorder` object with the specified highlight and shadow colors.

`public EmptyBorder(int top, int left, int bottom, int right)`

Constructor for creating a new `EmptyBorder` object. An empty border is essentially space around the component. The arguments give the size, in pixels, of the four border areas.

`public LineBorder(Color theColor, int thickness)`

Constructor for creating a new `LineBorder` object. A line border is a colored border of a given thickness. The thickness is given in pixels.

`public LineBorder(Color color, int thickness,`
                              `boolean roundedCorners)`

Creates a line border with the specified color, thickness, and corner shape. The thickness is given in pixels. If `roundedCorners` is `true`, rounded corners are produced. If `roundedCorners` is `false`, then right-angle corners are produced. If the third argument is omitted, right-angle corners are produced.

`public MatteBorder(`
        `int top, int left, int bottom, int right, Color theColor)`

Constructor for creating a new `MatteBorder` object. A `MatteBorder` is similar to a `LineBorder`, but you can specify the size (in pixels) of each of the four borders. (You should also read the box entitled "Icons in a `MatteBorder`.")

extra code on
CD

Quick Reference: Icons in a `MatteBorder`

The class `MatteBorder` has a constructor that lets you specify an icon instead of a color. The constructor is as follows:

```
public MatteBorder(
    int top, int left, int bottom, int right, ImageIcon theIcon)
```

This constructor will create a new `MatteBorder` object that is tiled with copies of `theIcon` (like a wallpaper pattern). A sample of a program using this constructor is in the file `BorderDemoWith-Icon.java` on the accompanying CD.

▲ *Gotcha*

Forgetting to Import `javax.swing.border`

If the compiler says that it cannot find the border classes you are using, you have undoubtedly forgotten the following `import` statement, which you need when dealing with borders:

```
import javax.swing.border.*;  △
```

FAQ: Are There More Border Classes?

Yes, there are more border classes. You can check the Java documentation on Sun's Web site for descriptions of these classes. However, the border classes we have presented here will serve you well for most situations.

FAQ: Can I Change the Look and Feel of a Swing GUI?

look and feel

The **look and feel** of a GUI refers to its general appearance. It includes such things as the shape and exact placement of buttons, default colors, and almost anything that affects the way a GUI looks without affecting what it does. You can change the look and feel of a Swing GUI, but that is beyond the scope of this book. For now, you will have to settle for the default look and feel provided on your system.

? Self-Test Questions

16. Can you use a border just to add space around a component?

17. Will the following line give your program access to the border classes?

```
import javax.swing.*;
```

14.3 MORE LAYOUT MANAGERS

box n. 1. A container typically constructed with four sides perpendicular to the base and often having a lid or cover. ... - The American Heritage Dictionary of the English Language, third edition

A GUI often needs a panel for a horizontal or vertical array of items, such as an array of buttons. If a horizontal array is needed, then a JPanel with a FlowLayout manager will do. If a vertical array is needed, then a JPanel with a GridLayout manager with only a single column will do. However, the BoxLayout manager class and the Box container class allow you to produce such panels and layout managers in a way that is perhaps simpler and that offers some very handy extra features. The extra features include good ways to create invisible components in order to separate other components, so that you can, for example, add space between buttons. A Box container is essentially a panellike class that uses the BoxLayout manager in a convenient way. We will first discuss a program that uses the BoxLayout manager with JPanels, and then we will discuss a second program that does the same thing, but that uses the Box container class to simplify and automate some of the programming. Both programs will produce the same GUI, which is shown in Display 14.9.

The GUI in Display 14.9 has buttons labeled "Red" and "Green" along the bottom and two other buttons labeled "Red" and "Green" along the right side of the GUI. The center is initially blue. If either "Red" button is clicked, the center panel turns red. Similarly, if either "Green" button is clicked, the center panel turns green. There is nothing very new here in terms of what the GUI does. What is new is the use of a BoxLayout manager.

The BoxLayout Manager Class

The program in Display 14.10 will produce the GUI in Display 14.9 when it is run. It uses the BoxLayout manager class. The code in the program is, in many ways, just more of what you have already seen. The content pane of the JFrame is divided into three sections, each containing a panel. The buttons are created and added to the panels in the same manner as you have already seen. The method actionPerformed is almost identical to similar actionPerformed methods that you saw before in this chapter and in Chapter 12. In fact, all the code that is not highlighted uses only techniques you have seen before.

■ DISPLAY 14.9 **A GUI Built with BoxLayout Managers**

■ DISPLAY 14.10 The BoxLayout Manager *(Part 1 of 2)*

```java
import javax.swing.*;
import java.awt.*;
import java.awt.event.*;
```

The resulting GUI is shown in Display 14.9.

```java
/**
 Simple demonstration of BoxLayout manager class and the use of
 struts to separate components (in this case, buttons). (For an
 alternative implementation, see BoxClassDemo in Display 14.11.)
*/
public class BoxLayoutDemo extends JFrame
                               implements ActionListener
{
    public static final int WIDTH = 300;
    public static final int HEIGHT = 200;
    public static final int HORIZONTAL_STRUT_SIZE = 15;
    public static final int VERTICAL_STRUT_SIZE = 10;

    private JPanel colorPanel;

    public BoxLayoutDemo()
    {
        setSize(WIDTH, HEIGHT);
        addWindowListener(new WindowDestroyer());
        setTitle("Box Demonstration");
        Container content = getContentPane();
        content.setLayout(new BorderLayout());

        colorPanel = new JPanel();
        colorPanel.setBackground(Color.BLUE);
        content.add(colorPanel, BorderLayout.CENTER);

        //Horizontal buttons at bottom of frame:
        JPanel horizontalPanel = new JPanel();
        horizontalPanel.setLayout(
                new BoxLayout(horizontalPanel, BoxLayout.X_AXIS));

        Component horizontalStrut =
                Box.createHorizontalStrut(HORIZONTAL_STRUT_SIZE);
        horizontalPanel.add(horizontalStrut);

        JButton hStopButton = new JButton("Red");
        hStopButton.addActionListener(this);
        horizontalPanel.add(hStopButton);

        Component horizontalStrut2 =
                Box.createHorizontalStrut(HORIZONTAL_STRUT_SIZE);
        horizontalPanel.add(horizontalStrut2);
```

■ DISPLAY 14.10 **The BoxLayout Manager** *(Part 2 of 2)*

```java
        JButton hGoButton = new JButton("Green");
        hGoButton.addActionListener(this);
        horizontalPanel.add(hGoButton);

        content.add(horizontalPanel, BorderLayout.SOUTH);

        //Vertical buttons on right side of frame:
        JPanel verticalPanel = new JPanel();
        verticalPanel.setLayout(
            new BoxLayout(verticalPanel, BoxLayout.Y_AXIS));

        Component verticalStrut =
            Box.createVerticalStrut(VERTICAL_STRUT_SIZE);
        verticalPanel.add(verticalStrut);

        JButton vStopButton = new JButton("Red");
        vStopButton.addActionListener(this);
        verticalPanel.add(vStopButton);

        Component verticalStrut2 =
            Box.createVerticalStrut(VERTICAL_STRUT_SIZE);
        verticalPanel.add(verticalStrut2);

        JButton vGoButton = new JButton("Green");
        vGoButton.addActionListener(this);
        verticalPanel.add(vGoButton);

        content.add(verticalPanel, BorderLayout.EAST);
    }

    public void actionPerformed(ActionEvent e)
    {
        if (e.getActionCommand().equals("Red"))
            colorPanel.setBackground(Color.RED);
        else if (e.getActionCommand().equals("Green"))
            colorPanel.setBackground(Color.GREEN);
        else
            System.out.println("Error in button interface.");
    }

    public static void main(String[] args)
    {
        BoxLayoutDemo gui = new BoxLayoutDemo();
        gui.setVisible(true);
    }
}
```

One minor point that you may not have seen before is that there are two buttons with "Red" written on them, and it is irrelevant to the `actionPerformed` method which one is clicked, because they have the same action command, namely, the string "Red". The situation with the two "Green" buttons is similar.

The really new material in Display 14.10 is in the highlighted code. The panel named `horizontalPanel` holds the buttons at the bottom of the screen. This panel uses a `Box-Layout` manager. The syntax for creating a `BoxLayout` manager is slightly different from what you have used for other layout managers, as illustrated by the following statement from Display 14.10:

BoxLayout

```
horizontalPanel.setLayout(
        new BoxLayout(horizontalPanel, BoxLayout.X_AXIS));
```

Note that, unlike the layout-manager classes you saw in Chapter 12, the constructor for the `BoxLayout` manager takes arguments; in fact, it takes two arguments. The first argument is the container for which it is the layout manager. This information is clearly redundant, because when used in this way it is the same as the calling object. But redundant or not, that first argument is required. The second argument must be one of the two constants `BoxLayout.X_AXIS` or `BoxLayout.Y_AXIS`. The constant specifies whether the layout will be vertical (X_AXIS) or horizontal (Y_AXIS).

X_AXIS and
Y_AXIS

When the second argument to the `BoxLayout` constructor is `BoxLayout.X_AXIS`, the layout is a horizontal panel with components added from left to right. Thus, the previously displayed layout manager is almost equivalent to the following:

```
horizontalPanel.setLayout(new FlowLayout());
```

At first, you might not notice any difference between these two layout managers (horizontal `BoxLayout` and `FlowLayout`). Thinking of the horizontal `BoxLayout` as being the same as the `FlowLayout` is a good first approximation of what a horizontal `BoxLayout` manager does. However, there are subtle, but sometimes important, distinctions between the two layout-manager classes. As you will see, a horizontal `BoxLayout` manager does exactly what you tell it to do. If you say to leave 15 pixels at the beginning of the panel, it will always leave exactly 15 pixels. On the other hand, a `FlowLayout` manager "thinks" it "knows better" than you do and may add extra pixels to make the display "look better."

Note that with a `BoxLayout` manager, you add components by using the add method in the way you are used to for a `FlowLayout` manager. If the layout is horizontal, as we have been discussing, the components are laid out from left to right in the order in which they are added. If the layout is vertical, which we will discuss next, the components are laid out from top to bottom in the order in which they are added.

Wow, that was a lot of work and a lot of explanation to describe something that is little more than a `FlowLayout` manager! But a payoff is coming. The rest of the program in Display 14.10 shows some of the real power of the `BoxLayout` manager class.

We have just discussed how you can get a horizontal layout of components by using the `BoxLayout` manager class. To get a vertical layout with a `BoxLayout` manager, you simply use `BoxLayout.Y_AXIS`, instead of `BoxLayout.X_AXIS`, as the second argument to the `BoxLayout` constructor. This approach is illustrated by the panel that displays buttons along the right side of the GUI in Display 14.9. The program in Display 14.10 specifies that the panel is a vertical panel via the following code:

```
verticalPanel.setLayout(
        new BoxLayout(verticalPanel, BoxLayout.Y_AXIS));
```

This layout manager will arrange the buttons vertically from top to bottom, rather than horizontally from left to right.

Note that a `FlowLayout` manager does not have anything equivalent to a vertical layout. You can get a rough approximation of a vertical `BoxLayout` manager with a `GridLayout` manager that has only one column, but the spacing will be different. With a `BoxLayout` manager, you have more control over spacing. With other layout managers, you usually can only make suggestions to the layout manager, but you cannot count on the instructions being followed. For example, with a `GridLayout` manager, the components are always stretched so that they are of equal size, and they are always placed right next to each other.

We said that a `BoxLayout` manager gives you more control over the spacing of components, but to take advantage of this control, you need to use invisible components known as struts and glue components. We discuss these kinds of components in the next subsection.

Struts and Glue

Part of the importance of the `BoxLayout` manager class comes from some of the static methods contained in the related class named `Box`. Some of these static methods can produce invisible components that can be added to a container. These invisible components can be used to add space between the visible components. For example, consider the following code from Display 14.10:

```
Component horizontalStrut =
            Box.createHorizontalStrut(HORIZONTAL_STRUT_SIZE);
 horizontalBox.add(horizontalStrut);
```

The method `createHorizontalStrut` is a static method in the class `Box`. It creates an object of type `Component` that is known as a **strut.** A strut is an invisible component that has a fixed horizontal size. For example, the method invocation

strut

```
Box.createHorizontalStrut(HORIZONTAL_STRUT_SIZE);
```

produces a strut whose horizontal size is `HORIZONTAL_STRUT_SIZE` pixels, which happens to be 15 pixels in the program in Display 14.10. A layout manager can change the vertical size of this strut, but it cannot change the horizontal size (i.e., cannot change the width). The strut is always exactly 15 pixels wide, so if this strut is added to a container with a `BoxLayout` manager, it will always produce a space of 15 pixels between components.

There are two kinds of struts: **horizontal struts** and **vertical struts.** We have just discussed horizontal struts. A horizontal strut is created with the method `createHorizontalStrut` and has a fixed width that cannot be changed. The layout manager can change the height of the strut, but not its width. A vertical strut is similar, except that it is the height that is fixed. A vertical strut is created with the method `createVerticalStrut`. The layout manager can change the width of a vertical strut, but not its height. Think of a strut as a stick of a fixed length that is used to separate visible components. That is, in fact, the root meaning of the word *strut* and is why the designers of Swing used the word *strut* for these components.

horizontal
strut

vertical
strut

Glue components are invisible component that are similar to struts, except that they are not rigid. They are used to separate visible components. The word *glue* is actually misleading and was a poor choice for these components. Glue components do not glue

glue
components

anything to anything else. The word *glue* is meant to convey the idea that these components are not rigid like struts, but squishy like glue. (Perhaps a better name would have been *goo*, but we are stuck with *glue*, no pun intended.)

horizontal and vertical glue

The layout manager can make a glue component larger or smaller. There are both **horizontal** and **vertical glue** components. They are created with the static methods `create-HorizontalGlue` and `createVerticalGlue`, respectively. Both of these methods are in the `Box` class. For example, the following lines create a horizontal and a vertical glue component:

```
Component horizontalGlue = Box.createHorizontalGlue( );
Component verticalGlue = Box.createVerticalGlue( );
```

You do not specify a size for a glue component.

extra code on CD

Glue components are added to a container by using the method `add` in the same way that struts are added. An example of a program that uses glue components is provided in the file `GlueDemo.java` on the accompanying CD.

? Self-Test Questions

18. Suppose `myPanel` is a `JPanel`. How do you give `myPanel` a vertical `BoxLayout` manager?

19. What is the difference between the following two ways of setting a layout manager?

```
horizontalPanel.setLayout(
        new BoxLayout(horizontalPanel, BoxLayout.X_AXIS));
```

and

```
horizontalPanel.setLayout(new FlowLayout( ));
```

20. Give a statement that will create a horizontal strut named `horizontalSpace` that has a width of 20 pixels.

21. What is the difference between a strut component and a glue component?

▲ *Gotcha*

Using Struts and Glue with Other Layout Managers

Struts and glue components are designed to be used with a `BoxLayout` manager. You can use them with other layout managers, but they usually do not realize their intended purpose when you do so. If a horizontal strut that is 15 pixels wide is added with some other layout manager, such as the `FlowLayout` manager, its width is still technically 15 pixels, but the layout manager may add extra space around it. Because a strut is invisible, adding extra space is pretty much equivalent to changing the size of the strut. Problems also arise with glue components used with layout managers other than a `BoxLayout` manager.

In a subsequent subsection, we discuss `Box` containers. A container object of the `Box` class automatically comes with a `BoxLayout` manager. So it is perfectly fine to add struts and glue components to a `Box` container. △

Setting the Spacing between Components

The `BoxLayout` manager and the `Box` container class discussed in the next subsection have struts and glue to provide spacing between components. All the other layout managers we discuss in this book use the following two methods to set horizontal and vertical spacing between components:

```
/**
 Sets the horizontal gap between components.
 The argument is the gap expressed in pixels.
*/
public void setHgap(int hgap)

/**
 Sets the vertical gap between components.
 The argument is the gap expressed in pixels.
*/
public void setVgap(int vgap)
```

These two methods do not work for the `BoxLayout` manager or for the `Box` class.

You can also separate components by using the `EmptyBorder` with each component. This technique works with any kind of layout manager, because the space is part of the component.

The Box Container Class

We have already discussed the static functions `createHorizontalStrut`, `create-VerticalStrut`, `createHorizontalGlue`, and `createVerticalGlue`, which are in the class `Box`. In this subsection, we discuss objects of the class `Box`. An object of the class `Box` behaves just like a panel that has a `BoxLayout` manager. The details are illustrated by the program in Display 14.11. That program will produce the GUI in Display 14.9. So the program in Display 14.10 and the one in Display 14.11 are equivalent. However, the program in Display 14.11 uses `Box` containers—that is, objects of the class `Box`— rather than `JPanel`s to hold the buttons. The details that involve new material are discussed in the rest of this subsection.

Box container

If you look at the programs in Displays 14.11 and 14.10, you will see that the only difference between them is that the panel `horizontalPanel` in Display 14.10 is replaced by the `Box` object `horizontalBox` in Display 14.11, and the panel `verticalPanel` in Display 14.10 is replaced by the `Box` object `verticalBox` in Display 14.11.

The object `horizontalBox` is created with the following statement from Display 14.11:

createHorizontalBox

```
Box horizontalBox = Box.createHorizontalBox();
```

Similarly, the object `verticalBox` is created with the following statement from Display 14.11:

createVerticalBox

```
Box verticalBox = Box.createVerticalBox();
```

Note that the way you create a box is different than you might expect. To create an object of the class `Box`, you use the static method `Box.createHorizontalBox` or the static method `Box.createVerticalBox`. The difference between these two methods is, of course, that the first creates a horizontal box and the second creates a vertical box.

■ DISPLAY 14.11 **The Box Container Class** *(Part 1 of 2)*

```java
import javax.swing.*;
import java.awt.*;
import java.awt.event.*;
/**
 Simple demonstration of Box container class and the use of struts
 to separate components (in this case, buttons). For an alternative
 implementation, see BoxLayoutDemo in Display 14.10.
*/
public class BoxClassDemo extends JFrame implements ActionListener
{
    public static final int WIDTH = 300;
    public static final int HEIGHT = 200;
    public static final int HORIZONTAL_STRUT_SIZE = 15;
    public static final int VERTICAL_STRUT_SIZE = 10;

    private JPanel colorPanel;

    public BoxClassDemo()
    {
        setSize(WIDTH, HEIGHT);
        addWindowListener(new WindowDestroyer());
        setTitle("Box Demonstration");
        Container content = getContentPane();
        content.setLayout(new BorderLayout());

        colorPanel = new JPanel();
        colorPanel.setBackground(Color.BLUE);
        content.add(colorPanel, BorderLayout.CENTER);

        //Horizontal buttons at bottom of frame:
        Box horizontalBox = Box.createHorizontalBox();

        Component horizontalStrut =
            Box.createHorizontalStrut(HORIZONTAL_STRUT_SIZE);
        horizontalBox.add(horizontalStrut);

        JButton hStopButton = new JButton("Red");
        hStopButton.addActionListener(this);
        horizontalBox.add(hStopButton);
        Component horizontalStrut2 =
            Box.createHorizontalStrut(HORIZONTAL_STRUT_SIZE);
        horizontalBox.add(horizontalStrut2);

        JButton hGoButton = new JButton("Green");
        hGoButton.addActionListener(this);
        horizontalBox.add(hGoButton);
```

The resulting GUI is shown in Display 14.9.

■ DISPLAY 14.11 **The Box Container Class** *(Part 2 of 2)*

```
        content.add(horizontalBox, BorderLayout.SOUTH);
        //Vertical buttons on right side of frame:
        Box verticalBox = Box.createVerticalBox();
        Component verticalStrut =
            Box.createVerticalStrut(VERTICAL_STRUT_SIZE);
        verticalBox.add(verticalStrut);

        JButton vStopButton = new JButton("Red");
        vStopButton.addActionListener(this);
        verticalBox.add(vStopButton);

        Component verticalStrut2 =
            Box.createVerticalStrut(VERTICAL_STRUT_SIZE);
        verticalBox.add(verticalStrut2);

        JButton vGoButton = new JButton("Green");
        vGoButton.addActionListener(this);
        verticalBox.add(vGoButton);

        content.add(verticalBox, BorderLayout.EAST);
    }
    public void actionPerformed(ActionEvent e)
    {
        if (e.getActionCommand().equals("Red"))
            colorPanel.setBackground(Color.RED);
        else if (e.getActionCommand().equals("Green"))
            colorPanel.setBackground(Color.GREEN);
        else
            System.out.println("Error in button interface.");
    }
    public static void main(String[] args)
    {
        BoxClassDemo gui = new BoxClassDemo();
        gui.setVisible(true);
    }
}
```

You do not need to use the method `setLayout` in order to give a layout manager to a Box object. In fact, you should not use the method `setLayout` with a Box object. An object of the class Box is automatically given a `BoxLayout` manager when it is created.

new
Box(...)

If you prefer, you can create a Box object by invoking the constructor for the class Box, using new in the usual way. For example, the following two statements are equivalent:

```
Box horizontalBox = new Box(BoxLayout.X_AXIS);
```

and

```
Box horizontalBox = Box.createHorizontalBox();
```

Similarly, the following two statements are equivalent:

```
Box verticalBox = new Box(BoxLayout.Y_AXIS);
```

and

```
Box verticalBox = Box.createVerticalBox();
```

Note that when you use the constructor for the class Box with new, you need to give the constructor an argument. If the argument is the constant BoxLayout.X_AXIS, a horizontal Box container is created. If the argument is the constant BoxLayout.Y_AXIS, then a vertical Box container is created.

? Self-Test Questions

22. Give two ways to create a vertical Box container named vBox. (*Hint*: One way uses a method, and one way uses a constructor.)

23. When coding for a Swing GUI that uses a Box container, should you use the set-Layout method to specify a layout manager for the Box container?

24. Struts and glue work with which of the layout managers discussed in this book?

25. The methods setHgap and setVgap work with which of the layout managers discussed in this book?

The CardLayout Manager

CardLayout is a layout-manager class that can add a dynamic element to your Swing GUIs. A CardLayout manager allows you to have a set of views that you can change, rather like a deck of cards that you flip through and view one at a time. With a CardLayout manager, you add any number of things to a container, but only one of those things is viewable at a time. You can go through the views in order or jump from one view to any other arbitrary view. So this layout manager does more than simply arrange the components in the container. Let's look at an example.

Display 14.12 shows a GUI that uses the CardLayout manager. The central portion of the GUI has three possible views. To move from one view to the other, the user clicks one of the buttons.

An object of the CardLayout class is created, and a container is given the layout manager, just as with any other layout-manager class. This procedure is shown in the following lines from Display 14.12, which give the panel deckPanel a CardLayout manager:

```
deckPanel = new JPanel();
dealer = new CardLayout();
deckPanel.setLayout(dealer);
```

■ DISPLAY 14.12 **The CardLayout Manager** *(Part 1 of 3)*

```java
import javax.swing.*;
import java.awt.*;
import java.awt.event.*;

public class CardLayoutDemo extends JFrame
                                implements ActionListener
{
    public static final int WIDTH = 300;
    public static final int HEIGHT = 200;

    private CardLayout dealer;
    private JPanel deckPanel;

    public CardLayoutDemo()
    {
        setSize(WIDTH, HEIGHT);
        addWindowListener(new WindowDestroyer());
        setTitle("CardLayout Demonstration");
        Container contentPane = getContentPane();
        contentPane.setLayout(new BorderLayout());

        deckPanel = new JPanel();
        dealer = new CardLayout();
        deckPanel.setLayout(dealer);

        JPanel startCardPanel = new JPanel();
        startCardPanel.setLayout(new FlowLayout());
        startCardPanel.setBackground(Color.LIGHT_GRAY);
        JLabel startLabel = new JLabel("Hello");
        startCardPanel.add(startLabel);
        deckPanel.add("start", startCardPanel);

        JPanel greenCardPanel = new JPanel();
        greenCardPanel.setLayout(new FlowLayout());
        greenCardPanel.setBackground(Color.GREEN);
        JLabel goLabel = new JLabel("Go");
        greenCardPanel.add(goLabel);
        deckPanel.add("green", greenCardPanel);

        JPanel redCardPanel = new JPanel();
        redCardPanel.setLayout(new FlowLayout());
        redCardPanel.setBackground(Color.RED);
        JLabel stopLabel = new JLabel("Stop");
        redCardPanel.add(stopLabel);
        deckPanel.add("red", redCardPanel);
```

■ DISPLAY 14.12 **The CardLayout Manager** *(Part 2 of 3)*

```java
        contentPane.add(deckPanel, BorderLayout.CENTER);

        JPanel buttonPanel = new JPanel();
        buttonPanel.setBackground(Color.WHITE);
        buttonPanel.setLayout(new FlowLayout());
        JButton stopButton = new JButton("Red");
        stopButton.addActionListener(this);
        buttonPanel.add(stopButton);
        JButton goButton = new JButton("Green");
        goButton.addActionListener(this);
        buttonPanel.add(goButton);
        JButton resetButton = new JButton("Reset");
        resetButton.addActionListener(this);
        buttonPanel.add(resetButton);
        contentPane.add(buttonPanel, BorderLayout.SOUTH);
        dealer.first(deckPanel);//Optional
    }

    public void actionPerformed(ActionEvent e)
    {
        String actionCommand = e.getActionCommand();

        if (actionCommand.equals("Red"))
            dealer.show(deckPanel, "red");
        else if (actionCommand.equals("Green"))
            dealer.show(deckPanel, "green");
        else if (actionCommand.equals("Reset"))
            dealer.show(deckPanel, "start");
        else
            System.out.println("Error in CardLayout Demo.");
    }

    public static void main(String[] args)
    {
        CardLayoutDemo demoGui = new CardLayoutDemo();
        demoGui.setVisible(true);
    }
}
```

■ DISPLAY 14.12 **The CardLayout Manager** *(Part 3 of 3)*

First GUI Displayed

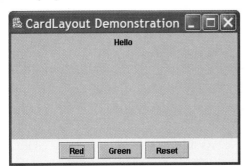

This is the view produced when the Reset button is clicked.

GUI Displayed When the Red Button Is Clicked

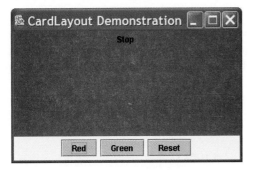

GUI Displayed When the Green Button Is Clicked

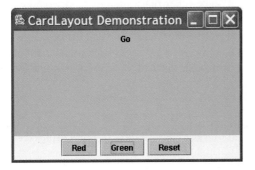

Note that we did not use an anonymous `CardLayout` argument to the `setLayout` method. The following lines while legal, is of little use:

```
deckPanel.setLayout(new CardLayout());//Do not use this!
```

We need a name (`dealer`) for the `CardLayout` manager so we can use it to change the "card" that is displayed. Moreover, we need to refer to the `CardLayout` manager in more than one method, so we've made `dealer` an instance variable of type `CardLayout`.

As illustrated in our GUI code, when you add an element to a container that uses a `CardLayout` manager, you give a string as the first argument and the component as the second argument. The string in the first argument serves as a name for the component:

```
deckPanel.add("start", startCardPanel);
    ...
deckPanel.add("green", greenCardPanel);
    ...
deckPanel.add("red", redCardPanel);
```

When the GUI is first displayed, it shows the first component that was added. To go to another view, your code uses the method `show`. For example, consider the following line from the definition of `actionPerformed` in Display 14.12:

show

```
dealer.show(deckPanel, "red");
```

When this statement is executed, the view (the "card") currently displayed changes to the view named `"red"`. In the GUI in Display 14.12, this means that when the user clicks the button labeled `"Red"`, the panel named `redCardPanel` is displayed. Note that the container is given as the first argument to `show`. (After all, the layout manager can manage more than one container.)

Two other methods that you can use to go to a new view (the new "card") are `first` and `next`. The following line, from the end of the constructor in Display 14.12, displays the first component added to the container:

first

```
dealer.first(deckPanel);//Optional
```

As indicated by the word `Optional`, the GUI will behave the same if you omit this particular invocation of `first`. This is because the container always starts with the first component (first "card") on view. However, at some other place, this method would change the display.

The method `next` goes to the next view (the next "card"), using the order in which the components were added. After the last component, `next` goes back to the first component. The following line is not used in Display 14.12, but if it were used, it would change the view from the current component to the next component.

next

```
dealer.next(deckPanel);
```

Some of the methods in the class `CardLayout` are summarized in Display 14.13.

Quick Reference: The CardLayout Manager Class

A `CardLayout` manager displays components added to its container one at a time, using the methods given in Display 14.13. Each component is assigned a string name when added to the component, as follows:

Syntax:

Container.add(*String_Name*, *Component*);

Example:

```
deckPanel.add("start", startCardPanel);
```

26. In Display 14.12, we added the layout manager to the panel deckPanel as follows:

    ```
    dealer = new CardLayout( );
    deckPanel.setLayout(dealer);
    ```

    Why didn't we add the layout manager by using the following code instead?

    ```
    deckPanel.setLayout(new CardLayout( ));
    ```

27. Write Java code that will display the next "card" in the deckPanel of Display 14.12.

■ DISPLAY 14.13 **Some Methods in the** CardLayout **Manager Class**

```
public void first(Container theContainer)
```
Causes the first "card" in theContainer to be displayed.

```
public void last(Container theContainer)
```
Causes the last "card" in theContainer to be displayed.

```
public void next(Container theContainer)
```
Causes the next "card" in theContainer to be displayed. The next card is the one that was added after the currently displayed card was added. If the currently displayed card is the last card, then next displays the first card.

```
public void previous(Container theContainer)
```
Causes the previous "card" in theContainer to be displayed. The previous card is the one that was added before the currently displayed card was added. If the currently displayed card is the first card, then previous displays the last card.

```
public void show(Container theContainer, String cardName)
```
Displays the "card" that was added with the cardName as its name.

28. Write Java code that will display the previous "cards" in the `deckPanel` of Display 14.12.

29. Suppose `dealer` is an object of the class `CardLayout` and `deckPanel` is a `JPanel` with `dealer` as its layout manager (as in Display 14.12). If the currently displayed card of `deckPanel` is the first card, which card will be displayed after the following statement is executed?

```
dealer.previous(deckPanel);
```

14.4   INNER CLASSES

Something deeply hidden had to be behind things. -Albert Einstein, note quoted in *New York Times Magazine* (August 2, 1964)

Inner classes are classes defined within other classes. Their use is not confined to programs and classes that use Swing. However, they are often used when programming with Swing. Although a full description of inner classes is beyond the scope of this book, some simple uses of inner classes can be both easy and helpful. We will describe one of the most useful applications of inner classes, namely, inner classes used as helping classes.

Inner classes were covered in Chapter 10, but since some readers may be reading this chapter before Chapter 10, we do not assume that you have read Chapter 10. (If you have read Chapter 10, you should still read at least the examples in this section.)

Helping Classes

All of our Swing windows used the class `WindowDestroyer` (Display 12.4) for closing the window. When doing things this way, we must always have the class `WindowDestroyer` around. Inner classes let us move the definition of a helping class, like `WindowDestroyer`, inside the class definition. For example, the class in Display 14.14 is a simple demonstration of an inner class used as a window listener. The GUI has essentially the same display as one of our very first Swing GUI classes (Display 12.2), but it uses the inner class `InnerDestroyer` rather than the class `WindowDestroyer`. Be sure to note that the definition of the class `InnerDestroyer` is inside the class `InnerClassDemo` (Display 14.14), so that the entire program is in one class definition (with another class definition inside of it).

There are two big advantages to inner classes. First, because they are defined within a class, they can be used to make the outer class self-contained or more self-contained than it would otherwise be. The second advantage was not used in Display 14.14, but can be very helpful. When you define an inner class, the methods in the inner class have access to all the instance variables and methods of the class in which it is defined, even if they are private. For this second reason, inner classes are very useful helping classes, because they can do things more easily than a class defined outside of the class they are helping. Because of these convenient features, inner classes are frequently used as listeners to handle events fired by the outer class or by a component of the outer class. For a longer example and one that uses more of the power of inner classes, see the program `InnerClassDemo2.java` on the accompanying CD.

extra code
on CD

■ DISPLAY 14.14   **An Inner Class** *(Part 1 of 2)*

```java
import javax.swing.*;
import java.awt.*;
import java.awt.event.*;

public class InnerClassDemo extends JFrame
{
    public static final int WIDTH = 300;
    public static final int HEIGHT = 200;

    /**
     Creates and displays a window of the class InnerClassDemo.
    */
    public static void main(String[] args)
    {
        InnerClassDemo sampleGUI = new InnerClassDemo();
        sampleGUI.setVisible(true);
    }

    public InnerClassDemo()
    {
        setSize(WIDTH, HEIGHT);
        setTitle("Inner Class Demo");
        Container contentPane = getContentPane();
        contentPane.setLayout(new BorderLayout());

        JLabel label = new JLabel(
                        "Please don't click that button!");
        contentPane.add(label, BorderLayout.CENTER);

        addWindowListener(new InnerDestroyer());       An inner class
    }

    //An inner class with the same functionality
    //as the class WindowDestroyer.
    private class InnerDestroyer extends WindowAdapter
    {
        public void windowClosing(WindowEvent e)
        {
            System.exit(0);
        }
    }
}
```

■ DISPLAY 14.14 **An Inner Class** *(Part 2 of 2)*

Resulting GUI

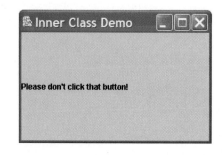

There is yet one more advantage to inner classes. The name of the inner class is local to the class in which it is defined. You could have another class named `InnerDestroyer` that is defined outside of the class in Display 14.14, and the program in Display 14.14 would completely ignore that other class named `InnerDestroyer`. Similarly, the class named `InnerDestroyer` that was defined outside would completely ignore the inner class of the same name.

We have made the inner class `InnerDestroyer` private because it is a helping class. It is possible to have a public inner class, but there are some subtleties involved in using public inner classes. We will not go into that topic in this book.

Remember: **Invoking a Method of the Outer Class**

Java makes it easy to invoke a method of an outer class within the definition of an inner class. If there is a method invocation and the inner class has no method of that name, but the outer class does have a method of that name, then Java interprets the invocation to be an invocation of the method for the outer object (that is, the calling object is the `this` of the outer class, not the `this` of the inner class.) An illustration of such invocations is given in the file `InnerClassDemo2.java` on the accompanying CD.

extra code
on CD

14.5 MORE ON EVENTS AND LISTENERS

A man may see how this world goes with no eyes.
Look with thine ears. . . . -William Shakespeare, *King Lear*

The `WindowListener` Interface

When we placed buttons in a window, we made the window itself the button-listener class. On the other hand, when we wanted a window listener to respond to window-closing events, we made the window listener a separate class, named `WindowDestroyer` (or an inner class named `InnerDestroyer`). In this subsection, we show you how to make the window itself the window listener.

You have made a window itself a button listener by making it implement the interface named `ActionListener`. There is also an interface named `WindowListener` that is used in a similar way. For example, in Display 12.14, we made the window class `Button-Demo` an action listener by adding `implements ActionListener` as follows:

```
public class ButtonDemo extends JFrame
                         implements ActionListener
```

If we wanted to make `ButtonDemo` a window listener instead of an action listener, the definition would begin

```
public class ButtonDemo extends JFrame
                         implements WindowListener
```

If, as is more likely, we wanted to make `ButtonDemo` both an action listener and a window listener, it would begin

```
public class ButtonDemo extends JFrame
                 implements ActionListener, WindowListener
```

Note that when a class implements more than one interface, we use the keyword `implements` only one time, and we separate the interface names with commas.

The reason we tend to avoid making a window its own window listener is that when a class implements an interface, such as the `ActionListener` or `WindowListener` interfaces, it must include definitions for *all* of the methods specified for the interface. The interface `ActionListener` has only the single method `actionPerformed`, so this requirement is not onerous for this case. The interface `WindowListener`, however, has the 7 methods given in Display 14.15. These are the first 7 of the 10 methods in the class `WindowAdapter`, which we discussed in Chapter 12. If a class implements the `Window-Listener` interface, it must have definitions for all 7 of these methods. If you do not need all of these methods, then you can define the ones you do not need to have empty bodies, as follows:

```
public void windowDeiconified(WindowEvent e)
{}
```

If you need only one or two methods in the `WindowListener` interface, this requirement is a nuisance, although it is not difficult to fulfill.

There are advantages to using the `WindowListener` interface. If you make the window class a derived class of the class `JFrame` and have it implement the `WindowLis-tener` interface, then it is easy to call a method in the window class within the window-listener class (because they are the same class).

For example, the program in Display 14.16 is a variant of the program we gave in Chapter 12 (Display 12.14). In Display 14.16, the GUI class is its own window listener. That allows it to have the following invocation in the method `windowClosing`:

```
this.dispose();
```

dispose

■ DISPLAY 14.15 **Methods in the `WindowListener` Interface**

```
public void windowOpened(WindowEvent e)
```
Invoked when a window has been opened.

```
public void windowClosing(WindowEvent e)
```
Invoked when a window is in the process of being closed. Clicking the close-window button causes an invocation of this method.

```
public void windowClosed(WindowEvent e)
```
Invoked when a window has been closed.

```
public void windowIconified(WindowEvent e)
```
Invoked when a window is iconified. When you click the minimize button in a `JFrame`, the window is iconified.

```
public void windowDeiconified(WindowEvent e)
```
Invoked when a window is deiconified. When you activate a minimized window, it is deiconified.

```
public void windowActivated(WindowEvent e)
```
Invoked when a window is activated. When you click in a window, it becomes the activated window. Other actions can also activate a window.

```
public void windowDeactivated(WindowEvent e)
```
Invoked when a window is deactivated. When a window is activated, all other windows are deactivated. Other actions can also deactivate a window.

The method `dispose` is a method in the class `JFrame`, and the class `WindowListenerDemo` is a derived class of the class `JFrame`, so it inherits the method `dispose`. The method `dispose` releases any resources used by the window. In a program this simple, the call to `dispose` is not really needed, because the resources are automatically released when the program ends, but if the program had several windows and was going to run longer and eliminate only this one window, then the call to `dispose` (without the call to `System.exit`) might prove useful. We used `dispose` only to have a simple example. (In the Java Tip "Programming the Close-Window Button," we present a more realistic use of the `dispose` method.)

Why bother to have both `WindowListener` and `WindowAdapter`? The reason is that `WindowAdapter` is a variant of `WindowListener` that is provided solely for the convenience of the programmer. `WindowAdapter` is a class that implements the interface `WindowListener` by giving every method an empty body. That way, when you define a derived class of `WindowAdapter`, you do not have to put in those empty definitions. So why not use `WindowAdapter` all the time? Often, you want a listener class to be a derived class of some class, such as `JFrame`, as well as a window listener. A class cannot be a derived class of two classes, such as `JFrame` and `WindowAdapter`. So in this situation, you make the class a derived class of the class `JFrame`, and you make it implement the `WindowListener` interface. A class can be a derived class of only one class, but it can also implement one or more interfaces.

■ DISPLAY 14.16   **A Window Listener** *(Part 1 of 2)*

```java
import javax.swing.*;
import java.awt.*;
import java.awt.event.*;
public class WindowListenerDemo extends JFrame
                    implements ActionListener, WindowListener
{
    public static final int WIDTH = 300;
    public static final int HEIGHT = 200;

    public static void main(String[] args)
    {
        WindowListenerDemo demoWindow = new WindowListenerDemo();
        demoWindow.setVisible(true);
    }

    public WindowListenerDemo()
    {
        setSize(WIDTH, HEIGHT);

        addWindowListener(this);
        setTitle("Window Listener Demonstration");
        Container content = getContentPane();
        content.setBackground(Color.BLUE);

        content.setLayout(new FlowLayout());

        JButton stopButton = new JButton("Red");
        stopButton.addActionListener(this);
        content.add(stopButton);

        JButton goButton = new JButton("Green");
        goButton.addActionListener(this);
        content.add(goButton);
    }

    public void actionPerformed(ActionEvent e)
    {
        Container content = getContentPane();
        if (e.getActionCommand().equals("Red"))
            content.setBackground(Color.RED);
        else if (e.getActionCommand().equals("Green"))
            content.setBackground(Color.GREEN);
        else
            System.out.println("Error in WindowListenerDemo.");
    }
```

This version does not need the class `WindowDestroyer` *or any similar class.*

■ DISPLAY 14.16 A Window Listener *(Part 2 of 2)*

```
        public void windowOpened(WindowEvent e)
        {}

        public void windowClosing(WindowEvent e)
        {
            this.dispose();
            System.exit(0);
        }

        public void windowClosed(WindowEvent e)
        {}

        public void windowIconified(WindowEvent e)
        {}

        public void windowDeiconified(WindowEvent e)
        {}

        public void windowActivated(WindowEvent e)
        {}

        public void windowDeactivated(WindowEvent e)
        {}
}
```

Resulting GUI

Quick Reference: **The** `WindowListener` **Interface**

You can make any class a window listener by either making it a derived class of the class `Window-Adapter`, as discussed in Chapter 12, or having it implement the `WindowListener` interface. One common example of a kind of class that implements the `WindowListener` interface is a `JFrame` class that is the window listener for its own close-window button. However, any kind of class can implement the `WindowListener` interface. The class need not be a `JFrame`.

In order for a class to implement the `WindowListener` interface, the class must have the following at the start of the class definition (after `extends JFrame` if the class is a `JFrame` class):

```
implements WindowListener
```

The class must also implement all the method interfaces given in Display 14.15.

Quick Reference: **The `dispose` Method**

The class `JFrame` has a method named `dispose` that will dispose of the `JFrame` without ending the program. When `dispose` is invoked, the resources consumed by the `JFrame` are returned for reuse, so the `JFrame` is gone, but the program does not end. The method `dispose` is often used in a program with multiple windows in order to eliminate one window without ending the program.

Syntax:

```
JFrame_Object.dispose();
```

The *JFrame_Object* is often an implicit `this`. A complete example of the use of `dispose` can be seen in Display 14.16.

---

30. When you define a class and make it implement the `WindowListener` interface, what methods must you define? What do you do if there is no particular action that you want one of these methods to take?

31. Can a class be a derived class of more than one class?

32. Can a class implement more than one interface?

33. If you want a Swing program to end completely, you can invoke the method `System.exit`. What if you want a window to go away, but do not want the program to end? What method can you invoke?

■ **Java Tip**
Programming the Close-Window Button

You can program the close-window button to end a Swing program by using the `WindowListener` interface, as we did in Display 14.16, or you can use the method `WindowDestroyer`, as we did in most of our Swing class definitions. However, sometimes you want something else to happen when the user clicks the close-window button.

If you wish to program the close-window button of a `JFrame` class to do something other than cause the window to go away or end the program, you should add the following invocation of the method `setDefaultCloseOperation` to the constructor:

```
setDefaultCloseOperation(WindowConstants.DO_NOTHING_ON_CLOSE);
```

setDefault-
Close-
Operation

Such an invocation is used in the class definition in Display 14.17. That class programs the close-window button so that when the user clicks the close-window button, a second window appears and asks the user if she or he wants to end the program. If the user clicks "No", the second window goes away, but the first window remains. If the user clicks "Yes", the program ends, and both windows go away. Let's look at some of the details in the class definition in Display 14.17.

The method setDefaultCloseOperation does what its name implies. It sets the default behavior for what happens when the user clicks the close-window button. If you do not invoke setDefaultCloseOperation, the default behavior is that the window disappears, but the program does not end. Note that simply reprogramming the method windowClosing does not cancel the default action. If you reprogram windowClosing and do not invoke the method setDefaultCloseOperation, then when the user clicks the close-window button, the window will probably do what you programmed into the method windowClosing, but it will also go away. If you do not want the window to go away, you must first reset the default action with the method setDefaultCloseOperation.

In addition to the invocation of setDefaultCloseOperation, the close-window button for the class CloseWindowDemo (Display 14.17) is programmed by registering the inner class InnerDestroyer as the window listener with the following line from the constructor for CloseWindowDemo:

```
addWindowListener(new InnerDestroyer( ));
```

To see what action is being programmed, you need to look at the definition of the method windowClosing in the inner class InnerDestroyer. That method definition is reproduced as follows:

```
public void windowClosing(WindowEvent e)
{
    ConfirmWindow askWindow = new ConfirmWindow( );
    askWindow.setVisible(true);
}
```

When the user clicks the close-window button of the outer class CloseWindowDemo, method windowClosing is invoked. This method then creates an object named askWindow of the class ConfirmWindow and makes it visible.

The behavior of the window askWindow is described in the actionPerformed method of the class ConfirmWindow. The relevant code is reproduced as follows:

```
if (e.getActionCommand( ).equals("Yes"))
    System.exit(0);
else if (e.getActionCommand( ).equals("No"))
    dispose( );//Destroys only the ConfirmWindow.
```

As indicated in the preceding code, if the user clicks the "Yes" button, the program ends and both windows disappear. If the user clicks the "No" button, the invocation of dispose eliminates the second window, but the first window remains.

(The class ConfirmWindow is an inner class of the class CloseWindowDemo. That makes the class CloseWindowDemo self-contained. However, the program would behave exactly the same if the class ConfirmWindow were defined as an independent class outside of the class CloseWindowDemo.) □

■ DISPLAY 14.17 **Programming the Close-Window Button** *(Part 1 of 3)*

```java
import javax.swing.*;
import java.awt.*;
import java.awt.event.*;
/**
 Demonstration of programming the close-window button.
*/
public class CloseWindowDemo extends JFrame
{
    public static final int WIDTH = 300;
    public static final int HEIGHT = 200;

    public static void main(String[] args)
    {
        CloseWindowDemo gui = new CloseWindowDemo( );
        gui.setVisible(true);
    }

    public CloseWindowDemo( )
    {
        setSize(WIDTH, HEIGHT);
        setDefaultCloseOperation(
                WindowConstants.DO_NOTHING_ON_CLOSE);
        addWindowListener(new InnerDestroyer( ));
        setTitle("Close Window Demo");
        Container contentPane = getContentPane( );
        contentPane.setLayout(new BorderLayout( ));

        JLabel message = new JLabel(
                        "Please don't click that button.");
        contentPane.add(message, BorderLayout.CENTER);
    }
```
An inner class

```java
    //Displays a window that checks if the user wants to exit.
    private class InnerDestroyer extends WindowAdapter
    {
        public void windowClosing(WindowEvent e)
        {
            ConfirmWindow askWindow = new ConfirmWindow( );
            askWindow.setVisible(true);
        }
    }
}
```

■ DISPLAY 14.17   **Programming the Close-Window Button** *(Part 2 of 3)*

```java
//Designed to be used with the inner class InnerDestroyer.
//Checks if the user wants to exit.
private class ConfirmWindow extends JFrame
                            implements ActionListener
{                                                          Another inner
    public static final int WIDTH = 200;                   class
    public static final int HEIGHT = 100;

    public ConfirmWindow( )
    {
        setSize(WIDTH, HEIGHT);
        Container confirmContent = getContentPane( );
        confirmContent.setBackground(Color.WHITE);
        confirmContent.setLayout(new BorderLayout( ));

        JLabel msgLabel = new JLabel(
                      "Are you sure you want to exit?");
        confirmContent.add(msgLabel, BorderLayout.CENTER);

        JPanel buttonPanel = new JPanel( );
        buttonPanel.setLayout(new FlowLayout( ));

        JButton exitButton = new JButton("Yes");
        exitButton.addActionListener(this);
        buttonPanel.add(exitButton);

        JButton cancelButton = new JButton("No");
        cancelButton.addActionListener(this);
        buttonPanel.add(cancelButton);

        confirmContent.add(buttonPanel, BorderLayout.SOUTH);
    }

    public void actionPerformed(ActionEvent e)
    {
        if (e.getActionCommand( ).equals("Yes"))
            System.exit(0);
        else if (e.getActionCommand( ).equals("No"))
            dispose( );//Destroys only the ConfirmWindow.
        else
            System.out.println("Error in Confirm Window.");
    }
}
}
```

■ DISPLAY 14.17   **Programming the Close-Window Button** *(Part 3 of 3)*

Resulting GUI

When you click this button, the second window appears.

Quick Reference: **Programming the Close-Window Button**

If you want to program the close-window button of a JFrame to do anything more complicated than either ending the program or making the window go away, then you need to add the following invocation to the constructor (or add it someplace that has the same effect as adding it to the constructor):

```
setDefaultCloseOperation(WindowConstants.DO_NOTHING_ON_CLOSE);
```

■   **Java Tip**
   More about setDefaultCloseOperation

You can use any of the following constants with the method setDefaultCloseOperation:

WindowConstants.DO_NOTHING_ON_CLOSE: Do nothing. The programmer should program any desired action in the definition of the windowClosing method of a registered WindowListener object.

WindowConstants.HIDE_ON_CLOSE: Automatically hide the frame after invoking any registered WindowListener objects.

WindowConstants.DISPOSE_ON_CLOSE: Automatically hide and dispose the frame after invoking any registered WindowListener objects.

JFrame.EXIT_ON_CLOSE: Exit the application using the System.exit method.

Sometimes, using setDefaultCloseOperation with one of these arguments is all you need to program the close-window button of a JFrame.

If setDefaultCloseOperation is not invoked, then the default action is the one for WindowConstants.HIDE_ON_CLOSE.

Almost all our Swing GUIs could be reprogrammed to have no window listener and still get the correct action for the close-window button by means of the following invocation of setDefaultCloseOperation:

```
setDefaultCloseOperation(JFrame.EXIT_ON_CLOSE);
```

This invocation would be used in place of

```
addWindowListener(new WindowDestroyer());
```

However, our technique of using window listeners provides you with more tools so that you can program any other actions that you may want.

In the next programming example, we will use

```
setDefaultCloseOperation(JFrame.EXIT_ON_CLOSE);
```

in place of WindowDestroyer, as we just discussed. ☐

? Self-Test Questions

34. Suppose you define a windowing GUI and do absolutely nothing to specify what happens when the close-window button is clicked. What happens when the user clicks the close-window button?

35. If you want to program the close-window button of a JFrame to do something other than cause the window to go away or end the program, what method invocation do you add to the constructor?

36. Suppose you make a JFrame into a window listener so that it can be the listener for its own close-window button. And suppose you define the method window-Closing for the JFrame as follows:

```
public void windowClosing(WindowEvent e)
{
    dispose();
}
```

Should you add the invocation given as the answer to Self-Test Question 35 to the constructor for the JFrame?

37. What is `WindowConstants.DO_NOTHING_ON_CLOSE`? Is it a method invocation? A class? Something else?

Programming Example
Components with Changing Visibility

Display 14.18 gives an example of a Swing GUI with components (in this case, labels) that change from visible to invisible and back again. When a suitable button is clicked, one label disappears and the other appears. When the button labeled "Up" is clicked, the label "Here I am up here" becomes visible at the top of the frame, and the label "Here I am down here!" disappears. When the button labeled "Down" is clicked, the label "Here I am down here!" becomes visible at the bottom of the frame, and the label "Here I am up here!" disappears.

The two labels are added and set to be invisible in the constructor. The relevant code from Display 14.18 is reproduced as follows:

```
upLabel = new JLabel("Here I am up here!");
contentPane.add(upLabel, BorderLayout.NORTH);
upLabel.setVisible(false);
downLabel = new JLabel("Here I am down here!");
contentPane.add(downLabel, BorderLayout.SOUTH);
downLabel.setVisible(false);
```

Note that you can make a component invisible without making the entire GUI invisible. The labels `upLabel` and `downLabel` are private instance variables, so they can be referenced in both the constructor and the method `actionPerformed`.

In this GUI, a label becomes visible or invisible when a particular button is clicked. For example, the following code from the method `actionPerformed` in Display 14.18 determines what happens when the button with the text "Up" on it is clicked:

```
if (e.getActionCommand().equals("Up"))
{
    upLabel.setVisible(true);
    downLabel.setVisible(false);
    validate();
}
```

The two statements

```
        upLabel.setVisible(true);
        downLabel.setVisible(false);
```

make `upLabel` visible and `downLabel` invisible in the representation of the GUI inside the computer. However, to make this change show on the screen requires a call to the method `validate`.

■ DISPLAY 14.18   **Invisible Labels** *(Part 1 of 2)*

```java
import javax.swing.*;
import java.awt.*;
import java.awt.event.*;

public class VisibilityDemo extends JFrame
                            implements ActionListener
{
    public static final int WIDTH = 300;
    public static final int HEIGHT = 200;

    private JLabel upLabel;
    private JLabel downLabel;

    public VisibilityDemo()
    {
        setSize(WIDTH, HEIGHT);
        setDefaultCloseOperation(JFrame.EXIT_ON_CLOSE);

        setTitle("Visibility Demonstration");
        Container contentPane = getContentPane();
        contentPane.setLayout(new BorderLayout());
        contentPane.setBackground(Color.WHITE);

        upLabel = new JLabel("Here I am up here!");
        contentPane.add(upLabel, BorderLayout.NORTH);
        upLabel.setVisible(false);
        downLabel = new JLabel("Here I am down here!");
        contentPane.add(downLabel, BorderLayout.SOUTH);
        downLabel.setVisible(false);

        JPanel buttonPanel = new JPanel();
        buttonPanel.setBackground(Color.WHITE);
        buttonPanel.setLayout(new FlowLayout());
        JButton upButton = new JButton("Up");
        upButton.addActionListener(this);
        buttonPanel.add(upButton);
        JButton downButton = new JButton("Down");
        downButton.addActionListener(this);
        buttonPanel.add(downButton);
        contentPane.add(buttonPanel, BorderLayout.CENTER);
    }
```

■ DISPLAY 14.18 **Invisible Labels** *(Part 2 of 2)*

```java
    public void actionPerformed(ActionEvent e)
    {
        if (e.getActionCommand( ).equals("Up"))
        {
            upLabel.setVisible(true);
            downLabel.setVisible(false);
            validate( );
        }
        else if (e.getActionCommand( ).equals("Down"))
        {
            downLabel.setVisible(true);
            upLabel.setVisible(false);
            validate( );
        }
        else
            System.out.println("Error in VisibilityDemo interface.");
    }

    public static void main(String[] args)
    {
        VisibilityDemo demoGui = new VisibilityDemo( );
        demoGui.setVisible(true);
    }
}
```

Resulting GUI (Two views of the same GUI)

validate   Every container class has the method `validate`. An invocation of `validate` causes the container to lay out its components again. It's a kind of "update" method that makes changes in the components actually happen on the screen. Simple changes that are made to a Swing GUI, like changing color or changing the text in a text field, happen automatically. Other changes, such as the addition of components or changes in visibility, require an invocation of `validate` (or some other "update" method.) Although it can make your program less efficient, it will have no other ill effects on your GUI if you mistakenly include an extra invocation of `validate` when it is not needed. ∎

Quick Reference: **The `validate` Method**

The class `Container`, and hence every container class, has a method named `validate`, which is a method for updating the container. An invocation of `validate` will cause the container to lay out its components again and redisplay them on the screen. As we discussed in the text, certain changes to a Swing GUI require an invocation of `validate` in order to update the screen and make the changes show on the screen.

Syntax:

Container_Object.`validate( );`

The *Container_Object* is often an implicit `this`. A complete example of the use of `validate` can be seen in Display 14.18.

? Self-Test Questions

38. In Display 14.18, we made text come and go by making labels visible and invisible, respectively. This process required an invocation of the method `validate`. Suppose that we had used an object of the class `TextField` instead of labels and had changed the text in the text field in order to make it look as though one word went away and other word appeared. Would we need an invocation of `validate` for the text-field changes to show on the screen?

39. Rewrite the program in Display 14.18 so that when you click the "Up" button, it becomes invisible and the "Down" button becomes visible, and similarly, when you click the "Down" button, the "Down" button becomes invisible and the "Up" button becomes visible. When the GUI is first displayed, both buttons are visible. (This program is long, but it does not require that you add very much code to the program in Display 14.18.)

Some More Details on Updating a GUI

repaint manager   With Swing, most changes to a GUI windowing system are updated automatically so that they are visible on the screen. This operation is done by an object known as the **repaint manager.** The repaint manager works automatically, and you need not even be aware of its presence. However, there are a few updates that the repaint manager will not do for you.

You have already seen that you need to update the screen with an invocation of the method validate when your GUI changes the visibility of a component, as in Display 14.18.

Two other updating methods that you will often see when looking at Swing code are pack and repaint. The method pack causes the window to be resized, usually to a smaller size, but, more precisely, to an approximation of a size known as the preferred size. (Yes, you can change the preferred size, but we do not have room to cover all of the Swing library in these few chapters.) The method repaint repaints the window.

pack

repaint

We do not have room in this book to go into all the details of how a GUI is updated on the screen, but these few remarks may make some code you find in more advanced books a little less puzzling.

14.6 ANOTHER LOOK AT THE SWING CLASS HIERARCHY

All men are mortal.
Aristotle is a man.
Therefore, Aristotle is mortal. -Common example of a syllogism

Buttons, Menus, and Abstract Buttons

Display 14.19 shows a portion of the Swing class hierarchy. Note that the classes JButton and JMenuItem are both derived from the class AbstractButton. All of the basic properties and methods of the classes JButton and JMenuItem are inherited from the class AbstractButton. That is why objects of the class JButton and objects of the class JMenuItem are so similar. All of the methods (other than constructors) that are listed for the class JButton in Display 14.3 are inherited from the class AbstractButton. The class JMenuItem also inherits all these same methods from the class AbstractButton, so a JMenuItem has all of the methods (other than constructors) that are listed for the class JButton in Display 14.3. (Some of these methods were inherited by the class AbstractButton from the class JComponent, so you may sometimes see some of the methods listed as "inherited from JComponent.")

Abstract-
Button

The class AbstractButton is an abstract class. As we said in Chapter 12, you cannot directly create objects of an abstract class. The only reason the class AbstractButton was defined was so that classes such as JButton and JMenuItem could be derived from it. This configuration provides for a unified view of JButton objects and JMenuItem objects, and it means that the designers of Swing did not have to write duplicate code, once for the class JButton and again for the class JMenuItem; they just wrote the code one time for the class AbstractButton.

abstract class

As we presented them, the classes JLabel and JButton are also very similar. However, they are not as much alike as the classes JButton and JMenuItem are. These degrees of similarity are also reflected in the Swing class hierarchy shown in Display 14.19. All three classes are descendant classes of the class JComponent, but only JButton and JMenuItem are descendants of the class AbstractButton.

There are a number of other things that you can see in the hierarchy shown in Display 14.19. Note that JMenu is derived from JMenuItem. This means that a menu is also a menu item, and that is why you can add a JMenu to another JMenu just as you add a more ordinary JMenuItem to a JMenu. This condition makes it possible to have nested menus.

■ DISPLAY 14.19 **Portion of the Swing Class Hierarchy**

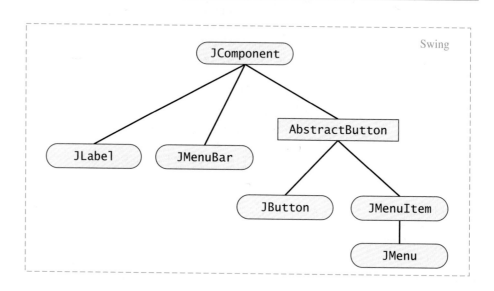

If there is a line between two classes, the lower class is a derived class of the higher class.

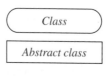

Note also that the class JMenuBar is a derived class of the class JComponent. This means that you can add a JMenuBar to a container, such as a panel or the content pane of a JFrame, just as you can add any other JComponent, such as a label or button. Therefore, with a suitable layout manager, you can have as many JMenuBars as you want, and you can place them almost anyplace in the container.

■ **Java Tip**
   More Constructors for the Class JMenuItem

As we discussed in Section 14.1, the class JMenuItem has all of the methods (other than constructors) that are listed for the class JButton in Display 14.3. The class JMenuItem also has constructors similar to those listed for the class JButton in Display 14.3. We list those constructors as follows:

```
public JMenuItem( )
```

Creates a menu item with no text or icon. (Presumably, you will later use `setText` or `setIcon` with the menu item.)

`public JMenuItem(String text)`

Creates a menu item with the `text` on it.

`public JMenuItem(ImageIcon picture)`

Creates a menu item with the icon `picture` on it.

`public JMenuItem(String text, ImageIcon picture)`

Creates a menu item with both the `text` and the icon `picture` on it. ☐

■ **Java Tip**

There Are a Lot More Swing Classes and Methods

In Chapter 12 and this chapter, you've learned a good amount of Swing, enough to do most of the basic things you might want to do it. However, Swing is too large a subject to permit us to cover it in exhaustive detail. A typical book on Swing for experienced Java programmers is longer than this entire book and usually is still not complete. If you feel that there is some method, class, or other facility that should be in Swing and that we have not covered in this book, there is a good chance that it is in Swing someplace. In most cases, we have given only the most important methods in a class, not all of the methods.

A good place to explore for new Swing classes and methods is the documentation that comes with Java 2. (Look for version 1.4 or any higher number.) If you have downloaded Java 2, you probably already have this documentation on your machine. If you do not have the documentation, you can get it from the Sun Java Web site. At the time this book went to press, the Web address for downloading was as follows:

`http://java.sun.com/j2se/1.4/download.html`

For on-line reading, the address was the following:

`http://java.sun.com/j2se/1.4/docs/api/`

If these addresses do not work, find Sun's Java Web site and follow the links to the documentation. ☐

? Self-Test Questions

40. Is the following line legal in Java?

    `AbstractButton b = new AbstractButton();`

41. Is a `JButton` an `AbstractButton`? Is a `JLabel` an `AbstractButton`? Is a `JMenuItem` an `AbstractButton`? Is a `JMenu` an `AbstractButton`? (*Hint*: The last question is a little harder than the other three.)

CHAPTER SUMMARY

- A menu item is an object of the class JMenuItem, a menu is an object of the class JMenu, and a menu bar is an object of the class JMenuBar.

- You can add icons to JButtons, JLabels, and JMenuItems.

- A JMenuBar can be added to a JFrame with the method setJMenuBar. It can also be added by using the method add just as any other component can be added.

- Both buttons and menu items fire action events and thus should have an action listener registered with them to respond to the events.

- You can use the class JScrollPane to add scroll bars to a text area.

- You can define a window-listener class by having it implement the WindowListener interface.

- You can reprogram the close-window button of a JFrame to do anything any other button can do. However, if you want to program it to do something other than close the window or end the program, you must use the method setDefaultCloseOperation.

- If you change the visibility of a component (or make certain other changes), you should use the method validate to update the GUI.

✔ Answers to Self-Test Questions

1. Clicking a JMenuItem fires an action event (that is, an object of the class ActionEvent). This situation is the same as with a JButton. There is no difference between the two in this regard.

2. To change the action command for a JMenuItem, you use the method setActionCommand just as you would for a JButton.

3. Yes, it is perfectly legal. It is, in fact, normal to add menus to menus. That is how you get nested menus.

4. As many as you want. Only one can be added with the method setJMenuBar, but any number of others can be added to the content pane, using the add method.

5. setJMenuBar

6. JMenuItem mItem = new JMenuItem("Choose Me!");
   or, equivalently,

   JMenuItem mItem;
   mItem = new JMenuItem("Choose Me!");

7. A menu item fires events of the class ActionEvent. Listeners for ActionEvent objects are action listeners. Note that this configuration is the same as for objects of the class JButton.

8.
```
m.add(mItem);
mBar.add(m);
setJMenuBar(mBar);
```

You could use the following instead of using `setJMenuBar`:

```
getContentPane( ).add(mBar);
```

In case you are wondering why we did not mention the class `MenusGalore`, it is because it is named implicitly. This will all take place inside a constructor named `MenusGalore`.

9. We list three solutions. There are other solutions as well. The first solution is

```
JButton myButton = new JButton("Push Me");
ImageIcon aliceIcon = new ImageIcon("alice.gif");
myButton.setIcon(aliceIcon);
```

The following will also work:

```
JButton myButton = new JButton("Push Me");
myButton.setIcon(new ImageIcon("alice.gif"));
```

The following will also work:

```
ImageIcon aliceIcon = new ImageIcon("alice.gif");
JButton myButton = new JButton(aliceIcon);
myButton.setText("Push Me");
```

10. We list two solutions. There are other solutions as well. The first solution is

```
ImageIcon aliceIcon = new ImageIcon("alice.gif");
JLabel alicePicture = new JLabel(aliceIcon);
picturePanel.add(alicePicture);
```

The following will also work:

```
picturePanel.add(new JLabel(
                   new ImageIcon("alice.gif")));
```

11.

```
ImageIcon aliceIcon = new ImageIcon("alice.gif");
JButton aliceButton = new JButton(aliceIcon);
aliceButton.setActionCommand("Curiouser and curiouser!")
```

The following will also work:

```
JButton aliceButton = new JButton(
                         new ImageIcon("alice.gif"));
aliceButton.setActionCommand("Curiouser and curiouser!")
```

12. No. The method `setMinimumSize` is only advisory to Java.

13. No. You can invoke both methods, invoke either one without the other, or invoke neither method.

14. No, there is no type violation. The class `JTextArea` is a descendant class of the class `Component`, so every `JTextArea` is also of type `Component`. If this concept is not clear, Display 12.18 and the accompanying text may help clarify things.

15. You add the `JTextArea` to the `JScrollPane`. You do this by giving the `JTextArea` as an argument to the `JScrollPane` constructor.

16. Yes, you can use the `EmptyBorder` class to add space around a component. For example, the following line adds 30 pixels of space to the left and right of the component b:

```
b.setBorder(new EmptyBorder(0, 30, 0, 30));
```

17. No, you need

```
import javax.swing.border.*;
```

18.

```
myPanel.setLayout(
          new BoxLayout(myPanel, BoxLayout.Y_AXIS));
```

19. There is no difference in how components are added and no difference in the ordering of components, but there is a difference in the spacing of components. With the `BoxLayout` manager, a strut will not have extra space added around it, but with the `FlowLayout` manager, it might have extra space added around it. Other differences in the spacing and sizing of components might also occur.

20.

```
Component horizontalSpace =
          Box.createHorizontalStrut(20);
```

21. A strut component has a fixed size in one dimension (either height or width), while a glue component can change size in either dimension.

22.

```
Box vBox = new Box(BoxLayout.Y_AXIS);
```

and the equivalent

```
Box vBox = Box.createVerticalBox();
```

23. No. A `Box` container automatically gets a `BoxLayout` manager. However, you do specify what kind of `BoxLayout` manager it gets (either vertical or horizontal) when you create the `Box` container.

24. Struts and glue work only with the `BoxLayout` manager (which includes the case of the `Box` container). You will get no compiler error if you use them with other layout managers, but they will not behave correctly for other layout managers.

25. The methods `setHgap` and `setVgap` work with any of the layout managers discussed in this book, except for the `BoxLayout` manager.

26. Because we needed a name for the layout manager so that we could switch the "card" displayed, as in the following line from the definition of the method `actionPerformed`:

```
dealer.show(deckPanel, "red");
```

27. `dealer.next(deckPanel);`

28. `dealer.previous(deckPanel);`

29. The last card will be displayed.

30. You must define all of the methods given in Display 14.15. Moreover, the number and types of the method parameters must be exactly as shown in Display 14.15. If you do not want to define a method to do anything special, you can give it an empty body, as follows:

```
public void windowIconified(WindowEvent e)
{}
```

31. No.

32. Yes, just list all of the interface names after the keyword `implements` and separate them with commas, as in the following example:

```
public class WindowListenerDemo extends JFrame
              implements ActionListener, WindowListener
```

You also need to implement all the methods in all the interfaces.

33. You can invoke `dispose()`, using the object you want to go away as the calling object.

34. The window goes away, but the program does not end. This is a problem if there are no other windows in the program, because then you have no nice way to end the program.

35.
```
setDefaultCloseOperation(
                  WindowConstants.DO_NOTHING_ON_CLOSE);
```

36. No, there is no need for it. (Although it would do no serious harm if you did add it.)

37. It is a constant named DO_NOTHING_ON_CLOSE that is defined in the class `WindowConstants`. You should be able to figure that out from the way it is written and the way it is used. (By the way, the class `WindowConstants` is in the package `javax.swing`. So the only `import` statement you need in order to use the class (and the constant) is

```
import javax.swing.*;
```

38. No. The method `setText`, which is used to set the text in a text field or text area, automatically takes care of updating the GUI.

39. You need names for the buttons. So add the following two instance variables:

```
private JButton upButton;
private JButton downButton;
```

The only changes to be made in the constructor are to replace

```
JButton upButton = new JButton("Up");
```

with

```
upButton = new JButton("Up");
```

and to replace

```
JButton downButton = new JButton("Down");
```

with

```
downButton = new JButton("Down");
```

The only other change is to change the nested if-then-else in the method ac-tionPerformed to the following:

```
if (e.getActionCommand( ).equals("Up"))
{
    upLabel.setVisible(true);
    downLabel.setVisible(false);
    upButton.setVisible(false);
    downButton.setVisible(true);
    validate( );
}
else if (e.getActionCommand( ).equals("Down"))
{
    downLabel.setVisible(true);
    upLabel.setVisible(false);
    downButton.setVisible(false);
    upButton.setVisible(true);
    validate( );
}
else
    System.out.println(
            "Error in VisibilityDemoExercise interface.");
```

extra code
on CD

The complete program is on the CD that accompanies this text, in the file Visi-bilityDemoExercise.java.

40. No, it is not legal. AbstractButton is an abstract class, and you cannot directly create an object of an abstract class. If you want an AbstractButton object, it must be an object of a more specific class, such as JButton or JMenuItem.

41. A JButton is an AbstractButton. A JLabel is not an AbstractButton. A JMenuItem is an AbstractButton. A JMenu is an AbstractButton. The first three answers are immediate from Display 14.19. To see that a JMenu is an Ab-stractButton, recall that a JMenu is a JMenuItem and that a JMenuItem is an AbstractButton. However, it is not always practical to use all the methods of an AbstractButton with a JMenu. So a JMenu is not a "typical" Abstract-Button.

● Programming Projects

1. Write a GUI that will let the user sample icons. It should have a menu named Icons that offers three choices: Smiley Face, Duke Waving, and Duke Stand-ing. When the user chooses a menu item, the corresponding icon is displayed (and

no other icons are displayed). When the GUI is first displayed, no icons are visible. The picture files for these icons are on the accompanying CD.

2. Enhance the memo saver GUI in Display 14.1 in all of the following ways:

■ Add another menu called `Scroll Bars`.

■ The menu named `Scroll Bars` should offer the user three choices: `Never`, `Always`, and `As Needed`. When the user makes a choice, the scroll bars are displayed according to the choice.

■ When the user clicks the close-window button, another window pops up and asks the user if she or he is sure she or he wants to end the program, as in Display 14.17.

3. Enhance the program you wrote for Programming Project 7 in Chapter 9 to give it a GUI interface that allows the user to write and read records of type `PetRecord` (Display 5.20 in Chapter 5) to a file. Include a menu with options to create a new file, read an existing one, or exit. Create two `PetRecord` files, named `dogPet-Records` and `catPetRecords`, and list them in a submenu under the read option. *Hint*: You can use this program to create the files `dogPetRecords` and `catPet-Records`. This project will require two testing phases, one before and one after creating `dogPetRecords` and `catPetRecords`, but that is not a major problem.

4. Write a GUI that will let the user sample borders. Include a menu named `Borders` that offers three options—bevel border, etched border, and line border—and sub-menus with the following options:

■ beveled-border options: raised or lowered;

■ etched-border options: raised or lowered;

■ line-border options: small, medium, or large.

■ Each line-border submenu should have a submenu with three color options black, red, and blue.

Put the borders around a `JLabel` containing text that describes the border, such as `"Raised Border"`, `"Lowered Etched Border"`, and so forth. Fix the high-light and shadow colors for the etched-border options to whatever colors you like, and make the small line border 5 pixels wide, the medium one 10 pixels wide, and the large one 20 pixels wide.

5. Redo or do for the first time Programming Project 3 in this chapter, but this time, use the `BoxLayout` manager (or the `Box` container class) to create the GUI, and put two buttons, one to write a file and the other to read a file, vertically on the left.

6. Write a "skeleton" GUI program that implements the `WindowListener` inter-face. Write code for each of the methods in Display 14.15 that simply prints out a message identifying which event occurred. Print the message out in a text field. Note that your program will not end when the close-window button is clicked (but will instead simply send a message to the text field saying that the `windowClos-ing` method has been invoked). Include a button labeled `Exit` that the user can click to end the program.

APPENDIX 1

Keywords

Keywords are also called *reserved words*. You may not redefine any of the keywords given in this appendix. Their meanings are determined by the Java language and cannot be changed. In particular, you cannot use any of these keywords for variable names, method names, or class names.

abstract	float	return
assert*	for	
		short
boolean	goto	static
break		strictfp
byte		super
	if	switch
case	implements	synchronized
catch	import	
char	inner*	
class	instanceof	this
const	int	throw
continue	interface	throws
		transient
		true*
default	long	try
do		
double	native	
	new	void
else	null*	volatile
extends		
		while
	package	
false*	private	
final	protected	
finally	public	

* According to the Sun documentation, these are not considered keywords. However, some authorities list them as keywords. For safety, this book considers them to be keywords, and you should as well.

APPENDIX 2

Precedence Rules

This appendix describes the rules that Java uses to determine the order in which operations are performed when evaluating an expression. In this list, operators on the same line are of equal precedence. As you move down the list, the operators in each line are of lower precedence than the ones on the previous line. When the computer is deciding which of two operations to perform first and the order is not dictated by parentheses, then it performs the operation of higher precedence before the operation of lower precedence. Some operators have equal precedence, and then the order of operations is determined by the sequence of the operators. Binary operators of equal precedence are performed in left-to-right order. Unary operators of equal precedence are performed in right-to-left order.

Highest Precedence

The dot operator, array indexing, and function call ., [ ], and ( )

The unary operators (+, −, ++, − −, !, and ~[1]), and type casts (*Type*)

The binary operators *, /, and %

The binary operators + and −

The binary operators (shift operators)[1] <<, >>, and >>>>

The binary operators <, >, <=, >=, and instanceof

The binary operators == and !=

The binary operator &

The binary operator (xor)[1] ^

The binary operator |

The binary operator &&

The binary operator ||

The ternary operator (conditional operator) ? :

The assignment operators =, *=, /=, %=, +=, −=, <<=, >>=, >>>>=, &=, ^=, and |=

Lowest Precedence

---

1. Not discussed in this book.

APPENDIX 3

Unicode Character Set

The characters shown in this table are a subset of the Unicode character set known as the ASCII character set. The numbering is the same whether the characters are considered to be members of the Unicode character set or of the ASCII character set. Character number 32 is the blank. Only the printable characters are shown in the table.

32		56	8	80	P	104	h
33	!	57	9	81	Q	105	i
34	"	58	:	82	R	106	j
35	#	59	;	83	S	107	k
36	$	60	<	84	T	108	l
37	%	61	=	85	U	109	m
38	&	62	>	86	V	110	n
39	'	63	?	87	W	111	o
40	(	64	@	88	X	112	p
41	)	65	A	89	Y	113	q
42	*	66	B	90	Z	114	r
43	+	67	C	91	[	115	s
44	,	68	D	92	\	116	t
45	–	69	E	93	]	117	u
46	.	70	F	94	^	118	v
47	/	71	G	95	_	119	w
48	0	72	H	96	`	120	x
49	1	73	I	97	a	121	y
50	2	74	J	98	b	122	z
51	3	75	K	99	c	123	{
52	4	76	L	100	d	124	|
53	5	77	M	101	e	125	}
54	6	78	N	102	f	126	~
55	7	79	O	103	g		

APPENDIX 4

SavitchIn

```java
import java.io.*;
import java.util.*;

/**
 Class for simple console input.
 A class designed primarily for simple keyboard input of the
 form "one input value per line". If the user enters an improper
 input, i.e., an input of the wrong type or a blank line, then
 the user is prompted to reenter the input and given a brief
 explanation of what is required. Also includes some additional
 methods to input single numbers, words, and characters, without
 going to the next line.
*/
public class SavitchIn
{
    /**
     Reads a line of text and returns that line as a String
     value. The end of a line must be indicated either by a
     new-line character '\n' or by a carriage return '\r'
     followed by a new-line character '\n'. (Almost all systems
     do this automatically. So you need not worry about this
     detail.) Neither the '\n' nor the '\r', if present, are
     part of the string returned. This class will read the rest
     of a line if the line is already partially read.
    */
    public static String readLine()
    {
        char nextChar;
        String result = "";
        boolean done = false;

        while (!done)
        {
            nextChar = readChar();
            if (nextChar == '\n')
                done = true;
            else if (nextChar == '\r')
            {
                //Do nothing.
                //Next loop iteration will detect '\n'.
            }
            else
                result = result + nextChar;
        }

        return result;
    }
```

```
/**
 Reads the first string of nonwhitespace characters on
 a line and returns that string. The rest of the line
 is discarded. If the line contains only whitespace,
 the user is asked to reenter the line.
*/
public static String readLineWord()
{
    String inputString = null,
           result = null;
    boolean done = false;

    while(!done)
    {
        inputString = readLine();
        StringTokenizer wordSource =
                        new StringTokenizer(inputString);
        if (wordSource.hasMoreTokens())
        {
            result = wordSource.nextToken();
            done = true;
        }
        else
        {
            System.out.println(
              "Your input is not correct. Your input must");
            System.out.println(
            "contain at least one nonwhitespace character.");
            System.out.println(
                        "Please try again. Enter input:");
        }
    }

    return result;
}

/**
 Precondition: The user has entered a number of type int
 on a line by itself, except that there may be
 whitespace before and/or after the number.
 Action: Reads and returns the number as a value of type
 int. The rest of the line is discarded. If the input is
 not entered correctly, then in most cases, the user will
 be asked to reenter the input. In particular, this
 applies to incorrect number formats and blank lines.
*/
public static int readLineInt()
{
    String inputString = null;
    int number = -9999;//To keep the compiler happy.
                       //Designed to look like a garbage value.
    boolean done = false;
```

```
        while (! done)
        {
            try
            {
                inputString = readLine();
                inputString = inputString.trim();
                number = Integer.parseInt(inputString);
                done = true;
            }
            catch (NumberFormatException e)
            {
                System.out.println(
                        "Your input number is not correct.");
                System.out.println(
                        "Your input number must be");
                System.out.println(
                        "a whole number written as an");
                System.out.println(
                         "ordinary numeral, such as 42");
                System.out.println("Minus signs are OK,"
                        + "but do not use a plus sign.");
                System.out.println("Please try again.");
                System.out.println("Enter a whole number:");
            }
        }

        return number;
    }

    /**
     Precondition: The user has entered a number of type long
     on a line by itself, except that there may be whitespace
     before and/or after the number.
     Action: Reads and returns the number as a value of type
     long. The rest of the line is discarded. If the input is
     not entered correctly, then in most cases, the user will
     be asked to reenter the input. In particular, this
     applies to incorrect number formats and blank lines.
    */
    public static long readLineLong()
    {
        String inputString = null;
        long number = -9999;//To keep the compiler happy.
                        //Designed to look like a garbage value.
        boolean done = false;

        while (! done)
        {
            try
            {
                inputString = readLine();
                inputString = inputString.trim();
```

```java
            number = Long.parseLong(inputString);
            done = true;
        }
        catch (NumberFormatException e)
        {
            System.out.println(
                    "Your input number is not correct.");
            System.out.println(
                        "Your input number must be");
            System.out.println(
                        "a whole number written as an");
            System.out.println(
                        "ordinary numeral, such as 42");
            System.out.println("Minus signs are OK,"
                        + "but do not use a plus sign.");
            System.out.println("Please try again.");
            System.out.println("Enter a whole number:");
        }
    }

    return number;
}

/**
 Precondition: The user has entered a number of type
 double on a line by itself, except that there may be
 whitespace before and/or after the number.
 Action: Reads and returns the number as a value of type
 double. The rest of the line is discarded. If the input
 is not entered correctly, then in most cases, the user
 will be asked to reenter the input. In particular, this
 applies to incorrect number formats and blank lines.
*/
public static double readLineDouble()
{
    String inputString = null;
    double number = -9999;//To keep the compiler happy.
                    //Designed to look like a garbage value.
    boolean done = false;

    while (! done)
    {
        try
        {
            inputString = readLine();
            inputString = inputString.trim();
            number = Double.parseDouble(inputString);
            done = true;
        }
        catch (NumberFormatException e)
        {
```

```java
                System.out.println(
                        "Your input number is not correct.");
                System.out.println(
                        "Your input number must be");
                System.out.println(
                        "an ordinary number either with");
                System.out.println(
                        "or without a decimal point,");
                System.out.println("such as 42 or 9.99");
                System.out.println("Please try again.");
                System.out.println("Enter the number:");
            }
        }

        return number;
    }

    /**
     Precondition: The user has entered a number of type float
     on a line by itself, except that there may be whitespace
     before and/or after the number.
     Action: Reads and returns the number as a value of type
     float. The rest of the line is discarded. If the input is
     not entered correctly, then in most cases, the user will
     be asked to reenter the input. In particular,
     this applies to incorrect number formats and blank lines.
    */
    public static float readLineFloat()
    {
        String inputString = null;
        float number = -9999;//To keep the compiler happy.
                        //Designed to look like a garbage value.
        boolean done = false;

        while (! done)
        {
            try
            {
                inputString = readLine();
                inputString = inputString.trim();
                number = Float.parseFloat(inputString);
                done = true;
            }
            catch (NumberFormatException e)
            {
                System.out.println(
                        "Your input number is not correct.");
                System.out.println(
                        "Your input number must be");
                System.out.println(
                        "an ordinary number either with");
```

```
            System.out.println(
                        "or without a decimal point,");
            System.out.println("such as 42 or 9.99");
            System.out.println("Please try again.");
            System.out.println("Enter the number:");
        }
    }

    return number;
}

/**
 Reads the first nonwhitespace character on a line and
 returns that character. The rest of the line is
 discarded. If the line contains only whitespace, the
 user is asked to reenter the line.
*/
public static char readLineNonwhiteChar()
{
    boolean done = false;
    String inputString = null;
    char nonWhite = ' ';//To keep the compiler happy.

    while (! done)
    {
        inputString = readLine();
        inputString = inputString.trim();
        if (inputString.length() == 0)
        {
            System.out.println(
                        "Your input is not correct.");
            System.out.println(
                        "Your input must contain at");
            System.out.println(
                        "least one nonwhitespace character.");
            System.out.println("Please try again.");
            System.out.println("Enter input:");
        }
        else
        {
            nonWhite = (inputString.charAt(0));
            done = true;
        }
    }

    return nonWhite;
}

/**
 Input should consist of a single word on a line, possibly
 surrounded by whitespace. The line is read and discarded.
 If the input word is "true" or "t", then true is returned.
 If the input word is "false" or "f", then false is
```

```
returned. Uppercase and lowercase letters are considered
equal. If the user enters anything else (e.g., multiple
words or different words), the user is asked
to reenter the input.
*/
public static boolean readLineBoolean()
{
    boolean done = false;
    String inputString = null;
    boolean result = false;//To keep the compiler happy.

    while (! done)
    {
        inputString = readLine();
        inputString = inputString.trim();
        if (inputString.equalsIgnoreCase("true")
                || inputString.equalsIgnoreCase("t"))
        {
            result = true;
            done = true;
        }
        else if (inputString.equalsIgnoreCase("false")
                    || inputString.equalsIgnoreCase("f"))
        {
            result = false;
            done = true;
        }
        else
        {
            System.out.println(
                    "Your input is not correct.");
            System.out.println("Your input must be");
            System.out.println("one of the following:");
            System.out.println("the word true,");
            System.out.println("the word false,");
            System.out.println("the letter T,");
            System.out.println("or the letter F.");
            System.out.println(
                    "You may use either upper-");
            System.out.println("or lowercase letters.");
            System.out.println("Please try again.");
            System.out.println("Enter input:");
        }
    }

    return result;
}
/**
 Reads the next input character and returns that character.
 The next read takes place on the same line where this
 one left off.
*/
```

```java
public static char readChar()
{
    int charAsInt = -1; //To keep the compiler happy.
    try
    {
        charAsInt = System.in.read();
    }
    catch(IOException e)
    {
        System.out.println(e.getMessage());
        System.out.println("Fatal error. Ending program.");
        System.exit(0);
    }

    return (char)charAsInt;
}

/**
 Reads the next nonwhitespace input character and returns
 that character. The next read takes place immediately
 after the character read.
*/
public static char readNonwhiteChar()
{
    char next;

    next = readChar();
    while (Character.isWhitespace(next))
        next = readChar();

    return next;
}

/**
 The methods given next are not used in the text, except
 for a brief reference in Chapter 2. No program code uses
 them. However, some programmers may want to use them.
*/

/**
 Precondition: The next input in the stream consists of
 an int value, possibly preceded by whitespace, but
 definitely followed by whitespace.
 Action: Reads the first string of nonwhitespace characters
 and returns the int value it represents. Discards the
 first whitespace character after the word. The next read
 takes place immediately after the discarded whitespace.
 In particular, if the word is at the end of a line, the
 next read will take place starting on the next line.
 If the next word does not represent an int value,
 a NumberFormatException is thrown.
*/
```

```java
public static int readInt() throws NumberFormatException
{
    String inputString = null;
    inputString = readWord();
    return Integer.parseInt(inputString);
}

/**
 Precondition: The next input consists of a long value,
 possibly preceded by whitespace, but definitely
 followed by whitespace.
 Action: Reads the first string of nonwhitespace characters
 and returns the long value it represents. Discards the
 first whitespace character after the string read. The
 next read takes place immediately after the discarded
 whitespace. In particular, if the string read is at the
 end of a line, the next read will take place starting on
 the next line. If the next word does not represent a long
 value, a NumberFormatException is thrown.
*/
public static long readLong()
                    throws NumberFormatException
{
    String inputString = null;
    inputString = readWord();
    return Long.parseLong(inputString);
}

/**
 Precondition: The next input consists of a double value,
 possibly preceded by whitespace, but definitely
 followed by whitespace.
 Action: Reads the first string of nonwhitespace characters
 and returns the double value it represents. Discards the
 first whitespace character after the string read. The
 next read takes place immediately after the discarded
 whitespace. In particular, if the string read is at the
 end of a line, the next read will take place starting on
 the next line. If the next word does not represent a
 double value, a NumberFormatException is thrown.
*/
public static double readDouble()
                    throws NumberFormatException
{
    String inputString = null;
    inputString = readWord();
    return Double.parseDouble(inputString);
}

/**
 Precondition: The next input consists of a float value,
 possibly preceded by whitespace, but definitely
 followed by whitespace.
```

```
    Action: Reads the first string of nonwhitespace characters
    and returns the float value it represents. Discards the
    first whitespace character after the string read. The
    next read takes place immediately after the discarded
    whitespace. In particular, if the string read is at the
    end of a line, the next read will take place starting on
    the next line. If the next word does not represent
    a float value, a NumberFormatException is thrown.
*/
public static float readFloat()
                    throws NumberFormatException
{
    String inputString = null;
    inputString = readWord();
    return Float.parseFloat(inputString);
}


/**
 Reads the first string of nonwhitespace characters and
 returns that string. Discards the first whitespace
 character after the string read. The next read takes
 place immediately after the discarded whitespace. In
 particular, if the string read is at the end of a line,
 the next read will take place starting on the next line.
 Note that if it receives blank lines, it will wait until
 it gets a nonwhitespace character.
*/
public static String readWord()
{
    String result = "";
    char next;

    next = readChar();
    while (Character.isWhitespace(next))
        next = readChar();

    while (!(Character.isWhitespace(next)))
    {
        result = result + next;
        next = readChar();
    }

    if (next == '\r')
    {
        next = readChar();
        if (next != '\n')
        {
            System.out.println("Fatal error in method "
                + "readWord of the class SavitchIn.");
```

```
                System.exit(1);
            }
        }

        return result;
    }

    /**
     Precondition: The user has entered a number of type byte
     on a line by itself, except that there may be whitespace
     before and/or after the number.
     Action: Reads and returns the number as a value of type
     byte. The rest of the line is discarded. If the input is
     not entered correctly, then in most cases, the user will
     be asked to reenter the input. In particular, this applies
     to incorrect number formats and blank lines.
    */
    public static byte readLineByte()
    {
        String inputString = null;
        byte number = -123;//To keep the compiler happy.
                    //Designed to look like a garbage value.
        boolean done = false;

        while (! done)
        {
            try
            {
                inputString = readLine();
                inputString = inputString.trim();
                number = Byte.parseByte(inputString);
                done = true;
            }
            catch (NumberFormatException e)
            {
                System.out.println(
                        "Your input number is not correct.");
                System.out.println(
                        "Your input number must be a");
                System.out.println(
                        "whole number in the range");
                System.out.println("-128 to 127, written as");
                System.out.println(
                        "an ordinary numeral, such as 42.");
                System.out.println("Minus signs are OK,"
                            + "but do not use a plus sign.");
                System.out.println("Please try again.");
                System.out.println("Enter a whole number:");
            }
        }

        return number;
    }
```

```java
/**
 Precondition: The user has entered a number of type short
 on a line by itself, except that there may be whitespace
 before and/or after the number.
 Action: Reads and returns the number as a value of type
 short. The rest of the line is discarded. If the input is
 not entered correctly, then in most cases, the user will
 be asked to reenter the input. In particular, this applies
 to incorrect number formats and blank lines.
*/
public static short readLineShort()
{
    String inputString = null;
    short number = -9999;//To keep the compiler happy.
                        //Designed to look like a garbage value.
    boolean done = false;

    while (! done)
    {
        try
        {
            inputString = readLine();
            inputString = inputString.trim();
            number = Short.parseShort(inputString);
            done = true;
        }
        catch (NumberFormatException e)
        {
            System.out.println(
                    "Your input number is not correct.");
            System.out.println(
                    "Your input number must be a");
            System.out.println(
                    "whole number in the range");
            System.out.println(
                    "-32768 to 32767, written as");
            System.out.println(
                    "an ordinary numeral, such as 42.");
            System.out.println("Minus signs are OK,"
                            + "but do not use a plus sign.");
            System.out.println("Please try again.");
            System.out.println("Enter a whole number:");
        }
    }

    return number;
}

public static byte readByte() throws NumberFormatException
{
    String inputString = null;
    inputString = readWord();
```

```
        return Byte.parseByte(inputString);
    }

    public static short readShort() throws NumberFormatException
    {
        String inputString = null;
        inputString = readWord();
        return Short.parseShort(inputString);
    }

    //The next class was intentionally not used in the code for
    //other methods, so that somebody reading the code could
    //more quickly see what was being used.
    /**
     Reads the first byte in the input stream and returns that
     byte as an int. The next read takes place where this one
     left off. This read is the same as System.in.read( ),
     except that it catches IOExceptions.
    */
    public static int read()
    {
        int result = -1; //To keep the compiler happy
        try
        {
            result = System.in.read();
        }
        catch(IOException e)
        {
            System.out.println(e.getMessage());
            System.out.println("Fatal error. Ending program.");
            System.exit(0);
        }
        return result;
    }
}
```

APPENDIX 5

Protected and Package Modifiers

In this text, we always use the modifiers `public` and `private` before instance variables and method definitions. Normally, these are the only modifiers you need, but there are two other possibilities that fall in between the two extremes of `public` and `private`. In this appendix, we discuss the modifier `protected` as well as the restriction that applies when you use no modifier at all.

If a method or instance variable is modified by `protected` (rather than `public` or `private`), then it can be directly accessed inside of its own class definition, and it can be directly accessed inside of any class derived from it. Moreover, if marked `protected`, then it can also be directly accessed in any method definition for any class in the same package. That is the extent of the access; the protected method or instance variable cannot be directly accessed in any other classes. Thus, if a method is marked `protected` in class *A*, and class *B* is derived from class *A*, then the method can be used inside any method definition in class *B*. However, in a class that is not in the same package as class *A* and is not derived from class *A*, it is as if the `protected` method were `private`.

The modifier `protected` imposes a peculiar sort of restriction, since it allows direct access to any programmer who is willing to go through the bother of defining a suitable derived class. Thus, it is like saying, "I'll make it difficult for you to use this item, but I will not forbid you to use it." In practice, instance variables should never be marked `protected`. On very rare occasions, you may want to have a method marked `protected`. However, if you want an access level that is intermediate between `public` and `private`, the access described in the next paragraph is often a preferable alternative.

You may have noticed that, if you forget to place one of the modifiers `public` or `private` before an instance variable or method definition, your class definition will still compile. If you do not place any of the modifiers `public`, `private`, or `protected` before an instance variable or method definition, then the instance variable or method can be directly accessed inside the definition of any class in the same package, but not outside of the package. This type of access is called **package access**, or **default access.** You use package access when you have a package of cooperating classes that act as a single encapsulated unit. Note that package access is more restricted than `protected` access and that package access gives more control to the programmer defining the classes. If you control the package directory, then you control who is allowed package access.

APPENDIX 6

The `DecimalFormat` Class

An object of the class `DecimalFormat` has a number of different methods that can be used to produce numeral strings in various formats. In this appendix, we describe some uses of one of these methods, named `format`. The general approach to using the `DecimalFormat` class is as follows:

Create an object of the class `DecimalFormat`, using a `String` pattern:

Syntax:

```
DecimalFormat Variable_Name = DecimalFormat(Pattern);
```

Example:

```
DecimalFormat formattingObject = new DecimalFormat("000.000");
```

The method `format` of the class `DecimalFormat` can then be used to convert a number of type `double` to a corresponding numeral `String`.

Syntax:

Decimal_Format_Object.`format`(*Double_Expression*)
produces a numeral string corresponding to the *Double_Expression*.
The *Decimal_Format_Object* is typically a *Variable_Name*.

Examples:

```
System.out.println(formattingObject.format(12.3456789));
String numeral = formattingObject.format(12.3456789);
```

Assuming that the object `formattingObject` is created as shown previously, the output produced by the foregoing `println` statement is

```
012.346
```

The format of the string produced is determined by the *Pattern* string that was used as the argument to the constructor that created the object of the class `DecimalFormat`.

For example, the pattern `"00.000"` means that there will be two digits before the decimal point and three digits after the decimal point. Note that the result is rounded when the number of digits is less than the number of digits available. If the format pattern is not consistent with the value of the number, such as a pattern that asks for two digits before the decimal point for a number like `123.456`, then the format will be violated so that no digits are lost.

You can create patterns such as `"#0.##0"`, in which the character `'0'` stands for a compulsory digit and the character `'#'` stands for an optional digit. Examples of patterns are shown in Display A6.1.

Percent Notation

The character `'%'` placed at the end of a pattern indicates that the number is to be expressed as a percentage. The `'%'` causes the number to be multiplied by 100 and have a percent sign (%) appended to it.

■ DISPLAY A6.1   **Demonstration of the** `DecimalFormat` **Class** *(Part 1 of 2)*

```java
import java.text.*;
public class DecimalFormatDemo
{
    public static void main(String[] args)
    {
        DecimalFormat twoDigitsPastPoint = new DecimalFormat("0.00");
        DecimalFormat threeDigitsPastPoint =
                          new DecimalFormat("00.000");

        double d = 12.3456789;
        System.out.println(twoDigitsPastPoint.format(d));
        System.out.println(threeDigitsPastPoint.format(d));

        double money = 12.8;
        System.out.println("$" + twoDigitsPastPoint.format(money));
        String numberString = twoDigitsPastPoint.format(money);
        System.out.println(numberString);

        DecimalFormat percent = new DecimalFormat("0.00%");

        double fraction = 0.734;
        System.out.println(percent.format(fraction));

        DecimalFormat eNotation1 =
            new DecimalFormat("#0.###E0");//1 or 2 digits before point
        DecimalFormat eNotation2 =
            new DecimalFormat("00.###E0");//2 digits before point

        double number = 123.456;
        System.out.println(eNotation1.format(number));
        System.out.println(eNotation2.format(number));

        double small = 0.0000123456;
        System.out.println(eNotation1.format(small));
        System.out.println(eNotation2.format(small));
    }
}
```

■ DISPLAY A6.1   **Demonstration of the** DecimalFormat **Class** *(Part 2 of 2)*

Sample Screen Dialog

```
12.35
12.346
$12.80
12.80
73.40%
1.2346E2
12.346E1
12.346E-6
12.346E-6
```

Scientific Notation (E-Notation)

E-notation is specified by including an 'E' in the pattern string. For example, the pattern "00.###E0" approximates the specification of two digits before the decimal point, three or fewer digits after the decimal point, and at least one digit after the 'E', as in 12.346E1. As you can see by the examples of E-notation in Display A6.1, the exact details of what E-notation string is produced can be a bit more involved than our explanation so far. Here are a couple more details:

The number of digits indicated after the 'E' is the minimum number of digits used for the exponent. As many more digits as are needed will be used.

The **mantissa** is the decimal number before the 'E'. The minimum number of significant digits in the mantissa (that is, the sum of the number of digits before and after the decimal point) is the *minimum* of the number of digits indicated before the decimal point plus the *maximum* of the number of digits indicated after the decimal point. For example, 12345 formatted with "##0.##E0" is "12.3E3".

To see how E-notation patterns work, it would pay to play with a few cases, and in any event, do not count on a very precisely specified number of significant digits.

APPENDIX 7
The `Iterator` Interface

The `Iterator` interface is designed to be implemented in conjunction with classes whose objects are collections of elements. In a good implementation, repeated execution of the method `next` would produce all elements in the collection. The `Iterator` interface might be implemented by the collection class itself or by another class whose objects are iterators for the collection class. The `Iterator` interface specifies the following three methods:

```
/**
 Returns the next element. Throws a
 NoSuchElementException if there is no next element.
**/
public Object next();

/**
 Returns true if there is an element left for next to return.
*/
public boolean hasNext();

/**
 Removes the last element that was returned by next.
 Throws an UnsupportedOperationException if the remove
 method is not supported by this Iterator. Throws an
 IllegalStateException if the next method has not yet
 been called or if the remove method has already been
 called after the last call to the next method.
*/
public void remove();
```

All the exception classes mentioned are derived classes of `RunTimeException`, so an object of any of these exception classes need not be caught or declared in a `throws` clause.

The `Iterator` interface is in the package `java.util`. So when defining a class that implements the `Iterator` interface, the file should contain the following `import` statement:

```
import java.util.*;
```

A sample implementation of the `Iterator` interface is given in the answer to Self-Test Question 23 in Chapter 10.

Cloning

clone

A **clone** of an object is (or at least should be) an exact copy of the object. The emphasis here is on both *exact* and *copy*. A clone should look as though it has the exact same data values as the object being copied, and it should be a true copy and not simply another name for the object being copied. In Section 5.6, entitled "Information Hiding Revisited," we discussed some of the problems involved in making copies of an object. You should read that section before reading this appendix.

A clone is made by invoking the method named `clone`. The method `clone` is invoked in the same way as any other method. The heading for the method `clone` is as follows:[1]

```
public Object clone()
```

Although the method `clone` returns a copy of an object of some class, it always returns it as an object of type `Object`. So you normally need a type cast. For example, consider the class `PetRecord` in Display 5.20 of Chapter 5. After you make suitable additions to the class definition, you can make a copy of an object of type `PetRecord` as follows:

```
PetRecord original = new PetRecord("Fido", 2, 5.6);
PetRecord extraCopy = (PetRecord)original.clone();
```

Be sure to notice the type cast (PetRecord).

The foregoing invocation of `clone` (or any invocation of `clone`) will not work unless the class implements the `Cloneable` interface. Thus, in order to make the preceding code work, you must do two things. First, you must change the beginning of the class definition for `PetRecord` to the following:

```
public class PetRecord implements Cloneable
```

Second, you must add a definition of the method `clone` to the class definition. In the case of the class `PetRecord`, the method `clone` would be defined as shown in Display A8.1. On the accompanying CD, we have included a copy of the class `PetRecord` that includes the definition of the method `clone` from Display A8.1.

extra code on CD

Note that the `Cloneable` interface and `clone` method behave in more complicated ways than most interfaces and inherited methods. Although the class `Object` has a method named `clone`, it is not inherited automatically. You must include `implements Cloneable` in the definition of the class, and you must include a definition of `clone`, even if it is defined as in Display A8.1, which, in effect, simply says that the method `clone` behaves as it would if it were inherited in the normal way.

If the instance variables are all of types whose objects cannot be changed by their methods, such as the primitive types and the type `String`, then the definition of `clone` shown in Display A8.1 will work fine. In that definition, the method `clone` invokes the version of

---

1. In the class `Object`, the method `clone` is `protected`, not `public`, but it normally makes more sense to make it `public` in the classes you define.

■ **DISPLAY A8.1   Implementation of the Method** `clone` **(Simple Case)**

```
public Object clone()
{
    try
    {
        return super.clone();//Invocation of clone in class Object
    }
    catch(CloneNotSupportedException e)
    {//This should not happen.
        return null; //To keep the compiler happy.
    }
}
```

Works correctly if each instance variable is of a primitive type or of the type `String`. Does not work correctly in most other cases.

`clone` in the class `Object`,[2] which simply makes a bit-by-bit copy of the memory used to store the calling object's instance variables. The `try-catch` blocks are required because the method `clone` can throw the exception `CloneNotSupportedException` if the class does not implement the `Cloneable` interface. Of course, in these classes, we are implementing the `Cloneable` interface, so the exception will never be thrown, but the compiler will still insist on the `try-catch` blocks. There is a bit of detail to worry about here, but as long as each instance variable is either of a primitive type or of type `String`, the definition of `clone` in Display A8.1 will work just fine and can simply be copied unchanged into your class definition.

If your class has instance variables of a class type (other than a class whose objects cannot change, like `String`), then the definition of `clone` in Display A8.1 is legal, but it probably does not do what you want a `clone` method to do. If the class contains an instance variable of some class type, the clone produced will have a copy of the instance variable's memory address, rather than a copy of the instance variable's data. For a class that cannot be changed, like `String`, this condition is not a problem. For most other classes, this condition would allow access to private data in the way we described in Section 5.6, entitled "Information Hiding Revisited." When defining a `clone` method for a class that has instance variables of a class type (other than the type `String` or a similar unchangeable class type), your definition of `clone` should make a clone of each instance variable of a changeable class type. Of course, this task requires that those class types for the instance variables have a suitable `clone` method themselves. The way to define such a `clone` method is illustrated in Display A8.2. Let's go over some of the details in the definition of that `clone` method.

---

2. If your class is a derived class of some class (other than `Object`), we are assuming that the base class has a well-defined `clone` method, since `super.clone` will then refer to the base class.

■ DISPLAY A8.2   **Outline of a Class with Cloning**

```java
public class Neighbor implements Cloneable
{
    private String name;
    private int numberOfChildren;
    private PetRecord pet;

    public Object clone()
    {
        try
        {
            Neighbor copy = (Neighbor)super.clone();
            copy.pet = (PetRecord)pet.clone();
            return copy;
        }
        catch(CloneNotSupportedException e)
        {//This should not happen.
            return null; //To keep the compiler happy.
        }
    }

    public PetRecord getPet()
    {
        return (PetRecord)pet.clone();
    }

        <There are presumably other methods that are not shown.>
}
```

The following line makes a bit-by-bit copy of the memory used to store the calling object's instance variables:

```java
Neighbor copy = (Neighbor)super.clone();
```

This sort of copy works fine for the instance variable numberOfChildren, which is of the primitive type int. It is also satisfactory for the instance variable name of type String. However, the value it gives to the instance variable copy.pet is the address of the pet instance variable of the calling object. It does not, as yet, give copy.pet the address of a *copy* of the calling object's pet instance variable. To change the value of copy.pet so that it names a copy of the calling object's pet instance variable, the clone method definition goes on to do the following:

```java
copy.pet = (PetRecord)pet.clone();
```

APPENDIX 9

Javadoc

The Java language comes with a program named `javadoc` that will automatically generate HTML documents that describe your classes. This documentation tells somebody who uses your program or class what she or he needs to know in order to use it, but omits all the implementation details, such as the bodies of all method definitions (both public and private), all information about private methods, and all private instance variables.

`javadoc` is normally used on packages, although it can also be used on single classes. Packages are discussed in Chapter 5. You need to have access to an HTML browser (a Web browser) so that you can view the documents produced by `javadoc`. However, you do not need to know very much HTML in order to use `javadoc`. Chapter 13 contains more HTML instruction than you need to know for this purpose.

In this appendix, we will first discuss how you should comment your classes so that you can get the most value out of `javadoc`. We will then discus the details of how you run the `javadoc` program.

Commenting Classes for Use with `javadoc`

To get a more useful `javadoc` document, you must write your comments in a particular way. All the classes in this book have been commented for use with `javadoc`.

The program `javadoc` will extract the heading for your class as well as the headings for all public methods, public instance variables, and certain comments. No method bodies and no private items are extracted.

For `javadoc` to extract a comment, the comment must satisfy two conditions:

1. The comment must *immediately precede* a public class definition or a public method definition (or other public item).

2. The comment must use the /* and */ style, and the opening /* must contain an extra *. So the comment must be marked by /** at the beginning and */ at the end.

All of the /* and */ style comments in this book are of this form. Note that both // style comments and comments preceding any private items will not be extracted.

You can insert descriptions of parameters and the value returned by a method into the comment preceding the method. The following code illustrates how this operation is done:

```java
/**
 Computes the total cost of multiple identical items.
 @param number number of items purchased
 @param price cost of one item
 @return total cost of number items at price for one
*/
public static double cost(int number, double price)
{
    return number*price;
}
```

Note that each @ **tag** is on a line by itself. The following are some of the @ tags allowed:

@param *Parameter_Name Parameter_Description*
@return *Description_Of_Value_Returned*
@throws *Exception_Type Explanation*

If an @ tag is included for an item, javadoc will extract the explanation for that item and include it in the documentation.

You can also insert HTML commands in your comments so that you gain more control over javadoc, but that is not necessary and may not even be desirable. HTML commands can clutter the comments, making them harder to read when you look at the source code.

Running javadoc

To run javadoc on a package, you must be in the directory (folder) that *contains* the package directory, not in the package directory itself. To phrase it another way, you must be one directory above the directory that contains the class (or classes) for which you want to generate documentation. Then all you need to do is give the following command:

javadoc −d *Document_Directory Package_Name*

The *Document_Directory* is the name of the directory in which you want javadoc to place the HTML documents it produces.

The accompanying CD has a package named javadocsample, which contains the two classes **Person** and **Student** from Chapter 7. It also contains the result of running the following command (look in the subdirectory ap09):

javadoc −d javadocsampledocs javadocsample

You can also run the javadoc program on a single class file. For example,

javadoc SavitchIn.java

The result of running javadoc on the file SavitchIn.java is in the file SavitchIn.html on the accompanying CD.

You can link to another set of Java documents so that your HTML documents include live links to standard classes and methods. The syntax is as follows:

javadoc -link *Link_To* −d *Document_Directory Package_Name*

Link_To is either a path to your local version of the Java documentation or the URL of the Sun Web site with standard Java documentation. As of this writing, that URL was

http://java.sun.com/j2se/1.4/docs/api/

APPENDIX 10

The JOptionPane Class

Chapters 12 through 14 describe the most common ways of creating windowing interfaces in Java. The class JOptionPane provides an alternative way of creating windowing interfaces that is simpler, but less versatile. (It is also possible to use JOptionPane as part of the windowing interfaces described in Chapters 12 through 14.) This appendix provides a description of some of the features of the JOptionPane class. This material can be covered anytime after Chapter 2 has been covered.

A Sample Program Using JOptionPane

Display A10.1 contains a demonstration Java program that uses JOptionPane. Following the program, we show the three windows produced by the program. The three windows are produced one at a time. The user enters a number in the text field of the first window and

■ DISPLAY A10.1 **A Java Program Using** JOptionPane *(Part 1 of 2)*

```java
import javax.swing.*;
public class JOptionPaneProgram
{
    public static void main(String[] args)
    {
        String appleString;
        appleString =
            JOptionPane.showInputDialog("Enter number of apples:");
        int appleCount;
        appleCount = Integer.parseInt(appleString);

        String orangeString;
        orangeString =
            JOptionPane.showInputDialog("Enter number of oranges:");
        int orangeCount;
        orangeCount = Integer.parseInt(orangeString);

        int totalFruitCount;
        totalFruitCount = appleCount + orangeCount;

        JOptionPane.showMessageDialog(
            null, "The total number of fruits = " + totalFruitCount);
        System.exit(0);
    }
}
```

■ DISPLAY A10.1 **A Java Program Using** `JOptionPane` *(Part 2 of 2)*

Window 1

Input

Enter number of apples:

10

OK   Cancel

When the user clicks the OK button, the window goes away, and the next window (if any) is displayed.

Window 2

Input

Enter number of oranges:

2

OK   Cancel

Window 3

Message

The total number of fruits = 12

OK

then clicks the OK button, using the mouse. When the user clicks the OK button, the first window goes away, and the second window appears. The user enters another number in the text field of the second window. When the user clicks the OK button in the second window, the second window goes away, and the third window appears. When the user clicks the OK button in the third window, the third window goes away, and that is the end of this sample program.

Any program that uses the class `JOptionPane` must have the following line at the beginning of the program:

```
import javax.swing.*;
```

This line tells Java where to find the definition of the `JOptionPane` class.

showInput-
Dialog

The following two lines from Display A10.1 are an invocation of the method `showIn-putDialog` of the class `JOptionPane`:

```
appleString =
    JOptionPane.showInputDialog("Enter number of apples:");
```

This statement produces a window for obtaining input. The string argument—in this case, `"Enter number of apples:"`—is displayed in the window in order to tell the user what to enter. This invocation of the method `showInputDialog` will produce the first window shown in Display A10.1. The user uses her or his mouse to click in the text field and then types in some input. If the user does not like what she or he typed in, the user can use the Backspace key to back up and retype the input. Once the user is happy with the input, the user clicks the OK button, and the window goes away.

The method invocation

```
JOptionPane.showInputDialog("Enter number of apples:")
```

returns (that is, produces) the input that the user typed into the text field. The rest of the statement specifies where that input goes in your program. The statement we are discussing,

```
appleString =
    JOptionPane.showInputDialog("Enter number of apples:");
```

is an assignment statement that sets the value of the `String` variable `appleString` to what is produced on the right side of the assignment operator (=). So it sets the variable `appleString` to the input string that the user typed into the text field of the first window.

The programmer who wrote this program wants the user to enter an integer into that first input window and wants the program to store this integer in the `int` variable named `appleCount`. However, the program has recovered the input that the user enters as a string, not as a value of type `int`. Let's say that the user types in 10, indicating that there are 10 apples. The window produces the string `"10"`. If you want your program to process the input from an input window as a number, your program must convert the string, like `"10"`, into the corresponding number (in this case 10). The program converts the string stored in the variable `appleString` to an `int` and stores the resulting `int` value in the variable `appleCount` as follows:

Integer.
parseInt

```
appleCount = Integer.parseInt(appleString);
```

The expression `Integer.parseInt` is explained in Chapter 5 in the subsection entitled "`Integer`, `Double`, and Other Wrapper Classes," but if you have not yet read Chapter 5, you can simply note that this expression converts a number string to the corresponding value of type `int`.

■ DISPLAY A10.2   **Methods for Converting Strings to Numbers**

Type Name	Method for Converting
byte	Byte.parseByte(*String_To_Convert*)
short	Short.parseShort(*String_To_Convert*)
int	Integer.parseInt(*String_To_Convert*)
long	Long.parseLong(*String_To_Convert*)
float	Float.parseFloat(*String_To_Convert*)
double	Double.parseDouble(*String_To_Convert*)

To convert a value of type String to a value of the type given in the first column, use the method given in the second column. Each of the methods in the second column returns a value of the type given in the first column. The *String_To_Convert* must be a correct string representation of a value of the type given in the first column. For example, to convert to an int, the *String_To_Convert* must be a whole number (in the range of the type int) that is written in the usual way, without any decimal point.

If you are converting from a string to a number value of some type other than int, you use the appropriate method from Display A10.2 instead of parseInt.

The following line from the program in Display A10.1 gives the program output, which is displayed as the third window:

```
JOptionPane.showMessageDialog(
    null, "The total number of fruits = " + totalFruitCount);
```

output window

The part showMessageDialog is another method in the class JOptionPane. This method displays a window for showing some output. The method showMessageDialog has two arguments, which are separated with a comma. For simple programs, you use null as the first argument. The constant null is discussed in Chapter 5. If you have not yet read Chapter 5, you can simply insert null in the first argument position. In this case, it is just a placeholder. The second argument is the string that is written in the output window. The output window stays on the screen until the user clicks the OK button, using the mouse, and then the window disappears.

showMessage-Dialog

null

Note that you can give the output string to a showMessageDialog in the same way that you give an output string as an argument to System.out.println—that is, as a quoted string; as a variable; as a constant; or as any combination of these formats, connected with plus signs.

The last program statement, shown as follows: simply says that the program should end:

```
System.exit(0);
```

System.exit

System is a predefined Java class that is automatically provided by Java, and exit is a method in the class System. The method exit ends the program as soon as it is invoked. In the programs that we will write, the integer argument 0 can be any integer, but by tradition we use 0, because 0 is used to indicate a normal ending of the program. When you write a program with a windowing interface, you always need to end the program with

```
System.exit(0);
```

The program will not end when there are no more statements to execute, unless you make a call to this exit method.

Quick Reference: JOptionPane for Windowing Input/Output

You can use the methods showInputDialog and showMessageDialog to produce input and output windows for your Java programs. When using these methods, you must include the following line at the start of the file that contains your program:

```
import javax.swing.*;
```

The syntax for input and output statements using these methods is given as follows:

Syntax (Input):

```
String_Variable = JOptionPane.showInputDialog(String_Expression);
```

Example:

```
String orangeString;
orangeString = JOptionPane.showInputDialog(
                              "Enter number of oranges:");
```

The *String_Expression* is displayed in a window that has both a text field in which the user can enter input and a button labeled OK. When the user types in a string and then clicks the OK button in the window, the method returns the string that was typed, and the string typed in by the user is stored in the *String_Variable*. The window also disappears when the user clicks the OK button. Note that when input is done in this way, all input is string input. If you want the user to input integers, for example, then your program must convert the input string numeral to the equivalent number.

Syntax (Output):

```
JOptionPane.showMessageDialog(null, String_Expression);
```

Example:

```
JOptionPane.showMessageDialog(
    null, "The total number of fruits = " + totalFruitCount);
```

The *String_Expression* is displayed in a window that has a button labeled OK. When the user clicks the OK button, using the mouse, the window disappears.

Multiline Output Windows

If you want to output multiple lines, using the method JOptionPane.showMessageDialog, you can insert the new-line character, '\n', into the string used as the second argument. If the string becomes too long, as it almost always does with multiline output, you can make each line into a separate string (ending with '\n') and connect the lines with the plus sign. If the lines are long or there are very many lines, the output window will be made larger so that it can hold all the output.

For example, the following code will produce the window shown in Display A10.3, provided that totalFruit is a variable of type int whose value is 12:

```
JOptionPane.showMessageDialog(null,
                    "The number of apples\n"
            + "plus the number of oranges\n"
            + "is equal to " + totalFruit);
```

■ DISPLAY A10.3   A Multiline Output Window

APPENDIX 11

Differences between C++ and Java

This appendix is for readers who have had some significant programming experience with either C or C++. Other readers can ignore this appendix.

Java and C++ appear to be very similar, but they have more differences than you might be led to believe by a casual examination of the two languages. We will not describe all of the differences in this appendix, but we will go over a few similarities and differences in order to help you make the transition from C++ (or C) to Java.

Primitive Types

Java has most of the same basic primitive types as C and C++ (`int`, `short`, `long`, `float`, `double`, and `char`), but Java adds the types `byte` and `boolean`. (Recent versions of C++ have the type `bool`, which corresponds to the Java type `boolean`.) Java has no type named `long double`. Unlike in C and C++, the size, in bytes, of a value for some specific primitive type is fully specified in Java and is not implementation dependent. See Chapter 2 for details.

Strings

Unlike in some versions of C and C++, strings in Java are not special kinds of arrays of characters. There is a predefined type `String` in Java. (Coverage of the `String` class starts in Chapter 2.) The Java `String` class is somewhat similar to the class `string` in recent versions of C++.

Flow of Control

Control structures (`if-else`, `switch`, `while`, `do-while`, and `for`) are the same in Java as in C and C++. However, there are some differences that can affect your use of control structures in Java. Specifically, Java has no comma operator, the type `boolean` in Java neither is a numeric type nor can have its values be type cast to a numeric type, and the assignment operator is better behaved in Java than in C and C++.

Java does not have the comma operator. However, the `for` statement in Java has been defined so as to allow use of the comma, as in the following code:

```
for (n = 1, product = 1; n <= 10; n++)
    product = product*n;
```

But this "comma operator" can be used only in a `for` statement.

In Java, the type `boolean` has the two values `true` and `false`, which cannot be interpreted as numeric values, even with a type cast.

A classic error in C and C++ is to use = in place of ==, as in the following code:

```
if (n = 42)
    . . .
```

In C and C++. the expression n = 42 returns the value 42, which either is or will be converted to a boolean value, depending on what version of C or C++ you are using. In Java, n = 42 also returns the value 42, but in Java, 42 is not of type `boolean`, nor will it convert to type `boolean`. So in Java, this mistake will produce a compiler error message.

Testing for Equality

Testing objects of a class type for equality can be troublesome in Java. With values of a primitive type, the == operator tests for equality, as you might expect. However, when you compare two objects of a class type with ==, the objects are tested for being in the same memory location, not for having the same data. Java classes often define a method called equals to test objects for our intuitive idea of being equal. You cannot overload the == operator (or any operator) in Java.

main Method (Function) and Other Methods

Functions are called **methods** in Java. The main method (function) serves the same purpose in Java as in C and C++. In Java, the main method heading is always as follows:

```
public static void main(String[] args)
```

In Java, all methods—indeed, all code of any kind—are defined inside of a class.

Files and Including Files

Java does not have a #include directive. Java does have an import statement that allows you to import an entire package (library) for use in a class (file).

The general layout of a Java program consists of a number of classes, each in a file by itself. If all the classes are in the same directory (folder), then Java will automatically find the class (file) it needs when it needs it. By using the import statement, it is also possible to combine classes (files) from different directories. See Section 5.7 for more details.

In Java, a class must be in a file that has the same name as the class, but with the suffix .java. For example, a class named MyClass must be in a file named MyClass.java. The compiled version of the class is automatically placed in a file named MyClass.class.

Class and Method (Function) Definitions

Java makes no distinction between defining a method and declaring it (or, as some authors phrase it, between a method prototype and a method definition). All methods (functions) have only their definition and no forward references. There is no "heading", or "signature", or "prototype" that is independent of the method definition.

All methods must be defined in some class.

All class definitions are fully defined in one file and do not have any kind of forward reference or interface file. In particular, all method definitions are given in their entirety in their class definition. See Chapter 4 for more details.

No Pointers in Java

There are no pointer types in Java. Java does have pointers. In fact, all objects are named by means of pointers. However, the pointers are called *references*, and they are handled automatically. For example, a variable of type String will contain a reference (pointer) to a string, but there is no type for a pointer to a String. See Section 4.3 for more details.

Method (Function) Parameters

Strictly speaking, Java has only one mechanism for parameter passing, namely, call-by-value. However, in practice, Java is usually viewed as having two kinds of parameter-passing mechanisms, one for primitive types (such as `int`, `double`, and `char`) and one for class types.

For primitive types, the only parameter-passing mechanism is call-by-value.

For class types, the parameter-passing mechanism is also call-by-value, but it is a reference (pointer) to the class object that is passed. This allows a method (function) to change the data in the object, so some people consider this mechanism to be a call-by-reference mechanism. It does not satisfy the most common definition of *call-by-reference*, but when doing most simple tasks, it behaves very much like call-by-reference. See Chapters 4 and 5 for more details.

Arrays

Java arrays are very much like C or C++ arrays, but there are some differences, and Java arrays are better behaved. An array in Java "knows" its range. If `a` is an array, then the instance variable `a.length` contains an integer equal to the number of elements that the array can hold. Java array indexes are checked for being out of range, and an exception is thrown if your code attempts to use an array index (subscript) that is out of range. See Chapter 6 for more details.

Garbage Collection

Memory management and garbage collection are automatic in Java. Java uses the `new` operator to create a new object of a class type (and thus this process is a form of memory allocation), but there is no other form of memory allocation. Java has no facility that the programmer can use to do garbage collection. Garbage collection is automatic.

Other Comparisons

Comments in Java and C++ are essentially the same.

There are no global variables in Java.

Java has no enumerated types.

Java has no `typedef`.

Java has no structures or unions.

You can overload method (function) names in Java, as you can in C++, but you cannot overload operators in Java.

Java has no multiple inheritance, but it does recover much of the functionality of multiple inheritance via something called an interface. See Chapter 7 for more details on interfaces.

Java has no templates, but it does recover much of the functionality of templates via interfaces.

In Java, a class can have a constructor with a parameter of the same type as the class, but this constructor has no special status, unlike a copy constructor in C++.

INDEX

Symbols

-- *see* decrement operator
! 110
" 68
% 59
& 168
&& 108
  quick reference 109
* 48
*/ 89
  quick reference 92
+
  with strings 69
  used in `System.out.println` 49
++ *see* increment operator
/ 59
/* 89
  quick reference 92
// 89
  comment
    quick reference 92
< 109
<= 109
=
  with arrays 366
  see assignment statement
== 25, 109
  with arrays 366
  dangers of 160
  with strings 111
  with class variables 235
> 109
>= 109
@ 917
[] *see* array
\" 77
\\
  escape character 77
\' 77
\n 77
\r 77
\t 77
{ 92
|| 110
  quick reference 110
} 92

A

`a href` 808, 812
`abs` 280
`Abstract Button` 883–884
Abstract class 452–454, 883
  quick reference 455
Abstract data type *see* ADT
Abstract Windows Toolkit *see* AWT
Accessor method 217
Action command 753
  for a `JMenuItem` 829
Action event *see* event, action
Action listener *see* listener, action
`ActionEvent` *see* event, action
  see also `actionPerformed`
`ActionListener` 746
  see also listener, action
`actionPerformed` 746–748
  parameter list 750
  quick reference 750
`add` 716
  quick reference 727, 760
  see also container class
  see also layout manager
  to a panel 758
`addActionListener` 746
`addElement` 615, 619
  quick reference 615, 617
Adder applet 800
Adding machine GUI 775–776
  source code 777
  with exception handling 780
Address 5, 7
`<address>` 808
`addWindowListener` 717
  quick reference 734
ADT 228
Algorithm 17–18
  quick reference 18
Alphabetical order 113–114
Ancestor 434, 437
And *see* `&&`, `&`
Anonymous object 732
API 227
Apple 8
Applet 21, 30, 797–819
  adding icons 803–805
  converting a Swing application to 803

927

B

X

END USER LICENSE AGREEMENTS

TERMS AND CONDITIONS OF THE LICENSE AND EXPORT FOR JAVA™ 2 SDK, STANDARD EDITION 1.4.0

SUN MICROSYSTEMS, INC.

BINARY CODE LICENSE AGREEMENT

READ THE TERMS OF THIS AGREEMENT AND ANY PROVIDED SUPPLEMENTAL LICENSE TERMS (COLLECTIVELY "AGREEMENT") CAREFULLY BEFORE OPENING THE SOFTWARE MEDIA PACKAGE. BY OPENING THE SOFTWARE MEDIA PACKAGE, YOU AGREE TO THE TERMS OF THIS AGREEMENT. IF YOU ARE ACCESSING THE SOFTWARE ELECTRONICALLY, INDICATE YOUR ACCEPTANCE OF THESE TERMS BY SELECTING THE "ACCEPT" BUTTON AT THE END OF THIS AGREEMENT. IF YOU DO NOT AGREE TO ALL THESE TERMS, PROMPTLY RETURN THE UNUSED SOFTWARE TO YOUR PLACE OF PURCHASE FOR A REFUND OR, IF THE SOFTWARE IS ACCESSED ELECTRONICALLY, SELECT THE "DECLINE" BUTTON AT THE END OF THIS AGREEMENT.

1. LICENSE TO USE. Sun grants you a non-exclusive and non-transferable license for the internal use only of the accompanying software and documentation and any error corrections provided by Sun (collectively "Software"), by the number of users and the class of computer hardware for which the corresponding fee has been paid.

2. RESTRICTIONS. Software is confidential and copyrighted. Title to Software and all associated intellectual property rights is retained by Sun and/or its licensors. Except as specifically authorized in any Supplemental License Terms, you may not make copies of Software, other than a single copy of Software for archival purposes. Unless enforcement is prohibited by applicable law, you may not modify, decompile, or reverse engineer Software. You acknowledge that Software is not designed, licensed or intended for use in the design, construction, operation or maintenance of any nuclear facility. Sun disclaims any express or implied warranty of fitness for such uses. No right, title or interest in or to any trademark, service mark, logo or trade name of Sun or its licensors is granted under this Agreement.

3. LIMITED WARRANTY. Sun warrants to you that for a period of ninety (90) days from the date of purchase, as evidenced by a copy of the receipt, the media on which Software is furnished (if any) will be free of defects in materials and workmanship under normal use. Except for the foregoing, Software is provided "AS IS". Your exclusive remedy and Sun's entire liability under this limited warranty will be at Sun's option to replace Software media or refund the fee paid for Software.

4. DISCLAIMER OF WARRANTY. UNLESS SPECIFIED IN THIS AGREEMENT, ALL EXPRESS OR IMPLIED CONDITIONS, REPRESENTATIONS AND WARRANTIES, INCLUDING ANY IMPLIED WARRANTY OF MERCHANTABILITY, FITNESS FOR A PARTICULAR PURPOSE OR NON-INFRINGEMENT ARE DISCLAIMED, EXCEPT TO THE EXTENT THAT THESE DISCLAIMERS ARE HELD TO BE LEGALLY INVALID.

5. LIMITATION OF LIABILITY. TO THE EXTENT NOT PROHIBITED BY LAW, IN NO EVENT WILL SUN OR ITS LICENSORS BE LIABLE FOR ANY LOST REVENUE, PROFIT OR DATA, OR FOR SPECIAL, INDIRECT, CONSEQUENTIAL, INCIDENTAL OR PUNITIVE DAMAGES, HOWEVER CAUSED REGARDLESS OF THE THEORY OF LIABILITY, ARISING OUT OF OR RELATED TO THE USE OF OR INABILITY TO USE SOFTWARE, EVEN IF SUN HAS BEEN ADVISED OF THE POSSIBILITY OF SUCH DAMAGES. In no event will Sun's liability to you, whether in contract, tort (including negligence), or otherwise, exceed the amount paid by you for Software under this Agreement. The foregoing limitations will apply even if the above stated warranty fails of its essential purpose.

6. Termination. This Agreement is effective until terminated. You may terminate this Agreement at any time by destroying all copies of Software. This Agreement will terminate immediately without notice from Sun if you fail to comply with any provision of this Agreement. Upon Termination, you must destroy all copies of Software.

7. Export Regulations. All Software and technical data delivered under this Agreement are subject to US export control laws and may be subject to export or import regulations in other countries. You agree to comply strictly with all such laws and regulations and acknowledge that you have the responsibility to obtain such licenses to export, re-export, or import as may be required after delivery to you.

8. U.S. Government Restricted Rights. If Software is being acquired by or on behalf of the U.S. Government or by a U.S. Government prime contractor or subcontractor (at any tier), then the Government's rights in Software and accompanying

documentation will be only as set forth in this Agreement; this is in accordance with 48 CFR 227.7201 through 227.7202-4 (for Department of Defense (DOD) acquisitions) and with 48 CFR 2.101 and 12.212 (for non-DOD acquisitions).

9. Governing Law. Any action related to this Agreement will be governed by California law and controlling U.S. federal law. No choice of law rules of any jurisdiction will apply.

10. Severability. If any provision of this Agreement is held to be unenforceable, this Agreement will remain in effect with the provision omitted, unless omission would frustrate the intent of the parties, in which case this Agreement will immediately terminate.

11. Integration. This Agreement is the entire agreement between you and Sun relating to its subject matter. It supersedes all prior or contemporaneous oral or written communications, proposals, representations and warranties and prevails over any conflicting or additional terms of any quote, order, acknowledgment, or other communication between the parties relating to its subject matter during the term of this Agreement. No modification of this Agreement will be binding, unless in writing and signed by an authorized representative of each party.

JAVA™ 2 SOFTWARE DEVELOPMENT KIT (J2SDK), STANDARD EDITION, VERSION 1.4.X SUPPLEMENTAL LICENSE TERMS

These supplemental license terms ("Supplemental Terms") add to or modify the terms of the Binary Code License Agreement (collectively, the "Agreement"). Capitalized terms not defined in these Supplemental Terms shall have the same meanings ascribed to them in the Agreement. These Supplemental Terms shall supersede any inconsistent or conflicting terms in the Agreement, or in any license contained within the Software.

1. Software Internal Use and Development License Grant. Subject to the terms and conditions of this Agreement, including, but not limited to Section 4 (Java Technology Restrictions) of these Supplemental Terms, Sun grants you a non-exclusive, non-transferable, limited license to reproduce internally and use internally the binary form of the Software complete and unmodified for the sole purpose of designing, developing and testing your Java applets and applications intended to run on the Java platform ("Programs").

2. License to Distribute Software. Subject to the terms and conditions of this Agreement, including, but not limited to Section 4 (Java Technology Restrictions) of these Supplemental Terms, Sun grants you a non-exclusive, non-transferable, limited license to reproduce and distribute the Software, provided that (i) you distribute the Software complete and unmodified (unless otherwise specified in the applicable README file) and only bundled as part of, and for the sole purpose of running, your Programs, (ii) the Programs add significant and primary functionality to the Software, (iii) you do not distribute additional software intended to replace any component(s) of the Software (unless otherwise specified in the applicable README file), (iv) you do not remove or alter any proprietary legends or notices contained in the Software, (v) you only distribute the Software subject to a license agreement that protects Sun's interests consistent with the terms contained in this Agreement, and (vi) you agree to defend and indemnify Sun and its licensors from and against any damages, costs, liabilities, settlement amounts and/or expenses (including attorneys' fees) incurred in connection with any claim, lawsuit or action by any third party that arises or results from the use or distribution of any and all Programs and/or Software. (vi) include the following statement as part of product documentation (whether hard copy or electronic), as a part of a copyright page or proprietary rights notice page, in an "About" box or in any other form reasonably designed to make the statement visible to users of the Software: "This product includes code licensed from RSA Security, Inc.", and (vii) include the statement, "Some portions licensed from IBM are available at http://oss.software.ibm.com/icu4j/".

3. License to Distribute Redistributables. Subject to the terms and conditions of this Agreement, including but not limited to Section 4 (Java Technology Restrictions) of these Supplemental Terms, Sun grants you a non-exclusive, non-transferable, limited license to reproduce and distribute those files specifically identified as redistributable in the Software "README" file ("Redistributables") provided that: (i) you distribute the Redistributables complete and unmodified (unless otherwise specified in the applicable README file), and only bundled as part of Programs, (ii) you do not distribute additional software intended to supersede any component(s) of the Redistributables (unless otherwise specified in the applicable README file), (iii) you do not remove or alter any proprietary legends or notices contained in or on the Redistributables, (iv) you only distribute the Redistributables pursuant to a license agreement that protects Sun's interests consistent with the terms contained in the Agreement, (v) you agree to defend and indemnify Sun and its licensors from and against any damages, costs, liabilities, settlement amounts and/or expenses (including attorneys' fees)

incurred in connection with any claim, lawsuit or action by any third party that arises or results from the use or distribution of any and all Programs and/or Software, (vi) include the following statement as part of product documentation (whether hard copy or electronic), as a part of a copyright page or proprietary rights notice page, in an "About" box or in any other form reasonably designed to make the statement visible to users of the Software: "This product includes code licensed from RSA Security, Inc.", and (vii) include the statement, "Some portions licensed from IBM are available at http://oss.software.ibm.com/icu4j/".

4. Java Technology Restrictions. You may not modify the Java Platform Interface ("JPI", identified as classes contained within the "java" package or any subpackages of the "java" package), by creating additional classes within the JPI or otherwise causing the addition to or modification of the classes in the JPI. In the event that you create an additional class and associated API(s) which (i) extends the functionality of the Java platform, and (ii) is exposed to third party software developers for the purpose of developing additional software which invokes such additional API, you must promptly publish broadly an accurate specification for such API for free use by all developers. You may not create, or authorize your licensees to create, additional classes, interfaces, or subpackages that are in any way identified as "java", "javax", "sun" or similar convention as specified by Sun in any naming convention designation.

5. Notice of Automatic Software Updates from Sun. You acknowledge that the Software may automatically download, install, and execute applets, applications, software extensions, and updated versions of the Software from Sun ("Software Updates"), which may require you to accept updated terms and conditions for installation. If additional terms and conditions are not presented on installation, the Software Updates will be considered part of the Software and subject to the terms and conditions of the Agreement.

6. Notice of Automatic Downloads. You acknowledge that, by your use of the Software and/or by requesting services that require use of the Software, the Software may automatically download, install, and execute software applications from sources other than Sun ("Other Software"). Sun makes no representations of a relationship of any kind to licensors of Other Software. TO THE EXTENT NOT PROHIBITED BY LAW, IN NO EVENT WILL SUN OR ITS LICENSORS BE LIABLE FOR ANY LOST REVENUE, PROFIT OR DATA, OR FOR SPECIAL, INDIRECT, CONSEQUENTIAL, INCIDENTAL OR PUNITIVE DAMAGES, HOWEVER CAUSED REGARDLESS OF THE THEORY OF LIABILITY, ARISING OUT OF OR RELATED TO THE USE OF OR INABILITY TO USE OTHER SOFTWARE, EVEN IF SUN HAS BEEN ADVISED OF THE POSSIBILITY OF SUCH DAMAGES.

7. Trademarks and Logos. You acknowledge and agree as between you and Sun that Sun owns the SUN, SOLARIS, JAVA, JINI, FORTE, and iPLANET trademarks and all SUN, SOLARIS, JAVA, JINI, FORTE, and iPLANET-related trademarks, service marks, logos and other brand designations ("Sun Marks"), and you agree to comply with the Sun Trademark and Logo Usage Requirements currently located at http://www.sun.com/policies/trademarks. Any use you make of the Sun Marks inures to Sun's benefit.

8. Source Code. Software may contain source code that is provided solely for reference purposes pursuant to the terms of this Agreement. Source code may not be redistributed unless expressly provided for in this Agreement.

9. Termination for Infringement. Either party may terminate this Agreement immediately should any Software become, or in either party's opinion be likely to become, the subject of a claim of infringement of any intellectual property right.

For inquiries please contact: Sun Microsystems, Inc. 901 San Antonio Road, Palo Alto, California 94303 (LFI#109998/Form ID#011801)

SUN(TM) ONE STUDIO 4, COMMUNITY EDITION LICENSE

Sun Microsystems, Inc. Binary Code License Agreement

READ THE TERMS OF THIS AGREEMENT AND ANY PROVIDED SUPPLEMENTAL LICENSE TERMS (COLLECTIVELY "AGREEMENT") CAREFULLY BEFORE OPENING THE SOFTWARE MEDIA PACKAGE. BY OPENING THE SOFTWARE MEDIA PACKAGE, YOU AGREE TO THE TERMS OF THIS AGREEMENT. IF YOU ARE ACCESSING THE SOFTWARE ELECTRONICALLY, INDICATE YOUR ACCEPTANCE OF THESE TERMS BY SELECTING THE "ACCEPT" BUTTON AT THE END OF THIS AGREEMENT. IF YOU DO NOT AGREE TO ALL THESE TERMS, PROMPTLY RETURN THE UNUSED SOFTWARE TO YOUR PLACE OF PURCHASE FOR A REFUND OR, IF THE SOFTWARE IS ACCESSED ELECTRONICALLY, SELECT THE "DECLINE" BUTTON AT THE END OF THIS AGREEMENT.

1. LICENSE TO USE. Sun grants you a non-exclusive and non-transferable license for the internal use only of the accompanying software and documentation and any error corrections provided by Sun (collectively "Software"), by the number of users and the class of computer hardware for which the corresponding fee has been paid.

2. RESTRICTIONS. Software is confidential and copyrighted. Title to Software and all associated intellectual property rights is retained by Sun and/or its licensors. Except as specifically authorized in any Supplemental License Terms, you may not make copies of Software, other than a single copy of Software for archival purposes. Unless enforcement is prohibited by applicable law, you may not modify, decompile, or reverse engineer Software. You acknowledge that Software is not designed, licensed or intended for use in the design, construction, operation or maintenance of any nuclear facility. Sun disclaims any express or implied warranty of fitness for such uses. No right, title or interest in or to any trademark, service mark, logo or trade name of Sun or its licensors is granted under this Agreement.

3. LIMITED WARRANTY. Sun warrants to you that for a period of ninety (90) days from the date of purchase, as evidenced by a copy of the receipt, the media on which Software is furnished (if any) will be free of defects in materials and workmanship under normal use. Except for the foregoing, Software is provided "AS IS". Your exclusive remedy and Sun's entire liability under this limited warranty will be at Sun's option to replace Software media or refund the fee paid for Software.

4. DISCLAIMER OF WARRANTY. UNLESS SPECIFIED IN THIS AGREEMENT, ALL EXPRESS OR IMPLIED CONDITIONS, REPRESENTATIONS AND WARRANTIES, INCLUDING ANY IMPLIED WARRANTY OF MERCHANTABILITY, FITNESS FOR A PARTICULAR PURPOSE OR NON-INFRINGEMENT ARE DISCLAIMED, EXCEPT TO THE EXTENT THAT THESE DISCLAIMERS ARE HELD TO BE LEGALLY INVALID.

5. LIMITATION OF LIABILITY. TO THE EXTENT NOT PROHIBITED BY LAW, IN NO EVENT WILL SUN OR ITS LICENSORS BE LIABLE FOR ANY LOST REVENUE, PROFIT OR DATA, OR FOR SPECIAL, INDIRECT, CONSEQUENTIAL, INCIDENTAL OR PUNITIVE DAMAGES, HOWEVER CAUSED REGARDLESS OF THE THEORY OF LIABILITY, ARISING OUT OF OR RELATED TO THE USE OF OR INABILITY TO USE SOFTWARE, EVEN IF SUN HAS BEEN ADVISED OF THE POSSIBILITY OF SUCH DAMAGES. In no event will Sun's liability to you, whether in contract, tort (including negligence), or otherwise, exceed the amount paid by you for Software under this Agreement. The foregoing limitations will apply even if the above stated warranty fails of its essential purpose.

6. Termination. This Agreement is effective until terminated. You may terminate this Agreement at any time by destroying all copies of Software. This Agreement will terminate immediately without notice from Sun if you fail to comply with any provision of this Agreement. Upon Termination, you must destroy all copies of Software.

7. Export Regulations. All Software and technical data delivered under this Agreement are subject to US export control laws and may be subject to export or import regulations in other countries. You agree to comply strictly with all such laws and regulation and acknowledge that you have the responsibility to obtain such licenses to export, re-export, or import as may be required after delivery to you.

8. U.S. Government Restricted Rights. If Software is being acquired by or on behalf of the U.S. Government or by a U.S. Government prime contractor or subcontractor (at any tier), then the Government's rights in Software and accompanying documentation will be only as set forth in this Agreement; this is in accordance with 48 CFR 227.7201 through 227.7202-4 (for Department of Defense (DOD) acquisitions) and with 48 CFR 2.101 and 12.212 (for non-DOD acquisitions).

9. Governing Law. Any action related to this Agreement will be governed by California law and controlling U.S. federal law. No choice of law rules of any jurisdiction will apply.

10. Severability. If any provision of this Agreement is held to be unenforceable, this Agreement will remain in effect with the provision omitted, unless omission would frustrate the intent of the parties, in which case this Agreement will immediately terminate.

11. Integration. This Agreement is the entire agreement between you and Sun relating to its subject matter. It supersedes all prior or contemporaneous oral or written communications, proposals, representations and warranties and prevails over any conflicting or additional terms of any quote, order, acknowledgment, or other communication between the parties relating to its subject matter during the term of this Agreement. No modification of this Agreement will be binding, unless in writing and signed by an authorized representative of each party.

These supplemental license terms ("Supplemental Terms") add to or modify the terms of the Binary Code License Agreement (collectively, the "Agreement"). Capitalized terms not defined in these Supplemental Terms shall have the same meanings ascribed to them in the Agreement. These Supplemental Terms shall supersede any inconsistent or conflicting terms in the Agreement, or in any license contained within the Software.

1. Software Internal Use and Development License Grant. Subject to the terms and conditions of this Agreement, including, but not limited to Section 4 (Java Technology Restrictions) of these Supplemental Terms, Sun grants you a non-exclusive, non-transferable, limited license to reproduce internally and use internally the binary form of the Software complete and unmodified for the sole purpose of designing, developing and testing your applets and applications ("Programs"). To the extent that you are designing, developing and testing Java applets and applications for a particular version of the Java platform, any executable output generated by a compiler that is contained in the Software must (a) only be compiled from source code that conforms to the corresponding version of the OEM Java Language Specification; (b) be in the class file format defined by the corresponding version of the OEM Java Virtual Machine Specification; and (c) execute properly on a reference runtime, as specified by Sun, associated with such version of the Java platform.

2. License to Distribute Software. Subject to the terms and conditions of this Agreement, including, but not limited to Section 4 (Java Technology Restrictions) of these Supplemental Terms, Sun grants you a non-exclusive, non-transferable, limited license to reproduce and distribute the Software in binary code form only, provided that (i) you distribute the Software complete and unmodified, (ii) you do not distribute additional software intended to replace any component(s) of the Software, (iii) if you are distributing Java applets and applications for a particular version of the Java platform, any executable output generated by a compiler that is contained in the Software must (a) only be compiled from source code that conforms to the corresponding version of the OEM Java Language Specification; (b) be in the class file format defined by the corresponding version of the OEM Java Virtual Machine Specification; and (c) execute properly on a reference runtime, as specified by Sun, associated with such version of the Java platform, (iv) you do not remove or alter any proprietary legends or notices contained in the Software, (v) you only distribute the Software subject to a license agreement that protects Sun's interests consistent with the terms contained in this Agreement, and (vi) you agree to defend and indemnify Sun and its licensors from and against any damages, costs, liabilities, settlement amounts and/or expenses (including attorneys' fees) incurred in connection with any claim, lawsuit or action by any third party that arises or results from the use or distribution of any and all Programs and/or Software.

3. License to Distribute Redistributables. Subject to the terms and conditions of this Agreement, including but not limited to Section 4 (Java Technology Restrictions) of these Supplemental Terms, Sun grants you a non-exclusive, non-transferable, limited license to reproduce and distribute the binary form of those files specifically identified as redistributable in the Software "RELEASE NOTES" file ("Redistributables") provided that: (i) you distribute the Redistributables complete and unmodified (unless otherwise specified in the applicable RELEASE NOTES file), and only bundled as part of Programs, (ii) you do not distribute additional software intended to supersede any component(s) of the Redistributables, (iii) you do not remove or alter any proprietary legends or notices contained in or on the Redistributables, (iv) if you are distributing Java applets and applications for a particular version of the Java platform, any executable output generated by a compiler that is contained in the Software must (a) only be compiled from source code that conforms to the corresponding version of the OEM Java Language Specification; (b) be in the class file format defined by the corresponding version of the OEM Java Virtual Machine Specification; and (c) execute properly on a reference runtime, as specified by Sun, associated with such version of the Java platform, (v) you only distribute the Redistributables pursuant to a license agreement that protects Sun's interests consistent with the terms contained in the Agreement, and (vi) you agree to defend and indemnify Sun and its licensors from and against any damages, costs, liabilities, settlement amounts and/or expenses (including attorneys' fees) incurred in connection with any claim, lawsuit or action by any third party that arises or results from the use or distribution of any and all Programs and/or Software.

4. Java Technology Restrictions. You may not modify the Java Platform Interface ("JPI", identified as classes contained within the "java" package or any subpackages of the "java" package), by creating additional classes within the JPI or otherwise causing the addition to or modification of the classes in the JPI. In the event that you create an additional class and associated API(s) which (i) extends the functionality of the Java platform, and (ii) is exposed to third party software developers for the purpose of developing additional software which invokes such additional API, you must promptly publish broadly an accurate specification for such API for free use by all developers. You may not create, or authorize your licensees to create, additional classes, interfaces, or subpackages that are in any way identified as "java", "javax", "sun" or similar convention as specified by Sun in any naming convention designation.

5. Java Runtime Availability. Refer to the appropriate version of the Java Runtime Environment binary code license (currently located at http://www.java.sun.com/jdk/index.html) for the availability of runtime code which may be distributed with Java applets and applications.

6. Trademarks and Logos. You acknowledge and agree as between you and Sun that Sun owns the SUN, SOLARIS, JAVA, JINI, FORTE, and iPLANET trademarks and all SUN, SOLARIS, JAVA, JINI, FORTE, and iPLANET-related trademarks, service marks, logos and other brand designations ("Sun Marks"), and you agree to comply with the Sun Trademark and Logo Usage Requirements currently located at http://www.sun.com/policies/trademarks. Any use you make of the Sun Marks inures to Sun's benefit.

7. Source Code. Software may contain source code that is provided solely for reference purposes pursuant to the terms of this Agreement. Source code may not be redistributed unless expressly provided for in this Agreement.

8. Termination for Infringement. Either party may terminate this Agreement immediately should any Software become, or in either party's opinion be likely to become, the subject of a claim of infringement of any intellectual property right.

For inquiries please contact: Sun Microsystems, Inc. 4150 Network Circle, Santa Clara, California 95054. (LFI#112968/Form ID#011801)

PEARSON EDUCATION LICENSE AGREEMENT AND LIMITED WARRANTY

READ THE FOLLOWING TERMS AND CONDITIONS CAREFULLY BEFORE OPENING THIS DISK PACKAGE. THIS LEGAL DOCUMENT IS AN AGREEMENT BETWEEN YOU AND PRENTICE-HALL, INC. (THE "COMPANY"). BY OPENING THIS SEALED DISK PACKAGE, YOU ARE AGREEING TO BE BOUND BY THESE TERMS AND CONDITIONS. IF YOU DO NOT AGREE WITH THESE TERMS AND CONDITIONS, DO NOT OPEN THE DISK PACKAGE. PROMPTLY RETURN THE UNOPENED DISK PACKAGE AND ALL ACCOMPANYING ITEMS TO THE PLACE YOU OBTAINED THEM FOR A FULL REFUND OF ANY SUMS YOU HAVE PAID.

1. GRANT OF LICENSE: In consideration of your payment of the license fee, which is part of the price you paid for this product, and your agreement to abide by the terms and conditions of this Agreement, the Company grants to you a non-exclusive right to use and display the copy of the enclosed software program (hereinafter the "SOFTWARE") on a single computer (i.e., with a single CPU) at a single location so long as you comply with the terms of this Agreement. The Company reserves all rights not expressly granted to you under this Agreement.

2. OWNERSHIP OF SOFTWARE: You own only the magnetic or physical media (the enclosed disks) on which the SOFTWARE is recorded or fixed, but the Company retains all the rights, title, and ownership to the SOFTWARE recorded on the original disk copy(ies) and all subsequent copies of the SOFTWARE, regardless of the form or media on which the original or other copies may exist. This license is not a sale of the original SOFTWARE or any copy to you.

3. COPY RESTRICTIONS: This SOFTWARE and the accompanying printed materials and user manual (the "Documentation") are the subject of copyright. You may not copy the Documentation or the SOFTWARE, except that you may make a single copy of the SOFTWARE for backup or archival purposes only. You may be held legally responsible for any copying or copyright infringement which is caused or encouraged by your failure to abide by the terms of this restriction.

4. USE RESTRICTIONS: You may not network the SOFTWARE or otherwise use it on more than one computer or computer terminal at the same time. You may physically transfer the SOFTWARE from one computer to another provided that the SOFTWARE is used on only one computer at a time. You may not distribute copies of the SOFTWARE or Documentation to others. You may not reverse engineer, disassemble, decompile, modify, adapt, translate, or create derivative works based on the SOFTWARE or the Documentation without the prior written consent of the Company.

5. TRANSFER RESTRICTIONS: The enclosed SOFTWARE is licensed only to you and may not be transferred to any one else without the prior written consent of the Company. Any unauthorized transfer of the SOFTWARE shall result in the immediate termination of this Agreement.

6. TERMINATION: This license is effective until terminated. This license will terminate automatically without notice from the Company and become null and void if you fail to comply with any provisions or limitations of this license. Upon termination, you shall destroy the Documentation and all copies of the SOFTWARE. All provisions of this Agreement as to warranties, limitation of liability, remedies or damages, and our ownership rights shall survive termination.

7. MISCELLANEOUS: This Agreement shall be construed in accordance with the laws of the United States of America and the State of New York and shall benefit the Company, its affiliates, and assignees.

8. LIMITED WARRANTY AND DISCLAIMER OF WARRANTY: The Company warrants that the SOFTWARE, when properly used in accordance with the Documentation, will operate in substantial conformity with the description of the SOFTWARE set forth in the Documentation. The Company does not warrant that the SOFTWARE will meet your requirements or that the operation of the SOFTWARE will be uninterrupted or error-free. The Company warrants that the media on which the SOFTWARE is delivered shall be free from defects in materials and workmanship under normal use for a period of thirty (30) days from the date of your purchase. Your only remedy and the Company's only obligation under these limited warranties is, at the Company's option, return of the warranted item for a refund of any amounts paid by you or replacement of the item. Any replacement of SOFTWARE or media under the warranties shall not extend the original warranty period. The limited warranty set forth above shall not apply to any SOFTWARE which the Company determines in good faith has been subject to misuse, neglect, improper installation, repair, alteration, or damage by you. EXCEPT FOR THE EXPRESSED WARRANTIES SET FORTH ABOVE, THE COMPANY DISCLAIMS ALL WARRANTIES, EXPRESS OR IMPLIED, INCLUDING WITHOUT LIMITATION, THE IMPLIED WARRANTIES OF MERCHANTABILITY AND FITNESS FOR A PARTICULAR PURPOSE. EXCEPT FOR THE EXPRESS WARRANTY SET FORTH ABOVE, THE COMPANY DOES NOT WARRANT, GUARANTEE, OR MAKE ANY REPRESENTATION REGARDING THE USE OR THE RESULTS OF THE USE OF THE SOFTWARE IN TERMS OF ITS CORRECTNESS, ACCURACY, RELIABILITY, CURRENTNESS, OR OTHERWISE.

IN NO EVENT, SHALL THE COMPANY OR ITS EMPLOYEES, AGENTS, SUPPLIERS, OR CONTRACTORS BE LIABLE FOR ANY INCIDENTAL, INDIRECT, SPECIAL, OR CONSEQUENTIAL DAMAGES ARISING OUT OF OR IN CONNECTION WITH THE LICENSE GRANTED UNDER THIS AGREEMENT, OR FOR LOSS OF USE, LOSS OF DATA, LOSS OF INCOME OR PROFIT, OR OTHER LOSSES, SUSTAINED AS A RESULT OF INJURY TO ANY PERSON, OR LOSS OF OR DAMAGE TO PROPERTY, OR CLAIMS OF THIRD PARTIES, EVEN IF THE COMPANY OR AN AUTHORIZED REPRESENTATIVE OF THE COMPANY HAS BEEN ADVISED OF THE POSSIBILITY OF SUCH DAMAGES. IN NO EVENT SHALL LIABILITY OF THE COMPANY FOR DAMAGES WITH RESPECT TO THE SOFTWARE EXCEED THE AMOUNTS ACTUALLY PAID BY YOU, IF ANY, FOR THE SOFTWARE.

SOME JURISDICTIONS DO NOT ALLOW THE LIMITATION OF IMPLIED WARRANTIES OR LIABILITY FOR INCIDENTAL, INDIRECT, SPECIAL, OR CONSEQUENTIAL DAMAGES, SO THE ABOVE LIMITATIONS MAY NOT ALWAYS APPLY. THE WARRANTIES IN THIS AGREEMENT GIVE YOU SPECIFIC LEGAL RIGHTS AND YOU MAY ALSO HAVE OTHER RIGHTS WHICH VARY IN ACCORDANCE WITH LOCAL LAW.

ACKNOWLEDGMENT

YOU ACKNOWLEDGE THAT YOU HAVE READ THIS AGREEMENT, UNDERSTAND IT, AND AGREE TO BE BOUND BY ITS TERMS AND CONDITIONS. YOU ALSO AGREE THAT THIS AGREEMENT IS THE COMPLETE AND EXCLUSIVE STATEMENT OF THE AGREEMENT BETWEEN YOU AND THE COMPANY AND SUPERSEDES ALL PROPOSALS OR PRIOR AGREEMENTS, ORAL, OR WRITTEN, AND ANY OTHER COMMUNICATIONS BETWEEN YOU AND THE COMPANY OR ANY REPRESENTATIVE OF THE COMPANY RELATING TO THE SUBJECT MATTER OF THIS AGREEMENT.

Should you have any questions concerning this Agreement or if you wish to contact the Company for any reason, please contact in writing at the address below.

Robin Short
Pearson Education
One Lake Street
Upper Saddle River, New Jersey 07458